WINDOWS SERVER 2003

IN A NUTSHELL

Other Microsoft Windows resources from O'Reilly

Related titles
Windows XP in a
 Nuthshell
Windows XP Annoyances
Windows XP Pro: The
 Mising Manual
Windows XP Home: The
 Missing Manual
Windows XP Pocket Guide
Windows 2000
 Administration in a
 Nutshell
Windows 2000
 Performance Guide

Windows 2000
 Commands Pocket
 Reference
Windows Server 2003 in a
 Nutshell
Active Directory
VBScript in a Nutshell
Word Pocket Guide
Outlook Pocket Guide
Access Database Design
 and Programming
Writing Excel Macros with
 VBA

Windows Books Resource Center
windows.oreilly.com is a complete catalog of O'Reilly's Windows and Office books, including sample chapters and code examples.

oreillynet.com is the essential portal for developers interested in open and emerging technologies, including new platforms, programming languages, and operating systems.

Conferences
O'Reilly & Associates brings diverse innovators together to nurture the ideas that spark revolutionary industries. We specialize in documenting the latest tools and systems, translating the innovator's knowledge into useful skills for those in the trenches. Visit *conferences.oreilly.com* for our upcoming events.

Safari Bookshelf (*safari.oreilly.com*) is the premier online reference library for programmers and IT professionals. Conduct searches across more than 1,000 books. Subscribers can zero in on answers to time-critical questions in a matter of seconds. Read the books on your Bookshelf from cover to cover or simply flip to the page you need. Try it today with a free trial.

WINDOWS SERVER 2003

IN A NUTSHELL

Mitch Tulloch

O'REILLY®

Beijing • Cambridge • Farnham • Köln • Paris • Sebastopol • Taipei • Tokyo

Windows Server 2003 in a Nutshell
by Mitch Tulloch

Copyright © 2003 O'Reilly & Associates, Inc. All rights reserved.
Portions of this book previously appeared in *Windows 2000 Administration in a Nutshell*, Copyright © 2001 O'Reilly & Associates, Inc. All rights reserved.
Printed in the United States of America.

Published by O'Reilly & Associates, Inc., 1005 Gravenstein Highway North, Sebastopol, CA 95472.

O'Reilly & Associates books may be purchased for educational, business, or sales promotional use. Online editions are also available for most titles (*safari.oreilly.com*). For more information, contact our corporate/institutional sales department: 800-998-9938 or *corporate@oreilly.com*.

Editors:	Debra Cameron and Robert Denn
Production Editor:	Mary Anne Weeks Mayo
Cover Designer:	Emma Colby
Interior Designer:	David Futato

Printing History:

September 2003:	First Edition.

ISBN: 0-596-00404-4
[M]

Table of Contents

Part III. Resources

Preface

This book is a quick desktop reference on administering the Windows Server 2003 (WS2003) operating system. It's not a tutorial; there are plenty of those around—big fat books full of screenshots and overblown procedures designed for beginners. Instead, this book is a *reference*—an A-to-Z compendium of concepts, tools, and tasks for basic administration of the WS2003 platform, small enough to sit handily on your *desktop* where you need it and condensed enough to be *quick* and easy to use—hence the description *quick desktop reference*. Let's unpack this a bit more.

Who This Book Is for

As I mentioned, tutorials are generally written for beginners, have lots of screenshots, and are generally quite wordy. This book has *no screenshots* (probably a first for a book on a Windows platform) and is highly condensed, packing tons of information into each page. So the individuals most likely to benefit from using this book are intermediate to advanced admins who are already familiar with either the Windows NT, Windows 2000 platform, or both. Not that beginners won't find this book useful as well, but it's definitely not a starting point for learning WS2003 administration—as I said, it's a reference not a tutorial. You don't learn a language by reading the dictionary, but for enhancing your fluency in a language, a dictionary is certainly essential. And my hope is that experienced NT/W2K admins will find this book just as essential.

How to Use This Book

To see how useful this book can be, check out the next few sections.

Part I: Transitioning

The first part of this book includes two chapters designed to help ease the pain of NT and W2K administrators as you transition to the new WS2003 platform.

Chapter 1, *NT → 2003*, is aimed mainly at NT admins and highlights important differences between administering NT and WS2003. The first part of the chapter lists the WS2003 counterparts to NT administrative tools, utilities, and commands. The rest of the chapter describes new features and provides various tips to help make the transition easier.

Chapter 2, *2000 → 2003*, targets W2K admins and highlights differences between W2K and WS2003. The chapter begins by describing significant changes to administrative tools, utilities, and the GUI. It concludes by summarizing the new features and enhancements that make WS2003 a more secure, powerful, and manageable platform than W2K.

Although Chapters 1 and 2 are intended for different audiences, I highly recommend that both NT and W2K admins read both chapters to get the most comprehensive view of the changes and enhancements in the new platform.

Part II: Alphabetical Reference

The second part is the meat of the book. It consists of three reference chapters whose topics are arranged in alphabetical order.

Chapter 3, *Task Map*, lists more than 600 different administrative tasks organized under more than a hundred different headings. Most entries provide task-oriented references to topics in Chapter 4 or commands in Chapter 5 where you can find detailed information. The remaining entries either outline the steps for performing the task or describe a Group Policy setting relating to its administration. Think of Chapter 3 mainly as a quick entry point for the reference material in later chapters, with some extra goodies thrown in for good measure.

Chapter 4, *GUI Reference*, covers the concepts, tools, and tasks for administering WS2003 from the GUI. The chapter is divided into broad topic areas ranging from Active Directory to WINS and, together with Chapter 5, forms the core of this book. You can either browse a topic in this chapter to learn more about its administration or look up a specific task in it using the Task Map in Chapter 3 or the Index.

Chapter 5, *Command Reference*, lists more than a hundred different commands and scripts that can be used to administer various aspects of WS2003 from the command line. Almost a third of these commands are new to WS2003. For each command, the syntax is presented together with examples, notes, and cross-references to topics in Chapter 4. The enhancements to commands in WS2003 mean that Windows now rivals Unix in the ability to manage the platform from the command line.

Part III: Resources

An appendix and an acronym list round out the book.

Appendix: Useful Sites, lists some web sites that those administering WS2003 may find useful.

Acronyms, helps you navigate the acronym maze for WS2003 from ACL to WPA.

What's New in This Edition

If you've been using my previous book, *Windows 2000 Administration in a Nutshell*, you'll quickly discover that this book represents a complete overhaul of that title and is not merely a cosmetic revision. The main changes in this new edition are as follows:

- The content has been thoroughly updated to cover the new features and enhancements of the WS2003 platform. This means coverage of new concepts, new tools, new procedures, and new commands has been added where appropriate. However, since my old book was almost 800 pages long, this means some old material had to be pruned to make room for the new, but I've tried to maintain all content important to everyday administration of the WS2003 platform.

- The content has also been completely reorganized to make it easier to use. In particular, all the alphabetical reference material in Chapters 3–6 of my old book, which covered concepts, tasks, consoles, and utilities, has now been blended into a single chapter (Chapter 4) to make it easier to use. This was done mainly in response to suggestions by readers of my earlier book. Thank you!

- Chapter 3, *Task Map*, has been added to this edition to help you quickly find useful information in Chapters 4 and 5 concerning specific administrative tasks you want to perform.

- Part I, called "The Lay of the Land" in my earlier book, has been expanded to help not just NT admins but also W2K admins transition to WS2003.

Conventions Used in This Book

To make things concise, tasks are presented in a condensed form throughout this book. For example:

> Start → Settings → Printers → right-click on a printer → Properties → Sharing → Share this printer → specify share name

is short for:

> Click the Start button, select Settings, then Printers. When the Printers folder opens, right-click on the printer you want to share and select Properties from the shortcut menu. Then click the Sharing tab, select the "Share this printer" option, and type a name for the share in the text box. Then click OK when you're finished to close the Properties sheet.

I'm sure you can appreciate my approach. Such "gestalt menus" are easy to follow if you're sitting at the computer and have even a smattering of experience with the Windows GUI.

Additional typographical conventions used include:

Constant width

> Command-line examples, code examples, and commands

Italic

> Filenames, directories, URLs, UNC paths, file extensions, utilities, and cross-references to topics in other chapters

Constant width italic

> Variables or user-defined elements such as username, which would be replaced by the user's logon name in gestalt menus or command examples

Constant width bold

> User input in gestalt menus or command examples

 This icon designates a note, which is an important aside to the nearby text.

 This icon designates a warning relating to the nearby text.

Comments and Questions

Please address comments and questions concerning this book to the publisher:

> O'Reilly & Associates, Inc.
> 1005 Gravenstein Highway North
> Sebastopol, CA 95472
> (800) 998-9938 (in the United States or Canada)
> (707) 829-0515 (international/local)
> (707) 829-0104 (fax)

There is a web page for this book, which lists errata, examples, or any additional information. You can access this page at:

> *http://www.oreilly.com/catalog/winsvrian/*

To comment or ask technical questions about this book, send email to:

> *bookquestions@oreilly.com*

For more information about books, conferences, Resource Centers, and the O'Reilly Network, see the O'Reilly web site at:

> *http://www.oreilly.com*

You can email the author directly at:

> *info@mtit.com*

Acknowledgments

Thanks first of all to Ingrid, my wife, for her support and encouragement while I worked on this project.

Thanks to Deb Cameron and Robert Denn, my editors on this project, for their support, encouragement, and friendly nagging.

Thanks to Robbie Allen, author of O'Reilly's *Active Directory*, who was my technical reviewer and provided many helpful suggestions and corrections.

Thanks to my agent, Neil Salkind, of Studio B Literary Agency (*http://www.studiob.com*) for his friendship and support.

Thanks to MTS Communications Inc. (*http://www.mts.ca*) for providing Internet services and web hosting for my web site (*http://www.mtit.com*).

Thanks to Orlando, owner of Ciao Caffe on Corydon Avenue (our Little Italy here in Winnipeg), whose espressos—the best in the city—kept me awake and inspired while writing this book.

And thanks finally to my readers for their helpful criticism and suggestions regarding my previous book.

Enjoy!

Disclaimer

Oh yeah, I almost forgot:

> Information contained in this work has been obtained from sources believed to be reliable. Although the author has made every effort to be accurate, neither the author nor the publisher assumes any liability or responsibility for any inaccuracy or omissions in this book or for any loss or damage arising from the information presented. In other words, the information provided in this book is presented on an "as is" basis.

So there. Have fun!

—Mitch Tulloch, MCSE, Cert. Ed.
Trainer, Consultant, Author, Nerd

Transitioning

1

NT → 2003

This brief chapter is designed to help Windows NT administrators quickly transition to Windows Server 2003 (WS2003) by highlighting some important differences between administering the two platforms. If you are a Windows 2000 (W2K) administrator looking for help transitioning, see Chapter 2. NT administrators are also encouraged to read through Chapter 2 because that chapter goes into greater depth regarding some features of WS2003.

New Tools, Old Tasks

If you are familiar with the Windows NT administrative tools and desktop, you may initially be thrown by WS2003 and its new Microsoft Management Console tools and enhanced desktop. Tables 1-1 through 1-3 help you bridge the gap between the two platforms, with the base Windows NT platform being Service Pack 4 or later.

To begin with, Table 1-1 lists the various Windows NT administrative tools and their counterparts in WS2003. Note that there is frequently no one-to-one correspondence between the old tools and the new. The steps for accessing administrative tools from the Start menu also differ slightly between the two platforms, namely:

Windows NT
> Start → Programs → Administrative Tools

WS2003
> Start → Administrative Tools

The above steps are implicit in Table 1-1.

There are often several ways of doing things in WS2003, but for simplicity and efficiency I usually describe only the most obvious method or the one involving the fewest number of steps.

Table 1-1. Administrative tools for Windows NT versus Windows Server 2003

NT tool	WS2003 counterpart
Administrative Wizards	Manage Your Server
Backup	Accessories System → Tools → Backup
DHCP Manager	DHCP[a]
Disk Administrator	Computer Management → Storage → Disk Management
DNS Manager	DNS[a]
Event Viewer	Event Viewer[a]
Internet Service Manager	Internet Information Services (IIS) Manager[a]
License Manager	Licensing
Migration Tool for NetWare	No counterpart
Network Client Administrator	Use \I386\Adminpak.msi to install WS2003 administrative tools on workstations Use Remote Installation Services (RIS) for network installation of workstations
Network Monitor	Network Monitor
Performance Monitor	Performance
Remote Access Admin	Routing and Remote Access
Server Manager	Computer Management → System Tools → Shared Folders (to manage shared folders and send console messages to connected users) Active Directory Users and Computers (to add a computer to a domain) Active Directory Sites and Services (to manually force directory replication between domain controllers)
System Policy Editor	Group Policy snap-in (can also be accessed from Active Directory Users and Computers and other consoles)
User Manager	Computer Management → System Tools → Local Users and Groups (to manage local accounts on standalone servers in a workgroup) Local Security Policy (to configure password restrictions, account lockout, audit policy, and user rights on standalone servers in a workgroup)
User Manager for Domains	Active Directory Users and Computers (to manage domain accounts and to configure password restrictions, account lockout, audit policy, and user rights through Group Policy) Active Directory Domains and Trusts (to manage trusts)
Windows NT Diagnostics	All Programs → Accessories → System Tools → System Information
WINS Manager	WINS[a]

[a] Can also be accessed under Computer Management → Services.

Table 1-2 compares special folders and utilities in Windows NT with their Windows Server 2003 counterparts.

Table 1-2. Special folders and utilities in Windows NT versus Windows Server 2003

NT folder or utility	WS2003 counterpart
My Computer	*My Computer*
Network Neighborhood	*My Network Places*
C:\Winnt (system folder)	*C:\Windows*
C:\Winnt\Profiles (location where local user profiles are stored)	*C:\Documents and Settings* (unless an upgrade from NT was performed, in which case it remains in its original location)
Default location where applications save their files varies in Windows NT	*My Documents* folder for compliant applications (unless an upgrade from NT was performed, in which case it remains in its original location)
Start → Find	Start → Search
Start → Help	Start → Help and Support
Start → Programs → Command Prompt	Start → Command Prompt
Start → Programs → Accessories → Windows NT Explorer	Start → Windows Explorer
Start → Settings → Active Desktop	Right-click on desktop → Active Desktop
Start → Settings → Folder Options	Control Panel → Folder Options
Accessories → Dial-up Networking	Control Panel → Network Connections
Accessories → Telnet	`telnet` command

Finally, Table 1-3 compares Control Panel utilities in Windows NT with their Windows Server 2003 counterparts.

Table 1-3. Control Panel utilities in Windows NT versus Windows Server 2003

NT Control Panel utility	WS2003 counterpart
Console	Command Prompt → right-click on Control Menu → Defaults
Devices	Computer Management → System Tools → Device Manager
Internet	Internet Options
Modems	Phone and Modem Options
Network → Network Identification	System → Computer Name
Network → {Services | Protocols | Adapters}	Network Connections → Local Area Connection → Properties
Network → Bindings	All Programs → Accessories → Communications → Network Connections → Advanced → Advanced Settings
ODBC	Administrative Tools → Data Sources (ODBC)
Ports	Computer Management → System Tools → Device Manager
Regional Settings	Regional and Language Options
SCSI Adapters	Computer Management → System Tools → Device Manager
Server	Computer Management → System Tools → Shared Folders
Services	Administrative Tools → Services
System → General	System → General
System → User Profiles	System → Advanced → User Profiles → Settings
System → Performance	System → Advanced → Performance → Settings
System → Environment	System → Advanced → Environment Variables
System → Startup/Shutdown	System → Advanced → Startup and Recovery
System → Hardware Profiles	System → Hardware → Hardware Profiles

NT Control Panel utility	WS2003 counterpart
Tape Devices	Computer Management → System Tools → Device Manager
Telephony	Phone and Modem Options → Dialing Rules
UPS	Power Options → UPS

Tips for Transitioning

The remainder of this chapter provides some quick tips for NT admins transitioning to WS2003. These are listed in alphabetical order rather than order of importance. This list is by no means exhaustive in coverage; for detailed information about common WS2003 administrative tasks, see the Task Map in Chapter 3 and the cross references listed here to various topics in Chapters 4 and 5.

Account Policy

Configuring account policy—password and account lockout restrictions—was relatively easy in Windows NT using User Manager for Domains. In WS2003, you have to use Group Policy if you are in a domain environment, and you need a good understanding of Group Policy before attempting this. In a simple workgroup environment with standalone servers, you can edit the local security policy directly instead, which is simpler. Either way, see *Group Policy* in Chapter 4 before you try experimenting with configuring account policy. If you want to dive in right away, you can find the account policy settings in either:

Local Security Policy
    Security Settings → Account Policies

Group Policy
    Computer Configuration → Windows Settings → Security Settings → Account Policies

Activation

If you've tried installing WS2003, you've already been prompted to activate your product, unless you're an enterprise client with a bulk volume licensing agreement with Microsoft. Activation is an antipiracy measure implemented by Microsoft on Windows XP and later; see *Installation* in Chapter 4 for more information.

Active Directory

Implementing Active Directory (AD) for an enterprise is not a trivial task. You can find information about administering various aspects of Active Directory in the topics *Active Directory*, *Domain*, *Domain Controller*, *Forest*, *OU*, *Site*, and *Trusts* in Chapter 4. You'll also find some tips on planning AD implementation scattered among these topics, but for a more thorough and systematic treatment of planning AD implementation, see *Active Directory* by Robbie Allen (O'Reilly).

Administration Tools Pack

Instead of walking over to a domain controller to run Active Directory Users and Computers from the local console, you can install a complete set of WS2003 administration tools on a Windows XP Professional workstation and then use that as your main administrator workstation. Note that you must have Windows XP Service Pack 1 or later installed before installing these tools on your workstation. To install the Windows Server 2003 Administration Tools Pack, double-click on *Adminpak.msi* in the \i386 folder on your WS2003 product CD.

In order to use a Windows XP Professional machine to administer Internet Information Services 6 (IIS 6) remotely, you need Windows XP Service Pack 2 or later.

Administrative Tools

If you're just starting out with WS2003, the two most important administrative tools you need to become familiar with here are:

Computer Management
Manages disks, shares, event logs, performance logs, services, and devices on a computer. You can use Computer Management to administer these things on either the local computer or on a remote computer—except that you can't update device drivers or uninstall devices on remote computers. (Device Manager operates in read-only mode when connected to a remote computer.)

Active Directory Users and Computers
Creates and manages domain user accounts and domain local, global, and universal groups. You can also use this tool to manage Group Policy settings.

For more information on these two tools, see *Administrative Tools* in Chapter 4. These two tools, and most administrative tools in WS2003, are implemented with the Microsoft Management Console (MMC), a management framework that uses snap-ins to create administrative tools with a common look and feel. The MMC can also build your own customized administrative tools, which can then be distributed to administrators by email or shared over the network; see *Microsoft Management Console* in Chapter 4 for more information.

Audit Policy

Configuring an audit policy was relatively easy in Windows NT using User Manager for Domains. In WS2003, you have to use Group Policy if you are in a domain environment, and you need a good understanding of Group Policy before you attempt this. In a simple workgroup environment with standalone servers, you can edit the Local Security Policy directly instead, which is simpler. Either way, see *Group Policy* in Chapter 4 before you try experimenting with configuring audit policy. If you want to dive in right away, you can find the audit policy settings in either:

Local Security Policy
Security Settings → Local Policies → Audit Policy

Group Policy
> Computer Configuration → Windows Settings → Security Settings → Local Policies → Audit Policy

Browsing the Web

The first time you open Windows Explorer on WS2003 to browse the Web, you'll see a dialog box saying:

> Microsoft Internet Explorer's Enhanced Security Configuration is currently configured on your server. This enhanced level of security reduces the risk of attack from Web-based content that is not secure, but may also prevent web sites from displaying correctly and restrict access to network resources.

This feature is one of the "secure out-of-the-box" enhancements of WS2003, which installs in a more-or-less locked-down state as opposed to NT which installs in a more-or-less wide-open state. In effect, this means that the security setting for the Internet zone is set to High, so if you want to browse a relatively benign site such as Google, you have a few choices:

- Add *google.com* to your Trusted Sites zone by entering the URL and then:

  File → Add this site to → Trusted Sites Zone

- Change the setting for the Internet zone to Medium so you can browse any Internet site:

  Internet Explorer → Tools → Internet Options → Security → Internet → Medium

- Disable the Internet Explorer Enhanced Security Configuration feature entirely:

  Control Panel → Add or Remove Programs → Add/Remove Windows Components → clear checkbox for Internet Explorer Enhanced Security Configuration

The best solution is the first one. In general, you shouldn't be browsing the Web on a server anyway; use a workstation instead to download drivers and perform similar tasks.

Computer Names

If you expect to have both Windows NT and WS2003 coexist for a while on your network, select NetBIOS computer names that will be compatible with both platforms (maximum 15 characters). Also, since WS2003 uses DNS as its name-resolution service when Active Directory is deployed, make sure your computer names are DNS-compatible as well (this means no underscores, periods, or spaces—only letters, numbers, and dashes).

Speaking of computer names, there is also the issue of share names to consider. When naming a shared folder or printer, it's a good idea to avoid using spaces or special characters if your network contains a mix of WS2003 and other computers (such as Windows NT, Unix, and so on). Otherwise, some clients might have difficulty connecting to your WS2003 shares.

By the way, if you change the name of a domain or domain controller using the *rendom* utility on the WS2003 product CD, this can cause problems if you have downlevel Windows NT servers on your network and are using WINS for name resolution for these servers. This is because the WINS databases maintains the former name of your domain controller for a period of time, which can cause name-resolution problems for clients unless the offending records are flushed from the database.

Delegation

Delegation is a powerful feature of WS2003 that helps administrators shuffle off some of their administrative responsibility to other trusted (trustworthy) users before overwork causes them to "shuffle off this mortal coil." For more information see *Delegation* in Chapter 4.

Desktop Stuff

One of the first things an NT admin will notice regarding the WS2003 desktop is that the standard NT desktop icons of My Computer, Network Neighborhood, Inbox, Internet Explorer, and My Briefcase are missing (only Recycle Bin is present). To get them back, do this:

> Right-click on desktop → Properties → Desktop → Customize Desktop → General → select the icons you want to appear on the desktop

You can also hide/display all desktop icons at any time by:

> Right-click on desktop → Arrange Icons By → Show Desktop Icons

The desktop for WS2003 is basically that of Windows XP, so if you're familiar with XP you should have no trouble with the basic desktop and navigation features of WS2003. For example, to select the Luna theme used by XP, first start the Theme service:

> Administrative Tools → Services → double-click on Themes → Startup Type → Automatic → Apply → Start

Now enable the Luna theme:

> Right-click on desktop → Properties → Themes → Theme → Browse → C:\ *Windows\Resources\Themes* → *Luna.theme* → Open → Apply

For more information on desktop stuff like this, see *Windows XP in a Nutshell* by David Korp, Tim O'Reilly, and Troy Mott (O'Reilly).

DHCP and APIPA

If you are going to deploy and manage IP addressing on WS2003 using DHCP, you may want to disable the Automatic Private IP Addressing (APIPA) feature on your machines. If a system is configured for DHCP but is unable to contact a DHCP server when it first starts up, APIPA automatically assigns it an IP address from the reserved address range, 169.254.0.1 through 169.254.255.254. No warning message appears to say that the system has used APIPA instead of DHCP to obtain its address. The effects can be nasty, resulting in an inability to access other machines on the network because they are on a different subnet. Chapter 4 includes more details on DHCP and APIPA; see *DHCP* for DHCP issues and for APIPA, see *TCP/IP*.

Disks and Disk Quotas

Microsoft has borrowed the concept of mounted volumes from Unix and implemented the ability to mount a volume in an empty folder on an NTFS volume in WS2003. This feature helps you get beyond the 24-letter limit for mapped drives in Windows NT (see *Disks* in Chapter 4 for details). Note that, if used carelessly, this feature can cause problems; nothing prevents you from mounting a volume in a folder on a mounted volume, or even mounting a volume in a folder on itself!

A good tip when implementing disk quotas is to configure global quotas only and not quotas for individual users. Not following this recommendation can make quota administration a real headache.

DNS and NetBIOS

DNS is used as the name-locator service for Active Directory in WS2003. This means you must have DNS servers implemented on your network if you want to connect to resources without specifying their IP address. For more information see *Active Directory* and *DNS* in Chapter 4.

NetBIOS is still an option for name resolution, however, and NetBIOS over TCP/IP is enabled by default (even in WS2003 functional-level domains) so downlevel (Windows NT/9x) computer names can be resolved if such systems are present. You can disable NetBIOS over TCP/IP using the Advanced TCP/IP settings box (see *TCP/IP* in Chapter 4). Note that, if you disable NetBIOS over TCP/IP, you can't restrict a user's access to specific workstations using the Account tab of the user account's property sheet because this feature requires NetBIOS over TCP/IP in order to work.

Domains and Domain Controllers

WS2003 domains are quite different from NT domains (see *Active Directory*, *Domain*, and *Forest* in Chapter 4 for details). For example, you no longer need to separate master (account) domains from slave (resource) domains or manually establish trusts between domains. New domains are created by promoting standalone or member servers to the role of domain controller using Manage Your Server, which is accessible directly from the Start menu. You can create three kinds of domains this way:

- The first domain controller of the root domain of the first tree in a new forest— in other words, the very first WS2003 domain controller on your network
- The first domain controller of a new root domain, creating a new tree in an existing forest, with a two-way transitive trust created automatically between the new root domain and the root domains of existing trees in the forest

- The first domain controller of a new child domain under an existing parent domain, with a two-way transitive trust created automatically between the parent and child domains

In Windows NT, one domain controller in each domain—the primary domain controller (PDC)—was special. The PDC was the only domain controller with a writable copy of the domain directory database, and all changes made to user, group, or computer accounts in the domain had to be made on the PDC. (If the PDC was unavailable, those changes could not be made.) All other domain controllers in the domain were backup domain controllers (BDCs), which contained read-only versions of the domain directory database.

With WS2003, domain controllers are all peers, and each domain controller contains a full writable copy of the Active Directory database. Replication between domain controllers follows a method called *multimaster replication* in which there is no single master domain controller. If you look under the surface, you find out that this is not quite the case. There are actually five special domain controller roles called *flexible single master of operations* roles or FSMO roles, which are found only on certain domain controllers in an enterprise. For information on these special roles, see *Domain Controller* in Chapter 4.

Speaking of PDCs and BDCs, the usual way to upgrade a Windows NT domain to WS2003 is to upgrade the PDC first, then the BDCs. The hitch is to make sure the former PDC is available on the network when you are upgrading the BDCs. If it isn't, the first BDC you upgrade will think it's the first domain controller in the domain and assume some of the operations master roles discussed earlier. Then when the former PDC comes back online, you will have a serious conflict between them, and the only way to resolve it is to wipe your former BDC and reinstall it from scratch.

Dual-Boot

I don't recommend dual-boot configurations except for playing around at home, and you should know that volumes formatted with the version of NTFS on WS2003 (called NTFS5) support dual boots only on Windows NT 4.0 with Service Pack 4 or higher. If you are using an earlier version of NT and want to maintain it on a dual-boot configuration, you will be unable to use advanced features of WS2003's NTFS, such as disk quotas and the Encrypting File System (EFS). Speaking of EFS, just because you encrypt a file or folder using EFS doesn't mean you can't accidentally delete it!

Emergency Repair Disk

There's no more ERD in WS2003. Instead, you can try Last Known Good Configuration, Safe Mode, the Recovery Console, and Automated System Recovery (pretty much in that order) if you have problems booting your system. See *Advanced Options Menu*, *Backup*, and *Recovery Console* in Chapter 4 for more information.

Event Logs

Event logs are pretty much the same as they were in Windows NT, although there are more of them on domain controllers and DNS servers, and an MMC console (Event Viewer) now manages them. If you run a high-security networking environment, you can configure a WS2003 system to halt when the event log becomes full. You need to configure a registry setting to do this; see *Event Logs* in Chapter 4 for more information. Also, when you install or upgrade a machine to WS2003, configure your event log size and wraparound settings immediately so you won't lose valuable data that might be useful for troubleshooting later on.

Hardware

WS2003 is forgiving of problems created when you update devices with incorrect or corrupt drivers. Such updates can sometimes prevent the system from booting to the point you can log on. If this is the case, simply press the F8 function key when the boot-loader menu prompts you to select an operating system to boot. This causes the Advanced Startup Options menu to appear. One of the menu items is the familiar Last Known Good Configuration, which restores the system to the state in which it last booted successfully. If this fails, you can select the Safe Mode option to boot using a minimal set of device drivers. For more information, see *Advanced Options Menu* in Chapter 4.

Speaking of the boot menu, in a normal Windows NT installation this menu displayed two options: Normal Boot and VGA Mode Boot. In WS2003, however, there is only one boot option: Normal Boot (there is no VGA Mode Boot menu option because safe mode takes care of this). As a result, in a normal WS2003 installation with only one operating system installed, the boot menu doesn't appear at all. In this case, to open the Advanced Startup Options menu, just press F8 while it says "Starting Windows" at the bottom of the screen. If the Recovery Console is installed on a machine, however, the boot menu does appear because the Recovery Console is essentially a different operating system (a command-line version of WS2003). See *Recovery Console* in Chapter 4 for details.

For general information about managing hardware devices and device drivers, see *Devices* in Chapter 4.

Installing and Upgrading

The Setup Manager wizard-based tool can perform unattended installations of WS2003; it's included in the *\SUPPORT\TOOLS* folder on your WS2003 product CD. It walks you through the process of creating an answer file; see *Installation* in Chapter 4 for more information.

If you plan to upgrade NT machines to WS2003, make sure their hardware supports it. Most shops will likely elect to install WS2003 on fresh machines instead and put their old NT boxes out to pasture afterward.

With Windows NT, some administrators chose to designate their boot partition as FAT while using NTFS to secure their data partitions. This enabled them to repair missing or corrupt system or driver files by booting from a DOS disk when these missing or corrupt files prevent successfully booting the system. This hack is no longer necessary with WS2003 because of Safe Mode and the Recovery Console, so the bottom line is that you should use only NTFS for your WS2003 boot volume because it is more secure than FAT or FAT32.

IntelliMirror

IntelliMirror is simply a buzzword for a hodge-podge of WS2003 features that enable users to access their desktops and data conveniently from any computer on (or off) the network. See *Files and Folders*, *Group Policy*, and *Users* in Chapter 4 for more information about offline folders, folder redirection, roaming user profiles, and other IntelliMirror technologies.

Permissions

Like Windows NT, WS2003 provides two sets of permissions for access to files and folders: NTFS permissions and shared-folder permissions. The basic approach for secure shared resources is the same as with NT, but NTFS permissions require some relearning in WS2003 because they are more complex than they were in NT. See *Permissions* in Chapter 4 for more information.

Printers

One new feature of WS2003 is remote management of printers across a network (or over the Internet) using a web browser; see *Printing* in Chapter 4 for more information. Otherwise, printing is much the same in WS2003 as it was in NT. By the way, always let WS2003 detect Plug and Play printers and install drivers for them automatically; if you install the driver manually and reboot your machine, you may end up with two printers for the same print device! Also, specify a location for your printer when you create it using the Add Printer Wizard. Users will then be able to search for printers by location when they search Active Directory using Start → Search.

Remote Access

If you have migrated a Windows NT domain to WS2003 but still have Windows NT member servers running RAS (or RRAS) on your network, note that they will be unable to communicate with Active Directory to authenticate users trying to initiate RAS sessions. Either upgrade the RAS servers to domain controllers, or weaken RAS permissions for your WS2003 domain by adding the Everyone built-in special identity to the Pre–Windows 2000 Compatible Access built-in group; this allows the RAS server to use NTLM for authenticating RAS users. For general information on remote access in WS2003, see *Routing and Remote Access* in Chapter 4.

Rights

Configuring user rights was relatively easy in Windows NT using User Manager for Domains. In WS2003 you have to use Group Policy if you are in a domain environment, and you need a good understanding of Group Policy before you attempt this. In a simple workgroup environment with standalone servers, you can edit the Local Security Policy directly instead, which is simpler. Either way, see *Group Policy* in Chapter 4 before you try experimenting with configuring user rights. If you want to dive in right away, you can find the user rights settings in either:

Local Security Policy
Security Settings → Local Policies → User Rights Assignment

Group Policy
Computer Configuration → Windows Settings → Security Settings → Local Policies → User Rights Assignment

Scheduling Tasks

Although the Windows NT 4.0 Server Resource Kit included a GUI utility to complement the at command-line scheduling tool, WS2003 carries this further with Task Scheduler, a wizard for scheduling tasks to be run (see *Tasks* in Chapter 4 for more information). The at command is still available for batch scripting purposes, but it is best not to use it because of compatibility issues between it and Task Manager. Instead, use the new schtasks command, which is covered in Chapter 5.

Secondary Logon

Best practice for administrators is to have two separate user accounts:

- An ordinary user account for browsing the Web, checking email, and doing other mundane stuff
- A Domain Admins account for performing administrative tasks

In Windows NT, if an administrator was logged on with her ordinary account and had to perform an administrative task, she had to log off, log on with her admin account, perform the task, log off, and log back on with her ordinary user account. WS2003 makes this easier with Secondary Logon, a way of performing a task with different credentials than those used for the current logon session.

To illustrate, say you are logged on with your ordinary user account and want to run some command-line scripts using Administrator credentials. First open a command-prompt window by:

Start → Command Prompt

Now type:

```
runas /user:domain\username cmd
```

where *username* is your Administrator account in *domain*. You'll be prompted to enter your password, after which a second command-prompt window opens up on top of the first that lets you execute commands using your Administrator credentials. The current directory of this new command prompt window is set to *%SystemRoot%\System32*, which is where most administrative tools (MMC consoles saved as *.msc* files) are located. For example, to open the Computer Management console as Administrator, type the following in the new window:

```
compmgmt.msc
```

Alternatively, you can type the following instead in your original window:

```
runas /user:domain\username "mmc %windir%\system32\compmgmt.msc"
```

You can also find the icon for the file *compmgmt.msc* in *C:\Windows\system32* using Windows Explorer, right-click on it, and select Runas from the shortcut menu. For more information on Secondary Logon, see *runas* in Chapter 5.

Sending Console Messages

In NT you could use Server Manager to send a console message to connected users before unsharing a shared folder or rebooting a server. In WS2003 you can use Computer Management to do the same; see *Shared Folders* in Chapter 4 for more information.

Shared Folders

If you have a lot of shared folders scattered across different file servers, there are two ways to make it simpler for your users to locate the shared resources they need:

- Use the Distributed File System (DFS) to combine your shared folders into one or more DFS trees. Users just connect to a DFS tree and browse the tree for the share they need, and they don't need to know the name of the file server on which the share is located. See *DFS* in Chapter 4 for more information.

- Publish the shares in Active Directory so users can search for them by location and by using friendly names. In this way users don't need to know the names of the file servers hosting the shares. You can also configure permissions on the shared folder object you publish to Active Directory—not to control access to the share but to control who can find and view the information you have published to Active Directory about the share. See *Active Directory* in Chapter 4 for more information.

For general information about how to manage shared folders, see *Shared Folders* in Chapter 4.

Sites

Managing directory replication between Windows NT domain controllers and sites connected by slow WAN links was a hit-and-miss procedure of juggling various registry entries such as ChangeLogSize, ReplicationGovernor, and so on. Things are simpler in WS2003: use Active Directory Sites and Service to create sites that map to the physical (geographical) topology of your network, map well-connected subnets to each site, and create and configure site links to join sites together and control directory replication between them. See *Site* in Chapter 4 for more information.

System Policy

If you have an NT network with System Policy implemented for locking down client desktops and other features, you should be aware that, when you upgrade your network to WS2003, these System Policies will not be upgraded to Group Policies. The reason is that Group Policy modifies special areas of the registry rather than the actual registry entries of the settings managed, whereas System Policy directly modifies the registry settings involved.

Likewise, if you migrate a portion of your network to WS2003, be aware that any Group Policies you configure will have no effect on your remaining NT machines. Therefore, you may want to continue using the NT System Policy Editor (*poledit. exe*) to create and manage System Policy on your downlevel machines (place the *Ntconfig.pol* file in the *sysvol* folder on your WS2003 domain controller for it to be applied). For more information, see *Group Policy* in Chapter 4.

Terminal Services

Terminal Services has been split in two in WS2003 into:

Terminal Services
   used for running applications from a central terminal server and requiring special licensing

Remote Desktop
   used for remote administration of WS2003 machines and supporting up to two concurrent connections

Administrators familiar with the Terminal Services Edition of NT will see many enhancements in WS2003, including improved display and sound capability.

Trusts

WS2003 domains are simpler to manage than NT domains because two-way transitive trusts are automatically established between parent and child domains in a domain tree and between the root domains of trees in a forest. However, the fine print is that these trusts are transitive only after you convert your domains to Windows 2000 native functional level—in other words, when you no longer have any remaining BDCs in your NT domains. For more information on functional levels, see *Domain* and *Forest* in Chapter 4.

Users and Groups

What NT called global users are called domain users in WS2003 (see *Users* in Chapter 4 for more information). Domain user accounts are created and managed using the Active Directory Users and Computers console, which is quite different from the old User Manager for Domains tool in NT. You can also use two command-line tools, csvde and ldifde, to simplify administration of large numbers of accounts through batch operations (see these topics in Chapter 5 for more info).

Groups are more complicated and flexible in WS2003, which now has three kinds of groups compared to NT's two, namely:

- Global groups (similar to global groups in NT)
- Domain local groups (similar to local groups in NT)
- Universal groups (not found in NT)

The new universal groups and the enhanced nesting functionality of domain local and global groups is available only for WS2003 domains running in Windows 2000 native or WS2003 functional level. For more information about functional levels and groups, see *Domain* and *Groups* in Chapter 4.

XP Professional

Upgrading your NT servers to WS2003 has clear advantages for enterprises, the most obvious being the improved scalability and manageability associated with Active Directory. But what about upgrading your desktop machines to Windows XP Professional? This is bound to be a costly exercise because hardware on existing machines will have to be beefed up or replaced entirely. Is it worth it? Probably, for several reasons:

- Remote management of XP Professional computers is a breeze using the Computer Management console, and it's bound to reduce your help-desk costs significantly.
- Group Policy enables enterprise-wide management of desktop settings, software installation, roving desktops, and other useful features.
- Costs for training users will be minimal if users are already familiar with the desktop features of Windows 95/98 and Windows NT 4.0.

I'll stop there lest I sound like an ad for Microsoft, but the fact is that there are compelling reasons why migrating desktop computers to XP Professional makes sense.

2

2000 → 2003

This brief chapter is designed to help Windows 2000 (W2K) administrators quickly transition to Windows Server 2003 (WS2003) by highlighting some important differences between administering the two platforms. For Windows NT administrators looking for similar help transitioning, see Chapter 1. W2K administrators may want to read through Chapter 1 also, because it covers a few points regarding WS2003 not covered in this present chapter.

What Changed?

I'll start by briefly summarizing a number of minor and often unnecessary changes that are likely to cause frustrated W2K administrators to say, "Why on earth did they do that?" Then I'll conclude the chapter with a quick summary of new features and enhancements that make WS2003 even better than W2K from the point of view of administering the platform. The changes listed here are more or less in the order you might encounter them as you begin administering the new platform.

If you're already familiar with the Windows XP Professional platform, the transition to WS2003 will be considerably easier because the desktop for the two platforms is almost identical, except that the (in my opinion) ugly Luna theme of XP is replaced by the standard Windows Classic theme in WS2003. For a good introduction to XP, see *Windows XP in a Nutshell* (O'Reilly).

Where Are the Icons?

By default, the only icon on the WS2003 desktop is Recycle Bin, which can be a bit unnerving the first time you log on to a WS2003 machine. To make icons for My Computer, My Network Places, My Documents, and Internet Explorer visible on the desktop, do the following:

Right-click on desktop → Properties → Desktop → Customize Desktop → General → select icons to make visible on desktop

You can also hide/display all desktop icons at any time by:

Right-click on desktop → Arrange Icons By → Show Desktop Icons

Display Properties

If you've opened the Display Properties using the earlier procedure, you'll immediately notice that they've renamed some of the tabs and rearranged where the settings are found. There's a lot of this renaming and rearranging in WS2003, and it can be frustrating to administrators who are used to the way they've been performing common tasks in W2K. Table 2-1 compares the Display Properties tabs and settings for the two platforms.

Table 2-1. Display properties tabs and settings in W2K versus WS2003

Old way (W2K)	New way (WS2003)
Appearance	Appearance
Background	Desktop
Effects	To change icons: Desktop → Customize Desktop → General
	Transitions and other effects: Appearance → Effects
N.A.	Themes
Screen Saver	Screen Saver
Settings	Settings
Web	Desktop → Customize Desktop → Web

System Properties

While we're right-clicking on desktop items, let's open the System Properties page by right-clicking on My Computer and selecting Properties. Again, note that some of the tabs and settings for this commonly used item have been renamed and rearranged as detailed in Table 2-2.

Table 2-2. System properties tabs and settings in W2K versus WS2003

Old way (W2K)	New way (WS2003)
Advanced → Environment Variables	Advanced → Environment Variables (moved to bottom of page)
Advanced → Performance	Advanced → Performance → Settings (lots more options for visual effects such as menu fade-outs and window shadows)
Advanced → Startup and Recovery	Advanced → Startup and Recovery → Settings
Control Panel → Automatic Updates (with Service Pack 3)	Automatic Updates
General	General
Hardware	Hardware
N/A	Advanced → Error Reporting
N/A	Remote → Remote Assistance
Network Identification	Computer Name

Table 2-2. System properties tabs and settings in W2K versus WS2003 (continued)

Old way (W2K)	New way (WS2003)
Use Add/Remove Programs to install Terminal Services, selecting Remote Administration Mode	Remote → Remote Desktop
User Profiles	Advanced → User Profiles → Settings

Network Connections

Right-click on My Network Places and select Properties. In W2K, this opens the Network and Dial-up Connections window, but in WS2003 this window is called Network Connections—another subtle name change. Exploring the various menu options available, note that:

> Advanced → Dial-up Preferences

now becomes:

> Advanced → Remote Access Preferences

even though it still refers only to dial-up connections. For more on network connections, see *Connections* in Chapter 4.

Start Menu

Let's continue by examining the changes to the Start menu, the launching point for running applications on W2K and WS2003. There are a few improvements here, but there are also a lot of unnecessary changes that will require you to perform familiar actions 200 times in totally different ways (since psychologists say it takes about 200 repetitions of an action to form a habit). The most frustrating change to me is placing the All Programs option at the *bottom* of the Start menu in WS2003, when in W2K the equivalent Programs option is found near the *top* of the menu. Argh! Anyway, Table 2-3 summarizes the main differences between the Start menu in the two platforms.

Table 2-3. Start menu in W2K versus WS2003

Old way (W2K)	New way (WS2003)
Start → Accessories → Windows Explorer	Start → Windows Explorer
Start → Documents → My Documents	Argh! It's gone! Right-click on Taskbar → Properties → Start Menu → Start menu → Customized → Advanced → Start menu items → My Documents → Display as a menu → OK then Start → Documents → My Documents
Start → Help	Start → Help and Support
Start → Programs	Start → All Programs
Start → Programs → Administrative Tools	Start → Administrative Tools
Start → Run	Start → Run
Start → Search → {For Files or Folders | On the Internet | For People}	Start → Search
Start → Settings → Control Panel	Start → Control Panel

Table 2-3. Start menu in W2K versus WS2003 (continued)

Old way (W2K)	New way (WS2003)
Start → Settings → Network and Dial-up Connections	Start → Control Panel → Network Connections
Start → Settings → Printers	Start → Printers and Faxes
Start → Settings → Taskbar and Start Menu	Right-click on Taskbar → Properties
Start → Shut Down	Start → Shut Down
Start → Windows Update	Start → Control Panel → System → Automatic Updates

Of course, you can also switch to the good old Classic Start menu if you prefer by doing the following:

> Right-click on Taskbar → Properties → Start Menu → Classic Start menu

Administrative Tools

Fortunately, the administrative tools haven't changed much from W2K to WS2003, but there are a few things that may trip you up initially. First, the default set of tools installed on a standalone server has changed somewhat, as Table 2-4 shows. The base platforms compared in this table are Windows 2000 Advanced Server and Windows Server 2003, Enterprise Edition.

Table 2-4. Default set of administrative tools installed on W2K versus WS2003

Old platform (W2K)	New platform (WS2003)
	Certification Authority
	Cluster Administrator
Component Services	Component Services
Computer Management	Computer Management
Configure Your Server	Configure Your Server
Data Sources (ODBC)	Data Sources (ODBC)
Distributed File System	Distributed File System
Event Viewer	Event Viewer
Internet Services Manager	
Licensing	Licensing
Local Security Policy	Local Security Policy
	Manage Your Server
	Microsoft .NET Framework 1.1 Configuration
	Microsoft .NET Framework 1.1 Wizards
	Network Load Balancing Manager
Performance	Performance
	Remote Desktops
Routing and Remote Access	Routing and Remote Access
Service Extensions Administrator	Service Extensions Administrator
Services	Services
Telnet Server Administration	

Table 2-4. Default set of administrative tools installed on W2K versus WS2003 (continued)

Old platform (W2K)	New platform (WS2003)
	Terminal Server Licensing
	Terminal Services Configuration
	Terminal Services Manager

While a few of these tools have been enhanced with new functionality in WS2003, some of them have also been changed in ways that might be more frustrating than helpful to administrators. A good example of this is the Routing and Remote Access console, in which the Routing and Remote Access Setup Wizard used to enable and configure RRAS has been completely redesigned without really adding that much new functionality (see *Routing and Remote Access* in Chapter 4 for more information).

Another seemingly arbitrary change in functionality is Computer Management: the useful System Information node under System Tools in the W2K version of this tool has disappeared in the WS2003 version. As a result, to access System Information you now have to do the following:

> Start → All Programs → Accessories → System Tools → System Information

Of course, you might consider starting System Information from the command line, but unfortunately its executable *msinfo32.exe* isn't in the default system path. To access it, you either have to type the full path (*C:\Program Files\Common Files\ Microsoft Shared\MSInfo\msinfo32.exe*) or add this path to your PATH environment variable. Alternatively, you can create a shortcut to the tool on your desktop or modify your Start menu. The point is, why make this change to Computer Management in the first place? Another seemingly arbitrary change is the omission of the Logical Drives node under Storage, but this is not as significant because the same information can be obtained from the Disk Management node anyway. For more on Computer Management, see *Administrative Tools* in Chapter 4.

Control Panel

There isn't much to trip you up regarding changes to Control Panel utilities, other than the following:

- Add/Remove Hardware is now called Add Hardware (but you can still remove it too).
- Add/Remove Programs is now called Add or Remove Programs (does Microsoft have something against forward slashes?).
- Date/Time is now called Date and Time (it seems they do in fact have something against slashes).
- Network and Dial-up Connections is now Network Connections (but you can still create dial-up connections too).
- Printers is now called Printers and Faxes (even if you aren't running a fax server).

- Regional Options is now called Regional and Language Options (which makes sense I suppose).
- Sounds and Multimedia is now called Sounds and Audio Devices (even though video codecs are included).

In addition, there are three new Control Panel utilities also found in XP, namely: Speech, Stored User Names and Passwords, and Taskbar and Start Menu.

Browse the Web

Let's try one more thing: start Internet Explorer and see what happens. You'll see a dialog box saying,

> Microsoft Internet Explorer's Enhanced Security Configuration is currently configured on your server. This enhanced level of security reduces the risk of attack from Web-based content that is not secure, but may also prevent web sites from displaying correctly and restrict access to network resources.

This feature is one of the "secure out-of-the-box" enhancements of WS2003, which installs in a more-or-less locked-down state as opposed to W2K which installs in a more-or-less wide-open state. Basically what it means is that the security setting for the Internet zone is set to High, so if you want to browse a relatively benign site like Google, you can either:

- Add *google.com* to your Trusted Sites zone by entering the URL and then:

  File → Add this site to → Trusted Sites Zone
- Change the setting for the Internet zone to Medium so you can browse any Internet site:

  Internet Explorer → Tools → Internet Options → Security → Internet → Medium
- Disable the Internet Explorer Enhanced Security Configuration feature entirely:

  Control Panel → Add or Remove Programs → Add/Remove Windows Components → clear checkbox for Internet Explorer Enhanced Security Configuration

The best solution is the first one, and in general you shouldn't be browsing the Web on a server anyway, use a workstation instead to download drivers and perform similar tasks.

While this new security feature is probably to be commended—who is going to read the Drudge Report on their server anyway—don't you think Microsoft could have at least added *.microsoft.com* to the Trusted Sites zone by default? After all, when you use Help and Support to search for information on some topic, the results list includes some links to Knowledge Base articles on *support.microsoft. com*. When you try to read those articles and all those security dialog boxes start popping up, it can be more than a bit annoying.

New Features and Enhancements

Anyway, now that I've vented my frustration a bit, I have to confess that I feel the new features and enhancements in WS2003 far outweigh the silly or unnecessary changes described earlier. Not only is WS2003 a more scalable platform than W2K, it's also more manageable and secure. Because this book focuses on the core tasks of everyday administration, this section highlights key new features W2K administrators should be aware of as you prepare to transition to WS2003, more or less in the order you might discover them as you start playing around with the new platform.

Activation

If you've tried installing WS2003, you've already been prompted to activate your product, unless you're an enterprise client with some sort of volume licensing agreement with Microsoft. Activation is an antipiracy measure implemented by Microsoft on Windows XP and later; see *Installation* in Chapter 4 for more information. Whether Activation is a plus or a minus is debatable, but it's a fact of life from now on.

Stay Current

When you first log on to WS2003 as Administrator, you'll be confronted with a notification bubble (or whatever they call it) that says "Stay current with Automatic Updates." This Automatic Updates feature was first included in Service Pack 3 for W2K, so you may already be familiar with it. If not, see *Automatic Updates* in Chapter 4 for more information about using this feature to automatically download and install the latest security patches from Microsoft as they are released.

Manage Your Server

When you first log on to WS2003 as Administrator, you'll also be confronted with the new Manage Your Server tool, which replaces (and incorporates) the old Configure Your Server Wizard in W2K. Manage Your Server lets you add roles to your server to turn it into a file server, print server, application (web) server, DHCP server, domain controller, and so on. Manage Your Server isn't the only way to add such roles however; for example, if you simply share a folder, your server automatically assumes the file server role.

My opinion is that Manage Your Server is great for initial server configuration tasks such as installing Active Directory on a smaller network, but beyond that the tool isn't really much use, mainly because of its layout. It's got way too much whitespace, which means you have to scroll to use it if you have more than a couple of roles configured on your server.

Administration Tools Pack

If you're really serious about managing your WS2003 servers, install the Windows Server 2003 Administration Tools Pack using the Windows Installer file

Adminpak.msi located in the \i386 folder on your WS2003 product CD. The Admin Tools pack installs a full slate of tools for managing any WS2003 machine including domain controllers, and by installing this pack on a Windows XP Professional machine, you can then use this machine as your main administrator workstation for managing WS2003 servers anywhere on your network. It's a big improvement on walking over to a domain controller in order to run Active Directory Users and Computers from the local console every time you have to reset some user's password. Note that you must have Windows XP Service Pack 1 or later installed before installing these tools on your XP machine and in order to use an XP machine to remotely administer Internet Information Services 6 (IIS 6), you need Windows XP Service Pack 2 or later.

Convenience Consoles

Tucked away on the Admin Tools Pack are three new MMC consoles that combine the functionality of a number of administrative tools to make life more convenient for administrators. These *convenience consoles* are:

Active Directory Management
> Combines the functionality of Active Directory Users and Computers, Active Directory Domains and Trusts, Active Directory Sites and Services, and DNS

IP Address Management
> Combines the functionality of DHCP, DNS, and WINS

Public Key Management
> Combines the functionality of Certification Authority, Certificate Templates, Certificates—Current User, and Certificates (Local Computer)

For more information on convenience consoles and other tools, see *Administrative Tools* in Chapter 4. In addition to the three convenience consoles described above, there is also a new File Server Management console that appears under Administrative Tools when you add the file server role to your WS2003 machine. File Server Management combines the functionality of Shared Folders, Disk Defragmenter, and Disk Management and is convenient for managing file servers, but for some reason it's not included in the list of convenience consoles in Help and Support.

Help and Support

Speaking of Help and Support, the old Help feature of W2K has been totally revamped as Help and Support in WS2003. In general, it's a huge improvement, but there are some frustrations, too. First, the pluses:

* The contents are well organized and enable you to quickly find general information about major topics like tools, tasks, users and groups, disks and data, and so on.

* If your server is connected to the Internet, Help and Support displays a list of Top Issues automatically downloaded from *support.microsoft.com* and allows you to search online for help regarding error messages, software compatibility information, and other information useful to administrators.

- Help and Support includes several additional tools that can be accessed by clicking on the Tools link and then selecting Help and Support Center Tools. These tools can display system, hardware, and software information; offer or obtain remote assistance; perform network diagnostics and more, displaying the results in a readable form.

What's the downside of Help and Support? The Search feature is slow, finicky, and sometimes hard to use. For example, say you want to learn how to create a scope on a DHCP server. If you simply type "scope" into the Search box, the result is zero Suggested Topics, 204 Help Topics, and (if you are connected to the Internet) up to 999 Microsoft Knowledge Base topics (or fewer if you've configured Help and Support to return fewer results). Browsing through the 204 Help Topics, the fifth topic, "Configuring Scopes: DHCP," has a useful discussion of what scopes are but doesn't actually explain the steps for creating one, nor does it contain a link to another topic containing such information. Scroll further down to topic 26, "Create a new scope: DHCP," and you find the information you are looking for. What makes it harder is that the 204 Help Topics displayed here are listed in seemingly random fashion and can't be sorted alphabetically.

Now compare this to using the old Help system in W2K. Start Help, switch to the Index tab, type "scope," and under "scopes" you see an alphabetical list of topics that includes "creating, how to create a scope," which is the desired information, quick and painless. To be honest, you can still use this Index method in WS2003 Help and Support by clicking the Index button on the toolbar, something I do often.

Remote Desktop

In W2K, another way to administer W2K servers was to use Terminal Services in Remote Administration Mode. In WS2003 this feature is now called Remote Desktop, is installed by default (yay!), and can be enabled with a few mouse clicks:

> Start → Control Panel → System → Remote → Remote Desktop →
> elect checkbox

If you have IIS installed on a WS2003 server (it isn't installed by default anymore), you can also use Remote Desktop Web Connection to remotely administer your server from a Windows computer with IE 5 or later using a downloadable ActiveX control. This is cool too. For more information on Remote Desktop and Remote Desktop Web Connection, see *Remote Desktop* in Chapter 4.

Enhancements to Tools

Speaking of administration, Table 2-5 briefly summarizes the enhanced functionality in the new platform for some commonly used administrative tools and other utilities.

Table 2-5. Enhancements to common tools in WS2003

Tool or utility	Enhancements
Active Directory Domains and Trusts	Lets you create external trusts more easily using the New Trust Wizard
Active Directory Sites and Services	Lets you drag and drop domain controllers between sites
	Displays replication intervals and site link costs in the Details pane
	Lets you simulate the effect of Group Policy for a domain or OU using the Resultant Set of Policy (RSoP) Wizard
Active Directory Users and Computers	Lets you drag and drop users between OUs.
	Lets you modify the properties of multiple selected objects simultaneously
	Lets you save Active Directory queries as XML files for later use
	Lets you simulate the effect of Group Policy for a site using the Resultant Set of Policy (RSoP) Wizard
Backup	Now starts in wizard mode by default
	On the Welcome tab, the Emergency Repair Disk option has been replaced by Automated System Recovery Wizard
netstat command	Includes a new option to display the process that owns a TCP or UDP port
Services	Has a new Extended view that describes the selected service and lets you stop or restart it
Task Manager	Includes a Networking tab to display network interface activity in real time
	Includes a Users tab to display, send a message to, log off, or disconnect connected users

Enhancements to Active Directory

While this book is not a detailed guide for implementing Active Directory in an enterprise, day-to-day Active Directory administration is an essential part of managing the WS2003 platform, and you can use this book to quickly look up how to perform common tasks in the following topics in Chapter 4: *Active Directory, Domain, Domain Controller, Forest, OU, Site,* and *Trusts*. Briefly, here are some of the enhancements to Active Directory in WS2003:

- Domains can now be renamed using free tools you can download from *www.microsoft.com/windowsserver2003/downloads/*. Note however, that while you can even rename the forest root domain, you can't change which domain is forest root.
- Forest/domain functional levels now replace the earlier W2K model of native/mixed modes and provide interoperability between NT, W2K, and WS2003 domain controllers. See *Domain* in Chapter 4 for more information.
- The Application Partition allows greater control over how directory information is replicated (DNS information is stored here now).
- Object quotas can be defined for restricting the maximum number of directory objects a user can create.
- Schema classes and attributes that are no longer needed can now be redefined.
- Compression of replication traffic can be disabled between selected sites.
- Global catalog servers are no longer required in each site to support logons, because WS2003 domain controllers now cache universal group membership information on a regular basis.

- Replication of updates to group membership is streamlined by replicating changes to only group membership, not the entire membership of a group.
- The Inter-Site Topology Generator (ISTG) has an improved algorithm that scales to forests containing much larger numbers of sites than W2K could support.
- Domain controllers can be deployed more quickly in remote sites using the new Install Replica From Media feature.
- Dcpromo does a better job of demoting domain controllers than it did in W2K.
- Active Directory client software is no longer provided for Windows 95 or for Windows NT 4.0 SP3 or earlier.
- Cross-forest authentication enables users in one forest to access resources in another forest.

Note that some of these tasks aren't described further in this book because they require advanced understanding of Active Directory, how to edit the schema, and so on—see O'Reilly's *Active Directory* for more information.

Enhancements to Command-Line Administration

Compared to the earlier W2K platform, there are huge improvements in managing WS2003 machines from the command line. To start with, there are numerous new commands for managing:

- Disks and disk quotas using the diskpart and defrag commands
- The boot loader menu using the bootcfg command
- Running processes using the tasklist and taskkill commands
- Active Directory using the dsadd, dsget, dsmod, dsmove, dsquery, and dsrm commands
- Scheduled tasks using the schtasks command (replaces the at command)
- Device drivers using the driverquery command
- Group Policy using the gpupdate and gpresult commands

Also, scripts such as *prncnfg* and *prnmngr* manage printers and print servers from the command line. These scripts (and similar ones for managing IIS) use the Windows Management Instrumentation (WMI) provider, which exposes almost every aspect of the platform for scripted administration. The power of WMI can really be harnessed only if you take the time and effort to learn VBScript or JScript in some depth, which is beyond the scope of this book. O'Reilly's *DNS on Windows 2003* by Robbie Allen, Matt Larson, and Cricket Liu, includes a chapter on using scripting to manage DNS programmatically.

Other Major Enhancements

Here are some additional enhancements that improve the manageability, scalability, and security of WS2003 over W2K:

- Automated System Recovery provides a last-resort method for recovering a failed system if other approaches such as Last Known Good Configuration, Safe Mode, or the Recovery Console don't work. See *Backup* in Chapter 4 for more information.

- The new volume shadow copy feature provides point-in-time copies of shared folders so you can restore earlier versions of files; see *Files and Folders* in Chapter 4 for more information. Of course, this feature doesn't replace regular backups.

- The Internet Information Services (IIS) component is totally revamped but is now not installed by default for greater security (you can even block its installation using Group Policy). To do justice to the capabilities of the new IIS 6 platform really requires an entire book, and I've written one called *IIS 6 Administration* (McGraw-Hill).

- The new Group Policy Management Console (GPMC) is an integrated tool for managing Group Policy on WS2003. Unfortunately, this tool was created too late in the development cycle and is not included on your WS2003 product CD, but you can find out how GPMC 1.0 works and download it from *www.microsoft.com/windowsserver2003/downloads/* along with other cool add-ons like the Domain Rename Tools and IIS 6 Migration Tool.

- The Distributed File System (DFS) now supports multiple DFS roots on a single server, but only on the Enterprise Edition of WS2003. This is good news for enterprise deployments that use DFS.

- The ACL editor (Security tab on a file's or folder's properties sheet) now includes a feature for displaying the effective permissions resulting from group membership; see *Permissions* in Chapter 4 for more information.

- The default permissions on the root directory of an NTFS volume used to be "Everyone has Full Control," but these defaults have been tightened considerably in WS2003 to make the platform more secure out of the box.

- The new Resultant Set of Policies (RSoP) snap-in can be used to analyze how GPOs combine to produce effective settings on the local machine.

Minor Enhancements

Here are some further enhancements in WS2003 that are perhaps less significant in terms of day-to-day administration but may be extremely useful in certain situations:

- Screensavers are now password-protected by default—a simple but effective security enhancement.

- An optional POP-3 mail server component to complement the existing SMTP component of IIS. I call this a minor enhancement because most admins will use Exchange Server anyway for such purposes.

- A new Protected Power Mode is available for hard drives to increase I/O performance, though at the expense of increased risk of data loss. This is accessed by:

  > Computer Management → Device Manager → Disk Drives → right-click on drive → Properties → Policies → Enable advanced performance

- The source IP address and port number are now included in all logon audit events.
- Performance now supports log files greater than 1 GB in size.
- The DHCP database can now be backed up while the DHCP service is running.
- DNS client settings can now be configured using Group Policy.
- A user's My Documents folder can now be redirected to his home directory using Group Policy.
- If your hardware supports it, you can add or remove RAM while the system is running.
- If your hardware supports it, you can use Emergency Management Services (EMS) to remotely manage certain aspects of WS2003 even when your server has crashed and is no longer available on the network.
- Application Compatibility mode ensures legacy Windows 9x/NT applications can run properly under WS2003. To use this feature, do the following:

    Windows Explorer → right-click on program icon → Properties → Compatibility
- The Shutdown Event Tracker records reasons for shutting down servers and displays when a user logs on after a server has unexpectedly rebooted. You can also force a shutdown or restart of a local or remote computer from the command line (see shutdown in Chapter 5).
- For improved security, the Telnet service is now disabled instead of being set to manual startup as it was in W2K.
- If an application hangs, you can now move or minimize its window and work on something else while you wait to see if it responds.
- Device drivers can now be rolled back to previously installed versions if new versions cause problems (see *Devices* in Chapter 4 for more information).
- Internet Connection Firewall (ICF) provides limited firewall functionality for TCP/IP connections. For your network card you can configure this by:

    Control Panel → Network Connections → Local Area Connection → Properties → Advanced

    You can also use ICF for securing VPN and dial-up connections; see *Connections* in Chapter 4 for more information.
- When you install WS2003, you are prompted (but not forced) to specify a strong password for the default Administrator account.

Alphabetical Reference

3

Task Map

This chapter lists more than 600 common administrative tasks for the Windows Server 2003 (WS2003) platform. For the majority of these tasks, cross-references to specific sections within topics in Chapters 4 and 5 are provided in which you can find useful information concerning the task and/or information about the tools for performing it. For a minority of these tasks, specific steps are outlined on how to perform the task, for example, configuring certain Group Policy settings to administer various aspects of WS2003.

This chapter is designed to make it easier for you to find useful information in Chapters 4 and 5, which constitute the main reference portion of this work. Of course, you can always turn directly to a topic in Chapter 4 or a command in Chapter 5 and browse to find what you're looking for if you prefer. What makes this chapter useful, however, is that the level of concepts here is more granular than in the other chapters. For example, information on FSMO roles in Chapter 4 is found within the more general topic *Domain Controller*, but in this chapter, there is a separate heading for FSMO roles that lists related tasks. Similarly, while the topic *Active Directory* in Chapter 4 contains a great deal of information, few tasks are listed here in this chapter under *Active Directory* because this heading is too broad. Look instead for more specific headings such as *Domains* or *Objects* or *Saved Queries* to find tasks relating to these specific aspects of Active Directory.

The tasks in this chapter are listed in alphabetical order according to the main and specific concept involved. For example, "Configure a user account" is listed here under *user* and not *account*. Similarly, "Create an object in Active Directory" is listed here under *Objects* and not *Active Directory*. Take a moment to browse through this chapter before you use it, and you'll quickly get the idea. Note that commonly abbreviated terms such as DNS and OU are found here in their abbreviated form instead of being spelled out; see, *Appendix: Useful Sites* for a quick list of abbreviations and acronyms.

Understanding the Entries

Because some entries in this chapter are cross-references to Chapters 4 or 5 while others are explicit procedures you can perform, their formatting is slightly different depending on what they are intended to convey. The examples in this section are taken mostly from the *DNS* section later in this chapter.

The fact that the elements in the following menu are in *italic* font means this is a cross-reference to the topic *DNS—Tasks* in Chapter 4. In other words, to perform this task, refer to the section *Configure a Forwarder* under *DNS—Tasks* in Chapter 4.

The following cross reference is to the subsection *Clients using Static Addresses* within the section *Configure DNS Clients* under *DNS—Tasks* in Chapter 4.

> Configure a name server to forward queries it can't resolve
> > DNS → Configure a Forwarder

> Configure DNS clients to use static addresses
> > *DNS → Configure DNS Clients → Clients using Static Addresses*

The following is a cross-reference to the section *Planning DNS* under *DNS—Concepts* in Chapter 4.

> Force a DNS client to reregister its hostname with name servers
> > `ipconfig /registerdns`

Compare this with the previous two examples, and you'll see that when the first element is simply *DNS*, it implicitly refers to *DNS—Tasks* in Chapter 4, while other sections in Chapter 4 like *DNS—Concepts*, *DNS—Tools*, and *DNS—Notes* are instead described explicitly. In other words, because Chapter 3 is a task map, references to tasks sections in Chapter 4 omit the *Tasks* designation to avoid belaboring the obvious.

> Plan an implementation of DNS on a network
> > *DNS—Concepts → Planning DNS*

The `constant width` font element in the previous example indicates it's a cross reference to the `ipconfig` command in Chapter 5, with focus on the `/registerdns` command option. If there's a particular section of the discussion you should refer to, its name is italicized, as it is in this reference to configuring a command window, taken from the heading *Command Prompt*:

> Configure a command prompt window
> > `cmd` → *Discussion → Configuring a command shell*

Here's a different kind of example that shows steps in a procedure rather than as cross references:

> Manage DNS clients using Group Policy
> > Group Policy Object Editor → Computer Configuration → Administrative Templates → Network → DNS Client

This example is an explicit description of how to find Group Policy settings that manage DNS clients using the Group Policy Object Editor. The key to recognizing

---

that this is a task and not a cross reference is that it isn't in *italics* or `constant width` font.

Here's one more example, taken from the heading *Error Reporting*, to illustrate one final type of menu in this chapter:

> Configure settings for sending error reports to Microsoft
> Control Panel → System → Advanced → Error Reporting

This is also not a cross reference but an explicit series of steps involving the System utility in the Control Panel. This task is listed here because it didn't fit under any of the broad administrative categories of Chapter 4, but it seemed important enough to include somewhere in this book.

To summarize, if the elements of a menu are in:

* *Italic* font, it's a cross-reference to Chapter 4.
* `Constant width` font, it's a cross-reference to Chapter 5.
* Normal font, it's either a series of steps to perform or a Group Policy setting to configure.

Alphabetical List of Tasks

Account Lockout Policy

Configure account lockout policy settings
> Group Policy Object Editor → Computer Configuration → Windows Settings → Security Settings → Account Lockout Policy
>
> *Group Policy—Concepts → Group Policy Settings → Security Settings*

Active Directory

See also *Domains, Forests, Objects, OUs,* and *Sites*

Install Active Directory on a network
> *Active Directory → Install Active Directory*
>
> *Active Directory → Upgrade to Active Directory*

Plan the deployment of Active Directory for an enterprise
> *Active Directory—Concepts → Planning Active Directory*

Administrative Shares

Connect to an administrative share on a remote machine as Administrator
> *Shared Folders—Notes → Administrative Shares*

Understand the purposes of the various administrative shares
> *Shared Folders—Concepts → Administrative Shares → see Table 4-51*

Task Map

Administrative Templates

Manage user environments with administrative templates using Group Policy
> Group Policy Object Editor → User or Computer Configuration → Administrative Templates
>
> *Group Policy—Concepts → Group Policy Settings → Administrative Templates*

Administrative Tools

Install the Administrative Tools Pack to manage WS2003 servers from a workstation
> *Administrative Tools → Install the Admin Tools Pack*

Launch an administrative tool
> *Microsoft Management Console—Concepts → Consoles*

Launch an administrative tool from the command line using its filename
> *Administrative Tools → Launch an Administrative Tool*
>
> *Microsoft Management Console—Concepts → Default Consoles → see Table 4-30*
>
> runas

Advanced Options Menu

Accessing the Advanced Options menu during startup
> *Advanced Options Menu → Accessing the Advanced Options Menu*

APIPA

Use Automatic Private IP Addressing (APIPA) to dynamically assign IP addresses to computers when no DHCP server is present
> *TCP/IP—Concepts → Automatic Private IP Addressing (APIPA)*

Auditing

Audit access to files and folders stored on NTFS volumes
> *Auditing → Audit File System Objects*

Audit access to global system objects
> *Auditing → Configure Security Options for Auditing*

Audit access to objects in Active Directory
> *Auditing → Audit Active Directory Objects*

Audit access to printers and printing documents
> *Auditing → Enable Auditing of Printers*

Audit use of backup and restore privileges
> *Auditing → Configure Security Options for Auditing*

Configure an audit policy
> *Auditing → Configure Audit Policy*
>
> *Auditing—Concepts → Audit Policy*

Enable audit logging for a DHCP server
DHCP → Configure Audit Logging for DHCP Servers

Manage audit policies using Group Policy
Group Policy Object Editor → Computer Configuration → Windows Settings → Security Settings → Local Policies → Audit Policy

Group Policy—Concepts → Group Policy Settings → Security Settings

Shut down system if unable to log security audits
Auditing → Configure Security Options for Auditing

Automated System Recovery (ASR)

Completely restore a system using Automated System Recovery
Backup → Perform a System Recovery

Recreate a missing ASR floppy disk
Backup → Re-create a Missing ASR Floppy

Automatic Updates

Configure Automatic Updates settings
Control Panel → System → Automatic Updates

Manage Automatic Updates settings using Group Policy
Group Policy Object Editor → User or Computer Configuration → Administrative Templates → Windows Components → Windows Update

Group Policy Object Editor → User Configuration → Administrative Templates → Windows Components → System

Use automatic updates to keep a system up to date with security patches
Automatic Updates → Configure Automatic Updates

Use Software Update Services SUS to keep a network of systems up to date with security patches
Automatic Updates—Concepts → Software Update Services (SUS)

Backups

Also see *Automated System Recovery*

Back up selected volumes or folders
Backup → Perform a backup

Restore selected files, folders, or volumes
Backup → Perform a Restore

Boot Logging

Enable boot logging to create *Ntbtlog.txt* file in *\Windows*
Advanced Options Menu → Accessing the Advanced Options Menu

Advanced Options Menu—Concepts → Enable Boot Logging

Boot Menu

View or modify the *boot.ini* file
> Control Panel → System → Advanced → Startup and Recovery → Settings → Edit
>
> `bootcfg`

Clock

Manage clock synchronization with Network Time Protocol (NTP) servers using Group Policy
> Group Policy Object Editor → Computer Configuration → Administrative Templates → System → Windows Time Service

Set the date on the system clock
> `date`

Set the time on the system clock
> `time`

Synchronize the system clock on the local machine with a time server
> `net time`

Command Prompt

Configure a command prompt window
> `cmd` → *Discussion* → *Configuring a Command Shell*

Executing multiple commands in a single line
> `cmd` → *Discussion* → *Running Multiple Commands*

Manage access to the command prompt using Group Policy
> Group Policy Object Editor → User Configuration → Administrative Templates → Windows Components → System

Open a command prompt window
> `cmd` → *Discussion* → *Opening a Command Shell*

Redirect the output of a command to the clipboard
> `clip`

Run a program or command
> `start`

View or set environment variables for current user or computer
> `cmd` → *Discussion* → *Environment Variables*
>
> `set`
>
> `setx`

Computers

See also *Domains*

Rename a computer
> Control Panel → System → Computer Name → Change

Connections

Also see *Direct Computer Connection, Network Bridge,* and *VPN*

Assign multiple phone numbers to a connection
Connections → Configure a Dial-up Connection → General

Configure a Local Area Connection
Connections → Local Area Connections → Configuring Local Area Connections

Configure an incoming connection on a standalone server
Connections → Incoming Connections → Configuring an Incoming Connection

Configure authentication protocols and data encryption for a connection
Connections → Configure a Dial-up Connection → Security

Configure DHCP settings for a connection
Connections → Configure a Dial-up Connection → Networking

Configure idle timeout for a connection
Connections → Configure a Dial-up Connection → Options

Configure permissions for an incoming connection on a standalone server
Connections → Incoming Connections → Allow/Deny Dial-in Permissions for a User

Configure redial attempts for a connection
Connections → Configure a Dial-up Connection → Options

Configure remote access preferences for an outbound dial-up connection
Connections → Configure Remote Access Preferences

Create a broadband connection for Internet access
Connections → Internet (Broadband) Connections → Creating an On-Demand Broadband Internet Connection

Create a dial-up connection for Internet access
Connections → Create a Dial-up Connection to the Internet

Create a dial-up connection for remote access
Connections → Create a Dial-up Connection to a Remote Access Server

Create an incoming connection on a standalone server
Connections → Incoming Connections → Create an Incoming Connection

Dial a connection
Connections → Dial a Dial-up Connection

Disconnect a connection
Connections → Disconnect a Dial-up Connection

Enable operator-assisted dialing for a dial-up connection
Connections → Enable or Disable a Connection → Enable Operator-Assisted Dialing

Enable or disable a connection
Connections → Enable or Disable a Connection

Manage network connections using Group Policy
Group Policy Object Editor → User Configuration → Administrative Templates → Windows Components → Network → Network Connections

Monitor the status of a connection
Connections → Enable or Disable a Connection → Monitor a Connection

Rearrange the order in which connections are accessed by network services
> *Connections* → *Enable or Disable a Connection* → *Configure Binding Order for Connections*

Repair a connection that has stopped working properly
> *Connections* → *Enable or Disable a Connection* → *Repair a Connection*

Share a dial-up connection to the Internet
> *Connections* → *Dial-up Connections* → *Configure a Dial-up Connection* → *Advanced*

Specify a modem used for a connection
> *Connections* → *Configure a Dial-up Connection* → *General*

Convenience Consoles

Install convenience consoles for integrated management of WS2003 systems and networks
> *Administrative Tools* → *Install the Admin Tools Pack*
>
> *Administrative Tools—Concepts* → *Convenience Consoles*

Delegation

Delegate limited administrative authority over a domain
> *Delegation* → *Delegate Authority over a Domain*

Delegate limited administrative authority over an OU
> *Delegation* → *Delegate Authority over an OU*

Delegate limited administrative authority over a site, subnet, or other site object
> *Delegation* → *Delegate Authority over a Site Object*

Modify Active Directory permissions that have been delegated or assigned
> *Delegation* → *Modify Delegated Permissions*

Plan delegation of limited administrative authority over a domain, OU, or site
> *Delegation—Concepts* → *Delegation Strategies*

Devices

See also *Device Drivers*

Add a new hardware device to a system
> *Devices* → *Add New Hardware*

Customize the view of Device Manager
> *Devices—Tools* → *Device Manager* → *Customizing Device Manager*

Disable a device
> *Devices* → *Disable a Device*

Display resource settings for a device
> *Devices* → *View or Modify Resource Settings for a Device*

Display system and hardware information
> systeminfo

Display the MAC address of a network interface card
> getmac

Display the status of COM, LPT, and console ports
> mode

Enable a device that is disabled
> *Devices → Enable a Device*

Manage devices using Group Policy
> Group Policy Object Editor → Computer Configuration → Windows Settings →
> Security Settings → Local Policies → Security Options

Reinstall a device that is behaving strangely
> *Devices → Reinstall a Device*

Scan your system to look for new PnP devices
> *Devices → Scan for Hardware Changes*

Troubleshoot problems with a device
> *Devices → Troubleshoot Device Problems*

Uninstall a device no longer needed
> *Devices → Uninstall a Device*

Device Drivers

See also *Devices*

Configure what Windows should do with unsigned device drivers
> *Devices → Configure Device Driver Signing*

Display drivers used by a device
> *Devices → Manage Device Drivers*

Display properties of installed device drivers
> driverquery

Install a new driver for a device
> *Devices → Manage Device Drivers*

Manage device drivers using Group Policy
> Group Policy Object Editor → Computer Configuration → Windows Settings →
> Security Settings → Local Policies → Security Options

> Group Policy Object Editor → User Configuration → Administrative Templates →
> Windows Components → System

Manage Windows File Protection settings using Group Policy
> Group Policy Object Editor → Computer Configuration → Administrative
> Templates → System → Windows File Protection

Roll back to a previous version of an installed driver
> *Devices → Manage Device Drivers*

Update the drivers for an installed device
> *Devices → Update Drivers for a Device*

DFS

Add a link
DFS → Add a Link

Add a new root
DFS → Add a Root

Add a new root target
DFS → Add a New Root Target

dfscmd /add

dfscmd /map

Configure DFS client support for different versions of Windows
DFS—Concepts → DFS Clients

Configure replication
DFS → Configure Replication

Implement DFS in a domain environment
DFS—Concepts → Implementing DFS

Manage how often DFS discovers domain controllers using Group Policy
Group Policy Object Editor → Computer Configuration → Administrative Templates → Network

Manage publishing of DFS roots using Group Policy
Group Policy Object Editor → User Configuration → Administrative Templates → Windows Components → Shared Folders

Monitor the status of a root or link
DFS → Monitor Status of a Root or Link

dfscmd /view

Publish a DFS tree in Active Directory
DFS → Publish DFS

DHCP

Activate a scope on a DHCP server
DHCP → Activate a Scope

Authorize a DHCP server in Active Directory
DHCP → Authorize a DHCP Server

Back up the DHCP database of a DHCP server
DHCP → Back Up a DHCP Server

Configure a DHCP relay agent
DHCP → Configure a DHCP Relay Agent

Configure a DHCP server to update DNS information for DHCP clients
DHCP → Configure Dynamic Updates

Configure multihomed DHCP server
DHCP → Configure Multihomed DHCP Servers

Configure DHCP clients for different versions of Windows
DHCP → Configure DHCP Clients

Configure DHCP options for a scope
> *DHCP → Configure Scope Options*

Configure DNS clients to obtain name server addresses using DHCP
> *TCP/IP → DNS Client Configuration*

Create a new scope on a DHCP server
> *DHCP → Create a Scope*

Create a reservation for a DHCP client
> *DHCP → Create a Reservation for a Scope*

Deploy DHCP relay agents on your network
> *DHCP—Concepts → DHCP Relay Agents*

Deploy DHCP servers on your network
> *DHCP—Concepts → Implementing DHCP*

Display the active leases for a scope
> *DHCP → Display Active Leases for a Scope*

Display the statistics for leases of a DHCP server
> *DHCP → Display DHCP Statistics*

Exclude addresses from a scope
> *DHCP·→ Create a Scope*

Manage DHCP servers from the command line
> `netsh DHCP context`

Release a leased address
> `ipconfig /release`

Renew a lease or request an address from a DHCP server
> `ipconfig /renew`

Direct Computer Connection

Configure the Guest computer of a direct computer connection
> *Connections → Direct Computer Connections → Configure a Direct Computer Connection*

Create a direct computer connection between two machines using serial or parallel ports
> *Connections → Direct Computer Connections → Create a Direct Computer Connection*

Establish a direct computer connection from the Guest computer
> *Connections → Direct Computer Connections → Establish a Direct Computer Connection*

Directory Services Restore Mode

Boot in Directory Services Restore Mode
> *Advanced Options Menu → Accessing the Advanced Options Menu*
>
> *Advanced Options Menu—Concepts → Directory Services Restore Mode*

Task Map

Disks

See also *Disk Quotas* and *RAID*

Add a new disk to a system
  Disks → Add a Disk

Assign a drive letter to a partition or volume
  Disks → Assign a Drive Letter

Change the label for a partition or volume
  label

Check a disk for errors or possible damage
  Disks—Tools → Error Checking

  chkdsk

Check a disk for free space
  freedisk

Clean up disks by deleting temporary files and other unneeded files
  Disks—Tools → Disk Cleanup

Configure how Disk Management displays information
  Disks—Tools → Disk Management

Convert a disk from basic to dynamic storage
  Disks → Convert a Disk

  diskpart

Convert a FAT partition or volume to NTFS
  convert

Create a logical drive within an extended partition
  Disks → Create a Logical Drive

Create a new partition
  Disks → Create a Partition

Create a new simple volume
  Disks → Create a Volume

Defragment a partition or volume
  Disks → Defragment a Disk

  defrag

Delete a partition or volume
  Disks → Delete a Partition or Volume

Display the status of a partition or volume
  Disks → View Status of Partition or Volume

Extend a volume by adding unallocated free space
  Disks → Extend a Volume

Format a partition or volume
  Disks → Format a Partition or Volume

  format

Implement disk quotas to control how much disk space users have
  Disks—Concepts → Implementing Disk Quotas

Manage partitions and volumes from the command line
    diskpart

Mount a partition or volume to an empty folder on an NTFS volume
    Disks → Assign a Drive Path

    mountvol

Reactivate a dynamic disk that is in a Missing or Offline state
    Disks → Reactivate a Disk

Repair a partition or volume that is in a Failed state
    Disks → Repair a Partition or Volume

Revert a dynamic disk back to basic type
    Disks → Revert a Disk

Schedule automatic checking of filesystem at startup
    chkntfs

Try to recover a file from a defective disk
    recover

Update the hardware information on all hard drives
    Disks → Rescan Disks

Disk Quotas

See also *Disks*

Copy quota entries between quota-enabled volumes
    Disks—Notes → Disk Quotas

Enable disk quotas on a partition or volume.
    Disks → Enable Disk Quotas

Log quota warning and/or quota exceeded events in event logs
    Disks → Log Disk Quota Events

Manage disk quotas from the command line
    dsadd quota

Manage disk quotas using Group Policy
    Group Policy Object Editor → Computer Configuration → Administrative Templates → System → Disk Quotas

Override a global quota limit with a user-specific quota limit
    Disks → Override Quota Limit

Set hard quota limits for users
    Disks → Enforce Quota Limit

Set soft quota limits for users
    Disks → Set Quota Limit

Set warning levels for quotas
    Disks → Set Quota Warning

View how much of their quotas users have used
    Disks → Monitor Quota Entries

DNS

Add a resource record to a zone
> *DNS → Add a Resource Record*

Clear the name server cache
> *DNS → Clear the DNS Server Cache*

Configure a name server as a caching-only name server
> *DNS → Configure a Caching-Only Name Server*

Configure a name server to forward queries it can't resolve
> *DNS → Configure a Forwarder*

Configure DNS clients to use static addresses
> *DNS → Configure DNS Clients → Clients Using Static Addresses*

Configure DNS clients to use DHCP
> *DNS → Configure DNS Clients → Clients Using DHCP*

Configure scavenging of stale resource records
> *DNS → Configure Scavenging*

Convert a zone from primary to secondary
> *DNS → Convert a Zone*

Configure zone transfer between name servers
> *DNS → Configure Zone Transfer/Replication*

Create a forward lookup zone
> *DNS → Create a Forward Lookup Zone*

Create a reverse lookup zone
> *DNS → Create a Reverse Lookup Zone*

Create a subdomain
> *DNS → Create a Subdomain*

Display the contents of the resolver cache
> *DNS → View the Resolver Cache*

> `ipconfig /displaydns`

Display the hostname of the local machine
> `hostname`

Enable a zone to be automatically updated using dynamic updates
> *DNS → Enable Dynamic Updates*

Flush the contents of the resolver cache
> *DNS → Flush the Resolver Cache*

> `ipconfig /flushdns`

Force a DNS client to reregister its hostname with name servers
> `ipconfig /registerdns`

Force updating a secondary zone from a master name server
> *DNS → Force Zone Transfer/Replication*

Force writing DNS updates to zone files
> *DNS → Update Server Datafiles*

Install a DNS name server
> *DNS → Install DNS Manually*
>
> *DNS → Install DNS Using Wizard*

Integrate BIND with WS2003 DNS
> *DNS—Concepts → Planning DNS → BIND and WS2003*

Manage DNS clients using Group Policy
> *Group Policy Object Editor → Computer Configuration → Administrative Templates → Network → DNS Client*

Monitor the status of a name server
> *DNS → Monitor a DNS Server*

Plan an implementation of DNS on a network
> *DNS—Concepts → Planning DNS*

Specify a boot method for a name server
> *DNS → Specify Boot Method*

Speed name queries by preloading entries from Hosts file
> *DNS → Preload Resolver Cache*
>
> `ipconfig`

Start, stop, pause, and resume the DNS service
> *DNS—Notes → General*

Troubleshoot problems with name servers and name resolution
> *DNS Notes → Troubleshooting*
>
> `nslookup`

Domains

See also *Domain Controllers*

Add a computer to a domain
> *Domain → Add a Computer to a Domain*
>
> `dsadd computer`
>
> `net computer`

Create a new domain
> *Domain Controller → Promote/Demote a Domain Controller*

Display domains and computers from the command line
> `net view`

Manage a domain
> *Domain → Manage a Domain*

Plan implementation of a domain
> *Domain—Concepts → Planning Domains*

Prepare a W2K domain for upgrading to WS2003
> `adprep /domainprep`

Raise the domain functional level of a domain
> *Domain → Raise Domain Functional Level*
>
> *Domain—Concepts → Domain Functional Level*

Rename a domain
    See *www.microsoft.com/windowsserver2003/downloads/domainrename.mspx*.

Upgrade an NT domain
    Domain Controller → *Upgrade Domain Controllers*

Domain Controllers

See also *FSMO Roles* and *Global Catalog*

Configure a domain controller
    Domain Controller → *Configure a Domain Controller*

Create a domain controller
    Domain Controller → *Promote/Demote a Domain Controller*

Deploy domain controllers at remote sites with no qualified administrators
    Domain Controller → *Install from Media*

Manage communication between domain members and domain controllers using Group Policy
    Group Policy Object Editor → *Computer Configuration* → *Windows Settings* → *Security Settings* → *Local Policies* → *Security Options*

Manage domain controllers using Computer Management
    Domain Controller → *Manage a Domain Controller*

Manage domain controllers using Group Policy
    Group Policy Object Editor → *Computer Configuration* → *Administrative Templates* → *System* → *Net Logon*

    Group Policy Object Editor → *Computer Configuration* → *Windows Settings* → *Security Settings* → *Local Policies* → *Security Options*

Domain Controller Security Policy

Configure a domain controller security policy on a domain controller
    Administrative Tools → *Domain Controller Security Policy* → configure settings as desired

    Group Policy—Concepts → *Security Policies* → *Domain Controller Security Policy*

Restore the domain controller security policy to its default state after installation
    dcgpofix

Domain Security Policy

Configure a domain security policy on a domain controller
    Administrative Tools → *Domain Security Policy* → configure settings as desired

    Group Policy—Concepts → *Security Policies* → *Domain Security Policy*

Restore the domain security policy to its default state after installation
    dcgpofix

EFS

Back up certificates and private keys used by EFS for current user
    cipher /x

Encrypt a file or folder on an NTFS volume
    Files and Folders → Encrypt a File or Folder

    Files and Folders—Concepts → Encryption → Strategies for Using Encryption

    cipher /e

Decrypt the contents of a file or folder
    Files and Folders → Decrypt an Encrypted File or Folder

    cipher /d

Generate a new recovery agent and private key
    cipher /r

Manage EFS using Group Policy
    Group Policy Object Editor → Computer Configuration → Windows Settings →
    Security Settings → Local Policies → Security Options

    Group Policy Object Editor → Computer Configuration → Windows Settings →
    Security Settings → Public Key Policies → Encrypting File System

Recover an encrypted file or folder using a designated recovery agent
    Files and Folders → Recover an Encrypted File or Folder

    Files and Folders—Concepts → Encryption → Recovery Policy

Error Reporting

Configure settings for sending error reports to Microsoft
    Control Panel → System → Advanced → Error Reporting

Manage error reporting settings using Group Policy
    Group Policy Object Editor → Computer Configuration → Administrative
    Templates → System → Error Reporting

Event Logs

Archive contents of an event log
    Event Logs → Archive an Event Log

Clear all events from an event log
    Event Logs—Notes

Configure size and retention settings for an event log
    Event Logs → Configure an Event Log

Configure system to shut down if security log becomes full
    Event Logs → Configure an Event Log

Display the events in an event log
    Event Logs → View an Event Log

Filter and search for events
    Event Logs—Tools

    eventquery /fi

Manage event logs using Group Policy
    Group Policy Object Editor → Computer Configuration → Windows Settings → Security Settings → Event Log

    Group Policy—Concepts → Group Policy Settings → Security Settings

---

File System

See also *EFS*, *NTFS*, and *Shared Folders*

Compress files and folders
    Files and Folders → Compress a File or Folder

    Files and Folders—Concepts → Compression

Copy or move a file or folder within or between NTFS volumes
    Files and Folders → Copy or Move a File or Folder

Customize the appearance of a folder in Windows Explorer
    Files and Folders → Customize a Folder

Define access permissions and audit settings for filesystem objects using Group Policy
    Group Policy Object Editor → Computer Configuration → Windows Settings → Security Settings → File System security settings

    Group Policy—Concepts → Group Policy Settings → Security Settings

Expand compressed files from distribution disks
    expand

Manage files and folders using Windows Explorer
    Files and Folders—Tools → Windows Explorer

Manage Windows Explorer functionality using Group Policy
    Group Policy Object Editor → User Configuration → Administrative Templates → Windows Components → Internet Explorer

Modify a file association
    Files and Folders → Modify a File Association

    assoc

    ftype

Open a file or folder
    Files and Folders → Open a File or Folder

Take ownership of a file or folder
    takeown

Transfer files or folders between machines or platforms or over the Internet
    ftp

    rcp

    tftp

View or modify the attributes of a file or folder
    Files and Folders → Display Attributes of a File or Folder

    Files and Folders—Concepts → Attributes

    attrib

View the properties of a file or folder
    Files and Folders → View Properties of a File or Folder

Folder Redirection

Redirect My Documents and other user folders to another network location
Group Policy Object Editor → User Configuration → Windows Settings → Folder
Redirection → right-click on a folder → Properties → Target → select target →
Settings
Group Policy—Concepts → Group Policy Settings → Folder Redirection

Forests

Add a UPN suffix to simplify logon credentials for users
Forest → Add a UPN Suffix

Plan a namespace for a forest
Forest—Concepts → Namespace

Prepare a W2K forest for upgrading to WS2003
adprep /forestprep

Raise a forest's functional level
Forest → Raise Forest Functional Level

Forest—Concepts → Forest Functional Level

FSMO Roles

Determine which domain controllers hold various FSMO roles
Domain Controller → Verify FSMO Roles

Domain Controller—Concepts → Operations Master Roles

Seize an FSMO role when a domain controller goes down
Domain Controller → Seize FSMO Roles

Transfer an FSMO role while a domain controller is available
Domain Controller → Transfer FSMO Roles

Global Catalog

Add new attributes to the global catalog to speed up search queries across domains
Domain Controller → Add an Attribute to the Global Catalog

Designate a domain controller as a global catalog server
Domain Controller → Assign a Global Catalog Server

Groups

Add members to a group
Groups → Domain Setting → Add Members to a Group

Groups → Workgroup Set ting → Add Members to a Local Group

Groups—Concepts → Domain Setting → Group Membership

Groups—Concepts → Workgroup Setting → Group Membership

Change the scope of a group to domain local, global, or universal
> *Groups → Domain Setting → Modify Properties of a Group → General*
>
> *Groups—Concepts → Domain Setting → Group Scopes*
>
> *Groups—Concepts → Domain Setting → Converting Scopes*

Change the type of a group to security or distribution
> *Groups → Domain Setting → Modify Properties of a Group → General*
>
> *Groups—Concepts → Domain Setting → Group Types*

Control group membership and nesting using Group Policy
> Group Policy Object Editor → Computer Configuration → Windows Settings → Security Settings → Restricted Groups

Create a new group
> *Groups → Domain Setting → Create a Group*
>
> *Groups—Concepts → Domain Setting → Group Types*
>
> *Groups—Concepts → Domain Setting → Group Scopes*
>
> *Groups → Workgroup Setting → Create a Local Group*
>
> *Groups—Concepts → Workgroup Setting → Local Groups*
>
> `dsadd group`

Delete a group
> *Groups → Domain Setting → Delete a Group*
>
> *Groups → Workgroup Setting → Delete a Local Group*

Display members of a group
> *Groups → Domain Setting → Modify Properties of a Group → Members*

Display nesting of groups
> *Groups → Domain Setting → Modify Properties of a Group → Members Of*
>
> *Groups—Concepts → Domain Setting → Nesting of Groups*

Find a group in Active Directory
> *Groups → Domain Setting → Find a Group*

Manage global and local groups from the command line
> `net group`
>
> `net localgroup`

Move a group to a different container
> *Groups → Domain Setting → Move a Group*

Plan implementation of groups in a domain setting
> *Groups—Concepts → Domain Setting → Using Groups*
>
> *Groups—Concepts → Built-in Groups → Domain Setting*

Plan implementation of groups in a workgroup setting
> *Groups—Concepts → Workgroup Setting*
>
> *Groups—Concepts → Built-in Groups → Workgroup Setting*

Rename a group
> *Groups → Domain Setting → Rename a Group*
>
> *Groups → Workgroup Setting → Rename a Local Group*

Send an email message to members of a group
> *Groups → Domain Setting → Send Mail to a Group*

Use groups to provide users with secure access to resources
> *Groups—Concepts*
>
> *Groups—Concepts → Domain Setting → Using Groups*

Group Policy

Back up a Group Policy Object
> *Group Policy → Manage Group Policy Using the GPMC → Back Up/Export a GPO*

Block the inheritance of Group Policy Objects from parent to child container
> *Group Policy → Manage Group Policy → Block GPO Inheritance*
>
> *Group Policy → Manage Group Policy Using the GPMC → Block GPO Inheritance*

Configure loopback for a Group Policy Object
> *Group Policy —Notes → General Notes*

Configure the settings of a Group Policy Object
> *Group Policy → Manage Group Policy → Open a GPO*

Copy a Group Policy Object
> *Group Policy → Manage Group Policy Using the GPMC → Copy a GPO*

Create a new Group Policy Object
> *Group Policy → Manage Group Policy → Create a GPO*
>
> *Group Policy → Manage Group Policy Using the GPMC → Create a GPO*

Delegate limited administrative control over a Group Policy Object linked to a container
> *Group Policy → Manage Group Policy → Delegate Control of a GPO*
>
> *Group Policy → Manage Group Policy Using the GPMC → Delegate Group Policy*

Delete a Group Policy Object
> *Group Policy → Manage Group Policy → Delete a GPO*
>
> *Group Policy → Manage Group Policy Using the GPMC → Delete a GPO*

Disable a Group Policy Object so you can modify settings without applying them
> *Group Policy → Manage Group Policy → Disable a GPO*
>
> *Group Policy → Manage Group Policy Using the GPMC → Disable a GPO*

Display a Resultant Set of Policies query report in HTML
> *Group Policy → Use RSoP → View an RSoP Report in HTML*

Display Resultant Set of Policies using the command line
> gpresult

Export a Group Policy Object
> *Group Policy → Manage Group Policy Using the GPMC → Back Up/Export a GPO*

Filter a Group Policy Object
> *Group Policy → Manage Group Policy → Filter a GPO*

Force a Group Policy Object to apply to an entire subtree of Active Directory
> *Group Policy → Manage Group Policy → Force a GPO*
>
> *Group Policy → Manage Group Policy Using the GPMC → Enforce a GPO*

Import a previously exported Group Policy Object
> *Group Policy → Manage Group Policy Using the GPMC → Import a GPO*

Link a Group Policy Object to a domain, site, or OU
   Group Policy → Manage Group Policy → Link a GPO

   Group Policy → Manage Group Policy Using the GPMC → Link a GPO

Manage Group Policy Objects in multiple forests using the GPMC
   Group Policy → Manage Group Policy Using the GPMC → Manage Multiple Forests

Manage the processing of Group Policy Objects using Group Policy
   Group Policy Object Editor → User or Computer Configuration → Administrative Templates → System → Group Policy

Modify a Resultant Set of Policies (RSoP) query
   Group Policy → Use RSoP → Change an RSoP Query

Modify the order in which multiple Group Policy Objects are linked to a container
   Group Policy → Manage Group Policy Using the GPMC → Modify GPO Link Order

Obtain the actual settings resulting from application of Group Policy
   Group Policy → Use RSoP (logging mode)

   Group Policy → Manage Group Policy Using the GPMC → Obtain Group Policy Results

Open a Group Policy Object in the Group Policy Object Editor
   Group Policy → Manage Group Policy → Open a GPO

   Group Policy → Manage Group Policy Using the GPMC → Open a GPO

Plan implementation of Group Policy
   Group Policy—Concepts → Planning Group Policy

   Group Policy—Concepts → Using Group Policy

Refresh Group Policy settings for a target user or computer
   gpupdate

Restore a GPO from backup
   Group Policy → Manage Group Policy Using the GPMC → Restore a GPO

Save a Resultant Set of Policies query
   Group Policy → Using RSoP → Save an RSoP Query

Search a forest for Group Policy Objects matching certain criteria
   Group Policy → Manage Group Policy Using the GPMC → Search for a GPO

Simulate the application of Group Policy without actually applying it
   Group Policy → Manage Group Policy Using the GPMC → Perform Group Policy Modeling

   Group Policy → Use RSoP (planning mode)

Specify which users and computers will receive the settings of a Group Policy Object
   Group Policy → Manage Group Policy Using the GPMC → Scope a GPO

Speed processing of Group Policy Objects by disabling User or Computer Settings
   Group Policy—Notes → General Notes

Understand Group Policy settings
   Group Policy—Concepts → Group Policy Settings

Use the downloadable Group Policy Management Console
   Group Policy —Tools → Group Policy Management Console (GPMC)

View which containers are linked to a Group Policy Object
> *Group Policy → Manage Group Policy → Display Links for a GPO*
>
> *Group Policy → Manage Group Policy Using the GPMC → Display Links for a GPO*

Hardware Compatibility

Check a system to ensure hardware compatibility before installing WS2003
> Insert Product CD → Check System Compatibility → Check My System Automatically
>
> *Installation—Concepts → Installation Windows Server 2003 → Before Installation*

Check the Hardware Compatibility List for WS2003
> *Devices—Concepts → Hardware Compatibility List (HCL)*

Hardware Profiles

Create new hardware profile
> *Devices → Create and Manage Hardware Profiles*

Enable or disable specific services for a given hardware profile
> *Devices—Notes → System*

Force a hardware profile to appear during startup
> *Devices → Create and Manage Hardware Profiles*

Select a hardware profile on startup
> *Devices → Create and Manage Hardware Profiles*

Specify the default hardware profile
> *Devices → Create and Manage Hardware Profiles*

Specify which devices are enabled in a given hardware profile
> *Devices → Create and Manage Hardware Profiles*

Hardware Requirements

View hardware requirements for installing WS2003
> *Installation—Concepts → Installation Windows Server 2003 → Before Installation*

Hibernation Mode

Configure a system to enter hibernation mode
> *Devices → Conserve Energy for Devices*

Enter hibernation mode
> *Devices → Conserve Energy for Devices*

Leave hibernation mode
> *Devices → Conserve Energy for Devices*

Manage password protection for hibernation mode using Group Policy
> Group Policy Object Editor → User Configuration → Administrative Templates → Windows Components → System → Power Management

Kerberos Policy

Configure Kerberos policy settings
   Group Policy Object Editor → Computer Configuration → Windows Settings → Security Settings → Kerberos Policy

   Group Policy—Concepts → Group Policy Settings → Security Settings

Installation

See also *Hardware Compatibility, Program Compatibility Mode, Software Installation, Upgrading,* and *Windows Product Activation*

Choose an installation method
   Installation—Concepts → Installation Windows Server 2003 → Installation Methods

Install optional components for WS2003
   Installation → Installation Optional Windows Components

   Installation—Concepts → Installation Optional Windows Components

Install third-party applications on WS2003
   Installation → Installation Third-Party Applications

   Installation—Concepts → Installation Third-Party Applications

Perform a clean install of WS2003 from a shared network distribution point
   Installation → Install from Network Distribution Point

Perform a clean install of WS2003 from the product CD
   Installation → Install from Product CD

Perform a clean install of WS2003 using disk imaging software
   Installation → Disk Imaging

Perform an unattended install of WS2003 using Setup Manager to create an answer file
   Installation → Unattended Install

Plan a clean install of WS2003
   Installation—Concepts → Installation Windows Server 2003 → Before Installation

Use the command-line switches for winnt.exe and winnt32.exe
   Installation → Install from Product CD

View the version information of the installed operating system
   ver

Internet Connection Firewall (ICF)

Configure ICF for a dial-up connection
   Connections → Dial-up Connections → Configure a Dial-up Connection → Advanced

Configure ICF for the Local Area Connection
   Network Connections → Local Area Connection → Properties → Advanced

Manage ICF using Group Policy
   Group Policy Object Editor → Computer Configuration → Administrative Templates → Network → Network Connections

Internet Connection Sharing (ICS)

Manage ICS using Group Policy
> Group Policy Object Editor → Computer Configuration → Administrative Templates → Network → Network Connections

Share a dial-up connection to the Internet with other computers on the network
> *Connections → Dial-up Connections → Configure a Dial-up Connection → Advanced*

Internet Explorer

Manage Internet Explorer settings using Group Policy
> Group Policy Object Editor → User Configuration → Windows Settings → Internet Explorer Maintenance

> Group Policy Object Editor → User or Computer Configuration → Administrative Templates → Windows Components → Application Compatibility

> *Group Policy—Concepts → Group Policy Settings → Internet Explorer Maintenance*

Work with Internet Explorer's Enhanced Security Configuration
> Chapter 2 → Whoops! → Browse the Web

Last Known Good Configuration

Boot using Last Known Good Configuration
> *Advanced Options Menu → Accessing the Advanced Options Menu*

> *Advanced Options Menu—Concepts → Last Known Good Configuration*

Licensing

Add client access licenses (CALs)
> Control Panel → Licensing

Read the End-User Licensing Agreement (EULA)
> Start → Run → **eula.txt**

Local Security Policy

Configure a Local Security Policy on a standalone server or member server
> Administrative Tools → Local Security Policy → configure settings as desired

> *Group Policy—Concepts → Security Policies → Local Security Policy*

Logon/Logoff Scripts

Manage logon/logoff scripts using Group Policy
> Group Policy Object Editor → Computer Configuration → Administrative Templates → System → Scripts

> Group Policy Object Editor → User Configuration → Administrative Templates → Windows Components → System → Scripts
>
> Group Policy Object Editor → User Configuration → Administrative Templates → Windows Components → Ctrl+Alt+Del Options
>
> Group Policy Object Editor → User Configuration → Administrative Templates → Windows Components → System → Logon

Specify scripts to be processed during logon or logoff
> Group Policy Object Editor → User Configuration → Windows Settings → right-click on Scripts → Properties
>
> *Group Policy—Concepts → Group Policy Settings → Scripts*

Specify the location where logon scripts are stored for a user
> *Users → Managing Domain Users → Configure a User → User Profile*
>
> *Users → Managing Local Users → Configure a Local User*

Logon

See also *Passwords* and *Secondary Logon*

Disable the display of the last user who logged on in the logon box
> *Logon → Disable Display of Last Logged-On User*

Enable automatic logon when a system is booted
> *Logon → Enable Automatic Logon*

Enable verbose system status messages during logon, logoff, startup, and shutdown for troubleshooting purposes
> *Logon → Enable Verbose Logon Messages*

Log off of a WS2003 network
> *Logon → Log Off*

Log on to a WS2003 network
> *Logon → Log On*
>
> *Logon—Concepts → Logon Names*

Manage interactive logons using Group Policy
> Group Policy Object Editor → Computer Configuration → Windows Settings → Security Settings → Local Policies → Security Options
>
> Group Policy Object Editor → Computer Configuration → Administrative Templates → System → Logon
>
> Group Policy Object Editor → User Configuration → Administrative Templates → Windows Components → System

---

MMC

Create a custom MMC console
> *Microsoft Management Console → Create a Console*

Customize an MMC console
> *Microsoft Management Console → Customize a Console*
>
> *Microsoft Management Console —Concepts → Snap-ins*

Manage MMC functionality using Group Policy
>   Group Policy Object Editor → User Configuration → Administrative Templates →
>   Windows Components → Microsoft Management Console

Save a console as an .msc file for distribution to appropriate personnel
>   *Microsoft Management Console → Saving Consoles*
>
>   *Microsoft Management Console → Distributing Consoles*

Set a console to author or user mode
>   *Microsoft Management Console → Setting Console Options*

Start a console from the command line
>   *Microsoft Management Console → Running Consoles from the Command Line*

Use keyboard accelerators for MMC consoles
>   *Microsoft Management Console → MMC Keyboard Accelerators*

Network Bridge

Bridge two or more LAN connections to join separate network segments
>   *Connections → Bridge Connections*

Manage network bridge settings using Group Policy
>   Group Policy Object Editor → Computer Configuration → Administrative
>   Templates → Network → Network Connections

NTFS

See also *EFS*

Assign standard permissions to a file to secure it
>   *Permissions → NTFS Permissions → Assign Standard Permissions to a File*
>
>   *Permissions—Concepts → NTFS Permissions → Standard Permissions → see Table
>   4-35*
>
>   `cacls`

Assign standard permissions to a folder to secure it
>   *Permissions → NTFS Permissions → Assign Standard Permissions to a Folder*
>
>   *Permissions—Concepts → NTFS Permissions → Standard Permissions → see Table
>   4-35*
>
>   `cacls`

Assign special permissions to a file for more granular control over its security than
standard permissions can provide
>   *Permissions → NTFS Permissions → Assign Special Permissions to a File*
>
>   *Permissions—Concepts → NTFS Permissions → Special Permissions → see Table 4-
>   34*
>
>   *Permissions—Concepts → NTFS Permissions → Standard Permissions → see Table
>   4-35*

Assign special permissions to a folder for more granular control over its security than
standard permissions can provide
>   *Permissions → NTFS Permissions → Assign Special Permissions to a Folder*

Permissions—Concepts → NTFS Permissions → Special Permissions → see Table 4-34

Permissions—Concepts → NTFS Permissions → Standard Permissions → see Table 4-35

Change the standard permissions on a file or folder
Permissions → NTFS Permissions → Modify Standard Permissions on a File or Folder

Change the special permissions on a file or folder
Permissions → NTFS Permissions → Modify Special Permissions on a File or Folder

Default permissions on a new NTFS volume
Permissions—Concepts → NTFS Permissions → Default NTFS Permissions → see Table 4-39

Display the effective permissions on a file or folder for a specified user or group
Permissions → NTFS Permissions → View Effective Permissions

Plan implementation of NTFS permissions for files, folders, and volumes
Permissions—Concepts → General Strategy for Assigning Permissions

Permissions—Concepts → NTFS Permissions → Working with NTFS Permissions

Take ownership of a file or folder
Permissions → NTFS Permissions → Take Ownership of a File or Folder

Permissions—Concepts → NTFS Permissions → Ownership

Objects

Create an object (user, group, computer...) in Active Directory
Active Directory → Create an Object

dsadd

Delete an object from Active Directory
Active Directory Users and Computers → right-click on object → Delete

dsrm

Display properties of an object in Active Directory
Active Directory Users and Computers → Right-click on object → Properties

dsget

Import multiple objects into Active Directory in a batch operation
csvde

ldifde

Modify properties of an object in Active Directory
Active Directory Users and Computers → Right-click on object → Properties → change settings

dsmod

Move an object to a different container
Active Directory → Move an Object

OU → Move an Object to a Different OU

dsmove

Search for an object in Active Directory based on specified criteria
    Active Directory Users and Computers → right-click on a container → Find → specify search criteria

    dsquery

Offline Files

Configure offline file settings on a file server
    Shared Folders → *Configure Offline Files on Server*

Configure synchronization, encryption, and disk space settings for offline files on a client
    Shared Folders → *Configure Offline Files on Client*

Enable or disable offline files for a shared folder
    Shared Folders → *Enable Offline Files on Server*

Enable the offline files feature on a client computer
    Shared Folders → *Enable Offline Files on Client*

Make a file, folder, or mapped network drive available offline using the Offline Files Wizard
    Shared Folders → *Make a File or Folder Available Offline*

Manage offline file settings using Group Policy
    Group Policy Object Editor → User or Computer Configuration → Administrative Templates → Network → Offline Files

Plan implementation of offline files
    Shared Folders—Concepts → *Offline Files*

Synchronize all or selected offline files either manually or according to schedule
    Shared Folders → *Synchronize Offline Files*

    Shared Folders—Tools → *Synchronize*

Work with offline files from a user's perspective
    Shared Folders → *Working with Offline Files*

OUs

Create a new OU
    OU → *Create an OU*

    dsadd ou

Move an OU
    OU → *Move an OU*

Plan a hierarchy of OUs for a domain
    OU—Concepts → *Using OUs*

Passwords

Change your password
    Logon → *Change Your Password*

Configure password policy settings
> Group Policy Object Editor → Computer Configuration → Windows Settings → Security Settings → Password Policy
>
> *Group Policy—Concepts → Group Policy Settings → Security Settings*

Manage stored usernames and passwords for network locations and web sites
> Control Panel → Stored User Names and Passwords
>
> cmdkey

Reset the password for a user in Active Directory
> *Logon → Reset Password for a User Account*

Specify password settings for a user
> *Users → Managing Domain Users → Configure a User → Account*

Power Options

Configure power options for portable computers
> *Devices—Notes → Power Options*

Permissions

See *NTFS* earlier in this chapter for tasks related to NTFS permissions and *Shared Folders* later in this chapter for tasks relating to shared-folder permissions.

Printers

Add a new local printer
> *Printing → Add a Printer → Install a Printer for a Local Print Device*

Add a new network printer
> *Printing → Add a Printer → Install a Printer for a Network-Interface Print Device*

Clear a print queue
> prnqctl -x

Connect to a printer to manage it
> *Printing → Connect to a Remote Printer*

Configure spooling settings for a printer
> *Printing → Configure Properties for a Printer → Advanced*
>
> *Printing → Configure a Print Server → Advanced*

Configure Windows client computers for printing to a printer
> *Printing → Configure Clients for Printing*

Control who has access to a printer
> *Printing → Assign Printer Permissions*
>
> *Printing—Concepts → Printer Permissions*

Display information about printers and configure them from the command line
> prncnfg

Find a printer published in Active Directory
> *Printing → Find a Printer*

Install a printer driver for a printer
> *Printing → Configure Properties for a Printer → Advanced*
>
> *Printing → Configure a Print Server → Drivers*

Manage a print queue and print jobs for a given printer
> *Printing → Manage a Print Queue*
>
> net print
>
> prnjobs

Manage printer drivers from the command line
> prndrvr

Manage printers from the command line
> prnmngr

Manage printers using Group Policy
> Group Policy Object Editor → Computer Configuration → Administrative Templates → Printers

Pause a printer to clear a paper jam
> *Printing → Pause a Printer*
>
> prnqctl -z

Pool multiple physical printers into a single logical printer
> *Printing → Configure Properties for a Printer → Ports*

Print a test page
> prnqctl -e

Print to a printer while it is offline
> *Printing → Use a Printer Offline*

Publish a downlevel shared printer in Active Directory
> *Active Directory → Publish a Resource*

Redirect jobs pending on a printer to another printer
> *Printing → Redirect a Printer*

Share a printer so users can print to it across the network
> *Printing → Share a Printer*

Specify a port for a printer
> *Printing → Configure a Print Server → Ports (for creating ports)*
>
> *Printing → Configure Properties for a Printer → Ports (for assigning ports)*

Specify paper feed settings for a printer
> *Printing → Configure a Print Server → Forms*
>
> *Printing → Configure Properties for a Printer → Device Settings*

Specify priority and available times for a printer
> *Printing → Configure Properties for a Printer → Advanced*

Take ownership of a printer
> *Printing → Take Ownership of a Printer*

Processes

Display running processes
> Task Manager → Processes

```
tasklist
```

Kill a process associated with a running application
   Tasks → Kill a Process Associated with a Task

```
taskkill
```

Manage processes using Task Manager
   Tasks → Open Task Manager

   Tasks—Tools → Task Manager

Terminate a running application
   Tasks → End a task

Program Compatibility Mode

Configure application compatibility settings to enable legacy software to run properly on WS2003
   Installation → Manually Configure Compatibility Settings

   Installation—Concepts → Install Third-Party Applications → Program Compatibility Mode

Manage application compatibility using Group Policy
   Group Policy Object Editor → User or Computer Configuration → Administrative Templates → Windows Components → Application Compatibility

Use the Program Compatibility Wizard to enable legacy software to run properly on WS2003
   Installation → Run the Program Compatibility Wizard

RAID

See also *Disks*

Compare NT and WS2003 RAID terminology
   Disks—Concepts → Advanced Disk Technologies

Create a new spanned, striped, mirrored, or RAID-5 volume
   Disks → Create a Volume

Recover a failed mirror volume
   Disks → Recover a Failed Mirrored Volume

Recover a failed RAID-5 volume
   Disks → Recover a Failed RAID-5 Volume

Restore a disk configuration to use NT RAID sets on WS2003
   Disks → Restore Disk Configuration

Recovery Console

Install the Recovery Console on a WS2003 system
   Recovery Console → Install the Recovery Console

Manage the Recovery Console using Group Policy
   Group Policy Object Editor → Computer Configuration → Windows Settings → Security Settings → Local Policies → Security Options

Remove the Recovery Console from a system on which it was installed
    Recovery Console → Remove the Recovery Console

Run the Recovery Console directly from the WS2003 product CD
    Recovery Console → Run the Recovery Console from the Product CD

Registry

Define access permissions and audit settings for the registry using Group Policy
    Group Policy Object Editor → Computer Configuration → Windows Settings → Security Settings → Registry security settings

    Group Policy—Concepts → Group Policy Settings → Security Settings

Edit the registry
    Start → Run → **regedit**

Manage access to registry editing tools using Group Policy
    Group Policy Object Editor → User Configuration → Administrative Templates → Windows Components → System

Remote Assistance

Enable Remote Assistance on the computer
    Control Panel → System → Remote → Turn on Remote Assistance

Invite someone to take control of the system using Remote Assistance
    Start → Help and Support → Remote Assistance → Invite

Manage Remote Assistance settings using Group Policy
    Group Policy Object Editor → Computer Configuration → Administrative Templates → System → Remote Assistance

Remote Desktop

See also *Remote Desktop Connection* and *Remote Desktop Web Connection*

Enable a WS2003 system to be remotely managed using Remote Desktop
    Remote Desktop → Enable Remote Connections

Grant a user the rights necessary to log on using Remote Desktop
    Remote Desktop → Add a User to Remote Desktop Users Group

Install Remote Desktop client software on downlevel Windows machines
    Remote Desktop → Install Remote Desktop Connection

Manage Terminal Services settings using Group Policy
    Group Policy Object Editor → User or Computer Configuration → Administrative Templates → Windows Components → Terminal Services

Open a remote console session that mirrors the session of the locally logged-on user on the server
    Remote Desktop → Connect to Console Session on Remote Server

Task Map

Remote Desktop Connection

Configure connection defaults for Remote Desktop Connections
Remote Desktop → Configure Remote Desktop Connection

Connect to a WS2003 machine using Remote Desktop Connection
Remote Desktop → Connect Using Remote Desktop Connection

Disconnect a connection and terminate the remote session
Remote Desktop → Terminate a Remote Session

Disconnect a connection without terminating the remote session
Remote Desktop → Disconnect without Terminating a Remote Session

Remote Desktop Web Connection

Install Remote Desktop Web Connection on the server
Remote Desktop → Install Remote Desktop Web Connection

Install Remote Desktop Web Connection on the client
Remote Desktop → Install Remote Desktop Web Connection

Rights

Assign rights to users and groups
Group Policy Object Editor → Computer Configuration → Windows Settings → Local Policies → User Rights Assignment

Group Policy—Concepts → Group Policy Settings → Security Settings

Roles

Add roles to a server using Manage Your Server
Administrative Tools—Concepts → Manage Your Server

Installation—Concepts → Install Windows Server 2003 → After Installation → Add Roles

RRAS

See also *Connections* and *VPN*

Add a server to the RRAS console
Routing and Remote Access → Add a Server

Configure and enable RRAS as a dial-up remote access server
Routing and Remote Access → Configure and Enable Routing and Remote Access → Remote Access (Dial-up or VPN)

Configure and enable RRAS in a plain vanilla configuration you can later customize
Routing and Remote Access → Configure and Enable Routing and Remote Access → Custom Configuration

Configure and enable RRAS to connect two networks together using PPPoE
Routing and Remote Access → Configure and Enable Routing and Remote Access → Secure Connection Between Two Private Networks

Configure and enable RRAS to provide Internet access through network address translation
Routing and Remote Access → Configure and Enable Routing and Remote Access → Network Address Translation (NAT)

Configure dial-up settings for remote access users
Users → Managing Domain Users → Configure a User → Dial-in

Create or edit a remote access policy and profile
Routing and Remote Access → Configure a Remote Access Policy

Routing and Remote Access—Concepts → Remote Access Policies

Disconnect a remote client with no warning
Routing and Remote Access → Configure RRAS → Manage Remote Access Clients

Display or modify the routing table
`route`

Display the status of a server and its ports
Routing and Remote Access → Configure RRAS → Monitor RRAS

Display the status of connected remote clients
Routing and Remote Access → Configure RRAS → Monitor Connected Clients

Enable RRAS for remote access (both dial-up and VPN)
Routing and Remote Access → Configure RRAS → Enable Remote Access

Enable RRAS for routing (LAN or demand-dial)
Routing and Remote Access → Configure RRAS → Enable Routing

Grant remote access permission to a user
Routing and Remote Access → Configure RRAS *→ Grant Remote Access Permission to a User*

Grant remote clients access to resources on the network
Routing and Remote Access → Configure RRAS → Configure IP Routing

Log specified remote access events in the System Log
Routing and Remote Access → Configure RRAS → Configure Logging

Manage demand-dial interfaces from the command line
`netsh– Interface`

Manage remote access servers from the command line
`netsh– RAS context`

Manage routers from the command line
`netsh– Routing`

Plan implementation of remote access
Routing and Remote Access—Concepts → Implementing Remote Access

Send a message to a remote client (e.g., to warn about impending disconnection)
Routing and Remote Access → Configure RRAS *→ Manage Remote Access Clients*
`net send`

Specify an address pool assigning IP addresses to remote clients
Routing and Remote Access → Configure RRAS → Configure an IP Address Pool for Clients

Specify a protocol for authenticating remote clients
> *Routing and Remote Access → Configure RRAS → Configure Security on an RRAS Server*
>
> *Routing and Remote Access—Concepts → Remote Access Terminology → WAN Authentication Protocols*

Troubleshoot remote access connection problems
> *Routing and Remote Access —Notes*

Use multilink for remote access connections
> *Routing and Remote Access → Configure RRAS → Enable Multilink*
>
> *Routing and Remote Access—Concepts → Remote Access Terminology → Multilink Protocols*

Work with the RRAS console
> *Routing and Remote Access —Tools*

Safe Mode

Boot in Safe Mode
> *Advanced Options Menu → Access the Advanced Options Menu*
>
> *Advanced Options Menu—Concepts → Safe Mode*

Boot in Safe Mode with Command Prompt
> *Advanced Options Menu → Access the Advanced Options Menu*
>
> *Advanced Options Menu—Concepts → Safe Mode with Command Prompt*

Boot in Safe Mode with Networking
> *Advanced Options Menu → Access the Advanced Options Menu*
>
> *Advanced Options Menu—Concepts → Safe Mode with Networking*

Saved Queries

Create a saved query against Active Directory
> *Active Directory → Create a Saved Query*

Secondary Logon

Enable the Secondary Logon service so you can use the runas command
> *Logon → Enable or Disable Secondary Logon*

Use Secondary Logon to run a program with different credentials from the logged-on user
> *Logon → Use Secondary Logon*
>
> runas

Security Configuration and Analysis

Compare the security configuration of a computer to a security configuration database
> *Security Templates → Apply a Security Template to a Computer*

Configure a computer to use an imported security template
Security Templates → Apply a Security Template to a Computer

Copy and modify an existing security template
Security Templates → Create a Custom Security Template

Create a new security template using the Security Templates snap-in
Security Templates → Create a Security Template

Import a security template into a security configuration database
Security Templates → Apply a Security Template to a Computer

Understand the differences between the various default security templates included with WS2003
Security Templates—Concepts

Use the Security Configuration and Analysis snap-in for analyzing and configuring security settings
Security Templates—Tools → Security Configuration and Analysis

View, create, or modify a security policy for a computer or network
Security Templates—Tools → Security Templates

Task Map

Services

Configure settings for the Workstation and Server services
`net config`

Configure the startup type, status, and security context for a service
Services → Configure a Service

Control startup mode and access permissions for services using Group Policy
Group Policy Object Editor → Computer Configuration → Windows Settings → Security Settings → System Services security settings

Group Policy—Concepts → Group Policy Settings → Security Settings

Pause a running service
Services → Pause a Service

`net pause`

Resume a service after pausing
Services → Resume a Service

`net continue`

Stop and start a service
Services → Restart a Service

`net start`

Stop a running service
Services → Stop a Service

`net stop`

View default startup type and description of each service
Services—Concepts → see Table 4-49

Shadow Copies

Enable shadow copies on a file server
  Shared Folders → Enable Shadow Copies

  Shared Folders—Concepts → Shadow Copies

Install client software to support shadow copies
  Shared Folders → Install Shadow Copy Client Software

  See *www.microsoft.com/windowsserver2003/downloads/*

Overwrite current version of file with a previous version
  Shared Folders → Restore a Previous Version of a File

Recover a file that was accidentally deleted
  Shared Folders → Copy a Previous Version of a File

Specify storage settings and schedule for shadow copies
  Shared Folders → Configure Settings for Shadow Copies

View previous versions of files if there are any
  Shared Folders → View a Previous Version of a File

Shared Folders

See also *Offline Files* and *Shadow Copies*

Assign shared-folder permissions to a shared folder to control access to it by users
  Permissions → Shared-Folder Permissions → Assign Shared-Folder Permissions

  Permissions—Concepts → Shared-Folder Permissions

Connect to a shared folder from a client machine
  Shared Folders—Concepts → Sharing Files → Connecting to Shared Folders

  Shared Folders—Tools → My Network Places

Display or disconnect files opened by users
  openfiles

Manage communication between network clients and file servers using Group Policy
  Group Policy Object Editor → Computer Configuration → Windows Settings →
  Security Settings → Local Policies → Security Options

Manage publishing of shared folders using Group Policy
  Group Policy Object Editor → User Configuration → Administrative Templates →
  Windows Components → Shared Folders

Manage shared folders using the command line
  net file

  net session

  net share

  net use

  net view

Manage shared folders using the File Server Management console
  Shared Folders—Tools → File Server Management

Manage shared folders using the Shared Folders snap-in for Computer Management
  Shared Folders—Tools → Shared Folders

Modify shared-folder permissions for a shared folder
Permissions → Shared-Folder Permissions → Modify Shared-Folder Permissions

Plan implementation of shared-folder permissions for controlling access to shared folders
Permissions—Concepts → General Strategy for Assigning Permissions

Permissions—Concepts → Shared-Folder Permissions → Working with Shared-Folder Permissions

Plan implementation of shared folders on a file server
Shared Folders—Concepts → Sharing Files → Planning Shared Folders

Publish a shared folder in Active Directory
Active Directory → Publish a Resource

Shared Folders → Publish a Shared Folder in Active Directory

Share a folder using the Shared Folders snap-in in Computer Management console
Shared Folders → Share a Folder using Computer Management

Share a folder using Windows Explorer
Shared Folders → Share a Folder using Windows Explorer

Shutdown

Force a shutdown of the local machine or a remote computer
shutdown

Manage shutdowns using Group Policy
Group Policy Object Editor → Computer Configuration → Windows Settings → Security Settings → Local Policies → Security Options

Troubleshoot shutdown problems
Advanced Options Menu → Troubleshoot Shutdown Problems

Sites

Associate a different site with a subnet
Site → Configure a Subnet

Configure a site link's cost and replication interval
Site → Configure a Site Link

Site—Concepts → Site Terminology

Configure a site's location and GPO links
Site → Configure a Site

Create a connection between domain controllers in different sites
Site → Create an Active Directory Connection

Create a new site for a remote branch office
Site → Create a New Site

Create a new site link using IP or SMTP as transport
Site → Create a New Site Link

Create a new subnet and associate it with a site
Site → Create a New Subnet

Designate a domain controller as a bridgehead server for replication with other sites
Site → Designate a Preferred Bridgehead Server

Force replication between domain controllers in different sites
Site → Force Replication over a Connection

Move a domain controller to another site to optimize logon and replication traffic
Site → Move a Server to a Different Site

Site—Concepts → Using Sites → Logon Traffic

Site—Concepts → Using Sites → Replication Traffic

Optimize the replication topology between sites
Site → Check the Replication Topology

Plan implementation of sites in a WAN environment
Site—Concepts → Using Sites → Planning Sites

Rename the default first site
Site → Rename the Default-First-Site-Name

Work with the Active Directory Sites and Services console
Site—Tools → Active Directory Sites and Services

Software Installation

Assign or publish software using Group Policy
Group Policy—Concepts → Software Installation

Group Policy Object Editor → User or Computer Configuration → right-click on Software Installation → Properties

Group Policy Object Editor → User or Computer Configuration → right-click on Software Installation → New → Package → select Windows Installer package (*.msi) to assign or publish

Create software restriction policies to protect systems against untrusted code
Group Policy Object Editor → User or Computer Configuration → Windows Settings → Security Settings → Software Restriction Policies

Group Policy—Concepts → Group Policy Settings → Security Settings

Manage Windows Installer settings using Group Policy
Group Policy Object Editor → User or Computer Configuration → Administrative Templates → Windows Components → Windows Installer

Special Identities

Work with built-in special identities
Groups—Concepts → Built-in Groups → Domain Setting → Built-in System Groups

Standby Mode

Configure a system to automatically enter standby mode
Devices → Conserve Energy for Devices

Enter standby mode
Devices → Conserve Energy for Devices

Leave standby mode
Devices → Conserve Energy for Devices

Manage password protection for suspend mode using Group Policy
> *Group Policy Object Editor → User Configuration → Administrative Templates → Windows Components → System → Power Management*

Password-protect a system running in standby mode
> *Devices → Conserve Energy for Devices*

Startup

Troubleshoot startup problems
> *Advanced Options Menu → Troubleshoot Startup Problems*

Startup/Shutdown Scripts

Manage startup/shutdown scripts using Group Policy
> *Group Policy Object Editor → Computer Configuration → Administrative Templates → System → Scripts*

Specify scripts to be processed during startup or shutdown
> *Group Policy Object Editor → Computer Configuration → Windows Settings → right-click on Scripts → Properties*
>
> *Group Policy—Concepts → Group Policy Settings → Scripts*

System Information

View System Information for a local or remote machine
> *Devices → View System Information*

System Restore

Manage System Restore for Windows XP Professional machines using Group Policy
> *Group Policy Object Editor → Computer Configuration → Administrative Templates → System → System Restore*

Tasks

Configure a scheduled task on the local machine
> *Tasks → Configure a Task*
>
> `schtasks /change`

Configure a scheduled task on a remote machine
> *Tasks → Configure a Remote Task*
>
> `schtasks /change`

Configure an additional schedule for a scheduled task
> *Tasks → Configure an Additional Schedule for a Task*

Configure the repeat interval for a scheduled task
> *Tasks → Configure How Often a Scheduled Task Runs*

Force a scheduled task on the local machine to run immediately
    Tasks → Run a Task Now

    schtasks /run

Force a scheduled task on a remote machine to run immediately
    Tasks → Run a Remote Task

    schtasks /run

Have a popup message appear when a scheduled task can't run
    Tasks—Tools → Scheduled Tasks

Manage task scheduling using Group Policy
    Group Policy Object Editor → User or Computer Configuration → Administrative Templates → Windows Components → Task Scheduler

Schedule a task to start at a particular time or during logon or reboot
    Tasks → Schedule a Task

    at

    schtasks /create

Schedule a task on a remote computer
    Tasks → Create a Remote Task

    schtasks /create

Specify the service account for running scheduled tasks
    Tasks—Tools → Scheduled Tasks

Stop or pause the Task Scheduler
    Tasks—Tools → Scheduled Tasks

    schtasks /end

Temporarily prevent a scheduled task from running
    Tasks → Disable a Scheduled Task

View all scheduled tasks
    Control Panel → Scheduled Tasks

    schtasks

View logged information concerning scheduled tasks that have run
    Tasks—Tools → Scheduled Tasks

TCP/IP

See also *APIPA*

Add an additional default gateway to a network connection
    TCP/IP → Add a Default Gateway

Add an additional IP address to a network connection
    TCP/IP → Add an IP Address

Assign a metric for a network connection to specify the cost of using the connection to route packets
    TCP/IP → Assign a Metric

Choose APIPA for assigning IP addresses if a DHCP server is not present
    TCP/IP → Configuration Method

Choose DHCP for assigning IP addresses if a DHCP server is present
  TCP/IP → Configuration Method

Choose static addressing for assigning IP addresses
  TCP/IP → Configuration Method

Configure packet filtering for a network connection
  TCP/IP → TCP/IP Filtering

Configure TCP/IP settings for local or dial-up connections
  TCP/IP → Configure TCP/IP

Troubleshoot TCP/IP communication problems
  TCP/IP—Concepts → Troubleshooting TCP/IP

  arp

  ipconfig

  nbtstat

  netstat

  pathping

  ping

  tracert

Trusts

Create an external trust within a forest
  Trusts → Create an External Trust → Create an External Trust Within a Forest

Create an external trust between forests
  Trusts → Create an External Trust → Create an External Trust Between Forests

Create a forest trust between two forests
  Trusts → Create an External Trust → Create a Cross-Forest Trust

  Trusts—Concepts → Forest Trust

Create a trust with an external Kerberos v5 realm
  Trusts ⟩ Create an External Trust → Create an External Trust to a Kerberos v5 Realm

Delete an external trust created earlier
  Trusts → Revoke an External Trust

Verify a trust to see if it is working properly
  Trusts → Verify a Trust

Upgrading

See also *Installation*

Installation of an NT domain controller to WS2003
  Installation → Upgrading from NT → Upgrading a Domain Controller

Plan an upgrade of a domain-based NT network to WS2003
  Installation—Concepts → Upgrading to WS2003 → Upgrade Process

Plan upgrades of NT or W2K machines to WS2003
  Installation—Concepts → Upgrading to WS2003 → Upgrade Paths

Task Map

Upgrade an NT machine to WS2003
Installation → Upgrading from NT

Upgrade a W2K domain controller to WS2003
Domain Controller → Upgrade Domain Controllers

Users

See also *User Profiles*

Copy a template user to create multiple users with similar attributes
Users → Managing Domain Users → Copy a User Account

Create a local user
Users → Managing Local Users → Create a Local User

Create a user in Active Directory
Users → Managing Domain Users → Create a User

dsadd user

Disable a user account so the user can't log on
Users → Managing Domain Users → Disable a User Account

Disconnect a user connected to a machine
Tasks → Disconnect or Log Off a User

Manage user accounts from the command line
net user

Modify the group membership for a user
Users → Managing Domain Users → Configure a User → Member Of

Users → Managing Domain Users → Add Users to a Group

Users → Managing Local Users → Configure a Local User

Permanently delete a user account
Users → Managing Domain Users → Delete a User Account

Rename a user account
Users → Managing Domain Users → Rename a User Account

Reset the password for a user account
Users → Managing Domain Users → Reset Password of a User Account

net accounts

Search for a user in Active Directory based on specified criteria
Users → Managing Domain Users → Find a User Account

Secure the Administrator and Guest accounts
Group Policy Object Editor → Computer Configuration → Windows Settings →
Security Settings → Local Policies → Security Options

Send a console message to a user connected to a machine
Tasks → Send a Console Message to a User

Specify account restrictions for a user
Users → Managing Domain Users → Configure a User → Account

Specify logon hours for a user
Users → Managing Domain Users → Configure a User → Account

Specify which computers a user can log on to
Users → Managing Domain Users → Configure a User → Account

Understand the various built-in user accounts
Users—Concepts → Built-in Accounts

Unlock a user account that has been locked out due to too many failed logons
Users → Managing Domain Users → Unlock a User Account

User Profiles

Create and configure a local user profile
Users → Manage User Profiles → Configure a Local Profile

Users—Concepts → User Profiles → Local User Profile

Create and configure a mandatory user profile
Users → Manage User Profiles → Create a Mandatory User Profile

Users—Concepts → User Profiles → Mandatory User Profile

Create and configure a roaming user profile
Users → Manage User Profiles → Create a Roaming User Profile

Users—Concepts → User Profiles → Roaming User Profile

Customize the default user profile
Users → Manage User Profiles → Customize the Default User Profile

Manage user profiles using Group Policy
Group Policy Object Editor → Computer Configuration → Administrative Templates → System → User Profiles

Group Policy Object Editor → User Configuration → Administrative Templates → Windows Components

Group Policy Object Editor → User Configuration → Administrative Templates → Windows Components → System → User Profiles

Specify the location of a user's home folder
Users → Managing Domain Users → Configure a User → User Profile

Users → Managing Local Users → Configure a Local User

Users—Concepts → Home Folders

Specify the location where a user profile is stored
Users → Managing Domain Users → Configure a User → User Profile

Users → Managing Local Users → Configure a Local User

Work with the My Documents folder
Users—Concepts → My Documents

VPN

Add additional WAN miniports for VPN connections
Routing and Remote Access → Configure RRAS → Enable Remote Access for a Device

Configure and enable RRAS as a VPN server
> *Routing and Remote Access → Configure and Enable Routing and Remote Access →*
> *Remote Access (Dial-up or VPN)*

Configure and enable RRAS as a VPN server that uses network address translation
> *Routing and Remote Access → Configure and Enable Routing and Remote Access →*
> *Virtual Private Network (VPN) Access and NAT*

Configure and enable RRAS to connect two networks using a tunneled connection
> *Routing and Remote Access → Configure and Enable Routing and Remote Access →*
> *Secure Connection Between Two Private Networks*

Configure a VPN client connection
> *Connections → Virtual Private Network Connection → Configure a VPN*
> *Connection*

Create a VPN client connection
> *Connections → Virtual Private Network Connection → Create a New VPN*
> *Connection*

Monitor the status of a VPN connection
> *Connections → Virtual Private Network Connection → Monitor a VPN Connection*

Plan implementation of a VPN
> *Routing and Remote Access → Concepts → Remote Access Terminology → Virtual*
> *Private Network (VPN)*

Windows Product Activation

Activate Windows after installing or upgrading to WS2003
> *Installation—Concepts → Install Windows Server 2003 → After Installation →*
> *Windows Product Activation*

WINS

Configure a WINS server
> *WINS → Install WINS*

Configure WINS clients
> *WINS → Configure WINS Clients*

Configure a WINS proxy agent for a subnet that has no WINS server
> *WINS → Configure a WINS Proxy*

Configure replication between WINS servers
> *WINS → Configure WINS Replication*

Create a static mapping for a non-WINS client
> *WINS → Create a Static Mapping*

Manage WINS servers from the command line
> `netsh`– WINS context

Work with the WINS console
> *WINS—Tools*

4

GUI Reference

Read This First!

A few words are probably in order before you start wading through the vast amount of material in this chapter. The topics in this chapter are organized alphabetically according to major themes of Windows Server 2003 (WS2003) administration. For example, if you want to find out about Active Directory and how to manage it, you'd begin by turning to *Active Directory*. Each topic begins with a description of basic concepts, followed by a description of the tools (if any) used to administer the feature, instructions on how to perform common or important administrative tasks, and notes providing extra insight on the topic. Many of the longer topics in this chapter follow this fourfold outline of concepts, tools, tasks, and notes, and knowing this will help you find the information you are looking for more quickly.

Concepts, Tools, Tasks, and Notes

Each topic generally begins with a *Concepts* section that provides you with the necessary background information for administering the aspect of WS2003 being discussed. Comprehensiveness of coverage varies with the subject matter; for example, the DNS topic includes a fair amount of basic material on DNS terminology. Readers who are coming from a Unix BIND background may want to skim through this material to see how Microsoft's take on DNS may differ from their own, while those familiar with Windows NT or Windows 2000 Server platforms can either skip all or portions of this material or use it as a refresher, depending on their level of expertise in the subject.

After *Concepts* may come a *Tools* section, if it's helpful to summarize the consoles, snap-ins, or other tools used to administer the topic under consideration. Usually there is a presentation of the basic features of each tool along with some tips on how to get the most out of using it. If a tool is covered elsewhere in the chapter, there may simply be a cross-reference instead to indicate this.

The *Tasks* section comes next. This section outlines, in condensed form, various administrative tasks related to the topic (unless the topic is informational only). In the DNS topic, for example, you can find out how to perform various tasks such as installing a DNS server, viewing or flushing the resolver cache, configuring a forwarder, and so on. The tasks presented are usually a selection of the most important or most common administrative tasks relating to the topic. Minor and infrequent tasks are generally omitted since wise readers can usually figure them out on their own.

After *Tasks* frequently comes *Notes* to detail some fine points and provide tips, gotchas, things that may not be obvious, and strategies for troubleshooting and administration. I recommend that you always read the *Notes* section even if you just look up a procedure for a simple task.

Finally, at the end of most topics is *See Also*, a brief list of cross-references to other sections to which the reader can turn for additional or related information. Note that cross-references that are capitalized and italicized, like *Active Directory*, *DNS*, or *Event Logs*, point to topics in this chapter, while those in lowercase and constant width font, like `adprep`, `dfscmd`, or `tasklist`, refer to commands described in Chapter 5.

Everyday Administration

To keep the size of this chapter at a (rather huge) minimum, I've tried to focus on common aspects of everyday WS2003 administration and have omitted end user experience stuff like enabling accessibility features, setting screen resolution, playing with desktop themes, and so on. Anyone who's worked with any version of Windows since Windows 95 either knows most of this stuff already or can easily pick it up by right-clicking all over the Windows desktop and selecting each available option. The GUI interface for WS2003 is almost identical to that of XP, so for a good overview of the WS2003 desktop, see a book on Windows XP such as *Windows XP in a Nutshell* by David A. Karp, Tim O'Reilly, and Troy Mott (O'Reilly). I've also omitted most things that are important only to developers, like ASP.NET, Authorization Manager, COM+, MSMQ, and the .NET Framework, as this is not the sort of stuff the average sysadmin needs to know for day-to-day administration of Windows-based networks. Specialized topics that are usually beyond the scope of day-to-day administration, like clustering, issuing and managing digital certificates, and Terminal Services, are also omitted (though Remote Desktop is covered).

Remember, this book is intended as a quick desktop reference for intermediate to advanced admins, and not as a beginner's tutorial. As a result, few readers will attempt to read this chapter through from beginning to end, and it really isn't intended to be used that way anyway. Instead, you will probably use this chapter to look up what you need to know about a specific topic you are interested in and to learn how to perform various administrative tasks commonly associated with the topic using the different tools the platform provides.

Help Finding Things

But what if you try to look up something in this chapter and can't find it? There are several things you can try:

- Use Table 4-1, which lists the topics in this chapter for quick reference.
- Use the Task Map in Chapter 3 to find out which topics in Chapters 4 and 5 relate to the specific feature you want to understand or administrative task you want to perform.
- Use the index at the back of the book.

Gestalt Menus

One more thing to note: procedures are generally shown as a series of steps separated by arrows (→) using what I call "gestalt menus." Steps in a procedure are described concisely and are often best understood when actually sitting at a WS2003 machine so you can follow along. For example, the procedure for sharing a printer is described as:

> Start → Settings → Printers → right-click on a printer → Properties → Sharing → Share this printer → specify share name

which, when working at the computer, is fairly easily understood to mean:

> Click the Start button, select Settings, then Printers. When the Printers folder opens, right-click on the printer you want to share and select Properties from the shortcut menu. Then click the Sharing tab, select the "Share this printer" option, and type a name for the share in the text box. Click OK when you're finished to close the Properties sheet.

Obvious steps are usually omitted, such as clicking OK to close a dialog box or Finish to end a wizard.

Topics Covered

Table 4-1 lists the topics covered in this chapter to help you quickly find the information you're seeking. If you have a more specific task in mind, consult the Task Map in Chapter 3, which points you to where you can find further information in the book on how to perform the task.

Table 4-1. Quick summary of topics covered in this chapter

Active Directory	Domain	Recovery Console
Administrative Tools	Domain Controller	Remote Desktop
Advanced Options Menu	Event Logs	Routing and Remote Access
Auditing	Files and Folders	Security Templates
Automatic Updates	Forest	Services
Backup	Groups	Shared Folders
Connections	Group Policy	Site
Delegation	Installing	Tasks

GUI Reference

Table 4-1. Quick summary of topics covered in this chapter (continued)

Devices	Logon	TCP/IP
DFS	Microsoft Management Console	Trusts
DHCP	OU	Users
Disks	Permissions	WINS
DNS	Printing	

Alphabetical List of Topics

Active Directory—Concepts

Active Directory is the central repository of information on a WS2003-based network. Active Directory stores information about where different resources are located on the network. These resources include user and group accounts, computers, printers, and shared folders. Active Directory can be used to locate these resources quickly so that administrators can create, delete, configure, and maintain them as needed, and ordinary users can access them if they have suitable permissions to do so. Active Directory gives administrators a great deal of flexibility in how their network resources should be administered. By managing resources from any location in the enterprise, you can centralize IT administration in a few users or a single location. On the other hand, Active Directory allows you to create structure using domains and OUs and then to delegate authority over these portions. This allows for decentralized administration in which certain administrative tasks are devolved to various trusted users throughout the enterprise. Active Directory is managed primarily through the GUI but can also be programmatically accessed through an API called the Active Directory Service Interface (ADSI). By writing scripts that use ADSI, administrators can automate most Active Directory administrative procedures, but this requires a good understanding of VBScript or JScript and is beyond the scope of this book.

Logical Structure of Active Directory

In its most abstract sense, Active Directory represents a company's network resources using a hierarchical structure of logical objects such as the following:

Forest
> The most encompassing logical construct in Active Directory. A forest is a collection of domain trees linked together at their roots by transitive trusts.

Tree
> Also called a domain tree, a hierarchical grouping of domains beginning with a root domain and branching out to child domains. Trees must form a contiguous DNS namespace, and a forest can consist of one or more trees joined at their roots by transitive trusts.

Domain
> The primary administrative boundary for WS2003 networks. Domains are named using DNS, and a tree consists of one or more domains hierarchically joined by transitive trusts.

Organizational unit (OU)

> Logical containers you can use to group objects in a domain for security and administration purposes. You can create hierarchical treelike structures of OUs to reflect your company's geographical, organizational, or administrative structure.

Object

> A user, group, computer, printer, shared folder, or anything else that can be "contained" within a domain or OU. For example, a user object represents an employee within your company, a computer object represents a physical computer, and so on.

Trust

> A secure communications channel between domains, domain trees, or forests. Trusts enable users in one domain to be authenticated by a domain controller in other domains and may be transitive, one-way, or cross-linked in nature.

For more information on these topics, see *Domain*, *Domain Controller*, *Forest*, *OU*, and *Trusts*. For more information on specific types of Active Directory objects, see *Groups*, *Printing*, *Shared Folders*, and *Users*.

Planning Active Directory

A big part of planning for an Active Directory deployment involves planning the logical structure that best meets your company's administrative and security needs. Figure 4-1 illustrates the logical structure of an Active Directory with domains represented by black dots, trees by shaded areas, and trusts by lines joining domains. The entire diagram represents the forest. In addition, domains may also contain organizational units. An OU is a logical container that can be created to enclose other Active Directory objects, such as users, computers, groups, printers, or even other OUs.

The typical approach to creating the logical structure for Active Directory is to create your domains and trees in a way that mirrors the geographical or administrative structure of your company. For example, you might create separate domain trees for your American and European offices with the root domain of each tree representing headquarters and child domains representing branch offices. Then you would create OUs within your domains to establish a more granular level of logical structure. For example, you could create separate OUs for your management, sales, human resources, and customer support departments. Then within your sales OU you could create additional OUs for different product groups. The key idea in planning the logical structure of Active Directory is that the domains and upper-level OUs you create should be relatively stable and unchanging in order to simplify administration through delegation and use of Group Policy.

The most important thing to remember when planning your Active Directory structure is to keep it simple—if you can get by using only one domain, then do so. On the other hand, there are sometimes advantages to having multiple domains (or even multiple trees) in your forest, the main one being that by partitioning Active Directory into multiple domains you have better control over replication traffic, an issue of particular importance in a company spanning several locations connected by slow wide area network (WAN) links. Planning an Active Directory implementation is a complex subject, however, and is beyond the scope of this book; for a good book on this subject, see *Active Directory* (O'Reilly).

DNS and Active Directory

Since Active Directory domains are named using DNS, planning Active Directory also involves planning the DNS names of the domains within your forest. The most

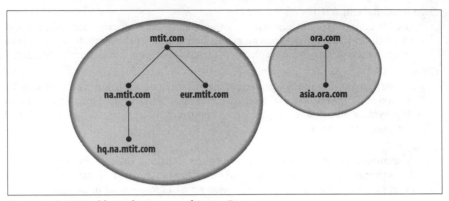

Figure 4-1. Typical logical structure of Active Directory

important choice is your root DNS name, the name of the first domain of your forest (called the forest root domain). You should generally select a root DNS name that reflects the largest scope of your entire organization, taking into account all of its branch offices, subsidiaries, partners, and even planned acquisitions and mergers. For more information on implementing a DNS WS2003 namespace for Active Directory, see *Planning DNS* under *DNS—Concepts* later in this chapter.

In Windows 2000 (W2K) it was important to plan your DNS naming scheme and domain structure carefully since you couldn't rename domains after you created them in Active Directory. W2K did allow you to restructure your forest by creating new domains and using the *MoveTree* utility from Support Tools to move objects from old to new domains, but this was not a trivial procedure. WS2003 takes things a little further and now allows you to rename your domains, including your forest root domain, and to restructure your forest more easily by repositioning domains within a tree or forest. To accomplish these tasks, Microsoft provides a Domain Rename tool that is available on its web site (use *search.microsoft.com* and search for "domain rename tool" to find the current URL for downloading it*). Note that this tool works only if all your domain controllers are running WS2003 and can't be used to change which domain is the root domain of your forest, to add or delete domains from your forest, or to change the name of a domain to the same name that another domain gave up in a previous restructuring. The main thing to remember is that the procedures involved are still complex and aren't intended for everyday administration; they should be used only for an exceptional event such as your company being acquired through a merger or changing its business identity.

Delegation and Group Policy

While a simple deployment of one domain could be managed by a single administrator, enterprises that have many domains and OUs can take advantage of two powerful features of WS2003 that simplify administering and securing Active Directory: delegation and Group Policy. Delegation lets an administrator assign limited administrative rights over domains and OUs to trusted users in order to distribute the burden of managing Active Directory. Group Policy allows policy-based management

---

* At this writing it is *http://www.microsoft.com/windowsserver2003/downloads/domainrename. mspx*.

of user and computer objects within Active Directory. See *Delegation* and *Group Policy* later in this chapter for more information.

New to WS2003 is the ability for administrators to set quotas limiting the number of objects that can be created in Active Directory by a user who has been delegated limited administrative authority. This new feature can be managed only from the command line; see dsadd, dsget, dsmod, dsmove, and dsquery in Chapter 5 for more information.

Schema

One final aspect of Active Directory's logical structure is the schema, which defines the classes of objects the directory may contain and the attributes these objects may have. Active Directory comes with a default schema that may be suitable for most companies, but the schema is also extensible for companies that need to create new object types and attributes. Modifying the schema is beyond the scope of this book.

Topological Structure of Active Directory

Besides logically representing your company's network resources, Active Directory can also topologically represent your company's IP internetwork. Large computer networks based on IP generally have a mesh-like structure in which smaller networks called subnets are joined together with routers into a single large internetwork. These subnets may be located at different geographical locations, in which case WAN links are used to connect locations. To ensure that Active Directory performs optimally over slower WAN connections, a topological structure can be created within Active Directory to reflect the WAN connections of your internetwork. The main elements of such a topology are sites. A *site* is a grouping of subnets that have high-speed (local area network—LAN) connections throughout. Sites are joined to other sites using site links (the logical counterpart in Active Directory to physical WAN links). Sites are important because domain controllers replicate portions of Active Directory with one another, and using sites allows replication traffic to be controlled so that it doesn't swamp the available bandwidth of slow WAN links. See *Site* later in this chapter for more information on these topics.

Physical Structure of Active Directory

From a physical perspective, Active Directory resides on special servers called *domain controllers*, which authenticate users and enable them to locate and access resources across the forest. To ensure scalability, Active Directory is partitioned into naming contexts (NCs), which are contiguous subtrees of directory objects and units of replication. Each domain controller has a replica of three directory partitions:

Schema NC
> Contains the classSchema and attributeSchema objects, which define the kinds of objects that can exist in the forest. Every domain controller in the forest contains a full replica of the same schema NC.

Configuration NC
> Contains objects that define the replication topology and other forestwide information. Every domain controller in the forest contains a full replica of the same configuration NC.

Domain NC
> Contains objects like users and computers that belong to the local domain. Every domain controller in a domain contains a full replica of the domain NC for that

domain, but domain controllers in one domain don't contain replicas of domain NCs for other domains.

Synchronization between domain controllers in a domain is maintained using multimaster replication, a process in which all domain controllers within a domain are peers and contain writable copies of the Active Directory partition for the domain (this is different from NT, in which only one domain controller, the PDC, contained a writable copy of the domain database). To speed queries across multiple domains in a forest, a subset of commonly used Active Directory objects called the global catalog is maintained by each domain.

Directories and Files

The Active Directory database and log files are located by default in the directory *%SystemRoot%\NTDS* and must be located on an NTFS partition. The main directory database file, or datastore, is *NTDS.dit*; it uses the Extensible Storage Engine (ESE) database engine in Microsoft's Exchange Server. The database can grow to a maximum size of 16 terabytes and can contain more than 10 million objects, which means Active Directory can support even the largest enterprise networks. The database defragments and repairs itself automatically, but it can also be taken offline and manually defragmented using the *ntdsutil* utility to reclaim unused space in the directory database. For better performance, Active Directory log files can be placed on a separate physical disk (these log files record transactions written to the datastore and can be used to help restore a system if the datastore volume is lost). A typical configuration might be:

- WS2003 operating system installed on a mirrored volume
- Datastore located on a RAID-5 volume with at least 4 GB to accommodate future datastore growth
- Log files located on a mirrored volume

 Make sure you back up Active Directory regularly. You can do this using the WS2003 *Backup* utility, which allows Active Directory and other system state information to be backed up while running. See *Backup* later in this chapter for more.

SYSVOL

Installing Active Directory creates and shares the directory *%SystemRoot%\sysvol\ sysvol* with the share name SYSVOL. The SYSVOL share contains NETLOGON shares, Group Policies, logon scripts, and other important files that are replicated by the File Replication Service (FRS) to all domain controllers in the domain. Other than placing your logon scripts into the correct subdirectory of SYSVOL, you shouldn't fool around with any of the files stored there.

Active Directory—Tools

The three main tools for administering Active Directory are the following MMC consoles, which are also the names of the corresponding MMC snap-ins:

Active Directory Domains and Trusts (domain.msc)
> Used to administer certain aspects of domains and trusts. This tool is discussed under *Domain—Tools* later in this chapter.

Active Directory Sites and Services (dssite.msc)
> Used to create sites and manage directory replication between them. This tool is discussed under *Site—Tools* later in this chapter.

Active Directory Users and Computers (dsa.msc)
> Used to create and manage Active Directory objects such as users, computers, groups, and printers. This tool is discussed later in this section.

You can access these tools several ways:

- Start → Programs → Administrative Tools → select the appropriate tool.
- Add the appropriate snap-in to a new or existing MMC console.
- Install the WS2003 Administrative Tools Pack on an XP or WS2003 machine and use the Active Directory Management convenience console, which contains all three of these snap-ins plus DNS.
- Type the filename associated with the tool (*domain.msc*, *dssite.msc*, or *dsa.msc*) at the command prompt or use Start → Run.

Other tools used to administer certain aspects of Active Directory include:

Active Directory Migration Tool (ADMT)
> An MMC snap-in used to simplify the migration of users, groups, and computers in NT 4.0 domains to Active Directory domains

Active Directory Schema
> An MMC snap-in used to add a new class or attribute to the Active Directory schema

adprep
> A command-line tool used to prepare an existing W2K forest or domain for upgrading to WS2003

dsadd, dsget, dsmod, dsmove, dsquery, and dsrm
> New command-line tools that enable you to find and manage users, groups, computers, and OUs

ldifde
> A command-line tool that enables you to batch import/export information to/from Active Directory using the LDAP Data Interchange Format (LDIF) standard

Ldp
> A GUI utility in *\SUPPORT\TOOLS* on the product CD that allows you to perform LDAP searches against Active Directory to view and modify information not visible in the GUI tools for managing Active Directory

ntdsutil
> A command-line tool used to perform maintenance on certain aspects of Active Directory, such as performing an offline defragmentation to compact the datastore

In addition, a number of command-line tools in the *\SUPPORT\TOOLS* folder on the WS2003 product CD can be used to administer certain aspects of Active Directory. These tools include *DCDiag, Dnscmd, DSAStat, MoveTree, Netdom, NETDiag, NLTest, Repadmin*, and several others that can be found in the *SUPPORT.CAB* cabinet file and can be installed using the *SUPTOOLS.MSI* Windows Installer package file.

Active Directory Users and Computers

Active Directory Users and Computers is one of the WS2003 tools you will use frequently as an administrator. You can use this tool to create Active Directory objects representing users, groups, computers, printers, and shared folders. You can also use it to create OUs, delegate authority over OUs to trusted users, link Group Policy Objects (GPOs) to domains and OUs, and manage certain aspects of domain controllers. The console tree of this tool displays the domain you have selected and the hierarchy of OUs (if any) that make up the logical structure of the domain. The console tree also includes a number of default containers:

Builtin
> Contains various domain local groups in the domain, such as Administrators and Users.

Computers
> Contains computer accounts for member servers and workstations in the domain.

Domain Controllers
> Contains domain controllers for the domain.

Foreign Security Principals
> Contains SIDs associated with objects from external trusted domains.

Users
> Contains built-in user accounts, global groups, and a few domain local groups. This container is also the default container for accounts upgraded from down-level NT domains.

There are also some additional hidden containers that are rarely used in day-to-day administration of Active Directory—later in this section I describe how to make these containers visible.

New to this version is the *Saved Queries* folder, which lets administrators create and save LDAP queries that search for specific types of Active Directory objects. For example, you can create queries to find all disabled user accounts, all users with nonexpiring passwords, and so on. When you execute a saved query, you can simultaneously modify all the objects found. This new bulk-edit feature of WS2003 is much easier than the W2K approach of creating custom ADSI scripts for similar purposes.

Action Menu

Here is a brief summary of the kinds of tasks you can perform using the Action menu once you select a node in the console tree or an object in the details pane:

Active Directory Users and Computers
> Select this node to connect to another domain or domain controller, view or change the operations masters for the domain, or raise the domain functional level.

Saved Queries
> Select this node to create a new query and create subfolders for organizing your queries. Select a query to edit it or export it as an XML file, which can then be imported into the *Saved Queries* folder of a different domain.

Any domain
> Select this node to delegate authority for the domain, apply Group Policy to the domain, invoke the Resultant Set of Policy (RSoP) Wizard, create OUs or other objects within the domain, and perform other tasks listed under *Active Directory Users and Computers* earlier in this section.

Any OU
> Select this node to delegate authority for the OU, move the OU within the domain, apply Group Policy to the OU, or invoke the RSoP Wizard.

Any user, computer, group, or other object
> The actions you can perform depend on the type of object you select. For example, right-clicking on a computer object and selecting Manage will open a Computer Management console with the selected computer having the focus.

View Menu

The View menu includes a few interesting options:

Users, Groups, and Computers as containers
> This option allows User, Group, and Computer objects to be displayed in the console tree as containers. You might think that selecting a Group object in the console tree would display the group's members in the details pane, but unfortunately, this is not so, so the feature has little usefulness.

Advanced Features
> This option toggles on or off various hidden containers, including LostAnd-Found, System, NTDS Quotas, and Program Data. The one of most interest here is System, which has subcontainers representing various networking services you have installed, such as DFS, DNS, RAS, and so on. Don't modify anything in these containers unless you really know what you're doing!
>
> Advanced Features also displays two hidden tabs on properties sheets of objects:
>
> *Object tab*
> > Displays the canonical name of the object or where it is logically located within Active Directory, in case you're interested.
>
> *Security tab*
> > Lets you modify the permissions of objects in Active Directory. Changing these without knowing what you're doing can really cause problems!

Filter Options
> This option lets you set up a filter to display one or more types of published objects—for example, to display user accounts only. Filters provide a quick way of narrowing the focus when you are looking for something and have thousands of objects to wade through.

Active Directory—Tasks

This section covers common (and not so common but important) administrative tasks concerning the general administration of Active Directory. For more specific tasks relating to administering domains, trusts, user accounts, and so on, refer to the related topics elsewhere in this chapter. For example, to learn how to manage domain controllers, see *Domain Controller*; to learn how to configure user accounts, see *Users*; and so on. Note that all tasks in this section involve using the Active Directory Users and Computers console unless otherwise indicated.

Audit Active Directory

You can use auditing to detect unauthorized attempts to access Active Directory:
> Right-click the Domain Controllers node → Properties → Group Policy → select Default Domain Controller Policy → Edit → Computer Configuration → Windows Settings → Security Settings → Local Policies → Audit Policy → right-click Audit Directory Services Access → Properties → select Define these policy settings → choose to audit success and/or failure events

Auditing of access to Active Directory on all domain controllers in the domain takes effect once the GPO settings have propagated to other domain controllers (usually within five minutes). Directory service access events are logged in the Security log on each domain controller and can be viewed with Event Viewer.

 For fresh installs of new WS2003 domain controllers in a new domain, Active Directory security auditing is enabled by default. If you upgraded from W2K domain controllers, you must enable auditing manually, as described earlier.

You can also audit specific objects within Active Directory. First, follow the steps described earlier, then make the Security tab visible on properties sheets of objects by View → Advanced Features, and then specify auditing for an object by:

Right-click on an object (such as a user or computer) → Properties → Security → Advanced → Auditing → Add → specify the user or group whose access to the object you want to audit → Object tab → select Successful and/or Failed for each type of access you want to audit for the object → Properties tab → select Successful and/or Failed for Read or Write actions you want to audit for the object

For more information, see *Auditing* later in this chapter.

Back Up Active Directory

See *Backup* later in this chapter for information on this.

Create an Object

Right-click a domain, container, or OU → New → select the type of object you want to create (user, group, computer...) → type a name and specify other common properties of the object

After you create an object in Active Directory, you can configure it further by opening its properties sheet. For more information on configuring Active Directory objects, see *Groups*, *Printing*, and *Users* later in this chapter.

Create a Saved Query

Saved queries let you quickly access a desired set of Active Directory objects. For example, you can create queries to display all disabled user accounts, all color printers, all computers whose names start with SRV, and so on.

Right-click Saved Queries → New → Query

Give the query a friendly name you can remember, specify a query root (the container on which the query runs, including its subcontainers), and define the type of query you want to create. For quick and dirty queries, select Common Query, which provides several options for user, group, and computer accounts. To execute a saved query later, just select it in the console tree and view the results in the details pane. You can edit queries after you create them and organize large numbers of queries in folders, sort of like Favorites in Internet Explorer but without the webbish look. If you're into LDAP, you can view the actual query string when you create the query.

Install Active Directory

Installing Active Directory means creating the first domain controller, the forest, and the forest root domain for your company's network. There are two ways to do this.

The first method starts with a freshly installed standalone WS2003 machine and is suitable mainly for new networks:

> Administrative Tools → Manage Your Server → Add or Remove a Role → Typical configuration for a first server → specify DNS name for your forest root domain (e.g., *mycompany.local*) → accept or modify default NetBIOS name for domain → specify IP address of DNS forwarder for external (Internet) name resolution

At the completion of this process, your server will have a static IP address (if it didn't have one already) and Active Directory installed on it. It will also be a DNS server and, if no DHCP server is detected on your network, a DHCP server as well. To verify the actions performed, check *Configure Your Server.log* in the *\Windows\Debug* folder.

Note that if you use this method on a member server already belonging to an existing WS2003 domain, the Typical configuration for a first server option is not displayed. Instead, you can select Manage Your Server → Add or Remove a Role → Domain Controller (Active Directory), which starts the Active Directory Installation Wizard, allowing you to convert your member server into a domain controller for the existing domain or to create a new child domain or root domain of a new tree (note that you need to be a member of the Enterprise Admins group to do this).

Before installing Active Directory together with DNS on W2K, it was necessary to ensure that your server's TCP/IP settings point to its own IP address as its DNS server. On WS2003, the process for installing Active Directory now takes care of this automatically.

A more flexible method for installing Active Directory is to use the Active Directory Installation Wizard:

> Insert product CD → Start → Run → dcpromo → Domain controller for a new domain → Domain in a new forest → specify DNS name for your forest root domain → accept or modify NetBIOS name for domain → accept or modify default location for *NTDS* and *SYSVOL* folders → Install and configure the DNS server on this computer and set this computer to use this DNS server as its preferred DNS server → specify default permissions for users and groups (select pre-W2K compatibility option only if you still have downlevel NT domain controllers on your network) → specify password for Directory Services Restore Mode

Either method makes the machine the first domain controller of the root domain of the forest. The machine is also a DNS server and a global catalog server for the domain. If you used the second method and want your users to have access to the Internet, you will need to manually configure a DNS forwarder to your ISP's name server; see *DNS* later in this chapter for directions.

You can also remove Active Directory by removing the Domain Controller role in Manage Your Server or by running the Active Directory Installation Wizard again. Removing Active Directory from all your domain controllers means your domain no longer exists, an action that of course has consequences for your users (they can no longer log on to the domain to access network resources).

GUI Reference

Move an Object

> Right-click an object → Move

You can create OUs and move objects to these OUs to facilitate delegation and application of Group Policy. See *Delegation* and *Group Policy* later in this chapter for more information.

New to the Active Directory Users and Computers console in WS2003 is the ability to drag and drop objects between containers. At last!

Publish a Resource

Publishing a resource means creating an object in Active Directory to represent the resource. This helps users locate the resource on the network in order to access it. Most resources, such as users, groups, computers, and printers, are published automatically in Active Directory. Two exceptions to this are shared folders on network file servers and downlevel shared printers that are managed by print servers not running WS2003 as their operating system; these resources must be published manually.

To publish a shared folder:

> Right-click on the OU where you want to publish the shared folder → New → Shared Folder → specify a friendly name for the resource → specify the UNC path to the shared folder

After publishing the folder, you can open its properties sheet and add a description and a list of keywords to help users find the folder when they need it.

To publish a downlevel shared printer:

> Right-click on the OU where you want to publish the printer → New → Printer → specify the UNC path to the printer

Once users find this printer in Active Directory, they can connect to it or manage its properties, depending on their permissions.

Upgrade to Active Directory

For information about upgrading from NT domains to Active Directory or from a W2K version of Active Directory to the WS2003 version, see *Active Directory* (O'Reilly).

Active Directory—Notes

This section provides some additional information about Active Directory; since this is a complicated topic, you'll definitely want to read this section.

Active Directory Users and Computers

If you try to connect to a domain controller using this console and receive an error message that the domain can't be contacted or doesn't exist, check to make sure the Windows Time Service is running on the domain controller.

If the console connects to a domain but performs slowly or hangs, you may have a DNS problem. Check to make sure your DNS server contains the proper SRV records for the domain. Another possibility is that your DNS server may have records pointing to nonexistent or unavailable domain controllers (check to make sure all your domain controllers are running too).

Normally, when you start Active Directory Users and Computers, it automatically connects to an available domain controller in the domain to which you are currently logged on. If desired, you can start this console from the command line to connect to a different domain or a specific domain controller. Suppose you are currently logged on to the *mtit.local* domain as Administrator. To open the console and connect to a domain named *usa.mtit.local*:

```
dsa.msc /domain=usa.mtit.local
```

To open the console and connect to a domain controller named *dc5* in the domain *canada.mtit.local*:

```
dsa.msc /server=dc5.canada.mtit.local
```

 WS2003 includes a revamped object picker that allows you to select multiple objects in the details pane of an MMC console, like Active Directory Users and Computers, in order to modify the properties of multiple objects simultaneously.

Client Computers

If you want Windows 98, Windows Me, or NT 4.0 post-SP3 computers to participate in an Active Directory–based network, you need to download and install the Active Directory Client Extensions for these operating systems from Microsoft's web site. This feature allows these machines to take advantage of advanced features like SMB signing that are available only when these extensions are installed. Computers running Windows 95 or NT 4.0 with SP3 or earlier can't log on to WS2003 domains unless SMB signing is disabled on WS2003 domain controllers by doing the following:

Default Domain Controller Policy → Computer Configuration → Windows Settings → Security Settings → Local Policies → Security Options → Microsoft network server: Digitally sign communications (always) → Disabled

Compacting Active Directory

Active Directory automatically performs periodic garbage collection to optimize its performance, but this online defragmentation process doesn't compact the datastore to reclaim disk space. If you frequently make changes to Active Directory, you may want to supplement this with occasional offline defragmentation. To do this, press F8 during startup to open the Windows Advanced Options Menu and select the option to start your domain controller in Directory Services Restore Mode. Then log on using the local Administrator account for the machine and use the *ntdsutil* utility to perform the offline defragmentation. Note that the password for the local Administrator account is set during dcpromo.

New in WS2003 is the ability to manually initiate an online defragmentation of Active Directory. To do this, first install the WS2003 Support Tools from *\SUPPORT\TOOLS* on the product CD. Run the *Ldp* tool, bind to your domain as an administrator, select Browse → Modify, and enter the following information:

Dn
    Leave this blank

Attribute
    DoOnlineDefrag

Value
    180

GUI Reference

Leave Add selected, click Enter → Run, and an online defragmentation process is initiated and is run once for 180 seconds.

Enable Diagnostic Logging

If you're experiencing problems with certain aspects of Active Directory, such as directory replication, you can enable various levels of diagnostic logging to help troubleshoot its operation. Open Registry Editor and select the following key:

```
HKLM\SYSTEM\CurrentControlSet\Services\NTDS\Diagnostics
```

Then open the appropriate value (in this case 5 Replication Events) and change the level of diagnostic logging from 0 (none) to 1 (minimum), 3 (medium), or 5 (maximum), as appropriate. Diagnostic events are recorded in the directory service log in Event Viewer. Be sure you don't enable too high a level of diagnostic logging for too many aspects of Active Directory or your log will fill rapidly and performance of your domain controller may degrade.

Failure During Active Directory Installation

Active Directory installation can fail if your server doesn't have network connectivity, so make sure your server's network card is securely attached to a switch or hub using a cable. If installation still fails, try uninstalling the following network components:

- Client for Microsoft Networks
- File and Printer Sharing for Microsoft Networks
- TCP/IP Protocol

Reinstall these components and try installing Active Directory again.

LDAP Queries

Note that Active Directory on WS2003 doesn't allow anonymous LDAP operations to be performed against it, with the exception of binds and rootDSE searches. Instead, you must be an authenticated user to successfully issue an LDAP request against Active Directory. You can override this behavior; see Knowledge Base article 326690 on *support.microsoft.com*.

Publishing Resources

If your network includes slow WAN links, publish only resources that change relatively infrequently to prevent unnecessary replication traffic from consuming valuable network bandwidth. If you move a published resource to a different server on the network, update the information about the resource in Active Directory to reflect this. In this way, users can still connect to the resource without needing to know its new location. This is really the main benefit of publishing resources in Active Directory: it frees users from the need to memorize which server the resource is located on in the network.

See Also

adprep, *Backup*, csvde, *Delegation*, DNS, *Domain*, *Domain Controller*, dsadd, dsget, dsmod, dsmove, dsquery, dsrm, *Groups*, *Forest*, *Group Policy*, ldifde, *OU*, *Printing*, *Site*, *Trusts*, *Users*

Administrative Tools—Concepts

WS2003 includes a number of administrative tools for performing day-to-day administration tasks on domain controllers and member servers. These tools are accessed from the Start menu and are mostly MMC consoles with a few wizards tossed in for good measure. However, the tools displayed in this menu are only those needed to administer the different WS2003 components installed on your server. For example, if you have not installed Certificate Services on your machine, the Certification Authority console is absent from the menu. Furthermore, most administrators prefer to manage their servers from a remote location such as their office instead of going to the server room every time they need to perform a task.

Administrative Tools Pack

To install the full slate of WS2003 administrative tools on your server or to install these tools on a different machine used for performing remote administration, install the WS2003 Administrative Tools Pack using the procedures outlined in the *Tasks* section for this topic. This pack is implemented as the Windows Installer file *adminpak.msi* and is found on your WS2003 product CD. You can install this pack on:

- Any member of the WS2003 family
- Windows XP Professional machines with Service Pack 1 installed

Using an XP/WS2003 machine with these tools installed, you can administer multiple WS2003 machines from a single location. If you have many tasks to perform on a single WS2003 machine, it may be simpler to use Remote Desktop instead.

 To perform administrative tasks on a domain controller using the WS2003 Administration Tools Pack installed on an XP or WS2003 machine, you must first join the machine to the domain. Also, if you plan to administer downlevel W2K domain controllers using these tools, you must either install W2K Service Pack 3 on these domain controllers or edit the registry to disable LDAP signing; see Knowledge Base article 325465 for more information.

Computer Management

Computer Management (*compmgmt.msc*) is a key administrative tool that contains a number of snap-ins organized into three categories:

System Tools
Event Viewer, Shared Folders, Local Users and Groups, Performance Logs and Alerts, and Device Manager snap-ins

Storage
Removable Storage, Disk Management, and Disk Defragmenter snap-ins

Services and Applications
Telephony, Services, WMI Control, and Indexing Service snap-ins

Computer Management may contain additional snap-ins such as Internet Information Services if such optional components are installed

Convenience Consoles

Three convenience consoles are included in the Administrative Tools menu when you install *adminpak.msi* on a machine. Like Computer Management, these convenience consoles contain multiple snap-ins. They can also be started from the command line using their *.msc* filenames. Table 4-2 provides details about the convenience consoles.

Table 4-2. Convenience consoles

Convenience console	Snap-ins
Active Directory Management (*ADMgmt.msc*)	Active Directory Users and Computers
	Active Directory Domains and Trusts
	Active Directory Sites and Services
	DNS
IP Address Management (*IPAddrMgmt.msc*)	DHCP
	DNS
	WINS
Public Key Management (*PKMgmt.msc*)	Certification Authorities
	Certificate Templates
	Certificates for Current User
	Certificates for Local Computer

Manage Your Server

Another key administrative tool is Manage Your Server, which lets you add different roles to your server and manage these roles by performing basic tasks using wizards and consoles. By default, WS2003 installs with no roles defined, and you can add any of the following roles with this tool:

File Server
Print Server
Application Server (IIS, ASP.NET)
Mail Server (POP3, SMTP)
Terminal Server
Remote Access/VPN Server
Domain Controller (Active Directory)
DNS Server
DHCP Server
Streaming Media Server
WINS Server

Here are a couple of examples of adding roles:

- Adding the File Server role lets you share folders using the Share a Folder Wizard and manage your file server using the File Server Management console (*filesrv. msc*), which contains the Shared Folders, Disk Defragmenter, and Disk Management snap-ins.

- Adding the Application Server role lets you use your server as a web server to host ASP.NET applications on the Internet. You can manage this role using the Application Server console (*appsrv.msc*), which contains the .NET Configuration 1.1, Internet Information Services (IIS) Manager, and Component Services snap-ins.

Administering Downlevel W2K Servers

The Administration Tools Packs for W2K Server and WS2003 have significant compatibility issues:

- The W2K Server version of *adminpak.msi* can be installed only on W2K machines. Similarly, the WS2003 version can be installed only on XP or WS2003 machines.

- Some W2K Server administrative tools are unable to display or configure certain settings of WS2003 machines, and vice versa for WS2003 admin tools.

The simplest solution (though not an elegant one) is for administrators to use two desktop machines to administer a mixed W2K/2003-based network: a W2K Professional machine with the W2K Server version of *adminpak.msi* installed on it and an XP machine with the WS2003 version installed. For IIS administrators, there is an additional problem: the WS2003 version of *adminpak.msi* doesn't include the Internet Service Manager console. Applying Service Pack 2 for XP and reinstalling *adminpak. msi* should correct this problem.

If you insist on having only one desktop for managing your whole network, it should probably be an XP system with the WS2003 version of *adminpak.msi* installed. In addition, make sure that Service Pack 3 for W2K is installed on all your W2K servers so you can use the new version of the Active Directory console to manage your downlevel domain controllers.

Administrative Tools—Tasks

Launch an Administrative Tool
To launch a tool like Computer Management from the Start menu, do this:

> Start → Administrative Tools → Computer Management

To launch the same tool using its filename:

> Start → Run → **compmgmt.msc** → OK

To launch the same tool from the command prompt, type **compmgmt.msc** and press Enter.

Some tools can be launched other ways as well. For example:

> Open Windows Explorer → Right-click on My Computer → Manage

Install the Admin Tools Pack
> Insert WS2003 product CD → open \i386 folder → right-click on *adminpak.msi* → Install

Alternatively, you can connect to a shared distribution point containing your source files (if you have one), or you can enter the path to *adminpak.msi* from the command line to start the installation. Note that you must be a member of the Administrators group both to install and to use these tools or have proper authority delegated by an administrator.

If you are using Active Directory, you can also assign or publish *adminpak.msi* to deploy it automatically when users log on or when they need these tools. See *Group Policy* in this chapter for information on how to assign or publish applications.

Installing *adminpak.msi* also installs a number of command-line tools used for server administration. These include directory service commands like dsadd and dsquery, IIS scripts like *IisBack.vbs* and *IisCnfg.vbs*, and many more. Note that these commands are accessible only from the command line and not from the Start menu.

Uninstall the Admin Tools Pack

To uninstall the Admin Tools Pack, use Add or Remove Programs in Control Panel.

Administrative Tools—Notes

Upgrading from W2K

If you have the W2K version of *adminpak.msi* installed on a W2K Professional or Server machine and then upgrade this machine to XP or WS2003, the previously installed tools aren't automatically upgraded and no longer work on the upgraded machine. It's best to uninstall the old version of *adminpak.msi* before performing the upgrade and install the new version afterward.

New Versions

Be sure to watch Microsoft's web site for updated versions of the WS2003 Administration Tools Pack that might correct some of the deficiencies and incompatibilities of the release version. Each installed version of *adminpak.msi* includes an *APVer.vbs* script that can be used to verify which version you have installed on your machine.

See Also

Commonly used administrative tools are covered in various places throughout this chapter. For example, the Active Directory Users and Computers console is discussed under *Active Directory—Tools,* while creating custom admin tools is covered in *Microsoft Management Console—Tasks.* In addition, see cmd, *Microsoft Management Console*, and runas.

Advanced Options Menu—Concepts

The Advanced Options Menu provides alternate methods for starting WS2003 in order to troubleshoot various kinds of startup problems. Using these options, you can usually bring up WS2003 to the point where you can make any repairs needed so that normal startup can then be achieved. This topic explains these advanced options and how to use them to troubleshoot startup and shutdown problems.

Safe Mode

Safe mode starts your system with drivers for mouse, keyboard, mass storage, base video, and essential system services. Safe mode doesn't enable network connections or services, and it bypasses any programs in the Startup menu. Safe mode also creates a boot log file, *Ntbtlog.txt,* in the */Windows* folder that records the success or failure of initialization of device drivers and system services and that may be useful for troubleshooting startup problems. If you can successfully boot your system to Safe Mode, you may be able to repair any problem preventing a normal boot. For example, you can remove or roll back a recently installed device driver, disable a service that is causing problems, or uninstall a faulty application.

Safe Mode with Networking

This is the same as Safe Mode except that networking support is included. A boot log file is also created. Use this option if a device driver or service is preventing a successful boot and you need to connect to shared network resources to resolve the problem.

Safe Mode with Command Prompt

This is the same as Safe Mode except that a command prompt is opened instead of the GUI interface. A boot log file is again created. You might use this option if a GUI problem is preventing a successful boot.

Enable Boot Logging

This performs a normal boot with the addition of creating a boot log file, *Ntbtlog. txt*, in *Windows*. This is not a toggle—you have to select this option each time you want to create a boot log for a normal boot.

Enable VGA Mode

This is the same as a normal boot except that a generic VGA video driver is used instead of the OEM or vendor driver that was installed. Use this option if a problem with your video driver is preventing a successful boot or preventing the GUI from appearing.

Last Known Good Configuration

This is the same as a normal boot except that it uses the registry settings and device drivers from your last successful boot. You might use this option if you made one or more configuration changes to your system such as installing new devices or updating device drivers, and the system failed to boot successfully afterward. If you select this option and the boot is successful, remove the device you installed or roll back the driver you updated that caused the problem. Alternatively, if you have some idea of which configuration change might be causing the problem, you can use Safe Mode instead to reconfigure your system the way it was previously and, if necessary, roll back any device drivers you installed to earlier versions.

 In WS2003, the Last Known Good feature restores not only previous working registry settings but also device drivers from your last successful boot. This is different from NT and W2K, in which only registry settings are rolled back.

Directory Services Restore Mode

Selecting this mode on domain controllers lets you boot without starting Active Directory so you can repair or restore Active Directory using command-line tools like *ndsutil.exe*. If you select this option on a member server or standalone server, the system simply boots to Safe Mode.

Debugging Mode

This option is used by qualified technicians to troubleshoot "stop" screens and other serious errors. It boots the system and transmits debugging information through a serial port to a second computer for debugging purposes. If you plan to use this option, use the System utility in Control Panel to specify which action should occur when a stop screen occurs, including what debugging information is saved. Such debugging information may be of use for Microsoft support specialists when trying to determine the cause of the crash. You can also use this utility to specify whether to

GUI Reference

automatically boot to the operating system or the Recovery Console if the Recovery Console is installed and how long the boot menu is displayed during startup. Note that no boot menu is displayed if only a single operating system is installed and there is no Recovery Console.

The other two menu options are Start Windows Normally and Reboot. If you installed your server using Remote Installation Services (RIS), there may be additional menu options related to this.

Advanced Options Menu—Tasks

You use the Advanced Options Menu to troubleshoot startup and shutdown problems.

Access the Advanced Options Menu

To access the Advanced Options Menu during the boot process, press F8 at the end of the BIOS startup just before the screen goes blank and Windows starts loading drivers. Once the menu appears, use the up and down arrow keys to select the option you want and then press Enter. Alternatively, you can press Esc to quit the menu without selecting any option and resume the normal boot process.

Troubleshoot Startup Problems

Here is a general procedure for troubleshooting startup problems that should help most of the time. By the way, you've backed up your system recently, haven't you?

You might start by checking the Event logs to see if an entry there identifies the source of the problem. If your boot problem arose after installing a new device, check the Hardware Compatibility List (HCL) for WS2003 at *www.microsoft.com/hcl* to see if the device is supported.

Another useful tool to consult is System Information, which you can access by Accessories → System Tools → System Information. You can use this tool to check for resource conflicts such as devices trying to share the same IRQ. If you discover a resource conflict, you can then use Device Manager to reconfigure, disable, or remove the problem device.

If System Information and Device Manager show no resource conflicts or device driver problems, you could try selecting the Last Known Good Configuration option from the Advanced Options menu. This should get the system booting normally again. You can then repeat one configuration change at a time until you discover what caused the problem.

If you've made several changes before you rebooted and you think you know which change caused the problem but don't want to use Last Known Good Configuration to roll back all your changes, you could boot to Safe Mode, roll back the change you think is causing the problem, and see if the system boots normally. It may also help to examine the boot log file (*Ntbtlog.txt*) created when you boot to Safe Mode, as this log lists all devices and services that load and don't load during the Safe Mode startup process.

If you still can't get your system to boot properly, you may have to try using the Recovery Console, a command-line version of Windows that you can either start from your product CD or select at startup if you previously installed the Recovery Console on your machine. One of the most useful things to do with this tool is to run chkdsk on your system to see if your startup problem is a result of a hard-drive failure. If this is the case, replace your hard drive and restore from backup. See *Recovery Console* later in this chapter for more information on how to use this advanced troubleshooting tool.

If you are unable to repair your system using the Recovery Console, you'll probably have to restore your system from backup. If you're lucky enough to have had the foresight to create an ASR disk set, you can use the new Automated System Recovery feature of WS2003 to restore your system to its pristine state and then restore your data volumes from backup media. For more information on Automated System Recovery, see *Backup* later in this chapter.

Another option you may consider is repairing your installation of Windows by running Setup in Repair Mode from the product CD, especially if you haven't previously created an ASR disk set. After performing the repair you'll still have to reinstall your applications and restore your data from backup. To repair your installation of Windows, follow these steps:

> Insert product CD → Boot machine → when prompted to boot from CD, do so → Enter → Enter → F8 → R

You are prompted for your product key, and then Setup runs without any further prompts while it reinstalls your operating system using its currently configured settings such as computer name and network settings. If something funny happens during the repair, check the *Setuperr.log* file in the *Windows* folder.

Note that I never mentioned using the Emergency Repair Disk (ERD). In NT and W2K, you could create an ERD together with a backup of registry hives in the *Winnt\Repair* folder. In WS2003, the ERD has been eliminated, perhaps because floppy disks are hardly needed anymore for systems with bootable CD-ROM drives. Instead, you can use the *Backup* utility to back up system state information, which includes the registry hives. Alternatively, you can use the *regback.exe* utility in the Resource Kit to back up your registry manually.

Troubleshoot Shutdown Problems

If your server hangs or displays an error message when you try to shut it down, you can use some of the procedures discussed earlier for troubleshooting the problem. First, try using Task Manager to see if any running applications are preventing your server from shutting down properly:

> Ctrl-Alt-Del → Task Manager → Application tab → right-click on application → End Task → try shutting down again → repeat if necessary with each application until the culprit is found

If your shutdown problem arose after you installed a new device, updated a device driver, or made some other system configuration change, you could either use Last Known Good Configuration or manually reverse your configuration steps if you can remember them. If this doesn't resolve the problem, you can see if your machine shuts down properly in Safe Mode, examine the boot log file, check the CMOS settings of your BIOS, run diagnostics on your machine, install a second machine with an identical configuration and applications to see if the problem is reproducible, reinstall drivers for all your devices, replace hardware components, call Microsoft Product Support Services (PSS), or swing your mouse overhead and yell for help.

Boot Disks

You can also create a boot disk for your server so you can boot from a floppy if your system can't start normally from its hard drive. This is done as follows:

1. Format a floppy disk on a WS2003 machine.

2. Copy the files *Ntldr* and *Ntdetect.com* from your WS2003 machine to the root directory of the floppy.

3. Use Notepad to create a file on the root directory of your floppy consisting of the following lines and save it with the name *Boot.ini*:

```
[boot loader]
timeout=30
default=multi(0)disk(0)rdisk(0)partition(1)\Windows
[operating systems]
default=multi(0)disk(0)rdisk(0)partition(1)\Windows="WS2003,
    Enterprise"
```

The last line may vary if you have SCSI instead of IDE for the drive on which your boot and system partitions reside or if you have Standard Edition instead. For more information on creating and editing *Boot.ini* files, search the Knowledge Base at *support.microsoft.com*.

See Also

Backup, bootcfg, *Devices*, *Event Logs*, *Recovery Console*, shutdown

---

Auditing—Concepts

Auditing records user and operating system activities as events (audit entries) in the Security log. A typical event records which action was performed, who performed it, whether the action succeeded or failed, which computer or user initiated the action, and so on. To view audit events, use the Event Viewer console in Administrative Tools.

Auditing is generally performed for either security or resource usage reasons. For example, by auditing failures of activities such as logon attempts or attempts to access a restricted share on the network, administrators can detect when unauthorized access is being attempted and thus protect the security of their systems. And by auditing successful attempts to access filesystem resources, administrators can track patterns of usage so they can determine when to upgrade their storage capacity.

Audit Policy

An audit policy is a type of security policy that specifies which kinds of user and system activities are audited. Before you enable auditing on a computer, you must configure the audit policy. You can configure nine types of audit policy settings:

Account logon events
> A user is authenticated by the security database on the local machine (if part of a workgroup) or by Active Directory on a domain controller (if part of a domain).

Account management
> An administrator creates, deletes, or modifies a user or group, resets a password, or performs some similar action.

Directory service access
> A user attempts to access an object in Active Directory.

Logon event
> A user logs on or off from the local computer or creates or terminates a network connection to the local computer. (This event is always recorded on the computer being accessed by the user, whether local or on the network.)

Object access
> A user attempts to access a file, folder, or printer.

Policy change
> A user changes a security setting, such as password options, user rights, or the audit policy itself.

Privilege use
> A user exercises a right to perform an action, such as modifying the system time or taking ownership of a file.

Process tracking
> An application performs some specific action (generally useful only to the developer of the application).

System
> A user shuts down or restarts the computer, or some other action occurs that impacts security in general on the machine.

Note that two of these audit policy settings (Object access and Directory service access) require specifying which objects (files, folders, printers, Active Directory objects) you actually want to audit and which type of auditing (read access, write access, object creation, and so on) you want to perform on them. This is sometimes called operations-based auditing because it involves specifying the operations (read, write, create) you want to audit for selected objects. For more information on how to audit object access, see *Auditing—Tasks*.

There are four possible ways to configure each of the nine audit policy settings: no auditing, success only, failure only, or both success and failure. For example, configuring the Logon event setting for Success means that successful logons are recorded in the security log but failed logons aren't. Table 4-3 summarizes the default for each audit policy setting.

Table 4-3. Default audit policy settings

Audit policy setting	Default
Account logon events	Success
Account management	Success (on domain controllers) No auditing (on member servers and workstations)
Directory service access	No auditing
Logon event	Success
Object access	No auditing
Policy change	No auditing
Privilege use	No auditing

GUI Reference

Table 4-3. Default audit policy settings (continued)

Audit policy setting	Default
Process tracking	No auditing
System	No auditing

Security Options for Auditing

You can configure three additional security options relating to auditing:

Audit the access of global system objects
> This option enables auditing of mutexes, semaphores, and other obscure operating system objects.

Audit the use of backup and restore privilege
> This can be useful as it generates an audit event for every file that is backed up or restored on the system. For this to work, the Audit privilege use setting must also be configured (see previous section).

Audit: Shut down system immediately if unable to log security audits
> In a high-security environment, this option shuts down the system when the Security log is full and overwriting of oldest events is disabled. When the system shuts down, a stop screen (blue screen of death) appears, displaying the message, "STOP: C0000244 Audit Failed." Only administrators can log on at this point, and they should back up and clear the Security log immediately to resolve the situation.

Auditing—Tasks

Before you can designate which objects to audit, you have to configure auditing. This section describes how to do this and related auditing tasks.

Configure Audit Policy

Audit policies can be configured on computers in several ways. For example, to configure auditing for standalone servers and workstations belonging to a workgroup:

> Administrative Tools → Local Security Policy → Security Settings → Local Policies → Audit Policy → double-click one of the nine audit policy settings → select Success, Failure, both, or neither for no auditing

For computers belonging to a domain, you can do the same for each machine by using the Domain Controller Security Policy on domain controllers and the Local Security Policy on member servers and workstations. Alternatively, you can use Group Policy to configure auditing at the domain, OU, or site level For example, to configure an audit policy for a domain by editing an existing GPO, do the following:

> Administrative Tools → Active Directory Users and Computers → right-click on the domain → Properties → Group Policy → select a GPO → Edit → Computer Configuration → Windows Settings → Security Settings → Local Policies → Audit Policy, etc.

Configure Security Options for Auditing

The three security options for auditing discussed in *Auditing—Concepts* are configured as follows:

> Administrative Tools → Local Security Policy → Security Settings → Local Policies → Security Settings

All three are disabled by default.

 Be sure to configure the Object access setting in your audit policy before auditing specific filesystem objects, or you'll get an error message.

Audit Active Directory Objects

First, configure your audit policy to enable Success and/or Failure auditing for Directory service access (see *Configure Audit Policy* earlier in this section) and then specify which AD objects you want to audit. For example, to audit access to the Users container in the *mtit.local* domain:

> Open Active Directory Users and Computers → View → toggle Advanced Features on → right-click on Users container → Properties → Security → Advanced → Auditing → Add → select user or group to audit → OK → select types of events to audit

 Auditing access to Active Directory objects can result in a considerable performance hit on your domain controllers.

Audit Filesystem Objects

First, configure your audit policy to enable Success and/or Failure auditing for Object access (see *Configure Audit Policy* earlier in this section) and then specify which files or folders you want to audit (these must be on an NTFS volume). For example, if you want to audit access to the file *C:\hello.txt*, you can use Windows Explorer to enable auditing of the file as follows:

> Windows Explorer → right-click on *C:\hello.txt* → Properties → Security → Advanced → Auditing → Add → select user or group to audit → OK → specify types of events to audit

Configuring auditing on many individual files is a lot of work. It's almost always better to configure auditing on folders instead. You can specify that the audit settings be applied to:

- This folder only
- This folder, subfolders, and files
- This folder and subfolders
- This folder and files
- Subfolders and files only
- Subfolders only
- Files only

The default is to pass audit settings down the entire subtree of files and subfolders beneath the folder you are configuring, which is the typical choice.

GUI Reference

Enable Auditing of Printers

To enable auditing of printers:

> Start → Settings → Printers → right-click on a printer → Properties → Security → Advanced → Auditing → Add → select a user or group to audit → OK → specify types of events to audit

Printer access can be audited for documents only, for the printer only, or for both.

Auditing—Notes

Don't audit everything: that's being paranoid and creates huge overhead on your system (your security log will be full in no time). Instead, be selective in what you audit, focusing on auditing failures for security tracking and on successes for resource access. Also, don't configure auditing on every computer in your network. Each computer has its own specific roles, resources, and vulnerabilities. You don't want to spend all your nights and weekends reviewing security logs!

If you're going to audit successes for tracking resource usage, you should probably archive your logs regularly. This saves disk space. Also, remember that auditing is of no use if you don't regularly check your security logs for problems. Schedule a time when you can do this or it won't get done!

Before configuring an audit policy, check the settings for the security log in Event Viewer, and check the available space on your disk to make sure that old log events aren't overwritten unexpectedly.

Audit access by the Everyone group if you are concerned about unauthorized users attempting to access file and print resources or Active Directory objects.

Permission to Audit

To configure an audit policy, you must either be a member of the Administrators group or be granted the "Manage auditing and security log" right in Group Policy.

Multiple Audit Policies

Domain-level audit policies override locally configured ones. See *Group Policy* later in this chapter for how different levels of policies combine.

See Also

Event Logs, Group Policy

Automatic Updates—Concepts

Automatic Updates is a feature of WS2003 that lets you automatically download and install updates to the operating system from the Windows Update web site. The types of updates available include critical updates like security fixes and roll-ups, updated device drivers, and operating system enhancements. In order for this feature to work, it must automatically collect certain information from your computer so it can identify your machine the next time it contacts the Windows Update site to see if new updates are available. The types of information collected include:

- Product ID number (to verify you are running a valid, licensed copy of Windows)
- Version numbers for the operating system, Internet Explorer, and other software running on the machine
- Plug and Play ID numbers of hardware devices

Once this information is collected from your machine, Windows Update generates a GUID that identifies your machine for future visits and stores this GUID on your machine. Note that Automatic Updates protects your anonymity as no personal information (name or email address) is collected.

Update Options

You can configure automatic updates to work using three different options:

Manual
> You are notified when updates are available and you decide whether to download them and which of them to download. If you choose to download them, you are notified again once they are downloaded and you can decide whether to install them and which of them to install. You have total control over the process—except that the icon in the notification area (bottom-right corner of desktop) keeps reminding you.

Semiautomatic
> Updates are automatically downloaded when they become available on the Windows Update web site, but you have to manually install them afterward. This is more convenient than the first option but still gives you control over which updates to install and which to ignore.

Automatic
> Updates are automatically downloaded when available and automatically installed according to a schedule you specify. This is probably the best approach for keeping your system up to date—as long as you trust every fix or patch Microsoft makes available on its site. On some occasions, a patch from Microsoft fixed one thing but broke another.

If you disable Automatic Updates entirely, you should either visit the Windows Update web site periodically to scan for new updates to download or use some other method like Microsoft Software Update Services (SUS) keep your servers up to date with critical security fixes.

Software Update Services (SUS)

The Automatic Updates feature included with WS2003 is really only for small networking environments with one or two servers connected to the Internet. In a large enterprise environment, administrators generally want more control over updating their machines, and for this purpose Microsoft has developed SUS.

SUS is a downloadable component that you install on a member server that resides within your firewall and has dedicated Internet connectivity. This SUS server automatically downloads updates from the Windows Update web site and allows administrators to test them before deciding which updates to approve for machines on their network. Servers running WS2003 or W2K Server with Service Pack 2 or later and desktops running Windows XP Professional or W2K Professional with Service Pack 2 or later can then use a downloadable, enhanced Automatic Updates client to connect to your SUS server and download any updates administrators have approved.

To download SUS server and client components, see *www.microsoft.com/ windows2000/windowsupdate/sus/*. Note that SUS can't be used to deploy service packs or custom updates—use Systems Management Server if you need that kind of functionality.

 In a large enterprise environment, Microsoft Systems Management Server (SMS) can be used instead of SUS to distribute critical updates to servers. SMS is a more powerful tool that can also be used to inventory software, install service packs, manage clients, and perform other systems management tasks across the enterprise; see *www.microsoft.com/smserver/* for more information.

Automatic Updates—Tasks

This section describes how to configure and work with automatic updates.

Configure Automatic Updates

Shortly after you install Windows on your machine, an icon appears in the notification area prompting you to keep your machine current with Automatic Updates. If you ignore it, it keeps bothering you until you decide to configure the feature or disable it. To configure Automatic Updates using this icon, do the following:

Click the Automatic Updates icon in the notification area → Next → choose an update option under Settings

If the notification icon isn't present, you can still configure Automatic Updates by:

Control Panel → System → Automatic Updates tab

Download Updates

When the notification icon appears indicating updates to download, do this:

Click the notification icon → clear checkboxes for updates you don't wish to download → Start Download

If you decide later that you wish to download updates you previously declined, do this:

Control Panel → System → Automatic Updates tab → Declined Updates

If you need to pause downloading for some reason, click the notification icon and select Pause, and then click it again later and select Resume. If Windows notifies you about available updates but you don't want to be bothered, do this:

Click the notification icon → Remind Me Later → specify a time from 30 minutes to 3 days

Install Downloaded Updates

When Windows notifies you that updates have been downloaded and are ready to install, do this:

Click the notification icon → Details → clear checkboxes for updates you don't wish to install → Install

If you don't want to install the updates you downloaded, click Remind Me Later instead of Details. If you decide later that you wish to install updates you previously downloaded but declined to install, do this:

Control Panel → System → Automatic Updates tab → Declined Updates

Disable Automatic Updates by:

Control Panel → System → Automatic Updates tab → clear the checkbox

If you disable Automatic Updates, you can still keep your system up to date by regularly visiting the Windows Update web site, *windowsupdate.microsoft.com*, and following the instructions displayed there.

Automatic Updates—Notes

Clicking the Declined Updates button restores all updates you have previously declined. The next time your system checks for new updates, you can still choose which updates you want to download or install.

Some (more likely most) updates you download will require you to reboot your machine for them to take effect.

Backup—Concepts

The single most important way to prepare for possible disasters is to back up your server and important data regularly. WS2003 includes a utility called *Backup* that lets you do this using either a wizard or standard interface. Using *Backup*, you can back up and restore the boot and system volumes, data volumes, individual folders and folder subtrees, and system state data to a tape drive, a file on a hard drive, or a removable disk. You can back up either local volumes or remote ones that are shared on the network to perform consolidated network backups of multiple machines to a single machine with tape drive attached.

The backup process can be configured using either a standard Windows interface or a wizard. You can back up using any of the common backup methods including normal, copy, differential, incremental, or daily copy (note that on domain controllers you can do only normal backups when backing up system state information). You can initiate a backup immediately or schedule a backup job to occur later or on a regular basis. Backups can also be verified as they are performed and compressed to save space on the backup media. You can restore individual files, folders, volumes, or entire backup sets to either the original or an alternate location, and the restore process can similarly be performed using a Windows interface or a wizard.

 New to WS2003 are volume shadow copy, which lets you back up files even while they are being written to, and Automated System Recovery, which simplifies restoring an entire system from backup after a catastrophic failure. These features are discussed later in this section.

Backup Terminology

A little Windows Backup terminology for you:

Backup job
> A single process of performing a backup.

Backup set
> A group of files, folders, and volumes backed up and stored as a *.bkf* file.

Catalog
> A summary of the files, folders, and volumes saved in a backup set.

Backup log
> A text file created while running Windows Backup that records the success or failure of each step of the backup operation.

System state
> Information that defines the configuration of the operating system on a WS2003 computer. It is essential for restoring the operating system after a disaster. System state data includes:

> - The registry
> - System startup (boot) files
> - Class registration database (for Component Services)
> - Certificate Services database (if the server is running Certificate Services)
> - Active Directory database (domain controllers only)
> - SYSVOL share (domain controllers only)

Volume Shadow Copy

Backup automatically uses the new Volume Shadow Copy Service (VSS) to let you perform backups of volumes when files are still open and in use by Windows, allowing users to continue working on files while Backup is running. VSS can also be used by administrators to configure Windows to save previous versions of files if users need them; see *Files and Folders* later in this chapter for more information.

Automated System Recovery (ASR)

ASR is a new feature that provides a last-resort method for recovering a failed system if other methods like Last Known Good Configuration, Safe Mode, or the Recovery Console don't work. ASR is incorporated into the Backup utility and lets you completely restore a failed system using a full backup of the system and boot partitions together with a special ASR floppy disk. If the hard drive on which your boot or system partition is installed fails, ASR is generally faster and easier than manually reinstalling Windows and restoring from backup media.

ASR works by automatically reinstalling Windows from your product CD using your previous configuration settings and then restoring your system and boot partitions from backup media. The backup media and associated ASR floppy are created at the same time and must be used together to perform a recovery. Note that ASR doesn't back up your data volumes; you have to do this separately.

Backup—Tasks

For most backup tasks, use the Backup or Restore Wizard.

Open the Backup or Restore Wizard

You can start the Backup or Restore Wizard in several ways:

Start → Programs → Accessories → System → Backup

Windows Explorer or My Computer → right-click on a drive → Properties → Tools → Backup Now

Computer Management → Storage → Disk Management → right-click on a drive → Properties → Tools → Backup

Open a command prompt → **ntbackup.exe**

Once the wizard is displayed, click Advanced Mode to open the standard interface for the program if desired.

Perform a Backup

To immediately create a backup of everything on your server, including an ASR floppy, do this:

Open the wizard → Back up files and settings → All information on this computer → select backup type (tape or file) → specify destination (if file) → specify name for backup set → Finish

To schedule a backup of selected volumes or folders, do this:

Open the wizard → Back up files and settings → Let me choose what to back up → Back up files and settings → select volumes, folders, system state, and/or network shares → select backup type (tape or file) → specify destination (if file) → specify name for backup set → Advanced → select backup type → optionally choose to verify backup and/or disable volume shadow copy → choose whether to append to or replace existing backup set → Later → specify job name → Set Schedule → Next → enter Administrator password

Backups can be scheduled to run daily, weekly, monthly, once, at startup, at logon, or when the system is idle. For more information on scheduling backups and other tasks, see *Tasks* later in this chapter.

Perform a Restore

To restore selected volumes, folders, or files, do this:

Open the wizard → Restore files and settings → select a backup set → choose what to restore → Finish

To restore an item to a different location, do this:

Open the wizard → Restore files and settings → select a backup set → choose what to restore → Advanced → choose Alternate Location or Single Folder as desired → choose whether to leave existing files, replace them always, or replace them if they are older than files being restored → specify whether to restore security settings → Finish

Perform a System Recovery

To completely restore a system using Automated System Recovery, do this:

> Insert your WS2003 product CD → Boot your machine → press F2 when prompted → insert ASR floppy → follow prompts

Make sure to remove your floppy and later your product CD when prompted to do so.

Recreate a Missing ASR Floppy

If you lose the ASR floppy for your backup set, you can recreate it as follows:

> Open the wizard → Restore files and settings → select backup set associated with missing disk → select \Windows\Repair folder → select Asr.sif and Asrpnp.sif files to restore → Advanced → Restore files to single folder → type A:\ → insert blank formatted floppy

---

Backup—Notes

General Tips

Only Administrators or Backup Operators can perform backups and restores.

Other backup options like compression may be available, depending on the type of backup device installed on your system.

Scheduled backup jobs appear in the *Scheduled Tasks* folder in the Control Panel and can be run immediately, deleted, or configured there. In order to schedule backups, the Task Scheduler service must be running (it is by default).

Backing Up to CD-R/RW

You can't use the Backup utility to back up directly to CD-R or CD-RW drives. A workaround is to back up to a file and then use the CD-burning capability of WS2003 to write the file to CD as follows:

> Insert blank writable CD into CD-R drive → open Windows Explorer → drag items to CD-R drive

Restoring System State

If you can't restore your system state, boot to Safe Mode and try again.

If you plan to restore system state data, be aware that the restore process overwrites the existing configuration information on your server, so if you restore from an old backup set, you lose any configuration changes made since that set was made.

To restore system state data on a domain controller, you must use the Advanced Options menu to start the computer in Directory Services Restore Mode.

See Also

Advanced Options Menu, dcgpofix

Connections—Concepts

In WS2003, a *connection* is a mechanism for connecting your computer to another computer, a remote access server, a dedicated network access device, or the Internet. Connections in WS2003 are classified in different ways. For example, you can create:

LAN connections
> These connections use a network interface card (NIC) to enable the computer to communicate with other computers on the local area network (LAN). Unlike other kinds of connections in WS2003, LAN connections are created automatically during Setup or when an additional NIC is installed.

WAN connections
> These include both dial-up and dedicated connections through wide area network (WAN) devices such as modems, ISDN terminal adapters, X.25 pads, or routers. They are also called remote access connections as they allow remote clients to access resources on the local network.

Direct computer connections
> These are special types of connections established between two computers using a serial (RS-232C) or parallel (ECP) file-transfer cable, or an infrared port. They are used only to establish a connection to transfer files between machines.

In addition, you can classify connections as incoming or outgoing:

Incoming connections
> These connections enable your computer to listen for and respond to connection attempts by remote clients. In an inbound connection your computer assumes the role of a server and can grant clients access to resources on the local computer or act as a secure gateway to allow them to access resources on the local network. WS2003 supports dial-in inbound connections using a modem, modem pool, ISDN adapter, serial or parallel cable, infrared port, or other hardware.

Outgoing connections
> These connections enable your computer to initiate or establish a connection with another computer, a remote network, or the Internet. WS2003 supports several different types of outbound connections:
>
> * Dial-up connections to the Internet using a modem or ISDN adapter
> * On-demand broadband connections to the Internet using a DSL or cable modem, sometimes called a PPPoE connections
> * Always-on broadband connections to the Internet using a DSL router or direct LAN connection
> * Dial-up connections to a remote private network using a modem or ISDN adapter
> * Virtual private network (VPN) connections that securely tunnel over the Internet to a remote private network
> * Direct connections to another computer using a null-modem cable, infrared transceiver, or other device

GUI Reference

Implementing Connections

On WS2003, outgoing connections are created using the New Connection Wizard, while inbound connections can be implemented two ways:

- If you need to allow incoming connections from only a few clients, you can use the Network Connection Wizard to create them. Use this approach if your network is small and clients need to connect only occasionally to access resources on your network.

- If you have a large, distributed network and want to support large numbers of remote clients, you're better off using the Routing and Remote Access Service (RRAS) to create a remote access server to manage your incoming connections. For more information on how to do this, see *Routing and Remote Access* later in this chapter.

Connections—Tools

To establish and configure connections, you can use the New Connection Wizard or, in the case of existing connections, the Network Connections Folder.

New Connection Wizard

This tool is used to create connections and can be opened several ways:

Start → Control Panel → Network Connections → New Connection Wizard

Start → All Programs → Accessories → Communications → New Connection Wizard

Windows Explorer → right-click on My Network Places → Properties → New Connection Wizard

Network Connections Folder → File → New Connection

Nework Connections Folder

This folder displays existing connections and allows you to enable, disable, rename, configure, and view the status of connections by right-clicking on them. Configuration options depend on the type of connection and are discussed in more detail under *Connections—Tasks*. Repairing a connection refreshes the stored configuration information concerning the connection and renews registration with network services. For example, if you repair a local area connection, it tries to refresh its DHCP lease; clears its ARP, NetBIOS, and DNS caches; and attempts to reregister with DNS and WINS servers.

You can open the *Network Connections* folder two ways:

Start → Control Panel → double-click Network Connections

Start → All Programs → Accessories → Communications → Network Connections

The Advanced menu option on the folder lets you specify TAPI location information, configure callback and other remote access features for incoming connections, display network identification information for the machine, rearrange network bindings, bridge LAN or high-speed Internet connections, and install optional networking services.

Connections—Tasks

The following tasks apply generally to most types of connections you can create.

Enable or Disable a Connection

Network Connections Folder → right-click on connection → Enable/Disable

Be sure to notify users before disabling a connection they are using.

Monitor a Connection

You can monitor the status of your connections a couple of ways:

Network Connections Folder → Right-click on an active connection → Status

Right-click on connection icon in system tray (if present) → Status

The General tab displays basic connection statistics. Some connections like VPN also have a Details tab that shows information like the IP address of the remote server, the authentication and encryption methods used, and so on.

You can also monitor the general status of all the connections on your machine by:

Network Connections Folder → View → Details

Share a Connection

See *Advanced* under *Configure a Dial-up Connection* later in this section.

Repair a Connection

If a connection stops working properly, you can try repairing it by:

Network Connections Folder → right-click on connection → Repair

This may fix simple issues like an expired DHCP lease or missing DNS server IP address. After repairing a connection, check it like this:

Network Connections Folder → right-click on connection → Status → Support → Details

If it still doesn't work, open its properties and check its configuration settings.

Configure Remote Access Preferences

For outbound dial-up connections to remote access servers, you can configure your client location information, autodial, and callback settings as follows:

Network Connections Folder → Advanced → Remote Access Preferences → specify your information → OK twice

Enabling autodialing starts an outgoing connection on demand when it's required to access the Internet or a remote access server. Callback lets a remote access server call back a remote client attempting to connect, either to avoid having the client pay the charges or to verify the identity of the client by its phone number. You can also enable connection logging here for troubleshooting purposes.

Callback can be enabled on the client, but it must also be required by the server in order for it to be used. The default setting causes a dialog box to be displayed on the client during the initial connection attempt, requesting that the user specify the phone number that the server should use to call the client back. Alternatively, you can require that the server always call the client back at a specified number to confirm the identity of the client by its location. The callback settings configured on the remote access server override any callback settings you configure for the outbound dial-up connection on your client computer. The server can require callback, deny callback, or allow the client to set the callback procedure.

To reconfigure location information or add additional locations, use Phone and Modem Options in Control Panel.

Enable Operator-Assisted Dialing

This feature is toggled on or off using:

> *Network Connections* Folder → Operator-Assisted Dialing

With this feature on, you can double-click on a connection, pick up the telephone, and manually dial the number or ask the operator to do it. Once the number has been dialed, click Dial, wait for the modem to take control of the line (the modem has gone silent at this point), and hang up.

Bridge Connections

You can easily bridge two or more LAN or high-speed Internet connections. Suppose your server has two NICs connected to different network segments. By bridging these connections, computers on each segment can communicate with each other. To bridge connections:

> *Network Connections* Folder → hold down Ctrl and select connections → right-click → Bridge

Configure Binding Order for Connections

If you have several connections of one type (such as remote access), you can rearrange the order in which they are accessed by network services and which network services they can use. Do this as follows:

> *Network Connections* Folder → Advanced → Advanced Settings → move connections or bindings up or down

Dial-up Connections

The following tasks are for outbound dial-up connections to private networks and the Internet.

Create a Dial-up Connection to the Internet

> New Connection Wizard → Connect to the Internet → Connect using a dial-up modem → specify ISP name and phone number → specify who can use the connection (only you or anybody) → specify credentials → enable/disable Internet Connection Firewall (ICF)

If you allow the connection to be used by anybody, you can select the "Use this account name and password when anyone connects to the Internet using this connection" option to use the specified credentials for all users.

Create a Dial-up Connection to a Remote Access Server

New Connection Wizard → Connect to the network at my workplace → Dial-up connection → specify company name and phone number → specify who can use the connection (only you or anybody)

An administrator on the remote network must grant remote access permissions for your user account before you can dial up and connect.

Dial a Dial-up Connection

Once a connection has been created, you can dial it by:

Network Connections Folder → double-click on connection → Dial

Note that the administrator on a remote private network must first grant dial-in permission to a user before the user can connect to a remote access server. See *Incoming Connections* later in this section for more information.

Disconnect a Dial-up Connection

To disconnect an established connection, you can do one of two things:

Double-click on connection → Disconnect

Right-click on connection icon in system tray (if shown) → Disconnect

Configure a Dial-up Connection

When you use the New Connection Wizard to create an outbound dial-up connection, you specify only minimal configuration information for the connection. If you need to further configure the connection, open its properties sheet by:

Right-click on connection → Properties

The configuration options are the same whether you are configuring a dial-up connection to a private network or to the Internet. The following are some of the more important settings on the five tabs of this properties sheet. Note that some remote access terminology is used in this discussion—for an explanation of PPP, BAP, PAP, CHAP, and similar terms, see *Routing and Remote Access* later in this chapter. Now I'll describe what each tabbed page of options does.

General

Click the Alternates button on the General tab if you want to assign multiple phone numbers to a connection. You can then have the connection try each number in order until it succeeds in establishing a connection. You can also configure it so that successful numbers are moved to the top of the list for future connection attempts.

Select the checkbox to make the connection icon visible in the system tray, as this simplifies the process of monitoring and terminating the connection. The connection icon blinks when data is being transferred, and you can double-click on it to display the status of the connection or right-click on it to terminate the connection.

If you have more than one modem installed, you have additional options on this tab that let you do the following actions.

- Specify which modem or modems will be used for this connection.
- Specify the order in which they are used to establish a connection. (If the first modem fails, then the next one in the list is used.)
- Specify whether they will all call the same numbers.

Options

The Options tab is where you specify redial attempts and whether the connection should automatically terminate after being idle for a period of time. You can also specify that the connection should automatically redial if it is dropped—this is useful for file transfers using FTP since WS2003 can resume a file transfer without needing to start all over.

If you have more than one modem installed and have enabled at least two of them for this connection on the General tab, you have the additional option of Multiple Devices on the Options tab. This new option can be specified as:

Dial all devices (the default selection)
> Use this to configure a PPP Multilink dial-up connection. (The remote access server you are dialing must also support PPP Multilink.)

Dial only the first available device
> Use this if you want to use multiple modems to provide fault tolerance for your connection.

Dial devices only as needed
> Use this to configure a BAP connection for dynamic multilinking. (The remote access server you are dialing must also support BAP.) After you make this selection, click Configure to specify the conditions under which lines are added or dropped to your connection.

Multilink dial-up connections usually don't work if callback is configured on the remote access server. This is because only one callback number can be stored on the server to call the client back, with the result that only the first line in a multilink connection is used. The exception is 2B+D ISDN connections in which both ISDN B channels can have the same number for callback.

Security

The Typical option on the Security tab gives you a series of preconfigured settings for authentication protocols and data encryption schemes. In any case, the remote access client and server will negotiate the highest degree of security for authentication and data integrity that they are both configured to support. The three settings here are (in order of increasing security):

Allow unsecured password (the default setting)
> Allows any authentication protocol including PAP but doesn't encrypt data

Require secured password
> Doesn't allow PAP but can encrypt data

Use smart card
> Allows only smart-card authentication and can encrypt data

If you want more granular control over which authentication protocols and data encryption schemes the dial-up client supports, select Advanced (custom settings) → Settings. For more information on these various schemes and protocols, see *Routing and Remote Access* later in this chapter.

 Since the default setting allows unsecured passwords to be transmitted over the connection, you may want to change this to provide greater security, especially when connecting to the Internet.

Also on this tab are options for opening an interactive terminal window and running a script during the connection establishment process. These options are usually needed only for legacy SLIP connections.

Networking

On the Networking tab you can specify that the ISP's modem bank or company's remote access server you are dialing into is either PPP or SLIP (it's almost always PPP nowadays). If it is PPP, click Settings to configure advanced PPP features, such as software compression, if they are supported by the server you are calling.

Usually, a dial-up connection to the Internet dynamically obtains a client IP address using DHCP, and this is configured by default for Internet Protocol (TCP/IP). If you need to specify a static IP address for your machine for this connection, you can do so here. Table 4-4 shows which networking components are enabled for Internet versus remote access dial-up connections.

Table 4-4. Network components enabled for outbound dial-up connections

Networking component	Type of dial-up connection	
	To a private network	To the Internet
Internet Protocol (TCP/IP)	Yes	Yes
Client for Microsoft Networks	Yes	No
File and Print Sharing for Microsoft Networks	No	No

Advanced

Formerly labeled "Sharing" in W2K Server, the Advanced tab is used to set up Internet Connection Firewall and configuring Internet Connection Sharing:

Internet Connection Firewall (ICF)
Integrated into WS2003 connections is an enhanced firewall feature that you can use to block dangerous traffic from your server. This firewall has been significantly improved over that in W2K Server. To configure ICF:

Advanced tab → select Internet Connection Firewall → Settings

Services
This tab essentially lets you configure which inbound ports to open on your connection to allow Internet users to access services on your network. For example, if you select Web Server (HTTP), it opens port 80 for inbound traffic. By default, all inbound network traffic is blocked.

GUI Reference

Secure Logging

This tab lets you log inbound packets that are either passed through or blocked by your firewall (or both). If you use ICF, you should review your firewall logs regularly.

ICMP

This tab lets you control which kinds of inbound ICMP packets are allowed through your firewall. ICMP packets are often used to probe networks, and a flood of them may be used in a denial-of-service (DoS) attack to prevent legitimate users from accessing services on your network. By default, all inbound ICMP traffic is blocked.

Internet Connection Sharing (ICS)

ICS lets your computer act as a gateway to the Internet so that other computers on your network can access the remote private network or the Internet by dialing up the connection to this server. Using the second checkbox, you can also specify that the connection be dialed automatically when another computer on your network tries to use it, a feature sometimes called on-demand dialing.

ICS is a great feature for the small office/home office (SOHO) environment, but it can cause problems in the enterprise. This is because when you enable this feature, WS2003 automatically reconfigures the TCP/IP settings on the computer to use Automatic Private IP Addressing (APIPA) to assign IP addresses based on a special reserved network ID of 192.168.0.0. As a result, you should not enable ICS on servers in networks that use DNS or DHCP or that have static IP addresses assigned to machines using a different network ID; otherwise, other computers on your network will be unable to communicate with your server. If you want to use ICS for your SOHO, first configure WS2003 computers on your LAN to obtain an IP address automatically using APIPA and then install and configure ICS. See *TCP/IP* later in this chapter for more information on how to use APIPA.

Direct Computer Connections

Direct computer connections are used mainly for file transfers between two computers over a null-modem (file-transfer) cable when no networking adapters are installed. However, you can share a direct computer connection, which gives you a way of connecting two networks together using a null-modem cable.

Create a Direct Computer Connection

To create a direct computer connection, you first need to configure either a COM port to use a serial RS-232C null-modem cable or a parallel port to use an ECP parallel file-transfer cable:

Control Panel → Phone and Modem Options → Modems → Add → select Don't detect my modem → select either cable option → select Port

Then decide which role your machine will assume:

Host machine

The computer that listens for and responds to direct computer connection attempts from a Guest machine:

New Connection Wizard → Set up an advanced connection → Connect directly to another computer → select Host → choose port (LPT or COM) → select users allowed to connect

Guest machine

The computer that attempts to initiate a direct computer connection with a Host machine:

New Connection Wizard → Set up an advanced connection → Connect directly to another computer → select Guest → choose port (LPT or COM) → specify who can use the connection (only you or anybody)

Note that when you create a Host connection, the RRAS service starts and the connection is displayed in the *Network Connections* folder as an Incoming Connection. However, when you create a Guest connection, it's displayed as a Direct Connection.

Establish a Direct Computer Connection

Make sure the null-modem cable is attached, then go to the Guest computer and do this:

Network Connections Folder → double-click on connection → Connect

Configure a Direct Computer Connection

Configuring Guest machines is similar to configuring dial-up connections, and the same five tabs are present on the properties sheet. There are a few differences, though:

* The General tab lets you choose only which device (COM or LPT port) is used for the connection.
* Advanced security settings are used instead of Typical ones used by dial-up connections, and these should generally not be changed.
* All default networking services are enabled for this connection.

The properties sheet for Host machines has only three tabs:

General

Here, you can configure the Host to listen for Guests on multiple ports—for example, COM and LPT. You can even use multilink to combine multiple connections from a single Guest machine, though you'd have to create multiple Guest connections on the Guest machine to do this.

Users

Here, you specify which users are allowed to establish direct computer connections with the Host machine. The information displayed depends on whether your machine belongs to a workgroup or domain.

Networking

Like Guest machines, all default networking services are enabled for this connection.

Incoming Connections

We'll focus here on creating incoming connections on a standalone server in a workgroup scenario. In a domain environment, you're more likely to use the Routing and Remote Access Service (RRAS) to create a full-fledged remote access server for your remote clients.

Create an Incoming Connection

> New Connection Wizard → Set up an advanced connection → Accept incoming connections → select devices to listen on → enable/disable VPN → select users allowed to connect → Properties → allow callback if desired → configure networking components for this connection

Note that the devices you can select depend on what's installed on your machine and may include COM and LPT ports (for direct cable connections), modems, ISDN adapters, and so on.

By enabling a VPN for your connection, you allow remote users to connect to your computer over the Internet—provided, of course, that your machine has a public IP address so packets can be routed to it from the Internet. This option is disabled by default for security reasons. If you enable it, Windows automatically configures ICF, but you should check the firewall configuration to make sure it's configured the way you want it.

The main networking component to configure for the connection is TCP/IP. By opening the properties of this component you can:

- Have clients use their own IP addresses or assign them using DHCP (the default) or from a pool of addresses
- Allow (the default) or deny clients access to other computers on your network

Allow/Deny Dial-in Permission to a User

When creating an incoming connection using the procedure described earlier, you specified the user accounts allowed to connect. By doing so, the remote access permissions for these accounts were set to Allow Access on the Dial-in tab of the properties sheet for each account. If you later want to allow additional users to use the incoming connection or decide to deny access to a user you previously granted it to, do the following:

> Computer Management → System Tools → Local Users and Groups → Users → right-click on user account → Properties → Dial-in → allow or deny access

You can also change the callback option for the user here.

Configure an Incoming Connection

> Right-click on connection → Properties

These settings discussed previously under *Direct Computer Connection* in reference to Host machines.

Internet (Broadband) Connections

In addition to dial-up Internet connections (discussed under *Dial-up Connections* earlier in this section), you can create two types of broadband Internet connections: always-on (LAN) or on-demand (PPPoE) connections.

Create an Always-on Broadband Internet Connection

First, make sure your DSL router is configured properly, is turned on, and your network cables are attached. Then do this:

> New Connection Wizard → Connect to the Internet → Connect using a broadband connection that is always on

That was easy!

Create an On-Demand Broadband Internet Connection

New Connection Wizard → Connect to the Internet → Connect using a broadband connection that requires a username and password → specify ISP name → specify who can use the connection (only you or anybody) → specify credentials → enable/disable ICF

Configure an On-Demand Broadband Internet Connection

The configuration options here are identical to those for dial-up Internet connections, except all references to modems and phone numbers are removed.

Local Area Connections

Local area connections (typically, Ethernet connections) can't be created manually using the New Connection Wizard. Instead, they're created automatically during Setup or when Windows detects a new network adapter. By selecting them in the *Network Connections* folder, they can be configured, disabled, enabled, and monitored like other connections, but they can't be deleted unless you remove the network card associated with the connection.

Configure Local Area Connections

To configure networking components and protocols for local area connections, do this:

Control Panel → Network Connections → select a local area connection → Properties → General

For information about configuring TCP/IP settings for local area connections, see *TCP/IP* later in this chapter. To configure firewall settings on your connection, do this:

Control Panel → Network Connections → select a local area connection → Properties → Advanced → Protect my computer → Settings

For wireless LAN (WLAN) connections, you can also configure authentication by:

Control Panel → Network Connections → select a local area connection → Properties → Authentication

Virtual Private Network Connection

These are outbound connections that securely tunnel over the Internet to a remote VPN server, such as a WS2003 machine with RRAS configured.

Create a New VPN Connection

First, make sure you have an Internet connection configured on your machine, either dial-up, on-demand broadband, or always-on, as described previously. Also, make sure the VPN server on the remote network is ready and listening so you can test your connection after you create it. Now proceed as follows if you have a dedicated Internet connection:

New Connection Wizard → Connect to the network at my workplace → Virtual Private Network connection → specify company name → specify IP address or DNS name of remote VPN server → specify who can use the connection (only you or anybody)

If you have a dial-up or on-demand Internet connection, do this instead:

New Connection Wizard → Connect to the network at my workplace → Virtual Private Network connection → specify company name → select a dial-up connection → specify IP address or DNS name of remote VPN server → specify who can use the connection (only you or anybody)

Instead of selecting a dial-up connection to automatically dial when you try to establish your VPN connection, you can choose *not* to automatically dial a connection. In this case, you have to manually establish your Internet connection before you open your VPN connection.

Configure a VPN Connection

The settings for configuring a VPN connection are the same as those for a dial-up connection to a private network (discussed previously), except for the following differences:

General

Instead of modem settings, you specify the IP address of the remote VPN server on this tab. If you have multiple dial-up or on-demand Internet connections available, you can also specify which one to try first when establishing your VPN connection.

Security

While the default security setting for dial-up connections to private networks is Allow Unsecured Password, the default setting for VPN connections is Require Secured Password with Require Data Encryption also enabled. These settings are necessary because the VPN connection travels over the Internet, which as everyone knows, is a dangerous place (just like the Wild West was in its heyday).

If you enable the option Automatically Use My Windows Name and Password, the credentials of the user currently logged on to your machine are sent to the remote VPN server for authentication.

Networking

File and Print Sharing is enabled for VPN connections (it wasn't for dial-up connections).

Monitor a VPN Connection

Network Connections Folder → Right-click on an active VPN connection → Status

The General tab shows bytes sent and received since the connection was initiated, as well as other network traffic information. The Details tab shows useful information about the type of server, IP address of server and client, type of authentication protocol used, and so on. Here's an example of what you might see on the Details tab if you were connected to another WS2003 machine configured as a VPN server:

```
Server type: PPP
Transports: TCP/IP
Authentication: MS CHAP V2
Encryption: MPPE 56
Compression: MPPC
PPP multilink framing: On
Server IP address: 172.16.11.128
Client IP address: 172.16.11.130
```

Connections—Notes

Dial-up Connections

If you have multiple private networks or ISPs to connect to using dial-up, you can make copies of an existing dial-up connection and rename and modify each copy as desired. Just right-click on the connection and select Create Copy. You can also copy direct and VPN connections.

Specifying a high value for "Idle time before hanging up" for a dial-up connection doesn't guarantee that the connection won't be terminated earlier by the remote access server, which typically has its own disconnect timer configured on it.

Direct Computer Connections

Direct computer connections can also work with modems, ISDN adapters, infrared ports, and other devices.

Incoming Connections

If you try to create a second incoming connection on a machine, it overwrites the existing connection.

Incoming connections can interfere with receiving incoming faxes from the Fax Service. The solution is to make sure you use a modem that supports adaptive answer.

Local Area Connections

On a multihomed computer with multiple network adapters installed, rename each local area connection to reflect the subnet to which it is connected.

If the system has more than one network adapter, make sure you disable any that aren't being used.

You can enable or disable a local area connection as desired in different hardware profiles for laptop computers that can't automatically detect the presence of a connection.

VPN Connection

WS2003, XP, W2K, NT 4.0, Windows 98, and Windows 95 client computers can establish VPN connections with a WS2003 remote access server, but note that:

* All of these clients have built-in support for PPTP except Windows 95, which requires the installation of the optional Windows Dial-Up Network 1.3 Performance & Security Upgrade component.

* Only WS2003, W2K, and XP support L2TP.

* NT 3.5x doesn't support VPN connectivity.

You can also create a VPN connection across a LAN between a VPN client and remote access server, which is becoming a popular way of making your local network secure against sniffing by insiders.

See Also

netsh, *Routing and Remote Access*, *TCP/IP*

Delegation—Concepts

Delegation is the process of granting users limited control over portions of Active Directory. This distributes the administrative burden of managing Active Directory to trusted users and groups in an enterprise, thus easing the workload for administrators.

Delegation Strategies

There are two ways to delegate authority over Active Directory:

Object-based delegation

> One way of delegating administrative privileges in Active Directory is to assign permissions over specific types of objects contained in sites, domains, or OUs to specific users or groups. These objects can include computers, users, groups, printers, and so on. For example, an administrator could delegate Full Control permission over computer objects in an OU called Web Servers to a Webmasters global group, giving members of this group full control over the servers in their department.

Task-based delegation

> Another way of performing delegation is to delegate the authority to perform a particular task for a site, domain, or OU to specific users or groups. For example, an administrator could delegate authority over a domain to a global group called CompAdmins to perform the task "Add a computer to the domain."

In addition, you can delegate the power to delegate by delegating the permission to assign permissions on objects to users and groups. By doing this, you can empower trusted users to entrust others with limited administrative privileges. This sounds like a good idea, but if not documented properly, you will soon lose track of who can do what on your network.

When delegating authority over objects or tasks, always delegate administrative authority over directory objects to groups, not to users. This simplifies Active Directory administration in the long run as your company grows and reorganizes. Nesting groups is a powerful technique that can simplify complex administration.

When choosing which directory objects to delegate authority over, note that delegating authority at the OU level is generally preferable to doing so at the site or domain level. When delegating authority at the OU level, do so at the highest level possible to take advantage of inheritance, which simplifies the assignment of Active Directory permissions. You can also override the permissions that a child object might inherit from its parent object. This is called blocking and prevents future changes to the parent's permissions from flowing to the child. Blocking makes permissions hierarchies more complicated and should be avoided unless absolutely necessary. Instead, it's better to move objects you want to block to a different OU and assign suitable permissions to that OU.

Delegation—Tasks

The console you use to perform delegation depends on which directory object you are delegating authority over:

- To delegate control over domains and OUs, use Active Directory Users and Computers. See *Active Directory—Tools* for more information about this console.

- To delegate control over sites, use Active Directory Sites and Services. See *Site— Tools* for more information about this console.

For both of these consoles, delegation is performed using the Delegation of Control Wizard.

Delegate Authority over a Domain

Active Directory Users and Computers → right-click on a domain → Delegate Control → Next → select users or groups → specify tasks to delegate

The three options here are:

- Join a computer to the domain.
- Manage Group Policy links.
- Create a custom task to delegate.

You can choose one or both of the first two options. If you choose the third option, the other two become unavailable and the wizard can continue two different ways:

Create a custom task to delegate → delegate control over all objects in this folder → specify permissions to delegate for the objects you selected

Create a custom task to delegate → delegate control over some objects in the folder → select objects to delegate authority over → choose whether to also delegate create/delete permissions for the objects you selected → specify permissions to delegate for the objects you selected

For example, you can grant specified users or groups Full Control permission over all Computer accounts in your domain.

Delegate Authority over an OU

Active Directory Users and Computers → right-click on an OU → Delegate Control

The wizard proceeds the same as before except that the list of tasks available for delegation is more extensive (and more useful) than when delegating authority over a domain. For example, you can delegate the right to:

- Create, delete, and manage user accounts
- Reset user passwords and force password change at next logon
- Read all user information
- Create, delete, and manage groups
- Modify the membership of a group
- Manage Group Policy links
- Generate Resultant Set of Policy

Delegate Authority over a Site Object

The term *site object* in this context refers to:

- The Sites container
- A particular site (including the Default-First-Site-Name object)
- A *Servers* folder beneath a particular site object
- The Inter-Site Transports container
- The Subnets container

GUI Reference

To delegate control over a site object:

> Active Directory Sites and Services → right-click on site → Delegate Control → Next → select users or groups → specify tasks to delegate

For any site object that is not a particular site, the only option you have is to create a custom task to delegate. For sites, you can also choose either to delegate Manage Group Policy Links or to create a custom task instead.

Modify Delegated Permissions

You can modify Active Directory permissions that have been assigned to users and groups using the Delegation of Control Wizard, but to do so for domains or OUs requires making the advanced portions of Active Directory visible:

> Active Directory Users and Groups → View → toggle Advanced Features on → right-click on domain or OU → Properties → Security → select user or group → modify permissions as desired

You really need to know what you're doing before you start playing around with Active Directory permissions this way! This also highlights a flaw in this wizard-based approach to delegation—you can use the wizard to delegate, but you can't use it to undo what you delegated—you have to do this manually!

Delegation—Notes

Delegation is a good reason why you might choose to adopt a single-domain model with multiple OUs instead of the more complex multiple-domain model. You can delegate authority over domains as well, but there are fewer administrative groups to manage with only one domain.

After you delegate authority over an object, it may take several minutes until the users or groups can perform the tasks delegated to them while Active Directory replicates the change across the network.

Delegation of authority over Group Policy Objects (GPOs) is different from delegation of authority over containers. See *Group Policy* in this chapter for more information.

You can't delegate control over the *Builtin* folder.

See Also

Active Directory, Delegation, Domain, OU, Site

Devices—Concepts

This topic covers managing hardware devices and device drivers, hardware profiles, and energy-saving options. Topics like how to configure display or mouse settings aren't covered—see *Windows XP in a Nutshell* (O'Reilly) for more information on basic stuff like that.

WS2003 supports a much wider range of hardware devices than the earlier NT Server operating system, including support for both Plug and Play (PnP) and legacy devices. When you install legacy devices on your system, you may have to manually specify resource settings like IRQ and I/O port settings. When you install PnP devices, Windows automatically assigns resources to the device. Should two devices end up with conflicting (overlapping) resource settings, one or both of the devices may fail to work. Using the tools described in this topic, you can troubleshoot such device conflicts—provided you also have a good understanding of PC hardware (see *PC Hardware in a Nutshell* by Robert Bruce Thompson and Barbara Fritchman Thompson from O'Reilly if you don't!).

Device Drivers

Device drivers are software components that enable hardware devices to work and communicate with the operating system. Using Device Manager you can update (install) new drivers and uninstall existing ones. If problems arise after updating drivers, you can also roll back to a previous version of the driver. Driver rollback is possible because of the new driver versioning feature of WS2003. You can also roll back drivers by selecting the Last Known Good Configuration option in the Advanced Menu Options, though Device Manager provides more granularity in performing this task.

To protect device drivers included with WS2003 against corruption or tampering, Microsoft digitally signs them to assure that the file has not been altered or overwritten. You can configure Windows to do one of three things when it finds a device driver that isn't digitally signed:

- Display a warning (default)
- Ignore the issue and install the driver
- Prevent the driver from being installed

Hardware Profiles

Hardware profiles specify which devices are enabled or disabled when your computer starts up. Hardware profiles were often used for laptop computers running NT, on which you could define one profile for mobile use and another for docked use. With PnP support for Windows Server, creating separate hardware profiles is usually unnecessary since a PnP-compliant laptop can automatically detect whether it is docked and enable or disable devices accordingly.

Hardware Compatibility List (HCL)

The HCL lists the hardware platforms and devices supported by WS2003 and can be found at *www.microsoft.com/hwtest/hcl/*.

Hardware Enhancements in WS2003

Other enhancements to hardware support in WS2003 include:

DualView

Display adapters supporting DualView have two video interfaces that allow you to connect two monitors to one adapter and display different output on each monitor. This feature is an extension to the multimonitor support of W2K that previously required two video adapters to do the same thing.

Headless server

The new Emergency Management Services (EMS) lets you install and manage a WS2003 machine remotely from the command line when no keyboard, mouse, display adapter, or monitor is connected to the server. Administrators can also use EMS to manage servers when Windows is not functioning, such as during the boot process or when a stop screen occurs. This feature is supported by only the latest hardware, and it would typically be used to manage rack-mounted servers in a data center. See bootcfg in Chapter 5 for more information.

Hot add memory
> On supporting hardware platforms, you can now add RAM without rebooting your system.

Large IDE drive
> OEM hardware that supports 48-bit block addressing for ATAPI allows you to use IDE drives larger than 137 GB. Support for new UDMA transfer modes is also included.

Devices—Tools

The main tools for managing hardware devices on WS2003 are:

- Device Manager, a snap-in that is part of Computer Management
- Add Hardware, Power Options, and System in Control Panel
- System Information under System Tools in Accessories

In addition, various Control Panel utilities we won't discuss are used to configure specific types of devices. These utilities include Display, Game Controllers, Keyboard, Mouse, Phone and Modem Options, Printers and Faxes, Scanners and Cameras, and Sounds and Audio Devices. A utility called *devcon.exe*, found in the WS2003 Support Tools, can be used to manage devices from the command line. Certain topics like managing disks and printers are covered under *Disks* and *Printing*.

Device Manager

Device Manager is used to display and manage device configuration settings, including:

- Enabling, disabling, and uninstalling devices
- Installing updated drivers for devices
- Diagnosing IRQ conflicts and other resource conflicts
- Manually reconfiguring IRQ and other resource settings to resolve conflicts
- Generating a printed report of your computer's hardware-configuration settings to aid in future troubleshooting efforts

Note that Device Manager can display devices on both local and remote machines, but it can configure settings only on the local machine—when you connect to a remote computer using Computer Management and try to access Device Manager, a message appears saying that Device Manager is acting in read-only mode.

Starting Device Manager

You can access Device Manager in several ways:

> Start → Programs → Administrative Tools → Computer Management → System Tools → Device Manager

> Start → Settings → Control Panel → System → Hardware → Device Manager

> Right-click on My Computer → Properties → Hardware → Device Manager

> Right-click on My Computer → Manage → System Tools → Device Manager

> Start → Run → **devmgmt.msc**

Device Manager displays a hierarchy of device types in the Details pane. Each device-type node contains nodes for each instance of that installed device type, and if a certain type of device is not installed on the computer, the container for that device type is not displayed.

Customizing Device Manager

In addition to being able to customize the MMC appearance, you can use the View menu to change the way in which devices are displayed in Device Manager. There are four different views:

Devices by type
> Groups devices by type. For example, all network adapters are grouped together under the Network Adapters node.

Devices by connection
> Groups devices by connection. For example, all devices connected to the PCI bus are grouped together under the PCI Bus node.

Resources by type
> Groups devices by type of resource used: IRQ, I/O, DMA, or memory.

Resources by connection
> Same as previous view except that a secondary grouping is included according to system board or PCI bus connection.

Two more options help you analyze your hardware configuration:

Show Hidden Devices
> Toggles the display of non–Plug and Play devices as well as devices that have been removed from the system but whose drivers have not been uninstalled.

Print
> Prints a report of your hardware devices and the resources they use. You have several different print options for different kinds of reports.

Add Hardware

This Control Panel utility opens a wizard that walks you through the process of installing new hardware devices or removing existing ones. Most of the time, this is not necessary with WS2003 as Plug and Play devices are usually detected and installed automatically without the need to reboot the system. Should the system require a reboot, Found New Hardware starts after the reboot and completes the installation.

Add Hardware is usually used for installing legacy (non–Plug and Play) devices, in which case you skip the Plug and Play option and manually specify the type and model of the device from a list displayed by the wizard. You can also run Add Hardware to unplug or eject a device such as a removable drive. If you need to do this frequently with a device, there is an option in the wizard to place an icon in the system tray, which can be used for this purpose.

Power Options

This Control Panel utility is used for:

- Configuring energy-saving features by selecting a power scheme to power down your disks and turn off your monitor when not in use
- Automatically switching your system into standby mode and enabling or disabling hibernation mode
- Configuring uninterruptible power supply (UPS) devices to protect your computer against sudden power loss

GUI Reference

Standby is the power-management mode in which both the display and hard drive are powered down to save power. Standby mode consumes minimal power for the processor and system board, as opposed to powering off, which causes your system to consume no power at all. The advantage is that the system can return from standby mode more quickly than rebooting from a powered-off condition.

Hibernation is a power-management option that powers off your display and hard disks, writes the contents of physical memory (RAM) to disk, and powers off your computer so that, when you restart, your desktop is exactly as you left it.

The Power Schemes tab lets you select a power scheme for your system (see Table 4-5). You can also create a custom scheme by modifying an existing scheme and saving it under a different name. Note that only a subset of these options may work if you have an older computer whose BIOS is not compliant with the Advanced Configuration and Power Interface (ACPI) standard supported by WS2003. By using the Advanced tab, you can place an icon in the system tray that can display your current power source (AC, battery, or UPS). See *Devices—Notes* for some recommendations for various kinds of systems.

Table 4-5. Default power schemes

Scheme	Turn off monitor	Turn off hard disks	System standby	System hibernates
Home/Office Desk	20 mins.	Never	Never	Never
Portable/Laptop	15 mins.	30 mins.	20 mins.	1 hr.
Presentation	Never	Never	Never	Never
Always On	20 mins.	Never	Never	Never
Minimal Power Management	15 mins.	Never	Never	Never
Max Battery	15 mins.	Never	20 mins.	45 mins.

System

This Control Panel utility is a catchall for a variety of different system-related configuration tasks. As far as managing hardware is concerned, you can use this tool to install hardware, configure devices, manage device driver signing, and create and manage hardware profiles. The first two tasks can be performed using Add Hardware and Device Manager, respectively; the remaining topics are discussed earlier under *Devices—Concepts*.

System Information

This utility under System Tools in Accessories can be used to display current system information for local or remote computers. System Information provides comprehensive information for troubleshooting problems with hardware and drivers and other software components on the connected computer. This information is either queried in real time or accessed from the registry, depending on the type of information needed. System Information displays hardware- and software-configuration information for a computer but can't be used to make changes to this information—use Device Manager to change hardware settings for a computer.

For administrators familiar with NT 4.0 Server, the System Information snap-in performs functions similar to those provided by the NT administrative tool called NT Diagnostics.

System Information displays five types of settings:

System Summary
Contains general information such as operating-system version, computer name, processor type, BIOS version, and memory.

Hardware Resources
Contains hardware information such as IRQ settings, I/O ports, DMA, and mapped memory. The Conflicts/Sharing node is useful for identifying possible device conflicts.

Components
Contains information about device drivers for keyboard, mouse, video, storage, network, modem, and multimedia. The Problem Devices node is useful for identifying devices with driver problems.

Software Environment
Contains detailed information about the software currently running on the computer, including device drivers, environment variables, pending print jobs, current network connections, tasks running (in more detail than that shown by Taskbar), and the status of installed services. It also displays the installed program groups and their shortcuts, programs in the Startup group, and OLE registration information.

Internet Settings
Contains information about the version, proxy configuration, cache settings, digital certificates, and security-zone settings for Internet Explorer.

Devices—Tasks

The following tasks for managing devices use the various tools covered in the previous section.

Add New Hardware

How you add a new hardware device depends on how fully your system and the device support the Plug and Play (PnP) standard:

PnP devices
When a PnP device is connected to a PnP system, WS2003 automatically detects a newly installed device and assigns it appropriate hardware resource settings (IRQ, I/O, memory, and DMA).

Legacy (non–PnP) devices
Use Control Panel → Add Hardware to install legacy devices or to install PnP devices into systems that aren't fully PnP-compliant. If the wizard can't detect the device, you must specify its settings manually.

Configure Device Driver Signing

To specify the action Windows should take when it encounters a device driver that has not been digitally signed, do this:

> Control Panel → System → Hardware → Driver Signing

Conserve Energy for Devices

To configure your system to enter standby mode automatically, do this:

> Control Panel → Power Options → Power Schemes → select a default scheme

To manually enter standby mode, do this:

> Start → Shutdown → Standby

You can also configure your system so that when the power button is pressed, the system enters standby mode instead of powering off completely:

> Control Panel → Power Options → Advanced → Power buttons → select Standby

To configure your system to enable hibernation mode, do this:

> Control Panel → Power Options → Hibernation → Enable hibernate support

Note that to support hibernation you must have free disk space greater than or equal to the amount of physical memory (RAM).

To manually enter hibernation mode do this:

> Start → Shutdown → Hibernate

Note that standby and hibernation mode are supported only on systems that are fully ACPI-compliant. You can password-protect your computer during standby by:

> Control Panel → Power Options → Advanced → Prompt for password when computer goes off standby

Note that the same password is used for both standby and hibernation modes.

To bring your system out of standby or hibernation, press the power button. You can also configure your keyboard or mouse to bring your system out of standby by doing the following:

> Device Manager → Keyboards or Mice → right-click on keyboard or mouse → Properties → Power Management → Allow this device to bring the computer out of standby

Some network cards that support Wake On LAN, such as 3C905-TX can be configured to automatically shut themselves off to save power. You may also be able to configure them to bring the computer out of standby when incoming traffic is detected or when a network management station tries to contact it. Some USB hubs can also be configured to turn themselves off to save power and bring the system out of standby mode.

Create and Manage Hardware Profiles

Use the System utility in Control Panel to create and manage hardware profiles, and use Device Manager to specify whether a particular device should be included in or excluded from the currently loaded hardware profile. To create a new hardware profile, do this:

> Control Panel → System → Hardware → Hardware Profiles → select an existing profile → Copy → provide a descriptive name for the profile (e.g., Mobile User)

To specify which devices are enabled or disabled in your new hardware profile, do this:

> Reboot → select the new hardware profile when prompted during startup → log on → Device Manager → right-click on a device → Properties

Then, under Device Usage, you can either enable or disable the device for the currently loaded hardware profile or disable it for all hardware profiles.

To specify which hardware profile is the default, do the following:

> Control Panel → System → Hardware → Hardware Profiles → use arrow buttons to move the desired profile to the top of the list

If a hardware profile doesn't appear in the menu during startup, you can force it to appear by:

> Control Panel → System → Hardware → Hardware Profiles → select profile → Properties → Always include this profile

If your machine is an older laptop and WS2003 can't detect that it is a laptop, do this:

> Control Panel → System → Hardware → Hardware Profiles → select profile → Properties → This is a portable computer → specify current docking state

To select a hardware profile when booting the machine:

> Boot your computer → select the new hardware profile when prompted during startup

Note that the Hardware Profile/Recovery Menu is not displayed if there is only one hardware profile configured on the system.

Disable a Device

> Device Manager → right-click on a device → Disable

This action prevents the device drivers from loading during startup—the device is still present but doesn't function.

Enable a Device

> Device Manager → right-click on a device → Enable

Manage Device Drivers

To view the drivers used for a device, do this:

> Device Manager → right-click on a device → Properties → Driver → Driver Details

To install a new or updated device driver for the device, do this:

> Device Manager → right-click on a device → Properties → Driver → Update Driver

Note that Microsoft may provide updated drivers for devices using its Windows Update site, and you can use the Automatic Updates feature of WS2003 to automatically download and install these updates.

If you install a new driver and the device stops working, try returning to the previous driver like this:

> Device Manager → right-click on a device → Properties → Driver → Rollback Driver

To manually uninstall the driver for the device, do this:

> Device Manager → right-click on a device → Properties → Driver → Uninstall Driver

Reinstall a Device

If a device is behaving strangely, you may want to try uninstalling it and then reinstalling it. To reinstall a PnP device, first make sure the device is connected and turned on. Then, if the device has not been properly uninstalled and the drivers for the device are still present on the system, do this:

Device Manager → right-click on computer → Scan for hardware changes

If the device has been properly uninstalled and the drivers for the device have been completely removed from the system, reboot your machine to autodetect the device.

For legacy devices or for systems that aren't fully PnP–compliant, use Control Panel → Add Hardware to reinstall the device.

Scan for Hardware Changes

Device Manager → right-click on computer node → Scan for hardware changes

This forces WS2003 to scan your system for new PnP devices that were not properly detected when you installed the hardware. You can also use it to scan your system when you have manually changed hardware settings on a device and want these changes recognized by the operating system. Normally, when you reboot, this hardware scan is performed automatically, but if you have installed hardware that doesn't require a reboot and the system did not detect it, forcing a scan could cause it to be detected properly. If hardware is detected, the Found New Hardware Wizard appears, leading you through a series of prompts. If this wizard doesn't appear, you can force its appearance using Control Panel → Add Hardware. Note that this method doesn't check for legacy devices.

Uninstall a Device

Device Manager → right-click on device → Uninstall → accept prompts → shut down → physically remove the device from your system → restart

Uninstalling a device removes the drivers for the device. You uninstall PnP devices simply by disconnecting them from the system (you may need to restart the system to free up resources).

Update Drivers for a Device

Device Manager → right-click on device → Properties → Drivers → Update Drivers

This starts the Update Device Driver Wizard, which steps you through the process of loading new drivers for the device.

View or Modify Resource Settings for a Device

Device Manager → right-click on device → Properties → Resources → deselect option for using automated settings → Change Setting → specify new resource settings

You generally can't modify the resource settings of PnP devices.

View System Information

Start → Programs → Accessories → System Tools → System Information

Start → Run → **msinfo32**

This displays the system information for the local machine. To connect to a remote computer, do this:

> View → Remote Computer

You can save your system information to a text file or print it out for documentation purposes by:

> File → Export or Print

To view information about network-related hardware and software, do this:

> Tools → Net Diagnostics

To check the integrity of system files, do this:

> Tools → File Signature Verification Utility

Troubleshoot Device Problems

First, view the icon for the device node in Device Manager, which may tell you something about the problem (see Table 4-6). Then try these steps:

> Device Manager → right-click on problem device → Properties → General → read Device Status message → Resources → read Conflicting Device List

If this fails, try:

> Device Manager → right-click on problem device → Properties → General → Troubleshoot

Table 4-6. Using device icons in Device Manager to troubleshoot devices

Device icon	Status of device
Normal	Working properly
Stop sign	Disabled due to resource conflicts
Exclamation point	Drivers missing or incorrect device configuration

Devices—Notes

Understanding some subtle points about devices can help alleviate (at least in some cases) the inevitable frustration caused by hardware that doesn't work properly due to improper configuration.

Device Manager

Exercise caution when using Device Manager: by making improper changes to your hardware resource settings, you can easily render your system inoperable. Make sure you have an understanding of computer hardware configurations before attempting to manually change these settings.

Make changes to hardware resource settings sparingly—when you manually change a device setting, the change becomes fixed and leaves WS2003 less flexibility when assigning remaining resources to PnP devices.

Don't use Device Manager to disable a device, such as your hard drive, that is necessary to start WS2003 or you could be in trouble!

Before you try uninstalling and reinstalling a PnP device that has stopped functioning, simply try rebooting the system to see if the problem corrects itself.

Uninstalling a device doesn't remove the device drivers from your hard disk.

Add Hardware

You may need to be logged on as an Administrator to install a PnP device if user inter-action is required during the installation process. You must be logged on as an Administrator to use Add/Remove Hardware to install a legacy (non–PnP) device.

If you encounter errors when installing a PnP device, check Event Viewer for more information on PnP events.

If you install a legacy device, you also manually specify the resource settings (IRQ, I/O, and so on) for the device. This means that if a resource conflict that involves the device arises afterward, WS2003 can't reconfigure the settings that you configured manually. This is a good reason for using only PnP hardware with WS2003.

Group Policy can prevent this wizard from running on a computer belonging to a certain domain.

Power Options

Additional tabs may be displayed by Power Options on certain machines. For example, laptop computers may show an Alarms tab that can be used to configure an alarm to warn you when your battery is about to run out.

On portables, you can specify one scheme for battery use and another for AC use.

Make sure that you save all your work before you enter (or allow your machine to enter) standby mode, since any data stored only in physical memory (RAM) is lost when standby occurs.

Servers should not generally be allowed to enter standby mode since they are often in demand 24 hours a day.

A command called `powercfg` can be used to configure power options from the command line. First introduced in XP SP1, this command is intended mainly for laptops.

System

If you specify that the Hardware Profile menu is displayed for zero seconds, the menu is not displayed and the default profile is loaded automatically. You can override this by pressing the spacebar during startup.

You can also enable or disable specific services for a given hardware profile by doing the following:

> Administrative Tools → Services → right-click on a service → Properties → Log On → select a hardware profile → Enable or Disable

System Information

When you first have your computer up and running, use System Information to print a complete report of the hardware configuration, and file this report somewhere safe. It may be useful later on should hardware problems occur. Make sure you update this report whenever you install new hardware or reconfigure existing hardware.

See Also

Administrative Tools, Automatic Updates, `bootcfg`, `date`, `driverquery`, `mode`, `net time`, `shutdown`, `systeminfo`, `time`

DFS—Concepts

DFS stands for Distributed File System, a feature that lets you create a logical tree of shared-disk resources that are physically located on different computers on the network. DFS simplifies the task of managing shared-disk resources across a network and makes it easier for users to find and access these resources. From a user's point of view, the DFS tree appears to be a single hierarchy of folders located on a single server while in actuality it may consist of shared folders on many different computers. Users don't need to know the computer on which a shared folder resides in order to access the folder—they simply connect to the DFS tree and access the folder. For example, documents for the sales department could be located on three different file servers on the network, but by implementing DFS, users can access these documents as if they were all stored on the same server.

DFS doesn't add any additional access control to the shared folders it manages. If users have suitable permissions to access a shared folder on the network, they can access it through DFS. However, when administrators add a DFS root or DFS link, they can specify who has permission to add new DFS links to the tree.

DFS Terminology

DFS trees consist of the following elements:

DFS namespace
Sometimes called a DFS tree, a hierarchical collection of shared resources consisting of a DFS root and one or more DFS links.

DFS target
The actual shared folder on the network to which a DFS root or link maps. The term "DFS target" replaces the term "DFS replica," which was used in W2K.

DFS root
The starting point for a DFS tree or namespace. Each DFS root maps to a DFS target, and clients can locate and access shared resources in DFS trees by browsing the root.

DFS link
A point beneath the root in a DFS tree or namespace. Each DFS link maps to one or more DFS targets.

In W2K Server, each machine could host only one DFS root. This is still the case for WS2003 Standard Edition, but machines running the Enterprise Edition can now host multiple DFS roots.

Types of DFS

There are two types of DFS you can use:

Standalone DFS
This method is used in small workgroup scenarios in which Active Directory has not been deployed. Configuration information for the DFS tree is stored on a single standalone server, and users locate and access shared resources by connecting to the DFS tree on the standalone server.

Domain-based DFS
Also called fault-tolerant DFS, this method is used in larger domain scenarios and stores DFS configuration information in Active Directory. Domain-based DFS automatically replicates this information to all domain controllers using standard

Active Directory replication. Note that in domain-based DFS, client computers must be members of the domain where the DFS root is located.

DFS Replication

DFS replication uses the File Replication Service (FRS) to replicate content across multiple DFS trees. By creating additional targets for DFS roots, you can replicate the content of your DFS tree. This is done for two reasons:

- To provide fault tolerance in case a server hosting a DFS root goes down
- To provide load balancing so clients can access the nearest DFS tree

New to DFS in WS2003 is the ability to choose from four possible DFS replication topologies:

Ring
This is the default method and is ideal for single-site DFS.

Hub and Spoke
You might use this approach to replicate DFS from corporate headquarters to branch offices.

Full Mesh
Distributed enterprises might adopt this approach, but it can be difficult to troubleshoot.

Custom
You design what you want DFS to do.

DFS Clients

It's not enough to set up DFS on a server for it to work: the client computers that users use must also support DFS. DFS clients are available for the following Microsoft Windows operating systems:

WS2003, XP, and W2K
Includes DFS 5.0 client (fully functional)

NT 4.0 with Service Pack 3 or higher
Includes DFS 4.x/5.0 client (works with standalone DFS servers only)

Windows 98
Includes DFS 4.x/5.0 client (works with standalone DFS servers only), but a DFS 5.0 client that supports domain-based DFS servers as well can be downloaded from Microsoft's web site

Windows 95
Allows a downloadable DFS 4.x/5.0 client (works with standalone DFS servers only)

To use DFS, users connect to the root of the tree using any standard method of accessing shared folders and then browse it to find the child node they want to access. To connect to the DFS root, the client uses the DNS name of the host server for the root. From the user's point of view, DFS is like a series of folders located within one shared folder on one file server. In order to connect to a DFS tree, however, the client computer must be running DFS client software.

Clients access DFS roots on standalone DFS host servers by specifying the UNC path to the root. For example, if the DFS root named *Files* points to the shared folder *Pub* on member server *George*, then you would access the DFS root using *George**Files*. By contrast, for domain-based DFS, you specify the DNS name of the domain in the UNC path (e.g., \\mtit com\Files).

Implementing DFS

To implement domain-based DFS, you might do this:

1. Create a DFS root on a domain controller or member server.
2. Add DFS links to shared folders on file servers in your domain.
3. Add a second DFS target to your root for fault tolerance and load balancing.
4. Configure replication between your DFS trees.

DFS—Tasks

The following procedures use the DFS console, which is opened by:

> Start → Programs → Administrative Tools → Distributed File System

> Command line → **dfsgui.msc**

You can also manage many aspects of DFS from the command line using dfscmd (see Chapter 5 for more information).

Add a Root

For standalone DFS, do this:

> Right-click on root node → New root → standalone root → specify server name → type a name for your new root → specify folder to share

The last step is required only if the name you typed is not that of a folder already shared on your system.

For domain-based DFS, do this:

> Right-click on root node → New root → domain root → specify domain → specify server name → type a name for your new root → specify folder to share

Add a New Root Target

This option is available on domain-based DFS only:

> Right-click on DFS root → New Root Target → specify host server → create or specify a folder to which the DFS root will point

The entire DFS root you select is now fault-tolerant—if a DFS client tries to connect to the root and the original host server is unavailable, DFS transparently redirects the client to the new host server where the replica of the root resides. Once you have created a root target, you should configure replication, as described later in this section.

Add a Link

For either standalone or domain-based DFS, first make sure the shared folder you want to target already exists somewhere on the network, and then:

> Right-click on DFS root → New Link → specify name for link → specify shared folder to which link points → specify DFS client cache time

By default, DFS client cache time is set to 1,800 seconds, or 30 minutes for DFS links, and to 300 seconds, or 5 minutes, for a DFS root. You may want to increase these

GUI Reference

times if clients need frequent access to shared folders and if you don't create or delete shared folders often on your file servers, as this reduces the network traffic associated with DFS.

Once you have created a DFS link, you can add additional DFS targets to it:

> Right-click a DFS link → New Target → specify shared folder to which link points

Then if one target becomes unavailable for the link, clients can connect to another target instead.

Configure Replication

You can configure replication only if you have added a new root target for your root. To configure replication, do this:

> Right-click on DFS root → Configure Replication → specify which root will be the initial master → select a replication topology

Configure your replication schedule by:

> Right-click on DFS root → Properties → Replication → Schedule → specify when replication should or should not be allowed to occur → exclude certain types of files or subfolders from replication

If you need to make major changes to your DFS setup, you should first stop replication by:

> Right-click on DFS root → Stop Replication

You'll then have to reconfigure replication to get things going again.

Monitor Status of a Root or Link

> Right-click on a DFS root or link → Check Status

A red circle with an X indicates that the root or link is unavailable. If a root or link points to multiple targets, it is still available as long as at least one of its targets is still available.

Publish DFS

For domain-based DFS you can publish your DFS setup in Active Directory to make it easier for users to locate and access DFS resources on the network:

> Right-click on DFS root → Properties → Publish

DFS—Notes

DFS shared folders don't need to be on WS2003 machines; they can be on downlevel NT or W2K servers or even client computers running Windows 95 or 98. However, to get the full advantages of DFS replication, use only WS2003 machines.

Using DFS eliminates the need to map network drives on client computers, making accessing network resources simpler for users.

If you want to use automatic replication with domain-based DFS, you must install DFS on NTFS.

You can't replicate between DFS shared folders on a single machine; the shared folders must be located on different machines.

DFS-link hierarchies can be only one level deep—you can't create links beneath links. A workaround is to target an existing link to a root on a different server, but this adds complexity.

For details about the integration of DFS with Active Directory, see *Active Directory* (O'Reilly).

See Also

dfscmd, *Shared Folders*

DHCP—Concepts

DHCP stands for Dynamic Host Configuration Protocol, a protocol used to simplify the management of TCP/IP clients on a network. With DHCP, a client can automatically obtain IP addresses, subnet masks, and other TCP/IP configuration settings from a DHCP server. This is easier than the alternative—manually configuring a static IP address for every client on your network.

 For a third method of configuring TCP/IP clients, see *Automatic Private IP Addressing (APIPA)* under *TCP/IP* later in this chapter.

How DHCP Works

When a DHCP client starts up, it contacts a DHCP server and asks to lease an IP address. The DHCP server responds by selecting an available IP address from a *scope*, a range of addresses that it manages. The server then leases the selected address to the client for a certain period of time (eight days by default), provides the client with the subnet mask associated with the address, and optionally provides the client with additional information such as a default gateway address, addresses of DNS servers, and addresses of WINS servers. Once the client has obtained a lease, the client has to renew the lease periodically with the server to maintain its current address. If the client shuts down properly, it releases its lease and the server may offer the same address to a different client unless the address has been specifically reserved for the original client.

To really understand DHCP, you need to know what's going on with DHCP at the packet level (you can view this information using a sniffer like Network Monitor, an optional network-monitoring component of WS2003). There are four types of DHCP packets:

DHCPDISCOVER
> This packet is broadcast by the client when it starts up. It contains the MAC address (physical or hardware address) and computer name of the client and essentially says, "If there is a DHCP server out there, please offer me a lease." This is repeated every five minutes until successful.

DHCPOFFER
> This packet is broadcast by a DHCP server in response to a DHCPDISCOVER packet. It contains the MAC address of the DHCP client that sent the DHCPDISCOVER packet, the IP address and subnet mask being offered to the client, the duration of the lease being offered, and the IP address of the DHCP server.

DHCPREQUEST

This packet is broadcast by the client in response to the first lease offer it receives. The DHCPREQUEST packet includes the IP address of the DHCP server offering the lease and basically says, "I'll take the lease you are offering me." Other available DHCP servers also hear this message but respond to it by withdrawing their offered leases (no message sent).

DHCPACK

This packet is broadcast by the server and tells the client, "The IP address is yours for so many days." At this point the client initializes its TCP/IP stack and can begin communicating over the network.

When 50% of the lease time has expired, the DHCP client sends a DHCPREQUEST packet directly to the DHCP server requesting a renewal. If the server is available, it responds with DHCPACK and the lease clock is reset.

If the server is not available, the client waits until 87.5% of the lease time has expired and then broadcasts a DHCPDISCOVER packet that basically says, "Is there any DHCP server out there that can renew my lease?" A different server can respond with DHCPOFFER if the scope of the server overlaps the scope of the client's original DHCP server.

If 100% of the lease time expires and the client hasn't heard from any DHCP servers, it releases its address and starts broadcasting DHCPDISCOVER packets to begin the lease process anew. In the meantime, it can't use TCP/IP to communicate on the network.

If a client is shut down properly, it releases its IP address. When it restarts, it tries to renew the same address it had before. If it can't contact a DHCP server, it continues to use the address until its current lease expires. If the lease expired while the client was offline, the lease process starts from the beginning.

DHCP Terminology

To understand how DHCP works on WS2003, you need to know the following terminology:

Scope

A set of IP addresses that a DHCP server issues to clients on a particular subnet. A scope is typically a contiguous block of addresses, possibly with certain addresses excluded, such as addresses that have already been manually assigned to servers. You can create three types of scopes:

Ordinary scope (or simply scope)

Specifies a range of IP addresses (with exclusions) that can be leased to DHCP clients on a connected subnet.

Multicast scope

Can issue a multicast address to a group of computers on the network. Multicasting is used for conferencing applications, such as Microsoft Windows Media Technologies, and can be used to "broadcast" information to a specific group of computers.

Superscopes

Consist of two or more scopes grouped together so they can be administered as a single entity. Any scope within a superscope can lease an address to any client on the subnet. Superscopes are useful when you planned for a certain number of DHCP clients on your network but later discovered you had more clients than you anticipated. You can create an additional scope for the extra clients and then combine this with the original scope to create a superscope without needing to delete your old scope and create a new one. Superscopes are also useful when you need to replace an existing range of IP addresses with a new range of addresses.

Scope options
Additional TCP/IP settings issued by the DHCP server to its clients. Scope options are specified by number, and the ones commonly used on Microsoft networks are as follows:

003 Router
IP address of default gateway

006 DNS Servers
IP address of a DNS server

015 DNS Domain Name
DNS name of the client's domain

044 WINS/NBNS Servers
IP address of a WINS server

046 WINS/NBT Node Type
Method used by client for NetBIOS over TCP/IP (NetBT) name resolution

047 NetBIOS Scope ID
Local NetBIOS scope ID of client

Scope options can also be configured at four different levels:

Server level
Options configured for this level are applied to all DHCP clients managed by the DHCP server. An example would be specifying the same WINS server (option 044) for all clients no matter which subnet they reside on. Server-level options are overridden by scope- or reserved client–level options.

Scope level
Options configured for this level are applied only to clients who lease their address from the particular scope. An example would be specifying a unique default gateway address (option 003) for each subnet/scope. Scope-level options are overridden by reserved client–level options.

Class level
Options configured for this level are applied only to clients belonging to a specified class. For example, you could assign the address of a DNS server to the class of client computers running WS2003 as their operating system.

Reserved client level
Options configured for this level are applied only to the client having the particular reservation.

Reservation
An IP address is reserved by a client whose network adapter has a particular MAC address. Instead of manually assigning static IP addresses to your network servers, you can create reservations for them so they can obtain their addresses from DHCP servers but always receive the same address from the servers.

Activation
Once a scope is created on a DHCP server, it must be activated (turned on) before the server can start leasing IP addresses from the scope to clients.

Authorization

Before a DHCP server running WS2003 can lease IP addresses to clients in an Active Directory environment, it must first be authorized by a member of the Enterprise Admins group. This gives administrators an extra level of control over their networks to prevent unauthorized DHCP servers from hijacking DHCP client machines.

Implementing DHCP

To implement DHCP using a DHCP server running WS2003, you can proceed as follows:

1. Manually specify a static IP address, subnet mask, and default gateway address on a member server.

2. Use Manage Your Server to add the DHCP Server role to your member server.

3. Authorize your DHCP server in Active Directory.

4. Create a scope on your DHCP server, excluding any IP addresses from the scope as necessary and configuring any scope options required by clients.

5. Create reservations for DHCP clients such as mail servers that must always lease the same IP address.

6. Activate the scope you created.

7. Configure client computers to obtain their IP addresses automatically from a DHCP server.

If you have configured your routers to forward DHCP traffic, you may need only one DHCP server for your entire network. Although DHCP traffic is mostly of the broadcast type, it's not very heavy unless you have a large number of DHCP clients and the lease period is very short. If your routers block DHCP traffic on UDP ports 67 and 68, you need either a DHCP server on each subnet or DHCP relay agents (described later in this section). For fault tolerance, it's a good idea to have two DHCP servers on your network, one with 80% of the available addresses and the other with 20%, something called the 80/20 rule.

 DHCP servers can work together with DNS servers to combine and simplify the administration of both IP addresses and DNS names for clients on your network. See *DNS* later in this chapter for more information.

Dynamic Updates

Dynamic updates link DHCP and DNS servers together to simplify the task of configuring DNS on DHCP clients. When a client is configured to use dynamic updates, it can either update its DNS information on the DNS server directly or ask the DHCP server to do this on its behalf. By default, WS2003 DHCP servers are configured to perform dynamic updates only when (and how) DHCP clients request such updates. They are also configured to discard such DNS information when DHCP leases expire. Versions of Windows that support dynamic updates include WS2003, XP, and W2K.

If you have downlevel (NT) or legacy (Windows 95/98) systems configured as DHCP clients, you can also configure DHCP servers to dynamically update DNS information for these clients as well, though this is not the default behavior for DHCP servers.

DHCP Relay Agents

DHCP relay agents are machines that listen for lease requests from DHCP clients on their own subnet and forward these requests to a DHCP server located on a different subnet. Consider a DHCP client on subnet A requesting a lease from a DHCP server on subnet B via a DHCP relay agent configured on subnet A:

1. The client on subnet A broadcasts a DHCPDISCOVER packet on its subnet.

2. The relay agent on subnet A hears the client's DHCPDISCOVER broadcast, picks up the packet, readdresses it using directed (not broadcast) IP to the DHCP server on subnet B, and sends it off.

3. The packet from the relay agent is forwarded by the router from subnet A to subnet B (since routers forward directed traffic but typically block broadcast traffic).

4. The DHCP server on subnet B receives the DHCPDISCOVER packet from the relay agent. Instead of responding with a broadcast DHCPOFFER packet, it sends the DHCPOFFER packet directly to the relay agent on subnet A.

5. The relay agent on subnet A receives the DHCPOFFER packet from the server, readdresses it as a local subnet broadcast, and broadcasts the packet to subnet A.

6. The client on subnet A hears the DHCPOFFER packet broadcast by the relay agent but interprets it as if it were broadcast by a DHCP server on its subnet. (The relay agent thus acts as a proxy for the DHCP server.)

7. The client responds by broadcasting a DHCPREQUEST packet and the process continues—with the relay agent acting as a proxy—until the client can lease an address.

DHCP—Tasks

The following procedures are performed using the DHCP console, which is opened by either:

Start → Programs → Administrative Tools → DHCP

Start → Run → **dhcpmgmt.msc**

Note that this console is available only if you have installed the optional DHCP component using Add or Remove Programs or added the DHCP Server role to your machine using Manage Your Server. You can also manage many aspects of DHCP servers from the command line using the netsh (Netshell) command (see Chapter 5 for more information).

Authorize a DHCP Server

If a DHCP server belongs to a domain, it must be authorized in Active Directory before it can be used. If you install the DHCP Server service on a domain controller, it should authorize itself automatically. If this doesn't occur or if the machine is a member server, authorize it manually as follows:

Right-click on DHCP server node → Authorize

After a minute or two, press F5 to refresh and see if authorization was successful. Note that you must be a member of the Enterprise Admins group to authorize a DHCP server. Unauthorizing a DHCP server causes it to ignore all lease and renewal requests from DHCP clients until it is reauthorized.

To connect to authorized DHCP servers and manage them or change their authorization status, do this:

Right-click root node → Manage authorized servers

Create a Scope

A DHCP server belonging to a domain must be authorized before you can create a scope. After creating a scope, you must activate it before clients can lease addresses from the DHCP server. To create an ordinary scope, do this:

Right-click on server node → New Scope → specify friendly name for scope → specify start and end IP addresses → specify subnet mask → specify individual addresses or blocks of addresses to exclude from scope → specify duration of lease → specify scope options such as default gateway address, DNS domain name, addresses of DNS servers, and addresses of WINS servers on your network

To reconfigure basic settings for your scope, do this:

Right-click on scope → Properties → General

Note that you can increase the range of IP addresses in a scope, but you can't decrease it. If you want to change the IP address range of the scope to a different subnet, you must first remove all exclusions and options that conflict with the new subnet. Otherwise, you will receive the error message "The specified range either overlaps an existing range or is not valid." An easier solution is usually to delete the scope entirely and create a new one. Be aware that you have to release and renew IP addresses from your DHCP clients afterward. It's essential to plan the DHCP configuration carefully before implementing it on your network.

To exclude additional IP addresses from an existing scope, do this:

Select scope → right-click on Address Pool → New Exclusion Range

Note that you can't exclude addresses that are actively leased to clients. To remove an existing exclusion, do this:

Select Address Pool → right-click on an exclusion → Delete

Configure Scope Options

You can configure scope options at several levels:

(Server level) Right-click on Server Options → Configure Options → General

(Scope level) Select scope → Right-click on Scope Options → Configure Options → General

(Reserved client level) Select scope → Select Reservations → right-click on reservation → Configure Options → General

The usual options to configure in Microsoft networks are 003, 006, and 015. If you are using WINS, configure 044 and 046 also. Each option requires you to specify information related to that option, as summarized in Table 4-7. For options involving IP addresses, you can optionally enter the name of the computer and click Resolve to determine its IP address. If you configure 044, then 046 must be configured as well. For 046, the typical choice is 0x8 if a WINS server is present on the network.

Table 4-7. DHCP scope options and the information you need to specify

Option	Information
003 Router	IP addresses of default gateways
006 DNS Servers	IP addresses of DNS servers
015 DNS Domain Name	DNS name of local domain
044 WINS/NBNS Servers	IP addresses of WINS servers
046 WINS/NBT Node Type	0x1 = B-node (broadcast) 0x2 = P-node (peer) 0x4 = M-node (mixed) 0x8 = H-node (hybrid)

Activate a Scope

Check the configuration of your new scope carefully before activating it, then do this:

Right-click on scope → Activate

Only an activated scope responds to DHCP lease and renewal requests from client computers. Activation allows you to selectively control which scopes are available on a DHCP server.

If you create a scope and later want to delete it (to create a new one), first deactivate the scope and leave it in that condition until half the configured lease time elapses. Otherwise, you have to manually release and renew IP addresses on each client using ipconfig once your new scope is created. Don't deactivate a scope unless you intend to retire it and remove it permanently from the server. A DHCP server whose scope is deactivated sends out DHCPNAK packets to clients who attempt to contact it, which commences a recall of DHCP addresses in the subnet.

Create a Reservation for a Scope

Select a scope → right-click on Reservations → New Reservation → enter the IP address and MAC address of the client computer for which you want to reserve an IP address.

You can determine a computer's MAC address using the getmac command; see getmac in Chapter 5 for more information. You can also type **ipconfig /all** at the command line to display the MAC address of the local machine.

Display Active Leases for a Scope

Select a scope → Select Address Leases → Select a scope

You can right-click on an active lease in the Details pane and delete it if you like. However, the client may request the address again unless you release the address on the client using ipconfig /release.

Display DHCP Statistics

Right-click on server node → Select a scope → Display Statistics

This window is manually refreshed by default. To cause it to refresh automatically, do the following:

Right-click on server node → Properties → General → Automatically update statistics

Reconcile a Scope

Right-click on Scope node → Reconcile → Verify

This option lets you fix any inconsistency in the DHCP database by comparing it with information stored in the registry. If everything is fine, you are prompted to click OK. If there are inconsistencies, the inconsistent addresses are displayed; select them and click Reconcile.

Configure DHCP Clients

The procedure for configuring DHCP clients depends on the version of Windows being used. For example, on WS2003, XP, or W2K, do this:

Control Panel → Network Connections → Local Area Connection → Properties → Internet Protocol (TCP/IP) → Properties → Obtain an IP address automatically → Obtain DNS server address automatically

If no DHCP server is available when a DHCP client starts up, a WS2003, XP, or W2K client autoconfigures its own IP address using Automatic Private IP Addressing (APIPA). See *TCP/IP* later in this chapter for more information.

Configure Dynamic Updates

To configure a DHCP server to update DNS information on behalf of DHCP clients, do this:

Right-click on server node → Properties → DNS → Enable DNS dynamic updates

By default, DHCP servers are configured to perform such updates only when clients request them and to discard DNS information when the client lease expires. WS2003 or XP clients request dynamic updates if they are configured as follows:

Control Panel → Network Connections → Local Area Connection → Properties → Internet Protocol (TCP/IP) → Properties → Advanced → DNS → Register this connection's suffix in DNS

To have your DHCP server register DNS information for downlevel (NT) or legacy (Windows 95/98) clients, do this:

Right-click on server node → Properties → DNS → Dynamically update DNS A and PTR records for DHCP clients that don't request dynamic updates

If necessary, you can specify credentials for the DHCP server to perform dynamic updates on DNS servers:

Right-click on server node → Properties → Advanced → Credentials

Note that you can also configure dynamic updates at the scope level instead of globally for all scopes. For example:

Right-click on scope → Properties → DNS

Configure Multihomed DHCP Servers

If your DHCP server has multiple LAN or WAN connections, you can specify on which connections the server should service DHCP clients as follows:

Right-click on server node → Properties → Advanced → Bindings

Configure Audit Logging for DHCP Servers

DHCP servers can be configured to record events in a DHCP audit log as follows:

Right-click on server node → Properties → General → Enable DHCP audit logging

These audit logs are named *DhcpSrvLog.xxx*, where the extension depends on the day of the week. The location of these logs can be configured on the Advanced tab.

Back Up a DHCP Server

You can back up the DHCP database on a DHCP server like this:

Right-click on server node → Backup

By default, DHCP database backups are binary files named *DhcpCfg* that are created in *\System32\dhcp\backup*. Note that creating a new backup simply overwrites the old one unless you choose a new location. Use the Restore option to restore a DHCP server database from backup, but note that this temporarily stops the DHCP service. Note that these backups don't include DHCP audit log settings.

 Advanced DHCP backup and restore can be performed using Net-Shell (netsh), a command-line utility included with WS2003. Using NetShell, you can move all or part of a DHCP server's database to another machine to balance the load or if it seems the original server might fail.

Configure a DHCP Relay Agent

DHCP relay agents are configured using the Routing and Remote Access Service (RRAS) as follows:

Open RRAS console → right-click on server node → Enable and configure routing and remote access ▸ Custom configuration → LAN routing → start the service when prompted → expand console tree → IP Routing node → right-click on General → New routing protocol → DHCP relay agent → right-click on DHCP Relay Agent → New Interface → select interface → configure hop count threshold → configure boot threshold → OK → right-click on DHCP relay agent → specify IP address of DHCP server to forward DHCP requests to

You enable the relay agent on each network connection or interface on which you want it to operate. If you have several DHCP servers on the network, you should specify which ones can service DHCP clients on the subnet on which your relay agent resides.

The boot threshold is the time in seconds the agent waits between receiving a DHCP client-broadcast request and forwarding it to a DHCP server. This useful feature allows you to provide backup for a local DHCP server. If the client broadcasts a DHCP message and the local DHCP server doesn't respond in the time specified, the message is forwarded by the agent to a DHCP server on a remote subnet. In this way, if the local DHCP server goes down, DHCP can still operate on the subnet.

DHCP—Notes

DHCP Servers

If a client tries to renew an address already owned by some other computer on the network, the DHCP server responds with a DHCPNAK packet that basically tells the client, "You can't have that address; give it up."

You can force a client to release its IP address before its lease expires by using the ipconfig /release command. You can force a client to attempt to renew a lease with ipconfig /renew. You might use this procedure when you physically move a computer from one subnet to another in your internetwork.

The DHCP lease and renewal process occurs separately for each network adapter that is configured for automatic TCP/IP addressing. Each adapter in a multihomed computer must have its own unique IP address to communicate using TCP/IP.

If a DHCP server has a network adapter with more than one IP address configured on it, only the first address is used to service DHCP clients.

If you want to reserve an IP address for a client but there is more than one DHCP server available to the client, you must configure the same reservation on each DHCP server.

The DHCP Server service is relatively disk-intensive, so take this into account when selecting the hardware for your server. RAID may be an option for DHCP servers that service a large number of clients.

If the configuration of your network rarely changes, you can increase the duration of DHCP leases or make it unlimited. If you frequently move computers around or have a lot of mobile computers, you can reduce the lease duration. Also, if you have a lot of extra, unassigned IP addresses, you can increase the duration of DHCP leases or make it unlimited. If you have barely enough addresses, reduce the lease duration. Note that dial-up clients should have leases of short duration, typically three days or less.

The DHCP Users group provides read-only access to the DHCP console. It can't modify the DHCP server settings. To give a user the ability to modify DHCP server settings, add the user to the DHCP Administrators group.

If your DHCP server stops unexpectedly, check the System log in Event Viewer. If this doesn't help, check the DHCP server audit log.

DHCP Relay Agents

WS2003 computers can be configured to operate as DHCP relay agents in two different ways:

- As a server on the subnet (for example, a file/print server) that also functions in the role of a DHCP relay agent

- As an IP router connecting two or more subnets (the computer must be multi-homed) that also functions on one or more network interfaces as a DHCP relay agent

Many third-party routers can also be configured as DHCP relay agents. You typically configure the agent by specifying the IP Helper Address of the DHCP server to which the agent forwards DHCP client traffic.

To view DHCP relay-agent statistics, select the DHCP Relay Agent node in the console tree and read the details pane.

See Also
DNS, netsh, *TCP/IP*

Disks—Concepts

Like previous versions of Microsoft Windows, WS2003 supports older, fixed-disk technologies, but it also supports some new technologies that increase performance and make disk management easier.

Types of Disk Storage

WS2003 supports two types of fixed-disk storage:

Basic storage
> This storage technology is the same as that of legacy versions of Microsoft Windows, including NT 4.0 and 3.51, Windows 98, and Windows 95. Basic storage divides disks into a limited number of partitions and logical drives and supports advanced features such as volume sets, stripe sets, stripe sets with parity, and mirror sets.

Dynamic storage
> This technology, available in WS2003 and W2K Server, divides disks into an unlimited number of volumes. Dynamic storage supports advanced features such as spanned volumes, striped volumes, RAID-5 volumes, and mirrored volumes.

In addition, WS2003 supports certain types of removable storage.

Basic Disks

When WS2003 is installed on a system, its disks are first configured to use basic storage. A disk that uses basic storage is called a basic disk. Basic disks are similar to disks in NT 4.0 and can consist of either:

- Up to three primary partitions plus one extended partition. The extended partition can have up to 24 logical drives, and each primary partition and logical drive is identified by a unique drive letter from C to Z.

- Up to four primary partitions and no extended partition or logical drives. Each partition is again identified by a unique drive letter.

Basic disks in WS2003 can be formatted using any of the following filesystems: FAT, FAT32, and NTFS. This is different from NT 4.0 Server, which supported only FAT and NTFS. The only real advantage of using basic storage is that you can dual-boot between WS2003 and legacy operating systems such as NT 4.0 Server or Windows 98—something you are unlikely to do on real production servers, however. The disadvantages of basic disks are:

- There is a limit of 4 primary partitions and 24 logical drives that you can create.

- Configuration information concerning the disk is stored in the registry rather than on the disk itself. If the registry becomes corrupted, the data on the disk becomes unusable.

- Basic disks in WS2003 can't be used to create the mirror sets, volume sets, stripe sets, and stripe sets with parity that you can create in NT. In order to use these advanced disk storage features, you must use dynamic storage instead of basic.

You can have mirror sets, volume sets, stripe sets, and stripe sets with parity on WS2003 systems using basic storage, but only if you upgraded the system from an earlier NT Server system that already had these storage technologies in place.

Dynamic Disks

WS2003 also supports a more advanced form of disk storage called dynamic storage. A disk that uses dynamic storage is called a dynamic disk. While basic disks contain partitions, dynamic disks contain volumes, and these volumes can be identified by either:

- Associating a volume with a drive letter. However, this can be used only to identify up to 24 different volumes (or 25 if you have no B: floppy drive in your system).
- Mounting a drive, which associates a volume with a folder on an existing volume. This method overcomes the drive-letter limitation and also enables friendly names like *My Volume* to be used to identify volumes.

The advantages of dynamic disks are:

- There is no limit to the number of volumes you can create on a dynamic disk (other than hardware limitations).
- Configuration information concerning the disk is stored on the disk instead of in the registry and is replicated to all other dynamic disks in the system for fault tolerance.
- You can extend a simple volume on a dynamic disk by adding unallocated space to it from the same disk (you can't extend partitions on basic disks).
- Dynamic disks support advanced disk technologies such as spanned, mirrored, striped, and RAID-5 volumes.

The disadvantage of dynamic disks is that you can't dual-boot between WS2003 and a legacy Windows operating system. Also, once you convert a disk to dynamic storage, you can't convert it back to basic without losing your data (unless you backed it up).

Advanced Disk Technologies

A volume is an area of storage on a dynamic disk, and a simple volume is a volume that occupies contiguous space on a single physical disk. Simple volumes are for dynamic storage as primary partitions and logical drives are for basic storage. Simple volumes can be extended with unallocated space from the same drive as long as they are formatted with NTFS. When extending a volume, WS2003 uses the smallest area of contiguous unallocated space it can find on the drive.

Other types of volumes supported by dynamic disks include:

Spanned volume
> Created from two or more areas of contiguous free space on the same or on different physical disks that are combined into a single, larger, logical storage area. Spanned volumes can be extended without losing existing data by adding further areas of contiguous free space, up to a maximum of 32 areas and up to 32 different disks. However, once extended, they can't be reduced in size. Data is written to the first area of the volume until it becomes full, whereupon further data is written to the next area. Spanned volumes aren't fault-tolerant, and if one disk fails, the entire spanned volume is unrecoverable.

Striped volume (RAID-0)
Created from two or more areas of contiguous free space on different physical disks that are combined into a single, larger, logical storage area. Like spanned volumes, striped volumes can consist of between 2 and 32 areas of contiguous free space. Unlike spanned volumes, however, each area of a striped volume must be on a different physical disk, all areas must be the same size, and data is written in an interleaved fashion across all areas instead of sequentially area by area. This generally provides better read performance than a spanned volume. Like spanned volumes, striped volumes are also not fault-tolerant.

Mirrored volume (RAID-1)
A fault-tolerant technology that consists of two separate simple volumes that are configured to be identical copies of each other and are located on different physical disks. When data is updated on one disk, it is automatically updated on the other as well, and the pair of volumes is identified to the system by a single drive letter or mount point. If one disk in a mirrored volume fails, you still have the complete data on the other disk.

RAID-5 volume
Created from three or more areas of contiguous free disk space on different physical disks that are combined into a single, larger, logical storage area. RAID-5 volumes are similar to striped volumes, except that error-correcting parity information is distributed across the set. The result is a popular fault-tolerant disk storage technology called RAID-5, which maintains data integrity in the event of failure of a single physical disk belonging to the set. RAID-5 volumes can use between 3 and 32 different disks.

The advanced disk technologies supported by Windows 2003 are similar to those supported by NT 4.0 Server but are named differently, as shown in Table 4-8.

Table 4-8. Disk terminology in WS2003 and NT Server

NT	WS2003	
Basic storage	Basic storage	Dynamic storage
Partition	Partition	Simple volume
Primary partition	Primary partition	Simple volume
Extended partition	Extended partition	N.A.
Logical drive	Logical drive	Simple volume
Mirror set	N.A.	Mirrored volume
Volume set	N.A.	Spanned volume
Stripe set	N.A.	Striped volume
Stripe set with parity	N.A.	RAID-5 volume

If you want to extend volumes or create striped, spanned, or fault-tolerant volumes, you first have to convert your disks from basic to dynamic storage. You can convert your disks without rebooting the system—unless the disk contains your system or boot partition or the active paging file.

To convert them to dynamic disks, basic disks must have a minimum of 1 MB of free space. This free space is used to store the database containing the configuration information concerning all the dynamic disks in the system. When you partition a basic

GUI Reference

disk, make sure you leave at least 1 MB of free (unallocated) space on the disk in case you later want to convert it to dynamic storage.

 The conversion of a disk from basic to dynamic storage should take place with no loss of data on the disk, but, to be safe, you should always back up a basic disk before converting it to dynamic.

Disk Quotas

Disk quotas manage the amount of disk space that users can utilize. Quotas are available only on NTFS partitions or volumes. Disk quotas can be configured several ways:

- Quota limits can be either enforced or not. If enforced, users who exceed their limits are denied access.
- Warnings can be issued when a user is nearing the configured quota limit.
- An entry can be logged in the event log when a warning is issued, when a limit is exceeded, or both.

Disk quota limits are based on file ownership and not on where the files are located on a quota-enabled NTFS volume; that is, they are established on a per-user basis. For example, if a user moves a file from one folder to another on the volume, she still shows the same amount of disk space used in My Computer or Windows Explorer. If a user takes ownership of a file on an NTFS volume, the file is charged against the user's quota.

In addition, disk quotas apply only to specific volumes and not to folders within volumes—that is, on a per-volume basis. If a physical disk has several volumes or partitions (or if you have multiple physical disks), each partition or volume may have quotas either enabled or disabled, and those on which quotas are enabled may have different quota limits set (unless it's a spanned volume).

Quota Limits

Disk quota limits can be one of two types:

Soft quotas
>When the user exceeds the limit, an event may be logged to the event log, but the user is not prevented from exceeding the quota.

Hard quotas
>When the user exceeds the limit, an event may be logged to the event log, and the user is prevented from using any additional space on the disk.

Once enabled on a volume, disk quota limits are tracked for all users who store files on that volume. However, different quota limits can be set for specific users to override the global settings for all users. Once quota limits have been established on a volume, users are monitored for any action that increases the amount of disk space used. These actions include:

- Copying or moving files to the disk
- Creating (saving) new files on the disk
- Taking ownership of existing files on the disk that belong to other users

User applications may respond differently when users try to create or save files on volumes on which a hard quota limit has been exceeded. In general, applications act as if the volume is full.

Implementing Disk Quotas

1. Begin by establishing realistic estimates of how much disk space users require on average and how these needs are likely to grow in the immediate future. To do this, you may want to classify users into three different categories, such as heavy users, moderate users, and light users.

2. Next, create partitions, volumes, and logical drives in such a way as to facilitate assigning space to different types of users. Allocate some volumes for heavy users, some for moderate, and some for light. Create home folders or data folders on these drives for each user or group of users, and assign NTFS permissions accordingly to restrict access. Make sure you leave unallocated space on the drives in case you need to increase the quota limits. Consider using dynamic storage so that you can extend simple volumes and create spanned volumes when simple volumes become full.

3. Assign disk quotas to each volume, partition, or logical drive according to the type of user storing data there. Use soft limits initially in case your estimates of user needs are too small.

4. Now share the folders for access over the network. Closely monitor disk quota entries over a period of time to see if realistic limits have been set.

5. Once you have determined that your quota limits are appropriate, make them hard quotas to prevent careless users from overutilizing disk space.

6. Monitor quotas periodically to determine whether they should be increased for all users. Check whether specific users might require individual quotas for special projects and so on.

7. If a user no longer needs to store data on a volume, remove the files (or take ownership of them) and then delete the user's quota entry to free up space on the volume.

 Make sure you enable quotas on a disk before any users have stored files on it. If a user has already stored a file and you then enable quotas and set quota limits, the user's quota limit is No Limit and you will have to change the quota entry manually for this user. Only new users who later store files on the disk are assigned the quota limits you expect them to have.

Disks—Tools

In addition to the tools for managing disks in WS2003, you can also use the `diskpart` and `defrag` commands to manage and defragment volumes and partitions from the command line or to schedule disk-management tasks.

Disk Management

Disk Management, a snap-in that is part of Computer Management, is the primary tool for managing disks on local or remote computers. It can be used to add and remove disks, create and manage partitions and volumes, change drive letters, mount volumes, create fault-tolerant volumes, configure disk quotas, and so on. The way Disk Management displays information can be changed using the View menu as follows.

View → Top
> Lets you display one of three views in the top portion of the righthand pane

Disk List
> Provides information about the physical disks (hard drives, CD-ROM drives, and so on) in your system

Volume List
> Provides information about the partitions, volumes, and logical drives on your hard disks

Graphical View
> Shows information about the partitions, volumes, and logical drives on your disks using color-coded regions

View → Bottom
> Lets you do the same and also lets you hide the bottom pane entirely, which is useful if you have a lot of disks or volumes on your system

View → Settings
> Lets you change the color coding and horizontal scaling of the regions in Graphical view

View → All Drive Paths
> Displays any drive paths (volume mount points) on a disk system that is configured for dynamic storage

Disk Defragmenter

This snap-in, also part of Computer Management, lets you manually defragment disks on the local computer to improve performance. Fragmentation is generally less of an issue with NTFS volumes than with FAT or FAT32 volumes since NTFS usually needs fewer disk accesses than FAT to locate all the fragments of a file. However, a significant performance improvement in disk access can be achieved by regularly defragmenting all volumes and partitions, including NTFS volumes and partitions, on a WS2003 computer. Disk Defragmenter achieves this performance gain by:

- Consolidating fragments of files and folders by moving them to one location so that each file and folder occupies a contiguous segment of space on the volume. Disk Defragmenter consolidates all fragments of each file into a single contiguous block of space, but different files may occupy different blocks of contiguous space after defragmentation. In other words, Disk Defragmenter doesn't cause all files on the volume to be grouped into a single contiguous region of space on the disk.

- Consolidating free space to make it less likely that new files become fragmented. Disk Defragmenter typically doesn't attempt to completely consolidate all free space on the volume, however, since this generally provides little improvement in performance.

You can run Disk Defragmenter in two modes:

Analysis
> Determines the amount of file fragmentation present and indicates whether defragmenting the disk is worthwhile. After analyzing a volume, the Analysis Display graphic box displays the volume's initial state of fragmentation using the color-coded legend at the bottom of the screen.

Defragmentation
> Defragments the disk and displays the progress in the Defragmentation Display graphic box.

You can pause or stop the analysis or defragmentation process at any time. Both the analysis and defragmentation processes produce reports you can view, save, and print. Note that only the report gives an accurate view of the defragmentation state of the volume; the graphical displays are only approximate since they can't resolve individual clusters into colored regions due to screen-resolution limits.

 Although it is possible to use your computer while a disk is being defragmented, this is generally not a good idea as the system will be slow to respond due to the overhead of the defragmentation process. Making changes to files during defragmentation can also considerably lengthen the defragmentation process. Instead, pause or stop defragmentation, perform the work you have to do, and then restart defragmentation.

Disk Cleanup

This utility can be used to delete unnecessary files from your disks, including temporary files, cached web pages, downloaded ActiveX controls, and so on. It can also be used to empty the Recycle Bin, compress files you haven't accessed for some time, and uninstall optional Windows components or applications you no longer need. The net result is more free space on your disk. To start Disk Cleanup, use one of the following methods:

Start → Programs → Accessories → System → Disk Cleanup

Windows Explorer or My Computer → right-click on a drive → Properties → General → Disk Cleanup

Computer Management ‣ Storage ‣ Disk Management → right-click on a drive → Properties → General → Disk Cleanup

Command prompt → **cleanmgr**

Error Checking

This option runs the Check Disk (chkdisk) command to scan a disk for possible damage. If you are encountering unknown data errors when reading files, you can try running this utility by:

Windows Explorer or My Computer → right-click on a drive → Properties → Tools → Error Checking

Computer Management → Storage → Disk Management → right-click on a drive → Properties → Tools → Error Checking

Command prompt → **chkdsk**

Disks—Tasks

Unless otherwise indicated, the procedures that follow use the Disk Management tool described earlier.

Add a Disk

The procedure for adding new disks to a system depends on whether the system supports hot swapping.

Hot swapping supported
> Install the new disks → right-click on disk → Rescan Disks

If the change is not detected, reboot the system.

Hot swapping not supported
> Install the new disks and reboot the system.

To remove disks from a system, follow the same procedures for adding a disk listed earlier.

 If the status of a new disk appears as Foreign, you must import the disk. Foreign disks are disks that were previously used in other WS2003 systems and may contain partitions or volumes with data on them. Right-click on a disk whose status is Foreign, select Import Foreign Disk, and follow the wizard. After this is complete, right-click on the disk → Rescan Disks, and you should be able to access the existing volumes on the new disk. If you want to add disks containing a RAID-5 volume or mirrored volume, you must add all the disks in the complete volume or you will be unable to access any of the data stored on the disks.

Assign a Drive Letter

Assign a new drive letter to a partition or volume this way:

> Right-click on a partition or volume → Change Drive Letter and Path → Change

If you are using a removable storage device, you should assign this device a drive letter that is beyond those used by permanent partitions, volumes, and drives on your system.

Assign a Drive Path

You can mount a partition or volume to an empty folder on an NTFS volume, a process also referred to as assigning a drive path to the partition or volume:

> Right-click on a partition or volume → Change Drive Letter and Path → Add → Mount in the following empty NTFS folder → specify folder

For example, if you create a second partition E: and then mount this partition to the empty folder C:\test, you can display the files in this partition in the right pane of Windows Explorer either by selecting E: drive or C:\test in the left pane. Mounting a drive to an empty folder on a local NTFS volume lets you do some fancy things. For example, you can create a C:\temp folder for temporary program files and mount it to a simple volume on another physical disk, allowing you to extend the volume when it runs low on space.

Convert a Disk

Converting a disk changes it from basic to dynamic storage. You need to do this if you want to use WS2003 fault-tolerant disk technologies such as mirrored or RAID-5 volumes or if you want to extend a volume, create a spanned volume, or create a striped volume. To convert a disk from basic to dynamic, first close any applications running or files open on the disk and then do this:

> Right-click any disk → Convert to dynamic disk → select disks to convert

---

You can also use diskpart from the command line to convert disks. If you convert the boot or system partition, the conversion process requires two reboots. Note that you must have at least 1 MB of unallocated space on the disk in order for conversion to be successful. This space is used to store the database that contains the configuration information of all physical disks in the system. Table 4-9 shows how partitions, logical drives in extended partitions, mirror sets, volume sets, stripe sets, and stripe sets with parity are upgraded when you convert your disk subsystem from basic to dynamic storage.

Table 4-9. What happens when basic storage is converted to dynamic

Previous basic storage type	New dynamic storage type
Primary partition	Simple volume
Extended partition with logical drives and free space	Simple volumes (from logical drives) and unallocated space (from free space)
Mirror set	Mirrored volume
Volume set	Spanned volume
Stripe set	Striped volume
Stripe set with parity	RAID-5 volume
Unallocated space	Unallocated space

Create a Partition

Right-click on unallocated space on a basic disk → Create Partition

This option launches the Create Partition Wizard, which lets you create either primary or extended partitions, assign them a drive letter, format the partitions, and so on.

Create a Logical Drive

Right-click on an extended partition → Create Logical Drive

This option starts the Create Partition Wizard. The only option available is creating a new logical drive and then specifying its size, drive letter, and filesystem.

Create a Volume

Right-click on unallocated space on a dynamic disk → Create Volume

This option launches the Create Volume Wizard, which lets you create simple, spanned, striped, mirrored, and RAID-5 volumes. Simple volumes can be formatted using FAT, FAT32, or NTFS, but other types of volumes require NTFS. The steps are different, depending on which type of volume you choose to create:

Simple volume
> The steps are similar to creating a partition except that volumes can either be assigned a drive letter or mounted to an empty folder.

Spanned volume
> To create a spanned volume, extend a simple volume with unallocated space from another disk. If you extend it with space from the same disk, it is still a simple volume.

Mirrored volume
> You can use the wizard to create a mirrored volume from scratch by selecting unallocated space from two different disks. You can also mirror an existing volume by right-clicking on the volume and selecting Add Mirror.

Striped volume

Select between 2 and 32 different disks that have sufficient unallocated space. The maximum size of the striped volume you create is determined by the disk with the smallest amount of unallocated space. (Striped volumes use equal amounts of unallocated space from each disk.)

RAID-5 volume

This is the same as striped volume, except that at least three disks must be used to create a RAID-5 volume.

Delete a Partition or Volume

Right-click on partition or volume → Delete

Note that you can't delete:

- The system partition where hardware-specific boot files such as *Ntldr* and *Ntdetect* reside
- The boot partition where the *\Windows* folder resides
- Any volume with an active paging file

To delete an extended partition, you must first delete any logical drives in the partition. Deleting a partition or volume is a permanent action and can't be undone.

Extend a Volume

Right-click on a simple volume → Extend Volume

This option launches the Extend Volume Wizard, which lets you add unallocated space to an existing volume to make it bigger. If you extend a simple volume using contiguous or noncontiguous unallocated space on the same disk, it is still a simple volume, only larger. If you extend it using space on another disk, it becomes a spanned volume.

Note that you can't extend FAT or FAT32 volumes, only NTFS. Furthermore, you can't extend the System or Boot volume or any volume that was formerly a partition before you upgraded your disks from basic to dynamic storage. You can extend only simple volumes that you created from unallocated space on dynamic disks using the Create Volume Wizard.

Format a Partition or Volume

To format a partition or volume, you can do the following:

Right-click on partition or volume → Format

You can also use My Computer or Windows Explorer to format disks. The only advantage of using Disk Management for formatting disks is that it provides more options for choosing the allocation unit size, although this is generally best left at Default.

Defragment a Disk

Note that this task uses the Disk Defragmenter snap-in, not Disk Management. Before defragmenting a disk, first analyze it to see if it needs defragmenting:

Disk Defragmenter → right-click on partition or volume → Analyze

If the result indicates that defragmenting the disk could improve its performance, click the Defragment button to start the process and watch the fun.

Reactivate a Disk

Should the status of a dynamic disk become Missing or Offline, first check to make sure the disk is attached properly and has power, and then:

> Right-click on the disk or volume → Reactivate Disk or Volume

The disk status should return to Online. Table 4-10 lists disk status indicators, their meanings, and what steps to take in each case.

Table 4-10. Disk status indicators

Status	Description
Online	Disk OK.
Online (Errors)[a]	I/O errors found on the disk. Try reactivating the disk in case the problem is transient; otherwise, remove the disk and replace it.
Offline	Disk is disconnected, powered down, or corrupted. Check controller and power cables, and then try reactivating the disk. If this fails, remove the disk and replace it.
Foreign	Disk has been moved to this system from another computer running WS2003. Import the foreign disk to use it.
Unreadable	Disk has I/O errors, hardware failure, or corrupted configuration database. Try rescanning disk or rebooting the system; otherwise, remove the disk and replace it.
Unrecognized	Unknown disk type, such as from a Unix system or with an OEM signature. Replace the disk.
No Media	No compact disc in CD-ROM drive, or no media in removable drive.

[a] Dynamic volumes only.

Recover a Failed Mirrored Volume

You can identify a failed mirrored volume in Disk Management as follows:

- The volume is marked as Failed Redundancy.
- The disk that failed is marked as either Missing, Offline, or Online (Errors).

If the status of the failed disk is Online (Errors), then:

> Right-click on disk marked Online (Errors) → Reactivate Disk

If all goes well, the mirrored volume regenerates and the volume status should read Healthy (see Table 4-11 for a list of partition and volume status indicators).

If the status of the failed disk is Missing or Offline, first make sure the disk is attached properly and has power, and then perform the steps listed earlier. If a disk doesn't reactivate (volume doesn't return to Healthy status), replace the failed disk. Break the old mirror by:

> Right-click on the mirrored volume on the failed disk → Remove Mirror

Create a new mirror by:

> Right-click on the good half of the broken mirror → Add Mirror

Recover a Failed RAID-5 Volume

You can identify a failed RAID-5 volume in Disk Management as follows:

- The volume is marked as Failed Redundancy.
- The disk that failed is marked as either Missing, Offline, or Online (Errors).

If the status of the failed disk is Online (Errors), then:

> Right-click on the disk marked Online (Errors) → Reactivate Disk

GUI Reference

If all goes well, the RAID-5 volume regenerates and the volume status should read Healthy. If the status of the failed disk is Missing or Offline, first make sure the disk is attached properly and has power, and then perform the steps listed earlier.

If a disk doesn't reactivate (volume doesn't return to Healthy status), replace the failed disk and then:

> Right-click on the RAID-5 volume on the failed disk → Repair Volume → select the disk to replace the failed one

This automatically regenerates the RAID-5 volume.

Repair a Partition or Volume

Should the status of a partition or volume become Failed, first check to make sure the physical disk on which the partition or volume resides is attached properly and has power. If the underlying disk has status Missing or Offline, see *Reactivate a Disk* earlier in this section for information about what to do. This should return the disk status to Online and the failed volume should return to Healthy. If the volume still indicates Failed, try:

> Right-click on the failed volume → Reactive Volume

Note that you can repair a failed volume only if it is on a dynamic disk, not a basic disk.

Table 4-11 shows the different possible partition/volume status indicators, their meanings, and what steps to take in each case.

Table 4-11. Partition and volume status indicators

Status	Description
Healthy	Volume OK.
Healthy (At Risk)[a]	Displayed by all volumes on a disk where I/O errors have been detected anywhere on the disk. Reactivate the disk.
Initializing	Normal at system startup.
Resynching	A mirrored volume is resynching its mirrors. don't make any configuration changes while this is happening.
Regenerating	A RAID-5 volume is being regenerated. don't make any configuration changes while this is happening.
Failed Redundancy	A disk has failed in a mirrored or RAID-5 volume. See *Recover a Failed Mirrored Volume* and *Recover a Failed RAID-5 Volume* earlier in this section.
Failed Redundancy (At Risk)[a]	A disk has failed in a mirrored or RAID-5 volume and I/O errors have also been detected. Reactivate the failed disk and proceed as described earlier.
Failed	A disk has failed or become corrupted. Check the disk cables, then reactivate the disk if necessary. If it still doesn't display Healthy status, try reactivating the volume.

[a] Dynamic volumes only.

Rescan Disks

> Right-click on Disk Management → Rescan Disks

This updates the hardware information on all hard drives and updates information about removable media, CD-ROM drives, volumes, partitions, filesystems, and drive letters. If you make configuration changes to your disks and this information doesn't show up properly in Disk Management, use Rescan Disks to rebuild the disk-configuration database on each disk. You should always perform this action after adding disks to or removing disks from your system. Rescanning disks can take a few minutes, so be patient.

Restore Disk Configuration

Use this procedure if you are installing WS2003 on a machine already running NT 4.0 Server. If you want to be able to use existing NT mirror sets, volume sets, stripe sets, or stripe sets with parity on the machine:

1. First use the NT administrative tool, Disk Administrator, to save the disk-configuration information for the system to a floppy disk.

2. Install WS2003 on the system.

3. Finally, open Disk Management, select Action → Restore Basic Disk Configuration, insert the floppy, and follow the instructions.

Disk Management should now be able to access the existing NT fault-tolerant volumes on the system.

Revert a Disk

To change a dynamic disk back to a basic disk, back up everything to tape, delete all volumes on the disk, and then:

> Right-click on a dynamic disk → Revert to Basic Disk

If your dynamic disk contains the System or Boot partition, you must reinstall WS2003 after the reversion process is complete.

Update Disk Information

After you have made changes to drive letters or filesystems or created or deleted partitions or volumes, you can do the following:

> Right-click on Disk Management → Refresh

View Status of a Disk

Use either Disk List or Graphical view and do this:

> Right-click on a disk → Properties

The Volumes tab shows the logical number of the disk (starting with Disk 0), the type (basic or dynamic), the status (online, offline, foreign, or unknown), and other useful information. The Policies tab can be used to turn write caching on or off—turning write caching on improves performance but could result in data loss, especially if you don't have a UPS device.

New to WS2003 is the Enable Advanced Performance setting on the Policies tab, which provides even more aggressive write caching called Power Protected Mode, but be careful enabling this unless you have a backup power supply for your system.

View Status of Partition or Volume

Use either Volume List view or Graphical view and do this:

> Right-click on a volume or partition → Properties

The properties sheet displays information concerning the volume or partition and lets you configure access disk maintenance tools, configure disk quotas, share disks, configure permissions, and so on. Most of these tasks are covered elsewhere in this book.

Enable Disk Quotas

Disk quotas need to be enabled before quota limits and warnings can be set. To enable and set disk quotas on a partition or volume:

> Right-click on partition or volume → Properties → Quota → Enable quota management

Note that if both "Enable quota management" and "Do not limit disk usage" are selected, quotas aren't tracked. The traffic light on the Quota tab of a disk's properties sheet indicates the status of disk quotas as follows:

Green light
> Disk quotas are enabled.

Red light
> Disk quotas aren't enabled.

Yellow light
> Disk quotas are enabled, but WS2003 is currently busy rebuilding the quota information.

Enforce Quota Limit

> Right-click on partition or volume → Properties → Quota → Deny disk space to users exceeding quota limit

Set Quota Limit

> Right-click on partition or volume → Properties → Quota → Limit disk space to

This sets a "soft limit" on the amount of disk space that can be used. The limit set here applies to all users individually. In order to make this a "hard limit," see the previous section.

Set Quota Warning

> Right-click on partition or volume → Properties → Quota → Set warning level to

You might typically set the quota warning level to about 50% or 75% of the quota limit value.

Log Disk Quota Events

> Right-click on partition or volume → Properties → Quota → Log event when a user exceeds his quota (or warning) limit

You can log quota warning events, quota limit exceeded events, or both. These events are logged to the System log where they can be viewed with Event Viewer.

Monitor Quota Entries

To view how much of their allotted space users have filled on a disk on which quotas have been enabled, do this:

> Right-click on partition or volume → Properties → Quota → Quota Entries

The information in this Quota Entries window is displayed as a flat-file database, so to keep things simple you should probably not mix users from different OUs or domains when having them store work on a specific partition, volume, or logical drive. If you must mix users from different OUs or domains, select View → Containing Folder to more easily distinguish users from different domains and OUs.

Note that quota entries are visible only for users who have stored files on the volume on which disk quotas have been enabled. The first time the Quota Entries window is opened for a volume, the computer must contact a domain controller to resolve user SID numbers (which are used by NTFS to record volume usage) to user logon names. This may take a few seconds if many users are using the volume. Once the SIDs have been resolved to logon names, this information is stored locally on the quota-enabled volume. If new users have been created and the list of users displayed from the information stored locally in the Quota Entries window becomes out of date, press F5 to refresh the user information from the nearest domain controller.

Override Quota Limit

Once a global quota limit has been established for all users, it may be overridden with specific quota limits for individual users. For example, if a user is given work on a special project and needs additional disk space, you can temporarily increase the quota specifically for that user by:

> Right-click on partition or volume → Properties → Quota → Quota Entries → select a user → modify quota limit and warning level

You can also use the Quota Entries box to set quotas for specific users who have not yet stored any files on the volume—for example, if you know in advance that a few selected users may require different quota limits from the rest. Do it like this:

> Right-click on partition or volume → Properties → Quota → Quota Entries → New Quota Entry

---

Disks—Notes

This section includes important information about basic and dynamic disks, RAID, drive letters, drive paths, disk quotas, and disk defragmenting.

Basic Versus Dynamic Disks

Disks must be either basic or dynamic; they can't contain a mixture of partitions and volumes. However, your computer can have a combination of basic and dynamic disks in its disk subsystem.

Dynamic disks can't be accessed by MS-DOS or earlier versions of Microsoft Windows. For example, if you physically move a dynamic disk from a W2K Server to an NT 4.0 Server computer, the new system will not be able to use it.

Dynamic storage is not supported on removable media. Only primary partitions are allowed on removable media.

You can't reinstall WS2003 on a volume that has been created from unallocated space on a dynamic disk. This is because under the hood there are really two types of volumes:

Volumes created from partitions when a basic disk was upgraded to a dynamic disk
> This type of volume has a partition table similar to that in a partition of a basic disk, and it can't be extended.

Volumes created after conversion of unallocated space on a dynamic disk
> This type of volume has no partition table and therefore can't be recognized by the Setup program of WS2003.

When you add a new disk to a computer, the disk is automatically configured as a basic disk. If you are using dynamic storage on your other disks, convert the new disk to dynamic after it has been recognized by the system.

You can't upgrade basic disks to dynamic when the sector size exceeds 512 bytes.

RAID

The system and boot partitions can't be part of a volume set, stripe set, or stripe set with parity. They can be part of a mirror set, however, which is a good way of providing fault tolerance for these partitions. However, hardware RAID can be used for system and boot partitions.

You can't extend a simple volume formatted with FAT or FAT32; you can do so only with NTFS.

You can't mirror a spanned volume that uses multiple physical disks; you can do so only with a simple volume that exists on a single physical disk.

You can't "unextend" a simple volume once you have extended it, and you similarly can't do so with spanned and striped volumes.

You can't extend a simple volume once you have mirrored it.

You can't extend or mirror a RAID-5 volume.

You can't extend the System or Boot volume, so make sure you give these volumes enough space when you install WS2003 on a machine.

Resynchronization is the process whereby a stale copy of a mirrored volume is brought up to date. Stale mirrors typically occur when one disk in a mirrored volume is temporarily disconnected or down. Mirrored volumes on dynamic disks are resynchronized automatically. If you have an older mirror set on your system (by virtue of installing WS2003 on an existing NT Server system), right-click on the volume and select Resynchronize Mirror to manually force resynchronization.

Breaking a mirror separates it into two simple volumes that are no longer fault-tolerant. Removing a mirror turns one half of a mirrored volume into unallocated space and the other half into a simple volume.

Drive Letters

Changing drive letters incautiously can drastically affect whether MS-DOS or legacy Microsoft Windows applications can continue running on the system.

Drive letters can't be changed for the System or Boot partitions.

You can't format a partition or volume that doesn't have either a drive letter or a mount point assigned to it.

Drive Paths

Partitions, volumes, and logical drives can be assigned multiple drive paths, but only one drive letter.

Assigning a drive letter or mounting a folder to a partition or volume doesn't make the partition or volume available on the network: you still need to share it.

To edit a drive path, you must first remove the path and then assign a new drive path to the partition or volume.

Disk Quotas

You should not set disk quotas on the system partition since problems may result if the operating system runs out of space. This occurs if you try to install new applications while logged on as a user who doesn't have administrative privileges. If you install these applications while logged on as an administrator, quota settings are ignored as members of the Administrators group aren't limited by any disk quota settings.

File compression is ignored when disk quotas are calculated. Compressed files are charged to the quota according to their uncompressed size.

Enabling disk quotas on a volume creates a small amount of overhead. As a result, file-system performance may degrade slightly.

Disk quotas can be assigned only to users, not to groups.

If a user tries to write to disk when her disk space has been exceeded, the error message "insufficient disk space" appears.

The quota limit is displayed for users as the capacity of the drive on which quotas have been configured. For example, if a quota limit of 25 MB is set on G: drive, any user who selects G: drive in Windows Explorer or My Computer sees that G: has a capacity of only 25 MB, regardless of the size of the physical disk on which G: exists.

Note that enabling and setting quota limits on a disk for all users doesn't actually divide the disk into segments of fixed size for each user. For example, user one and user two would both read the capacity of G: drive as 25 MB. If user one placed a 5 MB file named *stuff.dat* into the root of G: drive, the drive would show 5 MB of used space and 20 MB of free space. If user one then logged off and user two logged on, user two would also see the *stuff.dat* file in the root of G: drive, but this drive would display 0 bytes of used space and 25 MB of free space. So it's not enough to set quotas to manage disk space for users. You also have to create home folders where they should store their work and set appropriate permissions on these folders.

If a user finds he is reaching his limit and decides to delete files on the quota-enabled disk, he may discover after deleting that he still has the same space usage on the disk. This is because when a user deletes a file for the first time on a volume or partition, by default WS2003 creates a new Recycle Bin on the drive and simply moves the deleted files to the Recycle Bin, resulting in no net gain in free space. You can prevent this from occurring by configuring the Recycle Bin properties to restrict which drives can have a Recycle Bin on them.

You can sort the users in the Quota Entries window by using View → Arrange Items and then specifying the sort field. A good choice would be to sort by status to see quickly which users have exceeded their quotas, which are in a warning state, and which are still within limits. A quicker alternative is to click on the column title for the field you want to sort by.

You can copy quota entries from one quota-enabled volume to another in one of two ways:

- Use Quota → Export on the initial volume's Quota Entries window to save the settings to a file, then use Quota → Import on the destination volume's window to import the saved settings.
- Drag selected quota entries from one Quota Entries window to the other.

You can generate a report of disk quota usage by opening the Quota Entries window for a volume, choosing Edit → Select All, and dragging the highlighted entries into the window of a program such as Microsoft Excel or even Microsoft Word.

Disk Defragmenter

Use Disk Defragmenter during times of light or no usage—for example, late at night.

You can safely defragment the system and boot volumes, but do so when activity is light.

System files can't be defragmented using Disk Defragmenter. This includes the Master File Table (MFT), located at the beginning of each NTFS volume, and the paging file. Any other open files on the system are also not defragmented, so it is a good idea to close all running applications and files that may be open prior to starting defragmentation.

The key figure in an analysis or defragmentation report is the Average Fragments Per File, which should be as close to 1 as possible. A value of 1.25, for example, would indicate 25% defragmentation on the volume.

Always analyze a volume before defragmenting it—analyzing takes much less time and can determine whether defragmentation is really useful or not.

Volumes to which frequent file changes are written should be defragmented more frequently. An example would be the volume on a member server where users' home folders are stored.

See Also

Backup, chkdsk, chkntfs, convert, defrag, diskpart, *Files and Folders*, format, freedisk, label, mountvol, *Permissions*, recover, *Shared Folders*

DNS—Concepts

DNS is the backbone of Active Directory for two reasons: domains are named using DNS and domain controllers are located using DNS. So if DNS is not set up properly, client computers will not be able to locate domain controllers and users will be unable to log on to the network and access resources. Since DNS is critical to the operation of WS2003-based networks, I'll begin by briefly reviewing basic DNS concepts while keying in on various issues relating to DNS on WS2003. For a more detailed look at DNS on Microsoft platforms, see *DNS on Windows 2003* (O'Reilly).

How DNS Works

DNS is a client/server, Internet-standard protocol that implements a hierarchical naming system using a distributed database for associating names of hosts with IP addresses. This database is stored on DNS servers in the form of zones containing resource records, and DNS clients query these servers to resolve hostnames into IP addresses. DNS queries can be issued by DNS clients to DNS servers or by DNS servers to other DNS servers, and this system of queries is an essential part of the name-resolution process.

Let's unpackage that brief description in more detail.

DNS Namespace

The DNS namespace is hierarchical in structure and starts with a root domain represented by a period. Beneath the root domain are top-level domains, which are either functional (*.com*, *.org*, *.edu*, and so on) or geographical (*.us*, *.ca*, *.uk*, and so on). Beneath these top-level domains are second-level domains, usually simply called domains, which can be registered by individuals, companies, or organizations. An example is *microsoft.com*, which Microsoft Corporation has registered under the *.com* top-level domain. Organizations that have registered a domain name have the right to subdivide it any way they like into third-level domains, usually called subdomains. An example of a subdomain is *msdn.microsoft.com*, which Microsoft uses for the Microsoft Developer Network.

An individual host (a computer, router interface, network printer, or anything else having an IP address) is uniquely described within the DNS namespace by its fully qualified domain name (FQDN). For example, a computer whose hostname is *bob* and belongs to the *sales* subdomain of the *mtit.com* domain would have the FQDN *bob.sales.mtit.com*. FQDNs can consist only of the letters a–z and A–Z, the numbers 0–9, and the dash (-) symbol if they are to be RFC 1123–compliant, and this is important if your Microsoft DNS server needs to interoperate with another name server such as a Unix system running BIND.

DNS has several advantages over plain old IP addressing. FQDNs are easier to remember than IP addresses, and the hierarchical structure of the DNS namespace makes it easier to search for a particular host. Also, by organizing your hosts into a series of domains and subdomains, you can distribute management of your hosts across different DNS servers by creating zones. That way, instead of requiring that each DNS server contain and manage the entire DNS database, each DNS server can manage a portion of the distributed DNS database.

Resource Records

The DNS namespace is implemented as a distributed database containing resource records that map the FQDN of each host on the network to its IP address. They are called resource records because they are records of the resources (servers, gateways, and so on) on your network. Some important types of resource records include:

SOA (start of authority) record
> Each zone has one SOA record that identifies which DNS server is authoritative for domains and subdomains in the zone.

NS (name server) record
> An NS record contains the FQDN and IP address of a DNS server authoritative for the zone. Each primary and secondary name server authoritative in the domain should have an NS record.

A (address) record
> By far the most common type of resource record, an A record is used to resolve the FQDN of a particular host into its associated IP address.

CNAME (canonical name) record
> A CNAME record contains an alias (alternate name) for a host. For example, if a server functioned as both a web server and an FTP server, its A record might use the FQDN *www.mtit.com*, while the CNAME record might specify *ftp* as an alias for *www*. CNAME records can also be used to hide the true names of hosts on your network from external clients.

GUI Reference

PTR (pointer) record
> The opposite of an A record, a PTR record is used to resolve the IP address of a host into its FQDN.

SRV (service) record
> An SRV record is used by DNS clients to locate a server that is running a particular service—for example, to find a domain controller so you can log on to the network. SRV records are key to the operation of Active Directory.

MX (mail exchange) record
> An MX record points to one or more computers that process SMTP mail for an organization or site.

DNS Servers

The backbone of any DNS implementation is the collection of DNS servers (or name servers) that contain the distributed DNS database. The main job of a name server is to resolve the names of hosts into their IP addresses. There are four different types of DNS servers you can deploy:

Primary name server
> A name server that maintains the writable copy of the zone information for a zone. There can be only one primary name server for each zone.

Secondary name server
> A name server that has a read-only copy of the zone information for a zone. A secondary name server gets its zone information from a master name server by a process called zone transfer. Each zone can have zero, one, or several secondary name servers to provide fault tolerance in case the primary server goes down. Secondary servers can also be used to reduce the load on primary servers; they can be deployed at branch offices to prevent clients from trying to perform name resolution over slow WAN links using primary name servers at company headquarters.

Master name server
> Any name server configured to allow secondary name servers to download zone information. A master name server can be either a primary or secondary name server.

Caching-only name server
> A name server that doesn't have any zone information. Instead, these servers cache the results of name queries and use this information to answer other queries. Caching-only name servers are useful in reducing unwanted WAN traffic. For example, say you have a primary name server located at company headquarters and configure a caching-only name server at a smaller branch office that is connected to headquarters over a slow WAN link. If clients at the branch office use DNS to issue name queries, the caching-only name server receives the requests and uses the WAN link to query the primary name server for the information. When the primary server returns a response, the caching-only server passes it on to the client but caches it in case it is requested later by another client. This reduces the WAN traffic that would occur if no name server was located at the branch office.

Note that a master name server can be either a primary or a secondary name server. In other words, secondary name servers can download their zone file from either a primary name server or another secondary name server. Note also that a name server can be a primary name server for one zone while being a secondary name server for another zone. In other words, each DNS server can service multiple zones and have different roles in different zones.

Zones

A *zone* is a contiguous (unbroken) subtree of the DNS namespace managed by name servers authoritative for that zone. For example, a zone might include a domain (*mtit.com*) and several subdomains (*sales.mtit.com* and *marketing.mtit.com*) but exclude other subdomains (*accounting.mtit.com* and *support.mtit.com*). Each zone has one primary name server that is authoritative over the zone and zero, one, or more name servers that are associated with the zone but aren't authoritative.

Name servers that are member servers use standard zones that store their zone information in ASCII files called zone files. A standard primary zone has a writable copy of the zone file while a standard secondary zone has a read-only copy. Name servers that are also domain controllers running WS2003 can use either standard zones or Active Directory–integrated zones. An Active Directory–integrated zone stores its zone information in Active Directory, which has several advantages over standard zones:

- Zone transfers are subsumed into Active Directory replication, a process that is more efficient than traditional DNS zone transfers using standard zones. This also means there is only one replication topology to configure instead of two.

- All name servers are primary name servers and can therefore have zone information directly modified on them. This provides fault tolerance compared to traditional DNS where, if a primary name server goes down, you have to promote a secondary name server to take its place.

- Storing zone information in Active Directory is more secure as it prevents unauthorized clients from performing dynamic updates.

 Zone transfers can be performed between standard and Active Directory–integrated zones—for example, between WS2003 name servers and Unix BIND machines or legacy NT DNS servers.

Regardless of how zone information is stored, you can create three types of zones:

Forward-lookup zone
Contains mostly A records for resolving FQDNs into IP addresses when clients issue forward-lookup queries. Also contains an SOA record that defines the zone; NS records that specify authoritative name servers for the zone; and possibly other kinds of resource records such as SRV, MX, or CNAME.

Reverse-lookup zone
Contains mostly PTR records for resolving IP addresses into FQDNs when clients issue reverse-lookup queries (rare) or when administrators use nslookup to troubleshoot name-resolution problems (more common). Reverse lookups don't try to search all DNS namespaces to resolve their IP address into an FQDN; instead, they use a special DNS domain called *in-addr.arpa*, which uses a reverse ordering of the dotted IP address notation to identify hosts and stores this information in PTR records.

Stub zone
Contains only those resource records (SOA, NS, and possibly A records) needed to identify the authoritative name servers for that zone. Stub zones are new to WS2003. Stub zones help manage DNS query traffic by enabling local name servers to know the names and addresses of remote name servers authoritative for

GUI Reference

a given zone without requiring the local name server to have a copy of the information in that zone.

Zone Transfers

Zone transfer is the process by which zone information is replicated between name servers. Zone transfer ensures that all name servers for a zone have identical copies of the zone information, which enables clients to use any name server for the zone to perform name resolution. In DNS on NT, zone files were updated by a process called full zone transfer. This meant that when a DNS administrator updated one or more resource records in the primary zone, the full zone file would be replicated from the primary name server to any secondary name servers for the zone. This wasted network bandwidth, and WS2003 uses incremental zone transfer, in which only changes to the zone files are updated. Incremental zone transfer initiates when any of the following events occurs:

* The master server for a zone notifies all secondary name servers for the zone that records have changed in its zone file and that they need to request an update. The process used by the master name server to notify secondary name servers is called DNS Notify. The secondary name servers then contact their master name server requesting the updates for their zone files.

* The DNS Server service on a secondary name server starts up or is restarted. The secondary name server then contacts the designated master name server for the zone, requesting the updates for its zone file.

* The refresh interval configured on the secondary server expires. The secondary name server then contacts the master name server for the zone, requesting the updates for its zone file.

Note that name servers using incremental transfer require additional disk space to maintain a version history of their zone files—in effect, a DNS transaction log.

Resolvers

A *resolver* is software running on a client computer that enables the computer to communicate with name servers to resolve FQDNs into IP addresses. In other words, a name server represents the server side of DNS while a resolver represents the client side. The WS2003 resolver is a caching resolver service—when a name is resolved, the results are cached locally by the client in case it needs to resolve the name again in the immediate future (before the time-to-live—or TTL—of the resolved entry expires). WS2003 resolvers also cache negative name-query responses (failure to resolve a name).

Resolvers must be configured with the IP address of the name servers they will use to perform name resolution. This may be done either manually (for static IP addressing) or dynamically using DHCP.

Name Queries

A *name query* is a request for resolving a name into an IP address. Name queries may be issued by resolvers to name servers, or by name servers to other name servers. There are two types of queries:

Iterative query
When a DNS client or server issues an iterative query to a DNS server, the server must respond with its best current answer without contacting any other servers itself. This best answer is either:

- The requested information (typically the IP address associated with the FQDN sent in the query). If this response is returned, the client is satisfied because it has what it wants.

- A time-out or error message. If this is the case, the client is satisfied because an authoritative answer was received. However, since the answer was "I don't know," the desired network communications can't take place.

- A pointer to an authoritative DNS server that is located one level down in the hierarchical DNS namespace. This kind of response is known as a *referral*. If a referral is returned, the client goes on to interactively query the lower name server. This process continues until one of the two previous responses is received by the client.

Recursive query

When a client or server issues a recursive query to a DNS server, the server that receives the query takes on full responsibility for finding an answer to the client's request and does so iteratively querying other DNS servers until it has an answer or receives an error or time-out message. Whatever the result of the process, it is passed to the client.

Recursive queries are used by:

- DNS clients (resolvers), such as those running on XP Professional or other desktop Microsoft Windows operating systems.

- DNS servers that are configured to forward unresolved names to another DNS server. A DNS server that has been configured to perform recursive instead of iterative queries is called a forwarder because it forwards queries for resolving FQDNs outside of its domain to a different DNS server.

Dynamic Updates

Dynamic updates is a process that enables resolvers to automatically update their associated resource records on their zone's primary name server. This is a big improvement over traditional DNS, in which administrators had to manually create and update resource records in zone files. Dynamic DNS can be used with both standard and Active Directory–integrated zones and can be used in conjunction with DHCP to make administering DNS even easier. Depending on how dynamic updates have been configured, either the DHCP client itself updates its records on the DNS server or the DHCP server updates the client's records for it.

Using Dynamic DNS with Active Directory–integrated zones enables resource records on name servers to be automatically updated more securely than when using standard primary and secondary zones. This works because only clients and servers that have been authorized in Active Directory can update their own records on the DNS server.

Delegation

You can also create subdomains in a domain and then delegate authority over those subdomains to different name servers. This lets you delegate the task of administering DNS for each subdomain to different name servers. For example, in the large enterprise *mtit.com* domain, there might be several subdomains such as *ontario.mtit.com*, *quebec.mtit.com, bc.mtit.com*, and so on. You can have one or more DNS servers to service each geographical location within the enterprise and make them authoritative over their own subdomain.

Planning DNS

Let's now look at planning issues related to DNS and Active Directory. There are three basic approaches to implementing a DNS namespace with Active Directory. I'll examine each of them briefly.

Single-Name Approach

In this approach, your existing DNS name is used for both the forest root domain of your internal (Active Directory) network and for your external servers connected to the Internet. For example, if your company has the registered domain name *mtit.com* and you want to migrate your NT network to WS2003, you could choose *mtit.com* as the name of your forest root domain. The advantage of this solution is that it is the simplest form of namespace to adopt. The disadvantage is that you would need to consider carefully how to secure your private corporate network from the Internet since both your private and public servers use the same naming system. The solution is to implement a firewall/proxy server with identical DNS zones created on your internal and external name servers. Your internal DNS server needs resource records for all the IP hosts on your private network, including special records to support Active Directory. Using a WS2003 DNS server is a good choice for your private network, since it fully supports Active Directory's features. Your external DNS server needs only those web servers and other hosts that you maintain outside your firewall for public access, and it can be either Microsoft DNS or BIND. You can then configure your internal name server to forward client requests for Internet resources to your external name server.

The advantages of this approach are:

- Users need to remember only a single domain name when they want to access your company's resources, whether within the private corporate intranet or on your public Internet servers.
- You need to register only one company name with your domain name registrary.

The disadvantages are:

- The additional DNS administration work involved in making sure internal and external DNS servers contain only the records they are supposed to have
- The complexity of reconfiguring your firewall
- The fact that if you maintain some resources on both your internal and external networks, you need to figure out how to keep them synchronized properly

Double-Name Approach

In this approach, your existing DNS issued name for your public (external) servers connected to the Internet and a second DNS name for the forest root domain of your internal network is obtained. For example, you could use the DNS domain name *mtit. com* for your public web servers and register a new second name such as *mtitenterprises.com* to use for your internal network. You can then configure your internal name server to use your external server (typically your ISP's name server) as a forwarder for name resolution on the Internet. Note that when you use the Configure Your Server Wizard to install DNS on WS2003, it checks to see if your network is connected with the Internet. If it is, it creates a root hints file called *Cache.dns* that contains the addresses of the Internet's root name servers, and as a result you don't need to configure a forwarder to resolve hosts on the Internet. However, you may still want to configure a forwarder to increase performance and reduce DNS query traffic over your Internet connection.

If Configure Your Server can't detect an Internet connection, it may create a root (.) forward-lookup zone on your server to designate your server as a root name server! As a result, you may not be able to resolve hosts on the Internet even with a forwarder configured. The solution is to delete the root zone.

A variant of this approach is to use your existing DNS name (*mtit.com*) for your public presence and a local DNS name such as *mtit.local* for your internal network. The *.local* suffix is not part of the Internet's DNS system, and as a result clients on the Internet are unable to resolve and access hosts on your internal network and can resolve and access only public hosts on your DMZ. This provides an added layer of protection for your internal network by isolating it from the Internet, and if you use Manage Your Server to add the Typical First Server role to your first WS2003 machine, the Configure Your Server Wizard suggests this approach.

The advantages of this approach are:

- The DNS naming hierarchy of your private WS2003 domains, trees, and forests is hidden from external users on the Internet. The security of your network resources is greater because internal and external resources are clearly distinguished by belonging to different DNS domains.
- You can leave your existing corporate DNS naming hierarchy and zone files (if implemented) intact and simply upgrade your NT DNS servers to WS2003.

The disadvantages are:

- You may need to register a second DNS domain name for your company with ICANN (unless you use the *.local* approach).
- Some users might be confused by the fact that your company has two DNS domain names. Which one should they use?

Subdomain Approach

In this approach, your existing DNS domain name is used for your public servers connected to the Internet and for the legacy portion of your internal network that you don't plan to migrate to WS2003, and then a subdomain is created for the portion of your private network that you plan to upgrade to WS2003 and as the name for your WS2003 root domain in Active Directory. This might be the best approach in a heterogeneous network in which you migrate only a portion of your network to WS2003, especially if DNS is already configured on your existing network. For example, say your existing network uses the DNS name *mtit.com*, and you want to install Active Directory on a portion of your network. In this case you could create a DNS subdomain such as *windows.mtit.com* and make this the name of your new WS2003 root domain. Note that it might be better to use *windows.mtit.com* than *win2003.mtit.com* in case you decide to upgrade your network to Windows 2006 later on!

To make this happen, you need to:

- Create a DNS zone for *windows.mtit.com*, preferably on a WS2003 name server since it will support Active Directory.
- Create a delegation record on the existing name server that is authoritative for your *mtit.com* domain. The delegation record will indicate that authority for the *windows.mtit.com* subdomain is delegated to your WS2003 name server.
- Install Active Directory with *windows.mtit.com* as your forest root domain.

The advantages of this approach are:

- It provides a contiguous namespace for Active Directory, which you can easily administer.
- It doesn't necessitate the upgrade of your existing DNS servers, so you can keep your good old BIND servers if you like.
- You can leave your firewall pretty much the way it is right now.

The main disadvantage is that it takes longer for your DNS naming structure to name resources on your WS2003 network. This is only a minor bother, however, unless your domain name is something like *wishicouldthinkofabetterdomainnamethanthis.com*!

BIND and WS2003

Most name servers on the Internet and in large enterprises with heterogeneous networks are Unix machines running BIND, which stands for Berkeley Internet Name Domain. Recent versions of BIND are compatible with Active Directory, and you can elect to keep your existing BIND name servers if you like when deploying WS2003 on your network. The procedures for integrating BIND with Active Directory aren't trivial, however, and there are several ways you can approach the issue of integrating existing BIND name servers and Active Directory:

- You can use BIND exclusively, an approach your DNS administrator may prefer. You should use BIND 8.2.1 or later if you plan to keep your BIND servers and not implement WS2003 name servers. This is because BIND 8.2.1 supports Dynamic DNS (DDNS), SRV resource records, incremental zone transfers, and negative caching—all features supported by Active Directory. However, BIND doesn't support WINS or WINS-R records, which may be needed if you need to integrate WINS with DNS—for example, if part of your network will continue to use NT. If you want to use a BIND name server for the forest root domain of Active Directory, you need to create special subdomains like *_msdcs.<domainname>*, *_sites. <domainname>*, *_tcp.<domainname>*, and *_udp.<domainname>*, where *<domainname>* is the DNS name you registered for your company. These special subdomains are used by Active Directory to store various configuration information on the DNS server. See the *Deployment Planning Guide* of the *Windows Server 2003 Resource Kit* for more information.
- You can use WS2003 name servers exclusively. This is the simplest solution from the point of view of WS2003 but requires an upheaval of your existing BIND name servers and DNS administration scheme, plus the retraining of your DNS administrators. With the proven stability of BIND, your DNS administrators may try to talk you out of this approach.
- You can use Windows name servers for your internal network and BIND name servers for name resolution on the Internet. This might be the best solution, and it doesn't even require upgrading your BIND servers. What you can do here is register a second DNS name and use this as your forest root domain in Active Directory. You can then leave your BIND server to manage DNS for the portion of your network you don't plan to migrate to WS2003 and to manage DNS for your Internet hosts. Then create a secondary zone on your BIND name server for your WS2003 domain and a secondary zone on your WS2003 DNS server for your BIND server's domain.
- You can use BIND for both the internal and external network and configure your WS2003 root domain as a subdomain of your company's existing DNS domain. This might be a good solution if you are planning to migrate some (but not all) of

your network to WS2003. On the BIND server, you then delegate authority for the WS2003 subdomain to Active Directory, which manages the delegated portion of DNS namespace for the network. You must be running BIND 8.2.1 or later if you go this route, however. What you need to do is create a delegation record on your BIND name server for the new subdomain and then configure the WS2003 DNS server to use the subdomain as the root domain for Active Directory.

For more information on BIND, see *DNS and BIND* by Paul Albitz and Cricket Liu (O'Reilly).

DNS—Tasks

DNS administration tasks are performed using the DNS console, which can be opened by either:

> Start → Programs → Administrative Tools → DNS
>
> Command line → **dnsmgmt.msc**

In addition, many DNS administration tasks can also be performed from the command line using the following utilities found in *DEPLOY.CAB* in the *\SUPPORT\TOOLS* folder on your product CD:

Dnscmd
> Particularly useful for scripted administration of DNS servers

DNSLint
> Can be used to diagnose and repair problems caused by missing or incorrect DNS records in a domain environment

Install DNS Manually

On a standalone server, first open the TCP/IP Properties sheet for your Local Area Connection, assign your server a static IP address, and specify the server's own IP address as its preferred DNS server. Then install the DNS service using Add or Remove Programs in Control Panel. Finally, configure your new name server by creating forward- and reverse-lookup zones; adding A, PTR, or other records to your zones; configuring zone transfers with other DNS servers; and so on. These tasks are described later in this section.

Install DNS Using Wizard

> Start → Manage Your Server → Add or Remove Role

If your server is going to be the first server in your forest, select Typical Setup for a First Server as the role and follow the prompts. The wizard suggests a DNS name of the form *organization.local* for your root domain, where *organization* is the company name you specified when you installed WS2003 on your machine. The wizard also creates the necessary forward- and reverse-lookup zones automatically and allows you to specify the IP address of your ISP's name server as a forwarder for resolving hosts on the Internet.

If your server will be a standalone name server, select DNS Server as the role, and the Configure a DNS Server Wizard leads you through the process of creating forward- and reverse-lookup zones for your domain. If you abort the wizard, DNS is installed, but you have to create your zones manually using the DNS console.

Create a Forward-Lookup Zone

> Right-click on Forward Lookup Zones → New Zone

This starts the New Zone Wizard. The path through the wizard depends on the type of zone you create and whether Active Directory is installed. On standalone servers the process is simple. For example, to create a primary zone:

> Primary zone → specify DNS name → disable dynamic updates for optimal security

To create a secondary or stub zone:

> Secondary or stub zone → specify DNS name → specify IP address of master name server from which zone information will be obtained

If Active Directory–integrated zones are being used, extra steps are involved. For example, to create a primary zone:

> Primary zone → specify DNS replication scope → specify DNS name → enable dynamic updates for easiest administration

The replication scope defines the other name servers your machine will perform zone transfers with and can be forestwide, domainwide, domain controllers only, or an Active Directory partition. The default is all domain controllers in the local domain.

Secondary zones aren't stored in Active Directory, so the procedure is the same as for standalone servers. Stub zones may or may not be stored in Active Directory as desired.

Create a Reverse-Lookup Zone

> Right-click on Reverse Lookup Zones → New Zone

The rest is the same as creating a forward-lookup zone, except instead of specifying a zone name, you specify a network ID, and the wizard automatically creates the name for the zone in the standard *in-addr.arpa* format. For example, if you specify 172.16.13 as the network ID, the reverse-lookup zone is automatically named *13.16.172.in-addr. arpa*.

Convert a Zone

You can convert a zone from one type to another—for example, from primary to secondary—by:

> Right-click on zone → Properties → General → Change (Type) → specify new zone type

You can convert a primary zone to an Active Directory–integrated zone only if the name server is a domain controller.

Configure Zone Transfer/Replication

To manually configure zone transfer:

> Right-click on zone → Properties → Zone Transfers → enable zone transfer → specify who can request zone transfers

By default, zone transfers are enabled on standalone name servers but are allowed only for name servers listed on the Name Servers tab. If desired, you can instead specify IP addresses of servers allowed to request zone transfers or allow any server to request a zone transfer, which is a security risk. By default, your name server also notifies all servers on the Name Servers tab when updates are available. Additional configuration of zone transfer can be performed using the Start of Authority (SOA) tab, where you can specify:

Refresh interval
>This specifies how often a secondary name server contacts its master name server for zone updates, which by default is every 15 minutes.

Retry interval
>This specifies how long a secondary server waits before attempting to contact a master name server after a failed attempt at contacting it, which by default is every 10 minutes.

Expire interval
>This specifies how long the secondary server retries before it stops responding to client requests for name resolution, as the second server's DNS information is probably out-of-date. The default is one day.

Minimum TTL
>This specifies the amount of time during which the DNS server caches information it receives from other name servers in response to a recursive query it issues. Making the TTL smaller makes the DNS database information more consistent across the various DNS servers for the zone, but it also increases DNS network traffic and the load on the DNS servers. WS2003 DNS servers can also cache negative responses to name-query requests.

On stable networks whose configuration doesn't frequently change, you can try increasing the zone-transfer settings to reduce zone-transfer traffic. If name resolution starts to become erratic on the network, lower the settings again.

Zone transfer is configured differently for Active Directory–integrated zones:

>Right-click on zone → Properties → General → Change (Replication) → specify replication scope

In addition, you can manually specify zone transfers with name servers that don't use Active Directory–integrated zones.

Force Zone Transfer/Replication

To force a name server to update a secondary zone from a master name server:

>Right-click on secondary zone → Transfer from master

The option to reload from a master forces a full zone transfer instead of an incremental one. To force a master name server to notify its secondary name servers that they should contact it to initiate a zone transfer:

>Right-click on a zone → Properties → Start of Authority (SOA) → Increment

This increments the version number of the zone on the master name server, indicating to secondary servers that the zone has been updated and that they should initiate a zone transfer with the primary.

If you are using Active Directory–integrated zones exclusively (that is, all your DNS servers are domain controllers), you can force a zone transfer with another DNS server by forcing Active Directory replication to occur. To do this, open Active Directory

GUI Reference

Sites and Services from Administrative Tools and expand the following nodes in the console tree:

> Root node → Sites → select a site → Servers → select target DNS server (domain controller) → NDTS settings

Right-click on the object in the details pane that represents the link to the DNS server that you want to immediately replicate, and select Replicate Now.

Add a Resource Record

You can manually create resource records in a zone by right-clicking on a zone and specifying one of the following:

New Host
> Creates an A record for a host. This option is available only for forward-lookup zones, and you can optionally create an associated PTR record simultaneously.

New Pointer
> Creates a PTR record for a host. This option is available only for reverse-lookup zones.

New Alias
> Creates a CNAME record to map an alias to a host.

New Mail Exchanger
> Creates an MX record for an SMTP mail-forwarding host.

Other New Records
> Lets you create any type of resource record (use this mainly to create NS records).

Once you create a resource record, you can modify it by:

> Select zone → double-click on resource record

Create a Subdomain

> Right-click on zone → New Domain → specify name of subdomain

For example, if your existing zone is authoritative for the *mtit.com* domain, you can create a subdomain called *sales* within the same zone. You need to specify only the name *sales* for the new subdomain, not the full name *sales.mtit.com*. Creating subdomains is a way of adding structure to the DNS namespace of your company.

Configure a Forwarder

To configure a name server to forward queries that can't be resolved locally to a different name server (that is, to a forwarder):

> Right-click on DNS server → Properties → Forwarders → specify IP addresses of forwarders

If you specify more than one forwarder, they are tried in order until one is contacted within the specified forward time-out period. When a DNS server configured to use a forwarder receives a name query that it can't resolve itself, it sends the query to the forwarder to handle. If the forwarder can't resolve the name, it returns a failure message to the original DNS server. The original DNS server can then either:

- Simply pass the failure message to the client that issued the query (i.e., iterative behavior)
- Attempt to resolve the query itself from its own zone information (i.e., recursive behavior)

To choose the first option, on the Forwarders tab of the DNS server's properties sheet, select the checkbox "Do not use recursion." This makes your DNS server simply send all queries to the forwarder.

 Note that you can now specify that the forwarder be used only for specific DNS domains (the default is any domain). This feature, known as conditional forwarding, is new to WS2003. Conditional forwarders can be used to set up more efficient forwarding paths in your company if you support several zones.

Configure a Caching-Only Name Server

Simply install the DNS Server service on a WS2003 machine and don't configure any forward- or reverse-lookup zones on it!

Configure Scavenging

> Right-click on DNS server → Set Aging/Scavenging for all zones → Scavenge stale resource records

Scavenging removes stale resource records from the DNS database. This is important if you are using dynamic updates to maintain your DNS database. For example, if a DNS client configured to use dynamic updates shuts down improperly (for example, by turning the power off or removing the cable from its network card), the DNS server is not aware that the client is gone and still resolves names directed toward the client. If the client shuts down smoothly, its resource records are deleted from the DNS database when dynamic updates are used.

You can manually initiate scavenging by:

> Right-click on DNS server → Scavenge stale resource records

 Be careful with enabling scavenging. If it is not configured properly, you may end up deleting resource records that should have been retained. Scavenging can be enabled on a per-server, per-zone, or per-record basis. See the *Windows Server 2003 Resource Kit* for more information on configuring DNS scavenging.

Monitor a DNS Server

WS2003 DNS servers can perform self-monitoring actions on a scheduled basis to ensure they are functioning properly. To configure monitoring:

> Right-click on DNS server → Properties → Monitoring → select type of test → specify test interval

A simple query means the DNS server must return a response without querying any other name servers. Selecting recursive query means that your DNS server can recursively query other name servers if necessary, which is a more complex test to perform and interpret. You can also click Test Now to perform a test manually. Test results are PASS or FAIL.

Specify Boot Method

> Right-click on DNS server → Properties → Advanced → Load zone data on startup → select from where

Here are the possibilities:

From registry
> The default on WS2003 when Active Directory–integrated zones aren't used.

From file
> The option to store your name server configuration information in a boot file, an ASCII text file that uses BIND 4 format. You don't need this file for DNS on WS2003, but if you are importing your DNS information from an existing BIND 4.x.x name server, you can port the boot file from the BIND server to the WS2003 name server and then specify the setting described earlier.

From Active Directory and registry
> The default on WS2003 domain controllers.

Update Server Datafiles

At predefined update intervals, DNS servers automatically write changes in standard primary zones to their associated zone files on the server's disk. This information is also written to disk when a DNS server is shut down. To immediately write changes in standard primary zones to their associated zone files on the server's disk:

> Right-click DNS server → Update Server Data Files

When you make a change to an Active Directory–integrated zone, the information is written immediately to Active Directory—the Update Server Data Files option has no effect for these zones.

Clear the DNS Server Cache

> Right-click on DNS server → Clear cache

This removes all resolved names from the server cache. The server cache contains information received from other name servers in response to recursive queries it has issued. You might clear the server cache after you manually modify existing resource records within a zone (for example, if servers had their IP addresses changed). This will ensure that DNS clients querying the server will have names resolved from zone data and not from a stale server cache.

 The server cache on a DNS server and the resolver cache on a DNS client are two different things, although both are present on a DNS server (since every DNS server must also be a DNS client).

Configure DNS Clients

The procedure you will use to configure client computers to contact DNS servers for name resolution depends on the type of operating system on the client and whether DHCP or static IP addressing is used. The actual steps will vary, depending on which version of Microsoft Windows your clients are running, but some general guidelines are as follows.

Clients Using Static Addresses

Configure the following information on the client computer:

- Specify the IP address of the primary (and possibly a secondary) DNS server.
- Specify a list of DNS suffixes that should be appended to unqualified DNS names to try to resolve them (optional).

- Enable the client to register its IP address with the DNS server using DNS dynamic updates (W2K/2003/XP clients only).

On W2K/2003/XP clients, dynamic updates are configured by default.

Clients Using DHCP

Configure the following information on the client computer:

- Enable DHCP on the client.
- Enable dynamic updates on the client by selecting the checkbox to register the connection's addresses in DNS (W2K/2003/XP clients only).

Configure the following information on the DHCP server:

- Specify the IP addresses of primary and alternate DNS servers with DHCP option 6.
- If desired, specify a list of DNS suffixes that should be appended to unqualified DNS names to try to resolve them. Only one suffix can be assigned using DHCP option 15; others have to be manually assigned at the client.

New to WS2003 is the fact that Group Policy now lets you configure DNS on W2K/2003/XP clients by enabling/disabling dynamic updates, specifying a DNS suffix, and so on. These new policy settings are found under Computer Configuration → Administrative Templates → Network → DNS Client.

Enable Dynamic Updates

To allow a zone to be automatically updated by dynamic updates:

Right-click on a zone → Properties → General → Dynamic updates → select option

On standalone name servers your options are None (the default) or Nonsecure and Secure (not recommended). For Active Directory–integrated zones you have a third option, Secure Only, which is the default and is recommended. Once you enable dynamic updates on the name server, you also need to enable it on the client. W2K/2003/XP clients belonging to a Windows 2003/2000 domain and using DHCP are configured to use dynamic updates by default. This can be toggled on or off by:

Right-click on My Network Places → Properties → right-click on Local-Area Connection → Properties → select Internet Protocol (TCP/IP) → Properties → Advanced → DNS → select/deselect Register this connection's addresses in DNS

W2K/2003/XP machines dynamically reregister their A resource records with the DNS server every 24 hours or when a DHCP lease is renewed, a new lease is obtained, the TCP/IP configuration on the client changes, an IP address is added or removed for a static adapter, or a Plug and Play event occurs. If a DHCP lease expires, the client also deregisters its A record with DNS servers. You can force a client to reregister its A record with DNS servers with `ipconfig /registerdns` at the command line on the client. With NT clients that use DHCP to perform dynamic updates, use `ipconfig /release` and `ipconfig /renew` instead.

Preload Resolver Cache

You can speed up name queries to frequently accessed hosts by preloading the client resolver cache. On WS2003 clients, for example, open the *Hosts* file located in *%SystemRoot%\System32\drivers\etc* and add hostname-to-IP-address mappings using the format outlined in the file. When the client tries to resolve a name, it tries its local resolver cache first; if this fails, it then contacts a name server. You can verify that these entries have been preloaded into the client cache by using the `ipconfig /displaydns` command from a command prompt on the client. The downside of this procedure is that name-resolution data on your clients could become stale if you make changes to your server infrastructure often.

Flush the Resolver Cache

On a DNS client you can flush the contents of the resolver cache (the cached responses from a name query the client issued) using `ipconfig /flushdns` at the command line. You can do this if its contents become stale (for example, after you modify existing records on DNS servers).

View the Resolver Cache

In order to see what information is stored in the resolver cache on a DNS client, type **ipconfig /displaydns** at the command line. This displays both:

- Information received from name servers in response to recently issued name queries by the client
- Preloaded hostname-to-IP-address mappings from the client's local *Hosts* file

The entries in the cache age and expire when the TTLs associated with their records on the name server expire (entries in *Hosts* don't expire).

DNS—Notes

General

If the person responsible for administering a DNS zone should change, make sure you modify the SOA record for the zone to update the email address of the zone administrator. The DNS Server service sends email to this address automatically when query errors and other conditions arise. Note that the email address substitutes the usual at symbol (@) with a period (.); e.g., specify *info.mtit.com* instead of *info@mtit.com*.

DNS replaces the *Hosts* file, which was the original method for performing hostname–to–IP address name resolution on a TCP/IP network. However, the *Hosts* file can still be used in smaller WS2003 networks instead of DNS if desired, such as in a small intranet with no connection to the Internet.

You can start, stop, pause, and resume name servers by:

> Right-click DNS server → All Tasks → {Start | Stop | Pause | Resume | Restart}
> `net stop dns | net start dns | net pause dns | net continue dns`

Zones

Always have at least two DNS servers hosting each zone to provide fault tolerance for name resolution.

DNS servers and zones don't map one-to-one. In fact:

- One DNS server can manage one or more zones for efficiency and delegating administration of subdomains.
- One zone can be stored on one or more DNS servers for fault tolerance and load balancing.

It is generally best to have at least one secondary name server per zone. This way, if the primary name server for the zone goes offline, clients can still resolve names.

Standard zone files are stored in *%SystemRoot%\System32\dns* as a file with a *.dns* extension. For example, the forward-lookup zone for the *mtit.com* domain would, by default, be stored in the zone file *mtit.com.dns*.

Resolvers

You can stop or start the DNS Client service on a WS2003/2000/XP computer with net stop "dns client" or net start "dns client".

Stopping the DNS client also flushes the resolver cache.

Resolvers can query both remote name servers and the local computer if it is running the DNS Server service.

Troubleshooting

To troubleshoot DNS server problems, you can use:

- nslookup, which can be used to issue DNS queries and examine zone files on local and remote servers.
- ipconfig, which can be used to view and flush the resolver cache and force dynamic updates by WS2003 clients.
- Event Viewer, which manages the DNS server log.
- The optional DNS log *%SystemRoot%\System32\Dns\Dns.log*, which keeps track of DNS server activity. This log is enabled and configured by:

    Right click on DNS server → Properties → Logging → select logging options
- The DNS console to monitor the DNS server by:

    Right-click on DNS server → Properties → Monitoring → select a test

Here is a basic troubleshooting procedure for checking a DNS server if problems occur (stop at the step where the problem is resolved):

1. Check Event Viewer first.
2. Go to the client and try pinging the DNS server to test for basic network connectivity.
3. At the client, open a command prompt and type **nslookup 127.0.0.1**. If you get the name of the client in response to this, your server is OK. If it gives "Server failure" as a response, the server may simply be too busy (or the reverse-lookup zone in which the client's PTR record exists may be paused—check the General tab of the properties sheet for this zone on the server).
4. If the response is "Request to server timed out" or "No response from server," then go to the server, open a command prompt, and type **net start dns**. If DNS is already started, then check the Interfaces tab on the properties sheet of the server to make sure that the server is listening on the interface to which the client's subnet is connected.

If a client queries a DNS server and receives incorrect information (wrong IP address for the queried FQDN), then you can troubleshoot the problem like this:

1. Go to the client and flush the resolver cache by typing **ipconfig /flushdns** at a command prompt.
2. Type **nslookup *IPaddresstoresolve IPaddressofserver***. If you get a correct response, the problem was a stale cache entry. If not, the zone information on your authoritative name servers is in error. If you were querying the primary name server (or if your DNS is integrated with Active Directory), check the resource

records for your host and whether dynamic update is configured properly on the client. If you were querying a secondary name server, check if zone transfers are configured properly as well.

See Also

Active Directory, *DHCP*, nslookup

Domain—Concepts

A *domain* is a container in Active Directory that defines a logical boundary for objects that share common requirements for security, replication, and administration.

Security

A domain is a security boundary within which objects (users, groups, computers, printers, and so on) can be managed. For example, all users in a domain can log on to the domain using their usernames and passwords. Domains also have their own security policy, called a domain security policy, that defines account policies such as password and account lockout settings. See *Group Policy* later in this chapter for more information on domain security policies.

Replication

A new domain is created when you install the first domain controller for the domain. Domains are also units of replication, for all domain controllers in a domain automatically replicate their Active Directory updates to one another. See *Domain Controller* later in this chapter for more information.

Administration

Domains share common administration, and members of the Domain Admins group have broad rights and permissions for performing administrative tasks on objects in the domain. These administrators can also delegate aspects of domain administration to other trusted users using the Delegation of Control Wizard. Administrators can add further structure to a domain by creating a hierarchy of OUs within the domain. Administrators can delegate authority over OUs to trusted users to allow them to perform specific administrative tasks on the objects within the OUs. See *Delegation* and *OU* in this chapter for more information.

Domains can exist by themselves, or they can be grouped into multidomain hierarchical structures called trees. A tree consists of a root domain and one or more child domains joined by trusts to the root or to each other in hierarchical fashion. Elements of a tree share a common namespace. A forest consists of one or more trees joined at the roots by trusts. All domains in a tree or forest implicitly trust each other using two-way transitive trusts, allowing users to log on to a client computer anywhere in the enterprise and access shared resources on any server. For more information, see *Forest* and *Trusts* later in this chapter.

Domains aren't the same as sites. Domains are logical groupings of users, computers, and other Active Directory objects, while sites are physical divisions between networks connected by slow WAN links. One domain can span several sites, and one site can contain several domains. For more information, see *Site* later in this chapter.

Domains are named using DNS—for example, *mtit.com* or *sales.mtit.com*. The forest root domain is the first domain you create when you install Active Directory. When you promote your first domain controller, the forest root domain is created and is the root of both your first tree and the entire forest. Domains in a tree must form a contiguous namespace in Active Directory. For example, if the root domain of a tree is *mtit.com*, then *vancouver.mtit.com* and *seattle.mtit.com* would be two examples of child domains of *mtit.com*, while *support.vancouver.mtit.com* and *sales.vancouver.mtit. com* would be two more child domains whose parent domain is *vancouver.mtit.com*.

In W2K, domains could not be renamed—actually, there was a hack in which you could create a new domain with the desired DNS name and then use the *MoveTree* utility from Support Tools to move all the objects from your old domain to the new one, but this was tedious and somewhat risky. In WS2003, however, you can rename domains, reposition domains within a tree, and create new trees using the *Rendom* utility. This operation is still tedious, but it's no longer risky and can be used to restructure your forest after mergers and other major changes to your company.

Domain Functional Level

In W2K, domains could run in one of two domain modes:

Mixed mode
> Allowed downlevel domain controllers running NT to coexist with domain controllers running W2K by using NTLM authentication instead of Kerberos

Native mode
> Supported only domain controllers running W2K by requiring Kerberos authentication

You could switch W2K domains from mixed mode to native mode but not the reverse.

In WS2003 things are a little more complicated, for domains can now run in one of four different domain functional levels:

Windows 2000 mixed (default for new domains)
> Supports domain controllers running WS2003, W2K, and NT.

Windows 2000 native
> Supports domain controllers running WS2003 and W2K.

Windows Server 2003 interim
> Supports domain controllers running WS2003 and NT. This is a special domain functional level that exists only when you upgrade an NT-based network directly to WS2003.

Windows Server 2003
> Supports only domain controllers running WS2003.

By default, when you create a new domain, its domain functional level is Windows 2000 mixed, which gives it the greatest degree of interoperability with NT/2000 domain controllers. You can raise the domain functional level for your domain to Windows 2000 native if you have no more NT domain controllers or to WS2003 if you have no more W2K domain controllers, but you can't undo this operation afterward. Each time you raise the domain functional level, additional features that simplify the administration of your Windows-based network are supported; these are shown in Table 4-12.

Table 4-12. Features of different domain functional levels

Feature	Windows 2000 mixed	Windows 2000 native	Windows Server 2003
Universal groups	No	Yes	Yes
Group nesting	Partial nesting (global groups can belong to domain local groups)	Full nesting	Full nesting

Table 4-12. Features of different domain functional levels (continued)

Feature	Windows 2000 mixed	Windows 2000 native	Windows Server 2003
NT domain controllers	Allowed	Prohibited	Prohibited
W2K domain controllers	Allowed	Allowed	Prohibited
Rename domain controllers	No	No	Yes
Rename domains	No	No	Yes

Different domains within a forest can be assigned different domain functional levels, depending on how far your network migration has gone. Another type of functional level, called forest functional level, affects all domains in your forest. For more information, see *Forest* later in this chapter.

Planning Domains

When you are planning an Active Directory implementation, start by assuming that a single domain will suffice, create OUs within your domain to add additional structure mirroring the organization of your company, and then delegate authority over OUs to suitable users. Plan for additional domains only if necessary to separate administrative functions more sharply between business subsidiaries, locations, or departments. For example, the following security features are domainwide in scope:

> Password policy
> Account lockout policy
> Kerberos policy
> EFS recovery policy
> IPSec policy
> Public key encryption policy
> Certificate authorities

What this means is that if two departments in your company absolutely must have different password policies, then these departments must be different domains. Before you start creating additional domains, it might be time to consider harmonizing security policies across your company.

Here are some reasons to create multiple domains or trees in your forest:

- Your company is large enough to consider using the complexity of a multidomain implementation of WS2003 Active Directory. There is no hard and fast rule for how big a company should be, though; this is based essentially on your available IT resources and expertise, as well as on the other factors described later.

- Your company requires that IT administration be decentralized across multiple locations or divisions. Multiple domains are appropriate here because domains represent strong security boundaries for administration of users, groups, computers, and other resources. Domain Admins in one domain can't administer resources in other domains unless they are explicitly given permission to do so.

- Your company requires distinct Group Policy security settings (such as password and account lockout settings) for different locations or divisions. This might even be for legal reasons—for example, if some of your subsidiaries are in foreign countries with different legal security requirements.

- Your WAN links are slow, and you want to keep replication traffic between different locations to a minimum and to control it more tightly. You could make each location both a separate domain in the tree and a separate site. This is because the only Active Directory information replicated between domains in a tree are the schema, the configuration information, and the global catalog. If you use a single domain with multiple sites instead, the site links between the sites require enough bandwidth to support the greater traffic that occurs during intra-domain replication of Active Directory.

If you are migrating an existing NT-based enterprise to WS2003, the migration strategy you use depends on which of the four NT domain models your company currently employs:

Single-domain model

If you are currently using the single-domain model in your NT network, you simply upgrade the existing NT domain to create a root domain of a new WS2003 forest.

Single-master-domain model

This model consists of an account domain (the master domain) that is trusted by one or more resource domains (slave domains). You first upgrade the account domain to create the root domain of your new forest, then you upgrade the resource domains to become child domains of the root domain. This results in a single tree with one or more first-level child domains. An alternative is to upgrade your account domain to a root domain, create one top-level OU in the root domain for each existing resource domain, and then join the member servers and workstations to the OUs within the root domain, discarding the domain control-lers in the resource domains. This leaves you with a single domain to manage.

Multiple-master-domain Model

This model consists of two or more account domains (master domains), which trust each other, and one or more resource domains (slave domains), each of which trusts every account domain. A recommended procedure is first to create a new WS2003 domain as the root domain of your forest. This domain is left empty except for administrators belonging to the Enterprise Admins group. Next, you migrate the account domains to become child domains of the empty root domain. Finally, you migrate the resource domains to each become a child domain of the most appropriate, former account domain. The result is a tree with three levels of domains. Alternatively, you can create OUs in the former account domains and join servers and workstations in the resource domains to these former account domains, placing them in the appropriate OUs. The result is a tree with only two levels instead of three (a process called flattening the domains), which is easier to manage.

Complete-trust model

This model consists of two or more NT domains that trust each other. The recommended procedure here is first to create an empty root domain in a new forest and then migrate every NT domain to become a child domain of the root domain. For example, if MTIT Enterprises has the DNS domain name *mtit.com* and consists of two relatively independent offices in Vancouver and Seattle, you could create the forest root domain *mtit.com* in one of the two locations and add a few high-level Administrator accounts to the Enterprise Admins group in this root domain. Do not create any OUs or any other Active Directory objects such as users, groups, computers, or printers in this domain. In other words, this root domain is empty except for a few enterprise-level Administrator accounts. Then create the domains *vancouver.mtit.com* and *seattle.mtit.com* as child domains of the root domain *mtit.com*. Let the members of the Domain Admins group in each

GUI Reference

of these two child domains create the users, groups, computers, printers, OUs, and other directory objects for their own domains.

Domain—Tools

Administering domains is done using two consoles:

Active Directory Users and Computers
> Use this console to create and manage objects within a domain, such as OUs, users, computers, and so on. (This tool was discussed under *Active Directory— Tools* earlier in this chapter.) Most day-to-day administration of domains involves using this console to create users, reset user passwords, and similar stuff.

Active Directory Domains and Trusts
> Use this console to change the domain and forest functional levels, transfer the domain-naming master role, manage external trusts between domains (including trusts with downlevel NT domains), and specify alternative UPN suffixes for domains. These aren't everyday tasks and need to be performed only when required—for example, during different stages of migrating your NT network to WS2003.

In addition, the *Random* utility can be used to rename domains and restructure your forest, as described earlier. *Random* can be downloaded from Microsoft's web site at *www.microsoft.com/windowsserver2003/downloads/*.

Domain—Tasks

Unless otherwise indicated, the following tasks assume you already have the Active Directory Domains and Trusts console open. You must be a member of the Domain Admins group to perform these tasks.

Raise Domain Functional Level

Remember that this process is irreversible.

> Right-click on a domain → Raise Domain Functional Level

You can also raise the domain functional level by right-clicking on the domain in Active Directory Users and Computers. To change the forest functional level, see *Forest* later in this chapter.

Create a New Domain

See *Domain Controller* later in this chapter.

Add a Computer to a Domain

You can either join a Windows 2003/2000/XP computer to a domain when installing the operating system or afterwards. If afterwards, do this:

> Control Panel → System → Computer Name → Change → select Domain → type DNS name of domain → OK → specify credentials of a Domain Admin account → reboot

This creates a computer account in the domain. You can also create the computer account ahead of time using Active Directory Users and Computers.

Manage a Domain

Right-click on a domain → Manage

This opens the Active Directory Users and Computers console with the focus on the selected domain.

Domain—Notes

Whether you create one domain or many, the number of objects that Active Directory can hold is the same—10 million or so.

For information on how to delegate authority for a domain, see *Delegation* earlier in this chapter.

For information on creating a Group Policy for a domain, see *Group Policy* later in this chapter.

When specifying the name of the domain you want a computer to join, you can specify either the DNS name of the domain (for example, *mtit.com*) or the downlevel (pre–W2K) name of the domain (for example, *MTIT*). To display the DNS name for a domain, use Control Panel → System → Computer Name on a domain controller that belongs to the domain. To find the downlevel name for a domain, right-click on the domain node in the console tree of Active Directory Domains and Trusts and select Properties → General → Domain name (pre–Windows 2000). Other actions you can perform on computer accounts using Active Directory Users and Computers include the following:

Right-click on a computer → Disable

This breaks the computer's connection with the domain and prevents it from authenticating to the domain until you enable it. Disabling a computer account doesn't remove it from Active Directory (use → Delete to do that).

Right-click on a computer → Manage

This opens up Computer Management and connects to the selected computer to manage its resources.

Right-click on a computer → Reset Account

If you reset a computer account, you must first remove the computer from the domain if you want it to rejoin the domain.

See Also

Active Directory, adprep, *Delegation*, *DNS*, *Domain Controller*, *Forest*, *Group Policy*, net computer, net view, *Site*, *Trusts*

Domain Controller—Concepts

Domain controllers enable users to log on to the network and access resources for which they have suitable permissions. They also enable users to search Active Directory for shared folders, shared printers, and other published information. A domain must have least one domain controller—in fact, promoting a standalone WS2003 computer to the domain controller role is what creates the domain. However, for

GUI Reference

redundancy, a minimum of two domain controllers is recommended for each domain, for if you have only one domain controller and it goes down, no one will be able to log on. If your company has multiple sites separated by slow WAN links, you probably also want at least one domain controller at each site to reduce logon traffic over the WAN and to enable logons when the WAN goes down. See *Site* later in this chapter for more information.

Authentication

When a user wants to log on to the network from a client computer, the client computer first needs to find a domain controller to authenticate its logon request. What happens is that the client issues a DNS query to locate the nearest domain controller that the client can use. The client then contacts this domain controller, and authentication is performed using one of two authentication protocols:

Kerberos v5
> This protocol is used to authenticate computers running Active Directory client software, which is included with WS2003, W2K, and XP. Active Directory client extensions are also available for Windows 95, Windows 98, and NT.

NTLM
> This protocol is used to authenticate NT clients that don't have Active Directory client extensions installed and for communications with NT domain controllers in domains running in W2K mixed or WS2003 interim domain functional level.

Replication

Unlike the NT approach in which one domain controller (the PDC) in each domain was the master domain controller (the one containing a writable copy of the domain directory database), WS2003 and W2K use a multimaster approach in which all domain controllers in a given domain are peers and contain identical, writable copies of the directory database (Active Directory). Domain controllers within a domain automatically replicate their directory updates to every other domain controller in the domain. The result is that every domain controller in a domain essentially contains identical directory information. This replication process requires no special configuration unless the domain spans multiple sites.

In general, however, domain controllers in different domains don't replicate all their directory information with each other. Otherwise, in a large enterprise every domain controller in every domain would need to contain information about every directory object in the entire enterprise, and this might cause the directory database to grow too large to provide adequate performance when queries are issued against it. Also, the amount of replication traffic needed to keep domain controllers up to date could swamp other forms of normal network traffic.

To solve these problems, Active Directory is partitioned into several naming contexts, with the Schema and Configuration contexts being replicated to all domain controllers in the forest while the Domain context for each domain is replicated only to domain controllers in that domain. As a result, domain controllers in general have knowledge about objects (such as users and computers) only in their own domain and not in other domains. Of course, if this were strictly true then it would be difficult for a user to log on to a computer belonging to a different domain than her home domain. The solution to this problem is the global catalog.

Global Catalog

The global catalog is a partial replica of the most commonly searched attributes for all objects in all domains in the forest. The purpose of the global catalog is to help speed up search queries issued against Active Directory, especially forestwide queries and cross-domain logon attempts. This global catalog typically resides on one or more domain controllers in a domain or site. A domain controller that contains a copy of the global catalog is called a global catalog server. Global catalog servers thus contain the following Active Directory objects:

- A full replica of all objects in its own domain
- A partial replica of all objects in the forest in all naming contexts

By default, the first domain controller in the first domain (forest root domain) of a forest is automatically configured as a global catalog server, and any other domain controller can also be configured as a global catalog server. In W2K, it was critical in native mode domains to have one domain controller per site since domain controllers needed to contact a global catalog server to determine a user's universal group membership before they could authenticate the user's logon attempt, and, if no global catalog server could be found, the logon attempt would fail. As a result, administrators usually designated a global catalog server for each site, which led to increased WAN traffic due to global catalog replication. WS2003 resolves this situation; domain controllers can be configured to cache universal group membership for all users, with the result that global catalog servers are no longer needed for every site.

Operations Master Roles

Although in most senses no domain controller is more important than any other, there are a few special domain controller roles that stand out from the rest. These domain controllers are called FSMO (flexible single master of operations) roles and they are the only domain controllers that can be used to perform certain operations on Active Directory. There are five of these FSMO roles, of which two are forestwide in scope:

Schema master
> By default, this is the first domain controller installed in the forest root domain, and it is the only one on which the Active Directory schema can be modified. There can and must be only one schema master per forest; otherwise, conflicting modifications made to the schema on different machines could cause inconsistencies in Active Directory.

Domain-naming master
> By default, this is the first domain controller installed in the forest root domain. It controls the namespace and is the only one that allows domains to be added, removed, or renamed in your forest.

The remaining three FSMO roles are domainwide in scope:

Infrastructure master
> Responsible for maintaining references to objects located in other domains and for updating group information when groups are renamed or have their membership changed. In a single-domain scenario, this FSMO role is unnecessary.

RID master
> Ensures that globally unique security IDs (SIDs) are assigned to newly created objects (users, computers, or groups) in Active Directory.

GUI Reference

PDC emulator

Acts as a PDC for downlevel NT BDCs when the domain functional level is W2K mixed or WS2003 interim.

How these FSMO roles are assigned by Active Directory depends on the number of domains in your forest and the number of domain controllers in your domains:

Single domain with one domain controller

The domain controller automatically assumes all five FSMO roles.

Single domain with two domain controllers

The first domain controller installed automatically assumes all five roles. If maintenance is planned for the first domain controller, all five FSMO roles should first be transferred to the second domain controller. If the first domain controller goes down unexpectedly, the five FSMO roles can be seized by the second domain controller.

Two or more domains

The schema master and domain-naming master roles must remain in the forest root domain. In all other domains, the first domain controller in each domain automatically assumes the infrastructure master, PDC emulator, and RID master roles for that domain.

 In a multidomain environment, make sure the infrastructure master role is transferred to a domain controller that doesn't host the global catalog. Otherwise, domain controllers may end up with stale information concerning group membership.

Domain Controller—Tasks

Upgrade Domain Controllers

Upgrading W2K domain controllers to WS2003 is trivial since no modification of the namespace is required. Make sure all your W2K domain controllers have the latest service pack installed, use adprep to prepare the forest by extending the schema, and then run Setup on each domain controller to upgrade to WS2003.

If you are upgrading an NT domain, you need to upgrade the PDC first:

Synchronize all BDCs with PDC → take one BDC offline in case something goes wrong → insert WS2003 product CD into PDC → select Upgrade

Test your new mixed-mode domain, then upgrade the remaining BDCs, test, and once you're sure everything works, you can upgrade or decommission the BDC you set aside for an emergency.

Configure a Domain Controller

There's very little to configure on a domain controller:

Active Directory Users and Computers → Select domain → select OU → right-click on a domain controller → Properties

The "Trust computer for delegation" setting on the General tab enables services on the local machine running under the LocalSystem account to request services from other servers on behalf of clients. Since this can be a security concern, enable this only if you know it will be needed—for example, to allow the Message Queuing Service to run on the machine. None of the other settings on the properties sheet are really important, though a few—such as displaying the latest service pack installed on the machine—are informative.

Manage a Domain Controller

> Active Directory Users and Computers → choose domain → choose OU → right-click on a domain controller → Manage

This opens the Computer Management console with the focus on the selected domain controller.

Verify FSMO Roles

Various consoles are used to determine whether a particular domain controller in a particular domain has an FSMO role assigned to it. Specifically, to verify Infrastructure master, PDC emulator, or RID master roles:

> Active Directory Users and Computers → right-click on root node → Connect to a domain → right-click on root node → Connect to a domain controller → right-click on root node → All Tasks → Operations Masters

If an Infrastructure, PDC, or RID tab is visible, the selected domain controller in the selected domain has that FSMO role.

To verify the domain-naming master role:

> Active Directory Domains and Trusts → right-click on root node → Operations Master

To verify the schema master role:

> Active Directory Schema → right-click on root node → Operations Master

Transfer FSMO Roles

To transfer an FSMO role to a different domain controller, follow the procedure described in the previous section, *Verify FSMO Roles*, and:

> Change → select a different domain controller in the domain.

You can also transfer FSMO roles from the command line using the *ntdsutil* utility.

Seize FSMO Roles

If your domain controller goes down before you can transfer its FSMO roles to another domain controller, you'll have to seize these roles to assign them to another domain controller. This must be done from the command line using the *ntdsutil* utility.

Promote/Demote a Domain Controller

To promote a member server to the role of domain controller, you can:

> Manage Your Server → Add or Remove Role → Domain Controller

Alternatively, you can use *DCPromo*—for example, to create a child domain:

> Start → Run → **dcpromo** → Domain controller for a new domain → Create a new child domain in an existing tree → specify Enterprise Admin credentials and DNS name of forest root domain → specify parent domain → specify name for child domain → specify permissions → specify password for Directory Services Restore Mode → reboot

GUI Reference

Promoting and demoting computers to the role of domain controller has certain drastic effects:

- If you promote a standalone server, any local user accounts on the machine will be lost. If you demote a domain controller, any domain user accounts in Active Directory will be lost if this is the last domain controller in the domain.

- Any cryptographic keys stored on the computer will be lost after promotion or demotion and should be exported if necessary.

- Any EFS-encrypted files will be inaccessible after promotion or demotion and should therefore be unencrypted before the action is taken.

To demote a domain controller, either remove the role using Manage Your Server or run *DCPromo* again. If there are still other domain controllers in the domain, the domain controller you are demoting becomes a member server in the domain. If you are demoting the last domain controller in the domain, the domain controller becomes a standalone server. Note that you can't remove the last domain controller from a domain if your domain is a parent for other domains. To remove the last domain controller in the domain:

> Start → Run → **dcpromo** → specify the server as the last domain controller in the domain → specify an Enterprise Admins account for the forest → specify a password for a new local Administrator account → reboot

If you try to use *DCPromo* to demote a domain controller and the procedure fails for some reason, use dcpromo /forcedremoval to force the computer to return to the member server state.

Install from Media

If you need to deploy domain controllers at remote sites where qualified administrators aren't present, you can use the new Install From Media feature of WS2003. This new feature lets you prestage new domain controllers for an existing domain by installing them from the backup media created by backing up an existing domain controller. The procedure uses the Backup utility under System Tools in Accessories:

> Back up the system state of an existing domain controller in the domain → start Backup on the remote server → Restore Files and Settings → System State → Advanced → Alternate Location → specify a folder → Replace Existing Files → Finish → Start → Run → **dcpromo /adv** → Additional domain controller for existing domain → select restored backup files → specify administrator credentials → specify domain

WS2003 does a better job of demoting domain controllers than W2K and removes folders and files that were previously left behind.

Assign a Global Catalog Server

To assign the role of global catalog server to a domain controller:

> Active Directory Sites and Services → Site container → Servers container → right-click on domain controller → Properties → General → select Global Catalog

To remove the role of global catalog server from a domain controller:

> Active Directory Sites and Services → Site container → Servers container → right-click on domain controller → Properties → General → deselect Global Catalog

Add an Attribute to the Global Catalog

This procedure is useful to speed up search queries across domains for an attribute that is not included by default in the global catalog. For example, you might want to add the Phone Number attribute for user objects to the Global Catalog so users can search for other users' phone numbers easily in a multidomain forest:

> Active Directory Schema → expand Attributes container → right-click on attribute → Properties → Replicate this attribute to the Global Catalog

Domain Controller—Notes

When you promote a domain controller, there must be a DNS server available on the network. If you are creating a new forest root domain and you have no DNS server, you are prompted to have the wizard automatically install and configure your computer as a DNS server. The first domain controller of your forest should have its TCP/IP settings configured so that it points to itself as its preferred DNS server—otherwise, incorrect SRV records may be created. Additional domain controllers should also point to the first domain controller as their preferred DNS server and their own IP address as an alternate DNS server.

Domain controller objects are located by default in the Domain Controllers OU within a domain, and they can be managed, moved to different OUs, and configured using Active Directory Users and Computers.

If a domain controller you want to demote owns one or more of the FSMO roles, transfer these roles to other domain controllers in the domain before demoting it. If it is the last domain controller in your domain, this is not an issue.

You can't demote a domain controller if Certificate Services is running on it; you have to remove this service first.

Additional tabs are available on the properties sheet for a domain controller when View → Advanced Features is selected.

Don't create additional global catalog servers on a single domain unless you have multiple sites connected by slow WAN links. You should generally have one global catalog server per site if WAN connections between sites are slow because clients need to be able to access the global catalog in order to log on to the network (unless universal group caching is enabled).

In W2K, adding a new attribute to the global catalog resulted in a full synchronization of all Active Directory information for all domains in the forest, which created a lot of network traffic. This problem has been fixed in WS2003.

You can rename WS2003 domain controllers using the *netdom* utility.

See Also

Active Directory, Domain, Forest, Trusts

Event Logs—Concepts

An *event* is a specific occurrence of an activity of the WS2003 operating system, an installed component, or an application. Events are generated automatically and are recorded in event logs, which can then be viewed and analyzed using the Event Viewer console in Administrative Tools. The key is to use Event Viewer to regularly monitor the event logs on your servers and deal with any situations that arise. You can use Event Viewer to search for or filter particular types of events if the log becomes excessively large. It's also important to configure the size limit and retention period for event logs as soon as you set up a new server. Logs can wrap (newer events start overwriting older ones) once they reach a certain size, but this may cause important information to be lost. It's better to configure a decent chunk of disk space for each log and then archive and clear logs regularly, so that your information is saved but disk space is freed up.

Default Logs

Three event logs are present on every WS2003 computer:

System log

This log contains events generated by activities of the operating system. Examples of system events include the activities of services such as the Net-Logon service, failures of drivers to initialize properly, changes in the role of a server from member server to domain controller, and so on. System events come in three flavors:

Information events

These events simply describe normal activites that have occurred, such as the successful startup of the Event Log service itself, the establishment of a remote access connection, a browser forcing an election on the network, and so on. Some information events also record failures of certain activities that have no real consequence on network operations.

Warning events

These events describe occurrences that may be problems, such as failure of dynamic registration of a DNS name due to DNS client misconfiguration, failure of the Windows Time Service to find a domain controller, space running low on a disk, a scope on a DHCP server being 100% leased, and so on. You might be able to get by for a while with a warning, but you should resolve the problem as soon as you can.

Error events

These events describe critical occurrences that could result in loss of data or other significant problems. Error events include the failure of a required service such as failure of a workstation to initialize, the refusal of a dynamic DNS update from a DNS server, the PDC emulator of the forest root domain not having its time synchronized with a member server or clocking device, failure of a device driver, and so on.

Application log

This log contains events generated by applications running on the computer. The vendor must specifically code its applications to generate these events. Application events are usually helpful only when you give the information to the vendor to help troubleshoot problems you are encountering. However, some WS2003 system events are also logged here, such as Dr. Watson events for application failures, security events related to Group Policy, violations of export cryptography restrictions for IPSec, IIS activities involving Active Server Pages (ASP) functionality, and so on. Application log events are also either information, warning, or error events.

Security log

This log contains events generated when auditing is configured on the computer (for more information, see *Auditing* earlier in this chapter). A security log event is one of the following:

Success events

These indicate that the audited action occurred successfully—for example, a user successfully logged on to the network, successfully accessed a file on a share, or successfully exercised a system right he possesses.

Failure events

These indicate that the audited action failed in its attempt—for example, a user tried to log on but failed because she entered a wrong password, tried to access a mapped drive but couldn't because of permission problems, tried to access a printer object in Active Directory but was refused, and so on.

Additional Logs

Depending on which optional WS2003 components are installed on your computer, other event logs may be displayed by Event Viewer:

Directory service log

This log records the activities of Active Directory and is present on WS2003 domain controllers. Events are either information, warning, or error type.

DNS server log

This log records the activities of a WS2003 DNS server. Events are either information, warning, or error type.

File Replication Service log

This log records the activities of the File Replication Service (FRS) on a WS2003 on which DFS is configured. Events are information, warning, or error type.

Event Logs—Tools

You can start Event Viewer by:

Administrative Tools → Event Viewer

Computer Management → System Tools → Event Viewer

Under the Action menu, you can select the following:

Root node

Select this to connect to a remote computer whose event logs you want to monitor or to open an archived event log file.

Particular log

Select this to display its logged events in the details pane. Double-click on an event to display additional information concerning the event.

Under the View menu, you can select:

All Records

Displays all events recorded in the log (i.e., turns off any filter you created).

Filter

Lets you create a filter to display only certain kinds of events. This is a very useful feature, as event logs tend to grow unmanageably large otherwise.

Newest First or Oldest First
> Changes the order of the events (however, it is easier just to click the Date column header in the details pane).

Find
> Lets you search a log for a particular type of event. This is a powerful adjunct feature to Filter, and it's particularly useful if you are searching for all instances of a particular event in order to gauge its frequency (which may be a measure of its seriousness).

Event Logs—Tasks

These tasks assume that you already have Event Viewer open.

Configure an Event Log

To configure the size and retention settings of an event log, do the following:

> Right-click on an event log → Properties

The maximum log size can range between 64 KB and 4 GB (512 KB is the default). Monitor your logs, and if they grow too quickly, increase the maximum log size so events don't get lost. You can configure retention settings in one of three modes:

Overwrite events as needed
> This is the default setting and means that circular logging is configured. Once the log becomes full, old events are deleted to make room for new ones. This setting can result in loss of important information and should be changed as soon as your server becomes operational on the network.

Overwrite events older than seven days
> This is another form of circular logging. You can select this option if you know that your maximum log size is large enough to prevent your log from getting full, and if you regularly archive your log at the end of each logging interval and then clear the log to free up space for the next interval.

Do not overwrite events
> Use this setting if you have adequate disk space for the event log and when security and system functionality is a priority for your enterprise and you need to keep a long-life paper trail. You must monitor and archive the log periodically and manually clear the events before the log becomes full. Otherwise, if the log becomes full, WS2003 stops writing new events to the log.

If you have configured auditing on your system and security is a concern, you can configure your system to shut down when the Security log becomes full. Set the retention setting on the log to "Do not overwrite events," then use Registry Editor to create or assign the value of 1 to the `REG_DWORD` key called `CrashOnAuditFail` in:

> `HKLM\SYSTEM\CurrentControlSet\Control\Lsa`

and reboot your machine (use caution when editing the registry!). If the Security log fills up, the system will display a message saying "Audit failed" and will stop responding. To recover from this, reboot and log on as Administrator, open Event Viewer, archive the Security log if desired, and then clear it.

If you want your system to still be configured to stop when the log becomes full again, you need to recreate the CrashOnAuditFail registry key at this point.

View an Event Log

Select an event log in the console tree to display a list of events in the details pane. Recent events are listed at the top by default, but you can sort by type, date, and other attributes by clicking on the heading of each column in the details pane. Sorting by type lets you check for critical (error) events quickly; sorting by source helps you troubleshoot problems associated with specific services or devices; sorting by event ID helps you isolate specific conditions and system activities that cause problems. These methods help you quickly determine the frequency and severity of a problem. Use the up or down arrows to scroll through events and the other funny button to copy the details of the event to the clipboard so you can paste it into a document or email message. Note the event ID if you need to contact a Microsoft support technician. Double-click on a particular event in the details pane to display more information about the event.

To filter out unwanted events so you can focus on the problem at hand:

> Right-click on an event log → Properties → Filter

Note that the filter disappears when you connect to a different computer.

Archive an Event Log

> Right-click on an event log → Save Log File as → specify filename and file type

Event logs are located in *%SystemRoot%\System32\config*. They can be archived (saved) in one of three formats:

Log-file format (.evt file)
  Can be opened and viewed again only in Event Viewer

Comma-delimited text file (.csv file)
  Can be imported into a spreadsheet or database

Text-file (.txt file)
  Can be cut and pasted into a Word file or other application

Use the *.evt* format if you want to keep the binary information recorded in events, as this information is discarded with the other formats. Once a log has been archived, you can view it again by:

> Right-click on Event Viewer node → open Log File → select an archived log file → specify the type of log → specify a display name if desired → Open

---

Event Logs—Notes

Critical system events requiring immediate attention are usually displayed in a pop-up alert or warning box on the screen of the server. If the event is significant but doesn't require immediate attention, the event is logged instead to the System or Application log.

If you suspect your problem is hardware-related, filter your System log to show only those events generated by that component.

GUI Reference

If you right-click on an event log → Clear All Events, you can wipe out all the events in the log. The exception is the Security log: if you clear the events in this log, a single new event is generated in the log that records the user who cleared the Security log. You can't cover your tracks that easily!

You can also use archived security logs to track resource-usage trends over time to help in planning for hardware and software upgrades on your network.

See Also

Auditing, eventquery

Files and Folders—Concepts

This topic deals with various aspects of managing files and folders, including attributes, compression, encryption, and various ways of displaying and manipulating files and folders. For additional information, see *Disks*, *Permissions*, and *Shared Folders* in this chapter.

Attributes

Attributes are properties of a file or folder that indicate something about its state. The attributes you can set for files or folders depend on whether the underlying partition or volume is formatted using FAT, FAT32, or NTFS:

Read-only (NTFS and FAT)
> When applied to a file, this prevents the contents of the file from being modified. If applied to a folder, you can choose to make either the folder alone read-only or the folder and all its contents (including subfolders) read-only. Making the folder alone read-only isn't very useful since new files you create in the folder don't inherit this attribute. By default, operating-system files are always marked Read-only, Hidden, and System.

Hidden (NTFS and FAT)
> This hides the file or folder from normal view the next time you view the parent folder's contents. By default, operating-system files are marked Read-only and Hidden. To display hidden files in Windows Explorer, select Tools → Folder Options → View → Show hidden files and folders.

File/Folder is ready for archiving (NTFS and FAT)
> When marked, this indicates that the file or folder should be backed up during the next backup cycle. Once the file or folder has been backed up, the Archive attribute is automatically cleared. When a file or folder is created or its contents are modified, this attribute is automatically set.

For fast searching, allow Indexing Service to index this file/folder (NTFS only)
> The Indexing Service works automatically in the background to build a catalog that speeds up searching for files and folders. By default, all files and folders on NTFS volumes have this attribute marked, but the Indexing Service is not started by default on WS2003.

Compress contents to save disk space (NTFS only)
> This stores the file or folder in a compressed state on an NTFS volume.

Encrypt contents to secure data (NTFS only)
> This stores the file or folder in an encrypted state on an NTFS volume.

Compression

Files and folders stored on NTFS volumes can be compressed to minimize the amount of disk space they occupy. When these files are accessed, the operating system uncompresses them automatically so they can be read or modified; when the modified files are saved or closed, they are automatically compressed again. The whole process is transparent to the user. Both files and folders can be compressed. If a folder is compressed, the files within it don't need to be compressed—or some may be and others not. When a file is copied from one place to another, it is uncompressed, copied, and then compressed again. If there is insufficient disk space to hold the uncompressed file, an error message will occur and the copy will fail.

Certain file types can be effectively compressed, resulting in significant gains in disk space, while compressing other file types shows little gain in space. For example, a compressed bitmap (*.bmp*) may need only 25% or less of its uncompressed space, while compressing a binary executable program file (*.exe*) rarely results in a significant gain in space. You should not try to compress files that are already compressed, such as WinZip (*.zip*) files. This simply results in wasted processing power.

Data that is frequently modified, such as users' work files in their home folders, generally should not be compressed due to the overhead of the compression process. In addition, if you are using disk quotas to manage how much disk space is allocated to users, these disk quotas are calculated on the basis of the uncompressed size of users' files. So it really doesn't make sense to compress frequently accessed files. Instead, compress data that is relatively static in nature—for example, archived financial records stored on disk. This is really the only practical use for compression on NTFS volumes.

Encryption

NTFS permissions provide a way of securing files and folders from unauthorized local access. For example, if two users share a computer, assigning full control for each user to their own files prevents the users from accessing each other's files. However, administrators have the right to take ownership of any files on the system, but normally, users with Administrative privileges are considered trustworthy. A problem could occur if someone illicitly gained access to a user's computer and removed the hard drive from the system. The person could then install the NTFS drive in her own computer, log on as the local Administrator for that computer, and take ownership of any files on the stolen drive. Therefore, NTFS permissions themselves can't protect data from the theft of the hard drive itself. Additionally, third-party utilities have been developed that allow users to boot their computer from a floppy disk and access NTFS partitions directly. These utilities, though of some administrative use in troubleshooting situations, nevertheless pose a security risk for sensitive data stored on physically accessible systems.

To prevent such scenarios from occurring, WS2003 includes a feature called the Encrypting File System (EFS), which allows encryption of files and folders on NTFS volumes to protect them from unauthorized local access. When these files are accessed by their associated application, the operating system decrypts them automatically so they can be opened for reading or modification. When the modified files are saved or closed, they are automatically encrypted again. The whole process is transparent to the user. Both files and folders can be encrypted or unencrypted. If a folder is encrypted, the files within it don't need to be encrypted, or some may be and others not.

When a user encrypts his datafiles, only he can decrypt these files, and no other user can read them. To share an encrypted file's contents with another user in order to collaborate on work, the user must first decrypt the file so the other user can use it. Members of the Administrators group, however, have the right to decrypt any encrypted files.

 Never encrypt files in the system directory where the WS2003 boot files are located. Since the key for decrypting these files can't be accessed until the operating system has booted and a user has logged on, WS2003 will not be able to start. Of course, WS2003 safeguards against this by preventing you from encrypting files that have the System attribute set. But if you have removed the System attribute from these files using the `attrib` command (perhaps while troubleshooting startup problems) and failed to reset this attribute on the files afterward, the possibility of encrypting them exists.

How EFS Works

EFS is integrated into NTFS and uses private-key cryptography to ensure that data encrypted by users can be accessed only by that user (or by an administrator). For each file that a user encrypts, an associated private key called the file-encryption key is created, which can be used later to decrypt the file. This file-encryption key is itself encrypted in the form of an encryption certificate or EFS certificate, which is encrypted using both the user's public key and the public key of an authorized recovery agent (so the file can be decrypted after disaster recovery has been performed). The administrator by default is an authorized recovery agent.

To decrypt an encrypted file, the file-encryption key for the file must first itself be decrypted. This can be done using either:

- The private key corresponding to the public key that belongs to the user who encrypted the file (in other words, by the user herself)
- The private key of an authorized recovery agent (Administrator)

Once the file-encryption key for the encrypted file has been decrypted, the encrypted file itself can be decrypted.

Strategies for Using Encryption

Encryption is particularly useful for users with portable computers. Should your laptop be stolen while traveling, encryption provides a way of keeping your data safe from prying eyes. Otherwise, the decision to employ encryption on file servers throughout your enterprise should be weighed carefully. Since encryption results in additional overhead on file servers, a better solution might be to secure these servers physically in locked rooms.

On a system where you decide that encryption should be implemented, the following folders could be encrypted:

- *My Documents* and any other folders where the user regularly stores work
- *Temp* folders (such as *Winnt\Temp*), so that any temporary files that are created but not deleted by applications are encrypted

You generally should encrypt folders instead of files, since some applications create temporary files in odd locations that may not be encrypted.

Recovery Policy

By default, when an administrator logs on to the domain for the first time, a recovery policy is created to enable the administrator to perform the recovery of encrypted data during disaster recovery. Otherwise, encrypted data restored from backup media would not be decryptable if the users' private keys and the encryption certificates associated with the files happened to be lost when the disaster occurred. The recovery policy creates a special encryption certificate and private key that the recovery agent can use to decrypt files that were created and encrypted by domain users. As preparation for disaster recovery, the recovery agent should use the Export command in the Certificates console to make a copy of the recovery certificate and private key on a floppy disk and keep this in a safe location. After restoring the crashed system, this certificate and key can then be imported into the personal certificate store of the recovery agent, enabling the agent to decrypt the restored files.

Files and Folders—Tools

Files and folders can be accessed in numerous ways. For example, to access the file *compmgnt.msc* which opens the Computer Management Console, you can do any of the following and more:

- Start → Windows Explorer → browse the folder hierarchy in the lefthand pane until *C:\Winnt\System32* is selected → browse the righthand pane to find *compmgnt.msc*.
- Right-click on *System32* in Windows Explorer and select Search from the shortcut menu.
- Start → Search → Look in → Browse → select *System32* → All or part of the file name → **comp** → Search.
- Start → Run → **C:\Winnt\System32** → browse to find *compmgnt.msc*.
- Command prompt → **start C:\Winnt\System32** → browse to find *compmgnt.msc*.
- Computer Management → Disk Management → right-click on C: drive → select Open or Explore.
- Internet Explorer → type **C:\Winnt\System32** into the address box → press Enter .
- Make the *System32* folder a favorite if you want to access it again easily.
- Right-click on the desktop → New → Shortcut → **C:\Winnt\System32** → Next → Finish.

  This creates a shortcut on your desktop to the *System32* folder. Double-click on this shortcut to open the folder, and browse to find *compmgnt.msc*.
- Go to another computer in the forest, log on as Administrator, then do this:

  Start → Run → ***computername*\C$\Winnt\System32** and browse to find *compmgnt.msc*

  You can also enter this UNC path into Internet Explorer and get the same result.

Windows Explorer

The main tool for accessing files and folders is Windows Explorer, an all-in-one browsing tool that can be used to browse the filesystem of the local computer, shared folders and printers on the network, objects in Active Directory, and web content on the Internet. Other similar tools (My Computer and My Network Places) are simply

GUI Reference

different views of Windows Explorer. While Internet Explorer is a different tool, it cooperates seamlessly with Windows Explorer to give a unified browsing experience from the local computer to the Internet.

You can start Windows Explorer various ways:

Start → Windows Explorer

Start → Programs → Accessories → Windows Explorer

Right-click on My Computer → Explore

Right-click on My Network Places → Explore

Internet Explorer → type **C:** in Address bar → Enter → click Folders button on toolbar

Command prompt → **explorer.exe**

Windows Explorer displays resources in a familiar two-pane view called Explorer view, with the left pane showing the hierarchy of resources being browsed and the right pane displaying the contents of the folder, volume, or other container object selected in the left pane. Some of the more useful menu and toolbar options include:

Search button
This changes the left pane to the Search Assistant and searches for files or folders on local or remote computers.

History button
This changes the left pane to a *History* folder that lists files you have recently accessed.

View → Thumbnails
This new view displays a thumbnail image of files and is particularly useful for identifying images and web pages in a folder.

View → Customize This Folder
This starts a wizard to help you customize the folder by adding a background picture or folder comment or basing it on an HTML template. For example, you could modify an HTML template to customize it with your company's logo.

Favorites
This menu option is not just for web pages; it can also be used to provide fast access to local drives or folders and to shares on the network.

Tools → Folder Options
Use this to configure various options for displaying files and folders.

Tools → Synchronize
Use this to synchronize offline folders.

Command Prompt

The command interpreter *cmd.exe* can also be used to access files and folders. See cmd in Chapter 5 for details on using this tool.

Files and Folders—Tasks

Most of these operations on files and folders can be performed regardless of the underlying disk filesystem. For example, if you right-click on a folder, the same shortcut menu is displayed regardless of whether the underlying partition or volume is formatted using FAT, FAT32, or NTFS. Some tasks can be performed only on files and folders located on NTFS volumes, as indicated in the following descriptions.

Compress a File or Folder

> Right-click on file or folder → Properties → General → Advanced → Compress contents

If you compress a folder, you will be prompted to choose between the following:

Apply changes to this folder only
> Compresses the folder but doesn't compress any of the files in the folder. However, if you copy existing uncompressed files or save new files to this folder, they will be compressed automatically.

Apply changes to this folder, subfolders, and files
> Compresses the folder, all files within the folder, all subfolders within the folder, and all files within these subfolders. Use this option if you want to compress existing files within a folder.

To compress an entire drive, select the drive in Windows Explorer or Disk Management and:

> Right-click on drive → Properties → General → Compress drive

To display compressed files and folders using an alternate color, open My Computer or Windows Explorer and select:

> Tools → Folder Options → View → Display compressed files and folders with alternate color

Copy or Move a File or Folder

Copying or moving files within or between NTFS volumes can affect their NTFS permissions, compression state, or encryption state.

Effect on NTFS Permissions

A file or folder inherits the NTFS permissions of its destination folder when it is:

- Copied from one location to another within an NTFS volume
- Copied from one NTFS volume to another
- Moved from one NTFS volume to another

A file or folder retains its NTFS permissions when it is moved from one location to another within an NTFS volume.

Finally, if you save a new file in a folder, the file inherits the NTFS permissions assigned to the folder.

Effect on Compression State

The effect on the compression state is the same as the effect on NTFS permissions.

Effect on Encryption State

The rules are different here:

- An unencrypted file or folder moved or copied to an encrypted folder becomes encrypted, whether the destination folder is on the same NTFS volume or not.
- An encrypted file or folder moved or copied to an unencrypted folder remains encrypted, whether the destination folder is on the same NTFS volume or not.

Finally, if you save a new file in an encrypted folder, the file is saved as encrypted.

If you copy or move encrypted files and folders to a remote computer, your encryption certificate and private key must be available on the remote computer or you will not be able to decrypt them from the remote computer. To avoid this complicated process, decrypt files and folders prior to copying them over the network. Otherwise, you will have to export your certificate and key from the local computer as a *.pfx* file to a floppy disk and then import it into your personal store on the remote computer. The exception to this situation is if you have a roaming user profile configured on the network. In this case your encryption certificate and private key are stored on the file server where your profile is stored, and they are available from any machine you log on to.

Effect on Other Attributes

Other file and folder attributes, such as Read-only, Hidden, and so on, aren't affected in this way but are always retained whenever files are copied or moved.

Effect of Copy/Move to FAT/FAT32 Volumes

Copying or moving a file or folder from an NTFS volume to a FAT or FAT32 volume causes the file or folder to lose its NTFS permissions, become uncompressed, and be decrypted.

Customize a Folder

Select a folder in the left pane of Windows Explorer and:

Right-click on a blank spot in the right pane → Customize This Folder

You can customize the folder's appearance, icons, and other fun stuff.

Display Attributes of a File or Folder

Right-click on file or folder → Properties → General

On NTFS volumes, additional attributes are accessed using the Advanced button. You can modify attributes of files and folders on remote computers as follows:

- If the remote file or folder is in a shared folder, open Windows Explorer or My Network Places to find the share, and open the properties sheet for the file or folder.
- If the remote file or folder is not in a shared folder, first map a network drive to the hidden share name for the root of the remote drive on which the file or folder resides. Then when the window for the mapped drive opens, open the properties sheet for the file or folder.

This works with every attribute except encryption.

Encrypt a File or Folder

To encrypt a file or folder on the local machine, open Windows Explorer and:

Right-click on file or folder → Properties → General → Advanced → Encrypt contents

If you encrypt a file, you will be prompted to choose between the following:

Encrypt the file and the parent folder
This is the recommended choice, since files that are copied to or saved in encrypted folders are automatically encrypted.

Encrypt the file only
   By selecting "Always encrypt only the file," you can make this the default choice.

If you encrypt a folder, you will be prompted to choose between the following:

Apply changes to this folder only
   Encrypts the folder but doesn't encrypt any of the files in the folder. However, if you copy existing files or save new files to this folder, they will be automatically encrypted.

Apply changes to this folder, subfolders, and files
   Encrypts the folder, all files within the folder, all subfolders within the folder, and all files within these subfolders. Use this option if you want to encrypt existing files within a folder.

To encrypt a file or folder on a remote computer, first configure the remote computer for file encryption by:

   Active Directory Users and Computers → right-click on server name → Properties → General → Trust computer for delegation

Then open Windows Explorer on the local machine and:

   Tools → Map Network Drive → select mapped drive → right-click remote file or folder → Properties → General → Advanced → Encrypt contents to secure data

Decrypt an Encrypted File or Folder

To decrypt a file or folder that was previously encrypted:

   Right-click on file or folder → Properties → General → Advanced → deselect Encrypt contents

Recover an Encrypted File or Folder

If you are a designated recovery agent (like the default Administrator account), then restore the user's lost file or folder using the Backup utility in System Tools under Accessories. Then use Windows Explorer to decrypt the file or folder using the procedure just described and return the unencrypted version to the user.

To guard against permanent data loss, a designated recovery agent should back up the default recovery keys to a floppy as follows:

   Start → Run → **mmc** → add the Certificates snap-in → My user account → open the new console → Personal → Certificates → right-click the file recovery certificate → All Tasks → Export

The wizard then exports the certificate and its associated private key to floppy as a *.pfx* file. If you want to designate additional recovery agents for the local machine, do this:

   Local Security Policy → Public Key Policies → right-click Encrypting File System → Add Data Recovery Agent

To designate additional recovery agents for a domain, use Group Policy. New to WS2003 is the fact that you can configure domains so that recovery agents aren't required—also done using Group Policy.

Modify a File Association

Each file is associated with a default application that is used to open it. Double-clicking on the file opens the file using this program. To change the program that is invoked when you open the file:

   Right-click on file → Properties → General → Change → select application

GUI Reference

Changing the file association for a file changes the association for all files of the same type! For example, if you select a text file *Test.txt* and change its associated program from Notepad to Paint, all files ending with *.txt* will now invoke Microsoft Paint when you try to open them!

Open a File or Folder

To open a file using its default application or open a folder to display its contents, either double-click on it or:

> Right-click on file or folder → Open

If you want to open a file using a different program (for example, if you want to open an *.html* file using Notepad), do this:

> Right-click on file or folder → Open With

Secure a File or Folder

You can secure a file or folder using NTFS permissions (on NTFS volumes only, of course) by:

> Right-click on file or folder → Properties → Security

See *Permissions* later in this chapter for more information.

Send a File or Folder

> Right-click on file or folder → Send To → select destination

By default, there are four choices you can Send To:

3 1/2-inch Floppy
> Copies the selected file or folder to a floppy disk.

Desktop
> Creates a shortcut to the selected file or folder and places this shortcut on the desktop so you can access the file or folder more easily.

Mail Recipient
> Attaches the selected file or folder to a new email message in Microsoft Outlook Express and prompts you for the recipient. You should configure your Internet email settings using the Internet Connection Wizard before using this.

My Documents
> Copies (doesn't move) the selected file or folder to the *My Documents* folder for the logged-on user.

There may be other Send To options available when WS2003-compliant applications are installed. You can also create a custom Send To option by editing your user profile (unless it is mandatory). To do this, first open My Computer and go to:

> Tools → Folder Options → View → Show hidden files and folders

Then browse your profile to locate the *Send To* folder. For example, if you are logged on as Administrator, open the folder *C:\Documents and Settings\Administrator\SendTo*, right-click, and create a new shortcut to the program or location you want to send files or folders to. For example, to Send To → Notepad, create a shortcut to *C:\Winnt\ notepad.exe*; to Send To → the Pub share on *Server12*, create a shortcut to *\\Server12\ pub*.

Share a File or Folder

See *Shared Folders* later in this chapter for more information.

View Properties of a File or Folder

Right-click on a file or folder → Properties

Files and Folders—Notes

Attributes

By selecting multiple files or folders in My Computer or Windows Explorer, you can perform many of the previously mentioned tasks simultaneously on the selected files or folders. When multiple files are selected and their collective properties viewed, a checked attribute checkbox with a gray interior indicates that some of the selected files have the attribute set and others have it cleared.

If you set the Hidden attribute for a file on the desktop and My Computer is configured to hide hidden files from view, the file will remain visible but ghosted until you log off and then log on again, at which time it will be hidden from view.

There is another type of attribute called System on both FAT/FAT32 and NTFS volumes. The System attribute is not accessible from the GUI and can be accessed only from the command line using the attrib command. Critical operating-system files have their Read-only, Hidden, and System attributes all set by default.

If the Hidden attribute for a file has a checked attribute checkbox with a gray interior, it means the file has both its Hidden and System attributes set.

The term *attribute* has a different meaning in the context of Active Directory.

Compression

You can't both compress and encrypt a file at the same time.

You must have NTFS write permission on a file or folder in order to compress it. In order to compress a file, you need enough free space on the disk to hold the file in both its compressed and uncompressed states.

Encryption

You can't encrypt a file that is marked Read-only or System.

If you copy or move an encrypted file within or between NTFS volumes, it remains encrypted. If you copy or move it to a FAT/FAT32 volume or a floppy disk, it is decrypted.

Encrypt only datafiles; encrypting program files adds unnecessary system overhead.

When encrypted files are copied between computers over the network, the data is sent in an unencrypted state. To encrypt data sent over a network, you must use SSL or IPSec.

Remember, to read an encrypted file, you don't have to decrypt it manually—WS2003 does that automatically for you. You need to decrypt a file only when you want to share its contents with other users.

Folders are actually not encrypted themselves, just marked as such. The marker tells the operating system that any files that are later added to the folder should be encrypted, if they aren't already.

Encrypted files can't be accessed by Macintosh clients.

Backups of encrypted files are also encrypted, provided they are on NTFS volumes.

If you have partitions in a WS2003 system that are formatted using NTFS for NT 4.0 or earlier and you attempt to encrypt files on this volume, a chkdsk operation is run and the filesystem is converted to the WS2003 version of NTFS.

Users with roaming user profiles can use the same encryption key with trusted remote systems.

See Also

assoc, attrib, cipher, *Disks*, expand, ftype, *Permissions*, *Shared Folders*, takeown

---

Forest—Concepts

A forest is the largest entity in Active Directory. A forest consists of one or more trees joined together at their root domains by trusts. Each tree consists of one or more domains arranged in hierarchical fashion and also joined by trusts. All trees and domains in a forest share a common schema, configuration, and global catalog.

When you promote your first WS2003 domain controller, you automatically create a forest with a single domain. This first domain is the root domain of your first tree and the forest root domain of your entire forest. When you create additional WS2003 domains, you can choose whether to:

- Add the new domain to an existing tree of your forest
- Make the new domain the root domain of a new tree in your forest
- Create an entirely new forest

Namespace

While a tree has a contiguous DNS namespace, the namespace within a forest doesn't have to be contiguous. The root domain of each tree in a forest must have its own unique DNS name to identify it within the forest. However, the forest itself is uniquely identified with respect to other forests by the DNS name of its forest root domain—that is, the DNS name of the first domain created in the forest. For example, let's say that the Canadian company MTIT Enterprises (whose DNS domain name is *mtit.com*) decides to start a separate, worldwide operation called MTIT Enterprises Worldwide, whose domain name will be different (e.g., *mtitworld.com*). In this case the forest root domain and the root domain of the first tree could be *mtit.com* with subsidiaries *vancouver.mtit.com* and *toronto.mtit.com*, while the root domain of the other tree would be *mtitworld.com* with subsidiaries *mexico.mtitworld.com*, *france.mtitworld.com*, and so on.

You mght implement a multiple-tree forest if your company were very large and had multiple public identities. For example, you might create a multiple-tree forest if your company has one or more distinct subsidiaries in different locations or if your company and another company have recently merged, established joint ventures, or formed high-level partnerships. If two companies, which have already implemented a multiple-tree forest, merge with each other, you can now create transitive trusts between the roots of the two forests in order to grant users in one forest access to resources in the other forest. See *Trusts* later in this chapter for more information.

Forest Functional Level

In WS2003 forests can be configured to run in one of three different functional levels:

Windows 2000 (default for new forests)
> Supports domain controillers running WS2003, W2K, and NT.

Windows Server 2003 interim
> Supports domain controllers running WS2003 and NT. This is a special domain functional level that exists only when you upgrade an NT-based network directly to WS2003.

Windows Server 2003
> Supports only domain controllers running WS2003.

By default, when you create a new forest its forest functional level is W2K, which gives it the greatest degree of interoperability with NT/2000 domain controllers. You can raise the forest functional level to Windows Server 2003 if you have no more W2K domain controllers, but you can't undo this operation afterward. When you raise the forest functional level to Windows Server 2003, the following additional features are supported to simplify the administration of your network:

- Transitive trusts can be created between two forest roots so that all domains in one forest can trust all domains in the other forest.
- Per-value replication of attributes is enabled to reduce replication traffic when groups are modified.
- Deactivated schema classes and attributes can be redefined.

In addition, the new domain rename tool *Random* can restructure forests running in the WS2003 forest functional level.

Kerberos Authentication Within a Forest

When a user in one domain wants to access resources across a forest, the Kerberos v5 authentication protocol is used. Kerberos is a shared-secret authentication protocol in which both the client requesting access and a trusted intermediary called the Key Distribution Center (KDC) both share knowledge of the user's password. (Passwords are stored in Active Directory.) Kerberos thus uses mutual authentication in which both the user and the network services providing authentication must be mutually authenticated with each other to proceed. Every WS2003 domain controller is configured to run the Kerberos Key Distribution Center service and is thus a KDC.

Kerberos is the default WS2003 authentication service. It is more complex than NTLM (also called Challenge/Response or Windows Integrated) authentication, which is the earlier authentication protocol used by NT and which WS2003 uses for authenticating downlevel (Windows NT/98/95) clients that don't have the new Directory Services Client software installed on them. NTLM stored password information in the SAM database and authenticated only the client, not the network service providing authentication.

As an example, let's say a user on a client computer in *vancouver.mtit.com* wants to access resources on a server in *mexico.mtitworld.com*, which is part of the same forest. The process by which client authentication occurs happens automatically and is completely transparent to the user. Here is how it works (I've left out a few steps for simplification).

GUI Reference

1. The client submits the user's credentials to the KDC in its local domain, *vancouver.mtit.com*, to receive a Kerberos session ticket.

2. The client presents the session ticket to the KDC in the root domain, *mtit.com*, of the local tree, which then grants the client a second session ticket for the root domain, *mtitworld.com*, in the remote tree.

3. The client presents the second session ticket to the KDC in the *mtitworld.com* domain, which then grants the client a third session ticket for the *mexico.mtitworld.com* domain in the remote tree.

4. The client finally presents the third session ticket to the KDC in the *mexico.mtitworld.com* domain, which then grants the client access to the shared resources on the server that the client wants to access.

From this scenario you can see why it's good to try to "flatten" your domains in WS2003 and use only a single domain if that is at all possible: the more domains and trees you have in your enterprise, the more network bandwidth will be consumed by Kerberos authentication traffic.

Forest—Tasks

Add a UPN Suffix

Right-click on root node → Properties → specify an alternative UPN suffix for the domain → Add

Use this to simplify logon credentials for users—for example, by changing *mjones@sales.europe.mtit.com* to *mjones@mtitworld.com*.

Raise Forest Functional Level

Before you take this step, all your domain controllers must be running WS2003, and all your domains must have a domain functional level of either Windows 2000 native or Windows Server 2003. Also, you must be a member of the Enterprise Admins group to perform this step:

Active Directory Domains and Trusts → right-click root node → Raise Forest Functional Level

See Also

Active Directory, adprep, *Domain*, *Trusts*

Groups—Concepts

Groups allow user accounts to be logically grouped together for administrative purposes. For example, instead of granting Read access on a shared folder to three separate user accounts, create a group that contains these accounts and assign Read permission to the group. It may be more initial work to do things this way, but if you later want to change the users' access to Full Control, you can do it in one step by granting this permission to the group instead of granting it for each user individually. Also, if other users need these same permissions in the future, you just make them members of the group since members of a group receive whatever permissions have been assigned to the group (a user can belong to more than one group at a time).

The general strategy that Microsoft recommends for managing resource access by user accounts is called AGP: organize user Accounts into Groups to which suitable Permissions are assigned. A good way to begin is to determine which user accounts in your domain require access to the same file, printer, and other network resources. For example, users in the customer support department might need access to the FAQ share, so create a group called Support for this purpose.

However, in WS2003 it's a little more complicated than this: there are different types of groups, and these groups can have different scope. In addition, groups can contain not just user accounts but also computers and other groups. In fact, groups can be nested within groups in various ways, which can make for some rather complex administration scenarios.

We'll first consider groups in an Active Directory environment, followed by groups in a workgroup environment.

Domain Setting

In a domain environment groups are fairly complicated. There are two types of groups, three possible scopes, and complex rules for group membership and how groups may be nested.

Group Types

There are two basic types of groups in an Active Directory environment:

Security groups
> Used primarily to control the access that users have to network resources but can also be used to send email messages to users. Security groups in WS2003 correspond to the concept of groups in the earlier NT operating system.

Distribution groups
> Used only to send email messages to users—for example, as distribution lists for Microsoft's Exchange Server.

The rest of the discussion focuses solely on security groups.

Group Scopes

The scope of a group defines restrictions on the membership and use of the group. There are three different scopes that security groups can have:

Global groups
> These groups can be used to grant access to resources in any domain in the forest and are typically used to organize users who have similar needs for accessing resources. For example, you could create a Marketing global group and make all employees in the marketing department members of this group, since they all need to access the same file and print resources, web sites, applications, and so on. Global groups in WS2003 are similar to global groups in NT when used in domains whose domain functional level is W2K mixed.

Domain local groups
> These groups can be used to access resources in the local domain only. For example, if you want users in the *mtit.com* domain to be able to access the *Pub* shared folder in the same domain, you can create a domain local group called PublicUsers, make selected users or global groups members of it, and assign suitable permissions to it for accessing the resource. Domain local groups are similar to local groups in NT when used in domains whose domain functional level is W2K mixed.

Universal groups

> These groups can be used to access resources in any domain in the forest. They differ from global groups in that they are available only in WS2003 domains running in native mode, not mixed mode. Also, their membership can be drawn from any domain, whereas global group members can come only from the group's own domain. Universal groups are new to WS2003 and have no corresponding type in NT.

> WS2003 also has a fourth type of group scope called local groups. Local groups exist only in a workgroup environment and are discussed later in this section.

Group Membership

The membership that different group scopes are allowed depends on the domain functional level of the domain they are created in.

Windows 2000 Mixed

In the Windows 2000 mixed domain functional level, the rules for group membership are essentially the same as the rules in NT for backward compatibility (allowing for the fact that WS2003 trusts are transitive), specifically:

- Domain local groups can contain domain user and computer accounts from any domain in the forest and global groups from any domain in the forest.
- Global groups can contain only domain user and computer accounts from their own domains.
- Universal groups aren't available in mixed-mode domains.

Windows 2000 Native or Windows Server 2003

In the Windows 2000 native or Windows Server 2003 domain functional levels, the membership rules for different group scopes are much more complicated, as outlined in Table 4-13. As you can see, the membership restrictions for domain local and universal groups are the same. The difference is that domain local groups can be used only to access resources in the local domain while universal groups can access resources in any domain in the forest.

Table 4-13. Membership restrictions for group scopes in domains whose functional level is Windows 2000 native or Windows Server 2003

Scope	Can contain	
	From same domain	From other domains in the forest
Global	Domain users Computers Global groups	None
Domain local	Domain users Computers Global groups Universal groups	Domain users Computers Global groups Universal groups

Table 4-13. Membership restrictions for group scopes in domains whose functional level is Windows 2000 native or Windows Server 2003 (continued)

Scope	Can contain	
	From same domain	From other domains in the forest
Universal	Domain users Computers Global groups Universal groups	Domain users Computers Global groups Universal groups

Nesting of Groups

Nesting means making one group a member of another. Nesting lets you reduce the number of times permissions must be assigned in order to grant users access, but it can also make group permissions more hidden and obscure. Nesting groups in a multidomain environment can also help reduce replication traffic between domains. Rules for nesting groups also depend on the domain functional level.

Windows 2000 Mixed

The rules for nesting groups in domains running in Windows 2000 domain functional level are essentially the same as in NT—that is:

- You can nest global groups within domain local groups.
- You can't nest global groups within each other or domain local groups within each other.

In other words, groups don't really nest at all in mixed mode (or you could say they nest to one level only and, for global groups, within domain local groups only).

Windows 2000 Native or Windows Server 2003

Nesting is a much more powerful feature when domains are running in Windows 2000 native- or Windows Server 2003 domain functional level. Table 4-14 summarizes the various ways in which different group scopes can be nested in native mode domains. Note especially that:

- Global groups can now be members of global groups. This is different from how global groups worked in NT.
- Domain local groups still can't be members of other groups.

Table 4-14. Allowable nesting of groups in domains whose functional level is Windows 2000 native or Windows Server 2003

Scope	Can be nested within		
	Global	Domain local	Universal
Global	Yes (from same domain only)	Yes	Yes
Domain local	No	No	No
Universal	No	Yes	Yes

It's also important to realize that, where nesting is allowed, it can be performed to any level. In other words, you could have an Enterprise Managers global group, which contains Branch Managers global groups, which contain Division Managers global groups, which contain Department Managers global groups, and so on. This flexibility is almost too much of a good thing, and Microsoft recommends that groups be nested no more than one or two levels. Otherwise, permissions assignments may be difficult to track and troubleshoot if problems arise.

Converting Scopes

WS2003 lets you convert one type of group scope into another. This gives you greater flexibility than you had in NT. However, converting groups from one scope to another can be performed only on domains whose domain functional level is Windows 2000 native or Windows Server 2003. Otherwise, it would conflict with what you can do in NT, which is what mixed mode is designed to support. Table 4-15 shows the various kinds of scope conversions that can be performed on different groups in this scenario.

Table 4-15. Allowable scope conversions in domains whose functional level is Windows 2000 native or Windows Server 2003

Scope	Can be converted to		
	Global	Domain local	Universal
Global	No	No	Yes
Domain local	No	No	Yes
Universal	Yes	Yes	No

Using Groups

Careful planning is the key to effective use of the different WS2003 group scopes. Again, the key issue is which domain functional level is your domain running.

Windows 2000 Mixed

The mantra here is AGDLP, which means:

1. Create *Accounts* for your domain users within each domain.
2. Create *Global* groups within each domain to organize your domain users according to similar resource access needs or job description, and add your domain user accounts to your global groups as desired.
3. Create *Domain Local* groups in each domain to control access to specific sets of network resources within the domain, and assign appropriate *Permissions* for these resources to these groups.
4. Add global groups from various domains to domain local groups in each domain in order to grant access to these network resources to users everywhere in the forest.

This procedure is essentially the same as it was for NT-based networks, except that domain local groups were called local groups in NT (and thus the mantra was AGLP instead of AGDLP). Here is an example to illustrate the principles involved:

Users in the marketing department need access to the color laser printer to produce their flashy spreadsheets. Other users in other departments may also need access to the printer. To accomplish this, create a global group called Marketing, and make users in the marketing department members of this group. Create a domain local group called ColorPrinter, and assign Print permission for the shared printer to the ColorPrinter group. Add the Marketing group to the ColorPrinter group.

A tempting shortcut to this procedure is to eliminate either the global group or the domain local group from the process. Here's an example:

Create a global group called Marketing, and make users in the marketing department members of this group. Assign Print permission for the shared printer directly to the Marketing group. This strategy may be described as AGP.

Alternatively:

Create a domain local group called ColorPrinter, and assign Print permission for the shared printer to the ColorPrinter group. Make users in the marketing department members of this group. This strategy may be described as ADLP.

The problem with the second and third strategies is that they don't scale well if you later decide to add other domains to your enterprise. In the first case, if you want to allow users in a new domain access to the color printer in the local domain, you will have to explicitly assign permissions to the appropriate global group in the new domain instead of simply adding the global group to the ColorPrinter group in the local domain. This makes for somewhat more complicated administration. In the second place, if you want to grant permissions for a printer in the new domain to members of your local ColorPrinter group, you will again have to assign these permissions explicitly since domain local groups can't be members of any other groups.

Windows 2000 Native or Windows Server 2003

In native mode you can modify the AGDLP strategy somewhat since you can also use universal groups whose scope of membership and resource access span all domains in the forest. I call the mantra here AGUNP, which means:

1. Create *Accounts* for your domain users within each domain.
2. Create *Global* groups within each domain to organize your domain users according to similar resource access needs or job description, and add your domain user accounts to your global groups as desired.
3. Create *Universal* groups to organize enterprise-wide users according to similar enterprise-wide resource access needs, and add your global groups from each domain to your universal groups as desired.
4. If you have large numbers of global groups, consider *Nesting* universal groups within other universal groups to reduce the number of members in any individual universal group.
5. Assign appropriate *Permissions* for accessing network resources across the enterprise directly to your highest level of universal groups (or assign permissions to domain local groups and place universal groups within domain local groups if you want to keep it complicated).

Alternatively, you can take advantage of the fact that the performance issues relating to universal groups have been considerably improved in WS2003 as compared to W2K Server. As a result, you can often elect to use universal groups only when grouping users together for administration. The resulting mantra would then be AUNP, which means:

1. Create *Accounts* for your domain users within each domain.
2. Create *Universal* groups to organize users according to similar resource access needs, whether domain- or enterprise-wide in scope.
3. If you have large numbers of groups, consider *Nesting* groups within other groups to reduce the number of members in any individual group.

GUI Reference

4. Assign appropriate *Permissions* for accessing network resources across the enterprise directly to your highest level of universal groups (or assign permissions to domain local groups and place universal groups within domain local groups if you want to keep it complicated).

Workgroup Setting

In a workgroup environment, groups are simple: there is only one type of group with simple membership rules and no nesting.

Local Groups

Local groups allow local user accounts in a workgroup environment to be grouped together for administrative purposes. Local groups are created in the same local security database where local user accounts are created on a machine. Local groups are created within the *Groups* folder of the Local Users and Groups node under System Tools in Computer Management.

Since use of local user accounts is usually confined to standalone servers running WS2003 or client computers running XP, local groups are used only in small networks. One possible use of local groups is for several users to share a single standalone server or client computer, and you can then secure files and folders located on that machine. In this case you can create local groups to group local user accounts together in order to manage permissions more easily. Another use is to implement a WS2003 network using a workgroup model in which each machine manages its own security settings.

Group Membership

Here are the membership rules concerning local groups:

- Local groups can contain local user accounts from the computer on which the group resides and global or universal groups from any domain.
- Local groups can't be members of other groups.

One confusing difference between WS2003 and NT is in the use of the term *local groups*. On NT, local groups:

- Are used to assign permissions to resources in the domain
- Can contain user accounts and global groups from the local domain and trusted domains
- Can be created on domain controllers, member servers, and workstations

However, on WS2003, local groups:

- Are not recommended for use in domain-based networks
- Can contain local user accounts from the local machine and global or universal groups from any domain
- can't be created on domain controllers

The long and the short of it is, where you used to use local groups in NT, use domain local groups in WS2003 instead.

Built-in Groups

A number of special groups are created during the installation of WS2003. These built-in groups have predefined sets of rights that simplify the job of administering user accounts. For example, by adding a user account to the Administrators built-in group, that user gains all the rights and privileges that the special Administrator account has.

Different built-in groups are available, depending on whether you are working with member servers or domain controllers and whether you implemented your WS2003 environment as a workgroup or a domain.

Workgroup Setting

In a workgroup setting, each standalone server running WS2003 or client computer running XP has only one type of built-in group available—namely, built-in local groups. These built-in local groups can be used to simplify the job of administering the computer on which they exist. They control access to resources on the local computer on which they exist as well as granting users the rights to perform system tasks on this computer. Built-in local groups exist within the Local Security Database on standalone servers or client computers running WS2003. They are found within the *Users* folder of the Local Users and Groups node under System Tools in Computer Management. The six basic built-in local groups and their functions are as follows:

Administrators
> Members can perform any administrative task on the local computer.

Backup Operators
> Members can back up and restore the local computer.

Guests
> Members have no rights or permissions on the local computer unless they are specifically assigned.

Power Users
> Members can administer local user accounts, share folders and printers, and perform other limited administrative tasks on the local computer.

Replicator
> This special group supports file replication in a domain using DFS, and it needs no members added to it.

Users
> Members have the rights and permissions that are normally assigned to ordinary users of the local computer or other rights and permissions as they are specifically assigned.

Table 4-16 shows the initial membership of these built-in local groups on a standalone server or client computer that is part of a workgroup.

Table 4-16. Initial membership of built-in local groups

Built-in local group	Initial membership
Administrators	Administrator
Backup Operators	None
Guests	Guest
Power Users	None
Replicator	None
Users	None

Domain Setting

In a domain setting, four types of built-in groups are available:

> Built-in local groups
> Built-in domain local groups
> Built-in global groups
> Built-in system groups

The first type exists in the Local Security Database of member servers or client computers running WS2003 and is found within the *Groups* folder of the Local Users and Groups node under System Tools in Computer Management. The remaining three exist within Active Directory on domain controllers and are found in the Builtin and Users OUs of the Active Directory Users and Computers console. Let's look at each of these types separately.

Built-in Local Groups

Built-in local groups are found only on member servers or client computers in the domain; they are used to control access to resources on the local computer on which they exist and to grant users the rights to perform system tasks on this computer. Essentially, they function the same way in a domain-based network as they do in the workgroup setting described earlier. The only difference is that when a standalone server or client computer is moved from a workgroup to a domain, the membership of its built-in local groups changes from what is shown in Table 4-16 to that shown in Table 4-17. These changes give administrators, users, and guests in the domain appropriate rights and permissions to the resources on the computer.

Table 4-17. Initial membership of built-in local groups on a member server or client computer that belongs to a domain

Built-in local group	Initial membership
Administrators	Administrator, Domain Admins
Backup Operators	None
Guests	Guest, Domain Guests
Power Users	None
Replicator	None
Users	Domain Users

An example might help. When a standalone server running WS2003 and belonging to a workgroup joins a domain (and hence becomes a member server in that domain), the built-in global group Domain Admins (which is defined in Active Directory on domain controllers in the domain) becomes a member of the Administrators built-in local group on the member server. In this fashion, any users that belong to the Domain Admins global group also belong to the Administrators local group on all member servers in the domain, giving them full administrative rights and permissions on all member servers in the domain. Built-in global groups are discussed later.

An additional built-in local group called Pre–Windows 2000 Compatible Access is created when you promote a member server to a domain controller. This group lets you choose between stronger WS2003 security and weaker security that might be needed to continue running legacy applications, particularly for compatibility with NT 4.0 RAS servers. If you have problems running legacy applications after promoting a server to a domain controller, add the special group Everyone to this group and reboot your domain controllers.

Built-in Domain Local Groups

When a member server is promoted to a domain controller, the existing built-in local groups on the machine are changed to built-in domain local groups, and additional ones are created. Built-in domain local groups have predefined rights and permissions on domain controllers to simplify the task of administering domain controllers and the domain in which they reside. They are used to control access to resources on domain controllers and to grant users rights to perform system tasks on these computers. The standard built-in domain local groups on a WS2003 domain controller include:

Account Operators
> Members can create, modify, and delete user accounts and groups on domain controllers in the domain.

Administrators
> Members can perform any administrative task on domain controllers in the domain.

Backup Operators
> Members can bypass file security to back up and restore any files on any domain controllers in the domain.

Guests
> Members have no rights or permissions on domain controllers in the domain, unless they are specifically assigned.

Print Operators
> Members can administer network printers on domain controllers in the domain.

Replicator
> This special built-in domain local group is used to implement file replication in a domain and doesn't need any members added to it.

Server Operators
> Members can share folders and backup domain controllers in the domain.

Users
> Members have the rights and permissions that are normally assigned to ordinary users for domain controllers in the domain or other rights and permissions as they are specifically assigned.

If the domain functional level of a domain is changed from Windows 2000 mixed to Windows 2000 native or Windows Server 2003, the built-in domain local groups are sometimes just called security groups. Additional built-in domain local groups may also be present, depending on which optional WS2003 components are installed. The following are optional built-in domain local groups.

GUI Reference

DHCP Users
    Members have read-only access to settings on a DHCP server.

DnsAdmins
    Members can administer DNS servers.

RAS and IAS Servers
    Members are servers that can access remote access properties of users.

WINS Users
    Members have read-only access to WINS servers.

Table 4-18 shows the initial membership of the standard built-in domain local groups on a member server that has just been promoted to the role of domain controller.

Table 4-18. Initial membership of standard built-in domain local groups on a domain controller

Built-in domain local group	Initial membership
Account Operators	None
Administrators	Administrator, Domain Admins
Backup Operators	None
Guests	Guest, Domain Guests
Print Operators	None
Replicator	None
Server Operators	None
Users	Domain Users

Here's another example to make things clear. A domain controller is configured as the print server for a network printer. Sally needs to be granted the necessary rights and permissions to manage the network printer. To do this, simply add Sally's user account to the Print Operators group on any domain controller in the domain.

Built-in Global Groups

Built-in global groups on domain controllers are used to group together domain users who have similar resource access needs, making it easier to assign permissions to them for shared network resources. Built-in global groups have no predefined rights or permissions; you typically grant them rights and permissions by making them members of domain local groups on domain controllers or local groups on member servers.

The standard built-in global groups on a domain controller are:

Domain Admins
    Members are users who need full administrative rights in the domain.

Domain Computers
    Members are member servers and workstations in the domain.

Domain Controllers
    Members are domain controllers in the domain.

Domain Guests
    Members are users who require only temporary access to resources in the domain.

Domain Users
> Members are ordinary users in the domain.

Enterprise Admins
> Members can administer any domain in the forest.

Additional built-in global groups may also be present, depending on which optional WS2003 components are installed. These optional built-in global groups include:

Cert Publishers
> Members are enterprise certification and renewal agents.

DnsUpdateProxy
> Members are DNS clients that are allowed to perform dynamic updates on behalf of other clients (typically DHCP servers).

Group Policy Creator Owners
> Members can modify Group Policy for the domain.

Schema Admins
> Members can administer the Active Directory schema.

> When the forest functional level is changed from Windows 2000 to Windows Server 2003, the scope of the Enterprise Admins and Schema Admins groups becomes universal instead of global. You could call these groups built-in universal groups if you like.

Table 4-19 shows the initial membership of the standard built-in global groups.

Table 4-19. Initial membership of built-in global groups

Built-in global group	Initial membership
Domain Admins	Administrator
Domain Computers	Varies
Domain Controllers	Varies
Domain Guests	Guest
Domain Users	None
Enterprise Admins	Administrator in the forest root domain

Built-in System Groups

Built-in system groups (also called special identities) exist on all computers running WS2003—whether they belong to a workgroup or a domain. You can't modify the membership of a built-in system group. Instead, users temporarily become members of different system groups, depending on the kind of system or network activity in which they are involved. In other words, it's not who you are but what you are doing that determines whether you belong to one or more of the built-in system groups on a computer.

For example, if you log on to the local computer using its keyboard and try to access a folder on that computer, you are considered a member of the Interactive system group as far as accessing that resource is considered. If the Interactive group is explicitly denied access to the folder, no one who logs on locally to the computer will be able to access the folder (a rather extreme example).

System groups aren't displayed as groups in the Local Users and Groups console or in the Active Directory Users and Computers console, but they are displayed and can be selected when you are configuring permissions on files and folders on NTFS volumes, on printers, or on objects in Active Directory.

The following are some of the more important built-in system groups on a WS2003 computer:

Authenticated Users
> All users who have valid user accounts on the computer or domain (the same as the Everyone group, except it doesn't include anonymous users or guests)

Creator Owner
> The user who owns the particular local or network resource under consideration

Everyone
> All network users, including users with valid user accounts on the computer or domain, users from other domains (trusted or untrusted), and guest users

Interactive
> The user who is currently logged on locally at the keyboard of the local computer and is accessing a resource on this computer

Network
> All users who are currently logged on to computers on the network and are accessing a resource on the local computer

Groups—Tasks

We'll consider separately tasks for administering groups in domain and workgroup environments.

Domain Setting

Domain local groups, global groups, and universal groups are administered using the Active Directory Users and Computers console. After opening this console, expand the console tree and select the OU in which the group is located or where it will be created. Then proceed with the steps described in the following sections.

Add Members to a Group

> Right-click on group → Properties → Members → Add → select domain → select members → Add

When adding members, you can select multiple user accounts by the usual methods (e.g., Shift-click or Ctrl-click). You can also drag and drop.

Create a Group

> Right-click on OU → New → Group → specify group name → specify type and scope

Group names must be unique within the domain in which the group resides. By default, when you specify the group name, this also becomes the Pre–Windows 2000 or downlevel group name as well, though these can be different if you desire. Downlevel group names are used in a mixed-mode environment to provide compatibility with NT and earlier computers.

To create groups in a given domain, you must be a member of either the Administrators or the Account Operators built-in groups for that domain. When creating a group, any of the two group types may be combined with any of the three group scopes to give a total of six possible kinds of groups you can create. Note, however, that you can't create universal groups unless the domain functional level for your domain is Windows 2000 native or Windows Server 2003.

Delete a Group

Right-click on group → Delete

Deleting a group doesn't delete the members of the group.

Be careful before deleting a group from your enterprise. If you already have various permissions assigned to a group and you delete the group, you can't regain those permissions by simply creating another group with the same name as the old group. This is because groups are internally represented within Active Directory by unique security identifiers assigned when the groups are created. When you create a new group with the same name as the deleted group, the new group will have a different SID, and the new group's permissions will need to be assigned again from scratch.

Find a Group

If you have a large number of groups, you can use the Find function of Active Directory Users and Groups to find the group you want to work with. You can find groups in a particular domain or OU by:

Right-click on domain or OU → Find

You can also change the focus of the Find Users, Contacts, and Groups box to search the entire directory. To find all the groups of which a particular user is a member, do the following:

Right-click on user account → Properties → Member Of

Modify Properties of a Group

Right-click on group → Properties

This opens a properties sheet with the following tabs.

General

Lets you change the type and scope of the group. You can always change the type of a group from security to distribution and vice versa, but there are restrictions on which scope conversions you can perform (see Table 4-20).

Table 4-20. Allowed conversions between group scopes

Scope of group	Can be converted to		
	Domain local	Global	Universal
Domain local	No	No	Yes
Global	No	No	Yes
Universal	Yes	Yes	No

Members

Lists the user accounts that belong to the group and lets you add new members or remove existing ones.

Members Of

Lists other groups of which this group itself is a member. This can be domain local groups and universal groups from the local domain or universal groups from other domains in the current domain tree or forest.

Managed By

Lets you specify the user account or contact that is responsible for managing the selected group. If you select an existing user account or contact, the personal information for that user is automatically imported into the fields on this sheet.

Move a Group

Right-click on group → Move → select destination OU

Rename a Group

Right-click on group → Rename → specify new name

Send Mail to a Group

Right-click on group → Send mail

This opens Outlook Express as your default mail client, unless you have other software installed, such as Office 2000. Make sure you configure your mail client before using this feature, or you will be prompted to do so the first time you try to send mail to a group.

Workgroup Setting

Local groups are managed using the Local Users and Groups node under System Tools in Computer Management. This snap-in is available only on member servers running WS2003 and client computers running XP. You can also create a console containing this snap-in as follows:

Start → Run → **mmc** → Add/Remove Snap-in → Add → select Local Users and Groups → Add → select Local Computer to install the snap-in

Now proceed as follows.

Create a Local Group

Right-click on Groups container → New Group → specify group name → Add → select members → Add → Create

The New Group box stays open after you click Create, enabling you to continue creating more local groups. You can create a group without any members and then add members later if you prefer.

Add Members to a Local Group

Right-click on group → Add to Group → Add → select members → Add

Delete a Local Group

Right-click on group → Delete

Deleting a group doesn't delete the members of the group. If you have various permissions assigned to a group and you delete the group, you can't regain those permissions simply by creating a new group with the same name as the old group. This is because groups are internally represented within the local security database by a unique SID assigned when then group is created. When you create a new group with the same name as the deleted group, the new group will have a different SID, so the group's permissions must be assigned again from scratch.

Rename a Local Group

Right-click on group → Rename

Groups—Notes

Domain Setting

If you make a user a member of a group in order to grant the user permissions on network resources but the user is currently logged on to a computer in the forest, the new permissions will not take effect until the user next logs on to the network.

You can change both the type and scope of a group after it has been created, which gives administrators a lot of flexibility.

Use simple and meaningful names for your groups to help other administrators locate them in Active Directory and to minimize the amount of time you spend documenting your arrangement. For example, if the parent domain is *mtit.com*, use Support for the global group used for customer support people in your domain. Child domains, such as *ny.mtit.com* and *sf.mtit.com*, could use Support NY and Support SF for their corresponding global groups in the New York and San Francisco branch offices.

Domain local, global, and universal groups are created by default within the Users folder of the Active Directory Users and Computers console, but they can also be created in any OUt you choose or in a user-defined OU.

You must be a member of the Enterprise Admins group to modify the membership of universal groups.

Workgroup Setting

Do not create local groups on computers that belong to a domain since local groups can be used to secure resources located only on the computer on which you create them.

You can't create local groups on a WS2003 domain controller since a domain controller has no local security database.

Built-in Groups

Members of the Guests built-in group can't permanently modify the desktop settings on their WS2003 computer.

If additional services like Internet Information Services or Terminal Services are installed on a standalone server, additional built-in user accounts will be created as members of the Guests group.

You can't change the scope (domain local, global, or universal) or the type (security or distribution) of a built-in group. This provides an easy way to determine whether a given group is built-in or user-defined.

Limit membership in the Domain Admins global group for each domain. Members of this group have powerful privileges, including the ability to define domainwide security policies and the ability to take ownership of any object in the domain. A good strategy is to keep membership in this group small and to delegate limited administrative authority over different OUs in the domain to specific groups of trusted users.

Use built-in groups wherever possible to simplify the task of granting users rights and permissions to use network resources, and add users only to those groups that give the users just enough rights and permissions to access the resources they need on the network.

In addition to user accounts and other groups, you can also make computer accounts and contacts into members of groups. Active Directory provides a great deal of flexibility in how groups can be used.

See Also

Domain, net group, net localgroup, *Users*

Group Policy—Concepts

Group Policy lets you centrally define various user and computer settings for WS2003, W2K, and XP computers on your network. These settings are then periodically refreshed to ensure their effect is maintained when changes occur in the objects to which they apply. The advantages of using Group Policy on your network include the ability to:

- Centralize all policy settings for your enterprise at the domain or site level to enforce uniformity across administrative and physical locations. Group Policy is defined in Active Directory, the central repository of computer and network configuration information in WS2003.

- Manage different sets of users and computers by applying different policies to different sites, domains, and OUs in Active Directory. Administrators can also reduce their own workload by delegating management over different portions of the Active Directory hierarchy to trusted users and groups.

- Manage users' desktop environments on their client computers to make users more productive and to reduce time spent troubleshooting configuration problems. This includes the ability to lock down users' machines to prevent them from making changes to their working environment and the ability to make users' data folders be accessible from any computer on the network.

- Manage the installation, update, repair, and removal of software on users' client computers. This can be used for applications, service packs, operating-system updates, and fixes and can ensure that the same applications are available to users regardless of the computer to which they log on.

- Manage the security of computers and users in your domain by creating and managing account policies, audit policies, EFS recovery settings, and other security features.

Group Policy Objects

Group Policy settings are contained within a Group Policy Object (GPO). There are two different ways of looking at a GPO: logical and physical.

Logical Structure

There are two main types of settings within a GPO:

Computer configuration
These settings are applied to any computer affected by the GPO.

User configuration
These settings are applied to any user affected by the GPO.

For more information on the different categories of Group Policy settings available under user and computer configuration, see *Group Policy Settings* later in this section.

Physical Structure

The information specified in a GPO is actually stored in two separate, physical locations on domain controllers:

Group Policy Container
This is a container within Active Directory where the attributes and version information of GPOs are stored. The Group Policy Container is used for two purposes:

Domain controllers use it to determine whether they have the most recent version of GPOs. For example, if you update a GPO on one domain controller and other domain controllers check the Group Policy Container during Active Directory replication and discover that the version they have is an old one, they then replicate the new GPO to themselves.

Client computers use it to locate the Group Policy Template (GPT) associated with each GPO that is being applied to them.

 The Group Policy container can be displayed in the Active Directory Users and Computers console by first using View → Advanced Features to display the hidden containers in Active Directory. Then expand the System → Policies container, which contains the different Group Policy Containers associated with each GPO. Each Group Policy Container is named using the globally unique identifier (GUID) of its associated GPO. You can view this information for interest's sake, but there is nothing for you to administer here.

Group Policy Template (GPT)
This is a hierarchy of folders in the SYSVOL share, which is located on domain controllers. Each GPO has an associated GPT folder hierarchy in the SYSVOL share, which is also named using the GUID of the GPO. This GPT contains the administrative templates, security settings, scripts, software installation settings, and folder redirection settings associated with the GPO. In order to obtain these settings when a GPO is being applied, the client computer connects with the SYSVOL share on a domain controller and downloads the settings.

Group Policy Settings

There are several different categories of Group Policy settings:

Administrative templates
Folder redirection
Scripts

Security settings
Software installation
Internet Explorer maintenance

Let's examine these different categories.

Administrative Templates

These settings are used primarily to manage user environments. Administrative templates enable administrators to control the appearance and functionality of user work environments (desktops) and can be used to lock down user and computer settings to prevent desktops from being altered. This is important because ordinary users sometimes try to reconfigure their desktop settings themselves, resulting in extra support calls to the IT department and wasted time and money. Specifically, administrative template settings can be used to:

- Prevent users from accessing certain operating-system functions such as the Control Panel or customization options for Internet Explorer
- Enforce a standard desktop and Start menu across an enterprise or department
- Prepopulate users' desktops with shortcuts to shared folders and network connections they will need
- Enable users to access their personal desktop settings from any computer on the network

Of the eight groups of administrative template settings, some are under User Configuration in a GPO, some under Computer Configuration, and some under both, as Table 4-21 shows. If a conflicting administrative template setting is found in both the User and Computer Configuration in a GPO, the Computer setting usually overrides the User setting even if these settings are from different GPOs, and the one with the Computer setting was applied first.

Table 4-21. Categories of administrative template settings

Type	Description	Configuration
Control Panel	Lets you hide all or part of the Control Panel and restrict access to Add/Remove Programs, Display, Printers, and Regional Options	User
Desktop	Lets you control the appearance of the user desktop, enable or disable Active Desktop, and limit user ability to query Active Directory	User
Network	Lets you configure and manage aspects of offline files, network connections, DNS clients, and SNMP	User and Computer
Printers	Lets you control web-based printing, the automatic publishing of printers in Active Directory, and other aspects of network printing	Computer
Shared folders	Lets you allow shared folders and DFS roots to be published (new to WS2003)	User
Start menu & taskbar	Lets you control the appearance and functionality of the Start menu and taskbar	User
System	Lets you control logon and logoff functionality, set disk quotas, specify a primary DNS suffix, control how Group Policy is applied, disable registry-editing tools, disable Autoplay, configure user profiles, configure power management, enable Remote Assistance, configure the Windows Time Service, and more	User and Computer
Windows components	Lets you control the functionally of Internet Explorer, NetMeeting, Task Scheduler, Windows Installer, Windows Explorer, Terminal Services, Messenger, Windows Update, and more	User and Computer

Administrative templates are implemented as settings that modify the registry on users' machines. These settings are stored in two files, both called *Registry.pol*, which are located within two folders in the GPT of the GPO in the SYSVOL share of domain controllers in the domain. Specifically, the paths to these two files within the SYSVOL share are:

- *sysvol\<domain>\Policies\<GUID_for_GPO>\MACHINE\ Registry.pol*
- *sysvol\<domain>\Policies\<GUID_for_GPO>\USER\ Registry.pol*

When administrative template settings are applied to a client computer (when the GPO is applied), these settings are written to the client computer in two registry locations:

- User configuration templates settings modify the HKEY_CURRENT_USER (HKCU) hive.
- Computer configuration template settings modify the HKEY_LOCAL_MACHINE (HKLM) hive.

These settings are saved to two special sections of these hives:

- *\Software\Policies*
- *\Software\Microsoft\Windows\CurrentVersion\Policies*

By saving GPO administrative template settings to these special areas of the registry, the original (default) registry settings are unchanged so that when the GPO settings are removed (for example, by unlinking the GPO from the OU containing the User or computer object), the default registry settings take effect. This allows you to free up desktops that had previously been locked down by Group Policy.

 If a resultant GPO setting stored in the registry areas described previously conflicts with the default registry setting for that same operating-system function, the GPO setting wins, of course (otherwise, Group Policy could never be applied!). If a resultant GPO setting is Not Configured, the default registry setting applies for that function.

Folder Redirection

A useful feature of Group Policy in WS2003 is folder redirection, which allows *My Documents*, *Start menu*, *Desktop*, and *Application Data* folders for each user to be centrally located on a network share instead of on each user's local machine. These folders are normally part of a user's profile and are stored locally in the *C:\Documents and Settings\<username>* folder on the client computer that the user uses.

The advantages to redirecting folders include:

- It makes users' work easier to back up since datafiles are stored in a central location on a network file server.
- The data in these folders can be accessed easily by users no matter which computers they use to log on to the network.

Folder redirection is an alternative to implementing roaming users on your network and has several advantages over implementing roaming users:

- *My Documents* and other special folders are normally part of a user's roaming profile, and when a roaming user logs on to a computer, his entire roaming profile (including *My Documents* and its contents) is copied to the local computer. This is done to create a local profile on the machine and can use up a lot of disk space on client computers if users have many files in *My Documents* and if many users share a single machine. In addition, the bigger the contents of *My Documents*, the longer it takes for a roaming user to log on to the network. If users make changes to their datafiles during a session and then log off, the changes are copied to the server and slow down the logoff process as well.

- By contrast, files stored in redirected folders aren't copied to the local computer when a user logs on, with the result that logon and logoff traffic is minimized. Network traffic is generated only when a user tries to access a file in a redirected *My Documents* folder.

You can choose to redirect all four folders for each user to the same share or to separate shares, and you can redirect some of the folders and not the rest if you choose. Here are some specific reasons why you might want to redirect each folder:

Application Data
This folder contains user-specific data for applications such as Internet Explorer and should be redirected if users need to access these applications from any client computer.

Desktop
This folder contains the shortcuts and files on the user's desktop and should be redirected if you want users to have standardized desktops.

My Documents
This folder contains the work files for the user and is the default location for commands such as Open and Save in WS2003-compliant applications. You should redirect this folder if you want users to be able to access their work files from any computer on the network and to centralize user work files for backup purposes.

Start menu
This folder contains the user's Start menu shortcuts and folders and should be redirected if you want users to have a standardized Start menu. (Redirect all users to the same share and assign them NTFS Read permission so they can't alter their common Start menu.)

Scripts

These are settings that let you automate how scripts (batch files, Windows Scripting Host scripts, or even executable program files) are run on client computers. Four types of scripts can be configured to run automatically using Group Policy:

Startup scripts
These run synchronously (one after another, not concurrently) when a client computer is booted up.

Logon scripts
These run asynchronously (you can run multiple logon scripts concurrently) when users log on.

Logoff scripts
These run asynchronously when users log off.

Shutdown scripts
These run synchronously when the system is shut down normally.

Security Settings

These settings can be used to secure various aspects of WS2003 computers on your network. Security policies may be configured at the site, domain, or OU level, but most commonly at the domain level. Security settings are found in a GPO in Computer Configuration → Windows Settings → Security Settings. If you have Certificate Services installed, then User Configuration → Windows Settings → Security Settings is used also for these services.

Eleven groups of security settings are available, all of them under User Configuration, with two of them (public key policies and software restriction policies) also under Computer Configuration:

Account policies

These include password, account lockout, and Kerberos policies that control the security of the logon process. Password policies include the minimum length, age, history, and complexity of user passwords. Note that changing a password setting by using Group Policy has no effect on current user passwords until users try to change their passwords, so it's a good idea to ensure that users regularly change their passwords if you implement password policies on your network. Account lockout settings determine how long and after how many attempts users are locked out when they fail to enter their correct password. Once a lockout policy is configured, it is applied immediately for all users. Kerberos policies are used to configure aspects of Kerberos authentication for cross-domain authentication. Account policy settings (password and account lockout) apply to all users and work only for a GPO linked to a domain, not to a site or OU. You can configure account policy settings on a GPO linked to a site or OU, but these settings are ignored. Furthermore, account policy settings configured for a domain can't be blocked by GPOs linked to OUs. You can, however, link one GPO to multiple domains to enforce account policy settings across a domain tree or forest. See *Group Policy—Tasks* later in this chapter for more information about linking and blocking GPOs.

Local policies

These include audit policies, user rights, and miscellaneous security settings that affect individual computers instead of the domain.

Event log

These settings allow you to configure the size and behavior of the system, security, and application logs.

Restricted group

These settings control the membership of specified groups using security policies.

System services

These settings can be used to configure the startup and security settings of WS2003 services running on all computers in a domain or OU.

Registry

These settings allow you to configure permissions on subtrees of registry keys on all computers in a domain or OU.

Filesystem

These settings allow you to set consistent NTFS permissions on selected files or folders on all computers in a domain or OU.

GUI Reference

Wireless network (802.11) policies
> These run the Wireless Policy Wizard to create policies for wireless networks. This feature is new to WS2003.

Public key policies
> These settings allow you to configure trusted certificate authorities and encrypted data recovery agents.

Software restriction policies
> Create software restriction policies to identify which software is allowed to run on your computer. This feature is new to WS2003 and helps you protect your computer against untrusted code.

IP Security policies on Active Directory
> These settings let you configure IPSec settings on all computers in a domain or OU.

Security settings are covered in more detail under *Security Policies* later in this section.

Software Installation

Group Policy can also be used in conjunction with Active Directory and Windows Installer to enable administrators to remotely install, upgrade, maintain, and remove software applications on client computers from a central location. Windows Installer consists of two components:

Windows Installer service
> A client-side service on WS2003 computers that allows the installation and configuration of software to be fully automated. The service can install applications either from a CD-ROM or network share (distribution point) directly, or it can be done using Group Policy.

Windows Installer package
> The packaged application to be installed or upgraded. It consists of a Windows Installer file (an *.msi* file), external source files, package summary information, and a reference to the location of the distribution point where the files reside.

Windows Installer has several benefits over traditional Setup programs for installing applications:

* It automatically fixes an application when one or more of its critical files become corrupt or missing.
* It cleanly removes all files and registry settings when an application is uninstalled.
* It allows software installation, upgrade, maintenance, and removal processes to be fully automated using Group Policy.

You can deploy software in two ways using Software Installation and Maintenance:

Assigning software
> Assigning software causes the software to be installed automatically when users require it. Software can be assigned either to:
>
> *Users*
>> This option places shortcuts on the desktop and Start menu of any computer that the user logs on to. When the user double-clicks on the desktop shortcut, selects the Start menu option, or even double-clicks on a file that has the specified file association, the application automatically installs on the computer to which the user is logged on. The advantage of assigning

software is that the software is available on an as-needed basis and doesn't fill up the hard drives of client computers unnecessarily.

Computers

This option causes the software to be installed automatically when the designated computers are booted up. When users log on to their machines, the software is already deployed and available.

 If an application that is deployed with assigning software becomes damaged, it is reinstalled automatically the next time the user logs on and activates a document associated with the application (Users option) or the next time the computer boots up (Computers option).

Publishing software

This option creates information in Active Directory telling client computers that the software is available from a network distribution point. When users open Add/Remove Programs in the Control Panel, the application appears as available for installation by the user. Alternatively, if users double-click on a file with the appropriate file association for the application, the client computer automatically contacts Active Directory, finds the published application, locates the distribution point, and begins the installation process.

Other options you can configure using Software Installation and Maintenance include:

Software modifications

Also called transform files, these *.mst* files can be used to deploy multiple configurations of an application for different groups in your enterprise.

Software categories

This lets you group published applications into different categories, making it easier for users to find and install them using Add/Remove Programs in the Control Panel.

Internet Explorer Maintenance

These settings are new in WS2003 and let you manage favorites, security zones, content rating, authenticode settings, proxy settings, and other aspects of Internet Explorer.

Using Group Policy

To implement Group Policy, you do two things:

Create a GPO

If there is an existing GPO that contains the settings you want to configure, you can modify that GPO instead of creating a new one. If you create a new GPO, then by default none of the settings in the GPO are configured.

Link the GPO

This associates the GPO with a container (site, domain, or OU) in Active Directory whose objects (users and computers) you want the GPO applied to. Once a GPO is linked to a container, the GPO settings will be applied to the users and computers in that container. Linking GPOs can be done in different ways:

- You can link one GPO to multiple containers in Active Directory.
- You can link multiple GPOs to a single container.

GUI Reference

Once you have linked a GPO to a container in Active Directory, any users and computers in that container will have the GPO's settings applied to them (see *When Group Policy Is Applied* later in this section). Simply moving a user or computer object into the container automatically applies the GPO's settings to it.

How Group Policy Is Applied

You must understand the rules that control how GPOs are applied to users and computers—otherwise, you may configure a GPO setting and never see it applied! Here are the key things to remember about how Group Policy is processed:

Order of application
> GPOs are applied in a specific order:
>
> *Local*
>> Group Policies applied to the local machine are processed first.
>
> *Site*
>> The GPO linked to the site in which the user or computer resides is applied next, if in fact there is a GPO linked to the site. (By default, sites don't have a GPO linked to them.)
>
> *Domain*
>> The GPO linked to the domain in which the user or computer resides is applied next. This may be the Default Domain Policy or some custom GPO you have created.
>
> *OU*
>> The GPO linked to the OU in which the user or computer resides is then applied, if there is a GPO linked to the OU.

Conflicting settings
> All GPO settings in all GPOs are applied in order to produce the resultant Group Policy settings for a user or computer object in Active Directory. The exception is if two or more GPOs are in the chain conflict on one or more settings. If conflicts arise, the settings from the last GPO in the conflict are applied. For example, if a GPO linked to the domain hides the Control Panel for all users in the domain, but the Vancouver OU has a GPO linked to it that displays (unhides) the Control Panel, then users logging on in Vancouver (i.e., user objects in the Vancouver OU) will see the Control Panel in their Start menu.
>
> The exception is that if a User setting and a Computer setting conflict, the Computer setting is usually the winner regardless of the order in which the GPOs are applied.

Multiple GPOs
> A site, domain, or OU may have multiple GPOs linked to it. If this is the case, these GPOs are applied in the order in which they are listed in the Group Policy Object Links list on the Group Policy tab of the properties sheet for that container.

Inheritance
> GPO settings are inherited from site to domain to OU. Child containers inherit the settings of parent containers and can have Group Policy applied to them even if no GPO is explicitly linked to them. For example, if the Canada OU contains the Vancouver OU and a GPO is linked to Canada, user and computer objects in Vancouver will have the GPO settings applied to them as well.

If a GPO is linked to an OU and a parent OU higher up in the Active Directory hierarchy, the GPO inherited from the parent will be applied first, after which the explicitly linked GPO will be applied.

Blocking

You can explicitly prevent Group Policy settings from being inherited from a parent container (OU, domain, or site) using blocking. Blocking is limited by two factors:

- If a parent container has a forced GPO linked to it, blocking on the child doesn't stop GPO inheritance from the parent.
- Otherwise, if you enable blocking on a container, it blocks all settings from all GPOs higher up in the Active Directory hierarchy.

Forcing

You can force GPO inheritance on objects in child containers, regardless of whether the inherited settings conflict with those from processed GPOs—even when blocking is configured on child containers.

Filtering

You can filter GPO settings to prevent inheritance by specific users, computers, and security groups in the container. This is done by suitably configuring Group Policy permissions on the container.

When Group Policy Is Applied

When a computer starts, Group Policy settings (if any GPOs are linked to the site, domain, or OU in which the associated computer object resides in Active Directory) are applied as follows:

- Computer settings are processed.
- Startup scripts (if any) are processed.

When a user logs on to a computer, Group Policy settings (if any GPOs are linked to the site, domain, or OU in which the associated user object resides in Active Directory) are applied as follows:

- User settings are processed.
- Logon scripts (if any) are processed.

 Logon scripts assigned in a GPO are executed before scripts specified in the user's profile.

Once a computer for which Group Policy is assigned is running (whether a user is logged on or not), the Group Policy settings on the computer are refreshed at regular intervals, as follows:

- Domain controllers refresh every five minutes. This ensures that domain-controller security settings are always fresh.
- Client computers refresh every 90 minutes, plus a random offset of up to 30 minutes. This ensures that client-computer lockdown settings are maintained.

Software-installation and folder-redirection policies are processed only during startup and logon and aren't refreshed periodically as other policies are.

Planning Group Policy

Group Policy can be used to configure and manage computer and user environments to any degree desired. A large enterprise might want to use Group Policy to manage network security, enforce desktop standards, configure offline folders, deploy software, and perform and manage other administrative functions. The site, domain, and OU structure of an organization must be structured carefully in order to optimize the use of Group Policy.

You need to be aware of certain considerations when using Group Policy at each of the site, domain, and OU levels in Active Directory:

Site level

A GPO linked to a site is applied to all computers and users that are physically located at that site but doesn't affect mobile users from that site that travel to a different site in your organization. If a site spans multiple domains, the site GPO affects all the domains in the site.

A typical use of a site GPO is to prevent software installation from occurring beyond site boundaries since sites are often connected by slow WAN links.

Do not use a site GPO if your organization has only one site and one domain. Use a domain GPO instead.

Domain level

A GPO linked to a domain is applied to all computers and users in the domain. A GPO in a parent domain doesn't affect a GPO in a child domain of the parent. A domain GPO can be configured only by a domain administrator; it can't be delegated to someone not in that group.

A typical use of a domain GPO is to specify security settings for the domain (password and account lockout policies).

You can link a GPO to more than one domain, but this is not recommended since it increases interdomain network traffic. Instead, create a separate GPO for each domain.

OU level

A GPO linked to an OU is applied to all computers and users in the OU. Group Policy settings are inherited from a parent OU by its child OUs. Administrators can reduce their workload by delegating management of OU GPOs to trusted users in the enterprise (see *Delegation* earlier in this chapter).

Some typical uses for OU GPOs include:

- Managing user rights, auditing, event log settings, and local security settings on OUs containing domain controllers and member servers

- Managing software deployment and local security settings on OUs containing workstations
- Managing desktop lockdown, folder redirection, and EFS policy on OUs containing users

Security Policies

We mentioned the security settings portion of Group Policy earlier, but this needs a bit more explanation. There are three different types of security policies:

Domain Security Policy
> This is actually a system policy (not a GPO) that can be configured on WS2003 computers that aren't domain controllers.

Domain Security Policy
> This is the Security Settings portion of the Default Domain Policy GPO, which is linked to the domain container in Active Directory Users and Computers.

Domain Controller Security Policy
> This is the Security Settings portion of the Default Domain Controller Policy GPO, which is linked to the Domain Controllers OU within a domain container in Active Directory Users and Computers.

Let's look at each of these policies in more detail.

Local Security Policy

Local Security Policy displays the security settings for the local machine. In a domain-based scenario, these settings are determined by Group Policy—don't edit these settings directly or they will be overwritten the next time Group Policy refreshes. On standalone servers in a workgroup, however, you can edit these settings to configure the following aspects of WS2003 security:

Account policies
> This includes password and account lockout policies. For example, you can specify a minimum password length or have the lockout counter reset itself after a specified number of minutes.

Local policies
> This includes audit policies, the rights assigned to different users and groups, and various other local security settings.

Public key policies
> This contains a certificate declaring that the Administrator is an EFS recovery agent.

IP Security policies
> This includes settings to configure IPSec for secure communications across a virtual private network (VPN).

Domain Security Policy and Domain Controller Security Policy

The Domain Security Policy and the Doman Controller Security Policy shortcuts in Administrative Tools open the Default Domain Security GPO for the domain in an MMC console window with the Group Policy snap-in installed. The entire GPO is not displayed, however. Only the policy subtree Computer Configuration → Windows Settings → Security Settings is displayed and available, providing a quick way to configure security settings for domains using Group Policy.

Group Policy—Tools

Together with the complexity of Group Policy comes a plethora of tools for administering it.

GUI Tools

First, let's summarize the various GUI tools included in WS2003 for managing Group Policy:

Active Directory Users and Computers
> This console can be used to create, delete, edit, and link GPOs to domains and OUs.

Active Directory Sites and Services
> This console can be used to create, delete, edit, and link GPOs to sites.

Group Policy Object Editor (GPOE)
> This MMC snap-in is used to edit the settings of existing GPOs, but you can't use it to create a new GPO. This snap-in was named Group Policy in W2K.

Local Security Policy
> This console can be used on standalone and member servers to verify the security settings on the local machine.

Domain Controller Security Policy
> This console can be used on domain controllers to verify the security settings for the domain controller.

Domain Security Policy
> This console can be used on domain controllers to verify the security settings for the domain.

Resultant Set of Policies (RSoP)
> This MMC snap-in is new to WS2003 and can be used to analyze how GPOs combine to produce effective settings on the local machine. RSoP can run in one of two modes:
>
> *Planning Mode*
>> Simulates the effect of Group Policy without actually applying it
>
> *Logging Mode*
>> Obtains the results of Group Policy that have been applied

Related Security Tools

The use of two other MMC snap-ins has a bearing on Group Policy:

Security Configuration and Analysis
> Analyzes and configures security on the local computer

Security Templates
> Defines security templates that can be applied to a GPO to define its security settings

These tools are discussed later in this chapter under *Security Templates.*

Command-Line Tools

Useful command-line tools for managing Group Policy include gpupdate, which refreshes Group Policy settings (replacing secedit used in W2K), and gpresult, which displays the RSoP settings for a target user on a specified computer. See gpupdate and gpresult in Chapter 5 for more information.

Group Policy Management Console (GPMC)

The fact that the GUI tools for managing Group Policy aren't well-integrated and have no provision for backing up, exporting, or copying GPOs can make managing Group Policy difficult in a large enterprise environment with multiple domains and sites and a large OU hierarchy. To alleviate this problem, Microsoft has released a new integrated tool for administering Group Policy called the Group Policy Management Console (GPMC). Unfortunately, this tool was developed too late to be included with the Gold Release of the WS2003 product CD, but it is downloadable from Microsoft's web site at *www.microsoft.com/downloads/* and is free, provided you comply with the licensing agreement, which requires that you have at least one WS2003 license. Note that you don't have to actually have a WS2003 machine installed; just having a license is sufficient. See the GPMC EULA for details.

Features of GPMC

The GPMC can be installed on either a WS2003 machine or on a client computer running Windows XP Professional with SP1 or later. Once installed, the GPMC replaces the Group Policy tab of the properties sheet with a domain or OU in Active Directory Users and Computers or with a site in Active Directory Sites and Services. If desired, GPMC can be uninstalled later by rerunning the downloaded *GPMC.msi* Windows Installer file to restore the original Group Policy tab for these consoles. The new GPMC console can be used to:

- Manage GPOs and GPO links for domains, sites, and OUs. The GPMC can also manage Group Policy across multiple forests even if there is no trust relationship between them.
- Model and report RSoP in HTML format.
- Back up and restore GPOs.
- Export and import GPOs.
- Copy GPOs.
- Perform script operations on GPOs (but not on actual GPO settings).
- Manage WMI filters for GPOs. WMI filters let administrators who write scripts for the Windows Management Interface dynamically determine the scope of GPOs based on attributes of the target computer. WMI is an interesting feature, but beyond the scope of this book.

The GPMC isn't used to configure actual GPO settings; this is still done using the Group Policy Object Editor (GPOE) snap-in (see *Configure a GPO* in *Group Policy— Tasks*).

GPMC Console Tree

The hierarchical structure of the GPMC console tree typically looks like this:

```
Group Policy Management
    Forest: DNS_name_of_forest
        Domains
        Sites
        Group Policy Modeling
        Group Policy Results
```

GUI Reference

The pattern repeats if there are additional forests under the root Group Policy Management node. The four nodes under Forest are described next in detail.

Domains

The Domains container displays a flat list of each domain in the forest regardless of its parent domain or tree. The container for each individual domain typically looks like this:

> Domain
> > GPO links to domain...
> > OUs...
> > Group Policy Objects
> > WMI Filters

At the minimum, the GPO link to the Default Domain Policy is displayed under the Domain node, which displays the domain using its DNS name. Each OU can also contain one or more GPO links to the OU (if there are any), while the Group Policy Objects container holds the actual GPOs created within the domain. Note that GPO links are displayed using shortcut icons to distinguish them from GPO objects.

Sites

The Sites container initially can be used to display a flat list of all sites in the forest. By default, however, the Sites container displays nothing when it is selected, since querying Active Directory across the enterprise to determine information about all sites in the forest can take some time if slow WAN links are involved. To make certain sites visible, right-click on the container and select Show Sites. Like domains, all sites are displayed as peers of one another.

Group Policy Modeling

This node provides similar functionality to RSoP running in planning mode and lets you simulate or model how Group Policy settings are applied to users and computers without actually applying the settings. Note that this node isn't present if a W2K forest is selected; the node is visible only if the selected forest has at least one WS2003 domain controller present in it—in other words, if the Active Directory schema of the forest is WS2003 level.

Group Policy Results

This node provides similar functionality to RSoP running in logging mode and lets you query target users and computers to obtain information about existing Group Policy settings. Note that while this node is present regardless of whether the schema is WS2003 or W2K, the node can display RSoP results only on target computers running either WS2003 or XP.

To see what the GPMC can actually do, see *Manage Group Policy Using GPMC in the* next section.

Group Policy—Tasks

We'll look at general tasks for managing GPOs first. I'll then describe how to configure different types of GPO settings. After that, we'll examine the RSoP tool and I'll explain how to use it. Finally, we'll look at how to use the new Group Policy Management Console (GPMC) that can be downloaded from Microsoft's web site.

Manage Group Policy

The procedures described here use different consoles in different situations:

To work with GPOs in a domain or OU
Open the Active Directory Users and Computers console → right-click on a domain or OU → Properties → Group Policy tab

To work with GPOs in a site
Open the Active Directory Sites and Services console → right-click on a site → Properties → Group Policy tab

If the context described is not clear in the procedures that follow, the console to be used is explicitly stated; otherwise, the appropriate console is assumed to be already open at the start of the procedure. You typically work with GPOs by creating and linking them to a specific container (site, domain, or OU) in Active Directory using the consoles, but you can also open GPOs directly using the Group Policy Object Editor (GPOE).

Create a GPO

To create a GPO, you must first decide which container you want it to be linked to in Active Directory. This can be either a site, domain, or OU. By default, a GPO is automatically linked to the container on which it is created. To create a new GPO, access the properties sheet for the desired container using the appropriate MMC console and:

Right-click on a container → Properties → Group Policy → New → specify a name

Once a GPO has been created, it must be configured (see *Configure a GPO* later in this section).

To see how to perform these tasks using the GPMC, see *Manage Group Policy Using the GPMC* later in this section.

Open a GPO

Open a GPO using an MMC console that has the Group Policy snap-in installed. You can do this in different ways:

- Open the Active Directory Users and Computers (or Sites and Services) console, right-click a domain or OU (or site) to which the GPO is linked, and then select:

  Properties → Group Policy → select the GPO → Edit

  This opens the GPOE console and displays the different configurable settings of your selected GPO.

- Add the Group Policy Object Editor snap-in to a new or existing MMC console, and then open the GPO in it. For example:

  Start → Run → **mmc** → OK → Console → Add/Remove Snap-in → Add → Group Policy Object Editor → Add → Browse → select a GPO

Link a GPO

When you create a new GPO, it is automatically linked to the site, domain, or OU that you selected for creating it (see *Create a GPO* earlier in this section). You can also link a selected container (Site, Domain, or OU) to a GPO as follows:

Right-click on a container → Properties → Group Policy → Add → select {Domain | OU | Sites | All} as focus → look in domain or different OU → select a GPO

The Group Policy Object Links listbox displays all the GPOs that are currently linked to your container. To unlink a GPO from a container, do the following:

> Right-click on the container → Properties → Group Policy → select a linked GPO → Delete → Remove this link from the list

Display Links for a GPO

You can view the containers your GPO is linked to in Active Directory as follows:

> Right-click on a container → Properties → Group Policy → select a GPO → Properties → Links → select domain → Find Now

Alternatively, you can find links by opening the GPO in a Group Policy console (see *Open a GPO* earlier in this section) and then:

> Right-click on the GPO's root node in the console tree → Properties → Links → select domain → Find Now

Filter a GPO

> Right-click on a container → Properties → Group Policy → Properties → Security → select {user | group | computer} you want the GPO not to apply to → clear the Read and Apply Group Policy checkboxes

Alternatively, you can filter a GPO in the Group Policy console (see *Open a GPO* earlier in this section) and then:

> Right-click on the GPO's root node in the console tree → Properties → Security → continue as before

Force a GPO

> Right-click on a container → Properties → Group Policy → select a GPO → Options → select No Override

Any settings in this GPO are now applied to the entire subtree of the Active Directory hierarchy beneath the selected container, regardless of any other GPOs linked to containers in the subtree.

Block GPO Inheritance

> Right-click on a container → Properties → Group Policy → select Block Policy Inheritance

Blocking GPO inheritance prevents settings from GPOs linked to parent containers from being inherited by the selected child container. The exception is if parent GPO settings are forced (see *Force a GPO* earlier in this section).

Delegate Control of a GPO

Administrators can give trusted users administrative control over a GPO linked to a container. These users can manage the GPO settings even if they don't have administrative privileges over the container itself. Management is limited to modifying GPO settings and not creating new GPOs linked to the container. To do this:

> Right-click on a container → Properties → Group Policy → select a GPO → Properties → Security → Add → select user account → Add → select user account → allow Read and Write permission

Or you can open the GPO in a Group Policy console and then:

> Right-click on the GPO's root node in the console tree → Properties → Security → continue as before

If a user has administrative privileges over a container, he can create and modify new GPOs linked to that container.

Disable a GPO

Right-click on the container → Properties → Group Policy → select a linked GPO → Options → select Disabled

Disabling a GPO lets you modify its settings without worrying about having these modifications applied until you are ready.

Delete a GPO

Right-click on the container → Properties → Group Policy → select a linked GPO → Delete → Remove the link and delete the Group Policy Object permanently

Deleting a GPO deletes all the links between that GPO and different containers.

Configure a GPO

To configure the settings of a GPO, first open it for editing and then configure settings by double-clicking on them. The kind of configuration you can perform on a setting depends on the type of setting involved.

 If you are going to play around with the configuration of a GPO, disable it first so that the new settings you specify aren't accidentally applied to your client computers while you are playing with them.

Configure Administrative Templates Settings

These settings usually have three states you can choose from:

Enabled
The setting is applied when Group Policy is applied.

Disabled
The setting is removed when Group Policy is applied.

Not configured
The setting is ignored when Group Policy is applied.

Of course, the actual results of configuring an administrative template setting depend on the number of different GPOs applied, the containers they are linked to, whether GPO inheritance is blocked or forced, and so on. In addition to specifying the state, many administrative template settings require further information as well, depending on the type of operating-system function being controlled.

Configure Folder Redirection Settings

Before you can configure the settings on a redirected folder, you need to redirect it as described in the following procedures. To configure a redirected folder:

User Configuration → Windows Settings → Folder Redirection → right-click on a folder to redirect → Properties → Settings

If you want a user to have exclusive rights to her redirected folder, select "Grant the user exclusive rights." If multiple users will be sharing the same redirected folder, clear this setting. If you later unlink the GPO containing the folder-redirection policies from

GUI Reference

the OU where the users reside in Active Directory, you can specify whether to leave folders in their present (redirected) location or restore them to the local user profile for each user.

Redirect All Users' Folders to the Same Share

User Configuration → Windows Settings → Folder Redirection → right-click on a folder to redirect → Properties → Target → Setting → Basic → \\<server>\<share>

For example, you could redirect the Start menu folder to \\<server>\<share> for all users and set the NTFS permission to Read for the Users group on the <share> folder. In this way, all your users will have a common, standard Start menu that they can use but not modify.

Redirect Each User's Folders to a Different Share

User Configuration → Windows Settings → Folder Redirection → right-click a folder to redirect → Properties → Target → Setting → Basic → \\<server>\<share>\ %<username>%

Using the %<username>% replaceable variable in this case causes a separate subfolder named %<username>% to be created for each user within <share>.

Redirect Folders Based on Group Membership

User Configuration → Windows Settings → Folder Redirection → right-click on a folder to redirect → Properties → Target → Setting → Advanced → Add → Security Group Membership → Browse → select a group → OK → Target Folder Location → \\ <server>\<share>\<folder>

The option "Move the contents of Application Data to the new location" should be selected on the Settings tab; otherwise, redirection will not occur!

Configure Script Settings

Use these three steps to implement a startup/shutdown/logon/logoff script using Group Policy:

1. Create the script file using Notepad or some other editor.
2. Copy the script file to the GPT for the GPO in the SYSVOL share. This is necessary because the script file must be stored in the GPT so the GPO can run it when Group Policy is applied to the client. A simple way to copy the script file to the correct GPT folder is to do the following:

   Right-click on the script file in Windows Explorer or My Computer → select Copy

   Open the GPO that will run the script (see *Open a GPO* earlier in this section) and:

   For startup/shutdown scripts
   Computer Configuration → Windows Settings → Scripts

   For logon/logoff scripts
   User Configuration → Windows Settings → Scripts

   Double-click on the appropriate policy in the details pane to open its properties sheet, and click Show Files to open a window for the script folder in the GPT. Then paste the script into the GPT window.

3. Finally, add the script to the GPO by opening the properties sheet of the scripts setting and:

> Add → Browse → select script → OK → specify parameters needed for the script to run (optional)

If a startup or logon script fails to terminate properly, it must time out before another startup script can execute. The default timeout value is 10 minutes, which means that if your startup script has a problem, users are going to be pretty frustrated. You can configure the timeout value using the following GPO setting which applies globally to all scripts:

> Computer Configuration → Administrative Templates → System → Logon → Maximum wait time for Group Policy scripts

If multiple startup scripts are configured, they execute in the order in which they are listed on the Script tab of Startup Properties.

 You can also assign a specific logon script to an individual user using the Profile tab of the properties sheet in Active Directory Users and Computers. See *Users* in this chapter for more information.

Configure Security Settings

You can configure security settings at the local, domain, or domain-controller level. The settings you configure may be overridden by Group Policy, however, depending on how Group Policy has been configured.

Configure a Local Security Policy

> Open the Local Security Policy console → expand console tree and select a policy container → double-click on a policy setting in details pane → configure setting as desired

The changes you make to a Local Security Policy are applied immediately to the local machine.

Configure a Domain Security Policy

> Start → Administrative Tools → Domain Security Policy → modify settings as desired

A better method is to create custom GPOs linked to the domain and selected OUs using Active Directory Users and Computers. You then configure the security settings in each GPO as desired by opening the GPO and:

> Computer Configuration → Windows Settings → Security Settings → modify settings as desired

Configure Software-Installation Settings

Prior to configuring your method of software deployment, you need to perform the following preparatory steps:

Create or obtain a Windows Installer package

> A Windows Installer package (an *.msi* file) must first be created or obtained for the application you want to remotely deploy on your client computers. You may obtain a package from Microsoft or a third-party vendor, or you may create your own package using a third-party packaging tool.

GUI Reference

If you need to deploy an application that doesn't come from the vendor with a Windows Installer package file (*.msi* file), you can obtain a third-party packaging tool such as WinINSTALL to create your own packages. WinINSTALL is available from OnDemand Software, Inc. at *http://www.ondemand.com*. WinINSTALL is also included in Microsoft Systems Management Server. WinINSTALL LE is included on the WS2003 CD for this purpose.

Create a software distribution point

Share a folder on a file server on your network, and assign users Read and Execute permissions on the contents of the share. Create a subfolder that has the same name as the application you want to deploy, and store the *.msi* package file and any other files required for the application in the subfolder.

Create or edit a GPO

If you want to deploy software for all user or computer objects within a container (a site, domain, or OU), you need to create a new GPO and link it to the container or edit an existing GPO that is linked to the container.

The remaining procedures assume that you have already opened the GPO for editing unless otherwise specified.

Add a New Package for Deployment

Select {Computer | User} Configuration → Software Settings → right-click on Software installation → New → Package → select package → Open

At this point you have three options:

Assigned

This causes the application to be automatically deployed the next time the user logs on (if User Configuration was chosen) or the client computer boots up (if Computer Configuration was chosen). You can further configure the package for deployment by right-clicking the package in the details pane to open its properties sheet.

Published

This causes the application to appear as available for installation in Add/Remove Programs in the Control Panel, as well as automatically installed if the user double-clicks on a file whose file association matches the application. You can further configure the package for deployment by right-clicking the package in the details pane to open its properties sheet.

Advanced published or assigned

This simply opens the properties sheet for the new package and lets you configure the deployment method (assigned or published) and other options.

After you add a new package, you can further configure the deployment method, add software modifications, or create software categories. See the relevant headings in this section for more details.

Add Software Modifications to a Package

You can add and remove software modifications only when you are preparing to deploy the package. You can't add software modifications to the application once it has been installed on the client machines. Transform files (*.mst* files) are typically supplied by the vendor that created the package:

Select {Computer | User} Configuration → Software Settings → Software installation → right-click a package → Properties → Modifications → Add → select an *.mst* file → Open

If you have multiple software modifications added, they are applied in the order displayed.

Change the Deployment Method for a Package

Select {Computer | User} Configuration → Software Settings → Software installation → right-click a package → select a new deployment method

If your package is assigned, you can change it to published. If it is published, you can either change it to assigned or leave it as published but enable or disable automatic installation by users double-clicking on the appropriate file association for the application.

Configure Default Deployment Settings for All Packages

Select {Computer | User} Configuration → Software Settings → right-click Software installation → Properties

The key options to configure on these tabs are:

General
You can change the location where your packages are assumed to be stored. The default location is on domain controllers in the relevant GPT within the SYSVOL share:

sysvol\<domain>\Policies\<GPT_GUID>\Machine\Scripts\Startup

You can configure deployment options so that new packages are automatically published or assigned by default, so that a dialog box prompts whether you want to assign or publish the packages, or so that the properties sheet for the package lets you configure its deployment options in detail.

The Basic installation, user-interface option enables automatic installation using the default, Windows Installer, package settings. Maximum allows users to manually specify the installation options instead. Most *.msi* packages support both of these options.

If you want the application to be uninstalled automatically when the GPO containing the software-installation policy no longer applies to the users and computers for which it was configured (either by unlinking the GPO from the OU or by moving users and computers to a different OU), select "Uninstall the applications when they fall out of the scope of management."

File extensions
See *Modify File-Extension Priorities* later in this section.

Categories
See *Create and Assign Software Categories* later in this section.

Configure Deployment Settings for a Package

Select {Computer | User} Configuration → Software Settings → Software installation → right-click a package → Properties

Here are the key options on the Deployment tab:

Deployment type
Lets you change how your software is deployed (either Assigned or Published). If you choose Published, you can enable or disable either or both of the two

GUI Reference

installation methods used to install published software (by document activation or by using Add/Remove Programs).

Deployment options

Lets you choose to have the application installed automatically when the GPO used to deploy software is unlinked from the OU or when the user or computer objects are moved to a different OU where the GPO doesn't apply.

Installation user-interface options

Basic installation provides automatic installation using the default Windows Installer package settings, while Maximum lets you specify installation options.

Advanced

Displays the product code for the application and advanced diagnostic information.

Create and Assign Software Categories

To create a new category for software you are publishing:

Select {Computer | User} Configuration → Software Settings → right-click on Software installation → Properties → Categories → Add → enter a category name

Once the category is created, you can assign it to a package:

Select {Computer | User} Configuration → Software Settings → Software installation → right-click on a package → Properties → Categories → select a category → Select

Modify File-Extension Priorities

If you are deploying two different versions of an application that creates files with the same file extension, you can specify which extension's priority will be used to deploy published software using document activation (i.e., double-clicking on a document). To do this:

Select {Computer | User} Configuration → Software Settings → right-click on Software installation → Properties → File extensions → use Up or Down buttons

The application at the top of the list is installed. This affects all users or computers that have the currently selected GPO applied to them.

Redeploy Software

Use this procedure to apply a fix (service pack or patch) to a deployed application. This works only if the fix comes as a Windows Installer package file (an *.msi* file). First, place the fix in the appropriate location (where the original package file was placed). To apply the fix, open the GPO that was used to deploy the application and:

Select {Computer | User} Configuration → Software Settings → Software installation → right-click on a package → All Tasks → Redeploy application → Yes

Remove Deployed Software

To remove deployed software:

Select {Computer | User} Configuration → Software Settings → Software installation → right-click on a package → All Tasks → Remove

You can either choose to have the application removed immediately (i.e., when users' client computers next reboot or users next log on), or you can leave existing deployments as they are and prevent any new deployments from occurring. Either action removes the policy for the package from the Software Installation container in the

GPO but doesn't delete the package itself from its distribution point. If you choose to leave existing deployments intact, users may be able to delete them manually using Add/Remove Programs in the Control Panel, depending on Group Policy settings for their domain or OU.

Upgrade Deployed Software

To deploy a newer version of software you have already deployed using Group Policy, add a new package for the upgraded version of the software (see *Add a New Package for Deployment* earlier in this section). Then do the following:

Select {Computer | User} Configuration → Software Settings → Software installation → right-click on the new package → Properties → Upgrades → Add → Browse → select package for previous version → OK → specify whether to uninstall previous application first or perform the upgrade over it

The previous version may have been selected automatically with the right uninstallation/upgrade option. At this point, if you select the option "Required upgrade for existing packages," then a mandatory upgrade will be performed, replacing the previous version with the new version when the client computers boot up next or the user logs on next. If you deselect this option, the upgrade is optional and users can choose whether to continue working with the previous version or upgrade to the new version.

Note that upgrading a deployed application to a new version is different from applying a service pack or a fix to the application. To apply a service pack or fix to a deployed application, see *Redeploy Software* earlier in this section.

Assign an Application

If you are deploying software on client computers using Windows Installer technologies, Windows Installer packages are published automatically in Active Directory when you add a new package to the Software installation container in a GPO. Some packages, however—particularly those you create using *.msi* files—must be published manually or assigned in Active Directory, as follows:

Right-click on the OU to which the GPO for deploying the application is linked → Properties → Group Policy → select the GPO → Edit → {User | Computer} Configuration → Software Settings → Software Installation → New → Package → specify UNC path to share on file server where *.msi* file resides → select *.msi* file → Open → select Assign

Assigning the application results in its appearance in Add/Remove Programs in the Control Panel for users or computers in the OU where the GPO is configured to deploy the application.

Use RSoP

RSoP queries can be run various ways to simulate the effect of Group Policy on a domain, OU, or site. For example, to run an RSoP query on a domain or OU:

Active Directory Users and Computers → right-click on domain or OU → All Tasks → Resultant Set of Policy (Planning)

This starts the RSoP Wizard that can be used to view simulated policy settings for a selected user and computer. You can either skip to the end of the wizard immediately to see the result of your policies or click Next to simulate slow WAN links or loopback processing, specify a site, simulate the groups to which the user and computer might belong, and specify WMI filters linked to the GPO. When the wizard completes, the results of the RSoP query are displayed in a new console.

Next, you can run an RSoP query on a user or computer:

> Active Directory Users and Computers → right-click on computer or user → All Tasks → Resultant Set of Policy (Planning) or Resultant Set of Policy (Logging)

Logging mode reviews the settings currently applied to a user or computer, while planning mode simulates the application of a Group Policy you are considering:

> Logging mode → specify computer → specify user → view results

> Planning mode → starts Resultant Set of Policy Wizard

You can also run an RSoP query on a site:

> Active Directory Sites and Services → right-click on a site → All Tasks → Resultant Set of Policy (Planning)

RSoP in planning mode lets you simulate the effect of Group Policy without actually applying it, allowing you to see what would happen if you selected the policy you are examining. You can also run RSoP in logging mode, which displays the settings that result from applying the current Group Policy to a specified user or computer. To do this, you first create a custom MMC console containing the RSoP snap-in:

> Start → Run → **mmc** → OK → Add/Remove Snap-in → Add → Resultant Set of Policy → Add

Now do the following:

> Right-click on Resultant Set of Policy node → Generate RSoP Data → Logging Mode → select {this computer | another computer (specify)} → optionally display resulting user settings only → select {this user | another user (specify)} → optionally display resulting computer settings only

Save an RSoP Query

You can save RSoP queries for later analysis:

> RSoP query → View → Archive data in console file → File → Save → specify filename

Change an RSoP Query

If you want to rerun RSoP with a different user or computer, do this:

> Right-click on RSoP query → Change Query → specify computer → specify user

View an RSoP Report in HTML

Finally, try this:

> Start → Help and Support → Support Tasks → Tools → System Information → View Advanced System Information → View Group Policy Settings Applied

You can print this!

Manage Group Policy Using the GPMC

This section provides a brief overview of Group Policy management tasks performed using Version 1.0 of the GPMC, an optional add-on for WS2003 that can be downloaded from Microsoft's web site. To open the GPMC console, do one of the following:

Administrative Tools → Active Directory Users and Computers → right-click on a domain or OU → Properties → Group Policy → Open

Administrative Tools → Active Directory Sites and Services → right-click on a site → Properties → Group Policy → Open

Administrative Tools → Group Policy Management

Start → Run → **gpmc.msc**

You can also add the Group Policy Management snap-in to a new or existing MMC console to create your own custom tool for managing Group Policy (see the "Microsoft Management Console" sections later in this chapter for more information).

 Note that the GPMC is used only for managing GPOs and GPO links and for modeling or evaluating how they are applied to domains, sites, and OUs in a forest. The GPMC is not used for editing GPO settings, which is done with the GPOE instead. For information about managing GPO settings, see the section *Configure a GPO* earlier in this section.

These tasks assume you have the GPMC console open.

Create a GPO

There are several ways to create new GPOs using the GPMC. For example, to create a GPO and link it automatically to a domain or OU, do this:

Right-click on domain or OU → Create and Link a GPO Here → specify name for new GPO

To create an unlinked GPO, do this:

Select a domain → right-click on Group Policy Objects → New → specify name for new GPO

Don't forget that the new GPO must first be linked to a domain, OU, or site before it can be used.

Open a GPO

To open a GPO in the GPOE from the GPMC, do this:

Right-click on GPO → Edit

You can also right-click on a GPO link to do this—note that GPO links have shortcut icons to distinguish them from GPOs. A dialog box appears when you click on a GPO link to remind you that actions you perform affect the GPO and all links for that GPO.

Here is a new way of displaying GPO settings in HTML format:

Select a GPO or GPO link → Settings → show settings as desired

Note that this displays only *defined* GPO settings, together with other information about the GPO itself. If the new Internet Explorer Enhanced Security Configuration component is enabled, the first time you follow this procedure, a dialog box appears prompting you to add the HTML page displayed to the Trusted Sites zone. To save the HTML file for later viewing, do this:

Right-click on a GPO or GPO link → Save Report

Link a GPO

To link an existing GPO to a domain, OU, or site, do this:

> Right-click on domain, OU, or site → Link an Existing GPO → select GPO(s) to link

You can also drag and drop a GPO onto a domain, OU, or site to link it. Once a GPO is linked, the link can be enabled or disabled anytime using this toggle:

> Right-click on GPO link → Link Enabled

Display Links for a GPO

To view which domains, OUs, or sites a GPO is linked to, do this:

> Select a GPO → Scope → specify location → Links

Modify GPO Link Order

To modify the order in which multiple GPOs linked to a domain, OU, or site are applied, do this:

> Select domain, OU, or site → Linked Group Policy Objects → move up or down

The GPO with a link order of 1 has the highest precedence for that domain, OU, or site.

Scope a GPO

To *scope* a linked GPO (specify which users and computers will receive the settings in the GPO), do this:

> Right-click on GPO → Scope → Security Filtering → Add users, groups, or computers

Enforce a GPO

To force a GPO to apply to the entire subtree of Active Directory beneath a domain, OU, or site, do this:

> Right-click on a GPO link → Enforced

To undo this, repeat. A GPO link that is enforced displays with a gray padlock on its icon. This procedure of enforcing a GPO link corresponds to the No Override option in the standard Group Policy interface that the GPMC replaces when it is installed.

Block GPO Inheritance

To prevent a domain, OU, or site from inheriting GPOs from any parent container, do this:

> Right-click on domain, OU, or site → Block Inheritance

To undo this, repeat. When this is enabled, the domain, OU, or site displays a blue exclamation point on its icon.

Delegate Group Policy

By default, the ability to create GPOs is a right of the Group Policy Creator Owners (GPCO) group, but an administrator can also delegate this right to any other user or group by adding the user or group to the GPCO group. Another way of granting this right is by:

> Select Group Policy Objects → Delegation → Add → select user or group

To delegate limited ability to manage specify aspects of GPOs, do this:

> Select a GPO → Delegation → Add → select user or group → specify permissions

Possible permissions are:

- Read
- Edit Settings
- Edit Settings, Delete, Modify Security

You can also assign custom permissions by clicking the Advanced button, which corresponds to the Security tab on the standard Group Policy interface.

To delegate the ability to manage certain aspects of GPOs and GPO links using the GPMC, do this:

> Select a domain, OU, or site → Delegation → Add → select user or group → select {This container | This container and all child containers} → select permission {Link GPOs | Perform Group Policy modeling analyses → Read Group Policy results data}

This procedure can assign only one permission at a time, but you can repeat it to assign multiple permissions to the same user or group.

Disable a GPO

You can disable all or part (user or computer configuration) of a GPO by:

> Right-click on a GPO → GPO Status → disable user, computer, or all configuration settings as desired

You can also do this by:

> Select a GPO › Details › GPO Status › disable user, computer, or all configuration settings as desired

Delete a GPO

To delete a GPO:

> Right-click on GPO → Delete

Manage Multiple Forests

By default, the GPMC displays only the forest to which the user account running the console belongs. To use this tool to manage another forest with which a two-way, cross-forest trust has already been established, do the following:

> Right-click on root node → Add Forest → specify DNS or NetBIOS name of remote forest

You can also remove a forest from the GPMC by right-clicking on the forest node and selecting Remove.

Back Up/Export a GPO

New to the GPMC is the ability to back up (or export) a GPO to a file:

> Right-click on a GPO → Backup → specify location → specify a name

To view the defined settings of a backed-up GPO, do this:

> Right-click on Group Policy Objects → Manage Backups → select a backed-up GPO → View Settings

You can also back up GPOs from the command line using the *BackupGPO.wsf* and *BackupAllGPOs.wsf* scripts installed with the GPMC.

GUI Reference

Restore a GPO

Restoring a backed-up GPO resets the GPO to the state it had before it was backed-up:

> Right-click on Group Policy Objects → Manage Backups → select a backed-up GPO → Restore

You can also do this by:

> Right-click on the GPO → Restore from Backup → follow wizard to select backup file

You can also restore GPOs from the command line using the *RestoreGPO.wsf* and *RestoreAllGPOs.wsf* scripts installed with the GPMC.

Import a GPO

You can import a GPO that was previously exported (backed up) to transfer GPO settings from a backed-up GPO to a different existing GPO. This operation can be performed within a domain, between domains, or between forests. To do this:

> Right-click on a GPO → Import → follow wizard to select backup file

You can also import GPOs from the command line using the *ImportGPO.wsf* and *ImportAllGPOs.wsf* scripts installed with the GPMC.

Copy a GPO

Copying a GPO is like backing it up or exporting it, except that the GPO is not saved as a file but instead is used to create a new (identical) GPO:

> Right-click on a GPO → Copy → right-click on the Group Policy Objects container in any domain in the forest → Paste → specify permissions {Use default permissions for the new GPO (default) | Preserve the existing permissions}

If you copy a GPO to the same container in which it resides, its resulting name will begin with "Copy of." You can also copy GPOs between forests that have two-way trusts established between them. You can also copy GPOs from the command line using the *CopyGPO.wsf* script installed with the GPMC.

Copying GPOs across domains is complicated by the fact that some information in a GPO may be specific only to the domain in which it was created. To make this work, you can create a migration table to map references to users, groups, computers, and UNC paths in the source GPO to the new values they will have in the target GPO. See the online help for the GPMC for more information.

Search for a GPO

New to the GPMC is the ability to search a forest for a GPO:

> Right-click on a forest → Search → specify search range and criteria

Perform Group Policy Modeling

Group Policy Modeling corresponds to RSoP planning mode and allows you to simulate how Group Policy will be applied to a user or computer before you actually try applying it. Group Policy Modeling uses a wizard as follows:

> Right-click on Group Policy Modeling → Group Policy Modeling Wizard → select a WS2003 domain controller → select a user or container and/or select a

computer or container → skip to end of wizard or configure advanced modeling options

The advanced options include:

- Slow WAN link simulation
- Loopback processing (replace or merge)
- Select a site
- Modify alternate Active Directory paths for user and/or computer containers
- Modify user's and computer's security group membership
- Specify WMI filters for users and computers

The result of running the wizard is a saved query in the Group Policy Modeling container. By right-clicking on this query, you can:

- Display the applied GPO settings in detail in RSoP console
- Rerun the query
- Create a new query based on the original one
- Save the results displayed in the details pane as an HTML report

Obtain Group Policy Results

Group Policy results correspond to RSoP logging mode and let you obtain the actual resultant Group Policy settings that have been applied to a user or computer (unlike Group Policy Modeling, which is only a simulation). You obtain Group Policy results using a wizard:

Right-click on Group Policy Results → Group Policy Results Wizard → select this computer or another computer → optionally display resulting user settings only → select {this user | another user (specify)} → optionally display resulting computer settings only

The results node is placed in the Group Policy Results container, and by right-clicking on it, you can:

- Display the applied GPO settings in detail in the RSoP console
- Rerun the query
- Save the results displayed in the details pane as an HTML report

Group Policy—Notes

General Notes

Design your domain and OU structure to use as few GPOs as possible. The more GPOs you use, the:

- Slower logons may become
- More network traffic is generated
- Greater the chance of conflict between settings in different GPOs, causing unpredictable results
- More difficult it is to troubleshoot problems associated with GPOs

Keep the number of GPOs that are applied to a given user account small (two or three, usually). It is generally better to merge policy settings from several GPOs into a single

GPO whenever possible to speed up the process by which GPOs are applied and refreshed.

Link each GPO you create to only a single site, domain, or OU. GPOs linked to several domains or sites can significantly slow logons, and linked GPOs generally make it difficult to troubleshoot GPO problems when they occur.

Use blocking when you have a special group of users or computers that needs unique Group Policy settings in your site, domain, or OU.

Use forcing sparingly, and then only for containers high up in the Active Directory hierarchy and for GPO settings that are critical throughout the enterprise, such as security settings.

Try not to use GPO filtering since this makes troubleshooting Group Policy problems complex. Create an additional GPO instead of filtering an existing one.

Disable the User or Computer Configuration portion of a GPO if it is not needed. This speeds up processing.

Use the default security templates included in WS2003 as a starting point for configuring security settings in domain GPOs.

Test your Group Policy settings by logging on to workstations using ordinary user accounts and see if the settings work as you expected.

Document your GPOs, where they are linked, and which settings have been configured.

Use the gpresult command-line tool in WS2003 to determine which Group Policy settings have been applied to a specific computer and to the user currently logged on to the computer. This is a useful tool for troubleshooting Group Policy problems on your network.

You can't link a GPO to any of the default containers in Active Directory (i.e., Builtin, Computers, and Users). This is because these containers aren't OUs but special containers that behave differently from OUs. This is a good reason to create your own custom OUs, even in a single-domain environment, so that you can place your users and computers in these custom OUs and apply Group Policy to them.

Only Domain Admins and Enterprise Admins can delegate administrative control over a GPO to another user.

Administrative template settings offer a feature called loopback, which ensures that the User settings of a GPO are always applied to any machines that the Computer settings of the GPO are applied to, regardless of which user logs on to the computer. (Computer settings are always applied after User settings, which means that Computer settings always take precedence when there is a conflict.) You can use this on a computer that is set up to perform a dedicated function for all users who access it. To configure loopback:

> Right-click on a container → Properties → Group Policy → Edit → Computer Configuration → Administrative Templates → System → Group Policy → double-click User Group Policy loopback processing mode → Enabled → {Merge | Replace}

Use Replace to replace the user settings that are typically applied when users log on to the computer; use Merge if you want to combine them (User settings prevail if there is a conflict).

For example, if you create a GPO to manage only User (or only Computer) setting,l you should disable it for Computer (or User) settings. To do this, open the GPO in a Group Policy console and then:

Right-click on the GPO's root node in the console tree → Properties → General → Disable {User | Computer} Configuration settings

To do this, you can also open the GPO in a Group Policy console and then:

Right-click on the GPO's root node in the console tree → Properties → General → continue as earlier

The advantage of performing this action is that your GPO is processed more quickly if the unnecessary part of it (User or Computer) is disabled.

Once you create, configure, or delete a GPO, the GPO must be replicated to the domain controllers in your domain before it takes effect for all users and computers in your enterprise. This typically takes five minutes, unless your domain is partitioned into sites connected by slow WAN links with site replication scheduled to occur at intervals you specify.

You can't configure a Scripts setting using secondary logon.

Administrators can delegate control to a trusted user over existing GPOs linked to a container. This step is not necessary, however, if the user has already delegated administrative authority over the container itself, as this automatically gives the user the privilege to create and modify GPOs as desired for the container. See *Delegation* earlier in this chapter for general information on the subject.

Only Enterprise Admins can create GPOs at the site level.

Notes on the GPMC

By default, the GPMC obtains all GPO and GPO link information from the PDC Emulator in the domain in which the tool is run, but you can also connect to any other available domain controller if required.

You can't restore a backed-up GPO to a different domain.

GPO backups can't be restored once a domain has been renamed.

For more information on the GPMC, see the white papers at *http://www.microsoft. com/windowsserver2003/gpmc/* on Microsoft's web site.

See Also

Active Directory, dcgpofix, gpresult, gpupdate

Installation—Concepts

This topic describes concepts and procedures for installing and upgrading to WS2003, installing optional Windows components, and installing third-party applications. Windows Product Activation and Windows Program Compatibility Mode are also covered.

Install Windows Server 2003

The way you deploy WS2003 depends on several factors:

Scope of deployment
> It's one thing to upgrade two or three servers from NT or W2K to WS2003 in a small company; it's another thing entirely when you have to upgrade thousands of servers across multiple locations in a large enterprise. In the first scenario, you would probably run Setup directly from the product CD, but when the number of servers exceeds about a dozen, automated installations become a more practical solution.

Hardware homogeneity
> With large numbers of servers having identical hardware configurations, disk imaging is a simple and efficient way of installing or upgrading them. If servers are from a multitude of different vendors and have customized hardware configurations, disk imaging is probably not much of a time-saver.

Staff availability
> If only a few staff members are performing the deployment, you need to consider some form of automated installation either using answer files and UDB files or using disk imaging. If the server-to-staff ratio is small, however, it may not be cost-effective to spend the time learning how to perform these types of installations. It may simply be better to install or upgrade from the CD or from a network distribution server.

Installation Methods

The standard deployment methods for installing or upgrading to WS2003 include the following:

Product CD
> Here, *Setup.exe* is run directly from the WS2003 CD to install or upgrade the system. You typically use this method when you have only a few servers to deploy in your network. You are limited mainly by the number of CDs you have and the number of staff members who are available to respond to the prompts as Setup is run.

Distribution point
> Setup can also be run over the network by copying the WS2003 installation files to a folder on a file server and sharing the folder. File servers that share the WS2003 installation files are called distribution servers, and a shared folder containing the installation files is called a distribution point. The machines to be installed or upgraded then connect to the distribution point to start Setup, either by creating a network boot disk (see *http://www.bootdisk.com*) or by mapping a drive to the share. This method can be used to simultaneously deploy dozens or even hundreds of servers. You are limited mainly by the speed of the distribution servers, the network bandwidth available, and the number of staff members available to respond to the prompts as Setup is run.

> It's not a good idea simply to insert the WS2003 CD into a machine and share it for network installation. The read-access time of a CD-ROM is much slower than that of the typical hard drive. So while it might take a bit longer than usual to perform a network installation of 10 servers from a shared folder, it will take forever to do the same from a shared CD-ROM!

Unattended installation

Using a tool called Setup Manager (*Setupmgr.exe*) that's included in *\SUPPORT\ TOOLS\DEPLOY.CAB* on your product CD, you can create answer files and UDB files for performing unattended installations either over the network or from the product CD. An answer file is a specially formatted text file that answers some or all of the prompts during installation. This allows installations and upgrades to be performed without any user interaction other than starting the Setup process. A uniqueness database file, or UDB file, is a specially formatted text file that supplements or overrides some of the information in the answer file. While the answer file provides responses to general prompts, such as which optional components to install or which domain to join, UDB files are typically used to provide system-specific information, such as the names of computers or their IP addresses if DHCP is not being used. You would typically have one answer file for a group of servers in the same department or with the same function, and each installation or upgrade of a server would require its own UDB file. Setup Manager can also be used to create a distribution point for unattended network installs and to create *Sysprep.inf* files for unattended installs using disk imaging.

Disk imaging

Disk imaging (also called disk duplication or disk cloning) is the process of making an exact bit image of a hard drive. You first create a master image of the system/boot disk of a template WS2003 system and then copy or clone this image to other systems. This can be a very efficient method for deploying a large number of new installations of WS2003, but only when the systems you are deploying have identical or very similar hardware configurations. One of the great advantages of disk imaging is that you can use it to install not just a bare-bones version of WS2003 but also a fully loaded server with numerous preinstalled applications. WS2003 includes a utility called the System Preparation Tool (*Sysprep.exe*), which can be used to prepare a system for cloning by ensuring that the cloned systems will have their own unique SIDs. *Sysprep* works by deleting the SIDS on your existing system, which generates unique SIDs on the target systems when they are restarted after the image has been cloned to them. WS2003 doesn't itself include disk-imaging software, so *Sysprep* must be used in conjunction with third-party disk-cloning software.

WinPE

The Windows Preinstallation Environment (WinPE) is a tool available to original equipment manufacturers (OEMs) that can be used to create bootable ISO images of customized WS2003 configurations for rapid, mass deployment of identical systems. If you are a large enterprise customer, you may be able to obtain WinPE from Microsoft and use it instead of disk imaging for mass deployments.

Before Installation

You need to consider some things and make some decisions prior to installing or upgrading a system to WS2003:

Read the release notes

Make sure you read *Relnotes.htm*, *Readme1st.txt*, and any other last-minute documentation on the product CD concerning installation issues.

Hardware compatibility

You must ensure that all your hardware is fully supported by WS2003. The quickest way to do this is to use the Check System Compatibility feature of Setup, which can be started from the product CD menu. You can also consult the

GUI Reference

WS2003 Hardware Compatibility List (HCL), which lists devices whose drivers have been tested for and comply with WS2003. Microsoft supports only hardware that is listed on the HCL, so be sure to comply with this list if you want to be eligible for Microsoft's technical support. The HCL can be found on Microsoft's web site at *http:www.microsoft.com/hwtest/hcl/*.

Hardware requirements

You must also meet the minimum hardware requirements for installing WS2003, though experience says you should go well beyond the recommended hardware requirements if you want satisfactory performance. Table 4-22 lists the minimum hardware requirements for different editions of WS2003, while Table 4-23 shows recommended hardware. Table 4-24 displays the maximum RAM and supported number of processors for each edition.

Table 4-22. Minimum hardware for WS2003

Requirement	Standard Edition	Enterprise Edition	Web Edition	Datacenter Edition
CPU speed	133 MHz	133 MHz	133 MHz	400 MHz
Memory	128 MB	128 MB	128 MB	512 MB
Disk space	1.5 GB	1.5 GB	1.5 GB	1.5 GB

Table 4-23. Recommended hardware for WS2003

Requirement	Standard Edition	Enterprise Edition	Web Edition	Datacenter Edition
CPU speed	550 MHz	733 MHz	550 MHz	733 MHz
Memory	256 MB	256 MB	256 MB	1 GB
Disk space	1.5 GB	1.5 GB	1.5 GB	1.5 GB

Table 4-24. Maximum RAM and support for SMP in WS2003

Requirement	Standard Edition	Enterprise Edition	Web Edition	Datacenter Edition
Max RAM	4 GB	32 GB	2 GB	64 –512 GB
Min CPUs	1	1	1	8
Max CPUs	4	8	2	32

Disk partitioning

Although a 2.5-GB partition will suffice for installing WS2003, use at least a 4-GB partition to leave room for additional WS2003 components you may want to install later. You can create and delete partitions during the text-based initial portion of Setup, but Microsoft recommends that you use Setup only to create the partition on which you plan to install WS2003 and then use the Disk Management console after the installation is complete to create and format other partitions. Besides speeding up Setup, using Disk Management gives you the option of converting your disk subsystem to dynamic storage so you can create extended and fault-tolerant volumes.

Filesystem

During the text-based portion of Setup, you can specify which filesystem formats the partition on which you install WS2003. You can choose between FAT, FAT32, and NTFS, but the logical choice is NTFS. NTFS provides additional security and manageability through NTFS file and folder permissions, EFS encryption, disk compression, and disk quotas. The only reason you might want to choose FAT or FAT32 is if you want to be able to dual-boot your system, but this is a highly unlikely choice with a production server.

Licensing mode

Decisions about how you want to license your server must be made prior to installation. The three aspects of WS2003 Licensing are:

- One server license is required to license your right to install and run WS2003 on the computer.

- Multiple client-access licenses (CALs) are required to license client computers with the right to connect to your server and access its services. (In addition to determining the number of CALs you require, you also need to decide whether you will license these CALs in a per-server or per-seat mode.)

- Additional licenses may be required if you have other Microsoft applications installed and running on your server.

Security model

You need to decide whether your server will be installed as a standalone server that is part of a workgroup or as a member server belonging to a domain. If you plan to join the computer to a domain during Setup, then you will need:

- The name of the domain you plan to join (e.g., *mtit.com*).

- A computer account to be created for your computer in the domain you plan to join. This can be done by creating the computer account ahead of time using Active Directory Users and Computers, or you can create the computer account during Setup, provided you have the credentials of an administrator in the domain (member of the Domain Admins group for the domain).

- An available domain controller and DNS server for the domain.

Dynamic Update

If your system is connected to the Internet during Setup, you can use the new Dynamic Update feature of WS2003 to automatically download the latest Setup files and device drivers during installation.

Other system preparation issues

If any existing partitions from a previous operating system have been compressed with DriveSpace or DoubleSpace, make sure you uncompress them. If you have a mirror set from a previous operating system, break the mirror prior to upgrading, then recreate the mirror set after the upgrade is complete. Finally, if you are using a UPS, disconnect it before installing WS2003 on a machine.

After Installation

After installation is complete, you can log on to your standalone server (if the server belongs to a workgroup) or member server (if the server belongs to a domain) and perform various postinstallation tasks.

Windows Product Activation

You must activate your software after installing it. Windows Product Activation (WPA) is a process that links your product key with your hardware configuration and is used by Microsoft to discourage software piracy. Activation can be performed over the Internet or using the telephone, and no personal information is collected—in fact, the hardware information itself is hashed so that Microsoft doesn't even know what hardware you are using. If you don't activate Windows in the required grace period

(30 days), you will be unable to log on to your system, so make sure you use WPA the first time you log on to your new system. Note that customers with enterprise volume licensing agreements don't have to activate their systems.

Verify Installation

You should check to see if everything went well during Setup:

- Check Event Viewer to see if there are any error or warning messages associated with the installation process. Also, configure your event log settings as desired.
- Use Services in Computer Management to check that all services set to Automatic have started successfully.
- Use Device Manager in Computer Management to ensure that your hardware devices have been detected properly and assigned appropriate resource settings.
- Verify your IP address, DNS, and WINS settings by typing **ipconfig /all** at the command prompt. Also, try connecting to a shared folder on the network to see if your network connection is working properly.

Additional Configuration

Additional configuration steps you may want to perform immediately include:

- Use Display in the Control Panel to configure your display for at least 800×600 screen resolution.
- Use Power Options in the Control Panel to configure your ACPI power scheme. Servers should generally have their hard drives configured *not* to power down during idle times.
- Use System in the Control Panel to configure your Startup and Recovery settings as desired.

Add Roles

When you first log on to your newly installed or upgraded system, the Manage Your Server Wizard runs, prompting you to add roles to your server. Supported roles include domain controller, file server, print server, application server, and so on.

Upgrade to WS2003

Upgrading W2K servers to WS2003 is basically trivial, so this section focuses mainly on upgrading NT servers.

Upgrade Versus Install

Installing means putting WS2003 on a newly formatted partition or putting it on a partition having another operating system to create a multiboot machine. Upgrading means replacing an earlier operating system with WS2003. Installing means that you have to specify all of the user- and computer-specific settings for your machine, either by answering prompts during Setup or by using answer files to perform automated installations. Upgrading means that the existing user- and computer-specific settings from the previous operating system are carried over as much as possible to WS2003. Upgrading also means that your existing applications don't need to be reinstalled and reconfigured, provided, of course, that these applications are fully compatible with WS2003.

Upgrade Paths

The supported upgrade paths for Standard and Enterprise Editions of WS2003 are shown in Table 4-25. Note also that:

- You can upgrade Standard Edition to Enterprise Edition.
- You can't upgrade any platform to Web Edition.
- If you want to upgrade to Datacenter Edition, you should contact your OEM.

Table 4-25. Supported upgrade paths to WS2003

Current platform	Upgrade to Standard Edition	Upgrade to Enterprise Edition
NT Server 3.51	Upgrade to NT 4 first	Upgrade to NT 4 first
NT Server 4.0	Yes	Yes
NT Server 4, Terminal Edition	Yes	Yes
NT Server 4, Enterprise Edition	No	Yes
W2K Server	Yes	Yes
W2K Advanced Server	No	Yes

Upgrade Process

When upgrading an NT Server–based network to WS2003, you have a choice of which servers to upgrade first:

Upgrade member servers first

> This approach provides your network with many of the advantages of WS2003, including new management tools, group policies, support for USB and Plug and Play hardware, an updated version of NTFS with support for encryption and disk quotas, new services, better printing support, and so on. Without Active Directory, however, you must maintain your old NT Server domains until you upgrade your domain controllers. Nevertheless, you may want to choose this method since it gives you many of the advantages of WS2003 while allowing you to buy time to learn the complexity of Active Directory.

Upgrade domain controllers first

> This approach immediately provides you with all of the WS2003 features described earlier, plus the power and scalability of having Active Directory on your network. The downside is that you really have to know how Active Directory works before you start implementing it since you don't want to create a directory structure only to have to tear it down and rebuild it later.

The key thing, of course, with upgrading your servers is always to make a full backup of your system before you upgrade. Apart from that, the methods and approaches for upgrading to WS2003 are identical to those for performing clean installs, as discussed previously in this chapter.

Install Optional Windows Components

After installing WS2003 and adding roles to your server, you can install optional Windows components using Add or Remove Programs in the Control Panel. The additional components you have vary a bit with the OS edition, but generally include:

> Accessories and Utilities
> Certificate Services
> Fax Services
> Indexing Service

Internet Explorer
Internet Information Services (IIS)
Management and Monitoring Tools
Message Queuing
Networking Services
Other Network File and Print Services
POP3 Service
Remote Installation Services
Remote Storage
Terminal Server
Terminal Server Licensing
UDDI Services
Update Root Certificates
Windows Media Services

Install Third-Party Applications

You can also use Add or Remove Programs to install third-party applications on your server from floppy, CD-ROM, DVD-ROM, or software distribution points on your network. It's best to make sure that your third-party applications are compatible with WS2003 before installing them. Programs that are fully compatible with WS2003 are certified as such through Microsoft's Certified for Windows (CfW) program. See Veritest's web site at *cert.veritest.com/CfWreports/server/* for a searchable database of CfW products.

Program Compatibility Mode

If you're upgrading instead of installing, you probably have legacy applications on your server that were designed for W2K, NT, or even Windows 95/98/Me. In this case, you can use a new feature of WS2003 called Program Compatibility Mode to configure these applications to run as well as possible on the new platform. What you can do is first test your applications to see if they run properly after the OS is upgraded, and if "issues" appear, try running them under one of the following compatibility modes:

Windows 95
Windows 98/Me
NT 4.0 with Service Pack 5
W2K

You can also configure the display settings to ensure compatibility as follows:

Run in 256 colors
Run in 64 × 480 screen resolution
Disable themes

The easiest way to test your programs is to run the Program Compatibility Wizard. Alternatively, you can manually try different compatibility settings to see the result. If your application still doesn't run well after this, you can visit the vendor's web site to see if there is a patch or update for the program to make it work under WS2003. You can also visit the Windows Update web site to ensure your system files and drivers are fully up to date, as driver problems may be affecting your third-party programs.

Installation—Tasks

Install from Product CD

To install or upgrade directly using the WS2003 product CD, first start the Setup program by one of these methods:

- Boot the system directly from the product CD if your CD-ROM drive supports this method.
- Start → Run → **D:\Setup.exe** to start Setup where *D:* is your CD-ROM drive.
- Type **D:\I386\Winnt.exe** at the command prompt to install or upgrade systems running MS-DOS or 16-bit Windows.
- Type **D:\I386\Winnt32**.exe at the command prompt to install or upgrade systems running 32-bit Windows.

The advantage of the last two methods is that there are a number of command-line switches that can be used to customize Setup in various ways, as shown in Tables 4-26 and 4-27.

Table 4-26. Switches for winnt.exe

Switch	Description
/a	Enables accessibility options.
/e:*command*	Specifies a command to be executed when Setup finishes its GUI portion.
/r:*folder*	Specifies an optional folder that will be installed.
/rx:*folder*	Specifies an optional folder to be copied.
/s:*sourcepath*	Specifies where the WS2003 source files are located. Here *sourcepath* can be either a mapped drive path (e.g., *drive:\path*) or a UNC path (e.g., *\\server\share\path*). By default, the current directory is used.
/t:*tempdrive*	Specifies the drive to which the temporary installation files will be copied and where WS2003 will be installed. By default, the partition with the most space is used.
/u:*answerfile*	Used for unattended installation using an answer file. (See *Unattended Install* in this section for more information.) The /s switch must also be used to specify the location of the source files.
/udf:*id {,UDBfile}*	Specifies the identifier (ID) used by Setup to specify how the uniqueness database (UDB) file will modify the answer file. If you don't specify a UDB file, you will be prompted to insert a disk that contains the *$Unique$.udb* file. Use this switch with the /u switch for unattended installations.

Table 4-27. Switches for winnt32.exe

Switch	Description
/checkupgradeonly	Checks whether your computer can be successfully upgraded (same as selecting Check System Compatibility from the product CD menu).
/copydir:*folder*	Copies the specified folder from the share point on the distribution server to the *%SystemRoot%* folder on your machine. For example, you can copy a folder called \ *ExtraDrivers* from the share point to *Winnt\ ExtraDrivers*. In an automated installation, these locally copied drivers could then be used during Setup or afterward. You can use multiple instances of this switch to copy multiple folders to your machine.
/copysource:*folder*	Same as /copydir except that when Setup is finished, the copied folder is deleted.
/cmd:*command*	Specifies a command to be executed after the second reboot of Setup (just before the final phase of Setup occurs).

GUI Reference

Table 4-27. Switches for winnt32.exe (continued)

Switch	Description
/cmdcons	Copies additional files to provide the option of loading a Recovery Console for repair and recovery actions once Setup is completed.
/debuglevel:*file*	Creates a debug log file at the specified level. Using /debug alone creates a level 2 (warning) file called *C:\Winnt\Winnt32.log*. The levels are cumulative in their collected information and can be 0 (severe errors), 1 (errors), 2 (warnings), 3 (information), or 4 (detailed information). This switch is normally used only in consultation with Microsoft support specialists.
/dudisable	Disables the running of Dynamic Update during Setup.
/duprepare:*pathname*	Prepares an installation share to use with Dynamic Update files previously downloaded from the Windows Update site.
/dushare:*pathname*	Specifies the share to which you previously downloaded and copied Dynamic Update files and on which you previously ran /duprepare.
/emsport:*port*	Enables or disables Emergency Management Services (EMS) during Setup and after Windows has been installed. Here, *port* can be com1, com2, usebiossettings, or off.
/m:*folder*	Specifies that Setup should look in an alternate location for replacement files to be used instead of the similar ones in the default location.
/makelocalsource	Specifies that the source files should be copied to your hard disk prior to beginning Setup. You can use this switch when installing from a CD so that the CD is free for other use once the files have been copied.
/noreboot	Specifies that Setup should not reboot after the file-copy phase is completed so you can execute additional commands at that point.
/s:*sourcepath*	Specifies the location of the WS2003 source files. You can specify multiple paths to simultaneously copy files from multiple share points, but if the first server specified is unavailable, then Setup fails.
/syspart:*driveletter*	Copies the Setup startup files to your hard disk and then marks the drive as active, after which you can install the hard disk in a different computer and continue Setup when you boot the computer. You must also use the /tempdrive switch.
/tempdrive: *driveletter*	Specifies the drive to which the temporary installation files will be copied and where WS2003 will be installed. By default, the partition with the most space is used.
/udf:*id* {,UDBfile}	Specifies the identifier (ID) used by Setup to specify how the uniqueness database (UDB) file will modify the answer file. If you don't specify a UDB file, you will be prompted to insert a disk that contains the *$Unique$.udb* file. Use this switch with the /unattend switch for unattended installations.
/unattend *num*: *answerfile*	Used for unattended installation using an answer file. (See *Unattended Install* later in this section for more information.) Use *num* to specify the number of seconds between when Setup finishes copying files to the machine and when it reboots to continue Setup. (*num* works only when upgrading from an earlier version of WS2003.)
	Use /unattend by itself without specifying an answer file to automatically upgrade from NT 3.51/4.0, Windows 95/98, or an earlier version of WS2003. No user intervention is required as all settings are taken from the previous operating system.

After Setup copies a minimal version of WS2003 into memory, the text mode (blue screen) portion of Setup commences. Here, you specify:

- The partition on which WS2003 will be installed (typically, C:)
- The filesystem with which the partition should be formatted (typically, NTFS)
- The directory where the operating-system files will be installed (typically, C:\ *Windows*)

You can also press F8 at the appropriate point to load device drivers for SCSI or RAID drives if these are needed.

When the text mode portion of Setup is completed, operating-system files are copied from the CD to your hard disk, after which your machine reboots and the GUI mode portion of Setup (the Setup Wizard) then commences. First, you specify the following general information:

- Regional settings for your geographical location
- Your name and organization
- The licensing mode you have chosen
- The name of your computer
- A password for the local Administrator account
- Any optional WS2003 components you may want to install
- The date and time

 Note that if you plan to promote your server to a domain control-ler, it is important that you set the correct date and time and that these settings agree for all domain controllers on your network. This is because the date and time settings are used for timestamp-ing directory-replication messages for Active Directory. If these set-tings are wrong, then replication errors may occur, potentially corrupting the directory and leading to serious problems.

Next, the Setup Wizard guides you through configuring different networking compo-nents for your machine. At this stage:

- Network adapters are detected and configured.
- Networking components are installed. In a Typical installation, the following components are installed by default:
  - Client for Microsoft Networks
  - File and Print Sharing for Microsoft Networks
  - TCP/IP protocol
- An IP address is obtained from a DHCP server if one is available on the network (or you can manually specify an IP address, subnet mask, and default gateway for your machine).
- You are prompted to join either a workgroup or a domain.

Finally, the various WS2003 networking and optional components you have specified are now installed, the configuration settings you specified are applied, temporary files created during Setup are deleted, and the computer reboots one final time to finish Setup.

Install from Network Distribution Point

To install or upgrade WS2003 over the network from a distribution server, start Setup by using your network-client software to connect to the shared folder on your distribu-tion server. This shared folder contains the WS2003 source files—that is, the contents of the \I386 folder on the WS2003 product CD. For example, if your target machine is already running NT 4.0 or Windows 95/98, you can simply browse Network Neigh-borhood to locate the shared folder on your distribution server and then double-click on the file *Winnt32.exe* to run the Setup program, or you can type **D:\I386\winnt32.exe** from the command prompt. The Setup program first copies the needed \I386 files from

GUI Reference

the distribution server to a temporary folder called *$Winnt$.~ls* on your computer. After the files are copied, the machine reboots and the text mode portion of Setup begins. From here on, you use the same steps as you would when installing from a CD.

Unattended Install

To install or upgrade using the unattended installation method, first use Setup Manager to create an answer file. You can find Setup Manager (*Setupmgr.exe*) on your product CD in \SUPPORT\TOOLS\Deploy.cab; just start it and follow the wizard to specify how your answer file should respond to prompts during Setup. There are several dozen steps to follow in the wizard, depending on the choices you make along the way. By default, the resulting answer file is called *unattend.txt*, and it is saved in the folder where *Setupmgr.exe* is located. Setup Manager also creates a batch file, *unattend.bat*, in the same directory. This batch file demonstrates the use of the /u switch with *Winnt.exe* and the /unattend switch with *Winnt32.exe* for performing automated installations. You can then customize this batch file for use in your WS2003 deployment. Finally, if you specified more than one computer name using the wizard, Setup Manager generates the necessary UDB files and saves them in the same directory. Note that Setup Manager is a powerful tool that can be used for much more than just preparing for automated installations using answer files. For more information on how to use it, double-click on *deptool.chm* in your *C:\SUPPORT\TOOLS* folder.

Then use the answer file and the installation files (either on the product CD or on a distribution server) to perform an unattended installation of WS2003. On MS-DOS or Windows for Workgroups machines, open a command prompt and type:

> winnt /u:*answerfile* /s:*sourcepath* /t:*targetdrive*

On Windows 95, 98, Me, NT, or 2000 machines, use:

> winnt32 /unattend:*answerfile* /s:*sourcepath* {/syspart:*targetdrive*}
> {/tempdrive:*targetdrive*}

 You can also use Setup Manager to create a *winnt.sif* file as your answer file. Copy the *winnt.sif* file to a floppy disk, insert the WS2003 CD, and power on the system. Immediately after the system starts to boot off the CD, you can insert the floppy and perform an unattended installation.

Disk Imaging

The following steps are involved in deploying WS2003 using disk-imaging software. However, since WS2003 doesn't include disk-imaging software, you must purchase a third-party disk-imaging product to perform the deployment. As a result, the steps may differ depending on the instructions included with the software you purchase.

1. Install the System Preparation Tool (*Sysprep.exe*) from the WS2003 Resource Kit or from the *\SUPPORT\TOOLS* folder on the WS2003 CD.

2. Install and configure WS2003 on the computer whose configuration you will use to clone a master disk image. Typically, you do this on a test computer, not a production server. Also, install any applications you want on your servers, but make sure that your disk-imaging tool supports cloning of these applications. (There can be problems cloning some applications that use security identifiers [SIDs] or some similar security mechanism to ensure the uniqueness on the network of their associated services.)

3. Run *Sysprep.exe* on your master computer. This utility prepares the hard disk on the master computer for cloning by deleting the SIDs and any other user- or computer-specific information from the machine.

4. If you want to perform unattended installations using disk imaging, you can run Setup to create a *Sysprep.inf* file, which is the equivalent of an answer file for performing automated installations using disk imaging (optional). Start the Setup Manager Wizard and proceed as follows:

   Create an answer file → Sysprep Install → WS2003 → Yes, fully automate the installation → specify answers for various prompts displayed during Setup

   The result of running the wizard is the creation of the file *Sysprep.inf*, which is used by the disk-imaging software to control the installation steps. *Sysprep.inf* is saved by default in a new directory called *\Sysprep*, which also contains the *Sysprep.exe* utility, a batch file, and other files and folders used in disk-imaging installations.

5. Now reboot your master computer and run your third-party disk-imaging software on the computer to create a master disk image. Save the disk image you create in a shared folder on a file server to prepare for network installation using disk imaging. You can also save the image on a CD if you want to be able to archive images more easily.

6. Finally, copy the image from the share point on the file server to the target computers that you want to clone the image to, and restart these computers to start the cloning process. This step may vary depending on the disk-imaging software being used. *Sysprep* is used during cloning to create new unique SIDs for each target computer the image is cloned onto. Sysprep also creates a "mini-Setup" program for the target computer, which runs the first time the target computer is booted. The mini-Setup takes only about 5 minutes instead of the 45 to 60 minutes of regular Setup, and the only prompts are for accepting the EULA, specifying the user and company, specifying the workgroup or domain, specifying regional settings and TAPI location, and specifying networking protocols and services to be used. (But if you are using a *Sysprep.inf* file, then this mini-Setup is bypassed entirely.) Once installation is complete, the *\Sysprep* folder is typically deleted from the target computers.

For more information on using *Sysprep*, double-click on the *deptool.chm* file in your *C:\SUPPORT\TOOLS* folder, or see the *Windows Server 2003 Resource Kit*.

Upgrade from NT

The Setup procedure is almost the same as for performing a fresh installation of WS2003, as described earlier in this topic.

Upgrade a Standalone Server

There are no special issues involved here.

Upgrade a Member Server

There are no special issues involved here.

Upgrade a Domain Controller

The Setup Wizard prompts you for whether you want to create:

- A new domain or a child domain of an existing domain. Choose New Domain for your first primary domain controller (PDC) since a PDC actually defines a

GUI Reference

domain. For the other PDCs, the choice you make depends on the domain model you want to create.

- A new forest or a domain tree within an existing forest. Choose New Forest for your first PDC. For the other PDCs, the choice you make depends on the domain model you want to create.

Setup prompts you for where you want to locate your *SYSVOL* directory and your Active Directory data and log file (must be an NTFS partition). Make sure you choose a partition with enough free space—when the SAM database on an NT domain controller is upgraded to Active Directory, it may occupy as much as 10 times the disk space as the original SAM database.

For backward-compatibility reasons, upgraded domain controllers are in WS2003 interim domain functional level by default. This means that:

- WS2003 member servers and XP desktop machines see the upgraded domain controller as a WS2003 domain controller.
- NT servers and workstations see it as an NT PDC.

Install Optional Windows Components

> Control Panel → Add or Remove Programs → Add/Remove Windows Components → select category → Details → select components

Categories that have grayed-out checkboxes have some but not all components already installed.

Install Third-Party Applications

> Control Panel → Add or Remove Programs → Add New Programs → {CD or Floppy | Windows Update}

Check Windows Update for the latest enhancements and fixes for your server. You can also use the new Automatic Updates feature to download and install updates automatically; see *Automatic Updates* earlier in this chapter.

Run the Program Compatibility Wizard

> Start → All Programs → Accessories → Program Compatibility Wizard → select program → select a compatibility mode for testing purposes → select display settings for testing → select user account privileges → test settings → try another mode if required → send results of test to Microsoft

Manually Configure Compatibility Settings

> Right-click on application or shortcut → Properties → Compatibility → select mode → select display settings → select user account privileges

---

Installation—Notes

If you join a workgroup during Setup, you can always join a domain later. (See *Domain* earlier in this chapter for how to join a computer to a domain.) For example, if a domain controller isn't available for some reason, install WS2003 as a standalone server that is part of a workgroup (any workgroup will do). When a domain controller becomes available, you can join the domain to become a member server in that domain.

If you create a computer account using Active Directory Users and Computers prior to installing WS2003 on your machine, you need to use the computer name you specified for this account when you are performing the installation, or it will not succeed.

In addition to the installation methods described earlier, administrators of enterprise-level networks can also perform simultaneous installations on multiple servers using push technologies such as Microsoft Systems Management Server (SMS).

If there is no DHCP server available on the network when you install Setup, an IP address is assigned to your machine using Automatic Private IP Addressing (APIPA). See *TCP/IP* later in this chapter for more information.

If after installing WS2003 you get a message saying "Failure of dependency service to start," then you may have made a mistake in specifying your networking settings (adapter and protocol). Check also that your computer name is unique to the network.

If you need to do a complete reinstall of WS2003 on a wiped machine using the same computer name as the old installation, be sure to delete and recreate the computer account, first using Active Directory Users and Computers.

Besides being used to create new answer files from scratch, Setup Manager can also be used to modify existing answer files by specifying the file and then walking through all the steps of the wizard, altering your previous selections.

You can also create and edit answer files and UDB files using Notepad or some other simple text editor, but this is not recommended, as any formatting errors may result in Setup failing to complete properly.

When using *Sysprep* to prepare a computer for cloning, you must ensure that:

- Both computers use the same type of mass storage controller (IDE or SCSI).
- The hard disk on the target computer is at least as large as that on the master computer.
- Drivers for any Plug and Play devices on the target machines are available. (These devices don't have to be the same on both machines, but it helps.)
- Both computers have the same BIOS version (recommended).

Many programs have their own installation utility—if so, use this utility instead of Add/Remove Programs to install, uninstall, or add/remove components of the program.

You must be logged on as an Administrator to install or remove optional Windows components.

When you run Add or Remove Programs during a Remote Desktop session as Administrator, it installs program files into the *%SystemRoot%* path instead of the *%homepath%* path for the logged-on user. This is done so that any user who logs on may use the installed program.

See Also

Automatic Updates, bootcfg

Logon—Concepts

WS2003 supports several kinds of logons.

Interactive logon

Logging on to the local machine from the console by pressing Ctrl+Alt+Delete and entering credentials (a logon name and password). On a standalone server in a workgroup, all console logons are interactive logons. In a domain scenario, all logons to a domain controller are network logons, but when you log on to a member server you have a choice of logging on to the:

- Local machine (interactive logon) by selecting the computer name in the Log On To box
- Logging on to the network (network logon) by selecting the domain name in the Log On To box

Network logon

Logging on to the network from the console by pressing Ctrl+Alt+Delete and entering a logon name and password. When you log on to the local machine (interactive logon), your credentials are authenticated by the SAM database on the standalone or member server. When you log on to the network, your credentials are authenticated by a domain controller, that is, by Active Directory.

Automatic logon

The process of automating the logon process by storing the user's credentials in the registry. While autologon is convenient, it can represent a security risk since anyone who can physically access the computer can gain access to information stored on it. Furthermore, when automatic logon is configured, the user's password is stored in clear text in the registry and users who can remotely connect to the machine may be able to view registry information if they have sufficient permissions.

Secondary logon

Also called Run As, this feature lets the currently logged-on user run programs using another set of credentials if he has them. For example, sysadmins typically have two sets of credentials:

- An ordinary user account (belonging to the Domain Users group) that they use for accessing their email, browsing the web, writing reports, and so on
- An administrator account (belonging to the Domain Admins group) that they use to perform administrative tasks such as installing programs, configuring services, creating shares, and so on

Using secondary logon, an administrator can run programs and perform tasks that require Administrator privileges while logged on to her desktop computer using her ordinary user account.

Logon Names

Consider a user named John Smith who has a user account with username *jsmith*. In a workgroup scenario, the logon name for John Smith is simply his username *jsmith*, and to log onto a standalone server John Smith enters *jsmith* and his password in the Log On To Windows box invoked by Ctrl+Alt+Delete. Things are somewhat different in a domain scenario when Active Directory is deployed—in this case, each user has two different logon names:

User logon name

This name is of the form *username@UPNsuffix*, where *username* is the name of the user's account and *UPNsuffix* is the DNS name of the domain in which the user's account resides. If John Smith belongs to a domain named *mtit.com*, his user logon name would be *jsmith@mtit.com*. Another name for this name is user principal name (UPN), and every user in the forest must have a unique UPN. For example, if there is another John Smith in the company but he belongs to the *sales.mtit.com* domain, then his UPN would be *jsmith@sales.mtit.com*, which is different from the UPN for the first John Smith. If a third John Smith was then hired to the same *sales.mtit.com* domain, then the administrator would have to assign him a different username such as *jsmith2* so that his UPN will be unique throughout the forest.

Downlevel logon name

This name is of the form *DOMAIN\username*, where *DOMAIN* is the downlevel domain name for the domain. For example, if the downlevel domain name for the *mtit.com* domain is *MTIT*, then the downlevel logon name for the first John Smith would be *MTIT\jsmith*. Downlevel domain names must also be unique across the forest, so in our previous example the downlevel domain name for the second John Smith would typically be *SALES\jsmith*, and for the third John Smith, it would be *SALES\jsmith2*. Downlevel domain names are supported primarily for interoperability with downlevel NT domain controllers in domains whose domain functional level is Windows 2000 mixed or Windows 2000 interim and for downlevel Windows 95/98/Me/NT clients.

While the UPN suffix is usually the DNS name of the domain where the user's account resides, it doesn't have to be—you can assign a different UPN suffix to all users in your forest if desired. See *Forest* earlier in this chapter for more information.

Logon—Tasks

Log On

To log on to Active Directory using your username, password, and domain name, do this:

Ctrl+Alt+Delete → enter your username in the User Name box → enter your password → choose your domain from the Log On To box → OK

To log on to Active Directory using your user logon name or UPN, do this:

Ctrl+Alt+Delete → enter your UPN in the User Name box → enter your password → OK

When you enter your UPN in the User Name box, the Log On To box grays out since you are already specifying your domain.

To log on to Active Directory using your downlevel logon name, do this:

Ctrl+Alt+Delete → enter *DOMAIN\username* in the User Name box → enter your password → OK

Here, *DOMAIN* is the downlevel name of your domain. Again, when you enter *DOMAIN\username* in the User Name box, the Log On To box grays out since you are already specifying your domain.

Log Off

Ctrl+Alt+Delete → Log Off

Logging off closes any foreground applications that are running on your machine but leaves the operating system and network services running. This means that other users on the network can still access resources on the machine if they are shared on the network.

Disable Display of Last Logged-On User

By default, when a user logs off from a WS2003 computer and then another user presses Ctrl+Alt+Delete on the same machine, the username of the first user is automatically displayed in the User Name box. In high-security environments, this behavior is not desirable, and you can prevent this from happening using Group Policy. On a standalone server, do this:

> Start → Run → **gpedit.msc** → OK → Computer Configuration → Windows Settings → Security Settings → Local Policies → Security Options → Interactive logon: Do not display last user name → Define this policy setting → Enabled

In a domain environment, do it this way:

> Active Directory Users and Computers → right-click on a domain or OU → Properties → Group Policy → New → specify a name → select new GPO → Edit → Configuration → Windows Settings → Security Settings → Local Policies → Security Options → Interactive logon: Do not display last user name → Define this policy setting → Enabled

Enable Verbose Logon Messages

You can cause Windows to display verbose status messages during logon, logoff, startup, and shutdown. This can sometimes be a valuable troubleshooting technique when startup, shutdown, or logon problems occur. On a standalone server, do this:

> Start → Run → **gpedit.msc** → OK → Computer Configuration → Administrative Templates → System → Verbose vs normal status messages → Enabled

In a domain environment, do it this way:

> Active Directory Users and Computers → right-click on a domain or OU → Properties → Group Policy → New → specify a name → select new GPO → Edit → Computer Configuration → Administrative Templates → System → Verbose vs normal status messages → Enabled

This enables verbose messages for all computers in the specified domain or OU.

Enable Automatic Logon

> Start → Run → **regedt32** → Enter

Find the following registry key:

> `HKLM\SOFTWARE\Microsoft\WindowsNT\CurrentVersion\Winlogon`

Open the entry named DefaultUserName and type the UPN or downlevel logon name for the user and click OK. Then open the entry named DefaultPassword and type the password for the user and click OK. If the DefaultPassword entry is not present in this registry key, create it first by Edit → new → String Value → **DefaultPassword** → Enter

Open the entry named AutoAdminLogon and type the value 1 and click OK. If the AutoAdminLogon entry is not present in this registry key, create it first by Edit → new → String Value → **AutoAdminLogon** → Enter

Close Registry Editor and reboot your computer, and the specified user should now automatically log on.

You can temporarily bypass automatic logon by holding down Shift after Windows boots.

Enable or Disable Secondary Logon

Secondary logon is enabled by default in WS2003, but you can disable it on a standalone machine by:

> Computer Management → Services and Applications → Services → Secondary Logon → Properties → General → Stop → Startup type → Manual

You can reenable secondary logon by:

> Computer Management → Services and Applications → Services → Secondary Logon → Properties → General → Startup type → Automatic → Start

Use Secondary Logon

To start a program using secondary logon, find the icon, shortcut, or executable for the program and:

> Right-click on program → Run as → The following user → specify username and password

You can also use secondary logon in a command prompt session; see runas in Chapter 5 for more information.

Change Your Password

> Ctrl+Alt+Delete → Change Password

You must know your old password before you can specify a new one.

Reset Password for a User Account

> Active Directory Users and Computers → right-click on a user → Reset Password

Specify the new password, then select "User must change password at next logon" if you want users to manage their own passwords. You may have to reset a user's password if the user has forgotten it or if the password has expired before the user has had a chance to change it.

Logon—Notes

To log on to a domain, you must have a domain user account defined in Active Directory for that domain. A local user account can be used only to log on to a local computer.

If your machine's domain is a child domain within a domain tree, you can log on to either your local domain or its parent domain within the tree by using the drop-down box. (Your credentials must be defined in the domain you want to log on to.)

If you don't specify which domain in a tree to log on to, you will be logged on to the domain you most recently logged on to.

Domain names are listed in the Log On To box using their old NT form (e.g., *SUPPORT*) instead of as domain names (e.g., *support.mtit.com*).

If there is no Options button on your Log On To Windows box, your machine belongs to a workgroup instead of a domain. You must first join your computer to a domain before you can log on to a domain (see *Domain* earlier in this chapter).

Secondary logon may not work with some programs.

If you try to run programs over the network using secondary logon, it will fail if the credentials you specify using Run As are different from those used to connect to the network share.

Secondary logon works only with password authentication; it won't work with smart card logons.

Passwords in WS2003 can be up to 128 characters long and can contain upper- and lowercase letters, numbers, and nonalphanumeric characters.

Here are some tips for using passwords in a WS2003 environment:

- Assign the Administrator account a complex password and keep it secure. If you are really paranoid (or believe that someone in your enterprise may be running password-cracking software), change the password every week or so.

- Let users control their own passwords. This frees administrators from maintaining lists of user passwords and places the onus of responsibility upon the user. It also removes the temptation for administrators to snoop in users' home folders.

- Educate users on how to select a password that is hard to crack. One suggestion is to think of an original and catchy phrase that is easy to memorize and then to form the password from the acronym generated by the phrase. For example, "I always brush my teeth two times per day" generates the password *iabmt2tpd*. Also, educate users on what makes a bad password, such as your dog's name, postal code, phone number, and so on.

- Prohibit users from changing their passwords if multiple users share the same user account. For example, do this for temporary employees using a temporary account or the Guest account for network access.

- Required passwords for services or applications should be nonexpiring.

See Also

Active Directory, *Domain*, `runas`, `shutdown`, *Users*

Microsoft Management Console—Concepts

WS2003 administration is based largely on a software framework called the Microsoft Management Console (MMC). The MMC is an application that in itself has no administrative functionality, but in which other software components called snap-ins can be installed and utilized. Each of these snap-ins provides basic administrative functionality for some component or aspect of WS2003. When one or more snap-ins are installed in the MMC, the result is called a console. WS2003 includes a number of preconfigured consoles and utilities called administrative tools. These tools can be launched by shortcuts found in the Administrative Tools program group.

Snap-ins

Table 4-28 lists the various snap-ins included with WS2003. If the table entry under "Component Required" is "None," the snap-in is present when a typical setup of WS2003 has been performed; otherwise, the associated Windows component must be installed before the snap-in becomes available in the Add/Remove Standalone Snap-in box.

Table 4-28. Snap-ins available with WS2003

Snap-in	Component required
.NET Framework 1.1 Configuration	None
Active Directory Domains and Trusts	None
Active Directory Sites and Services	None
Active Directory Users and Computers	None
ActiveX Control	None
Authorization Manager	None
Certificate Templates	None
Certificates	None
Certification Authority	None
Component Services	None
Computer Management	None
Device Manager	None
DHCP	DHCP
Disk Defragmenter	None
Disk Management	None
Distributed File System	None
DNS	DNS
Event Viewer	None
Fax Service Management	Fax Service
Folder	None
FrontPage Server Extensions	FrontPage Server Extensions
Group Policy Object Editor	None
Indexing Service	None
Internet Authentication Service (IAS)	None
Internet Information Services (IIS) Manager	IIS
IP Security Monitor	None
IP Security Policy Management	None
Link to Web Address	None
Local Users and Groups	None
Performance Logs and Alerts	None
QoS Admission Control	QoS Admission Control
Remote Desktop	None
Remote Storage	Remote Storage
Removable Storage Management	None
Resultant Set of Policy	None
Routing and Remote Access	None
Security Configuration and Analysis	None
Security Templates	None

GUI Reference

Table 4-28. Snap-ins available with WS2003 (continued)

Snap-in	Component required
Services	None
Shared Folders	None
Telephony	None
Terminal Services Client Creator	Terminal Services
Terminal Services Configuration	None
Terminal Services Licensing	Terminal Services Licensing
Terminal Services Manager	Terminal Services
WINS	WINS
Wireless Monitor	None
WMI Control	None

When you try to add a snap-in to an MMC console, a dialog box sometimes appears prompting you for further information. For example, if you try to add the Computer Management snap-in to a console, a dialog box appears prompting you to specify whether the console will be used to manage the local computer or a remote computer. As a different example, when you install the Shared Folders snap-in, you must specify whether to display all three subnodes (Shares, Sessions, and Open Files) or just one of them. Table 4-29 summarizes the options offered when installing various snap-ins. When no options are indicated, no dialog box appears when you try to add the snap-in.

Table 4-29. Options when installing a new snap-in into a console

Snap-in	Manage local or remote computer	Select computer from command line	Other options
Active Directory Domains and Trusts			
Active Directory Sites and Services			
Active Directory Users and Computers			
ActiveX Control			Starts the Insert ActiveX Control Wizard
Certificates			Can specify whether to manage the user, service, or computer account
Component Services			
Computer Management	Yes	Yes	
Device Manager	Yes		
Disk Defragmenter			
Disk Management	Yes		
Distributed File System			
DNS			
Event Viewer	Yes	Yes	
Fax Service Management	Yes		

Table 4-29. Options when installing a new snap-in into a console (continued)

Snap-in	Manage local or remote computer	Select computer from command line	Other options
Folder			
FrontPage Server Extensions			
Group Policy	Yes	Yes	
Indexing Service	Yes		
Internet Authentication Service	Yes		
Internet Information Services			
IP Security Policy Management	Yes		Can manage domain policy for current or different domain
Link to Web Address			Can specify URL
Local Users and Groups	Yes	Yes	
Performance Logs and Alerts			
QoS Admission Control			
Removable Storage Management	Yes	Yes	
Routing and Remote Access			
Security Configuration and Analysis			
Security Templates			
Services	Yes	Yes	
Shared Folders	Yes	Yes	Can also display one or all subnodes
System Information	Yes		
Telephony			
WMI Control	Yes		Can specify credentials when managing remote computers

Consoles

Let's examine one particular administrative tool as an example of a preconfigured MMC console. The tool we will look at is Computer Management, which is used to manage a variety of resources on both local and remote computers. You can launch the Computer Management console in several ways:

- Start → Programs → Administrative Tools → Computer Management
- By using My Computer or Windows Explorer to browse the *System32* folder and double-clicking on the file *compmgmt.msc*
- From the command line by typing **%SystemRoot%\system32\compmgmt.msc**
- By opening a new (blank) MMC console and adding the Computer Management snap-in to create a custom MMC console

Computer Management consists of a single window with two panes:

Left pane

Displays a treelike structure of different nodes called the console tree. The root node identifies the snap-in involved (Computer Management) and displays which computer is currently being managed (local computer). Beneath the root node are three containers (System Tools, Storage, and Services and Applications) whose only purpose is to group together the nodes under them according to function or usage—these nodes themselves being either leaf nodes (nodes that can't contain other nodes) or further containers.

Right pane

Also called the details pane. What is displayed in this pane depends entirely on which node is selected in the left pane of the console tree. For example, if you select Event Viewer under System Tools in the left pane, the right pane displays a simple list showing the various logs that are managed by this tool. The details pane can also contain more complex elements such as multiple subpanes, graphic elements, or web pages, depending on the node selected in the console tree.

Besides the other usual Windows gadgets (titlebar, control gadget, sizing gadgets, status bar), there is also a toolbar displayed in the console window. This toolbar is context-sensitive, meaning that it changes depending on which node you select in the console tree or which object you select in the details pane. The toolbar typically includes several drop-down menus such as Action and View, usually providing the same set of options you obtain in the shortcut menu when you right-click on a node in the console tree or an object in the details pane.

The real power of the MMC, however, resides in the capability of creating your own custom MMC consoles. Custom consoles can contain any snap-ins you wish and can be arranged into a console tree in any fashion you desire. Some of the reasons you might want to create custom consoles include:

• Creating a console that can be used to manage the resources on more than one computer at a time (the preconfigured administrative tool called Computer Management can connect to only one computer at a time)

• Creating a console that can be used to manage a limited subset of resources on a computer and then assigning this console to a junior-level administrator

• Creating a console with multiple windows arranged just the way you like it

• Creating a console with shortcuts to frequently used nodes and objects to facilitate easy administration of those nodes and objects

Default Consoles

Table 4-30 lists the various preconfigured consoles (*.msc* files) installed on WS2003. Some of these files are present only when certain optional Windows components like DHCP or DNS are installed. All of these are found in the *System32* folder except:

comexp.msc

system32\Com

iis.msc

system32\inetsrv

mscorcfg.msc

system32\Microsoft.NET\Framework\version

Table 4-30. WS2003 .msc files

File	Console
acssnap.msc	QoS Admission Control
appsrv.msc	Application Server
asman.msc	Authorization Manager
certmgr.msc	Certificates
certsrv.msc	Certification Authority
certtmpl.msc	Certificate Templates
ciadv.msc	Indexing Service
comexp.msc	Component Services
compmgmt.msc	Computer Management
dcpol.msc	Domain Controller Security Policy
devmgmt.msc	Device Manager
dfrg.msc	Disk Defragmenter
DFSgui.msc	Distributed File System
dhcpmgmt.msc	DHCP
diskmgmt.msc	Disk Management
dnsmgmt.msc	DNS
domain.msc	Active Directory Domains and Trusts
dompol.msc	Domain Security Policy
dsa.msc	Active Directory Users and Computers
dssite.msc	Active Directory Sites and Services
eventvwr.msc	Event Viewer
faxserv.msc	Fax Service Management
filesrv.msc	File Server Management
fsmgmt.msc	Shared Folders
gpedit.msc	Group Policy Object Editor
ias.msc	Internet Authentication Service
iis.msc	Internet Information Services
lusrmgr.msc	Local Users and Groups
mscorcfg.msc	.NET 1.1 Configuration
ntmsmgr.msc	Removable Storage
ntmsoprq.msc	Removable Storage Operator Requests
perfmon.msc	Performance
rrasmgmt.msc	Routing and Remote Access
rsadmin.msc	Remote Storage
rsop.msc	Resultant Set of Policy
secpol.msc	Local Security Settings
services.msc	Services
tapimgmt.msc	Telephony
tscc.msc	Terminal Services Configuration

GUI Reference

Table 4-30. WS2003 .msc files (continued)

File	Console
tsmcc.msc	Remote Desktops
winsmgmt.msc	WINS
wmimgmt.msc	Windows Management Infrastructure (WMI)

Microsoft Management Console—Tasks

We'll walk through the process of creating, customizing, and working with custom consoles.

Create a Console

Let's create a custom console that can be used to simultaneously manage resources on two computers running WS2003: the local computer and a remote computer. Begin by logging on as Administrator and open a blank MMC console using one of the following methods:

- Start → Run → **mmc** → OK.
- Type **mmc** at the command line.
- Open the *System32* folder and double-click on the *mmc.exe* file.

Now add a Computer Management snap-in for managing the local computer:

Console → Add/Remove Snap-in → Add

This opens the Add/Remove Standalone Snap-in dialog box, which lists the various standalone snap-ins available for installation on the system. You can add as many of these snap-ins to a console as you like, and you can add multiple instances of any snap-in to manage different computers or simply to give different views of the same snap-in. In the Add/Remove Standalone Snap-in dialog box, select the Computer Management snap-in and click Add. This opens a dialog box prompting you to specify the computer that the snap-in will manage. If you select "Another computer," you have to browse Active Directory to locate the remote computer you want to manage. In our example, we want to install two instances of the Computer Management snap-in into our console: one to manage the local computer and the other to manage a remote computer. After selecting "Local computer," accept the remaining prompts to install the snap-in for managing the local computer. Then, to add a snap-in for managing the remote computer, simply repeat the previous steps, except that instead of selecting "Local computer," select "Another computer" and browse Active Directory to locate the remote computer you want to manage.

You now have your finished console, but before you do any work with it, you should save it, so perform the following steps:

Console → Save → **Manage Two Computers** → Save

This saves the console as an *.msc* file, which stands for management saved console. By default, this file is saved in the personal Administrative Tools program group of the local user profile for the currently logged-on user. If you are logged on as Administrator, by default the saved file is located in the folder:

\Documents and Settings\Administrator\Start Menu\Programs\ Administrative Tools

If you close your console, you should be able to reopen it by selecting:

Start → Programs → Administrative Tools → Manage Two Computers

The administrative tools created when WS2003 is installed (or when optional components are added later) are located in the folder *Documents and Settings\All Users\Start Menu\Programs\Administrative Tools*. Administrative Tools in the Control Panel is a shortcut to this folder, which explains why, when you create your own custom console, it is not found in Administrative Tools in the Control Panel.

Customize a Console

Now that we've created a new console for managing the local and a remote computer, let's see what can be done to customize this console. Customizing a console is the process of personalizing and configuring it to make using it quick and simple.

Use the View Menu

You can use the View menu to:

- Change the default view of how objects in the details pane are displayed. You probably want to use View → Detail so that any columns of status information present in the console are displayed.

- Hide or remove various elements of the MMC window using View → Customize. For example, with some administrative tools, such as the Services console, there is only one node in the console tree, so hiding the console tree might be a good idea.

 One of the customization options under View → Customize is to remove the View menu itself! If you later decide that you want to bring it back, use Customize View under the System menu. (The System menu is accessed using the gadget at the top lefthand corner of a window.)

If you have selected Detail view, you can rearrange columns by dragging and can sort rows by clicking on column headers in the details pane (this doesn't work for all snap-ins). Some snap-ins also provide a Filter item on the View menu, which can be used to filter what is displayed in the details pane.

Customize the Console Tree

A Folder is a standalone snap-in that simply provides a container for other snap-ins; it doesn't have any inherent administrative functionality. You can add folders to the console tree to group together snap-ins according to computer, site, network, domain, department, and so on. For example, if we plan on adding more Computer Management snap-ins for managing additional remote computers, we might add a Folder snap-in for grouping together the remote computers we are managing, and rename this Folder snap-in Remote Computers. Continuing our previous example, do the following:

Console → Add/Remove Snap-in → Add → Folder → Add → Close → OK → right-click on New Folder → Rename → **Remote Computers**

The problem is that we now have our new container in the same level of the console tree as our two Computer Management snap-ins. We need to move the snap-in for the remote computer into the *Remote Computers* folder. Unfortunately, Microsoft made this process more complicated than it should be. In fact, there is no way to move snap-ins around the console tree once they have been added to the tree! Our only recourse is to remove the existing snap-in for the remote computer and add it again, this time making sure that we add it to the *Remote Computers* folder instead of to *Console Root*:

> Console → Add/Remove Snap-in → select Computer Management (remote computer) → Remove → select Remote Computers folder from Snap-ins added to folder listbox → Add → select Computer Management → Add → Another computer → Browse → select remote computer → OK → Finish → Close → OK

This now gives us what we want and tells us the clear moral of the story regarding customizing the console tree: plan what you want to do before you start! It's even a good idea to write out a custom MMC console on paper before you actually start building it. You can obviously use this process to build incredibly complex consoles (if you have nothing better to do).

Adding Favorites

A quick way of switching to specific places on a complex console tree is to add favorites to your console. Once you have selected the particular node in the console tree you want to bookmark, use Favorites → Add to Favorites from the toolbar to create a favorite to that node. Unfortunately, favorites map only to nodes in the console tree, not to specific objects in the details pane for that node. You can even group favorites in different folders if you have a lot of them. Once you have created your favorites, you can access them in two different ways:

Use Favorites on the toolbar
> This method expands the console tree until the bookmarked node is selected, displaying its associated objects in the details pane.

Use the Favorites tab in the lefthand pane
> Selecting this tab hides the console tree entirely and displays the list of favorites as hyperlinks. Clicking on a link will display the associated objects for that favorite in the details pane.

Create New Child Windows

You can create new child windows within the MMC main window and root these windows at any node within the console tree. For example, to create a new child window whose root node is System Tools under Computer Management (Local), do this:

> Right-click on System Tools under Computer Management (Local) → New Window from Here

You can tile or cascade multiple child windows. More importantly, you can use this procedure to create custom consoles for junior administrators by closing the original child window, thus restricting their access to peripheral portions of the console tree. In the previous example, closing the original child Window leaves a console whose root node is System Tools for the local computer.

Add Taskpad Views and Tasks

The real customization power of the MMC is found in taskpad views. A taskpad view is a page in the details pane of a console to which you can add shortcuts to performing specific tasks, such as running wizards, opening properties sheets, selecting menus, opening web pages, and running command-line utilities and scripts. Taskpad views can make life easier for junior administrators by providing a single location from which various administrative tasks can be performed. Taskpad views can also make complex administration tasks easier by providing a single location from which the properties sheets and menus from many different snap-ins can be accessed.

Let's walk through the process by creating a taskpad view. You first need to decide which node in the console tree your taskpad view will be attached to, and you should think about the various tasks you want to incorporate into that view. Then right-click on the selected node to start the New Taskpad View Wizard, which leads you through the following steps:

Taskpad Display
Select how the taskpad view will be displayed, including how (or whether) the objects in the details pane will be displayed and whether normal or pop-up text is used to caption shortcuts.

Taskpad Target
Select whether the taskpad view will apply only to the current node in the console tree or to all nodes of the same type as the selected one, and specify whether the taskpad view will become the default display in the details pane for all nodes of the selected type.

Name and Description
Specify a name for the taskpad view and a brief description.

Once the New Taskpad View Wizard is finished, you can then run the New Task Wizard and add tasks to your taskpad. The New Task Wizard starts automatically when the New Taskpad View Wizard ends. Let's walk through the process of adding new tasks to the taskpad view using the New Task Wizard:

Command type
Specify the kind of task you want to perform, which includes:

Menu command
Run a command from a menu. Specify any menu command available for any node in the console tree or from objects in the list in the details pane.

Shell command
Run a script, start a program, or open a web page. Specify the path and file for the command or script you want to run, a list of parameters, the directory to start in, and the type of window the command or script will run in. You can select any program files to run here (*.exe, *.com, *.bat, *.cmd, *.pif) or specify a URL.

Navigation
Select a view to display from your list of favorites. This also causes the selected node to receive the focus in the left pane of the console.

Name and Description/Task icon
Once you have specified the details of the task, identify the shortcut that launches the task by assigning it a name, a short description, and an icon. You can then launch the task by clicking its shortcut in the taskpad view.

Once you have created your taskpad view, you can modify it by selecting Action → Edit Taskpad View. This allows you to change the display options of the taskpad view, launch the New Task Wizard to create new tasks, or modify, remove, and rearrange existing tasks in the taskpad view. You can also delete your taskpad view to return to the normal details pane view.

You can switch between a taskpad view and the normal details pane by using the tabs at the bottom of the right pane—they are easy to miss. You can also create as many taskpad views as you like for a given node in the console tree and use these tabs to switch easily between them. However, keep the name of a taskpad view short so that

GUI Reference

the space used by these tabs will be minimized; if these tabs go to the edge of the console window, there is no gadget to scroll through them.

Set Console Options

Once you have created and customized a console, you should specify a console name, associated icon, and the mode in which the console will be opened. These options are specified using Console → Options, and the most important of these is specifying the console mode, of which there are four possibilities:

Author mode
> Users have full rights to customize the console as they desire, including adding or removing snap-ins, creating new child windows, creating taskpad views, and accessing all portions of the console tree. Author mode is typically used only for creating and customizing new consoles. Once they are configured appropriately, they should be assigned one of the user modes to prevent them from being modified by users. Consoles opened in author mode have a second menu bar with the options Console, Window, and Help—consoles opened in user mode don't have this menu.

User mode—full access
> Users have full access to the console tree but can't add or remove snap-ins or change console properties.

User mode—limited access, multiple window
> Users have access only to the visible portion of the console tree. Users can open new windows but can't close existing ones. Users can't add or remove snap-ins or change console properties.

User mode—limited access, single window
> Users have access only to the visible portion of the console tree. Users can't open new windows or close existing ones. Users can't add or remove snap-ins or change console properties.

In addition, when any of the user modes is selected, you can also toggle whether users can customize the console view or use context menus (right-click) in taskpads in the console.

If a console has been set to one of the user modes, it will have no Console menu when it is opened the next time. If you later want to make changes to your console, you need to open it in author mode. Since there is no Console menu, you can't do this using Console → Options; you need another way of opening the console in author mode. You have several choices:

- If the console is an existing administrative tool:

  > Right-click on Start button → Open All Users → Programs → Administrative Tools → right-click on selected shortcut → Author

- If the console is a custom console saved in the user's profile:

  > Right-click on Start button → Open → Programs → Administrative Tools → right-click on selected shortcut → Author

- You can also perform these steps on the actual *.msc* file for the console if you can find it in Windows Explorer.

- You can also open any console in author mode from the command line by using the /a switch:

  ```
  mmc path\console_name.msc /a
  ```

If you are logged in as an ordinary user and need to perform some quick administrative task using a console, you can run the console using your Administrator credentials as follows:

- Right-click on console shortcut → Run as → specify credentials.
- Use the runas command from the command line.

Save Consoles

If a console is in author mode, you are prompted to save any changes you have made when you try to close it. If it is in one of the three user modes, whether the changes you have made are saved or not depends on the setting:

Console → Options → Do not save changes to this console

If the checkbox is checked, changes made by users will not be saved when they close the console. Remember, this setting can be configured only when the console is in author mode!

Distribute Consoles

You can distribute custom consoles that you've created to other administrators by:

- Saving or copying them to a network share with appropriate permissions set to preclude access by anyone except administrators. You may also want to publish the location of the *.msc* file in Active Directory so they can search for it using the Search Assistant.
- Right-clicking on the *.msc* file in My Computer or Windows Explorer and using the Send To option to email the file to other administrators or to copy it to a floppy disk to hand around.
- Any other creative way you can think of.

Run Consoles from the Command Line

You can run a console from the command line as long as you know the directory where the *.msc* file is stored (see Table 4-30). To run a console, specify its name, omitting the *.msc* externsion. Open a command prompt and type either:

    mmc path\console_file

or:

    path\console_file

unless you are in the current directory where the *.msc* file is stored, in which case you can type either:

    mmc console_file

or just:

    console_file

There are some optional switches you can append to these commands:

/a   Opens a saved console in author mode so you can modify the console.

/computer=computer_name
       Opens the console and connects to the specified computer. This switch is supported by Computer Management (*compmgmt.msc*) and related consoles.

/server=domain_controller_name
> Opens the console and connects to the specified domain controller. This switch is supported by Active Directory Users and Computers (*dsa.msc*).

/domain=domain_name
> Opens the console and connects to a domain controller in the specified domain. This switch is supported by Active Directory Users and Computers (*dsa.msc*).

MMC Keyboard Accelerators

Finally, for the mouse-weary, there is an extensive set of keyboard shortcuts you can use to work with the main window, console tree, and active child window in the console. These are summarized in Tables 4-31 to 4-33.

Table 4-31. Keyboard accelerators for navigating the console window

Accelerator	Function
Tab or F6	Moves forward between panes in the active console window
Shift-Tab or Shift-F6	Moves backward between panes in the active console window
Ctrl-Tab or Ctrl-F6	Moves forward between console windows
Ctrl-Shift-Tab or Ctrl-Shift-F6	Moves backward between console windows
Plus sign (+) on the numeric keypad	Expands the selected item
Minus sign (-) on the numeric keypad	Collapses the selected item
Asterisk (*) on the numeric keypad	Expands the whole console tree below the root item in the active console window
Up arrow	Moves the selection up one item in a pane
Down arrow	Moves the selection down one item in a pane
Page up	Moves the selection to the top item visible in a pane
Page down	Moves the selection to the bottom item visible in a pane
Home	Moves the selection to the first item in a pane
End	Moves the selection to the last item in a pane
Right arrow	Expands the selected item
Left arrow	Collapses the selected item
Alt-right arrow	Moves the selection to the next item (same as the forward arrow on the toolbar)
Alt-left arrow	Moves the selection to the previous item (same as the back arrow on the toolbar)

Table 4-32. Keyboard accelerators for accessing menu commands that act on the main console window

Accelerator	Function
Ctrl-O	Opens a saved console
Ctrl-N	Opens a new (blank) console and closes the existing one
Ctrl-S	Saves the open console
Ctrl-M	Adds or removes a console item
Ctrl-W	Opens a new window
F5	Refreshes all console windows

Table 4-32. Keyboard accelerators for accessing menu commands that act on the main console window (continued)

Accelerator	Function
Alt-spacebar	Displays the MMC window menu
Alt-F4	Closes the active console window

Table 4-33. Keyboard accelerators for accessing menu commands that act on the active console window pane

Accelerator	Function
Ctrl-P	Prints the current page or active window pane
Alt-minus sign	Displays the window menu for the active console window
Shift-F10	Displays the Action (shortcut) menu for the selected item
Alt-A	Displays the Action (shortcut) menu for the active console window
Alt-V	Displays the View menu for the active console window
Alt-F	Displays the Favorites menu for the active console window
F1	Opens the Help topic (if any) for the selected item
F5	Refreshes the content of all console windows
Ctrl-F10	Maximizes the active console window
Ctrl-F5	Restores the active console window
Alt-Enter	Displays the Properties dialog box (if any) for the selected item
F2	Renames the selected item
Ctrl-F4	Closes the active console window (if there is only one console window, this closes the console)

See Also

Administrative Tools

OU—Concepts

An organizational unit (OU) is a type of container object in Active Directory that can contain other objects such as users, computers, groups, printers, or even other OUs. OUs are the smallest units in Active Directory to which:

- Permissions and tasks can be delegated (see *Delegation* earlier in this chapter)
- Group Policies may be applied (see *Group Policy* earlier in this chapter)

Using OUs

The general strategy for using OUs within a domain is to create a hierarchy of OUs that mirror the administrative functions and security needs of your company. When you're designing this structure, the top-level OUs should be carefully chosen so that they don't need to be changed afterward unless a major company restructuring occurs. Top-level OUs should reflect some relatively static aspect of your enterprise, such as the different departments, divisions, cities, states, or countries, or the different kinds of objects you administer in Active Directory, such as users, groups, computers, and printers. If your enterprise is multidomain in scope (such as those with a national or

GUI Reference

international presence), then consider standardizing top-level OU names for all domains in your forest.

Once you've standardized and created your top-level OUs in each domain, you can create child OUs beneath them, which represent more granular levels of administrative authority. You can then delegate authority to different branches of OUs or individual OUs and apply Group Policies to manage them. If you create a child OU within a parent OU, the child OU inherits the settings of the parent OU by default.

Here are a few examples that illustrate how you might structure OU hierarchies within a domain or across domains:

- A company that does business both locally and in other countries and that administers these two business functions with relative independence could have two top-level OUs called National and Foreign within its domain. Users, groups, computers, and printers could be placed in the appropriate OU, and authority could be delegated by administrators to trusted users in each business area.

- A similar arrangement could be set up for a company that deals locally with both the private sector (wholesale or retail) and the public sector (government): create two top-level OUs called Private and Public. Within Public you could create two second-level OUs called Wholesale and Retail. Place objects in different OUs; delegate authority and apply Group Policies as desired.

- A company that has several large stores in different locations could have a separate top-level OU representing each store. Within each store OU, you could create second-level OUs for Sales and Support. Within each second-level OU, you could create third-level OUs for Users, Groups, Computers, and Printers. Within the Printers OU, you could have two fourth-level OUs called Standard and Color. You could then delegate administrative authority over the Color OU to a trusted user who knows how to work with color laser printers.

A different way of hierarchically structuring Active Directory is to create a hierarchy of domains instead of OUs. You should:

- Use a domain hierarchy when different portions of your enterprise need complete administrative control over their local users and resources, as in a decentralized-administration model.

- Use an OU hierarchy within a domain when different portions of your enterprise need only limited administrative control over users and resources, as in a centralized-administration model.

You can, of course, use both methods and create OU hierarchies within domains that are part of a domain hierarchy. See *Active Directory* for more information on planning the structure of Active Directory.

OU—Tasks

The following procedures assume that you have the Active Directory Users and Computers console open.

Create an OU

Use these methods to create a hierarchical structure of OUs within a domain:

Right-click on a domain → New → Organizational Unit → specify name for new OU

Right-click on an OU within a domain → New → Organizational Unit → specify name for new OU

You can also rename or delete OUs.

Move an OU

Drag and drop it somewhere else in the hierarchy of OUs in a domain.

Move an Object to a Different OU

Drag and drop it into the destination OU.

OU—Notes

An OU can contain objects only from its own domain, not from other domains.

For information on how to delegate authority for an OU, see *Delegation* earlier in this chapter.

To apply Group Policy to an OU, see *Group Policy* in this chapter. Be sure to test your Group Policies and the tasks or permissions you have delegated to OUs as you implement them. This is especially important when several levels of OUs are involved, as the application of policies can become quite complex.

See Also

Active Directory, Delegation, Group Policy

Permissions—Concepts

To grant users access to files and folders on the local computer or network, you assign these users permissions. Two kinds of permissions can be used to secure access to these resources: NTFS permissions and shared-folder permissions. You need to understand both kinds of permissions and how they work together.

NTFS Permissions

NTFS is the primary WS2003 filesystem (FAT/FAT32 aren't recommended for most purposes), and partitions formatted with NTFS can have their files and folders secured using NTFS permissions. These permissions secure the filesystem for both local and network access. For example, if user Mary Jones is granted NTFS Read permission on folder *Pub* and its contents (which are stored on her C: drive), she can log on to her machine, view the contents of *Pub*, and open any file stored in it. If *Pub* is then shared with the shared-folder permissions of Full Control for Everyone, she can log on to a different machine and access the *Pub* share and its contents over the network. Whether Mary is trying to access a resource on an NTFS volume locally or over the network, NTFS permissions will apply.

Special Permissions

The most granular NTFS permissions are called special permissions. These permissions give administrators the highest degree of control over how users can access files and folders stored on NTFS volumes. By selecting different sets of special permissions, administrators can create custom permissions for files or folders that need special access control. The 18 NTFS special permissions are listed and described in Table 4-34.

Table 4-34. NTFS special permissions

Special permission	Description
Folders only	
Traverse Folder	Drill into the folder to other files and folders, even if you have no permissions on intermediate subfolders.
List Folder	View the names of subfolders and files in the folder.
Create Files	Create files in the folder.
Create Folders	Create subfolders within the folder.
Files only	
Execute File	Execute the file.
Read Data	Read the file.
Write Data	Modify the file.
Append Data	Append to the file (you can't modify existing data, only append).
Both folders and files	
Read Attributes	View the attributes of the file or folder (attributes include Read-only, Hidden, System, and Archive).
Read Extended Attributes	View custom attributes that may be defined by certain applications for the file or folder.
Write Attributes	Modify the attributes of the file or folder.
Write Extended Attributes	Modify custom attributes that may be defined by certain applications for the file or folder.
Delete Subfolders and Files	Delete subfolders or files.
Delete	Delete the file or folder (even if this permission is denied on a file, you can delete it if its parent folder has been granted Delete Subfolders and Files permission).
Read Permissions	View the permissions on the file or folder.
Change Permissions	Modify the permissions on the file or folder.
Take Ownership	Take ownership of the file or folder.
Synchronize	Let threads in multithreaded programs wait on the file or folder handle and synchronize with another thread that signals it.

Standard Permissions

Special permissions are really too granular for administrators to use to secure files and folders in day-to-day usage. To make life simpler, Microsoft has grouped these special permissions into two different sets:

Folder permissions
> Used to secure folders and their files and subfolders

File permissions
> Used to secure individual files within folders

Together, these two sets of permissions are called standard permissions, and they are described in Tables 4-35 and 4-36. The effect of combined standard and special permissions is shown in Tables 4-37 and 4-38.

Table 4-35. NTFS standard permissions for files

File permission	Description
Read	Open the file and view its permissions, attributes, and ownership.
Write	Modify the file, modify its attributes, and view its permissions, attributes, and ownership.
Read & Execute	Execute the file, plus do everything Read permission allows.
Modify	Delete the file and do everything Read & Execute and Write permissions allow.
Full Control	Take ownership, modify permissions, and do everything Modify permission allows.

Table 4-36. NTFS standard permissions for folders

Folder permission	Description
Read	View contents of folder and view its permissions, attributes, and ownership.
Write	Create new files and folders in the folder, modify its attributes, and view its permissions, attributes, and ownership.
List Folder Contents	View contents of folder only.
Read & Execute	Traverse subfolders within the folder plus do everything Read and List Folder Contents permissions allow.
Modify	Delete the folder and do everything Read & Execute and Write permissions allow.
Full Control	Take ownership, modify permissions, and do everything that Modify permission allows.

Table 4-37. Special file permissions as combinations of standard permissions

Special permission	Read	Write	Read & Execute	Modify	Full Control
Read Data	Yes	—	Yes	Yes	Yes
Read Attributes	Yes	—	Yes	Yes	Yes
Read Extended Attributes	Yes	—	Yes	Yes	Yes
Read Permissions	Yes	Yes	Yes	Yes	Yes
Synchronize	Yes	Yes	Yes	Yes	Yes
Write Data	—	Yes	—	Yes	Yes
Append Data	—	Yes	—	Yes	Yes
Write Attributes	—	Yes	—	Yes	Yes
Write Extended Attributes	—	Yes	—	Yes	Yes
Execute File	—	—	Yes	Yes	Yes
Delete	—	—	—	Yes	Yes
Delete Subfolders and Files	—	—	—	—	Yes
Change Permissions	—	—	—	—	Yes
Take Ownership	—	—	—	—	Yes

Table 4-38. Special folder permissions as combinations of standard permissions

Special permission	Read	Write	List Folder Contents	Read & Execute	Modify	Full Control
List Folder	Yes	—	Yes	Yes	Yes	Yes
Read Attributes	Yes	—	Yes	Yes	Yes	Yes
Read Extended Attributes	Yes	—	Yes	Yes	Yes	Yes
Read Permissions	Yes	Yes	—	Yes	Yes	Yes

GUI Reference

Table 4-38. Special folder permissions as combinations of standard permissions (continued)

Special permission	Read	Write	List Folder Contents	Read & Execute	Modify	Full Control
Synchronize	Yes	Yes	Yes	Yes	Yes	Yes
Create Files	—	Yes	—	—	Yes	Yes
Create Folders	—	Yes	—	—	Yes	Yes
Write Attributes	—	Yes	—	—	Yes	Yes
Write Extended Attributes	—	Yes	—	—	Yes	Yes
Traverse Folder	—	—	Yes	Yes	Yes	Yes
Delete	—	—	—	—	Yes	Yes
Delete Subfolders and Files	—	—	—	—	—	Yes
Change Permissions	—	—	—	—	—	Yes
Take Ownership	—	—	—	—	—	Yes

Working with NTFS Permissions

In order to configure NTFS permissions on a file, folder, or NTFS volume, at least one of the following must be true:

- You must be a member of the Administrators group.
- You must have Full Control permission for the file, folder, or volume.
- You must be the owner of the file, folder, or volume.

NTFS permissions must be explicitly applied to a file or folder in order to grant a user access to it. In other words, if a file has no permissions specified for a particular user or for the groups to which that user belongs, the user has no access to the file.

Having said that, however, when you explicitly assign permissions to a folder, by default all subfolders and files within that parent folder inherit the permissions assigned to the parent. Another way of saying this is that permissions automatically propagate from the parent to the child. This is done to simplify and speed up the job of assigning permissions.

If you like, you can later change the permissions to any subfolder or file within the parent folder without affecting the permissions assigned to the parent. In other words, you can prevent permissions inheritance at a given folder or file within the filesystem hierarchy. You can do this two ways:

- You can copy the permissions inherited from the parent folder to the subfolder or file under consideration and then explicitly modify these permissions as desired.
- You can remove the permissions inherited from the parent folder to the subfolder or file under consideration and then explicitly assign new ones as desired.

Either way, the subfolder or file under consideration now becomes the new parent from which the subtree of files and folders beneath it inherit their permissions (a file has no subtree beneath it, of course). An example might help here. Let's say that folder A contains folder B, which contains folder C, which contains file F. Begin by assigning Read permission to folder A for user Dennis. By default, this permission is automatically propagated to folders B and C and file F. Now prevent permissions inheritance from folder B by copying the permissions from its parent A. All folders and files still have Read permission for Dennis, but folder C and file F now inherit their permissions from folder B instead of A. Change the permissions on B from Read to Full Control. Folder C and file F now inherit Full Control permission from folder B, while folder A remains Read permission, as expected. In general, it simplifies things if you simply let permissions be inherited from their highest parent and don't try to prevent permissions at subfolders in the hierarchy unless absolutely necessary. Use the K.I.S.S. (Keep It Simple, Stupid!) principle when administering NTFS permissions, unless you're really good at keeping things documented. Otherwise, you may find yourself spending unnecessary time troubleshooting resource-access problems.

When you create a new file or folder on an NTFS volume, the new file or folder automatically inherits the permissions assigned to its parent folder. If the file or folder is created in the root directory of the volume, it inherits the permissions assigned to that root directory. By default, if you create a new NTFS volume by formatting a partition with NTFS, its root directory is assigned the permission Everyone has Full Control, so any new folder or file created in the root will automatically inherit Everyone has Full Control permission.

When you create an NTFS volume, it's generally a good idea to change the default Everyone has Full Control permission to Authenticated Users have Full Control before you start creating directories and storing files on the volume. This enhances the security of the volume since the Authenticated Users built-in system group represents all users who have valid domain user accounts on the network, while the Everyone group also includes untrusted users from other connected networks.

What you shouldn't do is try to modify the default permissions of system volumes like the C: drive or those on the \Windows or \Windows\System32 folders. These permissions are necessary for the proper functioning of the operating system, so don't change them.

If you assign a particular user or group permission on a folder, by default the user or group is granted the three permissions—Read & Execute, List Folder Contents, and Read—for the folder. You can then change these permissions to whatever kind of access you want the user or group to have. Similarly, if you assign a user or group permission on a file, by default the user or group is granted the two permissions—Read & Execute and Read—for the file. Change these permissions to whatever kind of access you want the user or group to have.

When you assign a particular NTFS permission to a file or folder, you can either explicitly allow the permission to grant the user or group access to the object, or you can explicitly deny the permission to prevent the user or group from accessing it. Most of the time, you explicitly allow permissions to enable users to access files and folders, but in certain situations you may want to explicitly deny a user permission on an object. For example, if Bob has Read permission to the Accounts folder and all its contents, you could deny Bob Read permission to the particular document in Accounts that describes the plans for Bob's upcoming surprise party to prevent him from reading it. Users can have multiple NTFS permissions assigned for the same file or folder. This is because users can belong to groups, and permissions are assigned separately to user accounts and groups. For example, Susan could have Read permission on the *Pub* folder, while the Marketing group to which she belongs has Modify permission on the same folder. In the case of multiple permissions, the effective permission for the user is determined by adding them together (logical OR). In this example Susan's cumulative level of access to *Pub* will be Modify. To determine the effective permissions in a given situation, use Tables 4-35 through 4-38.

The exception to this is that a permission denied always overrides a similar permission allowed. For example, if Susan is denied Read permission to *Pub* while the Marketing group to which she belongs is allowed Read permission, she is effectively denied Read permission on *Pub*.

Permissions for a file override those for the folder that contains the file. For example, if Susan has Read permission on *Pub* but has Modify permission on the file *Readme.txt* within *Pub*, Susan will be able to make changes to the file and save them.

Once you've explicitly assigned permissions to your parent folders on an NTFS volume and started creating subfolders and files, you need to know what will happen if you try to copy or move these files and folders. This is because the act of copying and moving files and folders can have an effect on the permissions assigned to them. The general rules are as follows:

Copying files or folders
>	Whether the destination parent folder is on the same or different NTFS volume, the copied file or folder inherits the permissions of the parent folder.

Moving files or folders
>	If the destination parent folder is on the same NTFS volume, the moved file or folder retains its original permissions. However, if the destination parent folder is on a different NTFS volume, the moved file or folder inherits the permissions of the parent folder (since a move to a different volume is really a copy followed by the delete of the original).

For both copies and moves, if the destination volume is formatted with FAT, all permissions are lost from the copied or moved file or folder. For more information on copying and moving files on NTFS volumes, see *Files and Folders* earlier in this chapter.

Default NTFS Permissions

In W2K the default permissions on a new NTFS volume included Full Control for Everyone. In WS2003 these permissions have been tightened for increased security, and the default permissions on new NTFS volumes are now those shown in Table 4-39. These permissions are the same whether the computer belongs to a workgroup or domain.

Table 4-39. Default permissions on NTFS volumes

Security principal	Standard permission	Additional special permissions	Applies to
Administrators (local user)	Full Control	None	This folder, subfolders, and files
CREATOR OWNER	None	All (equivalent to Full Control)	Subfolders and files only
Everyone	None	Traverse Folder/Execute File List Folder/Read Data Read Attributes Read Extended Attributes Read Permissions (equivalent to Read & Execute)	This folder only
SYSTEM	Full Control	None	This folder, subfolders, and files
Users (local group)	Read & Execute Create Folders/ Append Data Create Files/ Write Data	None	This folder, subfolders, and files This folder and subfolders Subfolders only

Ownership

Ownership is an aspect of permissions in WS2003. Every file or folder created on an NTFS volume has an owner. When a user creates a file, the user becomes the owner of that file and can set permissions on it to allow others access to the file. And when a user installs a printer, the user becomes the owner of the printer. Objects in Active Directory also have owners and can be assigned permissions as well.

Ownership can't be given; it can only be taken. In order to assume ownership of a file or other object, a user needs Take Ownership permission. If the owner grants this permission on a file to another user, that user can then take ownership of the first user's file. Administrators, however, have the power to take ownership of any object that they can manage (essentially, anything except system objects).

Shared-Folder Permissions

NTFS permissions are the primary means of securing filesystem resources on a computer or network. However, they can be used only on volumes formatted with NTFS and not on FAT or FAT32 volumes. Furthermore, assigning NTFS permissions to a folder doesn't make the contents of that folder available over the network. To do this, we have to share the resource, and this means we have to deal with a whole other set of permissions called shared-folder permissions and how these combine with NTFS permissions to secure shared network resources.

Shared-folder permissions are permissions assigned to folders or volumes that have been shared. These folders may be on NTFS, FAT, or FAT32 volumes, and any of these volumes may themselves be shared at their root directory. In fact, shared-folder permissions are the only permissions that can be used to secure resources on FAT and FAT32 volumes. Shared folders secure resources only at the network level, however, and not at the local level. For example, if you share the folder *Pub*, which is located on a FAT volume, you control which users can access the folder over the network and the level of access they can have, but anyone who can log on locally to the machine where the volume is located has unrestricted (full) access to the folder and all its contents. So if you are concerned about securing resources from local access, you must use NTFS instead of FAT or FAT32. Microsoft correctly recommends that all volumes on which applications, data, or users' home folders are located should be NTFS.

Another reason for always using NTFS is that shared-folder permissions aren't as granular as NTFS permissions for controlling access, as you can see from Table 4-40 (note that there is no equivalent in shared-folder permissions to the highly granular NTFS special permissions). Also, shared-folder permissions apply uniformly to the folder and all its contents; if you want to prevent shared-folder permissions at a subfolder of a shared folder, you must create a new share at the subfolder. Furthermore, shared-folder permissions can be applied only to folders and volumes, while NTFS permissions can also be applied to individual files.

Table 4-40. Shared-folder permissions

Permission	Description
Read	View contents of folder and traverse subfolders, open files and view their attributes, and run executable files
Change	Create new files and folders in the folder, modify and append data to files, modify file attributes, delete folders and files, plus do everything Read permission allows
Full Control	Take ownership and modify permissions of files (on NTFS volumes only), plus do everything Change permission allows

Working with Shared-Folder Permissions

In order to share a folder and configure its permissions, you must be a member of at least one of the following built-in groups:

> Administrators
> Server Operators
> Power Users

In addition, if the folder you want to share is on an NTFS volume, you must have a minimum NTFS permission of Read for the folder in order to share it.

Folders (or volumes) must be shared and permissions explicitly assigned in order to grant a user access to the contents over the network. If a folder is shared but no shared-folder permissions are explicitly assigned to it, users will be able to see the share in My Network Places, but they won't be able to access its contents. Sharing a volume simply means sharing the root folder on the volume.

When you assign a particular shared-folder permission from the list in Table 4-40, you can either explicitly allow the permission for the folder to grant the user or group access to the contents of the folder or explicitly deny the permission to prevent the user or group from accessing it. Most of the time you will explicitly allow permissions instead of denying them.

When you share a folder, the default shared-folder permission assigned to it is Everyone has Full Control. It's usually a good idea to change this to Users have Full Control before you start storing files in the folder. When you assign a particular user or group permissions on a shared folder, by default the user or group is granted only Read permission for the folder. You can then change the permissions to whatever kind of access you want the user or group to have.

Like NTFS permissions, users can have multiple shared-folder permissions for the same folder—for example, when the user account is assigned one permission while a group to which the user account belongs is assigned a different permission. The effective permission is determined again by adding the different permissions together (logical OR). Once again, a permission denied always overrides a similar permission allowed. Copying or moving files to other shared folders always gives them the permissions assigned to the destination folder. Copying the shared folder itself leaves the original folder shared but the new folder not shared. Moving a shared folder causes it to stop being shared.

General Strategy for Assigning Permissions

The general strategy for using permissions to secure shared-network resources is to proceed as follows:

1. Format the volume where the shared folder will be created using NTFS instead of FAT or FAT32. Create the folder you are going to share.
2. Assign NTFS permissions to the folder first. Grant your users and groups suitable levels of access to the folder, giving each user and group only as much access as they need. It generally simplifies administration if you assign permissions only to groups and not to individual users. Check your NTFS permissions assignments to make sure they are correct.
3. Now share the folder and leave its shared-folder permission set to the default Everyone has Full Control setting. You're done.

The advantage of doing things this way is that you really have to deal with configuring only one set of permissions, namely NTFS. For comparison, let's say you followed this strategy instead:

1. Format the volume using NTFS. Create the folder you are going to share and leave its NTFS permissions set to the default Everyone has Full Control setting.

2. Share the folder and grant your users and groups suitable levels of access to the folder using shared-folder permissions.

The problems with this scenario are:

- The folder is secure for network access but not for local access. So if someone is able to log on locally to the computer where the volume is located, they will have unrestricted access to the folder and its contents.

- Shared-folder permissions are limited to Read, Change, and Full Control, while NTFS folder permissions can be Read, Write, List Folder Contents, Read & Execute, Modify, and Full Control. NTFS permissions thus give you greater granularity in controlling access than shared-folder permissions.

- You can also use NTFS file permissions to control access to individual files or create custom permission lists using NTFS special permissions. You can't do any of these things using shared-folder permissions.

- Shared-folder permissions provide the same level of access for all files and subfolders within the folder, while NTFS permissions allow you to explicitly assign different permissions to subtrees of folders and files within the parent folder.

Let's take a look at one more strategy:

1. Format the volume using NTFS and create the folder you are going to share.

2. Assign NTFS permissions for the folder to users and groups to grant them different levels of access. For example, assign the Marketing group Read permission for the *Pub* folder.

3. Share the folder and assign shared-folder permissions for the folder to users and groups to grant them different levels of access. For example, assign the Marketing group Change permission for the *Pub* folder.

The problem is that now you have the administrative headache of managing two separate sets of permissions instead of just one. Also, you must be aware of how NTFS and shared-folder permissions combine. The general rule is: when NTFS and shared-folder permissions combine, the most restrictive permission applies. In other words, for the Marketing group:

Read (NTFS) + Change (shared folder) = Read (combined)

What use is this second set of permissions (shared-folder permissions) if our strategy will always be to carefully assign NTFS permissions but leave shared-folder permissions at their default of Everyone has Full Control? Simple: shared-folder permissions are the only permissions that can be used to control resources for data stored on FAT volumes. Why would you want to use FAT instead of NTFS? Possible reasons are:

- When you are setting up a peer-to-peer network using a workgroup model for a small business that can't afford an administrator to manage a domain controller

- When you want to dual-boot a machine between WS2003 and Windows 95/98, which requires that you install WS2003 on FAT instead of NTFS

Neither of these is a particularly compelling reason, however.

GUI Reference

Permissions—Tasks

NTFS Permissions

NTFS permissions are the primary means of controlling access to filesystem resources on WS2003. To assign or modify NTFS permissions on a file or folder, you must either:

- Be the owner (creator) of the file or folder
- Have Full Control permission on the file or folder
- Be a member of the Administrators group

To assign NTFS permissions, you can use Windows Explorer or My Computer. The following procedures assume you have already selected the file or folder whose permissions you want to assign or modify.

 New to WS2003 is Special Permissions. This box being checked indicates that standard permissions have been modified by adding or removing special permissions.

Assign Standard Permissions to a File

Right-click on file → Properties → Security → Add → select domain → select user or group → Add → allow or deny standard permissions

Unless you explicitly allow different permissions, when you assign NTFS standard file permissions to a user or group, the default permissions assigned are Allow Read & Execute.

When you try to allow or deny different combinations of NTFS standard permissions, you will discover that not all combinations are allowed. For example, if you try to allow Full Control, then all five checkboxes under Allow automatically become checked. Table 4-41 shows the permissible combinations of NTFS standard permissions that can be assigned using the Security tab.

Table 4-41. Allowable combinations of NTFS standard permissions

Selecting	Automatically selects				
	Full Control	Modify	Read & Execute	Read	Write
Full Control	Yes	Yes	Yes	Yes	Yes
Modify		Yes	Yes	Yes	
Read & Execute			Yes	Yes	
Read				Yes	
Write					Yes

Unfortunately, Table 4-41 doesn't tell the whole story and works only if you are allowing standard permissions and not denying them. If you both allow and deny permissions, other combinations are possible, while many aren't. Furthermore, the Security tab doesn't always show the whole picture. For example, if you first allow Full Control permission, which causes all five checkboxes under Allow to be checked and then deselect the checkbox for Modify, the result is a configuration not displayed in Table 4-41—namely, the combination of allowed Read & Execute, Read, and Write permissions. A message then appears beside the Advanced button saying, "Additional permissions are present but not viewable here. Press Advanced to see them." Finally, when special permissions (described later in this section) are assigned to a file or folder, this same message appears on the Security tab while the standard permissions for that user or group are displayed as unassigned. The moral of the story may be that the GUI here is simply too smart for its own good, and unless you have a good grasp of the 18 underlying NTFS special permissions, it's easy to get confused by what's going on.

If the checkboxes for standard permissions are checked but filled (grayed out), these permissions are inherited from the parent folder (or the volume if the file is in the root directory). When you create a file or save a document in a folder, it automatically inherits the permissions of its parent folder. When you assign new permissions to a file for a user or group, however, these permissions are never grayed out since they are assigned, not inherited.

If you deselect the checkbox labeled "Allow inheritable permissions from parent to propagate to this object" before clicking Apply or OK, a warning will appear saying that you are preventing permissions being inherited to the file from its parent folder. You are given two options:

Copy
> This copies the permissions of the parent folder to your file but breaks the chain of permissions inheritance from the parent to the child. If the child were a folder instead of a file, it would become the root of a new chain of inherited permissions.

Remove
> This removes the permissions of the parent folder from your file and breaks the chain of permissions inheritance. Again, if the child were a folder instead of a file, it would become the root of a new chain of inherited permissions.

Assign Standard Permissions to a Folder

> Right-click on folder → Properties → Security → Add → select domain → select user or group → Add → allow or deny standard permissions

Unless you allow or deny different permissions, when you assign NTFS standard folder permissions to a user or group, the default permissions assigned are Allow Read & Execute. Otherwise, the behavior here is similar to that in *Assign Standard Permissions to a File* earlier in this section, except that there are six standard folder permissions instead of only five standard file permissions (the sixth folder permission is List Folder Contents).

Assign Special Permissions to a File

> Right-click on file → Properties → Security → Advanced → Add → select domain → select user or group → allow or deny special permissions

Unlike assigning standard permissions where selecting one checkbox may cause others to magically become selected or deselected as well, assigning special permissions is more straightforward: you can assign any combination of these 13 special file permissions, the only caveat being that you can't allow and deny a permission at the same time.

Clearing the checkbox "Allow inheritable permissions from parent to propagate to this object" will break the chain of permissions inheritance from the parent folder to the selected file.

Assign Special Permissions to a Folder

> Right-click on folder → Properties → Security → Advanced → Add → select domain → select user or group → allow or deny special permissions

The behavior here is similar to that in *Assign Standard Permissions to a File* earlier in this section, except that with folders you have two additional options:

Apply onto
> Lets you apply your special permissions to either:
> - This folder, subfolders, and files (the default)
> - This folder only
> - This folder and subfolders
> - This folder and files
> - Subfolders and files only
> - Subfolders only
> - Files only

Apply these permissions to objects and/or containers within this container only
> You have to select this checkbox if you want your selection in the "Apply onto" listbox to actually work. This is an "Are you sure?" kind of checkbox.

As in *Assign Standard Permissions to a File* earlier in this section, clearing the checkbox "Allow inheritable permissions from parent to propagate to this object" breaks the chain of permissions inheritance from the parent folder to the selected folder.

An additional option for folders appears here: "Reset permissions on all child objects and enable propagation of inheritable permissions." Selecting this checkbox removes all explicitly defined permissions on all child objects (the tree of files and subfolders within your folder) and turns on inheritance between the selected folder and the child objects within it. Only inherited permissions propagated downward from your folder will be in effect. After you confirm the action, the checkbox automatically clears itself in case you need to apply it again later.

Modify Standard Permissions on a File or Folder

> Right-click on file or folder → Properties → Security → select name → allow or deny standard permissions

For more information, see the earlier *Assign Standard Permissions to a File*.

Modify Special Permissions on a File or Folder

> Right-click on file or folder → Properties → Security → Advanced → select name → View/Edit

For more information, see the earlier *Assign Standard Permissions to a File*.

Take Ownership of a File or Folder

> Windows Explorer → right-click on a drive, file, or folder → Properties → Security → Advanced → Owner → Other Users and Groups → choose a new owner

The only users listed on the Owner tab are the currently logged-on user and the Administrators group. You must have Take Ownership permission on the file or folder to be able to take ownership of it. When you take ownership of a folder, you can optionally take ownership of all subdirectories and their files.

View Effective Permissions

New to WS2003 is a feature that allows you to view the effective NTFS permissions on a resource for a specified user or group:

> Windows Explorer → right-click on a drive, file, or folder → Properties → Security → Advanced → Effective Permissions → Select → specify user or group → view effective permissions

This feature is useful for viewing the effective permissions when users belong to several groups and these groups are assigned different permissions on a resource.

Shared-Folder Permissions

To assign shared-folder permissions, you must first be able to access the icon of the shared folder. The following procedures assume you have already used Windows Explorer or some other tool to select the shared folder with the permissions you want to assign or modify.

Assign Shared-Folder Permissions

> Right-click on shared folder → Sharing → Permissions → Add → select domain → select user or group → Add → allow or deny shared-folder permissions

Unless you allow or deny different permissions, when you assign shared-folder permissions to a user or group, the default permission that is assigned is Allow Read.

When you try to allow or deny different combinations of shared-folder permissions, you will discover that not all combinations are allowed. For example, if you try to allow Full Control, then all three checkboxes under Allow automatically become checked. Table 4-42 shows the permissible combinations of shared-folder permissions that can be assigned using the Sharing tab. These combinations work only if you are allowing permissions; if you both allow and deny permissions, other combinations are possible.

Table 4-42. Allowable combinations of shared-folder permissions

Selecting	Automatically selects		
	Full Control	Change	Read
Full Control	Yes	Yes	Yes
Change		Yes	
Read			Yes

Modify Shared-Folder Permissions

> Right-click on shared folder → Sharing → Permissions → select name → allow or deny shared-folder permissions

Permissions—Notes

NTFS Permissions

Always give users and groups just enough access to meet their needs. For example, don't assign Modify permission to a folder if you want users only to read files in the folder and not to change or delete them.

Never assign Full Control permission to folders used by ordinary users (except their home folder). Otherwise, a user might modify the permissions on the folder and cause difficulties for other users. Use Modify permission instead when you want to give the widest range of access to a folder for ordinary users. Modify will allow them to create, modify, and delete files and subfolders within the folder under consideration, which is pretty well all they will ever need to do.

If you want users to be able to do everything except delete files, assign Read & Execute and Write permissions to the folder instead of Modify.

By assigning Full Control to Creator Owner, users who create a subfolder or file within the given folder will have Full Control over that subfolder or file and will thus be able to delete it even if the Users group is assigned Read & Execute and Write permissions, as described earlier.

A suitable NTFS permission for a folder where applications will be stored is Read & Execute. Folders used to store data shared by different users should have Modify permission (or Read & Execute and Write, as described earlier). Home folders for users should be owned by users, and they should have Full Control.

Assign the Administrators group Full Control of all folders except users' home folders, to which they should have no access.

Assign permissions to groups, not users. To grant a user access to a resource, add the user to the group that has the suitable permissions.

When you copy a file or folder on an NTFS volume, you become the owner of the copy.

Denying a permission for a user takes precedence over any allowed permissions assigned to groups to which that user belongs.

You can deny all access for a user or group to a folder or file by denying Full Control permission for that user or group.

Always assign NTFS permissions to a folder first before sharing it. If you share the folder first, there is a chance someone might access the share before you have properly secured its contents.

You can also use the built-in system groups called Network and Interactive to control access to shared resources:

- Any permissions you assign to the Network group apply to all users who try to access the resource from other machines over the network.

- Any permissions you assign to the Interactive group apply to all users who try to access the resource from the local machine where the resource is located.

If a user or group has Full Control permission on a folder, the user or group can delete any files within the folder regardless of the permissions on that file.

For information on what happens to NTFS permissions on a file when you copy or move the file, see *Files and Folders* earlier in this chapter.

Don't assign special permissions unless absolutely necessary. Keep permissions simple to ease troubleshooting when things go wrong.

In the Access Control Settings dialog box, which appears when you click Advanced on the Security tab, users or groups for which some permissions are allowed while others are denied show up twice, once with a key icon (allowed permissions) and once with a lock icon (denied permissions). Also, the permissions column either displays standard file or folder permissions or the word Special when special permissions have been assigned.

You can manage NTFS permissions on a remote computer as well. Either browse My Network Places for the file or folder (if shared) or map a drive to the hidden administrative share for the remote drive on which the file or folder whose permissions you want to manage is located. Once the file or folder icon is displayed, right-click on it and select Properties → Security in the usual way.

Shared-Folder Permissions

To assign shared-folder permissions, the folder must of course be shared.

Unlike NTFS and print permissions, there are no advanced (special) shared-folder permissions you can configure.

To learn more about how to create and manage shared folders on the network, see *Shared Folders* later in this chapter.

If you do modify the default shared-folder permissions, make sure you understand how NTFS and shared-folder permissions combine.

See Also

Files and Folders, Shared Folders

Printing—Concepts

Printing terminology in Microsoft Windows can be confusing for users familiar with other operating-system platforms:

Printer
> Not a printer in the usual sense, but instead a software interface on the client machine that manages the printing process. This is sometimes called a logical printer but is usually just referred to as a printer. A printer must first be created on a client machine for that machine to be able to print documents. Printers are also used to configure print devices by specifying things like print schedule, job priority, who to notify when the job is done, which paper tray to use, which print quality to use, and so on.

Print device
> A piece of hardware that generates printed documents; in common parlance, this is called a printer.

Print server
> The computer that is actually responsible for managing the print device. The print server receives print jobs from the client machines, formats them accordingly, and passes them to the print device to generate printed output. You need a print server in order for client computers to use a printer over the network.

Printer driver
> Software installed on the print server that processes jobs received from client computers and turns them into a series of printer commands, which can be understood by the particular type of print device being used.

Print queue
> Software utility used to view print jobs waiting to be printed by a particular print device.

Local Versus Network Printers

WS2003 supports the same two kinds of print devices that were supported by earlier versions of Microsoft Windows:

Local print device
> A printer directly connected to the print server using a serial, parallel, USB, or other physical port on a print server.

Network-interface print device
> A printer directly connected to the network using its own network card. The print server manages the print device but is not directly connected to it.

Windows Printing Terminology

Windows printing terminology can be confusing. A local print device is a print device that is connected directly to a print server, usually by a parallel cable. A local printer, however, is a software interface that is installed on a print server and can manage either a local or network interface print device.

In the same vein, a network print device is a print device that is connected directly to the network. A network printer, however, is a software interface that is installed on a client computer to enable it to send print jobs to the print server.

In other words, you need to create two printers able to print over the network:

1. First create a local printer on the print server to manage the print device (which may be either the local or network interface type). Make sure the local printer is shared so it can be seen by client machines on the network.

2. Now create a network printer on each client computer to which the user actually prints from the running application. The process of creating a network printer on the client makes a connection between the printer installed on the client computer and the printer installed on the print server.

When you add a printer and share it over a WS2003 domain-based network, the information about the printer is automatically published in Active Directory. Make sure you take the time to enter information into the Location and Comments fields when you run the Add Printer Wizard, since this information is also published in Active Directory and can be utilized when searching for specific printers on the network.

Network Printing Process

The basic process of printing over the network is:

1. The user clicks the Print button on an application or performs some other action to print a document.

2. The printer driver on the client computer creates a print job by rendering the document into a series of printer commands, and then it spools (temporarily stores) the job for printing. By default, on WS2003, the document is only partially rendered at this point, resulting in an enhanced metafile format (EMF) file. EMF

is a kind of universal printer-command format. Typically, non-Windows clients fully render the document into a RAW file consisting of actual machine-specific printer commands. EMF can be disabled in WS2003 to use RAW instead, but EMF is preferred because a spooled EMF job typically occupies less disk space than a similar RAW one.

3. The client computer forms a connection with the appropriate print server using remote procedure calls (RPCs) and then forwards the job to the print server.

4. The print server receives the job and spools it for further processing and until a print device becomes available.

5. The print provider (software on the print server) finishes processing the job by converting it from EMF into RAW format (if necessary).

6. When a print device becomes available, the job is despooled to the appropriate print monitor (more software on the print server), which then forwards the rendered document to the print device, which finally turns it into a printed document.

Printer Permissions

To manage user access to printers attached to the local computer or connected to the network, you assign printer permissions. These permissions can also be used to specify who is allowed to manage printers and their documents. There are three levels of printer permissions:

Print
> Assigns ordinary users permissions for connecting to printers, printing documents, and managing their own documents

Manage Documents
> Delegates the job of managing all documents to users with limited administrative privileges

Manage Printers
> Provides complete administrative control over all aspects of printers and the printing process

Table 4-43 gives more detail concerning the specific privileges conveyed by each of the previous three types of printer permissions. These permissions can be assigned to both users and groups, but assigning them to groups is preferred since it reduces the amount of administration needed. Note that printer permissions are effective only when the printer is shared for use over the network.

Table 4-43. Printer permissions

Printing task	Printer permission		
	Print?	Manage Documents?	Manage Printers?
Connect to a printer	Yes	Yes	Yes
Print a document	Yes	—	Yes
Pause, resume, restart—or cancel your own document	Yes	Yes	Yes
Manage job settings for all documents	—	Yes	Yes
Pause, resume, restart, or cancel any user's documents	—	Yes	Yes
Cancel all documents	—	Yes	Yes

Table 4-43. Printer permissions (continued)

Printing task	Printer permission		
	Print?	Manage Documents?	Manage Printers?
Pause or resume a printer	—	—	Yes
Take a printer offline	—	—	Yes
Share a printer	—	—	Yes
Delete a printer	—	—	Yes
Modify the properties of a printer	—	—	Yes
Change the printer permissions	—	—	Yes

Default Printer Permissions

The printer permissions assigned by default to a newly created printer are shown in Table 4-44. In order to modify these permissions, you must either be the owner of the printer or have the Manage Printers permission.

Table 4-44. Default printer permissions

Group	Default printer permission
Administrators	Manage Printers
Print Operators	Manage Printers
Server Operators	Manage Printers
Creator Owner	Manage Documents
Everyone	Print

Advanced Printer Permissions

The three basic printer permissions described previously are actually comprised of combinations of six advanced printer permissions, as shown in Table 4-45. This is a bit confusing since three of these advanced permissions have the same names as the basic printer permissions. Advanced permissions can be applied either to:

* This printer only
* Documents only
* This printer and documents

Advanced printer permissions can also be selectively modified to provide a group of users with special (custom) printer permissions, if desired. However, it is highly unlikely that you will need (or want) to do this.

Table 4-45. Advanced printer permissions

Advanced printer permissions	Basic printer permissions		
	Print?	Manage Documents?	Manage Printers?
Print	Yes	—	Yes
Manage Printers	—	—	Yes
Manage Documents	—	Yes	—
Read Permissions	Yes	Yes	Yes
Change Permissions	—	Yes	Yes
Take Ownership	—	Yes	Yes

Planning Printer Permissions

Like access to any other shared resource, access to print devices is controlled by assigning permissions to groups and users. The best way of doing this is to:

1. Create a domain local group for a print device. Give the group a recognizable name such as HP5L Users (using the type or model of the device) or Barney Users (if you give your printers friendly names).

2. Assign the local group Print permission.

3. Put global groups into the local group to give users access to the printer.

Also, be sure to assign suitable permissions to Administrators or Print Operators so they can manage the device and its print queues.

Printing—Tasks

Printers can be administered three ways:

- Use the Printers folder, which can be accessed on the local machine by Start → Printers and Faxes. New printers can be created in this folder using Add Printer, while existing ones can be administered by right-clicking on the printer icon. If you aren't physically located at the print server, don't despair: as long as you are logged on with Administrator credentials (or as a user with Manage Printers permission for the printers on your network), you can manage shared printers on remote print servers located anywhere on your network. First, find the printer using any of the methods outlined under *Find a Printer* later in this section, and then right-click on its icon to select a task or open its properties sheet.

- Use a web browser running on any computer. The functionality is more limited than using the Printers folder and uses a web-based interface instead of dialog boxes.

- Use the command line (very limited administrative capability this way).

While administering printers using the Printers folder is the faster and most familiar method, administration using a web browser has some advantages:

- Printers can be managed from any computer on the network regardless of which operating system it is running, as long as it is running a web browser.

- The web pages displayed can be printed out to generate reports that display the status of print devices managed by a given print server or display the contents of a printer queue.

- The web interface can be customized by creating additional HTML pages to display information such as a floor plan indicating where print devices and print servers are located.

But the disadvantages are:

- Only a few printer settings are displayed, and none of them can be modified. This will probably be corrected later in a service pack.

- Like most web interfaces, more mouse work is generally required to accomplish a task than by using the standard Windows dialog boxes and shortcut menus.

To install and configure a printer, you need to be a member of the Administrators group. To administer a printer, you need to have either Manage Printers or Manage

Documents permission for that printer, depending on the kind of administration you want to perform.

You can also control printer administration through the use of Group Policies. These policies can be used to do the following:

- Modify the default behavior of the Add Printer Wizard
- Prevent new printers from being published by default in Active Directory
- Disable web-based management of printers and Internet printing

For more information, see *Group Policy* earlier in this chapter. If you can't perform some administrative task involving printers, there may be a Group Policy defined to prevent you from doing so.

Add a Printer

Start → Printers and Faxes → Add Printer

This opens the Add Printer Wizard, which can be used to either:

- Install printer software directly on a print server. Microsoft calls this "installing a printer."
- Install printer software on a client computer. Microsoft calls this "making a printer connection."

In addition, when installing a printer on a print server, you can choose which of the following to install:

- A local print device, which is directly attached to the server using a serial, parallel, or USB cable
- A network interface print device, which is directly connected to a TCP/IP network using a network card installed in the printer

Install a Printer for a Local Print Device

Make sure the print device is attached to the print server and is turned on in case it is Plug and Play. Start the Add Printer Wizard, select "Local printer," then follow the steps that involve selecting a port to which the print device is attached (usually LPT1), selecting the manufacturer and model, specifying the name of the printer, and so on. Make sure you share the printer if you plan to allow client machines to connect to it and print from over the network.

Install a Printer for a Network Interface Print Device

Make sure the print device is connected to the network and is turned on. Start the Add Printer Wizard on the print server and select "Local printer" (clear the Plug and Play checkbox). On the Select the Printer Port page of the wizard, select Create a new port → Standard TCP/IP Port. This opens another wizard called Add Standard TCP/IP Printer Port. Specify the IP address of the print device (a port name is generated automatically from this information) and the type of network card the print device uses (try Generic if you're not sure). Clicking Finish closes this wizard and returns to the previous one, which you must then complete as in the previous section.

Connect to a Remote Printer

There are lots of ways you can connect a client computer to a shared printer that is managed by a remote print server (i.e., create a network printer on a client computer that lets users submit jobs to the print server). Once you have connected to the printer, you can print to it as if it was physically connected to your client computer. Once your

WS2003 Professional client computer connects to the remote print server, it automatically downloads the necessary printer driver files to create the connection.

You can connect to a remote printer in several ways. On the client computer:

Start → Printers and Faxes → Add Printer → Network printer

Then specify the remote printer you want to connect to by either locating it in Active Directory, browsing for it on the network, typing its name, or specifying its URL:

Start → Search → Other search options → Printers, computers, or people → Printers on the network → enter search criteria → Find Now → select desired printer → right-click → Connect

Open the Active Directory Users and Computers console and:

Right-click on a domain → Find → Find Printers → enter search criteria → Find Now → select desired printer → right-click → Connect

You can also do:

Start → Run → **http://*printservername*/printers** → OK → click on Printer link → Connect

Start → Run → **http://*printservername*/printer/printersharename/printer/** → Connect

where *printservername* is the DNS name of the remote print server. This lets you connect to printers over the Internet, provided you have appropriate permissions on that printer and the remote print server is running Internet Information Services (IIS).

You can also find the remote printer in Windows Explorer, right-click on it, and select Connect from the shortcut menu.

Finally, you can find the remote printer in Windows Explorer, and drag its icon into the Printers window.

Configure Clients for Printing

The configuration needed on client computers depends on the operating system installed on them:

WS2003/2000/XP/Me/98/95 clients

No client configuration is necessary. The first time the client computer makes a connection to the shared printer, it automatically downloads the appropriate printer driver (provided you have made this driver available on the print server).

NT/3.x and MS-DOS clients

First, you need to manually install the printer driver on the client computer.

Macintosh clients

Services for Macintosh must be installed and configured.

Unix clients

TCP/IP Printing (LPD) must be installed and configured.

NetWare clients

File and Print Services for NetWare must be installed and configured. (This must be obtained separately.)

Configure Properties for a Printer

Start → Printers and Faxes → right-click on printer → Properties

This opens the printer's properties sheet to allow you to configure various printer settings. The following are the most popular settings configured by administrators.

- Setting priorities between printers for different groups of users
- Creating a printer pool to handle increased load
- Sharing an additional printer to handle increased load

Let's look at some highlights from the various tabs. Note that some printers may have additional device-specific tabs. For example, a color printer will have an additional tab called Color Management. Other tabs may be supplied by the vendor's printer driver.

General

Printing preferences set on print servers will be default settings for all users. Users can override these settings by opening their own *Printers* folders, right-clicking on a printer icon, and selecting Printing Preferences. Assigning a location to a printer helps users find it in Active Directory.

Sharing

See *Share a Printer* later in this section.

Ports

This lets you specify and configure the port to which the print device is attached. To redirect a printer to a different port or device, see *Redirect a Printer* later in this section. To add a TCP/IP port for a network interface print device, see *Add a Printer* earlier in this section.

Printer pooling lets you connect one logical printer to multiple physical print devices. Jobs that are sent to the printer are then distributed between the different print devices according to availability. This might be an option if your users make heavy demands on an existing printer and are frequently standing in line to pick up jobs. To make use of printer pooling, you must ensure that all printers in the pool use the same printer driver. (The best is to use identical print devices, but similar devices that use the same driver are acceptable.) To enable printer pooling, check the "Enable printer pooling" checkbox and select the ports to which the print devices are attached.

Advanced

If several printers send jobs to the same print device, you can control what happens by specifying the printer priority and available print times for each printer. Priorities range from 1 (lowest) to 99 (highest), and jobs from printers with higher priority are printed first. To assign different printer priorities to two different groups of users, you must create a printer for each group, assign a priority to each printer, set permissions so each group can use only one of the printers, and then instruct each group concerning which printer to use.

Spooling documents returns control to the application sooner than printing directly to the printer, but you must ensure you have adequate disk space for the spooling process. Mismatched documents occur, for example, when a letter-size document is being printed to a device whose only tray contains legal-size paper. Keeping printed documents causes them to remain in the queue so they can be resubmitted, but this can use up disk space quickly (if you have this feature enabled, disabling it will purge the print queue). Enabling the advanced printing feature is recommended unless printing problems occur relating to page order, pages per sheet, or other advanced features.

Clicking the New Driver button starts the Add New Printer Driver Wizard, which lets you install new or updated printer drivers for your print device. Note that this is not the same as the Additional Drivers button on the Sharing tab, which lets you install drivers for clients running other versions of Windows. You can also update printer drivers over the Internet by using Windows Update (Start → Windows Update). Whatever way you do it, you need to be a member of the Administrators group to update a driver.

A separator page is a file that contains printer commands and is used to switch between different printing modes—for example, from PostScript to PCL—and to separate print jobs with a printed page identifying the document being printed. Table 4-46 lists the different types of separator pages available. Note that some printers can automatically detect which language a print job uses and switch modes accordingly.

Table 4-46. Separator pages

File	Function
Pcl.sep	Switch an HP print device to PCL mode. A page is printed before each document
Pscript.sep	Switch an HP print device to PostScript mode. A page is not printed before each document
Sysprint.sep	Used with PostScript print devices to print a page before each document
Sysprtj.sep	Same as *Sysprint.sep* but uses Japanese characters

In order to use the Printing Defaults button to set default choices for page orientation, default printer tray, number of copies, and other settings, you must have Manage Printers permission. However, users who have Print permission can override these default settings and configure their own personal printing settings by:

Start → Printers and Faxes → right-click on printer → Printing Preferences

Security
See *Assign Printer Permissions* later in this section.

Device Settings
A form is a paper size such as letter, legal, A4, envelope#10, and so on. If your printer has multiple trays, you can assign a form to a particular tray or let WS2003 automatically detect the paper tray for each form.

Find a Printer
To administer a printer, you first need to find it. Information about shared printers is stored in Active Directory and can be found by opening the Active Directory Users and Computers console, right-clicking on the OU or domain in which the printer is located (if known), and then:

Find → Find Printers → specify search criteria → Find Now

You can also find a printer simply by browsing My Network Places until you locate the remote print server managing the desired printer. Once you have found the appropriate server, double-click on its icon to see the shared printers on the server. Don't stop here, however, as opening the properties sheet for one of these shared-printer icons gives only minimal information. Instead, you need to double-click on the *Printers* folder that is displayed for the remote print server you are viewing, and then right-click on a printer icon to administer it or open its properties sheet.

GUI Reference

Once you've found the *Printers* folder on a remote print server in My Network Places, simply drag this folder into your own local *Printers* folder to provide a quick way of finding and administering remote printers on your network.

Pause a Printer

Start → Settings → Printers → right-click on printer → Pause Printing

Pause a printer if there is a problem with the device, such as a paper jam. Pausing a printer doesn't delete jobs pending in the queue. To resume or restart printing after you have fixed the problem, repeat the steps listed earlier.

Taking a printer offline also pauses printing. See *Use a Printer Offline* later in this section.

Redirect a Printer

If a print device fails, you can redirect the pending jobs to a different print device as long as the new printer uses the same printer driver as the current one. You can even redirect jobs to a print device managed by a different print server than the one you normally use. To do this, open the properties sheet for the printer and:

Ports tab → Add Port → Local Port → New Port → *printservername*\ *printsharename*

If the new print device is managed by the same print server as the current one, redirecting jobs is easier: just change the port selected to the port used by the new printer.

Share a Printer

WS2003 shares printers by default when you create them (XP Professional doesn't), but if you decided not to share the printer when you created it, you can share it later:

Start → Printers and Faxes → Printers → right-click on printer → Sharing → Shared As → specify share name

If your shared printer will be used not just by XP Professional client machines but also by client machines running legacy versions of Microsoft Windows (NT 3.1/3.51/4.0 or Windows 95/98), you will need to install additional drivers for these legacy operating systems on your shared printer. To do this, use the Additional Drivers button on the Sharing tab. The WS2003 CD includes printer drivers for WS2003, W2K, NT 4.0, XP, Windows 98, and Windows 95.

Select the List in the Directory checkbox if you want to publish the printer in Active Directory (which is what you probably want to do). This makes it easier for users to find specific printers on the network. You can't publish a printer unless it has been shared first.

If you are running a mixed-mode network with some computers running legacy versions of Microsoft Windows, you can publish information about non-WS2003 shared printers in Active Directory so that clients can search for them. To do this, open the Active Directory Users and Computers console, right-click the OU or other container in which you want to publish the printer, and proceed as follows:

New → Printer → enter UNC path to printer

There is also a sample script, *Winnt\System32\pubprn.vbs*, which shows how to use the Windows Scripting Host to publish non-WS2003 printers from the command line.

You can also stop sharing a printer. Be sure to notify users, however, so that their jobs aren't lost.

How printer drivers are updated on the client depends on the particular Windows client operating system being used:

- Every time an XP Professional or NT 4.0 Workstation client connects to the WS2003 print server to print a document, it checks to make sure that it has the latest version of the driver. If the server has a newer driver, the client automatically downloads and installs it.

- NT 3.51 Workstation clients check for new drivers on the server only when the local spooler service on the client is restarted (typically when the machine is rebooted).

- Windows 95 and Windows 98 clients can't automatically download new drivers from the server; you must install these drivers manually on the clients.

Take Ownership of a Printer

Start → Printers and Faxes → right-click on a printer → Properties → Security → Advanced → Owner → choose a new owner

The only users listed on the Owner tab are the currently logged-on user and the Administrators group. You must have Manage Printers permission on a printer to be able to take ownership of it. This permission is granted by default to Administrators, Print Operators, Server Operators, and Power Users.

Use a Printer Offline

Start → Printers and Faxes → right-click on printer → Use Printer Offline

This is similar to pausing a printer except that pending jobs remain in the print queue even if you shut down and restart the print server.

Assign Printer Permissions

Printer permissions are a means for controlling the level of access to shared printers on a WS2003 network. Printers must be shared on the network for printer permissions to be assigned to them. To assign printer permissions, you must first be able to access the icon of the shared printer. You can do this using Windows Explorer, My Network Places, or from the Search Results of the Search Assistant accessed through Start → Search → For Printers. The following procedures assume you have already located the icon for the shared printer whose permissions you want to assign or modify.

Assign Standard Printer Permissions

Right-click on shared printer → Properties → Security → Add → select domain → select user or group → Add → allow or deny printer permissions

Unless you allow or deny different permissions, when you assign printer permissions to a user or group, the default permission assigned is Allow Print.

When you try to allow or deny different combinations of printer permissions, you will discover that not all combinations are allowed. For example, if you try to allow Manage Printers, the Print checkbox under Allow also automatically becomes checked. Table 4-47 shows the permissible combinations of printer permissions that can be assigned using the Security tab. These combinations work only if you are allowing permissions; if you both allow and deny permissions, other combinations are possible.

Table 4-47. Allowable combinations of printer permissions

Selecting	Automatically selects		
	Print?	Manage Printers?	Manage Documents?
Print	Yes	—	—
Manage Printers	Yes	Yes	—
Manage Documents	—	—	Yes

Assign Special Print Permissions

> Right-click on shared printer → Properties → Security → Advanced → Add → select domain → select user or group → allow or deny special permissions

Like assigning standard print permissions, assigning a special printer permission by selecting one checkbox may cause others to magically become selected or deselected as well (i.e., not all combinations of special print permissions are possible). Furthermore, you can't allow and deny a permission at the same time.

You also have the option of applying your special permissions to:

- This printer and documents (the default)
- This printer only
- Documents only

Modify Standard Printer Permissions

> Right-click on shared printer → Properties → Security → select name → allow or deny printer permissions

For more information, see the previous section.

Modify Special Printer Permissions

> Right-click on shared printer → Properties → Security → Advanced → select name → View/Edit

For more information, see the earlier *Assign Special Print Permissions*.

Manage a Print Queue

To open a print queue for a given printer, do the following:

> Start → Printers and Faxes → double-click on the printer icon

Once the print queue window is open, you can manage documents pending for that printer. Select a document in the queue, then use the Documents menu to pause, resume, cancel, or restart a job. You might pause a document if there is a problem printing it (e.g., margins too small), while you pause the printer itself if a problem such as a paper jam occurs. Resuming a paused document starts printing it from where it left off, while restarting a paused document prints the entire document again from the beginning. You can also drag jobs to change their print order, depending on your permissions and whose jobs are in the queue.

Documents → Properties lets you specify a print priority and printing schedule for the selected job. This overrides the settings on the Advanced tab of the printer's properties sheet, which specifies the default priority and schedule for all jobs printed using that printer. You can also specify a logon name to indicate which user will be notified when the job is done (the logon name of the user who submitted the job is entered by default). Also, make sure that notifications are enabled on the print server.

Configure a Print Server

Start → Printers and Faxes → File → Server Properties

This opens the Printer Server Properties box. Here are some highlights of the various tabs.

Forms

In addition to displaying available forms for the device, you can create new ones by specifying the paper size. Be sure to save your form definition if you want to use it again.

Ports

Similar to the Ports tab on the properties sheet for a printer, but this lets you only create and configure ports, not assign them to a specific printer. The information shown in the three columns of the listbox here are:

Port
> The name of the available port

Description
> The port monitor associated with the port

Printer
> The printers that use the port

The types of ports you can add are as follows:

Local port
> Typically used to add a new local port when you want to redirect the jobs pending in the printer's queue to another print device. See *Redirect a Printer* earlier in this chapter for more information. We describe the types of local ports you can create later in this section.

Standard TCP/IP port
> Used for network interface print devices that have their own built-in Ethernet card.

LPR port
> Used for printers managed by Unix print servers. You must first install Print Services for Unix on the WS2003 computer before you can create an LPR port, and you must know the full DNS name or IP address of the network interface print device or the Unix server running LPD to which it is connected. See the sidebar "Print Services for Unix" for more information.

Hewlett-Packard network port
> Used for older HP network interface print devices with JetDirect cards that use DLC instead of TCP/IP. You must install the DLC protocol on the WS2003 computer before you can create a Hewlett-Packard network port.

AppleTalk printing device port
> Used for printing from Macintosh clients. You must install the AppleTalk protocol on the WS2003 computer before you can create an AppleTalk printing device port.

You can also add new ports when running the Add Printer Wizard.

You can create three kinds of local ports on a WS2003 print server as discussed in the following list.

A filename

> (e.g., *C:\path\filename*). Any job sent to this port is written to the specified file, overwriting previous ones (this is essentially printing to a file).

A shared printer

> (e.g., *\\printserver\printer*). Any job sent to this port is handled by the specified remote printer (this is essentially redirecting a printer).

NUL

> This sends jobs to never-never land. It's used mainly for testing purposes.

 Parallel and serial ports are also local ports, but WS2003 generally detects this hardware automatically.

Print Services for Unix

This WS2003 component provides line printer remote (LPR) and line printer daemon (LPD) services to allow cross-platform printing between Unix and WS2003. LPR is the client-side Unix printing utility that enables a user to send a job to a Unix print server running LPD. In WS2003, the two new services provided by Print Services for Unix are:

LPRMON

> Enables WS2003 print servers to send print jobs to Unix print servers running LPD. In other words, LPRMON enables Windows clients to print to Unix printers via the WS2003 print server running LPRMON.

LPDSVC

> Emulates LPD on WS2003 print servers. In other words, LPDSVC enables Unix clients to send print jobs to the WS2003 print server running LPDSVC.

Note that once you install these services, you must change the startup configuration of LPDSVC from Manual to Automatic. Use Services in the Computer Management console to do this.

Note also that not all Unix systems use the same LPR specification, so establishing printing interoperability between WS2003 and Unix platforms can sometimes be problematic.

Drivers

This lists the various printer drivers installed on the server. If a printer driver somehow becomes corrupt, you can update (reinstall) it here by clicking Add to start the Add New Printer Driver Wizard. You can also use this wizard to add (install) drivers for legacy Windows clients such as NT, 98, or 95.

Select an installed driver and click Properties to list the various files that make up the printer driver and see where they are stored on the server.

You can also install printer drivers from the Sharing tab of each printer's properties sheet. The main advantage of doing this here on the Drivers tab of Server Properties is that if your print server is used to manage multiple print devices of the same type, you can update drivers for these in one step.

Advanced

This lets you specify the location where jobs will be spooled. This is useful if your current drive is filling up and you want to move the spool folder to a different drive. Make sure you stop the spooler service prior to moving the spool folder, and restart the spooler service or reboot the server afterward. Use the Services node in Computer Management to stop and start the spooler service.

Don't locate the spool folder on the *%SystemRoot%* volume—that is, the volume where the *\Windows* folder is located (typically the *C:* drive). If users print lots of long jobs, it could fill up all available space on the drive and cause the system to hang.

By default, spooler events are logged to the System log in Event Viewer. You may want to turn off information events to reduce the amount of noise in the log. If you make changes to these settings, you must stop and restart the spooler service.

You can specify that notifications be sent when printing jobs are finished. These notifications can be sent to either the users or the computers submitting the jobs. If notifications are sent to computers and the user who submitted the job has logged off her client machine, the next user who logs on to the machine will receive the notification. So you should generally specify that users instead of computers be notified if roaming user profiles are configured on the network. Again, be sure to stop and restart the spooler service after changing this setting.

Printing—Notes

Printers

You can create multiple printers for a given print device. One reason for doing so is if you have two different groups with different needs and privileges who are using the same print device. Different permissions, print priority, print times, and so on may be assigned to each group. For example, managers may be allowed to print documents at any time with top priority, while the large jobs submitted by accounts have low priority and can be run only at night.

When viewing a print queue using a web browser, the page is automatically refreshed when jobs enter or leave the queue.

If a printer is added and then deleted from a print server, the printer driver is not deleted from the hard disk. If you then reinstall the printer, you have the option of either keeping the existing driver or replacing it with a new one. This can be useful for troubleshooting problems associated with printer drivers.

When adding a printer, keep the printer name short (no more than 31 characters) to ensure legacy applications will be able to print to it.

If you can't find a printer using the Find Printers box, you may have deselected the List in the Directory checkbox on the Sharing tab of the printer's properties sheet.

Many of the options available when you right-click on a printer icon in the Printers folder are also available from:

- The File menu of the Printers window when the desired printer is selected in that window
- The Printer menu of the print-queue window for the selected printer

You can't redirect selected jobs to a different print device; you can redirect only all jobs.

When enabling printer pooling for print devices having different speeds, add the port for the fastest print device first, since this will be the default device to which jobs are sent when all devices in the pool are idle.

If you configure a printer's port as File, jobs will be printed to a file on the client machine, and users will be prompted for a filename.

If you do use printer pooling, make sure the pooled devices are physically near each other, not on different floors—unless you want to give your users lots of exercise climbing stairs!

Using separator pages can be a good idea if you have multiple users printing to the same print device. These pages help users identify their jobs and can decrease the crowd around the device.

Selecting View → Details in the Printers window allows you to quickly see the status of all printers managed by the print server.

To pause or resume a printer, take a printer offline, share a printer, or perform many other common administrative tasks involving printers, you need Manage Printers permission.

The standard port monitor, which connects a WS2003 printer to a TCP/IP network interface print device, is a big improvement over the old LPRMON print monitor of NT. LPRMON must still be used, however, for printing to print devices connected to Unix print servers.

The Performance console (which replaces the NT tool called System Monitor) includes a Print Queue object, which can be used for remote monitoring of print queues, as well as giving administrators useful statistics about job errors, cumulative pages printed, and so on.

If printing fails because a job becomes stuck in the print spooler, you can try stopping and restarting the print spooler. If printing still fails, stop the spooler again and manually delete the print job from the spooler folder, then restart the spooler. To stop or restart the spooler you can open the Computer Management console and select Services and Information → Services → Print Spooler → Action → Start or Stop. Alternatively, you can open a command prompt and type **net stop spooler** or **net start spooler**. Stopping the print spooler may stop other services such as the Fax Service, which will need to be restarted afterward.

The document currently being printed can't be redirected.

When accessing a printer using a web browser to print over the Internet, WS2003 first tries to connect to the remote printer using RPCs (in case it is on the local LAN or intranet). If this fails, it uses the Internet Printing Protocol (IPP), which is encapsulated by HTTP. Either way, the end result is transparent to the user printing the document.

USB, IEEE 1394, and IR print devices are automatically detected by WS2003 when you connect them to the appropriate port on the computer. The Found New Hardware Wizard is then invoked to walk you through the process. You need to use Add Printer in the Printers folder only when your print device is not detected by the operating system. Ports for these devices aren't listed on the Ports tab unless the device is already installed.

Parallel-port print devices aren't automatically detected when you attach them to an LPT port on a WS2003 computer. However, when you run the Add Printer Wizard, make sure that "Automatically detect my printer" is selected, which should successfully detect and help install most modern, bidirectional, parallel-port print devices.

Printer Permissions

Printer permissions may be allowed or denied, and denied permissions override allowed ones. For example, if you deny Print permission to Everyone, then no one will be able to print to the printer.

All users are allowed to print by default, since Print permission is assigned to Everyone. You may want to remove this permission and assign Print permission to the Users group instead, so that only authorized users who have logged on to the network are allowed to connect to the printer and print to it.

Alternatively, you may want to limit access to some printers to specific groups of users. For example, you could grant Print permission to use the color laser printer to the Managers group only.

Printer permissions are most important with print devices used to print sensitive business information, such as payroll checks. Make sure you restrict permissions accordingly for such devices, and be sure to locate them in secure areas as well.

Users with Manage·Documents permission don't have the privilege of printing documents unless they are also explicitly given Print permission. Users with Manage Printers permission do, however, also have the privilege of printing documents.

If you have Macintosh clients on your network and Print Services for Macintosh is installed on your print server, these clients can print without restriction. In other words, there is no control of printer access for Macintosh clients.

Inheritance is not an issue with printer permissions.

Don't assign special permissions unless absolutely necessary. Keep permissions simple to ease troubleshooting when things go wrong.

Print Queues

The Printer menu is similar to what you get when you right-click on the printer icon within the Printers folder.

You can also right-click on a printer icon within the Printers folder if you want to pause or resume a printer instead of just a particular document or if you want to cancel all documents pending for a printer.

If you cancel all documents for a printer, the job currently printing will finish.

If you are an ordinary user, you will be able to manage only your own jobs within the print queue, not those of other users.

You need at least the Manage Documents printer permission if you want to configure priority, schedule, and notifications for all documents sent to the printer.

Double-clicking on a job in the queue also opens the properties for that document.

GUI Reference

If the spooler folder is located on an NTFS volume, make sure Change permission is assigned to the Users group. Otherwise, they won't be able to print.

To delete a form you created, you must first deselect Create a New Form.

See Also

lpq, lpr, net print, *Permissions*, prncnfg, prndrvr, prnjobs, prnmngr, prnqctl

Recovery Console—Concepts

The Recovery Console is a command-line tool that can be used to repair WS2003 systems that won't start properly. The Recovery Console should generally be used when the following steps have failed to resolve the problem:

- Last Known Good Configuration
- Safe Mode

Using the Recovery Console, you can perform system recovery tasks such as:

- Copy files from the WS2003 product CD to your hard drive to replace missing or corrupt system files
- Enable or disable device drivers or services that are preventing Windows from starting properly
- Create a new master boot record (MBR) or boot sector when existing ones are corrupt
- Access FAT or NTFS drives from the command line to move, copy, or delete files
- Create new partitions and format them using FAT or NTFS

The commands supported by the Recovery Console are:

attrib, batch, bootcfg, cd, chdir, chkdsk, cls, copy, del, delete, dir, disable, diskpart, enable, exit, expand, fixboot, fixmbr, format, help, listsvc, logon, map, md, mkdir, more, rd, ren, rename, rmdir, systemroot, type

Recovery Console—Tasks

Install the Recovery Console

You can install the Recovery Console on a system that already has WS2003 installed:

Insert product CD → Start → Run → **D:\i386\winnt32.exe /cmdcons** → follow prompts

Here, *D:* represents the CD-ROM drive. Installing the Recovery Console this way will add a line to the *boot.ini* file and display the Recovery Console as an option in the boot menu.

Run the Recovery Console from Product CD

If you haven't previously installed the Recovery Console and suddenly need it to troubleshoot a system that won't boot, do this:

Insert product CD → reboot → boot from CD-ROM → Enter → **R** → specify the number of the Windows installation you want to log on to (usually 1, except on multiboot systems) → Enter → specify Administrator password → Enter

This takes you to the command prompt with *C:\Windows* as your current directory. Type **help** to see which commands are available in the Recovery Console.

Remove the Recovery Console

To remove the Recovery Console from a system on which it was installed:

> Windows Explorer → Tools → Folder Options → View → Show hidden files and folders → deselect Hide protected operating system files → OK → select *C:* drive → delete *Cdmons* folder → delete *Cmldr* file → right-click on *C:\boot.ini* → Properties → clear Read-only attribute → OK → open *boot.ini* in Notepad → delete entry for Recovery Console → File → Save → Exit → right-click on *C:\boot.ini* → Properties → set Read-only attribute → OK

Recovery Console—Notes

You can't use winnt32 /cmdcons to install the Recovery Console if your system partition is mirrored.

The Administrator password used for the Recovery Console is the same one used for Directory Service Restore Mode and is stored in the SAM in the registry on the local machine. On domain controllers, however, this password may be different from the Administrator password stored in Active Directory. To change the Recovery Console password, you can press F8 during startup to enter Directory Service Restore Mode, log on, use Local Users and Groups to change the password, and reboot. (See *Advanced Options Menu* earlier in this chapter for more information.) You can also change the Recovery Console password using the *ntdsutil* utility while booted in normal mode.

See Also

Advanced Options Menu, attrib, chkdsk, diskpart, expand, format

Remote Desktop—Concepts

Remote Desktop in WS2003 is an enhanced version of Terminal Services in Remote Administration mode, one of two modes for running Terminal Services in W2K Server (the other being Application Server mode). Remote Desktop allows administrators to remotely connect to a WS2003 computer and perform administrative tasks as if they were sitting at the computer's console. While Terminal Services in W2K was an optional component, in WS2003 the Remote Desktop feature is installed (but not enabled) by default.

Remote Desktop Components

Several components work together to provide Remote Desktop functionality:

Remote Desktop for Administration
> This is the proper name of the server-side component of Remote Desktop and corresponds to the Terminal Services in the Remote Administration mode component of W2K Server. Remote Desktop for Administration supports two concurrent connections with Terminal Services clients and is intended mainly for remotely administering WS2003 computers.

Remote Desktop Connection
> This is the client-side component of Remote Desktop and replaces the Terminal Services Client in downlevel Windows platforms. Remote Desktop Connection software is available for all versions of Microsoft Windows to enable remote administration of servers from downlevel clients.

Remote Desktop Web Connection
> This is an ActiveX control that can be downloaded and installed in Internet Explorer to turn the browser into a web-based Terminal Services client. Using Remote Desktop Web Connection, an administrator can remotely manage WS2003 machines over the Internet—for example, from an Internet cafe in Siberia.

> Another feature of WS2003 is Remote Assistance, which allows remote users to connect to the server when specifically invited to do so. Once connected, the remote user can view the display, chat, and even mirror the mouse and keyboard if allowed. Remote Assistance is a good tool for support personnel as it allows them to take over a remote machine to troubleshoot issues.

Remote Desktop—Tasks

Add a User to Remote Desktop Users Group

You can grant users the rights necessary for them to log on to WS2003 machines using Remote Desktop in two ways:

Add them to the Administrators group
> This is not recommended as administrators have powerful rights, and membership in this group should therefore be restricted as much as possible.

Add them to the Remote Desktop Users group
> This is the preferred method of granting users the right to remotely manage servers on which Remote Connections has been enabled.

You can add users to the Remote Desktop Users group using Local Users and Groups in Computer Management, or you can do the following:

> Control Panel → System → Remote → Select Remote Users → Add → select user or group

Enable Remote Connections

> Control Panel → System → Remote → select Allow users to connect remotely to your computer

Your server can now be remotely managed using Remote Desktop.

Install Remote Desktop Connection

Remote Desktop Connection is included in WS2003 and XP but needs to be installed in downlevel Windows platforms. Here are two ways to install a Terminal Services Client on a downlevel Windows machine:

From the Internet
> Visit *www.microsoft.com/downloads* → search for Remote Desktop Connection Software → download and install appropriate client for your platform

From a shared folder on a WS2003 file server
> First, log on to the file server and create a *Tsclient* share:
>> Windows Explorer → right-click on *\System32\Clients\Tsclient* folder → Sharing and Security → Sharing → Share this folder
> Then log on to the downlevel Windows machine and do the following:
>> Start → Run → ***fileserver*\Tsclient\Win32\Setup.exe** → follow prompts

Connect Using Remote Desktop Connection

From a WS2003 or XP machine
> Start → All Programs → Accessories → Communications → Remote Desktop Connection → specify IP address or DNS name of server on which Remote Desktop for Administration has been enabled → Connect

From a downlevel Windows machine
> Install the appropriate Terminal Services Client → continue as above

Configure Remote Desktop Connection

> Start → All Programs → Accessories → Communications → Remote Desktop Connection → Options → specify remote computer → specify credentials → specify display settings → enable access to keyboard, sound, disks, printers, and ports → optimize experience for best performance → save connection settings in My Documents as *.rdp* file for later use

Disconnect Without Terminating a Remote Session

> Remote Desktop Connection window → Start → Shut Down → Disconnect

Alternatively, simply click the close gadget on the Remote Desktop Connection window. The next time you connect to the remote computer, you will be reconnected to your session.

Terminate a Remote Session

> Remote Desktop Connection window → Start → Shut Down → Log Off

Install Remote Desktop Web Connection

Do the following on a WS2003 machine on which IIS has been installed:

> Control Panel → Add or Remote Programs → Add/Remote Windows Components → Application Server → Details → Internet Information Services → Details → World Wide Web Service → Details → Remote Desktop Web Connection

The ActiveX control for Remote Desktop Web Connection is now installed on the web server. To install the control on the client, do the following:

> Internet Explorer → **http://webserver/tsweb/** → enter IP address or name of remote server on which Remote Desktop for Administration has been enabled → specify screen size and logon information → Connect → ActiveX control installs and you are connected to the remote machine

Connect to Console Session on Remote Server

A console session is a Remote Desktop session that mirrors the session of the locally logged-on user on the remote machine. For example, say you log on interactively to a server on which Remote Desktop for Administration has been enabled and open *msn.com* using Internet Explorer. Then, you go to a second machine and remotely connect to the first machine using a console session. You will see Internet Explorer open and display *msn.com* in your session window! If you then return to your first machine, you'll find that your session has been locked out. Press Ctrl+Alt+Delete to unlock the machine, go back to the second machine, and you'll find that your remote session has been disconnected! The moral of the story is that a WS2003 machine can have only one console session running at any time, whether a local console session or a remote one!

To open a remote console session, use the Remote Desktops Console in Administrative Tools:

> Administrative Tools Remote → Desktops Console → right-click on Remote Desktops → Add new connection → specify name or IP address of remote server on which Remote Desktop for Administration has been enabled → specify credentials for connecting remotely → OK → select new connection to open console session with remote server

Remote Desktop—Notes

Remote connections aren't supported when offline files are in use on the system.

The Remote Desktop Users group is a local group on the server and initially has no membership.

Make sure members of the Remote Desktop Users group have strong passwords to protect your servers.

If you have downlevel Windows clients on your network, install the latest version of Remote Desktop or Terminal Services Client on these machines to take advantage of the enhanced features of Terminal Services in WS2003.

Try to avoid remotely performing administrative tasks that require reboots. Although the tasks may work as expected, if you've left a floppy in the server, it won't be able to restart.

You can manage many aspects of Remote Desktop using Group Policy.

Routing and Remote Access—Concepts

Remote access enables remote clients such as mobile users with laptops to connect to the corporate network and access shared resources. Routing enables traffic on one network to pass to another. In WS2003, both of these functions are configured using a single tool: the Routing and Remote Access Server (RRAS) console. This section covers the different types of remote access supported by RRAS, including dedicated versus dial-up remote access, Internet access, and virtual private networking (VPN). It also includes using RRAS for direct computer connection using a null-modem cable. For an explanation of client-side remote access, see *Connections* earlier in this chapter.

How Remote Access Works

Apart from LAN connections, which are created automatically by WS2003, and direct computer connections, which are temporary connections used to transfer files between two machines, all other forms of connections establish or provide remote access to computers, networks, or the Internet. Remote access typically works as follows:

1. A remote access client attempts to connect to a remote access server (or remote access device) using a WAN connection such as a dial-up connection over a phone line using a modem.

2. The remote access server responds to the connection attempt from the client and negotiates a suitable WAN protocol, such as PPP, that both the client and server can understand. WAN protocols are discussed later in this section.

3. The client uses the WAN protocol to encapsulate the network-level data packets (usually IP packets). Typically, both client and server need to use the same LAN protocol, unless the server is performing LAN protocol conversion in addition to providing remote access to the client.

4. The server provides the client with access to its own resources only, or it acts as a gateway to allow the client to access resources on the server's connected network, depending on how remote access is configured on the server.

Implementing Remote Access

To implement remote access, you basically need to do two things:

- Configure a server to receive inbound connections from remote clients.
- Configure client computers with outbound connections for connecting to the server.

In addition, you need to:

- Grant the users of your client computers suitable permission to connect to your remote access server. This can be allowed or denied on a per-user basis by configuring each user's account, but it can also be managed by creating and implementing a remote access policy (see *Remote Access Policies* later in this section).

- Specify whether the clients can access only resources on the remote access server or also resources on the LAN connected to the server (gateway function of remote access server).

You can implement the server side of a remote access solution using a WS2003 computer in two primary ways: standalone and domain-based. Both types of remote access servers can accept dial-up, demand-dial, direct cable, or VPN connections from remote clients. You create and configure connections on WS2003 computers using Network Connections in the Control Panel; see *Connections* earlier in this chapter for more information.

Remote Access Terminology

Various kinds of protocols are associated with remote access; they include LAN, WAN, multilink, authentication, and encryption protocols. The following is a brief summary of the different types and functions of these protocols.

LAN Protocols

TCP/IP is the default LAN protocol on WS2003, and RRAS supports remote access to corporate IP networks and the Internet using TCP/IP over PPP or SLIP. The phrase *TCP/IP over PPP* means TCP/IP is the LAN protocol, PPP is the WAN protocol, and IP packets are encapsulated into PPP frames in order to send them over the WAN link between the client and server.

WS2003 also supports remote access connectivity for additional LAN protocols:

AppleTalk
> Supports remote access connections to Macintosh file and print servers using the AppleTalk Control Protocol (ATCP) over dial-up PPP connections.

IPX/SPX
> Supports remote access connections to legacy NetWare file and print servers using the IPX Control Protocol (IPXCP) over PPP.

NetBEUI
> Supports remote access connections to NT RAS and legacy LAN Manager servers configured as NetBIOS gateways. Note that NetBEUI is not available on WS2003 by default, but a workaround allows it to be installed by extracting appropriate files from the product CD.

For more information on LAN protocols, see *TCP/IP* later in this chapter.

WAN Protocols

Also called remote access protocols, the following WAN protocols are supported by WS2003:

PPP (Point-to-Point Protocol)
> The most common WAN protocol in use today. PPP is suitable for establishing WAN connectivity between different platforms such as Microsoft Windows, Unix, or Macintosh. PPP supports several methods for authenticating clients (discussed later) and supports data encryption and compression. WS2003 supports PPP for both inbound and outbound connections and for any LAN protocol, and PPP is the standard WAN protocol used in most RRAS implementations.

SLIP (Serial Line Internet Protocol)
> A legacy WAN protocol that is not used much anymore. WS2003 can function as a SLIP client but not as a SLIP server. WS2003 SLIP clients must use TCP/IP and communicate with SLIP servers via a serial COM port on the client machine.

Microsoft RAS (Microsoft Remote Access Service)
> A legacy WAN protocol used on NT 3.1, Windows for Workgroups 3.11, MS-DOS, and Microsoft LAN Manager. Microsoft RAS protocol requires that these clients use NetBEUI. WS2003 supports both client and server implementation of Microsoft RAS.

ARAP (AppleTalk Remote Access Protocol)
> ARAP can be used by Macintosh clients to connect to WS2003 remote access servers. WS2003 doesn't include an ARAP client.

Multilink Protocols

A multilink connection consists of multiple physical connections combined into a single logical connection. For example, you could use multilink to combine two 56 kbps dial-up modem connections into a single 112 kbps connection to provide increased bandwidth for remote access. WS2003 supports two protocols for multilink connections:

PPP Multilink (MP)
> Allows one or more dial-up PPP connections to be combined into a single logical connection. PPP Multilink can be used with modems, ISDN adapters, or X.25 cards to provide additional bandwidth for these connections.

BAP (Bandwidth Allocation Protocol)
BAP is a dynamic multilink protocol that allows physical links to be added or dropped as needed. This is particularly useful if service-carrier charges depend on bandwidth utilization by clients.

WAN Authentication Protocols

WAN connections can use any of several authentication protocols to authenticate remote access clients that are attempting to connect to a remote access server. The authentication protocols supported by outbound dial-up connections on WS2003 are (in order of increasing security):

PAP (Password Authentication Protocol)
An older scheme that transmits passwords as clear text.

SPAP (Shiva Password Authentication Protocol)
A variant of PAP developed by the Shiva Corporation that uses two-way (reversible) encryption for securely transmitting passwords. However, SPAP doesn't support data encryption, only password encryption.

CHAP (Challenge Handshake Authentication Protocol)
Uses the secure one-way hashing scheme, Message Digest 5. CHAP lets the client prove its identity to the server without actually transmitting the password over the WAN link, so it is more secure than the reversible scheme used in SPAP.

MS-CHAP (Microsoft Challenge Handshake Authentication Protocol)
A version of CHAP specifically tailored for Microsoft Windows remote access clients and servers. A newer version, MS-CHAP v2, requires both the client and the server to prove their identities to each other before allowing a connection. MS-CHAP v2 is supported only by WS2003, W2K, NT 4.0, and Windows 98 clients and servers.

In addition to these authentication protocols, WS2003 also supports Extensible Authentication Protocol (EAP), an extension to PPP that supports a wide range of additional security mechanisms including token cards, smart cards, MD5-CHAP, and TLS/SSL.

 WS2003 also supports Remote Authentication Dial-in User Service (RADIUS), a client/server authentication protocol widely used by ISPs. RADIUS is implemented on WS2003 using the Internet Authentication Service (IAS) and provides a way of centrally managing user authentication, authorization, and accounting functions.

Table 4-48 summarizes which multilink and authentication protocols are supported by different Microsoft Windows dial-up clients.

Table 4-48. Microsoft Windows client support for PPP authentication protocols

Client	Authentication protocols							
	PAP	SPAP	CHAP	MS-CHAP	MS-CHAPv2	EAP	PPMP	BAP
WS2003	Yes	Yes	Yes	Yes	Yes	Yes	Yes	Yes
Windows 2000	Yes	Yes	Yes	Yes	Yes	Yes	Yes	Yes
Windows XP	Yes	Yes	Yes	Yes	Yes	Yes	Yes	Yes
NT 4.0	Yes	Yes	Yes	Yes	Yes	—	Yes	—

Table 4-48. Microsoft Windows client support for PPP authentication protocols (continued)

Client	Authentication protocols							
	PAP	SPAP	CHAP	MS-CHAP	MS-CHAPv2	EAP	PPMP	BAP
NT 3.51	Yes	Yes	Yes	Yes	—	—	—	—
Windows 98	Yes	Yes	Yes	Yes	Yes	—	Yes	—
Windows 95	Yes	Yes	Yes	Yes	Yes	—	—	—

Encryption Protocols

In addition to the encrypted authentication protocols described earlier, WS2003 supports several protocols for encrypting data transmitted over remote access connections, including:

MPPE (Microsoft Point-to-Point Encryption)
A data encryption scheme that uses a 40-, 56-, or 128-bit RSA RC4 encryption algorithm (depending on export requirements for your country)

IPSec (Internet Protocol Security)
A scheme that uses a 56 bit DES or 168 bit Triple DES encryption algorithm

Be aware that data encryption is not supported for the following authentication protocols: PAP, SPAP, and CHAP.

Virtual Private Network (VPN)

WS2003 RRAS allows you to set up a VPN that provides secure remote access services to clients without the need to purchase additional hardware such as modems or multiport adapters. Instead, a VPN utilizes an Internet connection such as a DSL connection or T1 line to provide secure remote access services to clients. VPNs work by encapsulating LAN protocol packets, such as TCP/IP packets, into PPP frames. These PPP frames are then transported using a secure VPN protocol, such as PPTP or L2TP, over the WAN link. A common scenario for implementing a VPN is as follows:

1. Mobile users with laptops running XP Professional have an outbound dial-up VPN connection configured on their machines. These users want to securely access their company's intranet using an insecure Internet connection. From a remote location, a user dials up a regional ISP to gain access to the Internet to establish a VPN with their corporate intranet.

2. On the company side, a WS2003 system with a dedicated T1 connection to the Internet has an inbound VPN connection configured on it. This remote access server will use the insecure Internet for servicing remote clients, rather than using the traditional remote access solution—a modem bank (which typically adds the additional expense of leasing a number of additional phone lines for remote access purposes, and since our company already has a T1 line anyway to provide LAN users with Internet access, then why not make use of it for remote access as well?).

3. The client dials up his ISP and connects to the Internet. Once connected, the client uses PPTP or L2TP to establish a secure, encrypted communications session with the VPN server at corporate headquarters. In effect, the client securely becomes part of the corporate LAN by tunneling through the insecure Internet between them.

VPN connections can even be used within a LAN to provide secure network communications between a VPN client and a VPN server.

Here are the two WAN protocols supported by WS2003 for creating VPNs:

PPTP (Point-to-Point Tunneling Protocol)
Derived from PPP. It uses PPP encryption for data and works only with TCP/IP as the underlying network protocol. PPTP is generally viewed as less secure than L2TP but is easier to implement.

L2TP (Layer 2 Tunneling Protocol)
Derived from the Layer 2 Forwarding (L2F) protocol. L2TP supports data encryption and tunneled authentication using IPSec and works with TCP/IP, X.25, Frame Relay, ATM, and other point-to-point, packet-oriented WAN links (but the WS2003 version supports only TCP/IP natively). L2TP also supports header compression for more efficient transfer of data.

Remote Access Policies

A remote access policy is a collection of conditions and connection settings. Remote access policies simplify the administrative task of managing remote access for users and groups in your enterprise. Using remote access policies, you can:

- Allow or deny remote access depending on the time or day of the week, the group membership of the remote user, the type of connection (VPN or dial-up), and so on

- Configure remote access settings to specify authentication protocols and encryption schemes used by clients, maximum duration of a remote access session, etc.

Remote access policies consist of three parts:

Conditions
These are attributes that are compared to the settings of the remote connection to determine whether the connection attempt should be allowed or denied. If multiple conditions are specified in the policy, they must all match the settings of the client or the connection attempt will be refused. Examples of conditions include the phone number of the remote access server, date and time restrictions, domain-based groups the user belongs to, etc.

Remote access permission
If the specified conditions are met, then remote access permission is either granted or denied, depending on how you configure this setting in the policy. (By default, this is set to Deny when a new policy is created.)

Profile
These are settings applied to the connection once it has been authorized (in other words, once remote access permission has been verified—note that *authorization* is different from *authentication*, which has to do with the user's credentials being accepted at the server end). Profile settings can include maximum session time allowed, whether Multilink is enabled, types of authentication protocols and encryption schemes allowed, and so on. These policy settings must also match the settings of the client, or the connection attempt will be finally denied.

Remote access policies are configured using the RRAS console. They are contained within the Remote Access Policies container under the server node in the console tree.

GUI Reference

There is a default remote access policy created when the RRAS is installed on a computer. This policy is called "Allow access if dial-in permission is enabled" and specifies that users will be denied remote access permission by the policy if:

- Their user account has its remote access controlled by remote access policies (the default on a native mode, domain-based, or standalone WS2003 remote access server).

- Their account logon restrictions allow them to log on anytime (also the default).

In other words, the default remote access policy denies remote access to all users unless a user account explicitly has remote access allowed for it.

 Remote access policies are stored on their associated remote access servers in WS2003 rather than in Active Directory to facilitate application of these policies to client connections without generating additional network traffic.

How Remote Access Policies Work

Let's start by considering how remote access by users to a remote access server can be explicitly controlled without using remote access policies. You explicitly allow or deny a user remote access permission by using the Dial-in tab of the properties sheet for the user account, using:

- Local Users and Groups in the Computer Management console on a standalone WS2003 computer

- Active Directory Users and Groups on a WS2003 domain controller or a member server that belongs to a domain

However, if you want to control remote access for users using remote access policies, then instead of selecting Allow or Deny on the Dial-in tab for a user, specify that WS2003 should "Control access through Remote Access Policy." (This setting is configured by default for built-in and new users in WS2003 domains configured to run in native mode and on standalone WS2003 remote access servers.) In this case, the permissions setting of the policy will determine whether the user will be allowed to establish a connection with the remote access server.

If your WS2003 domain is running in mixed mode, you don't have the option of selecting "Control access through Remote Access Policy"—this option is grayed out on the user account's properties sheet. The reason is that mixed-mode domains may contain both WS2003 and NT domain controllers, and NT RAS servers don't support remote access policies. You should convert your domain from mixed mode to native mode if you want to use remote access policies on domain-based remote access servers (standalone WS2003 systems do support remote access policies, however). If you have a domain-based remote access server running in a mixed-mode domain, you should delete the default remote access policy if it is present.

By default, all built-in and new user accounts on native-mode, domain-based, and standalone remote access servers have "Control access through Remote Access Policy" selected in their properties (unless their setting was previously changed from Deny to Allow, in which case it becomes Deny). On mixed-mode domain-based servers, all built-in and new user accounts have Deny as their remote access permission.

Remote access policies are used to control connection attempts in the following way:

1. The remote client (with the user account set to "Control access through Remote Access Policy") tries to connect to a remote access server (here, a domain-based server where the domain is running in native mode).

2. The server checks its list of policies:

   - If there is no remote access policy configured, the connection is refused.

   - If there is only one policy, all conditions in the policy must match the user's connection settings in order to move on to Step 3.

   - If there are multiple policies, these are tested in order, one at a time, until one matches and you move on to Step 3, or all fail and the connection is refused.

3. If a policy whose conditions match the user is found, the server checks the remote access permission of the policy. If this is set to Deny, then connection is refused; otherwise, move on to Step 4.

4. If remote access permission has been allowed to the user through a policy, the server checks the profiles associated with the policy. If these profile settings match the user, the connection is established and the user connects to the server; otherwise, no other untried policies are tried, and the connection is finally refused.

Routing and Remote Access—Tools

The main tool for configuring remote access is the RRAS console, an administrative tool that can be used to configure:

- A dial-up networking server (remote access server)
- A virtual private networking server (VPN server)
- A demand-dial connection
- A firewall/NAT server
- A LAN router

By default, RRAS is configured for manual startup on WS2003, so the console tree initially looks like this:

        Routing and Remote Access
            Server Status
            Server Name

where Server Name is the local computer. To start the RRAS on the local computer, right-click on Server Name and select Configure and Enable Routing and Remote Access. This starts a wizard that leads you through the process of configuring the computer as a remote access server or router. Once the server has been configured, the console tree typically looks something like this:

        Routing and Remote Access
            Server Status
            Server Name
                Network Interfaces
                    Loopback
                    Local Area Connection
                    Internal
                Ports
                    WAN Miniport (PPTP) (64 of them)

> WAN Miniport (L2TP) (64 of them)
> Direct Parallel (LTP1)
> Remote Access Clients
> IP Routing
>> General
>>> Loopback
>>> Local Area Connection
>>> Internal
>> Static Routes
>> DHCP Relay Agent
>>> Internal
>> IGMP
>> NAT/Basic Firewall
> Remote Access Policies
>> Connections to Microsoft RRAS servers
>> Connections to other remote access servers
> Remote Access Logging
>> Local File
>> SQL Server

Depending on the role in which the server is configured (remote access server, VPN server, router, and so on), the available nodes may vary. This example shows the console tree when RRAS has been given a custom configuration with all functions installed on a single-homed server.

Action Menu

Under the Action menu (or by right-clicking on a node), you can select:

Routing and Remote Access

Select this to add additional remote access servers to the console tree and to configure the interval at which the console refreshes when Auto Refresh is enabled.

Server Status

Select this to see the status of your remote access servers in the details pane.

Server Name node

Select this to pause, start, and restart the RRAS on the server or disable the service (remove the remote access server configuration from the server). You can also change the role of the server, specify providers for authentication and accounting, and manage IP routing and PPP settings on the server.

Routing Interfaces

Select this to display the physical or logical interfaces over which packets are forwarded. These can be LAN, demand-dial, or IP-tunnel interfaces. (You can create new demand-dial or IP-tunnel interfaces, but LAN interfaces are created automatically when network adapters are installed.) Depending on the type of interface, you may be able to connect or disconnect it, enable or disable it, configure dial-out credentials and hours, change the device associated with the interface, configure which networking services function over the interface, and configure other properties of the interface.

Ports

Select this to display and configure the devices (modems, modem banks, logical WAN miniports, and so on) supported by the RRAS on the server. The details pane displays the point-to-point connections that are configured and their statuses. (If you have a single-port device such as a modem, the port and the device are indistinguishable.) Double-click on a port to display more details of its status.

Remote Access Clients
Select this to view the connected dial-up or VPN clients in the details pane and disconnect them or view their status.

IP Routing
Select this to configure a multihomed server as a router.

Remote Access Policies
Select this to create a new Remote Access Policy for controlling remote access for users. The details pane displays the Remote Access Policy created when the RRAS is enabled on the server.

Remote Access Logging
Select this to view the remote access log file, and double-click on the file to configure its logging settings.

Routing and Remote Access—Tasks

The RRAS console is used to configure WS2003 as a remote access server, VPN server, or basic NAT/firewall server. Unless otherwise specified, the tasks in this section assume that you have already opened the Routing and Remote Access console by:

Start → Administrative Tools → Routing and Remote Access

 To create and configure connections, use Network Connections in the Control Panel (see *Connections* earlier in this chapter for more information).

Configure and Enable Routing and Remote Access

In order to install and use the RRAS on a WS2003 computer so it can accept incoming connections from clients, you must first configure and enable the RRAS:

Right-click on server → Configure and Enable Routing and Remote Access

This starts the RRAS Setup Wizard, which prompts you to choose a role for your remote access server. You can select from five different roles:

Remote access (dial-up or VPN)
Network address translation (NAT)
Virtual Private Network (VPN) access and NAT
Secure connection between two private networks
Custom configuration

Once you've walked through the wizard and configured the RRAS, you can perform further configuration using steps outlined later in this topic. If you decide later that you want to change the role of your RRAS server, you can remove the existing configuration and then run the wizard again. To remove the existing configuration of a remote access server:

Right-click on server → Disable Routing and Remote Access

Alternatively, you can reconfigure the settings on your server to assume a new role if you have a deep enough understanding of these settings. It's generally easier to rerun the wizard, however.

Let's look at enabling and configuring the RRAS using the wizard for each of the five roles the RRAS supports.

Remote Access (Dial-up or VPN)

Select this option to configure your server as a basic remote access server that can accept incoming connections from dial-up clients using a modem and/or VPN clients over the Internet. To configure a dial-up remote access server, do this:

> Dial-up → select LAN for remote clients to access (this option is available only on multihomed servers) → select method for assigning IP addresses to clients (either DHCP or from a specified range of addresses) → select server that authenticates remote clients (either the RRAS server itself or a RADIUS server)

To configure a VPN server, first make sure your server has at least two network interfaces and then do this:

> VPN → select interface connected to Internet → enable security using static packet filters → select method for assigning IP addresses to clients (either DHCP or from a specified range of addresses) → select server that authenticates remote clients (either the RRAS server itself or a RADIUS server)

You can also select both options together to create a hybrid VPN/dial-up remote access server.

Network Address Translation (NAT)

Select this option to configure your server as an Internet connection server that connects your private network to the Internet using NAT. You must have a public IP address in order to choose this option. The next steps of the wizard depend on the number of existing network interfaces configured on your machine. If your server has only one interface (for example, the Local Area Connection), then you can use the wizard to create a demand-dial interface to connect to the Internet using either a dial-up modem or dedicated broadband device such as a DSL router. Follow these steps:

> Enable security on the selected interface using Internet Connection Firewall (ICF) → Create a demand-dial interface using the Demand Dial Interface Wizard

The Demand Dial Interface Wizard lets you choose between creating a dial-up VPN or broadband PPPoE (PPP over Ethernet) interface. If you choose VPN, specify the tunneling protocol used (PPTP or L2TP), the IP address of the remote router, and the connection credentials for the remote router. If you choose PPPoE, you specify the connection credentials for your service provider.

If you already have two interfaces on your machine (Local Area Connection and dial-up or broadband Internet connection), then follow these steps:

> Select the network connection with a public IP address and connected to the Internet → Enable security on the selected interface using ICF

At this point you can choose between the following two options:

Basic name and address service
> The RRAS assigns IP addresses automatically using Automatic Private IP Addressing (APIPA) and forwards DNS queries to your service provider's DNS server.

Set up name and address service later

The RRAS uses Active Directory and DNS/DHCP servers on your network.

The first option is designed mainly for small office/home office (SOHO) use as it assigns IP addresses using APIPA instead of DHCP. Selecting this option does the following:

- Configures your server's network adapter with the IP address 192.168.0.1 and subnet mask 255.255.255.0 with no default gateway.

- Enables routing on your dial-up port so that computers on your LAN can connect to the Internet through your server. If your Internet connection is not a dedicated connection, such as a leased line, the wizard enables dial-on-demand for the outbound connection on the server.

- Adds the NAT routing protocol and binds both the LAN and Internet interfaces on the server to the NAT protocol.

VPN Access and NAT

Select this option to configure your server as a VPN server using NAT. Make sure your server has at least two network interfaces and then do this:

Select interface connected to Internet → enable security using static packet filters → select method for assigning IP addresses to clients (either DHCP or from a specified range of addresses) → select server that authenticates remote clients (either the RRAS server itself or a RADIUS server)

The VPN server will accept incoming connections from VPN clients using the WAN miniports (virtual ports) on the server.

Secure Connection Between Two Private Networks

Select this option to configure your server to connect with another network using your server as a router. If your server already has two network interfaces (a LAN and a WAN interface), choose No and, after running the wizard, ensure your WAN interface has suitable IP address settings (and configure routing protocols if required). If demand-dial routing will be used instead (typically for branch office connections) and you need to set up a new demand-dial interface, choose Yes and then follow these steps:

Select method for assigning IP addresses to clients (either DHCP or from a specified range of addresses) → Demand Dial Interface Wizard starts → specify name for remote interface → select VPN or PPPoE

If you choose VPN, specify the tunneling protocol used (PPTP or L2TP), the IP address of the remote router, and the connection credentials for the remote router. If you choose PPPoE, you specify the connection credentials for your service provider.

Custom Configuration

Select this option to create a plain vanilla RRAS server with one or more of the following services:

VPN access
Dial-up access
Demand-dial connections
NAT and basic firewall
LAN routing

This starts the RRAS service on the server with all components installed. (See *Routing and Remote Access—Tools* earlier in this chapter to see what the console tree looks like in this case.) You can then manually configure RRAS settings as desired.

Configure RRAS

The following are some of the more common tasks for configuring RRAS servers.

Enable Remote Access

Right-click on server → General → Remote access server

Selecting this option enables your server to accept connections from both dial-up and VPN clients.

Enable Routing

Right-click on server → General → Router

You can choose between LAN routing only or LAN and demand-dial routing. LAN routing requires either two network adapters or a network adapter and a dedicated WAN device such as a CSU/DSU. Demand-dial routing requires a network adapter and a dial-up WAN device such as a modem or ISDN terminal adapter.

 Note that an RRAS server can be enabled for both remote access and routing roles.

Configure Security on an RRAS Server

Right-click on server → Properties → Security

You can configure security on a remote access server in a variety of ways. For example, your authentication provider, which determines how remote access clients are authenticated by your server, can be either:

Windows Authentication
Authentication is performed by Active Directory.

RADIUS Authentication
Authentication is performed by a RADIUS server. You can configure a WS2003 system as a RADIUS server by installing the optional Internet Authentication Service (IAS) component of WS2003.

Similarly, your accounting provider (which keeps track of remote access sessions and connection attempts) can be either:

Windows Accounting
Connections are logged in the Remote Access Logs folder.

RADIUS Accounting
Connections are logged by the RADIUS server.

Once you select your authentication and accounting providers, you can also configure which authentication protocols will be supported by your remote access server. Here's how to do this:

Right-click on server → Properties → Security → Authentication Methods

By default, for added security, only MS-CHAP, MS-CHAPv2, and EAP are enabled on an RRAS server. If your clients can use only weaker authentication protocols, you must enable them here.

Configure IP Routing

Remote access servers can grant remote clients access to resources on either the remote access server alone or on any server in the local network. In the second case, the remote access server functions as a network gateway, allowing remote clients to access other servers on the LAN through the remote access server. To enable your server as a network gateway for an IP-based remote access server:

> Right-click on server → IP → Enable IP routing → Allow IP-based remote access and demand-dial connections

Configure an IP Address Pool for Clients

> Right-click on server → IP → Static address pool → Add → specify Start and End IP addresses

You should select addresses whose range forms a standard subnet since there is no option here for specifying the subnet mask. If you specify an address in a subnet that is different from the address of the LAN adapter of the server, you must add static routes to the server's routing table to enable the server to forward packets between the LAN and WAN connections (or you could enable an IP routing protocol on the server instead).

 If you are using IPX or AppleTalk instead of IP, the IP tab of the server's properties sheet will be replaced with an IPX or AppleTalk tab.

Configure Logging

To configure which remote access events will be logged in the System log:

> Right-click on server → Properties → Event Logging → specify logging level

To configure settings for the IAS log file:

> Expand server node → select Remote Access Logging → right-click on Local File → Properties → specify log file settings

Enable Multilink

> Right-click on server → PPP → Multilink connections

If you are going to use Multilink (MP or BAP), you also need to specify the phone numbers for your device:

> Expand server container → right-click on Ports → Properties → select device → Configure → Phone number for this device

Enable Remote Access for a Device

> Expand server container → right-click on Ports → Properties → select device → Configure → Remote access connections (inbound only)

The difference between a port and a device is:

Port

A logical communications channel that supports a single point-to-point connection between two computers. A port can be considered a subdivision of a multiport device.

Device
> Either hardware (modem, DSL router, and so on) or software (WAN Miniport) that can be used to create a physical or logical point-to-point connection between two computers.

A WAN Miniport is a software driver that acts as a kind of virtual modem bank for VPN connections. When you enable the RRAS, Windows automatically creates 128 WAN Miniport virtual ports with 64 of PPTP type and 64 of L2TP type. These virtual ports are used to accept incoming connections from VPN clients. You can increase the number of virtual ports up to 1,000 to support more simultaneous connections from VPN clients by:

> Expand server container → right-click on Ports → Properties → select WAN Miniport (*type*) → Configure → specify Maximum ports → reboot

When a remote VPN client connects to your remote access server to establish a VPN connection with the server, it uses the highest-numbered virtual port available. The client first tries to connect to an L2TP port (which requires the client to have a digital certificate installed that the server can recognize) and, if this fails, it uses PPTP instead.

Configure a Remote Access Policy

You can either edit the existing default remote access policy or delete it and create a new one. To create a new remote access policy:

> Right-click on Remote Access Policies container → New Remote Access Policy → Use the wizard to set up a typical policy for a common scenario → specify a name for the policy → select an access method (VPN, dial-up, wireless, or Ethernet) → select users or groups to grant access → choose authentication methods to use → choose encryption levels (VPN or dial-up only)

The exact options in the wizard vary with the access method you select. An alternative approach is to set up a custom policy:

> Right-click on Remote Access Policies container → New Remote Access Policy → Custom policy → specify a name for policy → add new conditions or edit existing ones → choose whether to grant or deny remote access based on the policy → Edit Profile

When adding conditions to your policy, you can choose from numerous options. Some of the more common conditions you add might be:

Calling Station ID
> Specifies the remote client's phone number for callback-verification purposes

Day and Time Restrictions
> Indicates which days of the week and times of the day the policy will be applied

Windows-Groups
> Specifies which WS2003 domain-based (global or universal) groups the user must belong to in order for the policy to be applied

When deciding whether to grant or deny remote access based on your policy, remember that you can create multiple remote access policies with some granting access and others denying it. Policies are evaluated one at a time in the order in which they are listed until a policy is found that matches (doesn't conflict with) the user account and client connection settings.

The last step, Edit Profile, is optional and allows you to configure settings on six tabs:

Dial-in Constraints
> You can restrict the duration of user sessions if you have limited dial-in ports on your remote access server. It's also good to configure the connection to disconnect automatically if it is idle for more than about five minutes.

IP You should generally leave the IP Address Assignment Policy set to "Server settings define policy." Configuring packet filters is an extra layer of complexity that should be done carefully; otherwise, connections may be accepted, but users will not be able to access the resources they need on the remote corporate network.

Multilink
> Multilink settings can be left at "Default to server settings." If you are short of modems, you can disable Multilink using this profile setting.

Authentication
> Try to specify only the most secure authentication protocols that your remote clients can negotiate. Select only Unauthenticated Access for direct computer connections using null-modem cables.

Encryption
> The encryption schemes you select here can be negotiated by the server with the client. If your clients are WS2003 computers and use VPN connections, then deselect No Encryption and Basic Encryption, leaving only Advanced selected. This will enable MPPE 56 to be used for data encryption.

Advanced
> These settings are typically used when RADIUS is implemented on your network and should not be modified for basic remote access.

Click Finish to create your new remote access policy. To further edit the policy, double-click on it. If you have multiple policies created, right-click on them and select Move Up or Move Down to change the order in which they are matched.

Grant Remote Access Permission to a User

> Active Directory Users and Computers → select domain or OU → right-click on a user → Properties → Dial-in → Allow access

You can choose to control access through a remote access policy only if you have all domain controllers running WS2003—that is, if you are running in native mode. The same is true for assigning a static IP address to a remote access client.

Manage Remote Access Clients

> Expand server node → select Remote Access Clients → right-click on a user

You have two options:

- Select Disconnect to immediately disconnect the remote VPN client. No warning message appears on the client's machine.

- Select Send Message to send a brief message to the client—for example, to warn the client that you are about to disconnect it. A dialog box will pop up on the client to display this message. You can also select Send To All to send a message to all connected clients—for example, when you are going to take the VPN server offline for maintenance.

GUI Reference

Monitor Connected Clients

If you select the Remote Access Clients container for your server in the console tree, the details pane displays the names of connected clients in the form *domain\username*, the time since the user connected, and the number of ports in use by the user (which is 1 unless it is a multilink connection). Note that the information in the details pane doesn't refresh automatically by default, so you should do the following:

> Right-click on root node → toggle Auto Refresh on → right-click again on root node → Refresh Rate → specify refresh interval in seconds

You can display further information about a connected client by:

> Right-click on user → Status

This displays the username connected, bytes in and out and other network-traffic information, and the IP address given to the client. (If you have created a static IP pool on the server, then IP addresses are assigned to clients in round-robin order starting with the lowest available address, and a client that disconnects and then reconnects is assigned the next higher address above its previously assigned one.)

You can also select the Ports container for your server in the console tree and then right-click on an active port to view the status of the connection or disconnect the port.

Add a Server

You can manage additional RRAS servers by:

> Right-click on Server Status → Add Server → select server

Monitor RRAS

Select the Server Status node in the console tree to view the state of each server and the number of ports in use in the contents pane. Make sure the Details view is selected from the menu.

Routing and Remote Access—Notes

Clients that can connect to WS2003 remote access servers include WS2003, W2K, XP, NT, Windows 95/98, Windows for Workgroups, MS-DOS, and Apple Macintosh.

If dial-in or VPN clients can't connect to your remote access server, there are a number of things you can check:

- Check the modem, modem bank, or other hardware at both the client and the server.

- Make sure the Routing and Remote Access Service is started on the server by:

  > Routing and Remote Access console → select Server Status → check server in details pane

- To start a stopped server:

  > Routing and Remote Access console → select Server Status → right-click on server in details pane → All Tasks → Start

- Make sure the remote access server is enabled for remote access by:

    Routing and Remote Access console → right-click on server → Properties → General → Enable this computer as a remote access server

- Make sure your dial-in or VPN (PPTP/L2TP) ports are enabled for inbound connections by:

    Routing and Remote Access console → expand server container → right-click on Ports → select device → Configure → select Remote access connections

- If all your remote access ports are active, you can add additional ports (easy for VPN ports).

- Make sure you have allowed remote access for the client's user account and, if there is a remote access policy configured, that the policy doesn't deny the user access.

- Lots of things can go wrong with remote access. Make sure:

    - Your client supports the correct network protocol
    - You have assigned the client addresses from a correct pool
    - You have allowed sufficiently lax authentication and encryption methods on the server
    - That a connection can be successfully negotiated with the client
    - That the client is using appropriate credentials
    - That the client supports the correct tunneling protocol for VPN connections
    - That the phone number on the client is configured correctly for a dial-up connection

See Also

Connections, netsh, route, *TCP/IP*

Security Templates—Concepts

Security templates are text files that contain various settings that can be used to:

- Configure security for a standalone server using Local Security Policy
- Configure security for servers in a domain by importing them into Group Policy
- Analyze the security of a server in either a workgroup or a domain

WS2003 includes a number of predefined security templates in the form of *.inf* files that are found in the *\Windows\Security\Templates* folder:

setup security.inf
: Default security settings for freshly installed machine

dc security.inf
: Default domain controller security settings (settings are undefined)

compatws.inf
: Default security settings for workstations/servers (settings are undefined)

securedc.inf and securews.inf
: Enhanced security settings for domain controllers and workstations/servers

GUI Reference

hisecdc.inf and hisecws.inf
>High security settings for domain controllers and workstations/servers

rootsec.inf
>Reapplies default permissions to root of system drive

You can view the various settings of the different security templates using the Security Configuration and Analysis console.

Security Templates—Tools

Security Templates

This snap-in can be used to view, create, or modify a security policy for a computer or network. You can import predefined templates and modify them or create your own templates and then apply them to a standalone computer or import them into Group Policy to apply them to computers in a domain. The console tree typically looks like this:

>Security Templates
>>Template Search Path
>>>Template
>>>Template...

Right-clicking on each node makes different actions available, depending on the node.

Security Templates
>Select this to define a new template search path.

Template Search Path (C:\Windows\Security\Templates by default)
>Select this to create a new template or delete an existing one. You can use Save As to save a copy of an existing template under a different name and then modify it. This can take less time than defining a new template from scratch. If you do create a new template, be sure to save it.

Template
>Select a template to display and modify the template's security settings using the details pane.

Security Configuration and Analysis

This snap-in can be used to analyze and configure security settings on the local computer. For example, you can:

- Import security templates created using the Security Templates snap-in into a computer-specific datastore (database), merging or overwriting successive templates to create a composite template that you can save or export.

- Compare the current (effective) security settings on the local computer with settings stored in the database, displaying the differences for easy recognition. (A green check mark next to a setting means the current setting and the template setting agree; a red X means there is a difference; no mark means both the current setting and template setting are Not Defined.)

- Apply a security template to the Local Security Policy on the computer so that it takes effect immediately. If after performing analysis you choose to accept the current settings, the corresponding value in the database is modified to match.

To use this tool, select Security Configuration and Analysis to create a new database or open an existing one. To create a new database, you must first import a security template. You can then import additional templates into the database, either merging them with previously imported template settings or overwriting the existing settings. You can also directly modify security settings in the database once you have completed the analysis procedure described next.

You then analyze your computer to compare the settings in the database with the system's current local security settings. After analysis, select Security Configuration and Analysis again to display a logged description of the results of the analysis. Then, if desired, expand the different containers to display the differences between the database settings and the system's current security settings (differences marked with a red X, as explained earlier). For more information on these different security settings, see *Group Policy* earlier in this chapter.

Finally, you can do one of the following:

- Immediately apply the security template settings you imported into the database to the computer's local security policy by right-clicking on Security Configuration and Analysis and selecting Configure Computer Now. Choose this approach if you have only a few computers to configure. Changes will be applied when you reboot your computer. If your computers are part of a domain in which Group Policy is configured, however, be aware that the security settings you configure locally on your computers may be overwritten when Group Policy is applied.

- Export your database settings to a security template, which you can then import into a Group Policy Object (GPO). Choose this approach if you have a domain configuration with multiple computers to configure.

Security Templates—Tasks

Create a Security Template

To speed the process of configuring security settings, you can create a template containing predefined security settings. WS2003 includes a number of default templates, but you can also create your own security templates using the Security Templates snap-in. Add this snap-in to a new or existing MMC console and do the following:

> Right-click the template search path node → New Template → specify a name and description → select and expand the new template in the console tree → double-click on a policy → define this policy setting in the template → specify parameters → repeat for any policies that need to be configured

Once you create a new security template, you can import it into a GPO to apply it to computers in a domain or OU (see the next task) or use it to analyze security on a local computer (see the later task).

Import a Security Template

You can import into a GPO either one of the default security templates included in WS2003 or a custom template you have created. To do this, open the desired GPO using Active Directory Users and Computers and then:

> Computer Configuration → Windows Settings → right-click on Security Settings → Import Policy → select *.inf* file for template → Open

Apply a Security Template to a Computer

Several steps are involved. First, you create a security-configuration database and specify a template to be imported into the database:

> Security Configuration and Analysis console → right-click Security Configuration and Analysis → Open database → specify a database name to create a new database → Open → select a security template → select "Clear this database" before importing → Open

In the previous steps, if you don't select "Clear this database" before importing, then the settings you import will be merged with the existing security settings instead of overwriting them. If you already have a database, you can open it instead of creating a new one (specifying a new name creates a new database) and then import a template into the database. Next, you need to configure your computer to use the imported template:

> Right-click Security Configuration and Analysis → Configure Computer Now

A dialog box will show progress as the settings are applied. Once this is finished, you should analyze your settings as follows:

> Right-click Security Configuration and Analysis → Analyze Computer Now

This compares the security configuration of your machine with the information stored in the configuration database file (*.sdb* file). Once this process is finished, you can either read the log file created by doing this:

> Right-click Security Configuration and Analysis → View Log File

or you can view the comparison information by doing this:

> Expand the Security Configuration and Analysis container → view analysis results for each setting

A green check mark means a setting is consistent; a red flag means a discrepancy; nothing means the setting is not configured.

Create a Custom Security Template

You can either create a new template from scratch or copy an existing one, which may be less work if the configuration you desire is close to one of the default configurations included in the template search path, *C:\Windows\Security\Templates*.

To create a new template from scratch:

> Security Templates console → right-click on templates search path container → New Template → specify a name and description → configure settings for new template as desired

To copy an existing template and modify the copy:

> Security Templates console → right-click on a template to copy → Save As → specify a name for the copy → Save → configure settings for copied template as desired

---

Security Templates—Notes

You must be a member of the Administrators local group in order to configure the local security policy on a WS2003 computer.

If local policy settings are combined with domain settings, the results are effective settings, which are displayed in the details pane of the console.

The *Secedit.exe* command-line utility can be used to perform batch analysis on multiple computers in a domain, but you must view the results of the analysis using Security Configuration and Analysis.

See Also

Group Policy

Services—Concepts

A service is a process that runs in the background on a machine to perform actions in response to client requests. Services on Microsoft Windows platforms are the equivalent of daemons on Unix platforms. An example of a service is the World Wide Web (WWW) service, which runs on a server on which Internet Information Services (IIS) is installed. The WWW service runs in the background on the server, waiting to receive Hypertext Transfer Protocol (HTTP) requests from web browsers. When an HTTP request is received, the WWW service responds by sending the requested files or performing the requested action.

Table 4-49 provides a list of many of the services that can run on WS2003 machines, focusing on services important for everyday administrative functions and tasks. Note that installing optional Windows components or other Microsoft server applications such as Exchange Server or SQL Server adds additional services to your machine.

The following is a key to Table 4-49:

A   Enabled, starts automatically during bootup

M   Enabled, must be manually started by an administrator

D   Disabled, must be enabled before it can be started

Table 4-49. WS2003 services

Service	Startup type	Description
Alerter	M	Notifies selected users and computers of administrative alerts
Automatic Updates	A	Enables the download and installation of critical Windows updates
Background Intelligent Transfer Service (BITS)	M	Transfers data between clients and servers in the background
ClipBook	D	Supports ClipBook Viewer, which allows pages to be seen by remote Clip-Books
Computer Browser	A	Maintains an up-to-date list of computers on your network and supplies the list to programs that request it
DHCP Client	A	Manages network configuration by registering and updating IP addresses and DNS names
Distributed File System	A	Manages logical volumes distributed across a LAN or WAN
Distributed Link Tracking Client	A	Sends notifications of files moving between NTFS volumes in a network domain
DNS Client	A	Resolves and caches DNS names
Event Log	A	Logs event messages issued by programs and windows
File Replication Service	M	Maintains file synchronization of file-directory contents among multiple servers

Table 4-49. WS2003 services (continued)

Service	Startup type	Description
Indexing Service	M	Indexes contents and properties of files on local and remote computers; provides rapid access to files through flexible querying language
Internet Connection Firewall (ICF)/Internet Connection Sharing (ICS)	D	Provides Network Address Translation, addressing, and name-resolution services for all computers on your home network through a dial-up connection
Intersite Messaging	D	Allows messages to be sent and received between Active Directory sites
IPSec Services	A	Manages IP Security policy and starts the ISAKMP/Oakley (IKE) and the IP Security drivers
Kerberos Key Distribution Center	D	Generates session keys and grants service tickets for mutual client/server authentication
License Logging Service	D	Manages licenses
Logical Disk Manager	A	Logical Disk Manager watchdog service
Logical Disk Manager Administrative Service	M	Administrative service for disk-management requests
Messenger	D	Sends and receives messages transmitted by administrators or by the Alerter service
Microsoft Software Shadow Copy Provider	M	Manages software-based volume shadow copies
Net Logon	M	Supports pass-through authentication of account logon events for computers in a domain
Network Connections	M	Manages objects in the *Network and Dial-Up Connections* folder, in which you can view both local area network and remote connections
NT LM Security Support Provider	M	Provides security to remote procedure call (RPC) programs that use transports other than named pipes
Performance Logs and Alerts	M	Configures performance logs and alerts
Plug and Play	A	Manages device installation and configuration and notifies programs of device changes
Print Spooler	A	Temporarily stores files for later printing
Protected Storage	A	Provides protected storage for sensitive data, such as private keys, to prevent access by unauthorized services, processes, or users
Remote Registry	A	Allows remote registry manipulation
Removable Storage	M	Manages removable media, drives, and libraries
Routing and Remote Access	D	Offers routing services to businesses in LAN and WAN environments
SAP Agent	A	SAP agent
Secondary Logon	A	Enables starting processes under alternate credentials
Security Accounts Manager	A	Stores security information for local user accounts
Server	A	Provides RPC support and file, print, and named pipe sharing
System Event Notification	A	Tracks system events such as Windows logon, network, and power events; notifies COM+ Event System subscribers of these events
Task Scheduler	A	Enables a program to run at a designated time
TCP/IP NETBIOS Helper Service	A	Enables support for NetBIOS over TCP/IP (NetBT) service and NetBIOS name resolution
TCP/IP Print Server	A	Provides a TCP/IP-based printing service that uses the LPD protocol

Table 4-49. WS2003 services (continued)

Service	Startup type	Description
Telephony	M	Provides Telephony API (TAPI) support for programs that control telephony devices
Telnet	D	Allows a remote user to log on to the system and run console programs using the command line
Terminal Services	M	Provides a multisession environment that allows client devices to access a virtual XP Professional desktop session and windows-based programs running on the server
Uninterruptible Power Supply	M	Manages an uninterruptible power supply (UPC) connected to the computer
Volume Shadow Copy	M	Manages and implements volume shadow copies used for backups
Windows Installer	M	Installs, repairs, and removes Windows Installer Packages
Windows Management Instrumentation	A	Provides system-management information
Windows Management Instrumentation Driver Extensions	M	Provides system-management information to and from drivers
Windows Time	A	Maintains date and time synchronization of all servers and clients in the network
Workstation	A	Provides network connections and communications

Services—Tasks

The main tool for administering services on the local computer is the Services console in the Administrative Tools program group. For a tool that can administer services on both local and remote machines, use Computer Management. These tasks assume that you have one of these consoles open.

Configure a Service

Right-click on a service → Properties

The settings you can configure here include:

Status

The status of a service can be started, stopped, or paused. Pausing a service keeps existing client connections to the service open while preventing new client connections from forming, but with some services it may have a different effect.

Startup type

Services can be configured to start in three ways:

Automatic

The service starts running automatically when the system is booted. Most services have this setting, but services may fail to start should the associated files somehow become corrupted or if other services on which they depend fail to start properly. Use Services in Administrative Tools to view whether a service that has been configured for automatic startup has in fact started up and is running properly.

Manual

The service must be manually started by the user or by a dependent service that requires it. (A service that is listed as manual startup, but which is running, was started automatically by another service that required it.)

Disabled

The service doesn't start upon boot and can't be started by a user or dependent service.

Log On As

Services require a security context in which to run and must therefore be assigned an account for authentication and access purposes. By default, most services run within the context of a built-in account called the Local System account, which grants the services all the rights and privileges to run as part of the operating system.

Recovery

If a service fails (terminates unexpectedly or fails to start when configured for automatic startup), you can configure several levels of recovery actions. These actions include taking no action, attempting to restart the service, running a designated file, and rebooting the computer. By default, no recovery actions are specified.

You can also use the net config command to configure two important services: the Server service and the Workstation service.

Pause a Service

Right-click on a service → Pause

You can pause only a service that is running.

Resume a Service

Right-click on a service → Resume

You can resume only a service that has been paused.

Restart a Service

Right-click on a service → Resume

You can restart only a service that has been stopped.

Stop a Service

Right-click on a service → Stop

You can also start, stop, pause, resume, and configure services from the command line using the net command.

Services—Notes

You must be logged on as a member of the Administrators group to configure service settings.

Some services, such as the Plug and Play service, can't be paused or stopped.

Some services, such as the DNS Client service, can be stopped but not paused.

To quickly stop and restart a running service, right-click on running service → Restart.

If you pause a service on which other services depend, the dependent services aren't paused but may not function as expected.

If you stop a service that has dependent services, these dependent services will also be stopped. You will then have to restart all of the stopped services independently since, unfortunately, you can't select multiple services in Services and restart them.

The Server service, which is fundamental to file-sharing functionality, has some special behaviors to note:

- If you pause the service, users will be unable to form new connections with the server. The exception is that members of the Administrators and Server Operators groups will still be able to form new connections with the server.

- If you stop the Server service on a remote computer, you will no longer be able to administer it remotely using Computer Management. You will have to go to the console of the remote computer and restart the service locally.

Some services have additional settings that can be configured. For example, the SNMP service has settings for Agent, Traps, and Security, which you can configure from the properties sheet of the service.

If you modify services and the computer fails to boot properly upon restarting, try booting to Safe Mode.

When configuring reboot as a recovery action, you can create a custom message sent to remote users warning them of the impending reboot and can specify the time interval before it takes place. For example, you may want to warn connected users before stopping the Server service since this will terminate their connections, causing them to lose unsaved work.

The Services and Applications container in Computer Management contains not only the Services node but also other nodes enabling more detailed configuration of services such as DHCP, DNS, Indexing, IIS, Message Queuing, Telephony, WINS, and WMI Control.

Services are typically disabled for security reasons to prevent unauthorized users or services from starting them.

Services can be enabled or disabled for each hardware profile on the machine.

If you are using a custom Services console, you can hide the console tree using View → Customize → deselect Console Tree (or use the Show/Hide button on the toolbar). This gives you a better view of the settings of the various services.

Services doesn't refresh automatically—use Action → Refresh to display the current state of all services on your system.

See Also

`net config`, `net continue`, `net pause`, `net start`, `net statistics`, `net stop`

Shared Folders—Concepts

This topic covers various aspects of shared folders, including managing shared folders, offline folders, shadow copies, and administrative shares.

Sharing Files

A shared folder is a folder whose contents (files) are made available for network users. To share a folder, you can use Windows Explorer, and once a folder is shared, its icon is a hand holding a folder. A file server is a computer dedicated to the purpose of hosting shared folders, and WS2003 can function as a file server by adding the File Server role using Manage Your Server. Alternatively, simply share a folder on the machine and the File Server role will be automatically added.

However, simply sharing a folder isn't enough to make network resources securely accessible to users—you also need to assign suitable permissions to the folder to control who has access to it and what level of access they have. For folders on FAT or FAT32 volumes, you can use shared-folder permissions to do this, but shared-folder permissions aren't very granular and offer only a limited degree of control over users' access to the folder. Furthermore, they can be applied only to the folder and its contents as a whole and can't be applied to individual files within the folder.

A better way of securing shared folders is to locate them on NTFS volumes. This is because NTFS permissions are more granular than shared-folder permissions. NTFS permissions can also be assigned to individual files within a folder, giving administrators a much greater degree of access control. For more information about both NTFS permissions and shared-folder permissions, see *Permissions* earlier in this chapter.

Planning Shared Folders

When planning which folders to share, here are some tips to follow:

- Use share names that are intuitive to the users who will be accessing them. Examples are *Pub* for public folder, *Apps* for applications folder, *Home* for home folder, and so on. Be aware that certain share names could cause difficulties for client computers running specific Microsoft Windows operating systems that try to access them (see Table 4-50).

- Try to group folders according to security needs and then share their parent folder, instead of sharing each folder individually. For example, if you have three applications stored in the folders *App1*, *App2*, and *App3*, place each of these folders into a parent folder called *Apps* and then share the parent folder. The fewer shared folders there are, the easier it will be for users to locate them on the network, and the less browse-list traffic they will generate.

Table 4-50. Share names acceptable to Windows operating systems

Operating system	Maximum share name length (characters)
WS2003	80
XP	80
W2K	80
NT 3.51 and 4.0	80
Windows 98	12
Windows 95	12
Windows for Workgroups 3.11	8.3
Windows 3.1	8.3
MS-DOS	8.3

Connecting to Shared Folders

Once a folder has been shared on a file server, users can connect to it from their client computers in several ways:

- By browsing My Network Places if the icon is present on the desktop. This is probably the simplest way of finding a shared folder and connecting to it.

- By using Windows Explorer. This is really the same method as the first item, but using the hierarchical two-pane window interface of Windows Explorer instead of the one-pane window of My Network Places.

- By clicking Start, selecting Run, and then typing the UNC pathname to the shared folder. Note that if you type *\\servername\sharename*, you can open a window displaying the contents of the specific share, while if you type only *\\servername*, a window displaying all shares on the specified server will open.

- By mapping a drive letter to the shared folder. This method can be used if you need to access a shared folder from an application that doesn't support UNC pathnames, if you need to back up the contents of shared folders over the network, or if you simply need a convenient way to access a particular share that you use often. To map a drive, right-click on My Network Places and select Map Network Drive to start the Map Network Drive Wizard.

Offline Files

Offline files is a feature of WS2003 that lets users work with files in shared folders even when the network connection is unavailable. When users want to work with their files, they typically connect to shared folders on network file servers to retrieve these files. When they modify these files, they save their new versions to the shared folders. This procedure has several benefits:

- It centralizes management of users' files, allowing them to be easily backed up by administrators.

- It allows users to roam between different client computers and still be able to access their files from a central location on the network.

The downside is that when the network connection becomes unavailable—due to either a network problem or the file server being down—the users are unable to access their files and can't do their work. The solution is to use the offline-files feature of WS2003, which allows files stored in network shares to be cached on the user's local computer so that these files are always available for the user.

How It Works

When offline files are configured, the process of accessing network resources is the same whether the user is connected to the network or not. When the user logs on, the locally cached copies of her files are synchronized with the copies on the network file servers so that both files are identical. Once synchronization is complete, the user can begin working with her files. The user can access these locally cached files the same way she accesses the copies on the network—for example, by browsing My Network Places or Windows Explorer, entering the UNC path to the share in the Run box from the Start menu, or accessing a mapped network drive. The user works with the remote copy of the file in the shared folder on the network file server, but if the network connection to the file server becomes unavailable, the user is switched transparently to the locally cached version of the file on the user's client computer. The user still thinks she is accessing shared folders on the network, but she is actually working from her own offline-files cache. A notification can be configured to appear over the system tray

GUI Reference

to alert the user that she is working offline. When the user logs off, her locally cached files are again synchronized with the copies on the network file server if the connection has been restored.

How the user works on the files depends on how you configure offline files on the server:

- If you specify manual caching for documents, then the user must specifically designate remote files or shared folders for offline use. Changes to files not designated for offline use are made only on the file servers. If the network connection fails, the file or folder is automatically taken offline and the user works with only the cached version.

- If you specify automatic caching for documents, then any remote files or the shared folders they are in are automatically cached locally for offline use. Any changes made to the files are made to both the local and network versions of the files.

If the network connection is unavailable at the start of or during a user's session, the user can still work on her files locally. From the user's perspective, the process is the same as working with files stored on a network file server. This is particularly advantageous with computers that are, for the most part, only temporarily connected to the network, such as laptop computers.

If two users modify locally cached copies of the same file and one of them logs off (automatically synchronizing her files) when the second user logs off, a message will appear indicating that someone else on the network has modified the file and providing the user with the option of:

- Saving her version on the network
- Retaining the other version on the network
- Saving both versions on the network

In other words, changes made by two or more users aren't merged but are handled intelligently.

Implementing Offline Files

You must do two things to implement offline files on WS2003:

- Configure your file server for offline-file operation. WS2003 computers have offline files enabled by default, but you need to configure how this feature should operate. In addition, you need to configure how offline files will be synchronized.

- Enable local caching of files on the client computer.

Use offline files if users frequently need to work offline with files stored in shared folders on network file servers. If you occasionally need to transfer files between a laptop and a desktop computer using a direct cable connection, Briefcase will suffice.

Shadow Copies

New in WS2003, shadow copies are point-in-time copies of files in shared folders on file servers. You can use this feature to recover files that were accidentally overwritten or deleted and to compare different versions of a file. To view shadow copies, client computers must download special client software from the file server. You can also use Group Policy to assign this client software to users in your network.

Administrative Shares

WS2003 automatically shares certain volumes and folders to support remote administration and to enable access to network printers. Many of these administrative shares are hidden shares, and as a result they aren't visible in My Computer, My Network Places, Windows Explorer, or when you type **net view** at the command line, but they are visible in the Computer Management console under Shared Folders.

Table 4-51 lists common administrative shares and their functions. Depending on the configuration of your machine, not all of these shares may exist on your machine. For example, the SYSVOL share is present only on domain controllers.

Table 4-51. Administrative shares

Admin share	Function
<drive_letter>$	For example, *C$, D$*, and so on; these hidden shares allow administrators or server operators to connect to a drive's root directory on a remote machine for administration purposes.
ADMIN$	Hidden share name for the *\Windows* system directory; used to allow remote administration of WS2003 machines.
IPC$	Hidden share used for communication between machines using named pipes, an interprocess communication (IPC) method supported by Microsoft Windows operating systems.
NETLOGON	Share name for *\Windows\sysvol\sysvol\<domain_name>\scripts* on domain controllers, where *<domain_name>* is the DNS name of the WS2003 domain (e.g., *mtit.local*). This share is used to process domain logon requests and contains domain policies and logon scripts. If a network default user profile is configured, it should be stored here as well. Note that this administrative share is not hidden.
print$	Share name for *\Windows\System32\Spool\Drivers*, the location of the printer drivers; used for administration of network printers by providing a share point where client machines can download printer drivers. This folder is shared only if your server has the print server role added to it.
SYSVOL	Share name for *\Windows\sysvol\sysvol*, which is used to store the public files for a domain. This share is present only on domain controllers and is not a hidden share.

Shared Folders—Tools

There are several useful tools for managing shared folders:

Shared Folders
> This MMC snap-in can be used to create and manage shares on local and remote computers, stop and reconfigure shares, terminate user sessions, and close files.

File Server Management
> This console includes snap-ins for Shared Folders, Disk Management, and Disk Defragmenter.

Synchronize
> This utility is used to synchronize offline files.

Clients who need to connect to shared folders can use Windows Explorer, My Computer, My Network Places, and various other tools. We'll focus here on My Network Places, which has some unique functionality to explore.

Shared Folders

This snap-in can be found under System Tools in Computer Management and can be started by Start → Run → **fsmgmt.msc** → OK. The console tree has three nodes.

GUI Reference

Shares

Displays information about shared resources (folders, volumes, printers, directories, or named pipes) on the computer, including the share name, the path to the shared resource, the type of network connection (Windows, Macintosh, or NetWare), and the current number of connected users.

Sessions

Displays information about network users currently connected to shared resources on the computer, including the username and computer name of each connected user, the type of network connection, the number of files the user has open on the computer, how much time has elapsed since the user first connected to the computer, and the amount of time since her last activity on the computer.

Open Files

Displays information about files currently open on the computer by users connecting over the network, including the name of the file (or print job or named pipe), who has opened it, the type of network connection, the number of locks on the resource (if any), and the permission granted to the user for the resource.

Right-click on:

Shared Folders

To send a console message to users who have active sessions with that server.

Shares

To create a new file share on the server using the Create Shared Folder Wizard. You can also send a console message to all users who have active sessions with that server. Selecting an existing share in the details pane allows you to stop sharing the share and to access the properties of the share to modify shared-folder permissions, NTFS permissions, maximum number of sessions, and file-caching settings.

Sessions

To disconnect all sessions from the server. Selecting a particular session in the details pane lets you close that session alone.

Open Files

To disconnect all open files from the server. Selecting a particular open file in the details pane lets you close that file alone.

The capability to send a console message is actually implemented by means of a snap-in extension to Shared Folders called Send Console Message. If for some reason you wish to do so, you can create a custom Shared Folders console that doesn't have the capability to send a console message by:

Start → Run → **mmc** → OK → Console → Add/Remove Snap-in → Add → Shared Folders → Add → Finish → Close → Extensions → deselect Add all extensions → deselect Send Console Message → OK

One thing this snap-in is not useful for is managing shared-folder permisisons. You might think that if you wanted to modify the permissions on a share you could proceed as follows:

1. Send a console message to inform connected users to close files and disconnect from the share.

2. Stop sharing the share by right-clicking on share → Stop Sharing.

3. Modify the permissions on the share by right-clicking on share → Properties.

4. Restart sharing the share again by right-clicking on share → Restart Sharing.

Unfortunately, there is no Restart Sharing option on the Action or shortcut menu. When you stop sharing a share, it disappears from the list of shares under the Shares node, which means you need to recreate the share and all its permissions and settings using Windows Explorer or some similar tool.

File Server Management

This console can be started two ways:

Manage Your Server → File Server role → click Manage this file server

Start → Run → **filesrv.msc**

The functionality is essentially the same as for Shared Folders, with the addition of some friendly links to perform common tasks like backing up your file server, configuring shadow copies, and sending a console message.

Synchronize

This utility ensures that you have the most current version of files when working offline. It can be started two ways:

Start → All Programs → Accessories → Synchronize

Start → Run → **mobsync.exe**

If you configured your computer to use offline files (or if you are using Internet Explorer in offline mode), you can use Synchronize to ensure that the same versions of your offline files (or offline web pages) can be found on both the local computer and the network (or the Internet). Synchronize opens a dialog box listing the files and web pages you have marked for offline use. If you select an offline file and click Properties, the *Offline Files* folder opens, displaying the locally cached versions of the files and their synchronization status. Click Synchronize to manually synchronize the selected offline files, or click Setup to configure automatic synchronization of selected offline items:

- When you log off from or log on to your computer. Different actions can occur for each network connection in the *Network and Dial-up Connections* folder.

- When your computer is idle for a specified interval of time. (You can prevent synchronization from occurring on laptops running on batteries to conserve power.)

- On a scheduled basis that you specify.

If you select an offline web page in Synchronize and click Properties, a properties sheet opens, allowing you to reconfigure the offline settings for the page. To make a web page available for offline use, first open the page using Internet Explorer, then add it to your list of favorites, making sure you select the checkbox "Make available offline." Click the Customize button as you add the favorite to specify a link depth to download, whether you will synchronize content manually (using Tools → Synchronize in Internet Explorer or using Synchronize in the Accessories program group) or automatically (using a schedule you define). Once you finish adding the favorite, the web page will automatically be downloaded to the local cache. To view offline web pages with Internet Explorer, select File → Work Offline, and then select the page from your favorites list.

My Network Places

This tool can be used to find and connect to shared folders and other network resources. It can be accessed numerous ways:

Desktop → My Network Places (if icon is present)

My Computer (if icon is present) → click the My Network Places link (Web view must be enabled using Folder Options)

Windows Explorer → select My Network Places in left pane → click Folders button on toolbar

Internet Explorer → type **C:** in Address bar → Enter → click Up button on toolbar twice → double-click on My Network Places

Start → Run → **start c:** → Enter → click Up button on toolbar twice → double-click on My Network Places

Command prompt → **explorer** → Enter → click Up button on toolbar twice → double-click on My Network Places

My Network Places is an all-in-one browsing tool that can be used to browse the file-system of the local computer, shared folders and printers on the network, objects in Active Directory, and web content on the Internet. However, this tool is just another incarnation of Windows Explorer—as are My Computer and Internet Explorer! There the several kinds of icons that are displayed when you open My Network Places:

Add Network Place

This starts a wizard that can be used to create shortcuts to network resources such as shared folders (enter a UNC path) or web and FTP sites (enter a URL). Note that if you specify a URL, the wizard must be able to connect to the remote web or FTP site in order to create the shortcut. If you try to specify a resource by browsing for it instead of entering the path, you can also select the *Printers* or *Scheduled Tasks* folder on a local or remote computer. But when you try to complete the wizard, an error occurs telling you that the network name can't be found. This is a small bug in the wizard.

Entire Network

This browses the domains, workgroups, computers, shared folders, and printers on your network. Double-clicking Entire Network displays one or more of the following items, depending on the configuration of your network (if you have web content enabled in Folder Options under the Tools menu, you also have to click the "entire contents" link to display the following items):

Microsoft Windows Network

Displays the domains and workgroups in your network.

NetWare or Compatible Network

Displays the NetWare servers on your network.

Directory

Displays the publicly readable portions of Active Directory for the local forest. The folder initially shows only the root domains of each tree in the forest. Double-click on a root domain to display the OUs and default containers in that domain, along with any first-level child domains in that tree. Double-click on an OU to browse the objects within it, and double-click on an object to display its publicly readable properties. If you are logged on as an Administrator in the domain, you can modify the displayed properties for Active Directory objects. Double-clicking on a published shared folder opens the folder and displays its contents. Right-clicking on a computer object and selecting Manage opens Computer Management for the computer.

Network Share

This represents a shortcut to a shared folder, web, or FTP site you created using the Add Network Place Wizard described earlier. Note that WS2003 sometimes creates some network shares automatically—for example, the "SYSVOL on <server>" shortcut in My Network Places on domain controllers, where <server> is the first domain controller in the forest root domain.

Computers Near Me

This takes the place of Entire Network if your computer belongs to a workgroup instead of a domain.

Right-clicking on My Network Places on the desktop also does some useful things:

Open

Opens the selected item; for example, if you open a workgroup, you see the computers in it.

Explore

Does the same as Open except it displays the folder using the two-pane Windows Explorer view.

Search for Computers

Opens the Search Assistant with the focus on searching for computers in the forest.

Who Am I

Displays credentials of logged-on user (present only when NetWare connectivity is enabled using CSNW or GSNW).

Map Network Drive

Maps a drive letter to a shared folder on a local or remote computer.

Disconnect Network Drive

Deletes a drive-letter mapping created earlier.

Create a Shortcut

Creates a shortcut to My Network Places and places it on the desktop.

Rename

Renames My Network Places. It's a really good idea to rename My Network Places so it displays the DNS name of your domain.

Properties

Has the same result as Start → Control Panel → Network Connections.

Shared Folders—Tasks

To share a folder, you first create the folder and then share it. Afterward, you can modify the shared folder by changing the permissions assigned to it or by changing the name under which it is shared, change the caching setting for offline use, share the folder under additional names, or stop sharing it. You can create and manage shared folders in two different ways in WS2003.

GUI Reference

- By accessing folder properties from the desktop or using Windows Explorer. This method is analogous to how one worked with shared folders in NT 4.0.
- By using Shared Folders in Computer Management. This method is analogous to using the NT administrative tool, Server Manager, but is easier and more powerful.

The advantages of using the latter method are:

- You can connect to remote machines and share folders without having to know the absolute path to the folder on the machine's drive.
- You can view hidden and administrative shares that aren't visible in My Computer, My Network Places, or Windows Explorer.
- You are presented with a uniform view of all shares on a machine in a single window.
- You can view session information, open files for users connected to shared folders, send messages to those users, and disconnect all or selected sessions and open files.
- You can create custom consoles using the Shared Folders snap-in to allow users to manage shared folders on a specific machine.

Let's look at each method in detail.

Share a Folder Using Windows Explorer

Select the folder using Windows Explorer and:

Right-click on folder → Properties → Sharing → Share this folder

Share name (required)

This is the name by which the shared folder will be visible on the network, and it doesn't need to be the same as the folder's name itself. The maximum length for a share name is 80 characters.

User limit

The number of concurrent client connections possible to the shared folder depends on the number of client access licenses (CALs) you have purchased.

Permissions

The default permission assigned to a newly created shared folder is Full Control for Everyone. If you add an ordinary user to the access list for a shared folder, the default permission assigned to the user is Read. See *Permissions* earlier in this chapter for information on shared-folder permissions.

Offline Settings

Discussed later in this section.

New Share

You can share the folder under additional share names. For example, *C:\Public* could be shared first using the default share name *Public* and then shared a second time using the share name *Pub*. Note that this option is available only after you have shared the folder for the first time. Each time you share a folder, you can assign different permissions and connection limits to the new share.

To modify an existing shared folder:

Right-click on folder → Properties → Sharing

Then make changes to the folder's permissions, change the share name, change the caching settings for offline access, reshare the folder under additional names, or stop sharing the folder as desired.

Share a Folder Using Computer Management

To share a folder on the local machine using Computer Management, use the Share a Folder Wizard:

> Computer Management → System Tools → Shared Folders → right-click on Shares → New File Share → specify path to folder → specify share name → configure offline settings if desired → specify shared-folder permissions

Here are the four different options for assigning permissions using the wizard:

All users have read-only access
> Allow Read is assigned to Everyone.

Administrators have full access; other users have read-only access
> Allow Full Control is assigned to Administrators.

> Allow Read is assigned to Everyone.

Administrators have full access; other users have read and write access
> Allow Full Control is assigned to Administrators.

> Allow Change is assigned to Everyone.

Use custom share and folder permissions
> Click the Customize button and assign the permissions you want.

To share a folder on a remote machine using Computer Management, do this:

> Computer Management → Action → Connect to another computer → select computer → System Tools → Shared Folders → right-click on Shares → New File Share

> Note that you must be a member of either the Administrators, Server Operators, or Power Users group to be able to create or modify shared folders.

Publish a Shared Folder in Active Directory

Publishing shared folders in Active Directory makes it easier for users to locate shared resources on the network. You should share the folder first before you publish it. To publish a shared folder in Active Directory, open the Active Directory Users and Computers console and:

> Right-click on a domain → New → Shared Folder → specify name → specify UNC path to shared folder

You can also publish shared folders to an OU within a domain instead of to the domain itself. For example, you can create an OU called Shares to contain all published shared folders in a domain.

Enable Offline Files on Client

> Windows Explorer → Tools → Folder Options → Offline Files → Enable Offline Files

Once this feature is enabled on the client, you need to configure offline files on the server.

Enable Offline Files on Server

Offline files are enabled on all shared folders by default and can be enabled or disabled on a per-shared folder basis. To enable or disable offline files for a shared folder:

Right-click on shared folder in Windows Explorer → Sharing → Offline Settings

You can either make all files in the share available offline, let the user specify which files in the share will be made available offline, or disable offline files for the share.

Configure Offline Files on Client

Windows Explorer → Tools → Folder Options → Offline Files → configure synchronization → create shortcut on desktop → encrypt offline files for greater security → specify disk space reserved for offline files → view or delete files

If you choose to synchronize all offline files before logging off, you must schedule Synchronization Manager to synchronize offline files automatically when you log off. Enabling reminders and specifying a time interval for these will cause a Help balloon to appear over the system tray (bottom-right corner of desktop) when the network connection becomes unavailable.

WS2003 clients automatically utilize 10% of their available disk space for locally caching offline files. If this is not enough, you can change the value here. Clicking View Files opens a window that displays which files have been locally cached. (You can also put a shortcut on your desktop to the *Offline Files* folder, which is located within the user's profile in the *Documents and Settings* folder.) Clicking Delete Files will let you delete your cached files but has no effect on copies stored on network file servers.

The Advanced button gives you more granular control of caching when you are accessing files on multiple file servers on the network. You can specify a list of file servers whose files are never cached locally or allow files from any file server to be cached (the default).

Configure Offline Files on Server

Right-click shared folder in Windows Explorer → Sharing → Offline Settings → configure settings

For more information, see *Offline Files* under *Shared Folders—Concepts*.

Make a File or Folder Available Offline

Right-click on the remote file, shared folder, or mapped network drive in Windows Explorer → Make Available Offline

This starts the Offline Files Wizard, which lets you choose whether to:

- Automatically synchronize the file, folder, or network drive when you log off or on to your client computer
- Cause Help balloons to appear over the system tray to let you know when your network connection becomes unavailable
- Create a shortcut to your *Offline Files* folder on your desktop

When you make a file, folder, or network drive available for offline use, its icon displays a two-way arrow indicating that it will be synchronized. Marking a network drive or shared folder for offline use marks all of its subfolders and files for offline use as well. In addition, any new folders or files you create within it are marked for offline use. Using the Offline Files Wizard, you configure these three settings globally for all offline files, folders, and drives by using the properties sheet opened by Windows Explorer → Tools → Folder Options → Offline Files. If you didn't select any of these options on the property sheet but select them all in the wizard, the last two will automatically be selected on the properties sheet.

Synchronize Offline Files

If a file has been made available offline, then you can manually force the cached local copy of the file to synchronize with the network copy of the file by:

> Right-click on file or folder → Synchronize

You can synchronize all or selected offline files by opening Windows Explorer and:

> Tools → Synchronize → select/deselect shares to synchronize → Synchronize

This opens Items to Synchronize, and by clicking Setup you can control synchronization by:

- Configuring how synchronization occurs on different network connections. This is useful if your computer is a portable and is used on multiple LAN or WAN connections.

- Toggling whether the user should be prompted before synchronizing files.

- Specifying which offline files should be synchronized after events like:
  - User logs on or off from network
  - System idle for a period of time
  - System running on battery power

In addition, Scheduled → Add starts the Scheduled Synchronization Wizard, which lets you create synchronization tasks to schedule when and how often different offline files should automatically be synchronized. (You can even cause your system to automatically dial a WAN connection if it is offline at the scheduled time.) Once a synchronization task has been created, you can further edit it to specify what to do if the task runs for an excessive period of time, how it should behave under different power-management conditions, and so on.

When a file with different modified versions on the client computer and network file server is synchronized, a Resolve File Conflicts dialog box appears, asking you whether you want to:

- Keep both versions (the local one is renamed and saved on the file server)
- Replace the remote version with the local one
- Discard the local one

You can open both versions of the file for viewing to help you make your decision. You can also make your choice the default for all conflicts with offline files.

Working with Offline Files

When you are working offline (for example, when the network connection to a file server on which you have enabled offline files has gone down), you can have a computer icon appear in the system tray and a Help balloon message notify you (see *Configure Offline Files on Server* earlier in this section). This system-tray icon is helpful since you can right-click on it to check the status of your connection to the file server and attempt to force synchronization. When the connection is restored, you can go back to the online version of the file by double-clicking the system-tray icon and clicking OK. When files are offline, you can work with them and save changes. When

GUI Reference

your network connection is restored and you log off, these changes will be synchronized with the server.

Enable Shadow Copies

Shadow copies must be enabled before they can be used. To enable shadow copies on your server, do the following:

> Computer Management → System Tools → right-click on Shared Folders → All Tasks → Configure Shadow Copies → select the volume where the shadow copies will be stored → Enable

You can also do it this way:

> Windows Explorer → right-click on any fixed volume → Properties → Shadow Copies → select the volume where the shadow copies will be stored → Enable

Configure Settings for Shadow Copies

> Computer Management → System Tools → right-click on Shared Folders → All Tasks → Configure Shadow Copies → select the volume where the shadow copies will be stored → Settings → specify storage area → specify maximum size → specify schedule

Install Shadow Copy Client Software

To view shadow copies you must first install appropriate client software for your version of Windows. First, you need to share the client files on a WS2003 machine:

> Windows Explorer → right-click on *System32\clients\twclient* → Sharing and Security → Share this folder

Now the client can connect and install the software:

> Start → Run → *fileserver***Windows\system32\clients\twclient\x86\twcli32.msi** → OK

This installs the Previous Version Client on your machine, and you can now work with shadow copies on the file server.

View a Previous Version of a File

> Windows Explorer → right-click on file → Properties → Previous Versions → select a previous version of the file → View

If no previous versions are displayed, the file has not changed since the oldest copy was taken.

Copy a Previous Version of a File

> Windows Explorer → right-click on file → Properties → Previous Versions → select a previous version of the file → Copy → specify destination

You can use this to recover a file that was accidentally deleted.

Restore a Previous Version of a File

> Windows Explorer → right-click on file → Properties → Previous Versions → select a previous version of the file → Restore

This deletes the current version of the file!

Shared Folders—Notes

Sharing Files

If the folder you want to share is on an NTFS volume, you must have a minimum NTFS permission of Read for the folder in order to share it.

If you copy a shared folder, the copy is not shared. However, the original shared folder remains shared.

If you move a shared folder, the moved folder is not shared.

Folders can be shared multiple times, each time with a different share name and different shared-folder permissions.

To temporarily prevent all users from accessing a shared folder, stop sharing it. This will immediately disconnect any users who had connected to the folder to access its contents.

You can change the share name of a shared folder without stopping it from being shared first. If you change the actual name of the folder itself, however, it will no longer be shared.

You can also share printers over the network. See *Printing* earlier in this chapter for more information.

Shared folders and shared printers are often simply called *shares* in Microsoft parlance.

When you are mapping a network drive, you can connect as a different user if desired. For example, if you are an administrator working at an ordinary user's desktop machine and you need to access the contents of a share whose permissions are restricted to Administrators, you can connect to the share using your Administrator credentials and the Map Network Drive Wizard.

Keep the share name the same as the folder name to simplify administration of shared folders.

If you add a dollar sign ($) as a suffix to the share name for a shared folder, it becomes a hidden folder that doesn't appear in My Network Places or Windows Explorer. A user can still access the folder, though, if he knows the exact share name—so this method should not be used to secure a shared folder. Use permissions instead to control access to the folder.

To make things easier for users when there are a large number of shared folders on the network, specify a Comment for each shared folder that describes what the folder is used for or what it contains. These comments are visible to users in My Network Places and Windows Explorer.

A good suggestion is to create all shared folders on NTFS volumes. Then leave the shared-folder permissions at their default setting (Full Control for Everyone), and manage folder access using the more granular NTFS permissions. For more information on shared-folder and NTFS permissions and how they combine, see *Permissions* earlier in this chapter.

There is little reason to create multiple shares for a single folder using New Share. Keep things simple when you are creating and managing shared folders.

If you have shared a folder more than once, an additional option called Remove a Share appears on the Sharing tab of the folder's properties sheet.

Do not stop sharing a folder while users are connected to it, or they may lose their data. Instead, first send a console message to all users connected to the share, indicating that they should save their work. Do this by opening the Computer Management console and selecting System Tools → Shared Folders → Action → Send Console Message.

If you modify the permissions on a shared folder to grant users or groups access to the folder, but users complain that they still don't have the access you promised them, tell them to either:

- Log off and then log on again (simplest).
- Close all network connections from the client to the server where the share resides (for example, by disconnecting network drives to that machine), and then make new connections to the server.

Other things you can check if this doesn't work include:

- Their network connection.
- Which groups the user belongs to and the level of access to the resource these groups have.
- If the resource is located on an NTFS volume, make sure the user has NTFS permissions explicitly assigned to his user account or to a group to which he belongs.

Note that the information displayed in Shared Folders is not updated automatically. To update the display, use Action → Refresh.

If you stop sharing an administrative share, it may disrupt network communications with the server and remote management of the server. If you do stop an administrative share, you should reboot the server to restore the appropriate permissions on the share.

When you create a custom Shared Folders console, you specify in advance which computer this console will manage. You can't switch the focus to a different computer once the console has been created, though you have the option to do this if you launch the console from the command line. If you are using Shared Folders as part of Computer Management, however, you can switch the focus to a different computer using the Action menu.

When you create a custom Shared Folders console, you also have the option of displaying all three subnodes or any single subnode you specify. In this way, for example, you can create a Shared Folders console that displays only the open sessions on the server.

Open Files displays files opened by other users on the network but not files opened by yourself.

A *named pipe* is a mechanism by which local or remote processes can exchange information. Sessions display administrative connections to remote computers as named pipes, and these sessions can't be closed using Shared Folders (since to do so would interfere with the operation of the Shared Folders console itself).

Offline Files

Offline files let you make any shared files or folders on a Microsoft network available for offline use, provided the computer supports the Server Message Block (SMB) protocol for file sharing. This includes WS2003, W2K, XP, NT 4.0, Windows 98, and Windows 95 computers, but doesn't include Novell NetWare servers.

You can make shared folders, specific files within shared folders, or mapped network drives available for offline use on WS2003 clients.

Heavy use of offline files can slow down the logon and logoff process for users. Enable this feature only when needed, such as for laptop computers or when the network connection is unreliable.

To enable and configure offline files on the server, you need to be an administrator.

If a shortcut to a file is made available offline, you will be able to access that file offline. If a shortcut to a folder is made available offline, however, you will not be able to access the contents of that folder offline. To make the contents of a folder available offline, make the folder itself available offline.

To make a single file within a shared folder available offline, make the file available offline, and then create a shortcut to the file so you can access it even though you can't access the shared folder itself.

Shared folders made available offline on the server and configured for automatic caching are displayed as network folder icons within My Network Places on client computers once the client connects to them for the first time.

Offline files can also be managed centrally using Group Policy. Open the GPO linked to the OU containing the computers on which you want to enable and configure offline files, select Computer Configuration → Administrative Templates → Network → Offline Files, and configure the policies as desired.

Shadow Copies

A maximum of 64 shadow copies can be stored per volume. When this is exceeded, the oldest copies are deleted.

Shadow copies are read-only and can't be modified, but if you copy a shadow copy you can modify the copy!

When you restore a file from a shadow copy, its permissions are the same as they were originally.

Don't use shadow copies as a replacement for normal backups of your file server.

Choose a separate volume on a different disk drive as the storage area for your shadow copies.

Administrative Shares

You should not stop sharing or otherwise modify these administrative shares. If you do stop sharing one, it will be reshared when you reboot your system or when the Server service is restarted.

If you are an administrator, you can quickly display and access the contents of any drive (for example, the C: drive) on a remote machine (for example, *Server9*) by Start → Run → **\\Server9\C$** → OK.

In WS2003, the *%SystemRoot%* folder is named *Windows* by default. This has changed since W2K and NT, on which this folder was named *Winnt* by default.

See Also

Files and Folders, net file, net send, net session, net share, net use, net view, openfiles, *Permissions*

Site—Concepts

While a domain is a logical grouping of computers connected for administrative purposes, a site is a physical grouping of computers that are well-connected to one another from the point of view of network bandwidth. Specifically, a site must consist of computers that:

- Run the TCP/IP protocol and are located on one or more subnets
- Are joined by a high-speed network connection, typically a LAN connection of 10-Mbps or greater with a high available bandwidth, but in some cases slower dedicated WAN connections

Sites are created within Active Directory to mirror the physical layout of a large network. Sites consist of one or more subnets and should mirror the physical connectivity of your network. Computers joined by LAN connections typically form a site, while slower WAN connections form the boundaries between different sites. You thus might have a Vancouver site, a Seattle site, and so on within your enterprise. Sites and domains don't need to correspond in a one-to-one fashion. For example, one domain may span several sites, or one site may span several domains.

Site Terminology

You need to understand a few other concepts to work with sites:

Site link

A connection between two sites that involves:

Cost

This is a number used to determine which site link will be preferred for replication when two sites are connected by multiple site links. The higher the cost number assigned to a site link, the lower the priority of the link as far as replication is concerned. A cost of 1 represents the highest priority for replication.

Member sites

This specifies the names of the sites that are connected by the site link. Most site links join only two sites, but it is possible to create backbone site links that link more than two sites together.

Schedule

This specifies the times when replication will occur between the sites. You might typically use 15 minutes over fast WAN links and longer time intervals over slower links.

Transport

This is the method used for intersite replication and can be either:

RPCs over IP

Use this transport when your WAN links are dedicated (always on). RPC communication is supported only by dedicated network links. Typically, this means using a leased line, such as a T1 line, for your WAN connection.

SMTP over IP

Use this transport for asynchronous WAN connections such as dial-up ISDN links. SMTP is Simple Mail Transport Protocol, the mail protocol used on the Internet, and it allows replication updates to be stored and forwarded as email messages.

Site-link bridge

This is a connection between two or more sites using multiple site links. Each site link in a site-link bridge must have a site in common with another site link in the bridge. This enables the bridge to calculate the cost value between sites in different links of the bridge.

You shouldn't need to use site-link bridges in fully routed IP internetworks, as site links are transitive. As a result, all site links belong by default to a default site-link bridge, and this is sufficient. You can disable the transitive nature of site links if you are using IP as your transport, and this will require that site-link bridges be created, but this is a lot of extra work and usually offers little gain in performance.

Subnet

This is a collection of IP hosts with a common subnet mask and network ID. Each site can consist of one or more subnets on your network.

Bridgehead server

This is a single domain controller used in each site for replication with other sites. You can let WS2003 automatically select and configure a bridgehead server, or you can manually define one for each site transport. Once you decide to manually specify a bridgehead server, the Knowledge Consistency Checker (KCC) no longer selects another bridgehead server if the designated one becomes unavailable, which can cause intersite replication to the site to stop.

Using Sites

Creating sites can help optimize the performance of your WS2003 network in a number of ways.

Logon Traffic

When a user attempts to log on to the network, the user's client computer contacts a domain controller to accomplish this. By default, XP Professional client computers try to find a domain controller in their own site to authenticate the user. In this way, valuable WAN-link bandwidth is conserved by not attempting to authenticate the user by remote domain controllers in other sites.

Replication Traffic

Sites can be used to schedule Active Directory replication traffic so that it occurs during off-peak hours. This gives administrators more control over replication traffic on their network. The reason is due to how the replication process works within a site (intrasite) and between sites (intersite):

Intrasite replication

Replication has low latency within a site, with the result that all domain controllers within a site almost always tend to be fully synchronized. If you make an update to Active Directory on one domain controller, this update is replicated to other domain controllers in the site 15 seconds after the update was made (this used to be 5 minutes in W2K). The way it works is that the domain controller on which the update was made notifies its replication partners, which then pull the updates from it. The topology of intrasite replication between domain controllers in a site is configured automatically by the KCC, and it doesn't need any further

GUI Reference

manual configuration by administrators. (The KCC is usually smart enough to establish the optimal replication topology within a site.)

Intersite replication

Replication between sites can be scheduled to utilize slow intersite WAN links during off-peak hours. In addition, replication information is compressed by about a factor of 10 to make more efficient use of these slow links. Intersite replication doesn't use notifications the way intrasite replication does. Intersite replication is enabled by creating site links between different sites.

Compression is used for intersite replication traffic only when the information to be updated exceeds 50 KB.

Distributed File System (DFS)

If you implemented DFS on your network and have replicas of a shared folder located in different sites, users will be automatically directed to the replica in their own site first if one exists, again conserving valuable WAN-link bandwidth between sites. See *DFS* earlier in this chapter for more information.

Site-Enabled Applications

Finally, Active Directory–aware applications, such as Microsoft's Exchange Server, can take advantage of sites to optimize messaging and replication traffic.

Planning Sites

Implementing sites on your network requires planning. The following are some of the things you need to consider when planning sites:

Default-First-Site-Name

When you install your first WS2003 domain controller, creating a forest root domain in a new forest, a default site called the Default-First-Site-Name is also created. You can rename this site to something more descriptive before you start creating new sites.

Site boundaries

Start by identifying the slow WAN links between different physical locations of your network, and use this information to create your sites.

Subnets

Each site must consist of one or more IP subnets. Look for subnets that are joined by high-speed LAN or WAN connections in your enterprise, and use this information to create subnet objects in Active Directory Sites and Services, associating them with your site objects.

Site links

Sites must be connected to one another by site links in order for replication to occur between them. Select the appropriate transport, specify the cost, and schedule replication for your site links as desired.

Domain controllers

Domain controllers should be placed where client computers can easily access them over high-bandwidth connections. Usually, the best solution is to place at least one domain controller in a site for each domain that is part of the site. The exception is when your site is a small branch office with only a few computers, in which case using the slow WAN link for logons would be acceptable.

Site—Tools

Active Directory Sites and Services

Active Directory Sites and Services is used to create sites and subnets that mirror the physical and geographical topology of your network. You can then configure how and when Active Directory replication occurs between different sites to optimize bandwidth usage over slow WAN links between sites. If your implementation of WS2003 is at one physical location only, then you may not use this tool at all. If you have multiple branch offices or subsidiaries at different locations, however, expect to use this tool, especially during the implementation stage when you are tuning network traffic over slow WAN links.

The console tree for this tool displays the sites in your enterprise and the links between them. A typical console tree looks like this:

```
Active Directory Sites and Services
   Inter-Site Transports
      IP
         Site link
         Site link ...
      SMTP
         Site link
         Site link ...
   Site
      Servers
         Server
            NTDS Settings
               Active Directory connection
               Active Directory connection...
         Server ...
   Site ...
   Subnets
   Subnet
   Subnet...
```

The three first-level containers here are:

Inter-Site Transports

This contains the various site links between your different sites, grouped together depending on whether they use RPCs or SMTP messages to replicate directory information between sites.

Sites

These are one or more containers for the various sites in your enterprise. The Default-First-Site-Name is created by default when you install your first domain controller in your forest root domain. Other sites are created using this tool to reflect the different physical or geographical locations of portions of your WS2003 network. Each site can contain one or more server objects, which are typically domain controllers. Each site also contains NTDS site settings for scheduling directory replication. Each server object contains an NTDS settings object, which represents the directory (*Ntds.dit* file). This file is located on an NTFS partition on the domain controllers and contains the Active Directory connections for the domain controller.

Subnets
> This contains the various subnets in your network, each of which is associated with one of your sites.

> The objects in the Server container for a site can also be member servers and not just domain controllers. This allows you to delegate authority over all servers (both domain controllers and member servers) in a given site.

Under the Action menu, you can select the following:

Active Directory Sites and Services node
> Select this to administer a target forest or to connect to a particular domain controller in the forest, thus retrieving the information needed to display the hierarchy of sites and subnets in the enterprise.

Sites, Inter-Site Transports, or Subnets container
> Select this in order to delegate authority to administer these portions of Active Directory to trusted users in your enterprise. You can also delegate individual sites or just the Servers container within a site. See *Delegation* earlier in this chapter for more information on the subject of delegation.

A site
> Select this to link a Group Policy Object (GPO) to that site. See *Group Policy* earlier in this chapter for more information.

A particular server within the Servers container in a site
> Select this if you want to move the server to a different site.

A particular Active Directory connection in the NTDS Settings container of any domain controller
> Select this to manually force directory replication to occur with that domain controller. For information on various tasks involving this tool, see *Domain Controller* earlier in this chapter and in the following section.

Site—Tasks

Sites, site links, and subnets are created and modified using the Active Directory Sites and Services console, which the following procedures assume is opened. Make sure you are logged on as a member of the Enterprise Admins group.

Create a New Site

> Right-click on Sites container → New Site → specify a name for the site → select a site link to associate with this site

Once you create a new site, you should add subnets for it to the Subnet container (see *Create a New Subnet* later in this section). You should then typically promote a member server in the site to the role of domain controller to facilitate user logons and specify the licensing computer for the site to ensure you're legal.

> You can delete any site you create, but you can't delete the Default-First-Site-Name—you can only rename it as something else. Note that you can, however, delete the DEFAULTSITELINK that was created for the Default-First-Site-Name.

Configure a Site

> Expand the Sites container → right-click on a site → Properties

The main thing to configure here is Location, which makes it easier to find sites in Active Directory when there are many of them. You can also apply Group Policy to the site (see *Group Policy* earlier in this chapter).

Create a New Site Link

> Right-click on Inter-Site Transports container → right-click on a transport (IP or SMTP) → New Site Link → specify a name → add sites to the site link

Once you create a new site link, you should configure its settings (see the next task).

Configure a Site Link

> Expand the Inter-Site Transports container → select transport (IP or SMTP) → right-click on a site link → Properties

The key settings here are on the General tab:

Cost
> Choose a lower cost value for a WAN connection with higher bandwidth and reliability to give preference to that connection when there are multiple links between sites. Dial-up connections such as ISDN should have a relatively high cost value for similar reasons. The lower-valued cost will always be used unless it is unavailable.

Replication interval
> The minimum replication interval is 15 minutes, and the maximum is 10,080 minutes (1 week). A typical choice is every few hours or so. Click the Change Schedule button to specify times and days of the week when the link will be unavailable for replication if needed.

Create a New Subnet

> Right-click on Subnets → New Subnet → specify network ID and subnet mask → select a site to associate with this subnet

When you specify the network ID and subnet mask, it is automatically displayed in the form *w.x.y.z/n*, where *w.x.y.z* is the network ID and *n* is the number of ones in the binary form of the subnet mask.

Configure a Subnet

> Expand the Subnets container → right-click on a subnet → Properties

The main thing you can configure here is Site on the Subnet tab. This lets you associate the selected subnet with a different site if desired.

Create an Active Directory Connection

To manually create a connection between a domain controller in one site and one in a different site, you can do the following:

> Expand the Sites container → expand a site → expand the Servers container → expand a server → right-click on NTDS Settings → New Active Directory Connection → select target domain controller

GUI Reference

Manually creating Active Directory connections is not usually necessary, as Active Directory creates these connections automatically between domain controllers in different sites. It is generally better to check the replication topology instead, using the procedure described earlier, which creates additional Active Directory connections if they are needed to optimize intersite replication.

Designate a Preferred Bridgehead Server

Bridgehead servers are domain controllers used for replication with other sites:

> Expand the Sites container → expand a site → select Servers container → right-click on a server → Properties → select transport → Add

Check the Replication Topology

The following procedure can be used to check the existing replication topology to determine whether it is optimal. The process checks whether domain controllers are available in each site and whether new ones have been added to sites. It then uses site link cost values to recalculate an optimal topology for intersite replication. If new Active Directory connections are required, these will be automatically created by the process:

> Expand the Sites container → expand a site → expand the Servers container → expand a server → right-click on NTDS Settings → All Tasks → Check Replication Topology

Force Replication Over a Connection

Use this procedure to force a domain controller in one site to replicate with one in a different site. The first domain controller is the one selected in the Servers container of the first site, while the second domain controller is the one specified on the Active Directory Connection tab of the properties sheet for the selected connection:

> Expand the Sites container → expand a site (the first site) → expand the Servers container → expand a server (the first domain controller) → select NTDS Settings → right-click on a connection → Replicate Now

To view the second site and second domain controller:

> … → select NTDS Settings → Properties → Active Directory connection → read Site and Server information

Move a Server to a Different Site

> Expand the Sites container → expand a site → select Servers container → right-click on a server → Move → select target site

This procedure is typically used to move a domain controller from one site to another to optimize replication and logon traffic for the target site.

Rename the Default-First-Site-Name

> Expand Sites container → right-click on Default-First-Site → Rename → specify a friendly name for the site

Site—Notes

Don't create additional sites unless you need them, since they may result in inefficient use of network bandwidth or poor performance of domain controller logon and replication functions.

Every site must have at least one site link for each site it is connected to; otherwise, domain controllers in the site will never replicate with those in the other connected sites.

If you schedule your site links to replicate only once a day (say at 3 a.m.), then replication latency may be unacceptably high in environments in which frequent changes are made to user and group settings. Using a more aggressive schedule (once an hour) is recommended in most cases.

If you have both a high-speed backbone link, such as a T3 link, and a slow redundant backup link, such as a 56-Kbps link, between two sites, you might configure a cost value of 1 for the backbone link and 100 for the redundant link. That way, the redundant link will never be used unless the high-speed backbone link is down.

Multihomed computers can belong only to a single site.

When SMTP is used as the transport for site links, the replication schedule is ignored.

SMTP used as a replication transport consumes about twice the network bandwidth as RPCs over IP because updates need to be packaged in SMTP messages.

SMTP can be used to replicate schema, configuration, and global catalog information between sites, but it can't be used to replicate between domain controllers belonging to the same domain. If you use SMTP as your transport, then your sites should be separate domains.

To delegate control of sites, right-click on a site → Delegate Control. See *Delegation* earlier in this chapter for more information.

A site link must contain at least two sites.

If you have two or more site links configured as a site-link bridge, the cost of the bridge is calculated as the sum of the costs of the links within the bridge.

You can delegate authority over sites, subnets, and Inter-Site Transports (see *Delegation* earlier in this chapter). You can apply Group Policy to sites as well (see *Group Policy* earlier in this chapter).

Manually created Active Directory connections will not be affected when Check Replication Topology is used to optimize intersite communications.

You can't use SMTP as an intersite transport unless you have installed a certificate authority (CA) in your enterprise and certificates on your domain controllers. This is necessary to ensure the authenticity of SMTP replication messages as they may be sent over the unsecured Internet.

See Also

Active Directory, Delegation, Group Policy

Tasks—Concepts

This topic covers how to schedule and manage tasks (applications and processes) using Scheduled Tasks and Task Manager.

Managing Tasks

By creating tasks and scheduling them, administrators can cause programs to run automatically without user intervention. Examples of tasks that can be scheduled include running scripts, running applications, and opening documents. Scheduling tasks is made possible by the Task Scheduler service, which starts automatically and runs in the background. Using the Scheduled Tasks Wizard, administrators can create and configure tasks and schedule how and when they run on the computer.

Once a task runs and the associated program starts, the program can be managed using Task Manager. Using this tool, administrators can start or end tasks, switch between tasks, and kill the processes associated with tasks.

Tasks—Tools

Scheduled Tasks

The *Scheduled Tasks* folder in Control Panel displays any tasks that have been scheduled to run on the system. New tasks are added to the folder using Add Scheduled Task, which starts the Scheduled Task Wizard. The Advanced menu on the *Scheduled Tasks* folder has several useful options:

Stop Using Task Scheduler
Stops Task Scheduler from running. The next time you start your computer, however, Task Scheduler will not automatically start again, and you will have to use Services in Computer Management to reconfigure its startup settings.

Pause Task Scheduler
Pauses the service and prevents any tasks from running. To resume the service, select Continue Task Scheduler.

Notify Me of Missed Tasks
Configures Task Scheduler to notify you by a pop-up message when a task can't be run.

AT Service Account
Specifies an account other than the System account as a security context within which scheduled tasks are run.

View Log
Opens the Task Scheduler log in Notepad. This log includes information on both tasks and the state of the service itself. The most recent data is at the bottom of the file. Note that this file is described incorrectly as *SchedLog.txt* in WS2003 Help (it is actually *SchedLgU.txt* and is in *%SystemRoot%*). A quick way to check the status of a task is to make sure the *Scheduled Tasks* folder is set to Details view and scroll to the Status column.

Task Manager

Task Manager has been enhanced in WS2003 with two additional tabs, Network and Users. The tasks that can be performed on these tabs are:

Applications
Displays the foreground programs currently running on the computer and lets you switch to a program (bring it into the foreground), end a program, or find the process associated with the program. You can also launch a new program if you know its associated executable file.

Processes

Displays the processes currently running on the computer and lets you end a process, end the process tree of which this process is the root, or modify the priority of the process. Do not indiscriminately modify the priority of running processes or your system may stop responding. You can use the Options menu to hide or view 16 bit processes that are running and the View menu to change to display additional columns of information about running processes.

Performance

Graphically displays CPU and virtual-memory usage and gives various real-time statistics about processes and memory. Double-click on a graph to display CPU usage information only in expanded view. Use the View menu to change the update speed, display each CPU separately on multiprocessor machines, or display the activity of kernel processes.

Networking

Graphically displays network utilization for any local area connections on your machine. By default, only Bytes Total is displayed, but you can also display Bytes Sent and Bytes Received using the View menu. Double-click on a graph to display Task Manager in full screen mode.

Users

Displays users currently connected to the machine. Right-click on a user to disconnect or log off the user or send a console message to the user, including to remote users connected to the system using Remote Desktop.

You can use the View menu to change the speed at which the information displayed by Task Manager is updated.

Tasks—Tasks

Schedule a Task

Control Panel → Add Scheduled Task → choose a program or browse to select an executable or script → specify name for task → specify scheduling option → specify time and date → specify credentials required to run program

The available scheduling options are:

• Daily at a specific time, weekdays only, or every nth day

• Weekly on a specific day(s) at a specific time for n weeks

• Monthly on a specific month(s) at a specific day or date

• Only once (specify date and time)

• Whenever your computer restarts

• Whenever you log on

You can also schedule a task by dragging a program, script, batch file, or document into the *Scheduled Tasks* folder and then configuring the properties of the task.

Configure a Task

Control Panel → Scheduled Tasks → select task

Then modify the properties of the task as desired. The Settings tab is of particular interest and can be used to do a number of tasks.

- Delete a task not scheduled to run again
- Stop a task that runs too long
- Run the task when the system is idle
- Stop running the task when the system is no longer idle
- Prevent the task from running when batteries are used or when batteries are low
- Wake the system from hibernation to run the task

Disable a Scheduled Task

To temporarily prevent a scheduled task from running:

Control Panel → Scheduled Tasks → select task → General → clear Enable checkbox

Configure an Additional Schedule for a Task

Control Panel → Scheduled Tasks → select task → Schedule → Show multiple schedules → New → configure schedule 2

You can have only two schedules for a task.

Configure How Often a Scheduled Task Runs

Control Panel → Scheduled Tasks → select task → Schedule → Advanced → Repeat Task → specify settings

Run a Task Now

Start → All Programs → Accessories → System Tools → Scheduled Tasks → right-click on task → Run

Run a Remote Task

Windows Explorer → My Network Places → Entire Network → Microsoft Windows Network → select domain or workgroup → select remote computer → Scheduled Tasks → right-click on task → Run

This works on WS2003, XP, W2K, NT, and Windows 95/98 computers, except that on Windows 95/98 computers you need to enable remote administration for your account and share the drive where the *Scheduled Tasks* folder is located. You must have administrative privileges on the remote system to run tasks like this.

Configure a Remote Task

Windows Explorer → My Network Places → Entire Network → Microsoft Windows Network → select domain or workgroup → select remote computer → Scheduled Tasks → right-click on task → Properties

Create a Remote Task

Create the task on the local machine, open the *Schedule Tasks* folders on both the local and the remote machine, and drag and drop the task from the local folder to the remote one. You can also email a task (*.job* file) to a user and have her save it into her *Scheduled Tasks* folder.

Open Task Manager

Right-click on taskbar → Task Manager
Ctrl+Alt+Delete → Task Manager
Command prompt → **taskmgr.exe**

End a Task

Task Manager → Applications → End Task

Kill a Process Associated with a Task

Task Manager → Applications → right-click on task → Go To Process → End Process

Disconnect or Log Off a User

Task Manager → Users → select user → Disconnect or Logoff

Send a Console Message to a User

Task Manager → Users → select user → Send Message

Tasks—Notes

If shadow copies are enabled on a volume, a volume-shadow-copies task appears in the *Scheduled Tasks* folder.

The user who configures the task usually doesn't need to be logged on at the time the task runs unless user input is required when the task runs.

If task A has started task B and you end task A, task B will still run.

Removing a task doesn't remove the executable that the task runs.

Make sure your computer's internal clock is set to the correct date and time if you want your tasks to execute as expected. If a task executes at an unexpected time, check your computer's date and time settings.

Don't try to schedule the *Backup* system tool using Scheduled Tasks, as *Backup* has its own built-in scheduling feature. However, backup jobs that are scheduled using *Backup* are displayed in the *Scheduled Tasks* folder.

See Also

at, *Backup*, schtasks, taskkill, tasklist

TCP/IP—Concepts

TCP/IP is a protocol that was originally implemented on Unix platforms but has now become the default network protocol on Microsoft Windows, Novell NetWare, and Apple Macintosh computing platforms. TCP/IP is routable and can be used for both local area networks and wide area networks. You should use TCP/IP if:

- Your network is heterogeneous in character, consisting of different computing platforms and operating systems that all need to work together.

- You need connectivity with the Internet or want to deploy Internet technologies within a corporate intranet environment.

GUI Reference

- You want to use the Active Directory component of WS2003. (Active Directory requires TCP/IP.)

A full treatment of TCP/IP is beyond the scope of this book. What follows here is a brief summary of its important features. For more information, see *TCP/IP Network Administration* by Craig Hunt (O'Reilly).

Some of the advanced features of TCP/IP in WS2003 include:

- Support for APIPA, which allows client computers to be assigned IP addresses automatically without the need of a DHCP server. See *Automatic Private IP Addressing (APIPA)* later in this section for more information.

- Support for dynamic recalculation of TCP window size and the ability to use large TCP windows to improve performance when large amounts of data are transmitted during a session. See Request For Comment (RFC) 1323 at *www.ietf.org/rfc/* for more information.

- Support for selective TCP acknowledgments to reduce the time retransmitting lost packets. See RFC 2018 for more information.

- Support for the TCP Round Trip Time Measurement option of RFC 1323 to improve performance over slow WAN links.

- Support for caching of resolved DNS name queries on client resolvers.

- Support for ICMP Router Discovery for discovering router interfaces that aren't assigned manually or through DHCP. This feature is enabled using the Routing and Remote Access console, and a description of the feature can be found in RFC 1256.

- The ability to disable NetBIOS over TCP/IP (NetBT) for specific network connections. This feature improves performance when DNS is the only name-resolution method in use on the network. This is really an all-or-nothing decision, as a WS2003 computer with NetBT disabled can use Client for Microsoft Networks to connect to other WS2003 computers running File and Print Sharing for Microsoft Networks only if those computers also have NetBT disabled. Disabling NetBT means the computer can no longer use NetBIOS name-resolution methods such as WINS servers or *lmhosts* files. In most cases, you will not use this feature as most networks will consist of a mix of WS2003 and legacy Windows clients and servers. For information on how to disable NetBT, see *WINS* later in this chapter.

IP Addressing

Each host (computer, network printer, router interface, and so on) on a TCP/IP network is generally characterized by three pieces of information:

IP address
    A logical 32 bit address that uniquely identifies the host on the network. IP addresses are expressed in dotted decimal form and consist of four octets separated by decimals with each octet ranging from 0 through 255 (with some restrictions). An example of an IP address might be 172.16.11.245.

Subnet mask
    A 32 bit number that divides the IP address into two parts—a network ID, which uniquely identifies the network that the host resides on, and a host ID, which uniquely identifies the host on that particular network. For example, the subnet mask 255.255.0.0, when applied to the IP address 172.16.11.245, indicates that the network ID of the host is 172.16, while the host ID of the host is 11.245.

Default gateway

A 32-bit address that identifies the default router interface to which to send packets that are directed to another network (or, more accurately, that are directed to a different subnet on a TCP/IP internetwork) if no other route is specified. The default gateway is optional and is necessary only on networks consisting of more than one subnet or when packets are being sent between different networks.

Managing TCP/IP

One aspect of managing TCP/IP is managing IP addresses on your network. WS2003 lets you assign IP addresses and other TCP/IP settings in three different ways:

Manually by using static IP addresses

This method is suitable only for small deployments of fewer than a hundred machines or so. TCP/IP settings must be configured at the local console of each machine, so this method is unsuitable if the hosts are geographically separated. Since errors in assigning IP addresses can cause general problems with network communications, this method can be a lot of work to troubleshoot.

Automatically by using DHCP

This is the default method for assigning TCP/IP settings on WS2003 machines. It uses one or more Dynamic Host Configuration Protocol (DHCP) servers, which maintain pools of available IP addresses, which lease these addresses to client computers that request them. DHCP should always be used on medium- to large-scale networks that run TCP/IP. DHCP can also be used by legacy Microsoft Windows platforms to configure TCP/IP on machines.

Automatic Private IP Addressing (APIPA)

If your WS2003 machine is configured to obtain an IP address by DHCP but no DHCP server is available on the network, the machine opts for assigning itself an address using APIPA. This method is an alternative to using DHCP on small- to medium-scale networks that use WS2003 and run DHCP. For more information, see the next section.

Automatic Private IP Addressing (APIPA)

APIPA is an extension of DHCP that allows computers to self configure their IP address and subnet mask without a DHCP server. The way it works is that a computer uses APIPA to randomly select a unique IP address from a block of IP addresses reserved by Microsoft for this purpose. This reserved IP block covers the address range 169.254.0.1 through 169.254.255.254 and, together with the subnet mask 255.255.0.0, provides enough addresses for 64,024 hosts running on a single subnet. In real life, however, APIPA is intended for use on home or small business networks containing at most a few dozen machines, because:

- Only the IP address and subnet mask can be assigned using APIPA, and not default gateways or other TCP/IP settings that can be provided by DHCP servers and that are needed by TCP/IP networks connected to other networks or to the Internet.

- Only a single subnet can be created using APIPA, which is not of much use in an enterprise-level network.

To configure a computer to use APIPA, simply configure it to obtain an IP address automatically. Then, when the machine restarts, it first tries to contact a DHCP server, and if this fails, APIPA then kicks in and the machine selects an IP address for itself of the form 169.254.*x.y*. It then tests the uniqueness of the address on the network by broadcasting a DHCP-type message to the rest of the machines on the network to find out if any other machine is using this address. If no other machine responds saying that it has taken that address, it assigns the address to itself along with the subnet mask 255.255.0.0. If, however, another computer claims to already be using the address, APIPA generates another address at random until a usable one is found. Then, should a DHCP server later be installed on the network, computers that used APIPA to select an address will soon detect the DHCP server and request a new IP address and other TCP/IP settings from the server.

APIPA can cause problems on large networks, however. For example, if a DHCP server goes down and client computers can't renew their leases, they would start using APIPA to assign themselves addresses. This would result in communications on the network breaking down because the machines that acquired new addresses using APIPA would be on a different subnet from those still holding their leased DHCP addresses. The solution is to disable APIPA entirely, but, unfortunately, the only way to do this is to use the registry. You disable APIPA on a specific network adapter by creating a new key called `IPAutoconfigurationEnabled` of type `REG_DWORD` within the subkey:

```
HKLM\SYSTEM\CurrentControlSet\Services\Tcpip\Parameters\Interfaces\GUID_of_
network_adapter\
```

and assigning this new key the value 0. Change the value to 1 to reenable APIPA on the adapter. On a multihomed machine with multiple network adapters, you can disable APIPA on all adapters by placing the `IPAutoconfigurationEnabled` key within the subkey:

```
HKLM\SYSTEM\CurrentControlSet\Services\Tcpip\Parameters\
```

If there are network connections that aren't being used on servers (most importantly, domain controllers), they should either be disabled or have APIPA disabled. Otherwise, clients may get incorrect IP addresses when querying DNS.

Troubleshooting TCP/IP

WS2003 includes a comprehensive set of command-line utilities for testing and troubleshooting TCP/IP configurations and networks, including `arp`, `ipconfig`, `nbtstat`, `netstat`, `pathping`, `ping`, `route`, and `tracert`. For more information on these utilities, see Chapter 5.

TCP/IP—Tasks

Configure TCP/IP

To configure TCP/IP, open the Internet Protocol (TCP/IP) Properties sheet on your system:

- If you are configuring TCP/IP for a local-area connection, then do the following:

    Start → Control Panel → Network Connections → select a local-area
    connection → Properties → select Internet Protocol (TCP/IP) →
    Properties

- If you are configuring TCP/IP for a dial-up or VPN connection, then do the following:

    Start → Control Panel → Network Connections → select a dial-up or VPN
    connection → Properties → Networking → select Internet Protocol (TCP/
    IP) → Properties

- To use DHCP or APIPA for obtaining TCP/IP settings, select "Obtain an IP address automatically." APIPA will be used if a DHCP server can't be found. See *DHCP* earlier in this chapter for more information.

Use the Internet Protocol (TCP/IP) properties sheet to make various changes to your TCP/IP configuration. The remaining tasks assume that you have the Internet Protocol (TCP/IP) Properties sheet open on your system.

Add a Default Gateway

To assign additional default gateways to a network connection:

> Advanced → IP Settings → Default gateways → Add

Add an IP Address

To assign additional IP addresses and subnet masks to a network connection:

> Advanced → IP Settings → IP addresses → Add

You can assign as many IP addresses as you like to the connection. A typical use of this feature is creating multiple virtual servers for hosting different web sites on machines running Internet Information Services (IIS).

Assign a Metric

The metric for the network connection is the cost in hops of using this connection to route packets. The metric you specify using Advanced → IP Settings is entered into the routing table for the network interface. The default value is 1, and this should usually not be changed unless you want to shape the flow of traffic over your internetwork, and then only if you are dealing with a multihomed WS2003 system acting as a router.

Configuration Method

To manually assign an IP address, subnet mask, and default gateway, choose "Use the following IP address."

DNS Client Configuration

You can either manually specify the IP address of a preferred and alternate DNS server, or, if you are using DHCP, you can select "Obtain the DNS server address automatically." You can also add IP addresses for additional DNS servers, modify the order in which these servers are queried by resolvers, and perform other DNS client configuration actions by Advanced → DNS. See *DNS* earlier in this chapter for more information.

TCP/IP Filtering

> Advanced → Options → Properties → Enable TCP/IP Filter (all adapters) → Permit Only → specify {TCP ports | UDP ports | IP protocols}

TCP/IP filtering can be used to protect your computer or simply to manage the bandwidth utilized by incoming network traffic. You can control which types of incoming TCP/IP traffic are accepted by your computer. TCP/IP filtering works with broadcast, multicast, and directed packets. Note that on a multihomed machine (multiple network adapters), filter settings apply globally to all adapters. You can also filter traffic using the Routing and Remote Access Service or by installing a firewall or proxy server application on your machine.

GUI Reference

When configuring TCP/IP filtering, make sure you don't block traffic that is essential to your network's operation! For example, blocking UDP ports 67 and 68 would cause problems with DHCP.

TCP/IP—Notes

You should assign static IP addresses to servers and let DHCP assign addresses automatically to desktop computers.

XP, W2K, and Windows 98/Me also support APIPA.

Any TCP/IP settings you configure manually on a computer will override similar settings obtained from a DHCP server.

A good practice on multihomed machines is to configure only a default gateway on the first adapter. If both adapters have gateways configured, the second gateway is used only if the first one is unavailable.

Configure multiple default gateways for a single adapter if your network topology is complex enough to allow alternate routes between subnets. This way, if a router fails, communications can still be maintained.

If your computer is configured to obtain an IP address automatically from a DHCP server but the server doesn't provide your computer with a default gateway, you either need to reconfigure the DHCP server to provide a default gateway or manually configure a TCP/IP address and subnet mask on the client in order to assign it a default gateway.

You can manually specify the IP addresses of WINS servers on your network, or you can use DHCP to assign these addresses. You can also manually enable or disable NetBIOS over TCP/IP (NetBT), obtain NetBT settings from a DHCP server, and enable or disable NetBIOS name resolution using *lmhosts* files using Advanced → WINS. See *WINS* later in this chapter for more information.

If your network will be connected to the Internet, the best IP addressing scheme to follow is to assign addresses from the private IP address blocks reserved by the Internet Assigned Numbers Authority (IANA) and connect your network to the Internet using a firewall or proxy server that uses Network Address Translation (NAT). The private IP addresses reserved by IANA are shown in Table 4-52. You can use these addresses as long as you aren't directly connected to the Internet.

Table 4-52. IP address blocks reserved for private networks

Network ID	Subnet mask	Range of addresses
10.0.0.0	255.0.0.0	10.0.0.1 to 10.255.255.254
172.16.0.0	255.240.0.0	172.16.0.1 to 172.31.255.254
192.168.0.0	255.255.0.0	192.168.0.1 to 192.168.255.254

See Also

arp, *DHCP*, *DNS*, finger, ftp, getmac, hostname, ipconfig, nbtstat, netstat, pathping, ping, rcp, rexec, route, rsh, telnet, tftp, tracert

Trusts—Concepts

Trusts provide a mechanism for users in one domain to access resources in other domains. Active Directory supports several kinds of trusts, as described in the following sections.

Transitive Trust

Two-way transitive trusts are automatically created when new child domains are added to an existing tree or when a new root domain is added to an existing forest to form a new tree. *Transitive* means that downstream trusted domains can be trusted over the trust—for example, if A trusts B and B trusts C, then A trusts C if all trusts are transitive. Transitive trusts require no maintenance or configuration and allow users to be authenticated by domain controllers in any domain in the forest. Transitive trusts operate using the Kerberos v5 authentication protocol.

External Trust

Also called a one-way trust, this type of trust is unidirectional and nontransitive (similar to NT) and must be explicitly created using the Active Directory Domains and Trusts console. In an external trust, the trusting domain trusts the trusted domain, and users in the trusted domain can access resources in the trusting domain, provided they have suitable permissions assigned for the resources they are trying to access. You can explicitly establish an external trust between a WS2003 domain and another WS2003 domain, a W2K domain, or an NT domain. You can also create a nontransitive two-way trust by creating two one-way trusts in opposite directions between two domains.

External trusts are typically used:

- To establish an explicit trust between a WS2003 or W2K domain and a legacy NT domain
- To establish an explicit trust between two WS2003 or W2K domains in different forests

Cross-Link Trust

Also called shortcut trusts, these are simply external trusts created to shorten the trust path between two domains in a forest when the users in one or both of these domains frequently need to access the resources in the other domain. By creating a shortcut trust between two domains in a forest, the Kerberos authentication process by which users are granted access to resources in different domains is considerably shortened in terms of the number of domains it must traverse, reducing authentication traffic and speeding up the interdomain authentication process for users.

Forest Trust

New to WS2003 is the forest trust (also called cross-forest trust), which is available only for forests that are configured at the WS2003 forest functional level. Forest trusts allow users in one forest to access resources in another forest using either Kerberos or NTLM authentication. Forest trusts are transitive trusts that can be created manually between the forest root domains of two forests and add additional flexibility to planning an Active Directory implementation by providing enterprises with more options for upgrading their NT or W2K domains to WS2003.

Forest trusts are external trusts created between the forest root domains of two forests. Note that forest trusts work only between two forests—in other words, if a forest trust between forests A and B is created and then one is created between forests B and C, there is no implicit forest trust between forest A and C. In other words, the transitivity of forest trusts is valid only within the two forests connected by the trust.

Trusts—Tasks

Trusts are managed using the Active Directory Domains and Trusts console, which is discussed under *Site* earlier in this chapter. The following procedures assume that you have this console open.

Create an External Trust

External trusts are one-way trusts in which a trusting domain trusts a trusted domain. Before you create a one-way trust, you need to decide which domain is the trusting domain and which is the trusted one. The trusting domain typically contains the shared resources that need to be accessed, while the trusted one contains the user accounts that need to access these resources.

Create an External Trust Within a Forest

To create a one-way external trust between two domains in the same forest:

> Right-click on trusted domain → Properties → Trusts → New Trust → specify DNS or NetBIOS name of trusting domain → One-way incoming → Both this domain and the specified domain → specify administrator credentials

To create a two-way external trust between two domains in the same forest:

> Right-click on trusted domain → Properties → Trusts → New Trust → specify DNS or NetBIOS name of trusting domain → Two-way → Both this domain and the specified domain → specify administrator credentials

Create an External Trust Between Forests

To create a one-way external trust between two domains in different forests, first start in the forest where the trusted domain resides and do this:

> Right-click on trusted domain → Properties → Trusts → New Trust → specify DNS or NetBIOS name of trusting domain → One-way incoming → This domain only (specify a password for the trust)

Now go to the other forest and do this:

> Right-click on trusted domain → Properties → Trusts → New Trust → specify DNS or NetBIOS name of trusted domain → One-way outgoing → This domain only (specify same password as above for the trust) → specify level of access to grant users in the trusted domain for resources in the trusting domain

To create two-way trusts, simply create two one-way trusts in opposite directions.

Create a Cross-Forest Trust

To create a cross-forest trust between two forests, first either make sure DNS servers in each forest can resolve the name of the other forest or ensure NetBIOS is enabled so you can specify the NetBIOS name of the forest instead of its DNS name. Then do this:

> Right-click on a domain → Properties → Trusts → New Trust → specify DNS or NetBIOS name of trusting forest → continue as previously for Create an External Trust Between Forests

Create an External Trust to a Kerberos v5 Realm

You can also create one-way trusts with non-Windows Kerberos realms by:

> Right-click on trusted domain → Properties → Trusts → New Trust → specify name of trusting realm → Realm trust → Transitive | Non-transitive → One-way incoming → specify a password for the trust

Then go to the Kerberos realm and create the other end of the trust using the same password.

Verify a Trust

> Right-click on a domain → Properties → Trusts → select a trusted or trusting domain → Edit → Verify

If the trust is working, a dialog box will confirm this. If the trust has failed, a series of dialog boxes will lead you through the process of reestablishing the trust relationship between the domains. You can verify both implicit (transitive) and explicit (external or shortcut) trusts this way.

Revoke an External Trust

> Right-click on the trusted or trusting domain → Properties → Trusts → select trusted or trusting domain → Remove

You can't revoke the implicit two-way transitive trusts that are created and maintained automatically by Active Directory; you can revoke only external trusts that you have explicitly created.

Trusts—Notes

Upgrading an existing NT 4.0 network to WS2003 preserves all existing trusts; that is, one-way trusts remain one-way in nature.

If you install a new WS2003 domain and you want its users in your existing NT network to be able to access resources in the new domain (and vice versa), you must create explicit trusts between the NT and WS2003 domains using Active Directory Domains and Trusts.

An external trust displays as External in the Relationship column of the Trusts tab.

See Also

Active Directory, Forest

Users—Concepts

A user (or user account) is a security principle that allows an individual to log on to a computer or network. The two kinds of user accounts in WS2003-based networks are:

Local user account

> Enables a user to log on to a standalone server to access resources on that computer. Local users are stored on the computer on which they are created in the computer's local security database. Local users can't be created on domain controllers, but they can be created on member servers belonging to a domain.

GUI Reference

Domain user account

> Enables a user to log on to a domain to access resources on computers in the domain. Domain users are domainwide in scope and are stored within Active Directory. Domain user accounts are internally identified within Active Directory by their security identifier. If you delete an account and create a new account with the same name, it will have a different SID than the deleted account.

Built-in Accounts

In addition, a number of built-in user accounts are created when WS2003 is installed:

Administrator

> An account that has full administrative rights for the domain or computer.

Guest

> An account used to grant temporary access to network resources in the domain or computer. This account is disabled by default and should be enabled only when needed.

On a member server or client computer, the Administrator and Guest accounts are local user accounts and are stored in the local security database. For example, the Administrator account on a member server has full administrative rights on that member server and no rights on any other computer in the network. On a domain controller, however, these accounts are domain user accounts and are stored in Active Directory. Therefore, the Administrator account on a domain controller has full rights on every computer in the domain. Depending on which optional components of WS2003 are installed, there may be other built-in user accounts. Table 4-53 lists some of the most common of these accounts.

Table 4-53. Optional built-in user accounts

Account	Name	Description
Internet Guest account	IUSR	Used by Internet Information Services (IIS) to provide anonymous users with access to IIS resources
Launch IIS Process account	IWAM	Used by IIS to launch out-of-process web applications
TsInternetUser	TsInternetUser	Used by Terminal Services
krbtgt	krbtgt	Key Distribution Center service account (disabled by default)

User Profiles

A *user profile* is a collection of files that stores the desktop configuration and personal settings of a user. User profiles ensure that users have consistent desktop and application settings each time they log on to their machines. User profiles can also be stored on the network to enable users to access their desktop and personal settings from any machine on the network and can be configured either to allow or prevent users from modifying their settings. Specifically, a user profile stores information about a user's desktop settings, wallpaper, screen resolution, desktop icons, Start menu items, files stored in his *My Documents* folder, network connections, mapped drives, and network shortcuts to shared folders and printers located on network servers

The three types of user profiles are local, roaming, and mandatory. These three types allow administrators to control users' desktop environments in a variety of ways.

Local User Profile

This user profile is stored on the local machine. A local user profile (or local profile) for a user is created the first time a user logs on locally to a machine. These local profiles are stored by default in subfolders of *C:\Documents and Settings*. Each subfolder is named after the username of a user who has logged on locally to the machine at least once. For example, the local profile for Administrator is located in the folder *C:\Documents and Settings\Administrator* and consists of a series of subfolders and files within the *Administrator* folder.

When a user makes changes to her desktop (e.g., changes the wallpaper) and then logs off, the local profile is updated to reflect any changes made by the user during the session. When the user next logs on, the settings will reflect these changes made during the previous session. If multiple users use the same machine, each user will have his own, separate, local profile stored in the folder *C:\Documents and Settings\ <username>*. Each user's settings will be preserved regardless of what the other users do while they are logged on to the machine.

Roaming User Profile

By storing users' profiles on a network file server and configuring users' accounts with information about where their profiles can be found, you give users the ability to roam around the network, log on to any client machine, and retrieve their own personal desktop settings for use on that machine. This is known as roaming user profiles (or roaming profiles) and is useful when users need to perform their work at multiple client computers.

When a user logs on to a machine using the roaming profile and makes changes to the desktop environment, these changes are saved when the user logs off. If the user then logs on to a different machine, the changes made on the first machine are reflected on the second. In other words, users can make changes to their roaming profiles, unless mandatory user profiles are implemented, as described next.

Roaming profiles are typically used when users share their computers. For example, if you have 15 sales personnel sharing five computers (since most of the time they should be out drumming up contracts anyway), then you could implement roaming profiles for these users so they can use whichever of the five computers is currently free. Another example would be if you had 10 trainers who need to access their email during coffee break. You could give them two computers to share and assign them roaming profiles (the cost-effective solution) or give them each a laptop (my own preference, but no one ever listens to me).

Mandatory User Profile

A mandatory user profile (or mandatory profile) is a form of roaming user profile in which the user can't make changes. The user can, however, make changes to the desktop environment while logged on. But when she logs off, the mandatory profile is not updated to reflect these changes. Mandatory user profiles are also sometimes referred to as mandatory roaming profiles and roaming mandatory profiles!

You might use mandatory profiles for naive users to prevent them from making changes to their desktop. Users sometimes like to install shareware and other software they have downloaded off the Internet, and sometimes such software can cause problems that necessitate costly intervention from technical support staff. Mandatory profiles prevent such changes to users' desktops and thus reduce the costs of supporting these users.

Another use for mandatory profiles might be to create a customized user profile that you assign to several users who need to perform the same type of tasks on their computers. You can create a default user profile that reflects the kind of desktop environment most conducive to their productivity, make this profile mandatory, and then assign it to each user.

How User Profiles Work

When a user logs on to a WS2003 client computer for the first time, the following procedure occurs:

1. WS2003 checks whether a roaming profile has been specified for the user by the administrator. If so, it downloads this roaming profile from the appropriate network file server and applies it to the user's desktop environment. When the user logs off, the roaming profile is updated on the file server to reflect any changes the user has made during the session.

2. If not, WS2003 checks whether there is a network-default user profile. A default user profile is a kind of template from which all other user profiles are created. It is called the network-default user profile if it has the name Default User and is stored in the NETLOGON administrative share on all domain controllers.

3. If such a default profile exists on the domain controller that the client computer contacts, WS2003 downloads this profile and applies it to the user's desktop environment. When the user logs off, a local profile is created on the client computer for the user. The next time the user logs on, the local profile is used instead of the network-default profile.

4. If not, WS2003 loads the default local user profile and applies it to the user's desktop environment. When the user logs off, a local profile is created on the client computer for the user. The next time the user logs on, the local profile is used instead of the local default profile.

Home Folders

A user's home folder is a centralized location on a network file server where he can store his personal documents. Home folders were a feature of NT that allowed users to store their personal files on network file servers, which could be backed up easily, instead of on their local machines. While WS2003 still supports home folders for backward compatibility with legacy applications, the default location for users to store their personal files is now the *My Documents* folder. By default, this folder is located on a user's local machine and is part of the user's profile.

My Documents

My Documents is a special folder that is part of a user profile. The *My Documents* folder is the default location for users to store their personal and work files. When you select File → Open from the menu of a "designed for WS2003" application, the application looks by default in the *My Documents* folder for the currently logged-on user. Similarly, when a user selects File → Save As to save work, it goes into the *My Documents* folder.

Each user who logs on to a WS2003 machine has his own separate *My Documents* folder for storing files. Each user also has an icon on the desktop that allows him easy access to his files. The *My Documents* folder for a user is contained within the user profile for that particular user. For example, if a user named Bob has his local user profile stored in *C:\Documents and Settings\Bob* on his machine, Bob's personal and work files will be stored in the subfolder *C:\Documents and Settings\Bob\My Documents*.

My Documents and other important user profiles can also be redirected to a network share using Group Policy. This ensures that users have their data available no matter which client computer they log on with. See *Group Policy* earlier in this chapter for more information.

Users—Tools

The two main tools for managing users are:

Active Directory Users and Computers
> Used to manage domain user accounts stored in Active Directory. See *Active Directory* earlier in this chapter for an overview of this tool.

Computer Management
> Contains the Local Users and Groups snap-in under System Tools, which is used to manage local user accounts on a standalone server.

In addition, the Advanced tab on System in the Control Panel can be used to manage user profiles.

Users—Tasks

Managing Domain Users

Domain user accounts are administered using the Active Directory Users and Computers console. After opening this console, expand the console tree and select the OU in which the account is located or where it will be created. Then proceed with the steps described in the following sections. Note that built-in user accounts such as Administrator and Guest are located in the default Users container.

Create a User

> Right-click on OU → New → User

Then specify first and/or last name (at least one of these is required) and the user logon name. The full name and downlevel (Pre–Windows 2000) logon name are then generated automatically from this information, but you can also define them differently if desired. The wizard's second screen asks you to specify a password and account restrictions (see *Configure a User* later in this section for more information).

 You can also create multiple user accounts by importing a specially formatted *.csv* file using the bulk-import utility *csvde.exe*.

On the first screen of the wizard, specify:

User logon name
> This is the name that the user will use to log on to the network, which might be something like *marys* or *msmith* for user Mary Smith. User logon names must always be unique within the domain. What's confusing is that there is an unlabeled listbox to the right of the text box for user logon name. This listbox displays the name of the currently selected domain, but this domain name begins with an

@ sign. The idea implied here is that the user logon name consists of two parts, an alias such as *marys* and a domain such as *@mtit.com*.

To create the account in a different domain, use the drop-down arrow in the listbox. Note that you must be a member of the Administrator or Account Operators group in a domain to be able to create accounts in the domain.

User logon name (Pre–Windows 2000)

This is the logon name that the same user will use when logging on to client computers running NT Workstation, Windows 98, or earlier versions of Microsoft Windows. Once again, the confusion is that there are two text boxes for this logon name: the first one is already populated with the older NetBIOS name of the domain followed by a backslash, and the second one is populated with the user logon name or alias you typed in the previous step. For example, if *HEADQUARTERS* is the NetBIOS domain name associated with the domain *mtit.com*, then Mary Smith's downlevel logon name would be *HEADQUARTERS\ marys*.

A user's downlevel logon name must also be unique within the domain. The NetBIOS domain name is determined when Active Directory is installed using the Active Directory Installation Wizard. This NetBIOS domain name can be found later using Active Directory Users and Computers by right-clicking on the domain node → Properties → General.

Full names must be unique within the OU in which the account resides. For example, there can be an account named Mary Smith in both the Accounting and Sales OUs within the *mtit.com* domain, provided that these accounts have different user logon names. You can do this by assigning Mary Smith in Accounting the logon name *marys@mtit.com* and Mary Smith in Sales the logon name *marys2@mtit.com*.

Accounts in different domains within a domain tree can also have identical full names. For example, there can be an account named Mary Smith in both the *mtit.com* and *ny. mtit.com* domains, where *mtit.com* is the parent domain and *ny.mtit.com* is the child domain. In this case, the logon name for Mary Smith in *mtit.com* would be *marys@mtit.com*, while that for Mary Smith in *ny.mtit.com* would be *marys@ny.mtit. com*, ensuring their uniqueness.

Configure a User

Right-click on user → Properties

This opens the properties sheet for the account, which has a number of tabs.

General, Address, Telephones, and Organization

These tabs let you specify personal information about the user. You should take time to populate these fields so you can search for users in Active Directory using search criteria such as name, address, organization, email, and so on.

Account

These settings are a superset of the account settings you specified when you created the account.

Logon Hours

Lets you specify when users can log on to the domain. This can help prevent accounts from being misused during off-hours. If users are logged on and their

---

hours expire, they can't form new connections to shared resources in the domain, but they aren't bumped off resources they are already connected to.

Log On To

Lets you specify the NetBIOS names of client computers in the domain with which the user is permitted to log on to the domain. This can help prevent users from trying to access information stored on computers that belong to other users. By default, users can log on to the domain using any client computer in the domain.

Account Options

These are more commonly known as account restrictions. Note that selecting some options prevents others from being selected. The more commonly enabled options include:

User must change password at next logon

This is a good choice in low- to medium-security environments because it forces users to take responsibility for managing their passwords and removes this burden from the administrator. In high-security environments, complex passwords may be created and assigned to users by the administrator.

User can't change password

Again, this is generally used in high-security environments or, at the other end of the scale, it can be used to prevent careless users from denying themselves access.

Password never expires

Note that an expired password and an expired account are two different things.

Account is disabled

See *Disable a User Account* later in this section.

Account Expires

By default, new accounts never expire.

User Profile

This lets you specify the network location of the user profile, the user's home folder, and a logon script that runs when the user logs on.

Another way to configure logon scripts for users is to use Group Policy, which allows administrators to centrally manage startup, shutdown, logon, and logoff scripts for all users and computers in a domain. See the earlier section *Group Policy* for more information.

Remote Control

This lets you enable administrators to remotely observe and control a Terminal Services session being run by the user.

Member Of

This displays the groups to which the user belongs and lets you modify which groups the user belongs to. See *Groups* earlier in this chapter for more information on the different kinds of groups that can be created in WS2003.

Leave the Primary Group as Domain Users unless you have Macintosh or POSIX clients and there is a reason you need to specify a different group.

Dial-in

This lets you control whether and how the user can remotely connect via a dial-up connection to a remote access server. See *Routing and Remote Access* earlier in this chapter for more information.

Environment, Sessions, Terminal Services Profile

This lets you specify the startup environment, Terminal Services profile, and time-out and reconnection settings for Terminal Services.

Add Users to a Group

This option is obscurely worded and means simply "add the selected account(s) to a group you specify":

Right-click on account(s) → Add members to a group → select group

Multiple accounts can be selected by the usual methods.

Copy a User Account

Right-click on account → Copy

Similar to adding a user account as shown earlier, except that when you copy an account, the new account has many of the same properties as the original one. Properties that are copied for the new account include the account restrictions, account expiration date, user profile, home folder, logon script, group membership, RAS, and Terminal Services settings of the original account. It's convenient when creating a large number of accounts to create a series of account templates for the different categories of users in your enterprise. Then copy each template as needed to create accounts for your users, entering only the personal information needed for each user. Make sure you disable account templates, as they should not be used to log on to the network.

Disable a User Account

Right-click on account → Disable Account

When an account is disabled, it still exists, but the user can't log on using the account. Disabled accounts in Active Directory Users and Computers have a red X icon on them. To enable an account that has been disabled, right-click on the account → Enable Account.

Delete a User Account

Right-click on account → Delete

Deleting an account is an irreversible action. It's usually better to disable an account instead. For example, if Bob is leaving the company and Susan is coming to replace him, disable Bob's account when he leaves, rename it Susan, and enable it when Susan arrives to take Bob's place. This way, Susan will have access to all the network resources that Bob had access to.

The problem with deleting rather than disabling accounts is that when you delete an account, its security identifier becomes unusable. (The SID is the internal way by which WS2003 identifies the account.) Thus, if you delete the account bobsmith and

---

then create a new account called bobsmith, the new account has a different SID from the old one and hence doesn't automatically inherit all the settings and access privileges that the old one had.

Find a User Account

If you have a large number of user accounts, you can use the Find function of Active Directory Users and Groups to find the account you want to work with. You can find accounts in a particular domain or OU by:

Right-click on domain or OU → Find

You can also change the focus of the Find Users, Contacts, and Groups box to search the entire directory.

Rename a User Account

Right-click on account → Rename → specify new name, display name, user logon name, and Pre–Windows 2000 user logon name

Renaming an account allows you to transfer all the rights, permissions, and group memberships of an account to another user. You may want to do this when an employee is leaving the company and will be replaced by someone new who will take over her job. Simply rename the account with the new employee's username, then change the personal information on the account's properties sheet to that of the new employee.

Reset Password of a User Account

Right-click on account → Reset Password

If a user forgets his password or it expires before he can change it, he will be unable to log on to the network with his user account.

 Checking "Force user to change password at next logon" doesn't get replicated immediately like the password. Therefore, it is best to reset the password and check this setting on a domain controller in the site where the user is located.

Unlock a User Account

Right-click on account → Properties → Account → clear Account Is Disabled

A user account is locked out when the user has violated the security policy for the domain. For example, if a user exceeds the number of failed logon attempts permitted by a policy, the user will receive an error message when she attempts to log on, informing her that her account has been locked out and must be unlocked by an administrator.

Managing Local Users

Local user accounts are administered using Local Users and Groups under System Tools in Computer Management.

Create a Local User

Local Users and Groups → right-click on Users → New User

The minimum to specify here is the username for the user. This will automatically make the full name the same as the username.

GUI Reference

Naming Conventions

Before you start creating user accounts for your enterprise, it is important to establish guidelines for naming conventions. These guidelines are needed to ensure that:

- Account names are simple and easy to remember for users.
- Users with identical names will have unique accounts.

Here are some considerations and recommendations for establishing naming conventions:

- User logon names can be up to 20 characters long and can include any characters except the following:

    "/\[ ]:;|=,+#?<>

- User logon names can have spaces in them, but this is generally not a good practice, since it may lead to unusable email addresses. For example, Bob Smart of the *mtit.com* domain could have the user logon name *bob smart@mtit.com*, but this would be unusable as an SMTP email address. Since email addresses are a separate attribute of a user's account, you could assign *bobsmart@mtit.com* as Bob Smart's email address, but this could confuse good old Bob ("Why do I use bob smart to log on to my machine but bobsmart in my email address?").

- Common naming conventions include: first name plus last initial, first initial plus last name, full name with spaces, full name without spaces, initials underscore department/OU, T- prefix for temporary employees, and so on. Use your imagination, but think of the users who will be using your accounts.

Configure a Local User

Local Users and Groups → Users → right-click on a user → Properties

You can change the group membership of the user (which by default is the Users built-in local group) and specify a home folder, logon script, and profile path for the user if desired. Most of these settings aren't very useful in a workgroup setting, however, which is what local user accounts are mainly designed for.

Manage User Profiles

The following tasks deal with default, local, roaming, and mandatory user profiles.

Customize the Default User Profile

1. Log on to a WS2003 computer as an ordinary user (e.g., Bob).
2. Configure the computer to reflect the desktop environment you wish all your users to have.
3. Log off the client computer to create a local user profile *C:\Documents and Settings\Bob*.
4. Log on as Administrator and make hidden files visible by:

Windows Explorer → Tools → Folder Options → View → Show hidden files and folders

This step is necessary to access the hidden Default Users profile in the next step.

5. Replace the existing default user profile with the newly configured one by:

Control Panel → System → Advanced → User Profiles → Settings → select newly configured profile → Copy To → select *C:\Documents and Settings\ Default User* → Permitted to use → Change → Everyone

When a user logs on to the computer for the first time, he will be assigned the customized default profile.

Configure a Local Profile

Log on with your user account, make changes to your desktop settings, then log off. Your local profile will be updated with any changes you have made.

Create a Roaming User Profile

First you need to create and customize the profile:

Log on as Administrator → Computer Management → System Tools → Local Users and Groups → right-click on Users → New User → specify name and password → clear User must change password at next logon → Create → Close → Log off → Log on as the newly created user → configure desktop settings as desired → log off

Your new profile is now stored in *C:\Documents and Settings\<username>*. Now create a share called Profiles on a file server on your network and create a folder called *<username>* within this share to store the new profile. Now copy your customized profile to the file server as follows:

Control Panel → System → Advanced → User Profiles → Settings → select the customized profile you created → Copy To → *fileserver\Profiles\<username>* → Permitted to use → Change → specify name of customized user account you created

Finally, assign the profile to the user by:

Computer Management → System Tools → Local Users and Groups → right-click on Users → Properties → Profile → Profile Path → *fileserver\Profiles\<username>*

Create a Mandatory User Profile

First, create a roaming user profile as described earlier, then open the profile using Windows Explorer and rename *Ntuser.dat* as *Ntuser.man*.

Users—Notes

A good security practice is to rename the Administrator account. Make sure you also assign the Administrator account a complex password and protect this password carefully.

Do not use the Administrator account as your everyday user account if you are a network administrator. Instead, create an ordinary user account for yourself and use this account to check your email, work on documents, and so on. Use the Administrator account (or any account that belongs to the Domain Admins group) only when performing network and system administration tasks that require this level of privilege.

Review permissions assigned to the Guest account (and Guests group) for shared network resources before enabling this account.

If you select multiple user accounts in an OU, you can simultaneously perform any of the following tasks on them:

> Add members to a group
> Delete account
> Disable account
> Enable account
> Move account
> Open home page
> Send email

When you create a new domain user account, it is automatically added to the Domain Users built-in global group, regardless of whether the new user account is created in the default Users OU or in some other OU you created.

As a security precaution, you should disable a user account when the user is going to be absent for an extended period—for example, on vacation. This is especially important for users who have some level of administrative access to network resources.

Make sure accounts for temporary employees have an expiration date.

Even if your ordinary users don't require the ability to roam, you may want to give your administrators this capability so they can perform administrative tasks from any machine in the network. On the other hand, in high-security environments you may want to restrict administrative logon to a few selected machines.

You don't need to make copies of mandatory profiles—multiple users can be assigned the same profile. If you do assign a single roaming profile to multiple users, make sure you configure the profile as mandatory. Otherwise, one user will change the wallpaper, and another user will complain about it!

Legacy (Windows NT/9X) applications may not be aware of the *My Documents* folders, in which case administrators may need to instruct users how to locate and store their work manually in their *My Documents* folders for these applications.

If roaming user profiles have been configured for your users, they may experience a delay when they log on or log off the network. This is caused by the contents of the *My Documents* folder being copied to and from the network file server where their roaming profiles are stored. Overall network performance can be degraded for other users as well when many megabytes of files are copied across the network. In a situation like this, implementing home folders might be a better way to store user files on the network.

See Also

Active Directory, *Logon*, net accounts, net user

WINS—Concepts

WINS stands for Windows Internet Name Service and is used to support NetBIOS name resolution for downlevel Windows clients. In a mixed environment in which you still have some NT servers or workstations, you may need to implement WINS on one or more servers in your network. WINS enables downlevel (Pre–Windows 2000) computers to resolve NetBIOS names into IP addresses without the need to use broadcasts. In addition, some legacy/downlevel applications may rely on NETBIOS and may still require WINS even if legacy or downlevel systems no longer exist on the network.

How WINS Works

WINS centralizes the registration of computer and domain NetBIOS names into a central WINS database on one or more WINS servers on your network. When NetBIOS computers start up, they register their name and IP address with the WINS servers. NetBIOS clients can then contact the WINS servers to resolve the registered computer's NetBIOS name into its IP address to establish network communications with it.

WINS Requirements

To implement WINS on your network, you need to meet the following requirements:

WINS server requirements
   A server with a static IP address and with the WINS service installed. A single WINS server can support up to about 5,000 WINS clients. Networks that require WINS should have at least two WINS servers for fault tolerance in case one becomes unavailable. WINS database replication can be configured to allow WINS servers to share a common WINS database.

WINS client requirements
   All Microsoft Windows versions can function as WINS clients. The client must be configured with the IP address of at least one WINS server on the network.

Note that when WINS is installed on WS2003, the WINS console in Administrative Tools can be used to manage only WS2003 or W2K WINS servers—it can't be used to manage downlevel NT WINS servers.

WINS Terminology

Static mapping
   A NetBIOS name-to-IP-address mapping that is manually created in the WINS database of a WINS server. Static mappings can be configured for servers that don't support WINS to allow WINS clients to resolve their names and access them.

WINS proxy
   A proxy that listens to broadcasts from non-WINS clients, forwards them to a WINS server for name resolution, then broadcasts the result to the clients.

Pull partner
   A WINS server that is configured to request WINS database updates from its replication partner at specific intervals. Pull partners are often configured over slow WAN links.

Push partner
   A WINS server that is configured to notify its replication partners when it has accumulated the threshold number of WINS database updates it wants to pass on to its partners. Push partners are generally configured when fast LAN links connect WINS servers.

Push/pull partner
   A WINS server that is configured as both a push and a pull partner.

WINS—Tools

The WINS console is added to Administrative Tools when the optional WINS service is installed. The console tree typically looks like this:

> WINS
>> Server Status
>> WINS Server
>>> Active Registrations
>>> Replication Partners

Using the Action menu you can select:

WINS
> Select this to add a new WINS server to the console, toggle the display of servers by name or IP address, show the DNS names of WINS servers, or validate the WINS cache on startup.

Server Status
> Select this to display the status of connected WINS servers in the details pane and to configure the refresh interval for this display.

A WINS server
> Select this to display server statistics, scavenge the WINS database for expired records, initiate WINS replication with another WINS server, back up the WINS database, and configure various WINS server settings.

Active Registrations
> Select this to display WINS database records by name or by owner, create a static mapping for non-WINS clients, import an *lmhosts* file, and perform other actions. Double-click on an active registration (WINS database record) in the details pane to display more information about it.

Replication Partners
> Select this to add a new WINS replication partner, configure replication settings, and force replication to occur.

WINS—Tasks

Install WINS

First, make sure that your server has a static IP address and that it points to itself as its preferred WINS server. Then use Add or Remove Programs in the Control Panel to install WINS.

Configure WINS Clients

You can configure WINS clients either manually or automatically using DHCP. To do this manually on WS2003 computers:

> Control Panel → Network Connections → right-click on Local Area Connection → Properties → Internet Protocol (TCP/IP) → Properties → Advanced → WINS → NetBIOS Setting → Enable NetBIOS over TCP/IP → Add → specify IP addresses of primary and secondary WINS servers

To use DHCP instead, first configure DHCP scope options 044 and 046 on your DHCP server (see *DHCP* earlier in this chapter). Then verify that the client is configured to use this option by:

> Control Panel → Network Connections → right-click on Local Area Connection → Properties → Internet Protocol (TCP/IP) → Properties → Advanced → WINS → NetBIOS Setting → Default

Configure WINS Replication

> WINS console → select a WINS server → right-click on Replication Partners → New → Replication Partner → specify the IP address of the replication partner

You can specify whether your replication partner is a push, pull, or push/pull partner using the Advanced tab on the properties sheet for the replication partner.

Create a Static Mapping

> WINS console → select a WINS server → right-click on Active Registrations → New → Static Mapping → specify computer name and IP address of non-WINS client

If you make an error entering a static mapping, delete it and recreate it.

Configure a WINS Proxy

To configure a WS2003 to act as a WINS proxy, use *regedt32.exe* to change EnableProxy from 0 to 1 in the following registry key:

    HKLM\System\CurrentControlSet\Services\NetBT\Parameters

You should have no more than two WINS proxies per subnet. Make sure you also configure the WINS proxy computer as a WINS client.

WINS—Notes

You can specify up to 12 WINS servers when configuring a WS2003 computer as a WINS client. The first two are the primary and secondary WINS servers, and the rest are backup WINS servers.

If you manually configure the addresses of WINS servers on WINS clients, the settings take precedence over WINS settings obtained using DHCP.

See Also

DHCP, netsh

5

Command Reference

Read This First!

Command-line administration has been greatly enhanced in Windows Server 2003 (WS2003). Dozens of new commands and scripts have been added for administration of Active Directory, disks, event logs, Group Policy, IIS, network diagnostics, the *pagefile*, printers, processes, shared folders, and the registry. The result is a Windows operating-system platform that now rivals Unix in its ability to support command-line and scripted administration. Windows Management Instrumentation (WMI), though beyond the scope of this book, adds an additional level of programmatic administration capability to almost every aspect of the operating system.

This chapter is an alphabetical reference to command-line tools in WS2003 including their syntax and use. Examples are provided to illustrate the power of each command, and extensive notes provide additional insights and gotchas concerning their use. The commands and scripts in this chapter include general Windows commands, net commands, netsh commands, TCP/IP troubleshooting utilities, and other miscellaneous commands useful for WS2003 administration. Also included is a description of how to use the Windows command interpreter (cmd) itself and a list of environment variables.

Command coverage in this chapter is comprehensive but not exhaustive; as in Chapter 4, the focus here is on the core tasks of everyday administration of WS2003. As a result, certain commands have been omitted; those omitted include:

- Commands such as certreq and change for administering optional Windows components such as Certificate Services and Terminal Services.

- Commands such as ipxroute for administering legacy networking components such as NWLink.

- Commands such as dir and copy that have been around since MS-DOS days and with which most readers are familiar.
- Commands such as choice and echo used only in DOS-style batch files.

Creating scripts for programmatic administration using the Windows Script Host (WSH) is also not covered; see *VBScript in a Nutshell* by Paul Lornax, Matt Childs, and Ron Petrusha (O'Reilly) for more information on this subject.

 All commands and scripts are listed here in strict alphabetical order for faster reference. Commands new to WS2003 are marked as such.

The following example (sample_command) illustrates the format used for most entries in this chapter. Exceptions to this format include commands that have multiple modes (nslookup), multiple contexts (netsh), or various subcommands (ftp). In addition, the net and bootcfg commands are broken down into a series of separate commands for easier reference.

sample_command

Brief explanation of what sample_command does.

Syntax

    Summary of syntax for running the command.

Options

Summary of syntax options and switches for the command.

Examples

Examples of how to use the command.

Notes

Additional hints, tips, and tricks for using the command.

See Also

Cross-references to topics in Chapter 4 are capitalized and in *italics* while cross-references within this chapter are in constant width font and lowercase.

If a Command Won't Run

Some commands in this chapter such as eventquery.vbs or prncnfg.vbs are actually admin scripts written in VBScript. The first time you try to run one of these scripts from the command line, you will see the following message:

    This script should be executed from the command prompt using CSCRIPT.EXE.
    For example: CSCRIPT %windir%\System32\EVENTQUERY.vbs <arguments>
    To set CScript as the default application to run .vbs files, run the
    following: CSCRIPT //H:CSCRIPT //S

```
You can then run %windir%\System32\EVENTQUERY.vbs <arguments> without
preceding the script with CSCRIPT.
```

This message is displayed because there are actually two versions of the Windows Script Host:

WSCRIPT
> The Windows-based version that provides a properties sheet for configuring how your script will run.

CSCRIPT
> The command-line version that uses switches to configure script properties.

By default, WS2003 uses WSCRIPT as its default script host, but the scripts in this chapter require CSCRIPT instead, so you can either use CSCRIPT each time you want to run one of these scripts, like this:

```
cscript eventquery.vbs
```

omitting "%windir%\System32\" since *eventquery.vbs* is already in the system path, or you can type:

```
cscript //h:cscript //s
```

to change the default script host from WSCRIPT to CSCRIPT, after which you can then run the script simply by typing its filename, like this:

```
eventquery.vbs
```

If this applies to a particular command in this chapter, the "Notes" section reiterates this information for your convenience.

Alphabetical List of Commands

adprep
new in WS2003

Prepares W2K domains and forests for upgrading to WS2003 by extending the schema, updating security descriptors, and adding new directory classes and attributes.

Syntax
```
adprep [/forestprep | /domainprep]
```

Options
/forestprep
> Prepares a W2K forest for upgrading to a WS2003 forest

/domainprep
> Prepares a W2K domain for upgrading to a WS2003 domain

Examples
Use adprep to prepare a W2K forest for upgrading to WS2003:

> Apply SP2 or later to all W2K domain controllers in your forest → back up schema master → take schema master offline → log on to schema master using an

account that belongs to both the Enterprise Admins and Schema Admins groups → open command prompt → change to \I386 folder on CD-ROM drive → type **adprep /forestprep**

If adprep /forest runs without errors and nothing in the event logs indicates a problem, wait until the schema changes effected by adprep /forest replicate to all domain controllers in your forest and then upgrade your domains as follows:

Log on to infrastructure for a domain using an account that belongs to either the Domain Admins or Enterprise Admins group → insert WS2003 product CD → change to \I386 folder on CD-ROM drive → **adprep /domainprep** → wait for effect of this command to replicate to other domain controllers in the domain → upgrade other domain controllers in the domain to WS2003 as desired → repeat process for other domains in the forest

Notes

- This command-line tool can be found in the \I386 folder on the WS2003 product CD. Note that adprep depends on several files in this directory, so you can't simply pull it off the CD and run it by itself.

- Check the adprep log files in \System32\Debug\Adprep\Logs each time you run adprep.

- For information about schema master, infrastructure master, and other FSMO roles, see *Domain Controller* in Chapter 4.

- Replication of schema changes within a site takes only 15 minutes, but if your enterprise has multiple sites, it may take longer. It may be best to wait a day or so after each use of adprep to ensure the effects have been replicated properly. If you try running adprep /domainprep without waiting long enough after running adprep /forestprep, a warning message indicates that the replication process has not finished. And if you try upgrading a W2K domain controller to WS2003 after running adprep /domainprep in the domain, a similar warning message is displayed.

- Once you prepare your forests and domains by running adprep, the remaining domain controllers can continue running W2K as long as you like until you decide to upgrade them.

- Consider installing SP3 on your W2K domain controllers before using adprep. If W2K domain controllers are running SP3, they are easier to administer remotely from Windows XP Professional or WS2003 machines using the WS2003 Administration Tools Pack. Also consider adding any post-SP3 hot fixes to your WS2003 SP3 domain controllers prior to running adprep, and search the Knowledge Base on *support.microsoft.com* for any issues regarding adprep before using it, especially if you have any Exchange 2000 servers in your forest.

See Also

Active Directory, Domain, Domain Controller, Forest, Installation

arp

Resolves IP addresses into media access control (MAC) addresses and caches them for reuse.

Syntax

```
arp -s IPaddress MACaddress [interfacenumber]
arp -d IPaddress [interfacenumber]
arp -a [IPaddress] [-N interfacenumber]
```

Options

-a [IPaddress]

Resolves the specified IP address into its associated MAC address by querying the Address Resolution Protocol (ARP) cache on the local machine. (If no address is specified, all cached IP-to-MAC address mappings are displayed.)

-g [IPaddress]

Same as -a.

-N interfacenumber

Specifies the network adapter whose ARP cache is to be queried. (Each network adapter has its own ARP cache on a multihomed machine.) Use arp -a to determine the number of each interface. If arp is used without -N on a multihomed machine, the first interface found is used.

-d IPaddress [interfacenumber]

Removes the IP-to-MAC address mapping from the local ARP cache for the specified IP address and interface. If no *IPaddress* is specified, the top entry in the ARP cache is removed.

-s IPaddress MACaddress [interfacenumber]

Adds a static IP-to-MAC address mapping to the local ARP cache for the specified interface. The MAC address must be expressed in hexidecimal form as 12 characters, in groups of 2, separated by dashes. Static ARP mappings are persistent until the system reboots.

Examples

View the ARP cache on the local machine:

```
arp -a
Interface: 172.16.11.104 on Interface 0x2
  Internet Address      Physical Address      Type
  172.16.11.100         00-40-95-d1-29-6c     dynamic
```

Ping the host named *Leonardo* to determine its IP address, and add a mapping for it to the local ARP cache:

```
ping -n 1 leonardo
Pinging leonardo [172.16.11.39] with 32 bytes of data:
Reply from 172.16.11.39: bytes=32 time<10ms TTL=32
Ping statistics for 172.16.11.39:
  Packets: Sent = 1, Received = 1, Lost = 0 (0% loss),
Approximate round trip times in milli-seconds:
  Minimum = 0ms, Maximum =  0ms, Average =  0ms
```

Verify that an IP-to-MAC address mapping for *Leonardo* (172.16.11.39) has been added to the local ARP cache:

```
arp -a
Interface: 172.16.11.104 on Interface 0x2
  Internet Address      Physical Address      Type
  172.16.11.39          00-40-95-d1-32-90     dynamic
  172.16.11.100         00-40-95-d1-29-6c     dynamic
```

Add a static mapping for *Leonardo* to the local ARP cache:

```
arp -s 172.16.11.39 00-40-95-d1-32-90
```

Verify the static mapping:

```
arp -a
Interface: 172.16.11.104 on Interface 0x2
  Internet Address      Physical Address     Type
  172.16.11.39          00-40-95-d1-32-90    static
  172.16.11.100         00-40-95-d1-29-6c    dynamic
```

Notes

- For one host to communicate with another on a TCP/IP network, the first host uses arp to resolve the second host's IP address into its corresponding MAC address. This MAC address then provides a destination address for Ethernet or token ring frames sent from the first host to the second. arp caches these IP-to-MAC address mappings for a short time (from 2 to 10 minutes) to reduce the number of ARP broadcasts needed.

- arp is a useful tool for troubleshooting TCP/IP networks because it can be used to find the MAC address of any host on the local subnet, provided that the IP address for the host is known.

- arp can be used to view the ARP cache only on the local machine, not on remote ones.

- To reduce broadcast traffic and speed up TCP/IP communications, you can add static mappings to the ARP cache on client machines. This lets clients resolve IP addresses of commonly used servers on the network from the clients' local ARP caches instead of using ARP broadcasts.

- To make static ARP cache mappings persistent across reboots, add arp commands to a batch file and run the file at system startup.

- Gratuitous ARP (or "courtesy ARP") is a TCP/IP mechanism used by hosts to announce their IP address, which avoids duplicate IP addresses on the network. You can disable gratuitous ARP by editing the registry and specifying 1 for the following value:

```
HKLM\System\CurrentControlSet\Services\TcpIp\Parameters\ArpRetryCount
```

See Also

ipconfig, pathping, ping, *TCP/IP*, tracert

---

assoc

Displays or modifies file extension associations.

Syntax

```
assoc [.ext[=[filetype]]]
```

Options

.ext

    Specifies the file extension

filetype

    Specifies the file type you want to associate with the specified file extension

Examples

Used without options, assoc displays a list of all current associations:

```
assoc
.323=h323file
.386=vxdfile
.aca=Agent.Character.2
.acf=Agent.Character.2
.acs=Agent.Character2.2
.aif=AIFFFile
.aifc=AIFFFile
.aiff=AIFFFile
.ani=anifile
.asa=aspfile
.asf=ASFFile
.asp=aspfile
.
.
.
.xml=xmlfile
.xsl=xslfile
.zap=zapfile
.ZFSendToTarget=CLSID\{888DCA60-FC0A-11CF-8F0F-00C04FD7D062}
.zip=CompressedFolder
```

A better way to do this is to redirect the current list of associations to a text file:

```
assoc > assoc.txt
```

and change the association for *.xml* files from XML documents (xmlfile) to text documents (txtfile):

```
assoc .xml=txtfile
.xml=txtfile
```

Now if you double-click on an XML document, it opens in Notepad instead of Internet Explorer.

Associate the extension *.xxx* with XML documents (xmlfile):

```
assoc .xxx=xmlfile
.xxx=xmlfile
```

View the newly created association:

```
assoc .xxx
.xxx=xmlfile
```

Remove the previously created association for *.xxx* files:

```
assoc .xxx=
.xxx=
```

Note there is a space after the equals sign.

Notes

- To view or modify file associations in the GUI, use Windows Explorer:
  Windows Explorer → Tools → Folder Options → File Types
- To view file types with open command strings defined, use ftype instead.

See Also

Files and Folders, ftype

---

at

Schedules tasks (commands or programs) to run on a computer at a specified time/date and manages scheduled tasks.

 Note that in WS2003 the schtasks command replaces the at command for managing and scheduling tasks from the command line (the at command is maintained only for backward compatibility with W2K/NT). See schtasks in this chapter for more info.

Syntax

```
at [\\computername] [ [id] [/delete] | [/yes] ]
at [\\computername] time [/interactive] [/every:date[,...]] |
/next:date[,...] ] command
```

Options

None
> Displays scheduled jobs.

\\computername
> Specifies the name of the remote computer on which the job is run. (If omitted, the job executes on the local computer.)

id   Is the identification number assigned to the scheduled job.

/delete
> Removes a job from the list of scheduled jobs. (If *id* is omitted, all scheduled jobs on the specified computer are canceled.)

/yes
> Executes the scheduled job without prompting for confirmation.

time
> Specifies when the command is to run (syntax is *hours:minutes* in 24-hour notation).

/interactive
> Lets the scheduled job interact with the desktop of the user logged on when the job runs.

/every:date[,...]
> Runs the job on specified day(s) of the week or month. Use M,T,W,Th,F,S,Su for days or the numbers 1 through 31 for dates, and separate them with commas. (If omitted, the current date is used.)

/next:date[,...]
> Runs the job on the next occurrence of the specified day or date.

command
> Is the command, program (*.exe* or *.com* file), or batch file (*.bat* or *.cmd* file) scheduled to run. Enclose the command in quotes if it includes spaces. If a path is required, use an absolute path for commands run on the local machine and a

UNC path (\\\server\share) for remote computers. (Don't use mapped drive letters because these may depend on the user who is logged on.)

Examples

Display all scheduled jobs on server *Bob*:

```
at \\Bob
```

Typical output might be:

```
Status ID   Day           Time      Command Line
-----------------------------------------------------
        1   Each M W F    2:00AM    \\Bob /yes c15.bat
```

Display information about job 12 on *Bob*:

```
at \\Bob 12
```

Delete job 4 on the local server:

```
at 4 /delete
```

To execute a command that isn't a simple executable, precede it with cmd /c because the at command doesn't automatically load the command interpreter (*cmd.exe*) prior to executing commands. For example, to synchronize the clock of the current server with *Bob* daily at 3 a.m.:

```
at 03:00 /every:M,T,W,Th,F,S,Su "cmd net time \\Bob /set /yes"
```

Notes

- For a GUI command scheduler, see *Tasks* in Chapter 4. For a more powerful command-line task scheduler, see schtasks later in this chapter.

- Note that jobs scheduled with at are displayed in the *Scheduled Tasks* folder, but if you then modify the parameters of the job using Scheduled Tasks, you can no longer access it from the command line using at.

- You need to be a member of the local Administrators group to use this command.

- The Task Scheduler service must be running to use this command. Use the Services console to start this service if necessary. (By default, this service is set to start automatically when the system is booted.)

- Scheduled jobs are stored in the registry and aren't lost if you restart the Scheduled Tasks service.

- The current directory for executing a scheduled command is *%SystemRoot%*.

- Scheduled jobs run as background processes, and no output is displayed on the screen. You can redirect screen output to a file instead by using the redirection symbol (>).

- If you change the system time on a computer after scheduling a job to run on it, be sure to synchronize the command scheduler with the new time by typing at without options.

- If a scheduled job uses a mapped drive letter to connect to a network share, be sure to schedule a second job that disconnects the drive when you are finished using it; otherwise, the drive letter will not be available from the command prompt.

See Also

schtasks, *Tasks*

---

attrib

Displays, modifies, or removes file attributes such as Read-only, Archive, System, and Hidden.

Syntax

```
attrib [+r | -r] [+a | -a] [+s | -s] [+h | -h] [ [drive:] [path] filename]
    [/s [/d] ]
```

Options

+r Sets Read-only attribute (useful for protecting users from themselves).

-r Clears Read-only attribute.

+a Sets Archive attribute (indicates files that have changed since the last backup was performed).

-a Clears Archive attribute.

+s Sets System attribute. (System files are generally protected operating-system files.)

-s Clears System attribute.

+h Sets Hidden attribute. (By default, hidden files aren't displayed in Windows Explorer.)

-h Clears Hidden attribute.

/s Sets or clears attributes recursively, starting from the current directory and extending to all subdirectories.

/d Sets or clears attributes on directories only.

[drive:][path] filename
  Indicates location and name of the directory, file, or set of files whose attributes you want to set or clear. (The wildcards ? and * can also be used.)

Examples

Display the attributes of all directories and files in the current directory:

```
attrib
A          C:\AUTOEXEC.BAT
A   SH     C:\boot.ini
A          C:\CONFIG.SYS
A   SHR    C:\IO.SYS
A   SHR    C:\MSDOS.SYS
A   SHR    C:\NTDETECT.COM
A   SHR    C:\ntldr
A   SH     C:\pagefile.sys
```

List the attributes of *C:\boot.ini* (used to create the Boot Loader menu):

```
attrib C:\boot.ini
A   SH     C:\boot.ini
```

Note that the Archive (A), System (S), and Hidden (H) attributes are set on this file.

Remove the System and Hidden attributes of *boot.ini* so the file can be modified (leave the Archive attribute unchanged):

```
attrib C:\boot.ini -s -h
```

View the attributes again:

```
attrib C:\boot.ini
A          C:\boot.ini
```

Notes

- The file with the System or Hidden attribute set must have these attributes cleared before you can change any other attributes for that file.

- To display or view advanced attributes such as encryption and compression state, see cipher in this chapter.

- attrib is also available from the Recovery Console.

See Also

cipher, *Files and Folders*, *Recovery Console*

---

bootcfg   new in WS2003

Views, modifies, and rebuilds the boot menu (*boot.ini*) file using information obtained by scanning your hard drives for installations of Windows 2003/XP/2000/NT.

Syntax

```
bootcfg
bootcfg /option [/s Computer [/u Domain\User /p Password]]
    [/id OSEntryLineNum]
```

Options

Since bootcfg has multiple command options, each with its own syntax, these options are treated separately in entries following this one. Here's a quick summary of the command options available:

addsw
> Adds load options for a specified OS entry

copy
> Copies an existing OS entry

dbg1394
> Configures IEEE 1394 port debugging for a specified OS entry

debug
> Modifies the debug settings for a specified OS entry

default
> Designates an OS entry as the default

delete
> Deletes an OS entry

ems
> Lets the user configure redirection of the Emergency Management Services (EMS) console to a remote machine

query
> Displays the boot loader and operating systems sections of *boot.ini*

raw
> Adds a specified string to a boot entry in the operating systems section of *boot.ini*

---

rmsw
> Removes load options for a specified OS entry

timeout
> Modifies the time-out value for the boot loader menu

Note that the following switches can be used with most of the bootcfg command options and are therefore not included in the syntax for the entries following this one:

/s Computer
> Specifies the name or IP address of a remote computer whose *boot.ini* file you wish to manage (if switch is absent, then defaults to local computer). This switch is available with all preceding command options and is therefore omitted from the entries following this one.

/u Domain\User /p Password
> Specifies credentials for running the command (defaults to logged-on user). This switch is available with all preceding command options and is therefore omitted from the entries following this one.

/id OSEntryLineNum
> Specifies a line number in the operating systems section of *boot.ini* in order to specify additional load options for the OS entry (first line after operating systems section header is line 1). This switch is available with all preceding command options except query and timeout.

Examples

To display the settings in the *boot.ini* file, use bootcfg with no options (same as using bootcfg /query):

```
bootcfg
Boot Loader Settings
--------------------
timeout:30
default:multi(0)disk(0)rdisk(0)partition(1)\WINDOWS
Boot Entries
------------
Boot entry ID:     1
OS Friendly Name: WS2003, Enterprise
Path:             multi(0)disk(0)rdisk(0)partition(1)\WINDOWS
OS Load Options:  /fastdetect
```

Note that this isn't the actual content of the *boot.ini* file, which in this example looks like this:

```
[boot loader]
timeout=30
default=multi(0)disk(0)rdisk(0)partition(1)\WINDOWS
operating systems
multi(0)disk(0)rdisk(0)partition(1)\WINDOWS="WS2003, Enterprise" /fastdetect
```

To perform other tasks using bootcfg, see the following entries.

Notes

- bootcfg is also available from the Recovery Console.
- You can also configure certain boot menu options (default OS, timeout) from the GUI or edit *boot.ini* directly:

  Control Panel → System → Advanced → Startup and Recovery → Settings → select default OS | modify timeout | click Edit to directly edit *boot.ini*

See Also

Recovery Console

---

bootcfg /addsw   new in WS2003

Adds load options for a specified OS entry in *boot.ini*.

Syntax

```
bootcfg /addsw [/mm MaximumRAM] [/bv] [/so] [/ng] /id OSEntryLineNum
```

Options

/mm MaximumRAM
> Specifies maximum amount of RAM the operating system can use

/bv Adds the /basevideo option to OS entry specified by *OSEntryLineNum* to force use of standard VGA mode

/so Adds the /sos option to OS entry specified by *OSEntryLineNum* to display names of device drivers as they load

/ng Adds the /noguiboot option to OS entry specified by *OSEntryLineNum* to hide the progress bar that appears before the logon prompt

Examples

Disable the boot progress bar for OS entry 1 in the operating systems section of *boot.ini*:

```
bootcfg /addsw /ng /id 1
SUCCESS: Added the switch to OS entry for line "1" in the BOOT.INI file.
```

Verify the result:

```
bootcfg
Boot Loader Settings
--------------------
timeout:30
default:multi(0)disk(0)rdisk(0)partition(1)\WINDOWS
Boot Entries
------------
Boot entry ID:    1
OS Friendly Name: WS2003, Enterprise
Path:             multi(0)disk(0)rdisk(0)partition(1)\WINDOWS
OS Load Options:  /fastdetect /noguiboot
```

Notes

To remove boot entry switches after adding them, use the bootcfg /rmsw command.

See Also

bootcfg, *Recovery Console*

---

bootcfg /copy

Copies an existing OS entry specified by *OSEntryLineNum*.

Syntax

```
bootcfg /copy [/d Description] /id OSEntryLineNum
```

Options

/d Description
> Specifies a description (must be in quotes) for the new OS entry.

Examples

Copy OS entry 1 in operating systems section of *boot.ini* and give it the description "WS2003 Enterprise":

```
bootcfg /copy /d "WS2003 Enterprise" /id 1
SUCCESS: Made a copy of the boot entry "1".
```

Verify the result:

```
bootcfg
Boot Loader Settings
--------------------
timeout:30
default:multi(0)disk(0)rdisk(0)partition(1)\WINDOWS
Boot Entries
------------
Boot entry ID:     1
OS Friendly Name:  WS2003, Enterprise
Path:              multi(0)disk(0)rdisk(0)partition(1)\WINDOWS
OS Load Options:   /fastdetect /noguiboot
Boot entry ID:     2
OS Friendly Name:  WS2003 Enterprise
Path:              multi(0)disk(0)rdisk(0)partition(1)\WINDOWS
OS Load Options:   /fastdetect /noguiboot
```

See Also

bootcfg, *Recovery Console*

---

bootcfg /dbg1394

Configures IEEE 1394 port debugging for a specified OS entry.

Syntax

```
bootcfg /dbg1394 {ON | OFF} [/ch Channel] /id OSEntryLineNum
```

Options

{ON | OFF}

> Enables/disables remote debugging support by adding/removing /dbg1394 switch to OS entry specified by *OSEntryLineNum*.

/ch Channel

> Indicates channel used for debugging (must be integer between 1 and 64). Omit if OFF is specified.

Examples

Enable IEEE 1394 debugging by adding the /dbg1394 switch with channel 8 to OS entry 2 in *boot.ini*:

bootcfg /dbg1394 ON /ch 8 /id 2
```
SUCCESS: The OS load options have been changed for the BootID: 2.
```

Verify the result:

bootcfg
```
Boot Loader Settings
--------------------
timeout:30
default:multi(0)disk(0)rdisk(0)partition(1)\WINDOWS
Boot Entries
------------
Boot entry ID:    1
OS Friendly Name: WS2003, Enterprise
Path:             multi(0)disk(0)rdisk(0)partition(1)\WINDOWS
OS Load Options:  /fastdetect /noguiboot
Boot entry ID:    2
OS Friendly Name: WS2003 Enterprise
Path:             multi(0)disk(0)rdisk(0)partition(1)\WINDOWS
OS Load Options:  /fastdetect /noguiboot /debug /debugport=1394 /channel=8
```

Now turn off IEEE 1394 debugging:

bootcfg /dbg1394 OFF /id 2
```
SUCCESS: The OS load options have been changed for the BootID: 2.
```

Verify:

bootcfg
```
Boot Loader Settings
--------------------
timeout:30
default:multi(0)disk(0)rdisk(0)partition(1)\WINDOWS
Boot Entries
------------
Boot entry ID:    1
OS Friendly Name: WS2003, Enterprise
Path:             multi(0)disk(0)rdisk(0)partition(1)\WINDOWS
OS Load Options:  /fastdetect /noguiboot
Boot entry ID:    2
OS Friendly Name: WS2003 Enterprise
Path:             multi(0)disk(0)rdisk(0)partition(1)\WINDOWS
OS Load Options:  /fastdetect /noguiboot
```

Notes

Use bootcfg /debug if COM port debugging is required instead.

See Also

bootcfg, *Recovery Console*

---

bootcfg /debug   new in WS2003

Modifies the debug settings for a specified OS entry.

Syntax

```
bootcfg /debug {ON | OFF | EDIT} [/port {COM1 | COM2 | COM3 | COM4}]
[/baud {9600 | 19200 | 38400 | 57600 | 115200}] /id OSEntryLineNum
```

Options

{ON | OFF | EDIT}
> ON/OFF enables/disables remote debugging by adding /debug switch to OS entry specified by *OSEntryLineNum* while EDIT lets you modify the port or baud rate settings

/port {COM1 | COM2 | COM3 | COM4}
> Indicates which COM port should be used for debugging (omit if OFF is specified)

/baud {9600 | 19200 | 38400 | 57600 | 115200}
> Indicates the baud rate that should be used for debugging (omit if OFF is specified)

Examples

Enable debugging on COM2 at 115200 baud for OS entry 2 in *boot.ini* file:

> **bootcfg /debug ON /port COM2 /baud 115200 /id 2**
> SUCCESS: Changed the OS entry switches for line "2" in the BOOT.INI file.

Verify the result:

> **bootcfg**
> Boot Loader Settings
> --------------------
> timeout:30
> default:multi(0)disk(0)rdisk(0)partition(1)\WINDOWS
> Boot Entries
> ------------
> Boot entry ID: 1
> OS Friendly Name: WS2003, Enterprise
> Path: multi(0)disk(0)rdisk(0)partition(1)\WINDOWS
> OS Load Options: /fastdetect /noguiboot
> Boot entry ID: 2
> OS Friendly Name: WS2003 Enterprise
> Path: multi(0)disk(0)rdisk(0)partition(1)\WINDOWS
> OS Load Options: /fastdetect /noguiboot /debug /debugport=com2
>   /baudrate=115200

Change that to COM1 instead:

> **bootcfg /debug EDIT /port COM1 /baud 115200 /id 2**
> SUCCESS: Changed the OS entry switches for line "2" in the BOOT.INI file.

Verify:

```
bootcfg
Boot Loader Settings
--------------------
timeout:30
default:multi(0)disk(0)rdisk(0)partition(1)\WINDOWS
Boot Entries
------------
Boot entry ID:     1
OS Friendly Name: WS2003, Enterprise
Path:              multi(0)disk(0)rdisk(0)partition(1)\WINDOWS
OS Load Options:  /fastdetect /noguiboot
Boot entry ID:     2
OS Friendly Name: WS2003 Enterprise
Path:              multi(0)disk(0)rdisk(0)partition(1)\WINDOWS
OS Load Options:  /fastdetect /noguiboot /debug /debugport=COM1
    /baudrate=115200
```

Notes

Use bootcfg /dbg1394 if IEEE 1394 debugging is required instead.

See Also

bootcfg, *Recovery Console*

---

bootcfg /default

new in WS2003

Designates an OS entry as the default.

Syntax

```
bootcfg /default /id OSEntryLineNum
```

Options

/id OSEntryLineNum
Specifies line number of OS entry that should be designated as default OS to boot from

Examples

Display current boot menu:

```
bootcfg
Boot Loader Settings
--------------------
timeout:30
default:multi(0)disk(0)rdisk(0)partition(1)\WINDOWS
Boot Entries
------------
Boot entry ID:     1
OS Friendly Name: WS2003, Enterprise
Path:              multi(0)disk(0)rdisk(0)partition(1)\WINDOWS
OS Load Options:  /fastdetect /noguiboot
Boot entry ID:     2
```

```
OS Friendly Name: WS2003 Enterprise
Path:             multi(0)disk(0)rdisk(0)partition(2)\WINDOWS
OS Load Options:  /fastdetect /noguiboot
```

Note default OS listed in line 4. Now change default OS to boot entry 2:

bootcfg /default /id 2
```
SUCCESS: Changed the default OS entry in the BOOT.INI.
```

Verify the result:

bootcfg
```
Boot Loader Settings
--------------------
timeout:30
default:multi(0)disk(0)rdisk(0)partition(2)\WINDOWS
Boot Entries
------------
Boot entry ID:    1
OS Friendly Name: WS2003 Enterprise
Path:             multi(0)disk(0)rdisk(0)partition(2)\WINDOWS
OS Load Options:  /fastdetect /noguiboot
Boot entry ID:    2
OS Friendly Name: WS2003, Enterprise
Path:             multi(0)disk(0)rdisk(0)partition(1)\WINDOWS
OS Load Options:  /fastdetect /noguiboot
```

Note the change in line 4 and the reversed boot entries.

Notes

You can also use the GUI to specify which OS entry should be the default for booting:

Control Panel → System → Advanced → Startup and Recovery → Settings → select default OS

See Also

bootcfg, *Recovery Console*

---

bootcfg /delete   new in WS2003

Deletes an OS entry.

Syntax

```
bootcfg /delete /id OSEntryLineNum
```

Options

/id OSEntryLineNum

Deletes the OS entry with line number *OSEntryLineNum* in the operating systems section of *boot.ini* file

Examples

Display current *boot.ini* info:

bootcfg
```
Boot Loader Settings
```

```
--------------------
timeout:0
default:multi(0)disk(0)rdisk(0)partition(1)\WINDOWS
Boot Entries
------------
Boot entry ID:    1
OS Friendly Name: WS2003, Enterprise
Path:             multi(0)disk(0)rdisk(0)partition(1)\WINDOWS
OS Load Options:  /fastdetect /noguiboot
Boot entry ID:    2
OS Friendly Name: WS2003 Enterprise
Path:             multi(0)disk(0)rdisk(0)partition(2)\WINDOWS
OS Load Options:  /fastdetect
```

Delete the second boot entry:

bootcfg /delete /id 2
```
SUCCESS: OS entry "2" has been deleted.
```

Verify the result:

bootcfg
```
Boot Loader Settings
--------------------
timeout:0
default:multi(0)disk(0)rdisk(0)partition(1)\WINDOWS
Boot Entries
------------
Boot entry ID:    1
OS Friendly Name: WS2003, Enterprise
Path:             multi(0)disk(0)rdisk(0)partition(1)\WINDOWS
OS Load Options:  /fastdetect /noguiboot
```

See Also

bootcfg, *Recovery Console*

bootcfg /ems   new in WS2003

Lets the user configure redirection of the Emergency Management Services (EMS) console to a remote machine.

Syntax

```
bootcfg /ems {ON | OFF | EDIT} [/port {COM1 | COM2 | COM3 | COM4 | BIOSSET}]
[/baud {9600 | 19200 | 57600 | 115200}] /id OSEntryLineNum
```

Options

{ON | OFF | EDIT}

ON|OFF enables/disables sending output to a remote computer by adding/ removing a /redirect switch to the specified *OSEntryLineNum* and a redirect=comX setting to the boot loader section, while EDIT lets you modify port settings by changing the redirect=comX setting.

/port {COM1 | COM2 | COM3 | COM4 | BIOSSET}
> Indicates COM port used for redirecting output to remote computer. The BIOSSET option configures EMS to query BIOS to determine which port to use for redirection. Omit this switch if OFF is specified.

/baud {9600 | 19200 | 57600 | 115200}
> Indicates baud rate for redirection. Omit this switch if OFF is specified.

Examples

Enable EMS output redirection on COM2 at 57600 baud for OS entry 2:

```
bootcfg /ems ON /port COM2 /baud 57600 /id 2
SUCCESS: Changed the redirection port in boot loader section.
SUCCESS: Changed the redirection baudrate in boot loader section.
SUCCESS: Changed the OS entry switches for line "2" in the BOOT.INI file.
```

Verify the result:

```
bootcfg
Boot Loader Settings
--------------------
timeout:          30
default:          multi(0)disk(0)rdisk(0)partition(1)\WINDOWS
redirect:         COM2
redirectbaudrate:57600
Boot Entries
------------
Boot entry ID:    1
OS Friendly Name: WS2003, Enterprise
Path:             multi(0)disk(0)rdisk(0)partition(1)\WINDOWS
OS Load Options:  /fastdetect /noguiboot
Boot entry ID:    2
OS Friendly Name: WS2003 Enterprise
Path:             multi(0)disk(0)rdisk(0)partition(2)\WINDOWS
OS Load Options:  /fastdetect /noguiboot /redirect
```

Note the additional entries in the boot loader settings section. Now remove the settings just applied:

```
bootcfg /ems OFF /id 2
SUCCESS: Changed the OS entry switches for line "2" in the BOOT.INI file.
SUCCESS: The redirection port has been removed from BOOT LOADER section.
SUCCESS: The redirection baudrate has been removed from BOOT LOADER section.
```

Notes

You can also enable and configure EMS using optional switches for *winnt32.exe* on the product CD; see *Installation* in Chapter 4 for more info.

See Also

bootcfg, *Installation, Recovery Console*

---

bootcfg /query
new in WS2003

Displays the boot loader and operating systems sections of *boot.ini*.

Syntax

```
bootcfg /query
```

Examples

Display the results of using the bootcfg /query command:

```
bootcfg /query
Boot Loader Settings
--------------------
timeout:30
default:multi(0)disk(0)rdisk(0)partition(1)\WINDOWS
Boot Entries
------------
Boot entry ID:    1
OS Friendly Name: WS2003, Enterprise
Path:             multi(0)disk(0)rdisk(0)partition(1)\WINDOWS
OS Load Options:  /fastdetect /noguiboot
Boot entry ID:    2
OS Friendly Name: WS2003 Enterprise
Path:             multi(0)disk(0)rdisk(0)partition(2)\WINDOWS
OS Load Options:  /fastdetect /noguiboot
```

Now compare this with the actual contents of the *boot.ini* file:

```
[boot loader]
timeout=30
default=multi(0)disk(0)rdisk(0)partition(1)\WINDOWS
operating systems
multi(0)disk(0)rdisk(0)partition(1)\WINDOWS="WS2003, Enterprise" /fastdetect
/noguiboot
multi(0)disk(0)rdisk(0)partition(2)\WINDOWS="WS2003 Enterprise" /fastdetect
/noguiboot
```

Note that:

- The Boot Loader Settings part of the output for bootcfg /query displays the information for each entry in the boot loader section of the *boot.ini* file.

- The Boot Entries part of the output for bootcfg /query shows the Boot entry ID, Friendly Name, Path, and OS Load Options for each OS entry in the operating systems section of the *boot.ini* file.

Notes

Using bootcfg without switches produces the same result as bootcfg /query.

See Also

bootcfg, *Recovery Console*

---

bootcfg raw   new in WS2003

Adds a specified string to a boot entry in the operating systems section of *boot.ini*.

Syntax

```
bootcfg /raw "OSLoadOptionsString" [/id OSEntryLineNum] [/a]
```

Options

OSLoadOptionsString
> Specifies load options to add to the OS entry specified by *OSEntryLineNum* (the string must be enclosed in quotes and no validation is performed)

/a   Indicates that the load options being added should be appended to existing load options (if /a switch is omitted, any existing load options associated with the entry are replaced)

Examples

Append the /crashdebug option to OS entry 2:

bootcfg /raw "/crashdebug" /id 2 /a
```
SUCCESS: Added the switch to OS entry for line "2" in the BOOT.INI file.
```

Verify the result:

bootcfg
```
Boot Loader Settings
--------------------
timeout:30
default:multi(0)disk(0)rdisk(0)partition(1)\WINDOWS
Boot Entries
------------
Boot entry ID:      1
OS Friendly Name: WS2003, Enterprise
Path:               multi(0)disk(0)rdisk(0)partition(1)\WINDOWS
OS Load Options:  /fastdetect /noguiboot
Boot entry ID:      2
OS Friendly Name: WS2003 Enterprise
Path:               multi(0)disk(0)rdisk(0)partition(2)\WINDOWS
OS Load Options:  /fastdetect /noguiboot /crashdebug
```

Notes

Use bootcfg /raw to add additional switches to *boot.ini* OS entries. Examples of such switches are /fastdetect, /nodebug, /baudrate, /crashdebug, and /sos.

See Also

bootcfg, *Recovery Console*

---

bootcfg /rmsw   new in WS2003

Removes load options for a specified OS entry.

Syntax

```
bootcfg /rmsw [/mm] [/bv] [/so] [/ng] /id OSEntryLineNum
```

Options

/mm Removes /maxmem switch with its associated maximum memory value from OS entry specified by *OSEntryLineNum*

/bv Removes /basevideo switch from OS entry specified by *OSEntryLineNum*

/so   Removes /sos switch from OS entry specified by *OSEntryLineNum*

/ng   Removes /noguiboot switch from OS entry specified by *OSEntryLineNum*

Examples

Display current *boot.ini* info:

```
bootcfg
Boot Loader Settings
--------------------
timeout:30
default:multi(0)disk(0)rdisk(0)partition(1)\WINDOWS
Boot Entries
------------
Boot entry ID:    1
OS Friendly Name: WS2003, Enterprise
Path:             multi(0)disk(0)rdisk(0)partition(1)\WINDOWS
OS Load Options:  /fastdetect /noguiboot
Boot entry ID:    2
OS Friendly Name: WS2003 Enterprise
Path:             multi(0)disk(0)rdisk(0)partition(2)\WINDOWS
OS Load Options:  /fastdetect /noguiboot
```

Remove the /noguiboot switch from boot entry 2:

```
bootcfg /rmsw /ng /id 2
SUCCESS: Removed the switches from the OS entry for line "2" in the BOOT.
INI.
```

Verify the result:

```
bootcfg
Boot Loader Settings
--------------------
timeout:30
default:multi(0)disk(0)rdisk(0)partition(1)\WINDOWS
Boot Entries
------------
Boot entry ID:    1
OS Friendly Name: WS2003, Enterprise
Path:             multi(0)disk(0)rdisk(0)partition(1)\WINDOWS
OS Load Options:  /fastdetect /noguiboot
Boot entry ID:    2
OS Friendly Name: WS2003 Enterprise
Path:             multi(0)disk(0)rdisk(0)partition(2)\WINDOWS
OS Load Options:  /fastdetect
```

Notes

The bootcfg /rmsw command has the opposite effect of the bootcfg /addsw command.

See Also

bootcfg, *Recovery Console*

---

bootcfg /timeout   new in WS2003

Modifies the time-out value for the boot loader menu.

Syntax

```
bootcfg /timeout TimeOutValue
```

Options

/timeout TimeOutValue
> Specifies the time (from 0 to 999 seconds) the boot menu is displayed before booting with the default OS entry

Examples

Change the default time-out value from 30 to 5 seconds:

bootcfg /timeout 5
```
SUCCESS: Changed the timeout value in the BOOT.INI.
```

Verify the change:

bootcfg
```
Boot Loader Settings
--------------------
timeout:5
...
```

Disable the boot loader menu entirely:

bootcfg /timeout 0
```
SUCCESS: Changed the timeout value in the BOOT.INI.
```

Notes

You can also modify the time-out value using the GUI:

> Control Panel → System → Advanced → Startup and Recovery → Settings → modify timeout

See Also

bootcfg, *Recovery Console*

---

cacls

Displays or modifies access control lists (ACLs) of files and directories on NTFS volumes.

Syntax

```
cacls filename [/t] [/e] [/c] [/g username:perm] [/r username [...] ]
[/p username:perm [...] ] [/d username [...] ]
```

Options

filename [filename...]
> Displays ACLs of specified file(s)

/t Recursively applies changes to ACLs of specified files, starting from the current directory and extending to all subdirectories

/e Merges changes into an ACL instead of overwriting it

/c Ignores errors during the process of modifying an ACL

/g username:perm
>   Grants *username* one of the following permissions:
>
>   N   None
>
>   R   Read
>
>   C   Change (Write)
>
>   F   Full Control

/r username
>   Revokes all permissions for *username*

/p username:perm
>   Replaces one of the following permissions for *username*:
>
>   N   None
>
>   R   Read
>
>   C   Change (Write)
>
>   F   Full Control

/d username
>   Explicitly denies access to *username*

Examples

Display the ACL for the directory *C:\WINDOWS*:

cacls C:\WINDOWS

```
C:\WINDOWS NT AUTHORITY\Authenticated Users:R
           NT AUTHORITY\Authenticated Users:
               (OI)(CI)(IO)(special access:)
                   GENERIC_READ
                   GENERIC_EXECUTE
           BUILTIN\Server Operators:C
           BUILTIN\Server Operators:(OI)(CI)(IO)C
           BUILTIN\Administrators:F
           BUILTIN\Administrators:(OI)(CI)(IO)F
           NT AUTHORITY\SYSTEM:F
           NT AUTHORITY\SYSTEM:(OI)(CI)(IO)F
           BUILTIN\Administrators:F
           CREATOR OWNER:(OI)(CI)(IO)F
```

Table 5-1 explains the various symbols used in the output of cacls.

Table 5-1. Symbols used in cacls command

Symbol	Description
C	Container (directory)
O	Object (file)
I	Inherit (taking on the permissions of the parent directory)
OI	Object inherit (any files created in this directory inherit this ACL)
CI	Container inherit (any subdirectories created in this directory inherit this ACL)
IO	Inherit only (ACL doesn't apply to the directory, only to subdirectories)

Notes

- cacls can't be used to create special permissions, only standard permissions. In this sense it is less granular than the GUI.
- You can specify more than one file or user in a command.
- cacls can't be used to set permissions on the root of an NTFS volume that is mounted to a folder on a different NTFS volume.
- To use cacls in a batch file, you need to provide a way to automatically answer prompts it may generate. Since calcs doesn't have a /y switch to do this, use the Echo command to pipe y as input in response to an "Are You Sure?" message that cacls might generate. To do this, use:

      Echo y | cacls filename /g username:perm

- A practical use for cacls is to add the Administrators group automatically to the ACL for users' home directories. See Knowledge Base article Q180464 on Microsoft TechNet for several scripts for doing this.

See Also

Permissions

---

chkdsk

Verifies and fixes the integrity of a filesystem on a disk.

Syntax

      chkdsk [volume [[[path] filename]]] [/f] [/v] [/r] [/x] [/i] [/c]
      [/l[:size]]

Options

None
>   Displays status of current drive.

volume
>   Specifies drive to check. This can be a drive letter followed by a colon, a volume mount point, or a volume name.

[path] filename
>   Lists specific file(s) to check using chkdsk (wildcards are acceptable).

/f   Fixes any disk errors found.

/v   Verbose mode (displays the name of each file checked).

/r   Recovers readable information from bad sectors.

/x   Forces volume to dismount first if necessary (NTFS only) and fixes any disk errors found. Note that all open handles to the disk are then invalid. You can't force-dismount the system volume.

/i   Performs a quick check of index entries only (NTFS only).

/c   Speeds check by ignoring cycles within folder structure (NTFS only).

/l[:size]
>   Specifies log-file size (NTFS only). Current size is displayed if no size is specified.

The following options are available only when running the Recovery Console (see *Recovery Console* in Chapter 4):

/p   Performs an exhaustive check on the drive regardless of whether chkdsk is marked to run (doesn't fix errors).

/r   Recovers readable information from bad sectors (implies /p).

Examples

Check C: drive but don't fix any errors found:

```
chkdsk C:
```

Typical output might be:

```
The type of the file system is NTFS.

WARNING!  F parameter not specified.
Running CHKDSK in read-only mode.

CHKDSK is verifying files (stage 1 of 3)...
File verification completed.
CHKDSK is verifying indexes (stage 2 of 3)...
Index verification completed.
CHKDSK is verifying security descriptors (stage 3 of 3)...
Security descriptor verification completed.
CHKDSK is verifying Usn Journal...
Usn Journal verification completed.
Windows found problems with the file system.
Run CHKDSK with the /F (fix) option to correct these.

   2096450 KB total disk space.
   1758220 KB in 23870 files.
      8056 KB in 1407 indexes.
         0 KB in bad sectors.
     72348 KB in use by the system.
     12544 KB occupied by the log file.
    257826 KB available on disk.

      2048 bytes in each allocation unit.
   1048225 total allocation units on disk.
    128913 allocation units available on disk.
```

Note that errors were found. To try to correct these, run:

```
chkdsk C: /f
```

The output is now:

```
The type of the file system is NTFS.
Cannot lock current drive.

Chkdsk cannot run because the volume is in use by another
process.  Would you like to schedule this volume to be
checked the next time the system restarts? (Y/N)
```

Press Y to schedule chkdsk to run at the next reboot. Note, however, that running chkdsk on the active partition may generate spurious errors. (On NTFS volumes, chkdsk identifies unreferenced security descriptions as errors, whereas they simply take up space.)

Notes

- You must be a member of the Administrators group to use chkdsk.

- chkdsk can take hours (or days) to run on very large volumes. To speed up chkdsk, use the /i and /c options, which omit certain checks on the volume.

- If you choose to fix errors using chkdsk /f, there is a possibility of data loss (especially on FAT partitions), so you are prompted to confirm whether chkdsk should make the necessary changes to the file-allocation table. Also, always make a full backup of volumes containing important data before running chkdsk /f on them.

- The file *%SystemRoot%\System32Autochk.exe* is required by chkdsk in order to run. Autochk writes a message to the application log for each drive checked.

- You can also check a disk for errors from the GUI using the Check Disk button on the Tools tab of a disk's properties sheet (see *Disks* in Chapter 4 for more information).

- chkdsk can't repair corruption in the master file table (MFT) for an NTFS volume. If you have a file or directory that you can't open, rename, copy, or delete from an NTFS volume, back up the volume to tape—excluding the problem file from the backup job—and then restore the volume.

- See the recover command later in this chapter for information about recovering physically damaged files.

See Also

chkntfs, convert, defrag, diskpart, *Disks*, format, label, mountvol

---

chkntfs

Displays or specifies whether to schedule automatic filesystem checking (using chkdsk) to be run at startup.

Syntax

```
chkntfs volume [...]
chkntfs /d
chkntfs /t[:time]
chkntfs /x volume [...]
chkntfs /c volume [...]
```

Options

volume [...]
:   Displays the filesystem of the volume(s) and, if automatic file checking is scheduled, whether the volume has been corrupted. (If so, then run chkdsk /f.) The volume may be identified by a drive letter with colon, a volume mount point, or a volume name.

/d
:   Restores default behavior—except countdown time—for automatic file checking (use this switch alone). In other words, all drives are checked at startup, and those found to be dirty have chkdsk run against them.

/t[:time]
:   Displays or specifies countdown time for automatic filesystem checking.

/x   Excludes specified volume from being checked (even if volume is marked for running chkdsk). To exclude multiple volumes, list them in one command. (This option isn't accumulative.)

/c   Checks the specified volume at startup. (This option is accumulative.)

Examples

Display the filesystem on drive *C:* and its current state:

```
chkntfs c:
The type of the file system is NTFS.
C: is not dirty.
```

Show the countdown time for automatic filesystem checking:

```
chkntfs /t
The AUTOCHK initiation count down time is set to 10 seconds.
```

Change the countdown time to 60 seconds:

```
chkntfs /t:60
```

Specify that only *C:* be checked at startup on a system that also has *D:* and *E:* as fixed drives:

```
chkntfs /d
chkntfs /x C: D: E:
chkntfs /c C:
```

In this example:

- The first command resets the default setting, which causes all volumes to be checked at startup.
- The second command excludes all volumes from being checked.
- The third command schedules *C:* alone for checking.

Notes

- You must be a member of the local Administrators group to use the chkntfs command.
- The default behavior of chkntfs is to check all volumes at startup.
- Don't set the countdown time to zero, as checking the filesystem can be very time-consuming and the user will be unable to cancel this operation. (chkdsk can't be stopped once it is running.)

See Also

chkdsk, convert, defrag, diskpart, *Disks*, format, label, mountvol

---

cipher

Displays or modifies the encryption state of files and directories on NTFS volumes.

Syntax

```
cipher [/e | /d] [/s:directory] [/a] [/i] [/f] [/q] [/h] [/k] [/u[/n]]
[pathname [...]]
cipher /r:pathnamewithoutextension
```

```
cipher /w:pathname
cipher /x[:pathname] pathnamewithoutextension
```

Options

None
> Lists encryption state of current directory and its files.

pathname [...]
> Specifies files or directories to be processed.

/e   Encrypts specified directories.

/d   Decrypts specified directories.

/s:directory
> Recursively processes all subdirectories in specified directory (can't be used more than once in a single command).

/a   Processes specified files. (If there is no matching file, the switch is ignored.)

/i   Ignores errors during processing.

/f   Forces encryption/decryption of specified files even if they have already been encrypted/decrypted.

/q   Switches to quick (nonverbose) output.

/h   Shows files with Hidden or System attributes. (These files aren't encrypted or decrypted.)

/k   Creates a new EFS key for the current user (use this switch alone).

/u   Updates all encrypted files with new file encryption key or recovery agent key (use this switch by itself or with /n)

/n   When used with /u, this option finds all encrypted files on local drives.

/r:pathnamewithoutextension
> Generates a new recovery agent certificate and private key, which are then written to the specified file (this option must be used by itself).

/w:pathname
> Removes data stored on unused portions of a volume (this option must be used by itself).

/x[:pathname] pathnamewithoutextension
> Identifies and backs up certificates and private keys used by EFS for currently logged-on user, with the resulting file having a *.pfx* extension.

Examples

View the encryption state of files and directories in the root of *H:* drive:

cipher h:*
```
Listing h:\
New files added to this directory will not be encrypted.

U doc1.txt
E doc2.txt
U pub
```

Encrypt the *pub* folder shown earlier:

cipher /e h:\pub
```
Encrypting directories in h:\
```

Command Reference

```
    pub                    [OK]
```

```
1 directorie(s) within 1 directorie(s) were encrypted.
```

New files added to *pub* now will be encrypted. To encrypt only the file *doc3.txt* in *pub*:

cipher /e /a h:\pub\doc3.txt
```
Encrypting files in h:\pub\
```

```
    doc3.txt               [OK]
```

```
1 file(s) [or directorie(s)] within 1 directorie(s) were encrypted.
```

Notes

- Wildcards work with files but not directories.
- You can't encrypt system or compressed files.

See Also

Files and Folders

---

clip   new in WS2003

Redirects the output of a command to the clipboard.

Syntax

```
clip
```

Examples

Redirect the output of bootcfg to the clipboard:

bootcfg | clip

Now copy the clipboard to Notepad:

Start → Notepad → Edit → Paste

View the results:

```
Boot Loader Settings
--------------------
timeout:0
default:multi(0)disk(0)rdisk(0)partition(1)\WINDOWS
Boot Entries
------------
Boot entry ID:    1
OS Friendly Name: WS2003, Enterprise
Path:             multi(0)disk(0)rdisk(0)partition(1)\WINDOWS
OS Load Options:  /fastdetect /noguiboot
```

See Also

cmd

---

cmd

Runs a new instance of the command-line shell.

Syntax

```
cmd [/a | /u] [/q] [/d] [/e:on | /e:off] [/f:on | /f:off] [/v:on |
/v:off] [ [/s] [/t:bf] [/c | /k] command]
```

Options

None
> Opens a new command shell.

command
> Runs the specified command in the current command shell.

/c Executes command and then exits the shell. (The remainder of the command following the /c switch is processed as a command line.)

/k Executes command and continues running the shell. (The remainder of the command following the /k switch is processed as a command line.)

/s If the first character after /c or /k is a quote and the /s switch is used, strips the leading and final closing quotes and retains any other quotes in the line as part of the command.

/q Disables local echo.

/d Disables running AutoRun commands, which are stored in the registry and executed by default whenever cmd is run. The registry locations are:

```
HKLM\Software\Microsoft\Command Processor\AutoRun
HKCU\Software\Microsoft\Command Processor\AutoRun
```

/a Sets output to ANSI.

/u Sets output to Unicode.

/t:bf
> Specifies background and foreground colors using hexadecimal numeric codes of the color command (type **color /?** for a list of codes).

/e:[on | off]
> Enables or disables command-shell extensions (enabled by default), which extend the functionality of the following commands: del (erase), color, cd (chdir), md (mdir), prompt, pushd, popd, set, setlocal, endlocal, if, for, call, shift, goto, start, assoc, and ftype.

/f:[on | off]
> Enables or disables filename and directory name completion characters (disabled by default), which use Ctrl-D and Ctrl-F for directory and filename completion, respectively.

/v:[on | off]
> Disables delayed environment-variable expansion (disabled by default). If enabled, you can use the exclamation character (!) to substitute the value of environment variables at runtime.

Examples

Turn autocompletion on:
> **cmd /f:on**

Change to the *C:\Program Files* directory using autocompletion:
> **cd p**

Then press Ctrl-D several times until "Program Files" appears, and then press Enter.

Discussion

Because understanding cmd is essential to running all other commands in this chapter, it's worth taking a deeper look at how it works.

Opening a Command Shell

To launch the command interpreter from the GUI:

> Start → All Programs → Accessories → Command Prompt
> Start → Run → **cmd** → OK

To start a new instance of the command interpreter from an existing instance:

> Command interpreter → **cmd** (opens a nested command shell in the same window)
> Command interpreter → **start cmd** (opens a new command shell)

Tip: to quit a nested shell, type **exit**.

Configuring a Command Shell

To configure the properties of a command prompt window, right-click on the titlebar of the window and select Properties. This opens a properties sheet with four tabs. The key settings here are:

Options
> Switches the command interpreter between full screen and a window (you can switch between them using Alt-Enter), enables QuickEdit (which lets you cut and paste using a mouse instead of the tedious Edit menu), enables Insert mode (which lets you insert text at the present cursor position instead of overwriting previous text there), and configures the number of commands that can be remembered in the command-history buffer (you access previously typed commands by using the up and down arrow keys).

Font
> Specifies a font size and name for use in the command-interpreter window.

Layout
> Lets you specify the window and buffer size. Window size refers to the width in characters and height in lines of the command-interpreter window. Buffer size refers to the virtual size of the window when you use the horizontal and vertical scrollbars. It's a nice touch that the default buffer size is now 300 lines instead of the 25 lines it was in Windows NT.

Colors
> Lets you specify colors for the screen text and background and for pop-up text and background.

When you change the properties of a command-prompt window and click OK, a dialog box appears asking you whether you want to apply the properties to the current command-interpreter window only (in which case the settings vanish when you close this window) or to future windows of the same title or started from the same shortcut (in which case the changes you made are persistent). If you want your settings to be persistent, you can avoid this annoyance by selecting Defaults instead of Properties when you right-click on the titlebar of the command-prompt window.

Running Multiple Commands

You can use conditional processing symbols to run multiple commands as a single command, with a command to the right of a conditional processing symbol processing the results of the command to the left of the symbol. Table 5-2 lists the conditional processing symbols that are available.

Table 5-2. Conditional processing symbols

Symbol	Syntax	Comment
& [...]	Command1 & Command2	Runs the first command, then the second.
&& [...]	Command1 && Command2	Runs the second command only if the first completed successfully.
‖ [...]	Command1 ‖ Command2	Runs the second command only if the first command failed.
() [...]	(Command1 & Command2)	Group commands together.
; *or* ,	Command1 Parm1;Parm2	Separates command parameters.

Environment Variables

An environment variable is a string that contains information used to control some aspect of the operating system or application, such as the path to an important system file or directory, the number and type of processors on the motherboard, and so on. The two types of environment variables are:

System variables
> These are the same for all users who log on to the computer, and their effect applies to the whole operating system. Only members of the Administrators group can create or modify system variables, and some default ones can't be modified at all.

Local variables
> These differ for each user who logs on to the computer, and users can create and modify their own user variables and assign them values. Local variables were formerly called user variables in W2K and earlier.

Table 5-3 lists the system environment variables defined in WS2003 together with their default values, while Table 5-4 does the same for local environment variables.

Table 5-3. System environment variables and their default values

Variable	Description	Default value
%CMDEXTVERSION%	Version number of current command processor extensions	2
%COMPUTERNAME%	Name of computer	—
%COMSPEC%	Exact path to *cmd.exe*	*C:\Windows\system32 \cmd.exe*
%DATE%	Current date (see date)	—
%ERRORLEVEL%	Error code of most recently executed command (nonzero value indicates error)	—
%HOMEDRIVE%	Drive letter connected to user's home directory	—
%HOMEPATH%	Full path of user's home directory	—
%HOMESHARE%	Network path to user's shared home directory	—
%NUMBER_OF_PROCESSORS%	Number of processors in computer	—
%OS%	Operating system name	*Windows_NT*

Table 5-3. System environment variables and their default values (continued)

Variable	Description	Default value
%PATH%	Search path for executable files	*C:\Windows\system32;* *C:\Windows;* *C:\Windows\system32* *\Wbem*
%PATHEXT%	List of the file extensions considered executable	*.COM;.EXE;.BAT;.CMD;* *.VBS;.VBE;.JS;.JSE;.* *WSF;.WSH;.VBS*
%PROCESSOR_ ARCHITECTURE%	Chip architecture of the processor	—
%PROCESSOR_ IDENTFIER%	Description of the processor	—
%PROCESSOR_ LEVEL%	Model number of the processor installed on the computer	—
%PROCESSOR_ REVISION%	Revision number of the processor	—
%RANDOM%	Random decimal number between 0 and 32767	—
%SYSTEMDRIVE%	System root drive	*C:*
%SYSTEMROOT%	Location of OS root directory	*C:\Windows*
%TIME%	Current time (see time)	—
%WINDIR%	Location of OS directory	*C:\Windows*

Table 5-4. Local environment variables and their default values

Variable	Description	Default value
%ALLUSERSPROFILE%	Location of all users profile	*C:\Documents and Settings* *\All Users*
%APPDATA%	Default location where applications store data	*C:\Documents and Settings* *\current_user* *\Application Data*
%CD%	Current directory string	—
%CMDCMDLINE%	Exact command used to start current command shell	—
%LOGONSERVER%	Name of domain controller that validated current logon session	—
%PROMPT%	Command prompt settings for current command shell	—
%TEMP% and %TMP%	Default temporary directories used by applications for currently logged-on user	*C:\Documents and Settings* *\current_user* *\Local Settings* *\Temp*
%USERDOMAIN%	Name of domain containing currently logged-on user's account	—
%USERNAME%	Name of currently logged-on user	—
%USERPROFILE%	Location of profile for currently logged-on user	—

Working with Environment Variables

To set (create, delete, or modify) environment variables using the GUI:

Control Panel → System → Advanced → Environment Variables → {New | Edit | Delete}

To set a variable from the command line, use the set command (see set later in this chapter).

Only a member of the Administrators group can add, delete, or set the value of a system environment variable. Changes made by the currently logged-on user affect the user environment variables only for that user. You may have to reboot your system or close and reopen your application for the new value of an environment variable to take effect.

System variables may be used to define paths for logon scripts, home directories, and user profiles. They may also be used within logon scripts or in commands executed at the command prompt. To use an environment variable, enclose it in percent signs. For example, typing the command:

```
C:\> cd %windir%
```

produces the following result:

```
C:\Windows>
```

You can easily display the value of an environment variable from the command line. For example, to display the name of the installed operating system using the OS system variable, just type:

```
C:\>echo %os%
```

which produces the result:

```
Windows_NT
```

Who says WS2003 isn't really just Windows NT disguised?

Notes

- Use double quotes to enclose commands that contain spaces.
- Use && to separate multiple commands surrounded by quotes in a single command line.
- Note that /x is the same as /e:on and /y is the same as /e:off for backward compatibility with the Windows NT command shell.
- Installing new operating-system components or applications may create additional environment variables or modify existing ones such as PATH.

See Also

runas, set

---

cmdkey
new in WS2003

Manages stored usernames and passwords.

Syntax

```
cmdkey /add:TargetName /user:UserName /pass:Password
cmdkey /add:TargetName /smartcard
cmdkey /generic:TargetName /user:UserName /pass:Password
```

```
cmdkey /delete{:TargetName | /ras}]
cmdkey /list[:TargetName]
```

Options

/add:TargetName /user:UserName /pass:Password
> Adds the specified username and password for the specified computer or domain to the stored credentials list

/add:TargetName /smartcard
> Retrieves credentials from a smart card and adds them to the stored credentials list

/generic:TargetName /user:UserName /pass:Password
> Adds the specified generic credentials (not associated with a specific computer or domain) to the stored credentials list

/delete{:TargetName | /ras}
> Deletes the specified username and password or remote access entry from the stored credentials list

/list:TargetName
> Lists the stored credentials for the specified computer or domain (if TargetName is omitted, all stored credentials are listed)

Examples

Add credentials for Bob Smith to the stored credentials list in the *mtit.local* domain:

cmdkey /add:mtit.local /user:bsmith@mtit.local /pass:password
```
CMDKEY: Credential added successfully.
```

Display list of stored credentials:

cmdkey /list
```
Currently stored credentials:
    Target: mtit.local
    Type: Domain Password
    User: bsmith@mtit.local
```

Delete stored credentials for *mtit.local* domain:

cmdkey /del:mtit.local
```
CMDKEY: Credential deleted successfully.
```

Verify the result:

cmdkey /list
```
Currently stored credentials:
* NONE *
```

Add credentials for Bob Smith to the stored credentials list on the standalone server named *esrv230d*:

cmdkey /add:esrv230d /user:esrv230d\bsmith /pass:password
```
CMDKEY: Credential added successfully.
```

Notes

You can also manage stored credentials from the GUI using the Stored usernames and Passwords utility in the Control Panel.

See Also

Logon

---

convert

Converts FAT and FAT32 volumes to NTFS.

Syntax

```
convert volume /fs:ntfs [/v] [/nametable:filename]
```

Options

volume

  Specifies the volume to convert. A drive letter with colon, a volume mount point, or a volume name can identify this volume.

/fs:ntfs

  Converts the volume to NTFS (required).

/v Verbose.

/nametable:filename

  Creates a temporary table of the filenames that need to be changed when converting to NTFS. (Use this if you have strange filenames that prevent conversion from completing properly.)

Examples

Convert *F:* drive from FAT32 to NTFS:

```
convert F: /fs:ntfs
The type of the file system is FAT32.
Enter current volume label for drive F: F32
Determining disk space required for file system conversion...
Total disk space:            614400 KB
Free space on volume:        613160 KB
Space required for conversion:   6083 KB
Converting file system
Conversion complete
```

Note that for safety purposes, you have to enter the volume label of the volume you want to convert. If you type the convert command and then open Windows Explorer or My Computer to determine the necessary volume label, be sure to close that tool before entering the label or you might get this:

```
convert f: /fs:ntfs
The type of the file system is FAT32.
Enter current volume label for drive F: F32
Convert cannot gain exclusive access to the F: drive,
so it cannot convert it now.  Would you like to
schedule it to be converted the next time the
system restarts (Y/N)?
```

Notes

- The current drive can't be converted.
- If a drive is almost full, convert may not run successfully. Delete some files, and try again.
- Check for Winlogon events in the application log if automatic conversion fails at boot.

See Also

chkdsk, chkntfs, defrag, diskpart, *Disks*, format, label, mountvol

---

csvde

Stands for comma separated value directory exchange, a utility for bulk import/export of data between comma-delimited (CSV) text files and Active Directory. csvde can be used to create multiple user accounts, groups, computers, printers, or other AD objects in a single batch operation.

Syntax

csvde *options*

Options

CSVDE options are either export-specific, import-specific, or general in nature. There are also options for how credentials are specified for accessing AD.

General Options

-c string1 string2
Replaces all occurrences of *string1* with *string2* (used to change the distinguished name of objects when importing data from one domain to a different domain).

-f filename
Indicates name of import/export file.

-i Switches to import mode (the default is export mode).

-j path
Specifies location of log file (default is current directory).

-s servername
Specifies the domain controller on which the import/export operation is performed.

-t portnumber
Specifies LDAP port number (the default is 389). The global catalog is port 3,268.

-u Specifies a CSV file is in Unicode format.

-v Specifies verbose mode.

Options for Export Only

-d baseDN
Specifies the distinguished name of the search base for exporting data.

-g Disables paged searches.

-l attributelist
  Lists attributes to export (the default is all attributes).

-m Omits attributes specific to Active Directory objects. (Examples include `ObjectGUID`, `objectSID`, `pwdLastSet`, and `samAccountType`.)

-n Don't export binary values.

-o attributelist
  Lists attributes to omit during export.

-p scope
  Specifies the search scope as `Base`, `OneLevel`, or `SubTree`.

-r filter
  Creates an LDAP search filter for exporting data.

Options for Import Only

-k Keep importing even if errors occur.

Options for Establishing Credentials

-a user-distinguished-name password
  Security context (credentials) within which the command runs

-b username domain password
  Same as -a but different format for credentials

Examples

First, create a properly formatted CSV file to create three new user accounts in Active Directory. The file *C:\newusers.txt* contains the following lines of information:

```
DN,objectClass,sAMAccountName,userPrincipalName,displayName,
userAccountControl
"cn=George Smith,ou=Support,dc=mtitcanada,dc=com",user,gsmith,
gsmith@mtitcanada.com,George T. Smith,514
"cn=Barb Smith,ou=Support,dc=mtitcanada,dc=com",user,bsmith,
bsmith@mtitcanada.com,Barbara Lynn Smith,514
"cn=Judy Smith,ou=Support,dc=mtitcanada,dc=com",user,
jsmith,jsmith@mtitcanada.com,Judy Ann Smith,512
```

The meaning of this information is as follows:

DN
  This is the distinguished name of object.

objectClass
  user specifies user account object.

sAMAccountName
  This is the pre-W2K/2003 user logon name.

userPrincipalName
  This is the W2K/2003 user logon name.

displayName
  This is the full name of the user.

userAccountControl
  512 means account is enabled; 514 means disabled.

Now use csvde to import *newusers.txt* and create the three user accounts:

```
csvde -i -f C:\newusers.txt
Connecting to "(null)"
Logging in as current user using SSPI
Importing directory from file "C:\newusers.txt"
Loading entries....
3 entries modified successfully.

The command has completed successfully
```

Use the Active Directory Users and Computers console to verify that the accounts were properly created.

A quick way to list all the possible attributes of user objects is to export all users and look at the first line:

```
csvde -f attribs.txt
Connecting to "(null)"
Logging in as current user using SSPI
Exporting directory to file attribs.txt
Searching for entries...
Writing out entries....................................
...................................................
...........
Export Completed. Post-processing in progress...
152 entries exported

The command has completed successfully
```

Notes

- A common use for csvde is creating multiple user accounts. To do this, the CSV file you import:
  - Must contain a first line called the attribute line, which specifies the name of each attribute defined in the file.
  - Must contain one additional line for each user account you want to create. The attributes in this line must match the sequence of those in the attribute line (first line). Use quotation marks to include values that have embedded commas.
  - Must contain the path to the user account in AD, the object type, and the user logon name (pre-W2K/2003) for each user.
  - Should contain the user principal name (UPN) for each user.
  - Should specify whether the account is enabled or disabled (the default is disabled).
  - Can include any personal information that is an attribute of a user account, such as address or phone number.
- Passwords aren't included in csvde files because these files are text files (*.csv* files) and are thus not secure. csvde creates new user accounts and assigns them a blank password. As a result, it is best to have accounts disabled when they are first created, because anyone can log on using the accounts and a blank password.

- csvde can be used only to add objects to AD; it can't modify or delete existing objects.
- Microsoft Excel is a good tool for creating csvde files because it can export spreadsheet data in CSV format.

See Also
Active Directory, ldifde

---

date

Displays or modifies system date.

Syntax
```
date [MM-DD-YY[YY]] [/t]
```

Options
None
> Displays current date and prompts you to specify a new date

MM-DD-YY[YY]
> Specifies a date

/t   Does not prompt for new date

Example
Display current date:
```
date /t
Wed 03/26/2003
```

Notes
Valid years are 80 through 99, or 1980 through 2099.

See Also
time

---

dcgpofix

A disaster recovery utility that restores default domain policy and/or default domain-controller policies to their default state after initial installation.

Syntax
```
dcgpofix [/target: {domain | dc | both}] [/ignoreschema]
```

Options
/target: {domain | dc | both}
> Specifies target domain, domain controller, or both (if omitted, defaults to both)

/ignoreschema
> Ignores Active Directory schema version number at your peril

Examples

dcgpofix

```
Microsoft(R) Windows(R) Operating System Default Group Policy Restore
Utility v5.1

Copyright (C) Microsoft Corporation. 1981-2003

Description: Recreates the Default Group Policy Objects (GPOs) for a domain

Syntax: DcGPOFix [/ignoreschema] [/Target: Domain | DC | BOTH]

This utility can restore either or both the Default DomainPolicy or the
Default Domain Controllers Policy to the state that exists immediately after
a clean install. You must be a domain administrator to perform this
operation.

WARNING: YOU WILL LOSE ANY CHANGES YOU HAVE MADE TO THESE GPOs. THIS UTILITY
IS INTENDED ONLY FOR DISASTER RECOVERY PURPOSES.

You are about to restore Default Domain policy  and Default domain
Controller policy for the following domainmtit.local

Do you want to continue: <Y/N>? y

WARNING: This operation will replace all 'User Rights Assignments' made in
the chosen GPOs. This may render some server applications to fail. Do you
want to continue: <Y/N>? y

The Default Domain Policy was restored successfully
Note: Only the contents of the Default Domain Policy was restored. Group
Policy links to this Group Policy Object were not altered.
By default, The Default Domain Policy is linked to the Domain.

The Default Domain Controller Policy was restored successfully
Note: Only the contents of the Default Domain Controller Policy was
restored. Group Policy links to this Group Policy Object were not altered.
By default, The Default Domain Controller Policy is linked to the Domain
Controllers OU.
```

Notes

- When you run dcgpofix, you will lose any changes made to these Group Policy objects.
- The /ignoreschema switch enables dcgpofix to work with different versions of Active Directory, but make sure you use the version of dcgpofix included with your current version of Active Directory.

See Also

Group Policy

defrag

Defragments local drives.

Syntax

```
defrag Volume [/a] [/v] [/f]
```

Options

Volume
> The drive letter or mount point of the volume to defragment

/a Performs a fragmentation analysis only and displays a summary report

/v Verbose analysis report

/f Forces defragmentation even if free space is low

Examples

Check volume *E:* for fragmentation:

defrag e: /a
```
Windows Disk Defragmenter
Copyright (c) 2002 Microsoft Corp. and Executive Software International,
Inc.

Analysis Report
    502 MB Total,  60 MB (11%) Free,  1% Fragmented (2% file fragmentation)

You do not need to defragment this volume.
```

Get verbose information about fragmentation:

defrag e: /v
```
Windows Disk Defragmenter
Copyright (c) 2002 Microsoft Corp. and Executive Software International,
Inc.

Analysis Report

        Volume size                 = 502 MB
        Cluster size                = 512 bytes
        Used space                  = 442 MB
        Free space                  = 60 MB
        Percent free space          = 11 %

    Volume fragmentation
        Total fragmentation         = 1 %
        File fragmentation          = 2 %
        Free space fragmentation    = 0 %

    File fragmentation
        Total files                 = 781
        Average file size           = 611 KB
        Total fragmented files      = 8
        Total excess fragments      = 19
        Average fragments per file  = 1.02
```

```
    Pagefile fragmentation
        Pagefile size                = 0 bytes
        Total fragments              = 0

    Folder fragmentation
        Total folders                = 1,256
        Fragmented folders           = 1
        Excess folder fragments      = 36

    Master File Table (MFT) fragmentation
        Total MFT size               = 2 MB
        MFT record count             = 2,052
        Percent MFT in use           = 97
        Total MFT fragments          = 3
```
Defragment *E:* drive:

defrag e:
```
Windows Disk Defragmenter
Copyright (c) 2002 Microsoft Corp. and Executive Software International,
Inc.

Analysis Report
    502 MB Total,  60 MB (11%) Free,  1% Fragmented (2% file fragmentation)

Volume New Volume (E:) has only 11% free space available for use by Disk
Defragmenter.  To run effectively, Disk Defragmenter requires at least 15%
usable free space.  There is not enough disk space to properly complete the
operation.  Delete some unneeded files on your hard disk, and then try
again.
```
Force defragmentation even though free space is low:

defrag e: /f
```
Windows Disk Defragmenter
Copyright (c) 2002 Microsoft Corp. and Executive Software International,
Inc.

Analysis Report
    502 MB Total,  60 MB (11%) Free,  1% Fragmented (2% file fragmentation)

Defragmentation Report
    502 MB Total,  60 MB (11%) Free,  0% Fragmented (0% file fragmentation)
```

Notes

- You can't run the defrag command and the Defragmenter tool in Computer Management at the same time.
- A minimum of 15% free space is required on volumes to completely defragment them. Forcing a defragmentation when there is less free space often results in partial defragmentation.
- To stop the defragmentation process, type Ctrl-C.

See Also

chkdsk, chkntfs, convert, diskpart, *Disks*, format, label, mountvol

---

dfscmd

Configures an existing DFS tree.

Syntax

```
dfscmd options
```

Options

/add \\dfsname\dfsshare\path \\server\share\path [/restore]
: Adds a replica to a DFS volume. With /restore, don't check the destination server.

/map \\dfsname\dfsshare\path \\server\share\path [comment] [/restore]
: Creates a new DFS volume by mapping a DFS path to a shared folder. The /restore option causes no check to be performed to see if the destination server is available.

/remove \\dfsname\dfsshare\path \\server\share\path
: Removes a replica from a DFS volume.

/unmap \\dfsname\dfsshare\path
: Deletes a DFS volume and removes all its replicas.

/view \\dfsname\dfsshare [/partial | /full | /batch || / batchrestore]
: Views the volumes in the specified DFS tree. If no arguments are specified, only volume names are displayed. The /partial option displays the comments as well, and the /full option lists the full details of the tree. The /batch option is used to output the DFS tree configuration to a file, which allows the DFS tree to be re-created using the /batchrestore option if necessary.

Examples

Add a new DFS link named SALESREPORTS, which maps to the shared folder *Sales* on the server *Test* to the existing domain-based DFS root named *mtitcanada. com\ public*:

```
dfscmd /map \\mtitcanada.com\public\salesreports \\test\sales
The command completed successfully.
```

Add a second DFS link named CATALOGS, which maps to the shared folder *Cat* on server *Bach.mtitworld.com*:

```
dfscmd /map \\mtitcanada.com\public\catalogs \\bach.mtitworld.com\cat
The command completed successfully.
```

Add a DFS replica that maps the existing DFS link SALESREPORTS to the shared folder *Sales* on server 172.16.11.100:

```
dfscmd /add \\mtitcanada.com\public\salesreports \\172.16.11.100\sales
The command completed successfully.
```

View the full details of the domain-based DFS tree whose root is *mtitcanada.com\ public*:

```
dfscmd /view \\mtitcanada.com\public /full
\\MTITCANADA\public
        \\TEST\pub
\\MTITCANADA\public\salesreports
        \\test\sales
        \\172.16.11.100\sales
```

```
\\MTITCANADA\public\catalogs
     \\bach.mtitworld.com\cat
The command completed successfully.
```

Notes

- The `dfscmd` command can manage existing DFS trees (both domain-based and standalone) but can't be used to create a new DFS tree. You must use the Distributed File System console to create a new DFS tree by creating a new DFS root (see *DFS* in Chapter 4 for more information).

- Paths that have embedded spaces must be enclosed in quotes.

See Also

DFS

---

diskpart   new in WS2003

Manages disks, partitions, and volumes from the command line.

Syntax

```
diskpart
diskpart /s script
```

Options

None
> Enters interactive mode and displays the DISKPART> prompt, waiting for you to enter `diskpart` commands

/s Specifies a script containing a series of `diskpart` commands to execute sequentially

Commands

The following is a summary of `diskpart` commands that can be used either interactively or in scripts. Note that each command has its own unique syntax, which is summarized briefly.

active
> Marks the selected basic partition as active.

add disk=N
> Adds the specified disk as a mirror to the selected simple volume.

assign {letter=D | mount=path}
> Assigns the specified drive letter or mount point to the selected volume. If `assign` is used alone, the next available drive letter is used. Does not work with system/ boot volumes or volumes where a paging file resides.

automount [enable | disable]
> Enables and disables automatic mounting of basic volumes. Automounting is enabled by default and should be disabled only for storage area networks.

break disk=N [nokeep]
> Breaks a mirror set into two simple volumes and changes the focus to the specified volume so you can assign it a drive letter. The `nokeep` option causes the mirrored volume to be converted to free space instead.

---

clean [all]
>   Deletes the configuration information from the selected disk by overwriting the MBR. The all option sets every sector to zero to delete all data on the disk.

convert basic
>   Converts a dynamic disk to basic (must delete all volumes first).

convert dynamic
>   Converts a basic disk to dynamic.

create partition primary [size=N]
>   Creates a primary partition of size *N* megabytes and shifts focus to the new partition (if no size is specified, the partition is as large as possible).

create partition extended [size=N]
>   Creates an extended partition of size *N* megabytes and shifts focus to the new partition (if no size is specified, the partition is as large as possible).

create partition logical [size=N]
>   Creates a logical drive of size *N* megabytes within the extended partition and shifts focus to the new logical drive (if no size is specified, the partition is as large as possible).

create volume raid [size=N] disk=N,N,N[,N,...]
>   Creates a RAID-5 volume from simple volumes of size *N* megabytes on the specified dynamic disks. If no size is specified, the largest possible volume size is used. After the RAID-5 volume is created, it assumes the focus.

create volume simple [size=N] [disk=N]
>   Creates a simple volume of size *N* megabytes on the specified dynamic disk. If no size is specified, the partition is as large as possible, and if no disk is specified, the currently selected disk is used. After the volume is created, it assumes the focus.

create volume stripe [size=N] disk=N,N[,N,...]
>   Creates a striped volume from simple volumes of size *N* megabytes on the specified dynamic disks. If no size is specified, the largest possible volume size will be used. After the striped volume is created, it assumes the focus.

delete disk [override]
>   Deletes a missing dynamic disk from the disk list. The override option deletes all simple volumes on the disk but doesn't work if the disk is part of a RAID-5 volume.

delete partition [override]
>   Deletes the selected partition on a basic disk. The override option deletes nonstandard partitions.

delete volume
>   Deletes the selected volume (won't work for system/boot volumes or volumes containing the pagefile).

detail {disk | partition | volume}
>   Displays properties of disk, partition, or volume.

exit
>   Exits diskpart when running in interactive mode.

extend [size=N]
>   Extends the selected partition on a basic disk using adjacent contiguous free space (if any) from the disk on which the partition resides.

extend [size=N] disk=N
> Extends the selected volume on a dynamic disk using contiguous free space on the specified dynamic disk.

import
> Imports every disk that belongs to the foreign disk group to which the currently selected disk belongs.

inactive
> Marks the current basic partition as inactive.

list {disk | partition | volume}
> Lists the disks on the local machine or the partitions/volumes on the currently selected disk. If volume option is used with basic disks, logical volumes are displayed instead.

online
> Brings online a disk that is currently marked offline.

rem
> Used to comment scripts.

remove {letter=D | mount=path | all} [dismount]
> Removes the specified drive letter or mount point assignment or all drive letters and mount points. The dismount option closes all handles to the partition or volume before dismounting it. Does not work with system/boot volumes or volumes on which the pagefile resides.

repair disk=N
> Repairs a failed disk on a RAID-5 volume using the specified disk.

rescan
> Rescans the computer looking for new disks and volumes that may have been added.

retain
> Prepares a simple volume to be used as a system/boot volume during unattended Setup.

select disk=N
> Changes the focus of diskpart to the specified disk.

select partition=N
> Changes the focus of diskpart to the specified partition.

select volume=N
> Changes the focus of diskpart to the specified volume.

Examples

Run diskpart interactively:

```
diskpart
Microsoft DiskPart version 5.2.3763
Copyright (C) 1999-2001 Microsoft Corporation.
On computer: ESRV210D

DISKPART>
```

List the fixed disks on the computer:

list disk

```
Disk ###  Status      Size     Free    Dyn  Gpt
--------  ----------  -------  -------  ---  ---
Disk 0    Online      37 GB    27 GB
```

Select disk 0 to give it the focus for further diskpart commands:

select disk=0

```
Disk 0 is now the selected disk.
```

List the partitions on the selected basic disk:

list partition

```
Partition ###  Type              Size     Offset
-------------  ----------------  -------  -------
Partition 1    Primary            10 GB   32 KB
Partition 2    Primary           502 MB   10 GB
```

List the logical volumes on the selected basic disk:

list volume

```
Volume ###  Ltr  Label        Fs     Type        Size     Status    Info
----------  ---  -----------  -----  ----------  -------  --------- -----
Volume 0    D                        CD-ROM        0 B    Healthy
Volume 1    C                 NTFS   Partition    10 GB   Healthy   System
Volume 2    E    New Volume   NTFS   Partition   502 MB   Healthy
```

Note that the CD-ROM drive shows up as a logical volume because it has a drive letter assigned. Note also that volume 1 is the system volume.

Create a new primary partition 2 GB in size:

create partition primary size=2048

```
DiskPart succeeded in creating the specified partition.
```

Verify the result:

list volume

```
Volume ###  Ltr  Label        Fs     Type        Size     Status    Info
----------  ---  -----------  -----  ----------  -------  --------- -----
Volume 0    D                        CD-ROM        0 B    Healthy
Volume 1    C                 NTFS   Partition    10 GB   Healthy   System
Volume 2    E    New Volume   NTFS   Partition   502 MB   Healthy
* Volume 3                    RAW    Partition  2055 MB   Healthy
```

The asterisk beside volume 3 indicates that this newly created volume has the focus. Note also that volume 3 has no drive letter assigned, so let's assign one to it:

assign letter=G

```
DiskPart successfully assigned the drive letter or mount point.
```

Verify:

list volume

```
Volume ### Ltr  Label        Fs     Type        Size     Status     Info
---------- ---  -----------  -----  ----------  -------  ---------  -----
Volume 0   D                        CD-ROM         0 B   Healthy
Volume 1   C                 NTFS   Partition    10 GB   Healthy    System
Volume 2   E    New Volume   NTFS   Partition   502 MB   Healthy
* Volume 3  G                       RAW    Partition  2055 MB  Healthy
```

Change the focus to volume 2 so it can be deleted:

select volume=2

```
Volume 2 is the selected volume.
```
delete volume

```
DiskPart successfully deleted the volume.
```

Verify:

list volume

```
Volume ### Ltr  Label        Fs     Type        Size     Status     Info
---------- ---  -----------  -----  ----------  -------  ---------  -----
Volume 0   D                        CD-ROM         0 B   Healthy
Volume 1   C                 NTFS   Partition    10 GB   Healthy    System
Volume 3   G                 RAW    Partition  2055 MB   Healthy
```

Now no volume has the focus, so let's select volume 3 and extend it 1 GB:

select volume 3

```
Volume 3 is the selected volume.
```
extend size=1024

```
DiskPart successfully extended the volume.
```

Verify:

list volume

```
Volume ### Ltr  Label        Fs     Type        Size     Status     Info
---------- ---  -----------  -----  ----------  -------  ---------  -----
Volume 0   D                        CD-ROM         0 B   Healthy
Volume 1   C                 NTFS   Partition    10 GB   Healthy    System
* Volume 3  G                       RAW    Partition  3083 MB  Healthy
```

Display properties of selected volume:

detail volume

```
Disk ###  Status      Size     Free     Dyn  Gpt
--------  ----------  -------  -------  ---  ---
* Disk 0   Online       37 GB    24 GB
```

Display properties of selected disk:

detail disk

```
MAXTOR 6L040J2
Disk ID: C95AC95A
```

```
Type   : ATA
Bus    : 0
Target : 0
LUN ID : 0
```

```
  Volume ###  Ltr  Label        Fs     Type       Size    Status     Info
  ----------  ---  -----------  -----  ---------- -------  ---------  -----
  Volume 1    C                 NTFS   Partition   10 GB  Healthy    System
* Volume 3    G                 RAW    Partition  3083 MB Healthy
```

Quit diskpart interactive mode:

exit

```
Leaving DiskPart...
```

```
C:\>
```

Notes

- When running diskpart commands from a script, you can redirect the output to a text file to view later by:

  diskpart /s script > file.txt

- If you use more than one script with diskpart in a batch file, add timeout /t 15 before each diskpart /s script command to ensure the first tasks are completed before the next tasks are begun.

- If an error occurs while running a diskpart command, the task stops, and an error code is displayed. If you add a noerr option to the command, the command is processed as if the error never occurred. diskpart error codes are as follows:

  0 No errors. The script ran successfully.

  1 Fatal exception.

  2 Incorrect parameters for the diskpart command.

  3 Unable to open the specified script or output file.

  4 A service has returned an error.

  5 Invalid command syntax.

See Also

chkdsk, chkntfs, convert, defrag, *Disks*, format, label, mountvol

---

driverquery   new in WS2003

Displays properties of installed device drivers.

Syntax

```
driverquery  [/s Computer] [/u Domain\User /p Password] [/fo {TABLE | LIST |
CSV}] [/nh] [{/v | /si}]
```

Options

/s Computer
> Name or IP address of a remote computer (if omitted, defaults to local computer)

/u Domain\User /p Password
> Credentials for running the command (if omitted, defaults to currently logged-on user)

/fo {TABLE | LIST | CSV}
> Format for displaying driver properties (if omitted, default is TABLE)

/nh Omits header row from displayed information if /fo is set to TABLE or CSV

/v Displays verbose driver information

/si Displays properties of signed drivers

Examples

Display driver properties in table format:

driverquery

```
Module Name   Display Name              Driver Type   Link Date
============  ========================  ============  ==================  =========
ACPI          Microsoft ACPI Driver     Kernel        2/4/2003 9:09:10 PM
ACPIEC        ACPIEC                    Kernel        2/4/2003 9:09:15 PM
AFD           AFD Networking Support    Kernel        2/4/2003 9:34:39 PM
agp440        Intel AGP Bus Filter      Kernel        2/4/2003 9:09:19 PM
AsyncMac      RAS Asynchronous Media    Kernel        2/4/2003 9:07:37 PM
atapi         Standard IDE/ESDI Hard    Kernel        2/4/2003 9:01:09 PM
...
```

Display driver properties in list format:

driverquery /fo list

```
Module Name:    ACPI
Display Name:   Microsoft ACPI Driver
Driver Type:    Kernel
Link Date:      2/4/2003 9:09:10 PM

Module Name:    ACPIEC
Display Name:   ACPIEC
Driver Type:    Kernel
Link Date:      2/4/2003 9:09:15 PM

Module Name:    AFD
Display Name:   AFD Networking Support Environment
Driver Type:    Kernel
Link Date:      2/4/2003 9:34:39 PM

Module Name:    agp440
Display Name:   Intel AGP Bus Filter
Driver Type:    Kernel
Link Date:      2/4/2003 9:09:19 PM

Module Name:    AsyncMac
Display Name:   RAS Asynchronous Media Driver
```

```
    Driver Type:        Kernel
    Link Date:          2/4/2003 9:07:37 PM

    Module Name:        atapi
    Display Name:       Standard IDE/ESDI Hard Disk Controller
    Driver Type:        Kernel
    Link Date:          2/4/2003 9:01:09 PM
    ...
```

Create a comma-separated text file containing driver information with headers omitted:

driverquery /fo csv /nh > log.csv

Display verbose driver information in list format:

driverquery /fo list /v

```
    Module Name:        ACPI
    Display Name:       Microsoft ACPI Driver
    Description:        Microsoft ACPI Driver
    Driver Type:        Kernel
    Start Mode:         Boot
    State:              Running
    Status:             OK
    Accept Stop:        TRUE
    Accept Pause:       FALSE
    Paged Pool(bytes):  45,056
    Code(bytes):        106,496
    BSS(bytes):         0
    Link Date:          2/4/2003 9:09:10 PM
    Path:               C:\WINDOWS\system32\DRIVERS\ACPI.sys
    Init(bytes):        8,192

    Module Name:        ACPIEC
    Display Name:       ACPIEC
    Description:        ACPIEC
    Driver Type:        Kernel
    Start Mode:         Disabled
    State:              Stopped
    Status:             OK
    Accept Stop:        FALSE
    Accept Pause:       FALSE
    Paged Pool(bytes):  4,096
    Code(bytes):        8,192
    BSS(bytes):         0
    Link Date:          2/4/2003 9:09:15 PM
    Path:               C:\WINDOWS\system32\drivers\ACPIEC.sys
    Init(bytes):        4,096

    Module Name:        AFD
    Display Name:       AFD Networking Support Environment
    Description:        AFD Networking Support Environment
    Driver Type:        Kernel
    Start Mode:         Auto
    State:              Running
```

```
Status:              OK
Accept Stop:         TRUE
Accept Pause:        FALSE
Paged Pool(bytes):   139,264
Code(bytes):         12,288
BSS(bytes):          0
Link Date:           2/4/2003 9:34:39 PM
Path:                C:\WINDOWS\system32\drivers\afd.sys
Init(bytes):         16,384
...
```

Display info for signed drivers:

driverquery /si

```
DeviceName                       InfName       IsSigned Manufacturer
================================ ============= ======== =====
Advanced Configuration and Pow hal.inf       TRUE     (Standard computers)
Microsoft ACPI-Compliant Syste acpi.inf      TRUE     Microsoft
Processor                        cpu.inf       TRUE     (Standard processor types
ACPI Power Button                machine.inf TRUE     (Standard system devices)
System board                     machine.inf TRUE     (Standard system devices)
PCI bus                          machine.inf TRUE     (Standard system devices)
...
```

Notes

The GUI tool Device Manager in Computer Management can display driver informa-tion, update and roll back device drivers, configure hardware resource settings, and perform other administrative tasks relating to devices and device drivers.

See Also

Devices

---

dsadd   new in WS2003

Adds users, groups, and other objects to Active Directory and configures AD quotas.

Syntax

```
dsadd command switches [{-s Server|-d Domain}] [-u UserName]
[-p {Password|*}] [-q] [-dsec Description]
```

Options

command
   Any dsadd command (see later list).

switches
   Various switches that go with each command (see later list).

{-s Server | -d Domain}
   Connects to a specified server or domain to run the command (if omitted, defaults to domain controller in logon domain).

*[-u UserName] [-p {Password | *}]*
   Credentials for running the command. Specify *UserName* as *domain\user* or *user@domain*. If -p *, prompts for password.

-*q*   Runs in quiet mode to suppress standard output of command.

-desc Description
Specifies the description for the object.

Commands

Here is a list of supported dsadd commands with a brief description of their syntax (only the most commonly used switches are described):

dsadd computer ComputerDN
Adds a computer account to Active Directory with distinguished name `ComputerDN`.

dsadd contact ContactDN [-fn FirstName] [-ln LastName] [-email Email]
Adds a contact to Active Directory with distinguished name `ContactDN`.

dsadd group GroupDN [-secgrp {yes | no}] [-scope {l | g | u}]
Adds a group to Active Directory with distinguished name `GroupDN`. The `-secgrp` yes option creates a security group (the default) while the `-scope` option creates either a local, global, or universal group (default is global).

dsadd ou OrganizationalUnitDN
Adds an organizational unit to Active Directory with distinguished name `OrganizationalUnitDN`.

dsadd quota -part PartitionDN [-rdn RelativeDistinguishedName]
-acct SecurityPrincipalDN -qlimit Value
Configures an Active Directory quota for the security principal specified by `-acct` `SecurityPrincipalDN`, limiting how many directory objects the security principal can own in the specified partition. To specify an unlimited quota, use `-qlimit -1`.

dsadd user UserDN [-upn UserPrincipalName] [-fn FirstName] [-ln LastName]
*[-display DisplayName] [-pwd {Password | *}] [-memberof Group;...]*
[-tel PhoneNumber] [-email Email] [-title Title] [-company Company] [-hmdir
HomeDirectory] [-profile ProfilePath] [-pwdneverexpires {yes | no}] ...
Adds a user to Active Directory with distinguished name `UserDN` and properties specified by switches (there are many more).

Examples

Create a new computer account for the workstation DESK155 in the Sales organizational unit of the *mtit.local* domain using the Administrator account for that domain:

```
dsadd computer CN=DESK155,OU=Sales,DC=mtit,DC=local -u Administrator -p *
Enter Password:**********

dsadd succeeded:CN=DESK155,OU=Sales,DC=mtit,DC=local
```

If you open Active Directory Users and Computers, you can see the new computer account in the Sales OU.

Create a new domain local group named Human Resources in the Sales OU of *mtit.local*:

```
dsadd group "CN=Human Resources,OU=Sales,DC=mtit,DC=local" -scope l
dsadd succeeded:CN=Human Resources,OU=Sales,DC=mtit,DC=local
```

Note the quotation marks in the example (required due to the space in the group name).

Create the user Bob Jones and add him to the Human Resources group:

```
dsadd user CN=bjones,OU=Sales,DC=mtit,
DC=local -upn bjones@mtit.local -fn Bob -ln Jones
```

Command Reference

```
        -display "Bob Jones" -pwd Passw0rd -email bjones@mtit.com
        -memberof "CN=Human Resources,OU=Sales,DC=mtit,DC=local"
dsadd succeeded:CN=bjones,OU=Sales,DC=mtit,DC=local
```

Notes

If you omit the distinguished name of the object you are creating, it is obtained from standard input—STDIN—i.e., the keyboard, a redirected file, or piped output from another command. Use Ctrl-Z to indicate the end of file character for STDIN.

See Also

Active Directory, dsget, dsmod, dsmove, dsquery, dsrm, *Groups, Users*

---

dsget
new in WS2003

Displays properties of objects in Active Directory.

Syntax

```
dsget command switches [{-s Server|-d Domain}] [-u UserName]
[-p {Password|*}] [-q] [-c] [-l] [-desc]
```

Options

command
> Any dsget command (see below).

switches
> Various switches that go with each command (see below)

{-s Server | -d Domain}
> Connect to a specified server or domain to run the command (if omitted, defaults to domain controller in logon domain).

*[-u UserName] [-p {Password | *}]*
> Credentials for running the command. Specify *UserName* as *domain\user* or *user@domain*. If -p *, prompts for password.

-q
> Runs in quiet mode to suppress standard output of command.

-c
> Reports errors and then continues with next object in argument list if multiple objects are specified; otherwise exits upon error.

-l
> Displays output in list format instead of the default table format.

-desc
> Displays the description for the object.

Commands

Here is a list of supported dsget commands together with a brief description of their syntax (only the most commonly used switches are described):

dsget computer ComputerDN... [-dn] [-samid] [-sid] [-disabled] [-part PartitionDN]
[-qlimit] [-qused]]
> Displays properties of one or more computer accounts identifed by their distinguished names. Options include:
>
> *-dn* Displays the distinguished name of each computer
>
> *-samid*
>> Displays the SAM account name of each computer

-sid Displays the SID of each computer

-disabled
Displays whether computer account is enabled (yes) or disabled (no)

-part PartitionDN [-qlimit] [-qused]
Displays the configured and used quota values for the computer account in Active Directory

dsget computer ComputerDN [-memberof [-expand]]
This variation of dsget computer displays which groups the specified computer belongs to. The -expand switch recursively expands the list of groups to which the computer belongs.

dsget contact ContactDN... --dn] [-fn] [-ln] [-email] ...
Displays first name, last name, email address, and other info about one or more contacts identified by their distinguished names.

dsget group GroupDN... [-dn] [-secgrp] [-scope] [-samid] [-sid] [-part PartitionDN [-qlimit] [-qused]]
Displays properties of one or more groups identified by their distinguished names. See dsadd group earlier in this chapter for info about -secgrp and -scope options.

dsget group GroupDN [-memberof [-expand]]
This variation of dsget group displays which groups the specified group belongs to. The -expand switch recursively expands the list of groups to which the group belongs.

dsget ou OrganizationalUnitDN... [-dn]
Displays properties of one or more organizational units specified by their distinguished names.

dsget partition ObjectDN... [-dn] [-qdefault] [-qtmbstnwt] [-topobjowner N]
Displays properties of the specified partition object and their default quota and tombstone object count.

dsget quota ObjectDN [-dn] [-acct] [-qlimit]
Displays the properties of a quota specification defined in Active Directory. Here ObjectDN is the distinguished name of the quota object being viewed, -acct displays the DN of the accounts to which the quotas are assigned, and -qlimit the quota limits for the specified quotas.

dsget server ServerDN... [-dn] [-dnsname] [-site] [-isgc]
Displays properties of one or more domain controllers specified by their distinguished names. Options here include:

-dnsname
Displays the DNS names of the servers

-site
Displays the sites to which the servers belong

-isgc
Indicates whether the server is a global catalog server (yes) or not (no)

dsget server ServerDN -part PartitionDN
This variation of dsget server displays the distinguished names of the directory partitions on the specified domain controller.

dsget server ServerDN -topobjowner N

This variation of dsget server lists the *N* security principals that own the greatest number of directory ojects on the specified domain controller.

dsget site SiteDN... [-dn] [-autotopology] [-cachegroups] [-prefGCsite]

Displays properties of one or more sites specified by their distinguished names. The options here are:

-autotopology

Indicates whether automatic intersite topology generation is enabled (yes) or not (no)

-cachegroups

Indicates whether caching of universal group memberships is enabled (yes) or not (no)

-prefGCsite

Displays the preferred global catalog site used for refreshing universal group membership caching for domain controllers in this site

dsget subnet SubnetDN [-dn] [-site]

Displays properties of one or more subnets specified by their distinguished names.

dsget user UserDN... [-dn] [-samid] [-sid] [-upn] [-fn] [-ln] [-display] [-pwd] [-tel] [-email] [-title] [-company] [-hmdir] [-profile] [-pwdneverexpires] ...

Displays the properties of one or more user accounts specified by their distinguished names. See dsadd user earlier in this chapter for information on some of the switches here.

dsget user UserDN [-memberof] [-expand]

This variation of dsget user displays which groups the specified user belongs to. The -expand switch recursively expands the list of groups to which the user belongs.

Examples

Display the SAM account name and SID number of the computer named DESK155 located in the Sales OU of the *mtit.local* domain:

```
dsget computer CN=DESK155,OU=Sales,DC=mtit,DC=local -samid -sid
  samid       sid
  DESK155$    S-1-5-21-3989638602-2554627321-2483607968-1111
dsget succeeded
```

Use dsget in interactive mode to display the account status (enabled or disabled) for three computers in the Sales OU:

```
dsget computer -disabled
CN=DESK155,OU=Sales,DC=mtit,DC=local
CN=DESK156,OU=Sales,DC=mtit,DC=local
CN=DESK157,OU=Sales,DC=mtit,DC=local
^Z
  disabled
  no
  no
  yes
dsget succeeded
```

Display selected properties of Human Resources group in list format:

**dsget group "CN=Human Resources,OU=Sales,DC=mtit,
DC=local" -dn -secgrp -scope -samid -sid -l**
```
dn: CN=Human Resources,OU=Sales,DC=mtit,DC=local
samid: Human Resources
sid: S-1-5-21-3989638602-2554627321-2483607968-1112
scope: domain local
secgrp: yes

dsget succeeded
```

Display properties of user Bob Jones in the Sales department:

dsget user CN=bjones,OU=Sales,DC=mtit,DC=local -samid -sid -upn -l
```
samid: bjones
sid: S-1-5-21-3989638602-2554627321-2483607968-1114
upn: bjones@mtit.local

dsget succeeded
```

Display the groups to which Bob belongs:

dsget user CN=bjones,OU=Sales,DC=mtit,DC=local -memberof
```
"CN=Human Resources,OU=Sales,DC=mtit,DC=local"
"CN=Domain Users,CN=Users,DC=mtit,DC=local"
```

List the properties of a domain controller named ESRV210D located in Default-First-Site, in particular its DNS name and whether it is a global catalog server or not:

**dsget server CN=ESRV210D,CN=Servers,CN=Default-FirstSite,
CN=Sites,CN=Configuration, DC=mtit,DC=local -dnsname -isgc -l**
```
dnsname: esrv210d.mtit.local
isgc: yes

dsget succeeded
```

Note that here the distinguished name involved the location of the domain controller in the Configuration container.

See Also

Active Directory, dsadd, dsmod, dsmove, dsquery, dsrm, *Groups*, *Users*

---

dsmod

Modifies the properties of objects in Active Directory.

Syntax

```
dsmod command switches [{-s Server|-d Domain}] [-u UserName]
[-p {Password|*}] [-q] [-c] [-desc Description]
```

Options

command
> Any dsmod command (see below).

switches
> Various switches that go with each command (see below).

{-s Server | -d Domain}
> Connects to a specified server or domain to run the command (if omitted, defaults to domain controller in logon domain).

*[-u UserName] [-p {Password | *}]*
> Credentials for running the command. Specify *UserName* as *domain\user* or *user@domain*. If -p *, prompts for password.

-q   Runs in quiet mode to suppress standard output of command.

-c   Reports errors and then continues with next object in argument list if multiple objects are specified; otherwise, exits upon error.

-desc Description
> Modifies the description for the object.

Commands

Here is a list of supported dsmod commands together with a brief description of their syntax (only the most commonly used switches are described):

dsmod computer ComputerDN... [-disabled {yes | no}] [-reset]
> Modifies properties of one or more computer accounts identified by their distinguished names. Options include:

> *-disabled {yes | no}*
>> Enables (yes) or disables (no) the computer account

> *-reset*
>> Resets the computer account

dsmod contact ContactDN... [-fn] [-ln] [-email] ...
> Modifies the first name, last name, email address, and other attributes of one or more contacts identified by their distinguished names

dsmod group GroupDN... [-secgrp {yes | no}] [-scope {l | g | u}] [-samid SAMName] [{-addmbr | -rmmbr | -chmbr} MemberDN...]
> Modifies the properties of one or more groups identified by their distinguished names. See dsadd group earlier in this chapter for info about -secgrp and -scope options. The -samid SAMName option specifies the SAM account name, and the last option specifies members that should be added to, removed from, or replaced in the group.

dsmod ou OrganizationalUnitDN...
> Modifies properties of one or more organizational units specified by their distinguished names. The only thing you can modify is the description of the group.

dsmod server ServerDN... [-isgc {yes | no}]
> Modifies properties of one or more domain controllers specified by their distinguished names. The -isgc option specifies whether the server is a global catalog server (yes) or not (no).

*dsmod user UserDN... [-upn UserPrincipalName] [-fn FirstName] [-ln LastName] [-display DisplayName] [-pwd {Password | *}] [-tel PhoneNumber] [-email Email] [-title Title] [-company Company] [-hmdir HomeDirectory] [-profile ProfilePath] [-pwdneverexpires {yes | no}] ...*
> Modifies the properties of one or more user accounts specified by their distinguished names. See dsadd user earlier in this chapter for information on some of the switches here.

dsmod quota QuotaDN... [-qlimit Value]
> Specifies the distinguished names of one or more quota specifications to modify. Here -qlimit *Value* indicates the number of Active Directory objects that can be owned by the security principal to which the quota object is assigned.

dsmod partition PartitionDN... [-qdefault Value] [-qtmbstnw Percent]
> Specifies distinguished names of one or more directory partitions you want to modify, with -qdefault *Value* specifiying the default quota for the partition and -qtmbstnwt *Percent* specifying the percentage by which the tombstone object count should be reduced when calculating quota usage.

Examples

Use dsget to check whether computer account DESK157 in Sales OU of *mtit.local* domain is enabled or disabled:

```
dsget computer CN=DESK157,OU=Sales,DC=mtit,DC=local -disabled
  disabled
  yes
dsget succeeded
```

The account is disabled, so use dsmod to enable it:

```
dsmod computer CN=DESK157,OU=Sales,DC=mtit,DC=local -disabled no
dsmod succeeded:CN=DESK157,OU=Sales,DC=mtit,DC=local
```

Verify the result:

```
dsget computer CN=DESK157,OU=Sales,DC=mtit,DC=local -disabled
  disabled
  no
dsget succeeded
```

See Also

Active Directory, dsadd, dsget, dsmove, dsquery, dsrm, *Groups*, *Users*

---

dsmove

new in WS2003

Moves or renames an object in Active Directory.

Syntax

```
dsmove ObjectDN [-newname NewRDN] [-newparent ParentDN]
[{-s Server|-d Domain}] [-u UserName] [-p {Password|*}] [-q]
```

Options

ObjectDN
> The distinguished name of the object to be moved or renamed.

-newname NewRDN
> Renames the object using the specified relative distinguished name.

-newparent ParentDN
> Moves the object to the location specified by the distinguished name of its new parent container.

{-s Server | -d Domain}
> Connects to a specified server or domain to run the command (if omitted, defaults to domain controller in logon domain).

*[-u UserName] [-p {Password | *}]*
> Credentials for running the command. Specify *UserName* as *domain\user* or *user@domain*. If -p *, prompts for password.

-*q*   Runs in quiet mode to suppress standard output of command.

Examples

Move user account for Bob Jones from Sales OU to Customer Support OU:

> **dsmove CN=bjones,OU=Sales,DC=mtit,DC=local -newparent "OU=Customer**
> **Support,DC=mtit, DC=local"**
> dsmove succeeded:CN=bjones,OU=Sales,DC=mtit,DC=local

Rename username for Bob Jones from *bjones* to *bobj*:

> **dsmove "CN=bjones,OU=Customer Support,DC=mtit,DC=local" -newname bobj**
> dsmove succeeded:CN=bjones,OU=Customer Support,DC=mtit,DC=local

Notes

- You can move and rename an object in one step using -newparent and -newname switches in a single command.
- dsmove can move objects only within a domain. To move objects between domains, use *MoveTree* from Support Tools on the product CD.

See Also

Active Directory, dsadd, dsget, dsmod, dsquery, dsrm, *Groups*, *Users*

---

dsquery   new in WS2003

Search for a specific type of object within Active Directory.

Syntax

> dsquery *command switches* [{-s *Server*|-d *Domain*}] [-u *UserName*]
> [-p {*Password*|*}] [-desc *Description*] [-q] [-r] [-gc] [-limit *N*]

Options

command
> Any dsquery command (see below)

switches
> Various switches that go with each command (see below)

{-s Server | -d Domain}
> Connects to a specified server or domain to run the command (if omitted, defaults to domain controller in logon domain).

*[-u UserName] [-p {Password | *}]*
> Credentials for running the command. Specify *UserName* as *domain\user* or *user@domain*. If -p *, prompts for password.

-desc Description
> Description for the object.

-*q*   Runs in quiet mode to suppress standard output of command.

-*r*   Performs recursive search or follows referrals during search.

-*gc*   Performs the search using the global catalog.

-*limit N*
> Number of results to be returned (default is 1000).

Commands

Here is a list of supported dsquery commands together with a brief description of their syntax (only the most commonly used switches are described).

dsquery computer [{StartNode | forestroot | domainroot}] [-o {dn | rdn | samid}] [-scope {subtree | onelevel | base}] [-name Name] [-samid SAMName] [-inactive Weeks] [-stalepwd Days] [-disabled]
> Searches for computers within Active Directory. The switches here are:

> *{StartNode | forestroot | domainroot}*
>> Where to begin the search (default is domainroot)

> *-o {dn | rdn | samid}*
>> Output search results by distinguished name, relative distinguished name, or SAM account name of each object

> *-scope {subtree | onelevel | base}*
>> Scope of search to be entire subtree of start node, immediate children of start node, or start node only

> *-name Name*
>> Searches for computers with specified name (wildcards supported)

> *-samid SAMName*
>> Searches for computer accounts with specified SAM account name

> *-inactive Weeks*
>> Searches for computer accounts that have been stale (inactive) for a certain number of weeks

> *-stalepwd Days*
>> Searches for computers whose password has not been modified for a certain number of weeks

> *-disabled*
>> Searches for disabled computer accounts

dsquery contact [{StartNode | forestroot | domainroot}] [-o {dn | rdn}] [-scope {subtree | onelevel | base}] [-name Name]
> Searches for contacts within Active Directory. See dsquery computer earlier in this list for an explanation of switches.

dsquery group [{StartNode | forestroot | domainroot}] [-o {dn | rdn | samid}] [-scope {subtree | onelevel | base}] [-name Name] [-samid SAMName]
> Searches for groups within Active Directory. See dsquery computer earlier in this list for an explanation of switches.

dsquery ou [{StartNode | forestroot | domainroot}] [-o {dn | rdn}] [-scope {subtree | onelevel | base}] [-name Name]
> Searches for organizational units within Active Directory. See dsquery computer earlier in this list for an explanation of switches.

dsquery partition [-o {dn | rdn}] [-part PartitionCN]
> Searches for partitions matching the common name PartitionCN.

dsquery quota [{domainroot | ObjectDN}] [-o {dn | rdn}] [-acct Name] [-qlimit Filter]
> Searches for quota specifications within Active Directory. The switches here are:
>
> *domainroot | ObjectDN*
>> Specifies the starting point for the search, either the root of the domain or the distinguished name of a specified container
>
> *-o {dn | rdn | samid}*
>> Output search results by distinguished name, relative distinguished name, or SAM account name of each object
>
> *-acct Name*
>> The security principal to which the quota specifications queried are assigned
>
> *-qlimit Filter*
>> Searches for quota specifications matching the filter condition, for example, "=100" or "<=75" percent

dsquery server [-forest] [-domain DomainName] [-site SiteName] [-o {dn | rdn}]
[-name Name] [-hasfsmo {schema | name | infr | pdc | rid}] [-isgc]
> Searches for domain controllers within Active Directory. See dsquery computer earlier in this list for an explanation of some switches. Other switches include:
>
> *-forest*
>> Searches for domain controllers in the forest
>
> *-domain DomainName*
>> Searches for domain controllers in the specified domain
>
> *-site SiteName*
>> Searches for domain controllers in the specified site
>
> *-hasfsmo {schema | name | infr | pdc | rid}*
>> Searches for domain controllers with a specific FSMO role assigned
>
> *-isgc*
>> Searches for domain controllers that are global catalog servers

dsquery site [-o {dn | rdn}] [-name Name]
> Searches for sites within Active Directory. See dsquery computer earlier in this list for an explanation of switches.

dsquery user [{StartNode | forestroot | domainroot}] [-o {dn | rdn | samid | upn}]
[-scope {subtree | onelevel | base}] [-name Name] [-upn UserPrincipalName]
[-samid SAMName] [-inactive Weeks] [-stalepwd Days] [-disabled]
> Searches for user accounts within Active Directory. See dsquery computer earlier in this list for an explanation of these switches.

dsquery * [{StartNode | forestroot | domainroot}] [-scope {subtree | onelevel | base}]
[-filter LDAPFilter] [-attr {AttributeList | *}] [-attrsonly] [-l]
> Searches for objects in Active Directory by using an LDAP query.

Examples

Search for all computer accounts in the forest:

```
dsquery computer forestroot -o dn
"CN=ESRV210D,OU=Sales,DC=mtit,DC=local"
"CN=ESRV230D,CN=Computers,DC=mtit,DC=local"
"CN=DESK155,OU=Sales,DC=mtit,DC=local"
"CN=DESK156,OU=Sales,DC=mtit,DC=local"
"CN=DESK157,OU=Sales,DC=mtit,DC=local"
```

Restrict search to computers whose name begins with *D* and which reside in the Sales OU, displaying results as SAM account names:

```
dsquery computer OU=Sales,DC=mtit,DC=local -o samid -name d*
"DESK155$"
"DESK156$"
"DESK157$"
```

Search for the PDC Emulator in the local domain:

```
dsquery server -hasfsmo pdc
"CN=ESRV210D,CN=Servers,CN=Default-First-
Site,CN=Sites,CN=Configuration,DC=mtit,DC=local"
```

Display all partitions in Active Directory:

```
dsquery partition
"DC=TAPI3Directory,DC=mtit,DC=local"
"DC=DomainDnsZones,DC=mtit,DC=local"
"DC=ForestDnsZones,DC=mtit,DC=local"
"CN=Configuration,DC=mtit,DC=local"
"DC=mtit,DC=local"
"CN=Schema,CN=Configuration,DC=mtit,DC=local"
```

See Also

Active Directory, dsadd, dsget, dsmod, dsmove, dsrm, *Groups*, *Users*

---

dsrm

new in WS2003

Deletes objects from Active Directory.

Syntax

```
dsrm ObjectDN... [-subtree [-exclude]] [-noprompt] [{-s Server|-d Domain}]
    [-u UserName] [-p {Password|*}] [-c] [-q]
```

Options

ObjectDN...
The distinguished names of objects to remove from Active Directory.

-subtree [-exclude]
Deletes the specified object and all its children. If -exclude is used, all children are deleted, but the parent isn't.

-noprompt
Doesn't prompt for confirmation of each deletion.

{-s Server | -d Domain}
Connects to a specified server or domain to run the command (if omitted, defaults to domain controller in logon domain).

*[-u UserName] [-p {Password | *}]*
Credentials for running the command. Specify *UserName* as *domain\user* or *user@domain*. If -p *, prompts for password.

-c   Reports errors and then continues with next object in argument list if multiple objects are specified; otherwise, exits upon error.

-q   Runs in quiet mode to suppress standard output of command.

Examples

Delete the child objects within the Customer Support OU in the *mtit.local* domain:

> **dsrm "OU=Customer Support,DC=mtit,DC=local" -subtree -exclude**
> Are you sure you wish to delete all children of OU=Customer Support,DC=mtit,
>   DC=local (Y/N)? **y**
> dsrm succeeded:OU=Customer Support,DC=mtit,DC=local

See Also

Active Directory, dsadd, dsget, dsmod, dsmove, dsquery, *Groups*, *Users*

---

eventquery   new in WS2003

Displays events from event logs.

Syntax

```
eventquery [/s Computer [/u Domain\User [/p Password]]] [/fi Filter]
   [/fo {TABLE | LIST | CSV}] [/r EventRange [/nh] [/v]
   [/l [APPLICATION] [SYSTEM] [SECURITY] ["DNS server"] [UserDefinedLog]
   [DirectoryLogName] [*] ]
```

Options

/s Computer
  Name or IP address of remote computer (if omitted, defaults to local computer).

/u Domain\User /p Password
  Credentials for running the command (if omitted, defaults to currently logged-on user).

/fi Filter
  Filter for specifying types of events to search for (enclose in quotes). These can be:

```
Datetime {eq | ne | ge | le | gt | lt} {mm/dd/yy(yyyy) | hh:mm:ss{AM | PM}}
Type {eq | ne} {ERROR | INFORMATION | WARNING | SUCCESS | SUCCESSAUDIT |
FAILUREAUDIT}
ID {eq | ne | ge | le | gt | lt} ValidInteger.
User {eq | ne} ValidString
Computer {eq | ne} ValidString
Source {eq | ne} ValidString
Category {eq | ne} ValidString
```

/fo {TABLE | LIST | CSV}
  Format for command output.

/r EventRange
  Range of events to display. This can be:

  N   Lists *N* most recent events

  -N Lists *N* oldest events

  N1-N2
      Lists events *N1* to *N2*

/nh No headers for columns in output (TABLE and CSV format only).

/v   Verbose information should be displayed.

/l [APPLICATION] [SYSTEM] [SECURITY] ["DNS server"] [UserDefinedLog] [DirectoryLogName] [*]

One or more logs to query, with the default being wildcard (*). Reuse the /l switch if you want to query more than one log.

Examples

Display five most recent events from System log:

```
eventquery /l system /r 5
Microsoft (R) Windows Script Host Version 5.6
Copyright (C) Microsoft Corporation 1996-2001. All rights reserved.


-----------------------------------------------------------------------------
Listing the events in 'system' log of host 'ESRV210D'
-----------------------------------------------------------------------------

Type          Event  Date Time                  Source            ComputerName
------------  ------ -------------------------   ---------------   ------------
Warning       40961  3/26/2003 10:26:15 AM      LSASRV            ESRV210D
Warning       36     3/26/2003 10:25:55 AM      W32Time           ESRV210D
Warning       20     3/26/2003 9:51:41 AM       Print             ESRV210D
Error         1111   3/26/2003 9:51:17 AM       TermServDevices   ESRV210D
Error         1111   3/26/2003 9:51:17 AM       TermServDevices   ESRV210D
```

Search the System log for events with ID 36 and display the results in list format:

```
eventquery /fi "ID eq 36" /l SYSTEM /fo LIST
Microsoft (R) Windows Script Host Version 5.6
Copyright (C) Microsoft Corporation 1996-2001. All rights reserved.


-----------------------------------------------------------------------------
Listing the events in 'system' log of host 'ESRV210D'
-----------------------------------------------------------------------------

Type:         Warning
Event:        36
Date Time:    3/26/2003 10:25:55 AM
Source:       W32Time
ComputerName: ESRV210D

Type:         Warning
Event:        36
Date Time:    3/11/2003 11:42:32 AM
Source:       W32Time
ComputerName: ESRV210D
```

Repeat the command but display verbose output instead:

```
eventquery /fi "ID eq 36" /l SYSTEM /fo LIST /v
Microsoft (R) Windows Script Host Version 5.6
Copyright (C) Microsoft Corporation 1996-2001. All rights reserved.


-----------------------------------------------------------------------------
Listing the events in 'system' log of host 'ESRV210D'
-----------------------------------------------------------------------------

Type:         Warning
Event:        36
```

```
Date Time:    3/26/2003 10:25:55 AM
Source:       W32Time
ComputerName: ESRV210D
Category:     None
User:         N/A
Description:  The time service has not synchronized the system time for
86400 seconds  because none of the time service providers provided a usable
time  stamp.
 The time service is no longer synchronized and cannot provide the time to
other clients or update the system clock. Monitor the  system events
displayed in the Event  Viewer to make sure that a more  serious problem
does not exist.


Type:         Warning
Event:        36
Date Time:    3/11/2003 11:42:32 AM
Source:       W32Time
ComputerName: ESRV210D
Category:     None
User:         N/A
Description:  The time service has not synchronized the system time for
86400 seconds  because none of the time service providers provided a usable
time  stamp.
 The time service is no longer synchronized and cannot provide the time to
other clients or update the system clock. Monitor the system events
displayed in the Event  Viewer to make sure that a more serious problem does
not exist.
```

Notes

This command is a .*vbs* script and requires CScript to run. You can make CScript your default script host by typing the following at the command prompt:

```
cscript //h:cscript //s
```

See Also

Event Logs

---

expand

new in WS2003

Extracts compressed files from distribution disks.

Syntax

```
expand [-r] Source Destination
expand -r Source [Destination]
expand -d Source.cab [-f:Files]
expand Source.cab -f:Files Destination
```

Options

Source

Names of files to extract (can include path and wildcards).

Destination

Where to extract the files to (path). When extracting multiple files without the -r switch, the destination must be a directory.

-d Displays source files but doesn't extract them.

-f:*Files*

Specifies files in a cabinet (.*cab*) file that you want to expand (can use wildcards).

-r Renames files after extracting them.

Examples

Display the compressed files within the *DEPLOY.CAB* file in *SUPPORT\TOOLS* on the product CD:

```
expand D:\SUPPORT\TOOLS\DEPLOY.CAB -d
Microsoft (R) File Expansion Utility  Version 5.2.3763.0
Copyright (c) Microsoft Corporation. All rights reserved.

d:\support\tools\deploy.cab: cvtarea.exe
d:\support\tools\deploy.cab: oformat.com
d:\support\tools\deploy.cab: setupmgr.exe
d:\support\tools\deploy.cab: factory.exe
d:\support\tools\deploy.cab: setupcl.exe
d:\support\tools\deploy.cab: sysprep.exe
d:\support\tools\deploy.cab: deploy.chm
d:\support\tools\deploy.cab: readme.txt
d:\support\tools\deploy.cab: ref.chm

9 files total.
```

Expand Setup Manager to the *stuff* folder on *C*: drive:

```
expand D:\SUPPORT\TOOLS\DEPLOY.CAB -f:setupmgr.exe C:\stuff
Microsoft (R) File Expansion Utility  Version 5.2.3763.0
Copyright (c) Microsoft Corporation. All rights reserved.

Expanding d:\support\tools\deploy.cab to c:\stuff\setupmgr.exe.
```

Verify the result:

```
dir c:\stuff
Volume in drive C has no label.
Volume Serial Number is D405-058E

Directory of c:\stuff

03/26/2003  12:14 PM    <DIR>          .
03/26/2003  12:14 PM    <DIR>          ..
02/04/2003  07:08 PM           529,408 setupmgr.exe
               1 File(s)        529,408 bytes
               2 Dir(s)   8,047,779,840 bytes free
```

Notes

This command is also available from the Recovery Console.

See Also

Recovery Console

finger

Provides information about a user on a remote system.

Syntax

```
finger [-l] [username]@computername [...]
```

Options

-l   Verbose output.

[username]@computername
> The user you want to finger on the remote system—that is, the user about whom you want to obtain information. If *username* is omitted, finger obtains information concerning all users on the remote system.

Examples

In general, the output to the finger command depends on the system being queried. For example, here are the instructions displayed when using finger on a hypothetical Unix host at university *BlahBlah.edu* and the results of fingering a user named *mitch*:

```
finger help@blahblah.edu
[blahblah.edu]
Welcome to the finger daemon at blahblah.edu! By default, the finger command
displays in multicolumn format the following information about each logged-
in user:
    o   user Name
    o   Nickname, you can use this to send to nickname_lastname@blahblah.edu.
    o   The send_email_to field is the address to use to send this person
email.
    o   Campus address
    o   Campus phone
    o   Project
We don't show login info, or idle time since these IDs never actually login;
this is a client-server system.

Different types of queries:
    alias/netid lookup - finger jwh2@blahblah.edu
    name lookup - finger howell@blahblah.edu
                  finger jim@blahblah.edu
```

If you get a message that says "Too many returns for your query," refine your query:

```
finger mitch@blahblah.edu
[blahblah.edu]
Information from BlahBlah's Network Identity Directory...
-----------------------------------------------------

Your query returned   2 matches:

Name:         Mitchell K Sillyness
Nickname:     Mitch
Send Email To: mks@graphics.blahblah.edu
Campus Phone:  607-555-1212
Campus Address: 580 Smith Hall
Local Phone:
```

```
Local Address:
Project:

Name:           Mitch H. McNobody
Nickname:
Send Email To:  mhm12@blahblah.edu
Campus Phone:
Campus Address:
Local Phone:
Local Address:
Project:

...
```

Notes

The remote machine must be running the finger daemon or service. If it isn't, you'll get "Connection refused" in response to using the finger command. WS2003 doesn't include a finger service, only a command-line finger client.

See Also

TCP/IP

---

format

Formats a partition or volume.

Syntax

```
format Volume /fs:{FAT | FAT32 | NTFS} [/v:Label] [/a:UnitSize] [/q] [/c] [/x]
```

Options

Volume
> Drive letter, volume name, or mount point to format.

/fs:{FAT | FAT32 | NTFS}
> Type of filesystem to create.

/v:Label
> Label for volume.

/a:UnitSize
> Size of allocation unit (if omitted, the command chooses the optimal allocation unit based on the size of the volume).

/q
> Quick format (deletes file table and root directory but doesn't scan for bad sectors.

/c
> Files created on an NTFS volume are compressed by default.

/x
> Dismounts volume before formatting. All open file handles are closed.

Examples

Format *F:* drive using NTFS, assign it the label MYVOL, and compress the volume:

```
format f: /fs:NTFS /v:MYVOL /c
The type of the file system is RAW.
```

```
The new file system is NTFS.

WARNING, ALL DATA ON NON-REMOVABLE DISK
DRIVE F: WILL BE LOST!
Proceed with Format (Y/N)? y
Verifying 502M
Creating file system structures.
Format complete.
    514079 KB total disk space.
    509129 KB are available.
```

Format a mount point named *newvol* using FAT32:

```
format newvol /fs:FAT32
The type of the file system is RAW.
The new file system is FAT32.

WARNING, ALL DATA ON NON-REMOVABLE DISK
DRIVE C:\newvol WILL BE LOST!
Proceed with Format (Y/N)? y
Verifying 502M
Initializing the File Allocation Table (FAT)...
Volume label (11 characters, ENTER for none)? Budget
Format complete.

    525,373,440 bytes total disk space.
    525,369,344 bytes available on disk.

        4,096 bytes in each allocation unit.
    128,264 allocation units available on disk.

            32 bits in each FAT entry.

Volume Serial Number is A83C-2E40
```

Notes

When format is used with the Recovery Console, only the /fs and /q switches can be used.

See Also

chkdsk, chkntfs, convert, defrag, diskpart, *Disks*, label, mountvol

---

freedisk

Checks for free space on a disk.

Syntax

```
freedisk [/s Computer [/u [Domain\]User [/p [Password]]]] [/d Drive] [Value]
```

Options

/s Computer /u [Domain\]User /p [Password]
> Name or IP address of a remote computer (if omitted, defaults to local computer) and credentials for running the script (if omitted, defaults to SYSTEM built-in identity).

/d Drive
> Drive to check for free space.

Value
> Amount of free space to check for (can be in bytes, KB, MB, GB, TB, PB, or NB).

Examples

Check if *E:* drive has at least 100-MB free space:

```
freedisk /d e: 100MB
```

```
SUCCESS: The specified 104,857,600 byte(s) of free space are available on
"E:\" volume.
```

Notes

When performing unattended installations, use freedisk in a batch file to verify sufficient free space for the installation to proceed.

See Also

defrag, diskpart, *Disks*, format, freedisk

---

ftp

Transfers files to or from a computer running the FTP Server service.

Syntax

```
ftp [-v] [-n] [-i] [-d] [-g] [-s:filename] [-a] [-w:windowsize] [hostname]
```

Options

-a Uses any local interface for the endpoint of the FTP data connection. (The FTP data connection is used to transfer files and is different from the FTP control connection, which sends FTP commands between the client and server.)

-d Enables debugging mode, which displays all FTP commands sent between the client and server.

-g Disables globbing (filename expansion) so that wildcards can be used within local paths and filenames without being interpreted by the shell.

-i Disables interactive prompting when multiple files are being transferred.

-n Disables autologon to establish a control connection with the remote host but nothing else.

-s:filename
> Executes a series of FTP commands stored in a text file as a batch job.

-w:windowsize
> Specifies the amount of data that can be transferred before requiring that the receiving end issue a confirmation. The default transfer buffer size is 4,096 bytes.

-*v*   Disables showing responses of remote FTP connections.

hostname
> Identifies the computer name (DNS or NetBIOS name) or IP address of the remote computer you want to connect to using FTP (this must be the last parameter on the line).

Commands

You can select from a whole separate set of FTP-specific commands when you run ftp in interactive mode. Here are some of the more commonly used:

!   Escapes from an interactive FTP session to the command shell *cmd.exe* in order to execute the command, then returns to the FTP session.

ascii
> Sets file transfer type to ASCII for transferring text files. ASCII is the default type, the other being binary.

binary
> Sets file transfer type to binary for transferring binary files such as image files and Word documents.

bye, close, or quit
> Terminates an FTP session with the remote server and exits the FTP shell.

cd remotedirectory
> Changes to the specified directory on the remote server.

delete remotefilename
> Deletes the file from the current directory on the remote server.

dir [remotedirectory] [localfilename]
> Displays a directory listing of the specified remote directory (or the current remote directory if none is specified). If a filename is specified, the listing is saved with this name on the local machine instead of being displayed.

disconnect
> Terminates an FTP session with the remote server, but stays within the FTP shell.

get remotefilename [localfilename]
> Transfers the specified file from the remote server to the local machine, renaming it as well if *localfilename* is specified.

hash
> Displays one hash character (#) each time 2,048 bytes are transferred (useful for displaying the progress when downloading large files).

help [command]
> Lists the available FTP commands or displays a short description of the specified command.

lcd localdirectory
> Changes to the specified directory on the local computer.

ls [remotedirectory] [localfilename]
> Same as dir earlier in this list.

mget remotefilenames
> Gets multiple files (see get earlier in this list).

mput localfilenames
> Puts multiple files (see put later in this list).

open hostname [port]

Opens an FTP connection to the specified remote computer. *hostname* can be a computer name (DNS or NetBIOS name depending on the network) or IP address. *port* is required only if the remote server is listening on a different TCP port than the standard FTP port, which is 21.

prompt

Toggles prompting for confirmation by user (default is on).

put localfilename [remotefilename]

Transfers the specified file from the local machine to the remote server, renaming it as well if *remotefilename* is specified.

pwd

Displays the name of the current directory on the remote server.

remotehelp [command]

Displays a list of FTP commands understood by the remote server or describes a particular command.

user username

Logs on to the remote server as *username* and then prompts for a password.

Examples

Run FTP in interactive mode:

```
C:\>ftp
ftp>
```

Open a session with an FTP server:

```
ftp> open 172.16.11.104
Connected to 172.16.11.104.
220 test Microsoft FTP Service (Version 5.0).
```

Log on to the server as anonymous:

```
User (172.16.11.104:(none)): anonymous
331 Anonymous access allowed, send identity (e-mail name) as password.
Password: ********
230 Anonymous user logged in.
```

Display the current directory on the server:

```
ftp> pwd
257 "/" is current directory.
```

List the contents of the current directory on the server:

```
ftp> ls
200 PORT command successful.
150 Opening ASCII mode data connection for file list.
hello.txt
226 Transfer complete.
ftp: 11 bytes received in 0.04Seconds 0.28Kbytes/sec.
```

Download the file *hello.txt* from the server to the client:

```
ftp> get hello.txt
200 PORT command successful.
150 Opening ASCII mode data connection for hello.txt(12 bytes).
226 Transfer complete.
ftp: 12 bytes received in 0.00Seconds 12000.00Kbytes/sec.
```

Escape from the FTP shell momentarily and run the command type C:\hello. txt on the client, which should display the contents of the text file if it's successfully downloaded from the server:

```
ftp> !type C:\hello.txt
Hello there!ftp>
```

Note that the file contains the line of text "Hello there!"

Close the connection with the server and terminate the interactive FTP session:

```
ftp> quit
221
C:\>
```

Notes

- The ftp command is a client, as opposed to an FTP service or daemon, which resides on the server.
- WS2003 includes an FTP Server service as part of its Internet Information Services (IIS). By default, the home or root directory of this service is mapped to the directory *C:\Inetpub\ftproot* on the server.
- FTP is inherently insecure because it transmits passwords in clear text.

To use ftp in batch mode, do the following:

1. Go through an interactive FTP session, and copy it to a text editor such as Notepad.
2. Edit out the responses, leaving only the commands.
3. Use the -s switch to run the batch file with ftp.

See Also

TCP/IP

---

ftype

Displays or modifies file types for file extension associations.

Syntax

```
ftype [FileType[=[OpenCommand]]]
```

Options

None
    Displays all file types that have open commands defined

FileType
    Specifies the file type to display or change

OpenCommand
    Specifies the command used to open this type of file

Examples

Display all types that have open commands defined:

```
ftype
AIFFFile="C:\Program Files\Windows Media Player\wmplayer.exe" /Open "%L"
```

```
ASFFile="C:\Program Files\Windows Media Player\wmplayer.exe" /prefetch:7
    /Open "%L"
ASXFile="C:\Program Files\Windows Media Player\wmplayer.exe"  /Open "%L"
AUFile="C:\Program Files\Windows Media Player\wmplayer.exe"  /Open "%L"
AVIFile="C:\Program Files\Windows Media Player\wmplayer.exe" /prefetch:8
    /Open "%L"
batfile="%1" %*
Briefcase=explorer.exe %1
...
```

Display open command for txtfile file type:

ftype txtfile
```
txtfile=%SystemRoot%\system32\NOTEPAD.EXE %1
```

Notes

Use ftype FileType= to delete the open command string for the specified file type, then use the assoc command to create a new file association.

See Also

assoc, *Files and Folders*

---

getmac   new in WS2003

Diplays MAC address and network protocols for all network cards.

Syntax

```
getmac [/s Computer [/u Domain\User [/p Password]]] [/fo
{TABLE | LIST | CSV}] [/nh] [/v]
```

Options

/s Computer /u [Domain\]User /p [Password]
: Name or IP address of a remote computer (if omitted, defaults to local computer) and credentials for running the script (if omitted, defaults to SYSTEM built-in identity)

/fo {TABLE | LIST | CSV}
: Format for displaying driver properties (if omitted, default is TABLE)

/nh Omits header row from displayed information if /fo is set to TABLE or CSV

/v Displays verbose information

Examples

List MAC addresses for interfaces on local machine:

getmac /fo list

```
Physical Address: 00-02-1E-F3-28-36
Transport Name:   \Device\Tcpip_{59EC22D4-09DF-4720-B5B1-A9444E90CCD1}
```

Repeat in verbose mode:

getmac /fo list /v

```
Connection Name:  Local Area Connection
Network Adapter:  3Com EtherLink XL 10/100 PCI For Complete PC
   Management NIC
   (3C905C-TX)
Physical Address: 00-02-1E-F3-28-36
Transport Name:   \Device\Tcpip_{59EC22D4-09DF-4720-B5B1-A9444E90CCD1}
```

See Also

TCP/IP

---

gpresult

Displays the Resultant Set of Policy (RSoP) settings for a target user on a specified computer.

Syntax

```
gpresult [/s Computer [/u Domain\User /p Password]] [/user TargetUserName]
   [/scope {user | computer}] [{/v | /z}]
```

Options

None
> Displays RSoP settings for currently logged-on user

/s Computer /u [Domain\]User /p [Password]
> Name or IP address of a remote computer (if omitted, defaults to local computer) and credentials for running the script (if omitted, defaults to SYSTEM built-in identity)

/user TargetUserName
> User whose RSOP data is displayed

/scope {user | computer}
> Displays user or computer portion of Group Policy settings (if omitted, defaults to both)

/v Verbose output

/z Even more verbose output

Examples

While logged on as Administrator, display both user and computer Group Policy settings for self:

gpresult

```
Microsoft (R) Windows (R) Operating System Group Policy Result tool v2.0
Copyright (C) Microsoft Corp. 1981-2001

Created On 3/26/2003 at 3:26:20 PM

RSOP data for MTIT\Administrator on ESRV210D : Logging Mode
```

OS Type:	Microsoft(R) Windows(R) Server 2003, Enterprise Edition
OS Configuration:	Primary Domain Controller
OS Version:	5.2.3763
Terminal Server Mode:	Remote Administration
Site Name:	Default-First-Site
Roaming Profile:	
Local Profile:	C:\Documents and Settings\Administrator
Connected over a slow link?: No	

  COMPUTER SETTINGS

    CN=ESRV210D,OU=Sales,DC=mtit,DC=local
    Last time Group Policy was applied: 3/26/2003 at 3:22:32 PM
    Group Policy was applied from: esrv210d.mtit.local
    Group Policy slow link threshold: 500 kbps
    Domain Name: MTIT
    Domain Type: W2K

    Applied Group Policy Objects

        Default Domain Policy

    The following GPOs were not applied because they were filtered out
    ----
        Local Group Policy
            Filtering: Not Applied (Empty)

    The computer is a part of the following security groups

        BUILTIN\Administrators
        Everyone
        RAS and IAS Servers
        BUILTIN\Pre-W2K Compatible Access
        BUILTIN\Users
        Windows Authorization Access Group
        NT AUTHORITY\NETWORK
        NT AUTHORITY\Authenticated Users
        This Organization
        ESRV210D$
        Domain Controllers
        NT AUTHORITY\ENTERPRISE DOMAIN CONTROLLERS
        RAS and IAS Servers

  USER SETTINGS

    CN=Administrator,CN=Users,DC=mtit,DC=local
    Last time Group Policy was applied: 3/26/2003 at 2:57:06 PM
    Group Policy was applied from: esrv210d.mtit.local
    Group Policy slow link threshold: 500 kbps
    Domain Name: MTIT
    Domain Type: W2K

```
        Applied Group Policy Objects
        ----------------------------
            Default Domain Policy

        The following GPOs were not applied because they were filtered out
        --------------------------------------------------------------------
            Local Group Policy
                Filtering:  Not Applied (Empty)

        The user is a part of the following security groups
        ---------------------------------------------------
            Domain Users
            Everyone
            BUILTIN\Administrators
            BUILTIN\Users
            BUILTIN\Pre-W2K Compatible Access
            REMOTE INTERACTIVE LOGON
            NT AUTHORITY\INTERACTIVE
            NT AUTHORITY\Authenticated Users
            This Organization
            LOCAL
            Domain Admins
            Enterprise Admins
            Schema Admins
            Group Policy Creator Owners
```

Display verbose RSoP user settings for user *fsmith@mtit.local* on remote member server having IP address 172.16.11.230:

gpresult /s 172.16.11.230 /user mtit\fsmith /scope user /v

```
Microsoft (R) Windows (R) Operating System Group Policy Result tool v2.0
Copyright (C) Microsoft Corp. 1981-2001

Created On 3/26/2003 at 3:39:18 PM

   RSOP data for MTIT\fsmith on ESRV230D : Logging Mode
   -----------------------------------------------------

OS Type:                Microsoft(R) Windows(R) Server 2003, Enterprise
Edi
tion
OS Configuration:       Member Server
OS Version:             5.2.3763
Terminal Server Mode:   Remote Administration
Site Name:              Default-First-Site
Roaming Profile:
Local Profile:          C:\Documents and Settings\fsmith
Connected over a slow link?: No

USER SETTINGS
--------------
    CN=Frank Smith,OU=Sales,DC=mtit,DC=local
    Last time Group Policy was applied: 3/26/2003 at 3:30:41 PM
    Group Policy was applied from:      N/A
```

```
Group Policy slow link threshold:    500 kbps
Domain Name:                         MTIT
Domain Type:                         W2K

Applied Group Policy Objects
----------------------------
    Default Domain Policy

The following GPOs were not applied because they were filtered out
-----------------------------------------------------------------------
    Local Group Policy
        Filtering:  Not Applied (Empty)

The user is a part of the following security groups
-----------------------------------------------------
    Domain Users
    Everyone
    BUILTIN\Users
    NT AUTHORITY\INTERACTIVE
    NT AUTHORITY\Authenticated Users
    This Organization
    LOCAL

The user has the following security privileges
------------------------------------------------

    Bypass traverse checking

Resultant Set Of Policies for User
----------------------------------

    Software Installations
    ----------------------
        N/A

    Logon Scripts
    -------------
        N/A

    Logoff Scripts
    --------------
        N/A

    Public Key Policies
    -------------------
        N/A

    Administrative Templates
    ------------------------
        N/A

    Folder Redirection
    ------------------
        N/A
```

```
          Internet Explorer Browser User Interface
          ----------------------------------------
               N/A

          Internet Explorer Connection
          ----------------------------
               N/A

          Internet Explorer URLs
          ----------------------
               N/A

          Internet Explorer Security
          ---------------------------
               N/A

          Internet Explorer Programs
          ---------------------------
               N/A
```

See Also

gpupdate, *Group Policy*

---

gpupdate   new in WS2003

Refreshes Group Policy settings.

Syntax

```
gpupdate [/target:{computer | user}] [/force] [/wait:Value] [/logoff] [/boot]
```

Options

/target:{computer | user}
> Specifies whether to process computer or user Group Policy settings (if omitted, defaults to both).

/force
> Reapplies Group Policy settings.

/wait:Value
> How long policy processing waits to finish (if omitted, defaults to 600 seconds). Use -1 to wait indefinitely.

/logoff
> Logs off after refresh is finished to process Software Installation and Folder Redirection settings.

/boot
> Restarts computer after refresh finished to process Software Installation settings.

Examples

Refresh Group Policy in Active Directory:

```
gpupdate
Refreshing Policy...
```

```
User Policy Refresh has completed.
Computer Policy Refresh has completed.

To check for errors in policy processing, review the event log.
```

Notes
- This command can refresh Group Policy settings stored either on standalone computers or in Active Directory.
- The gpupdate command replaces secedit /refreshpolicy.

See Also
gpresult, *Group Policy*

---

hostname

Displays the hostname of the local machine.

Syntax
```
hostname
```

Options
None

Examples
Display the hostname of the computer whose full DNS name is *test.mtitcanada.com*:
hostname
```
test
```

See Also
DNS

---

ipconfig

Displays the current TCP/IP settings of the local machine.

Syntax
```
ipconfig [/all | /release [adaptername] | [/renew [adaptername] | /flushdns
| /displaydns | /registerdns | /showclassid adaptername | /setclassid
adaptername [newclassID]]
```

Options
None
    Displays the IP address, subnet mask, and default gateway for each interface on the machine.

/all
    Yields verbose output showing additional TCP/IP settings.

/release [adaptername]

> Releases an IP address acquired using DHCP. On a multihomed machine, specify an adapter name using the name that appears for the adapter when you type ipconfig without parameters.

/renew [adaptername]

> Requests a new IP address from a DHCP server (available only when the computer is configured as a DHCP client)

/displaydns

> Displays the contents of the local DNS name cache on the client. When DNS resolves a DNS name into an IP address, the results are temporarily cached.

/flushdns

> Flushes the list of locally cached DNS names on the client. Flushing the cache removes these mappings and can be useful when troubleshooting DNS-related problems. Flushing the DNS cache on the client doesn't remove mappings that have been preloaded from the local *Hosts* file. (You must remove these mappings from the *Hosts* file to do this.)

/registerdns

> Causes the client to reregister its hostname with DNS servers without restarting the client machine. This may also be used with Dynamic DNS.

/showclassid adaptername

> Displays all the DHCP class IDs allowed for the adapter. WS2003 DHCP clients support DHCP class options that can be viewed using this command and configured using ipconfig /setclassid.

/setclassid adaptername [newclassID]

> Changes the DHCP class ID for the adapter.

Examples

Display summary of TCP/IP settings on local machine:

```
ipconfig
Windows IP Configuration
Ethernet adapter Local Area Connection:
   Connection-specific DNS Suffix  . :
   IP Address. . . . . . . . . . . : 172.16.11.105
   Subnet Mask . . . . . . . . . . : 255.255.255.0
   IP Address. . . . . . . . . . . : 172.16.11.104
   Subnet Mask . . . . . . . . . . : 255.255.255.0
   Default Gateway . . . . . . . . : 172.16.11.196
```

Display full details:

```
ipconfig /all
Windows IP Configuration
   Host Name . . . . . . . . . . . : test
   Primary DNS Suffix  . . . . . . : mtitcanada.com
   Node Type . . . . . . . . . . . : Hybrid
   IP Routing Enabled. . . . . . . : No
   WINS Proxy Enabled. . . . . . . : No
   DNS Suffix Search List. . . . . : mtitcanada.com
Ethernet adapter Local Area Connection:
   Connection-specific DNS Suffix  . :
```

```
Description . . . . . . . . . . : Realtek
                 RTL8029(AS) PCI Ethernet Adapter
Physical Address. . . . . . . . : 00-00-B4-A0-47-74
DHCP Enabled. . . . . . . . . . : No
IP Address. . . . . . . . . . . : 172.16.11.105
Subnet Mask . . . . . . . . . . : 255.255.255.0
IP Address. . . . . . . . . . . : 172.16.11.104
Subnet Mask . . . . . . . . . . : 255.255.255.0
Default Gateway . . . . . . . . : 172.16.11.196
DNS Servers . . . . . . . . . . : 172.16.11.104
                                  172.16.11.100
```

Display contents of client DNS name cache:

ipconfig /displaydns
```
Windows IP Configuration

    localhost.
    ----------------------------------------------------
        Record Name . . . . . : localhost
        Record Type . . . . . : 1
        Time To Live  . . . . : 31338848
        Data Length . . . . . : 4
        Section . . . . . . . : Answer
        A (Host) Record . . . :
                        127.0.0.1


    1.0.0.127.in-addr.arpa.
    ----------------------------------------------------
        Record Name . . . . . : 1.0.0.127.in-addr.arpa
        Record Type . . . . . : 12
        Time To Live  . . . . : 31338847
        Data Length . . . . . : 4
        Section . . . . . . . : Answer
        PTR Record  . . . . . :
                        localhost


    bach.mtitworld.com.
    ----------------------------------------------------
        Record Name . . . . . : bach.mtitworld.com
        Record Type . . . . . : 1
        Time To Live  . . . . : 261
        Data Length . . . . . : 4
        Section . . . . . . . : Answer
        A (Host) Record . . . :
                        172.16.11.100


    test.mtitcanada.com.
    ----------------------------------------------------
        Record Name . . . . . : test.mtitcanada.com
        Record Type . . . . . : 1
        Time To Live  . . . . : 2665
        Data Length . . . . . : 4
        Section . . . . . . . : Answer
```

```
          A (Host) Record . . . :
                           172.16.11.104

          Record Name . . . . . : test.mtitcanada.com
          Record Type . . . . . : 1
          Time To Live  . . . . : 2665
          Data Length . . . . . : 4
          Section . . . . . . . : Answer
          A (Host) Record . . . :
                           172.16.11.105
```

Flush client DNS name cache:

```
ipconfig /flushdns
Windows IP Configuration
Successfully flushed the DNS Resolver Cache.
```

Verify that client DNS name cache has been flushed:

```
ipconfig /displaydns
Windows IP Configuration

   localhost.
   --------------------------------------------------
          Record Name . . . . . : localhost
          Record Type . . . . . : 1
          Time To Live  . . . . : 31338835
          Data Length . . . . . : 4
          Section . . . . . . . : Answer
          A (Host) Record . . . :
                           127.0.0.1
```

Note the mapping that remains in the cache. This is preloaded from the *Hosts* file on the client.

Reregister client's DNS information with DNS server:

```
ipconfig /registerdns
Windows IP Configuration
Registration of the DNS resource records for all adapters of this computer
has been initiated. Any errors will be reported in the Event Viewer in 15
minutes.
```

Display DHCP class IDs for the client on the "Local-Area Connection" adapter:

```
ipconfig showclassid "Local Area Connection"
Windows IP Configuration
DHCP Class ID for Adapter "Local Area Connection":
DHCP ClassID Name . . . . . . . . : Default BOOTP Class
DHCP ClassID Description  . . . . : User class for BOOTP Clients
```

Notes

The DNS name cache in WS2003 also supports negative caching of unresolved or invalid DNS names. However, these negative DNS responses are cached for only a short period of time.

See Also

DNS, ping, *TCP/IP*

label

Modifies a volume label for a disk.

Syntax

```
label [Drive:][Label]
label [/MP][Volume][Label]
```

Options

None
> Modifies or deletes the current volume label.

Drive:
> Drive letter.

Label
> Label for volume or disk.

/MP
> Treat the volume as a mount point.

Volume
> Drive letter, mount point, or volume name.

Examples

Assign the label TESTVOL to *E:* drive:

```
label e: TESTVOL
```

Switch to E: drive:

```
e:
E:\>
```

Change the label to BADVOL:

```
label
Volume in drive E: is TESTVOL
Volume Serial Number is 6EA7-D467
Volume label (32 characters, ENTER for none)? BADVOL

E:\>
```

See Also

chkdsk, chkntfs, convert, defrag, diskpart, *Disks*, format, mountvol

---

ldifde

Stands for Lightweight Directory Access Protocol Interchange Format (LDIF) Directory Exchange, a utility for bulk import/export of data between line-delimited (LDIF) text files and Active Directory. ldifde can add, delete, or modify multiple user accounts, groups, computers, printers, or other AD objects in a single batch operation.

Syntax

```
ldifde options
```

Options

These are the same as for the csvde command described previously in this chapter, except for the following additional import-specific option:

-y   Use "lazy writes" to improve disk performance for import process.

Examples

The following is a properly formatted LDIF file called *C:\newusers.txt*, which creates three new user accounts. The accounts created are identical to the ones created in the example for the csvde command earlier in this chapter:

```
dn: CN=George Smith,OU=Support,DC=mtitcanada,DC=com
objectClass: user
sAMAccountName: gsmith
userPrincipalName: gsmith@mtitcanada.com
displayName: George T. Smith
userAccountControl: 514
# Create user account for Barb Smith

dn: CN=Barb Smith,OU=Support,DC=mtitcanada,DC=com
objectClass: user
sAMAccountName: bsmith
userPrincipalName: bsmith@mtitcanada.com
displayName: Barbara Lynn Smith
userAccountControl: 514
# Create user account for Judy Smith

dn: CN=Judy Smith,OU=Support,DC=mtitcanada,DC=com
objectClass: user
sAMAccountName: jsmith
userPrincipalName: jsmith@mtitcanada.com
displayName: Judy Ann Smith
userAccountControl: 512
```

Use ldifde to import the previous file into AD to create the users:

```
ldifde -i -f C:\newusers.txt
Connecting to "test.mtitcanada.com"
Logging in as current user using SSPI
Importing directory from file "C:\newusers.txt"
Loading entries....
3 entries modified successfully.

The command has completed successfully
```

Notes

Unlike csvde, which can only to add new objects to AD, ldifde can add, delete, or modify them.

If an attribute is to be left unspecified in an LDIF file, use FILL SEP as the value for the attribute.

See *Notes* under csvde for more information.

See Also

Active Directory, csvde

lpq

Displays the status of a print queue on a TCP/IP print server running LPD.

Syntax

```
lpq -S servername -P printername [-l]
```

Options

-S servername
> The name or IP address of the LPD print server

-P printername
> The name of the print queue on the server

-l   Verbose output

Examples

Display status of print queue for the network printer *BROTHER* on *TEST*:

```
lpq -S 172.16.11.104 -P brother
   Windows LPD Server
   Printer \\172.16.11.104\brother

Owner Status Jobname Job-Id Size Pages Priority
-------------------------------------------------------
Administrator Printing Test Page 513 103793 0 0
```

Notes

lpq can query non-LPD print servers as well (for example, Microsoft Windows print servers). You can't use lpq to send jobs to these print servers, however.

You can query the TCP/IP print queue on the local machine by typing:

```
lpq -S localhost -P printername
```

See Also

lpr, *Printing*

---

lpr

Prints a file to a TCP/IP print server running LPD.

Syntax

```
lpr -S servername -P printername [-C classname] [-J jobname] [-o option] [-x] [-
d] filename
```

Options

-S servername
> Indicates the name or IP address of the LPD print server.

-P printername
> Indicates the name of the print queue on the server.

-C classname
> Specifies something to identify the output as your job (otherwise, the hostname of your computer is used). This appears on the banner page (if enabled on the print server).

-J jobname
> Specifies the name of your job (otherwise, the name of the file you are printing is used). This appears on the banner page (if enabled on the print server).

-o option
> Specifies the type of file being printed (the default is ASCII text). For example, specify .PS as the option when printing PostScript files.

-x Provides backward compatibility for printing to LPD servers running older versions of SunOS.

-d Transfers the datafile before the control file, if needed by the LPD server.

filename
> Indicates the file you are printing.

Examples

Send a job to queue *HPLASERJ* on LPD server 172.16.11.104:

```
lpr -S 172.16.11.104 -P hplaserj -C Mitchell -J Testing C:\hello.txt
```

Use lpq to check the queue to verify whether the job is pending.

See Also

lpq, *Printing*

---

mode

Displays status of COM, LPT, and console ports.

Syntax

```
mode /status
```

Examples

```
mode /status

Status for device LPT1:
-----------------------
    Printer output is not being rerouted.

Status for device COM2:
-----------------------
    Baud:            1200
    Parity:          None
    Data Bits:       7
    Stop Bits:       1
    Timeout:         OFF
    XON/XOFF:        OFF
    CTS handshaking: OFF
    DSR handshaking: OFF
    DSR sensitivity: OFF
```

```
        DTR circuit:    ON
        RTS circuit:    ON

   Status for device COM1:
   -----------------------
        Baud:             1200
        Parity:           None
        Data Bits:        7
        Stop Bits:        1
        Timeout:          OFF
        XON/XOFF:         OFF
        CTS handshaking:  OFF
        DSR handshaking:  OFF
        DSR sensitivity:  OFF
        DTR circuit:      ON
        RTS circuit:      ON

   Status for device CON:
   -----------------------
        Lines:          300
        Columns:        80
        Keyboard rate:  31
        Keyboard delay: 1
        Code page:      437
```

Notes

The mode command also includes options for configuring COM, LTP, and console ports; type **mode /?** for more info.

See Also

Devices

---

mountvol

Creates, deletes, or displays a volume mount point.

Syntax

```
mountvol [drive:]path volumename
mountvol [drive:]path /d
mountvol [drive:]path /l
```

Options

None

   Displays existing mount points (if any) and volumes that can be targeted for new mount points

[drive:]path

   Specifies a directory (must be empty and on an NTFS volume) where the mount point will reside

volumename
> Indicates the volume name targeted for the mount point (must be the GUID of the volume)

/d   Deletes the mount point

/l   Lists the mounted volume name for the specified directory

Examples

Display volumes on which empty directories can be targeted as mount points:

```
mountvol
Possible values for VolumeName along with current mount points are:

    \\?\Volume{efc6cef2-cd37-11d3-8139-806d6172696f}\
       C:\

    \\?\Volume{886dfe07-d034-11d3-8142-0000b4a04774}\
       E:\

    \\?\Volume{886dfe08-d034-11d3-8142-0000b4a04774}\
       F:\

    \\?\Volume{886dfe09-d034-11d3-8142-0000b4a04774}\
       G:\

    \\?\Volume{b5349550-d58e-11d3-8144-0000b4a04774}\
       H:\

    \\?\Volume{0b77be43-ccff-11d3-b77a-806d6172696f}\
       D:\

    \\?\Volume{0b77be42-ccff-11d3-b77a-806d6172696f}\
       A:\
```

Notice that the Help file for mountvol is also printed (here omitted). Let's now create the empty directory *C:\accounting* and mount the *H:* drive to this directory. Working in the current directory, which is *C:*, do the following:

```
md accounting
mountvol accounting \\?\Volume{b5349550-d58e-11d3-8144-0000b4a04774}
```

To see if it worked:

```
dir accounting
Volume in drive C has no label.
Volume Serial Number is D839-4CFA

 Directory of C:\accounting

06/22/2000  01:40p                    46 doc1.txt
06/22/2000  01:44p                    30 doc2.txt
06/22/2000  02:12p       DIR          pub
            2 File(s)             76 bytes
            1 Dir(s)     497,959,936 bytes free
```

This is the contents of the *H:* drive that's mounted to the empty folder *C:\accounting*.

Notes

- You can create mount points using Disk Management as well (see *Disks* in Chapter 4).

- Mount points can be used if you are running out of drive letters for local volumes and to expand the space on a volume without reformatting it or replacing the hard drive (just add a mount path to another volume). You can also use one volume with several mount paths to enable access to all your local volumes using a single drive letter.

- Don't delete a mount point using Windows Explorer or del /s because this removes the target directory and all its subdirectories. Use instead mountvol /d.

See Also

chkdsk, chkntfs, convert, defrag, diskpart, *Disks*, format, label

nbtstat

Displays statistics and current connections for NetBT (NetBIOS over TCP/IP).

Syntax

```
nbtstat [ [-a computername] [-A IPaddress] [-c] [-n] [-r] [-R] [-RR] [-s]
[-S] [interval] ]
```

Options

-a computername
　　Displays the NBT name table on the specified remote computer.

-A IPaddress
　　Same as -a except that IP address of remote computer is used.

-c　　Displays contents of NetBIOS name cache on local machine. This shows the NetBIOS names on the network that have been successfully resolved into IP addresses.

-n　　Lists the NetBIOS names registered by the local machine. The "registered" field shows whether the name has been registered using broadcasts (B-node) or WINS servers (other node types).

-r　　Displays statistics for NetBIOS name resolution on the local machine.

-R　　Purges all NetBIOS name-to-IP address mappings from the local NetBIOS name cache and then preloads mappings from the *lmhosts* file that have the #PRE specifier.

-RR　Releases and refreshes all NetBIOS names for the local machine.

-s　　Shows all current NetBIOS sessions, listing remote computers by NetBIOS names.

-S　　Shows all current NetBIOS sessions, listing remote computers by IP addresses.

interval
　　Causes the output to be refreshed the specified number of seconds until Ctrl-C is pressed.

Examples

Purge NetBIOS name-to-IP-address mappings in the local NBT name cache:

nbtstat -R
```
Successful purge and preload of the NBT Remote Cache Name Table.
```

View the local NBT cache:

nbtstat -c
```
Local Area Connection:
Node IpAddress: [172.16.11.104] Scope Id: [ ]
    No names in cache
```

Ping server *BACH* to resolve its NetBIOS name into its IP address:

ping bach
```
Pinging bach [172.16.11.100] with 32 bytes of data:

Reply from 172.16.11.100: bytes=32 time<10ms TTL=128
Reply from 172.16.11.100: bytes=32 time<10ms TTL=128
Reply from 172.16.11.100: bytes=32 time<10ms TTL=128
Reply from 172.16.11.100: bytes=32 time<10ms TTL=128

Ping statistics for 172.16.11.100:
Packets: Sent = 4, Received = 4, Lost = 0 (0% loss),
Approximate round trip times in milli-seconds:
Minimum = 0ms, Maximum =  0ms, Average =  0ms
```

Check if the resolved name (*BACH*) and its IP address mapping (172.16.11.100) have been cached on the local machine:

nbtstat -c
```
Local Area Connection:
Node IpAddress: [172.16.11.104] Scope Id: [ ]

            NetBIOS Remote Cache Name Table

Name    Type          Host Address     Life [sec]
---------------------------------------------------
BACH    <00>  UNIQUE    172.16.11.100       597
```

Display a list of NetBIOS names registered for the local machine:

nbtstat -n
```
Local Area Connection:
Node IpAddress: [172.16.11.104] Scope Id: [ ]

            NetBIOS Local Name Table

        Name               Type       Status
    ---------------------------------------------
    TEST            <00>  UNIQUE      Registered
    MTITCANADA      <00>  GROUP       Registered
    MTITCANADA      <1C>  GROUP       Registered
    TEST            <20>  UNIQUE      Registered
    MTITCANADA      <1B>  UNIQUE      Registered
    TEST            <03>  UNIQUE      Registered
    NETSHOWSERVICES<03>  UNIQUE      Registered
    MTITCANADA      <1E>  GROUP       Registered
```

```
MTITCANADA    <1D>  UNIQUE     Registered
.._MSBROWSE__.<01>  GROUP      Registered
INet~Services <1C>  GROUP      Registered
IS~TEST........<00>  UNIQUE     Registered
```

The fact that one of the previous NetBIOS names has the <1C> suffix indicates that the local machine is a domain controller.

Display the list of NetBIOS names registered by the remote machine called *BACH* (this is also a handy way of obtaining the MAC address of *BACH*):

```
nbtstat -a bach
Local Area Connection:
Node IpAddress: [172.16.11.104] Scope Id: [ ]

          NetBIOS Remote Machine Name Table

      Name              Type         Status
    ---------------------------------------------
    BACH          <00>  UNIQUE     Registered
    BACH          <20>  UNIQUE     Registered
    MTITWORLD     <00>  GROUP      Registered
    MTITWORLD     <1C>  GROUP      Registered
    MTITWORLD     <1B>  UNIQUE     Registered
    BACH          <03>  UNIQUE     Registered
    MTITWORLD     <1E>  GROUP      Registered
    INet~Services <1C>  GROUP      Registered
    IS~BACH........<00>  UNIQUE     Registered
    MTITWORLD     <1D>  UNIQUE     Registered
    .._MSBROWSE__.<01>  GROUP      Registered
    ADMINISTRATOR <03>  UNIQUE     Registered

    MAC Address = 00-40-95-D1-29-6C
```

Display current NBT session statistics on the local machine:

```
nbtstat -S
Local Area Connection:
Node IpAddress: [172.16.11.104] Scope Id: [ ]

              NetBIOS Connection Table

LocalName  State     In/Out  RemoteHost   Input   Output
---------------------------------------------------------
TEST  <00>Connected  Out  172.16.11.39   320KB   721KB
TEST  <00>Connected  Out  172.16.11.94   711KB   185KB
TEST  <00>Connected  Out  172.16.11.100    5KB     8KB
TEST  <03>Listening
```

Notes

nbtstat is most useful when troubleshooting name-resolution problems in mixed WS2003/W2K/NT networks where NetBIOS is still being used. (NetBIOS can be disabled in the TCP/IP properties of WS2003 machines and isn't really needed in pure WS2003 networks.) Here are the various fields of the output from nbtstat.

Input
> Bytes received over the connection

Output
> Bytes sent over the connection

In/Out
> Whether the connection is inbound or outbound

Life
> How long the entry remains in the name table cache before being purged

LocalName
> The local NetBIOS name associated with the connection

RemoteHost
> The name or IP address of the remote computer

Type
> The type of the NetBIOS name, which can be either a unique name or a group name

State
> Current state of the connection (see Table 5-5)

Table 5-5. Possible states of an NBT connection

State	Description
Accepting	An inbound session is in the process of being accepted.
Associated	A connection endpoint has been created and associated with an IP address.
Connected	A session has been established.
Connecting	A session is in the connecting phase during which the name–to–IP address mapping of the destination is being resolved.
Disconnected	The local machine has issued a disconnect and is waiting for confirmation from the remote machine.
Disconnecting	A session is in the process of disconnecting.
Idle	An endpoint has been opened but can't receive a connection.
Inbound	An inbound session is in the connecting phase.
Listening	An endpoint is available for an inbound connection.
Outbound	A session is in the connecting phase during which the TCP connection is being formed.
Reconnecting	A session is attempting to reconnect after failure to connect.

See Also

TCP/IP, WINS

net

Allows command-line administration of certain aspects of network connectivity and security.

Syntax

```
net [option]
```

Options

net.exe must be used with one of the following services to give it a specific focus:

accounts
Manages password and logon requirements for user accounts

computer
Adds or removes computer accounts from the domain

config
Displays whether Server and Workstation Services are running and configures these services

continue
Continues paused services

file
Displays a list of shared files that are open and closes them

group
Creates global groups or modifies their membership

help
Provides quick help for a net command from the command line

helpmsg
Provides information on net command error messages

localgroup
Creates local groups or modifies their membership

name
Adds or removes an alias for the computer

pause
Pauses a service

print
Manages printer queues and print jobs

send
Sends a message to users or computers on the network

session
Manages sessions between a server and connected clients

share
Manages shared folders

start
Manages services

statistics
Displays statistics for the Workstation or Server service

stop
Stops a service

time
Synchronizes the clock on the local machine with a time server

use
Manages connections with shared resources

user
> Manages user accounts

view
> Lists domains, computers, and shared resources

Because these options are independent of one another and can't be combined in a single command, you can think of them as a family of net commands instead of a single command with distinct options. The individual members of this family are considered in detail in the following entries.

Notes

- To see the syntax of a net command from the command line, type **net help** followed by the option that defines the command. For example, to see the syntax for net accounts, type **net help accounts**.

- All net commands also accept the following options:

  /y Automatically answers yes to any prompt generated by the command (useful in batch files)

  /n Automatically answers no to prompts

See Also

net accounts, net computer, net config, net continue, net file, net group, net help, net helpmsg, net localgroup, net name, net pause, net print, net send, net session, net share, net start, net statistics, net stop, net time, net use, net user, net view

---

net accounts

Manages password and logon requirements for user accounts.

Syntax

```
net accounts [/forcelogoff:{minutes | no}] [/minpwlen:length]
[/maxpwage:{days | unlimited}] [/minpwage:days] [/uniquepw:number]
[/domain]
```

Options

None
> Current password and logon settings.

/forcelogoff:[minutes | no]
> Time to wait before terminating a user session when account or password expires. (The default is no, which means user isn't forced to log off.) A warning is sent to the user telling her to save her work.

/minpwlen:length
> Minimum number of characters required for password. (The default is 6, and the allowed range is 0–127.)

/maxpwage:[days | unlimited]
> Maximum number of days passwords are valid before expiring. (The default is 90, and the allowed range is 1–49,710.) unlimited means passwords never expire. The value of /maxpwage must exceed /minpwage.

/minpwage:days
>   Minimum number of days before a user is allowed to change his password. (The default is 0, and the allowed range is 0–49,710.) Choosing 0 means users can change their passwords anytime.

/uniquepw:number
>   Specification of password history by requiring users to not repeat a password for number password changes. (The default is 5, and the allowed range is 0–24.)

/domain
>   On member servers and workstations, an indication that net accounts settings apply to domain accounts rather than local ones. (On WS2003 domain controllers, this is the default setting anyway and isn't needed.)

Examples

Display the current password and logoff settings:

```
net accounts
Force user logoff how long after time expires?: Never
Minimum password age (days): 0
Maximum password age (days): 42
Minimum password length: 0
Length of password history maintained: 18
Lockout threshold: Never
Lockout duration (minutes): 30
Lockout observation window (minutes): 30
Computer role: PRIMARY
The command completed successfully.
```

Notes

- The Netlogon Service must be running to use net accounts.
- To manage password and logon restrictions for a domain, see *Group Policy* in Chapter 4.
- If net accounts displays the computer role as PRIMARY, the computer is a domain controller; if SERVER, it is a standalone server.

See Also

Groups, Group Policy, Users

---

net computer

Adds or removes computer accounts to or from the domain.

Syntax

```
net computer \\computername {/add | /del}
```

Options

\\computername
>   Indicates name of computer to add to or remove from the domain

/add
> Adds a computer account

/del
> Removes a computer account

Examples

Add a computer account for the server *GEORGE*:

```
net computer \\george /add
The command completed successfully.
```

If you now open the Active Directory Users and Computers console, you will find a new computer account for *GEORGE* in the Computers container for the current domain.

Notes

- Using this command, you can create computer accounts for member servers and workstations, but not for domain controllers.
- Computer accounts are created on the PDC emulator.

See Also

net

---

net config

Displays whether Server and Workstation services are running.

Syntax

```
net config {server | workstation}
```

Options

None
> Verifies whether Server and Workstation services are running

Notes

To configure the Server and Workstation services, see net config server and net config workstation.

See Also

net config server, net config workstation

---

net config server

Control settings for the Server service.

Syntax

```
net config server [/autodisconnect:minutes] [/srvcomment:"text"]
[/hidden:{yes | no}]
```

Options

None

    Shows current settings.

/autodisconnect:minutes

    Sets the maximum idle time before disconnecting user sessions. (The default is 15, and the allowed range is 1–65,535.) Specify -1 to never disconnect a user.

/srvcomment:"text"

    Displays the comment when the net view command is used (up to 48 characters). Be sure to use the quotes.

/hidden:[yes | no]

    Hides the server name from the net view command. (The default is no.)

Examples

Display the configuration of the Server service on the local machine:

```
net config server
Server Name                      \\TEST
Server Comment                   Hello
Software version                 WS2003
Server is active on
    NetBT_Tcpip_{54414D01-02DA-4783-B931-C9AC7A70EDDD}
      (0000b4a04774)
    NetBT_Tcpip_{54414D01-02DA-4783-B931-C9AC7A70EDDD}
      (0000b4a04774)
    NetbiosSmb (000000000000)
    NetbiosSmb (000000000000)
    Nbf_{54414D01-02DA-4783-B931-C9AC7A70EDDD}
      (0000b4a04774)
    Nbf_NdisWanNbfOut{0D374F9E-C395-4C81-BDFA-
      FC1503D82B34} (f46f20524153)
    Nbf_NdisWanNbfIn{AEDAF533-9187-477C-BDF7-
      07B657D13D4F} (f25920524153)
    NwlnkNb (0000b4a04774)
    Nbf_NdisWanNbfOut{0FC56659-6FD4-4E8A-BF83-
      146D25681D8B} (f6f420524153)
    Nbf_NdisWanNbfIn{160A090E-ACA6-4D63-95E3-
      6E111EB3A6D4} (f2e620524153)
    Nbf_NdisWanNbfOut{033CCCCB-D120-4913-A25F-
      3DD13FE9E915} (f46f20524153)
    NwlnkIpx (000000000001)

Server hidden                    No
Maximum Logged On Users          Unlimited
Maximum open files per session   16384
Idle session time (min)          15
The command completed successfully.
```

Table 5-6 shows the fields displayed.

Command Reference

Table 5-6. Displayed in net config server command output

Field	Description
Server name	UNC name of server
Server comment	"Text" value specified
Software version	WS2003
Server is active on	Protocols bound to service
Server hidden	Yes or no
Maximum logged-on users	Unlimited
Maximum open files per session	16,384
Idle session time (minutes)	15 minutes by default

Disconnect user sessions after five minutes of inactivity:

```
net config server /autodisconnect:5
The command completed successfully.
```

Notes

- Changes made using this command take effect immediately and are permanent.
- It's better to modify Server service parameters by editing the registry directly instead of using this command with any of its three switches. The reason is that using this command permanently saves the current settings of the Server service to the registry and disables autotuning of the Server service. Autotuning is a mechanism by which WS2003 tries to maintain optimum performance for the Server service. For example, if you add more memory to your server after running net config server /autodisconnect:5, the result is that WS2003 will be unable to automatically configure itself to make best use of the additional memory. Note, however, that using net config server without any additional parameters doesn't have this negative effect. To learn how to undo this problem should it occur, see Knowledge Base article 128167.
- To configure the Workstation service, use net config workstation.

See Also

net config, net config workstation

---

net config workstation

Control settings for the Workstation service.

Syntax

```
net config workstation [/charcount:bytes] [/chartime:msec]
[/charwait:sec]
```

Options

None
    Shows current settings.

/charcount:bytes

> Number of bytes buffered before sending data to a COM device. (The default is 16, and the allowed range is 0–65,535.) If /chartime:*msec* is specified, the first one satisfied is used.

/chartime:msec

> Time in milliseconds data is buffered before sending it to a COM device. (The default is 250, and the allowed range is 0–65,535,000.) If /charcount:*bytes* is specified, the first one satisfied is used.

/charwait:sec

> The maximum time WS2003 waits for a COM device to become available when it has data to send. (The default is 3,600, and the allowed range is 0–65,535.)

Examples

Display the configuration of the Server service on the local machine:

```
net config workstation
Computer name                      \\TEST
Full Computer name                 test.mtit.com
usernames                          Administrator

Workstation active on
    Nbf_{54414D01-02DA-4783-B931-C9AC7A70EDDD}
       (0000B4A04774)
    Nbf_NdisWanNbfIn{AEDAF533-9187-477C-BDF7-
       07B657D13D4F} (F25920524153)
    Nbf_NdisWanNbfIn{160A090E-ACA6-4D63-95E3-
       6E111EB3A6D4} (F2E620524153)
    Nbf_NdisWanNbfOut{0D374F9E-C395-4C81-BDFA-
       FC1503D82B34} (F46F20524153)
    Nbf_NdisWanNbfOut{033CCCCB-D120-4913-A25F-
       3DD13FE9E915} (F46F20524153)
    Nbf_NdisWanNbfOut{0EC56659-6FD4-4E8A-BF83-
       146D25681D8B} (F6F420524153)
    NwlnkNb (0000B4A04774)
    NetbiosSmb (000000000000)
    NetBT_Tcpip_{54414D01-02DA-4783-B931-C9AC7A70EDDD}
       (0000B4A04774)

Software version                   WS2003
Workstation domain                 MTITCANADA
Workstation Domain DNS Name        mtitcanada.com
Logon domain                       MTITCANADA
COM Open Timeout (sec)             0
COM Send Count (byte)              16
COM Send Timeout (msec)            250
The command completed successfully.
```

Table 5-7 shows the fields displayed.

Table 5-7. Fields displayed in net config workstation command output

Field	Description
Server name	UNC name of computer
Username	Currently logged-on user
Server active on	Lists protocols and interfaces bound to the service
Software version	WS2003
Workstation domain DNS Name	Domain workstation belongs to
Logon domain	Domain of currently logged-on user
COM open timeout (sec)	Value of charwait
COM send count (byte)	Value of charcount
COM send timeout (msec)	Value of chartime

Notes

- Changes made take effect immediately and are permanent.
- To configure the Server service, use net config server.

See Also

net, net config server

net continue

Continues paused services.

Syntax

    net continue *service*

Options

service
   The paused service to continue

Examples

Continue the Server service:

net continue server
The Server service was continued successfully.

Notes

- Service names with embedded spaces require double quotes around them.
- This command restarts only paused services, not stopped ones.

See Also

net pause, net start, net stop, *Services*

net file

Displays a list of shared files that are open and closes them.

Syntax

```
net file [id [/close] ]
```

Options

None
> Lists the shared files on the server that are open

id   Represents the identification number of the file

/close
> Closes the file

Examples

Display a list of shared files open on the server:

```
net file
ID      Path                    usernames           # Locks
--------------------------------------------------------
15      \PIPE\lsarpc            BACH$               0
2765    G:\pub\mydoc.txt        ADMINISTRATOR       0
The command completed successfully.
```

Close the open file:

```
net file 2765 /close
The command completed successfully.
```

Notes

- `net file` should be typed on the console of the server on which the shared file is located.
- `net files` has the same effect as `net file`.
- Closing a file removes any locks on the file.
- Use the Shared Folders node in Computer Management to manage shared files with the GUI (see *Shared Folders* in Chapter 4).

See Also

`net session`, `net share`, `net use`, `net view`, *Shared Folders*

---

net group

Creates global groups or modifies their membership.

Syntax

```
net group [groupname [/comment:"text"] ] [/domain]
net group groupname {/add [/comment:"text"] | /delete} [/domain]
net group groupname username [...] {/add | /delete} [/domain]
```

Options

None
> Lists global groups on the server.

groupname
> Shows the name of a group to create, delete, or modify the membership of.

/comment:"text"
> Describes a group (up to 48 characters).

/domain
> If omitted, performs the command on the local computer (which must be a domain controller). Use this switch to manage groups from a workstation.

username[...]
> Adds or removes user account(s) from the group (separate with spaces).

/add
> Creates a new group or adds existing users to an existing group.

/delete
> Deletes a group or removes users from a group.

Examples

List all global groups in the domain:

```
net group
Group Accounts for \\TEST
-----------------------------------------------------
*Cert Publishers
*DnsUpdateProxy
*Domain Admins
*Domain Computers
*Domain Controllers
*Domain Guests
*Domain Users
*Group Policy Creator Owners
The command completed successfully.
```

Create a new global group called Support, and give it the description "Support staff":

```
net group support /add /comment:"Support staff"
The command completed successfully.
```

Add users *sally* and *mktulloch* to Support:

```
net group support sally mktulloch /add
The command completed successfully.
```

View the membership of Support:

```
net group Support
Group name      Support
Comment         Support staff
Members

-----------------------------------------------------
mktulloch               sally
The command completed successfully.
```

Notes

- net group can also be typed **net groups**.
- Use double quotes around group names with embedded spaces, such as "domain users."
- In the output of net group, an asterisk preceding a group name indicates that it includes both users and groups.

See Also

Groups, net accounts, net localgroup, net user

---

net help

Provides quick help for a net command from the command line.

Syntax

```
net help command
net command /help
```

Options

None
> Shows a list of net commands

command
> Represents the net command you need help with

Examples

Get help information on the net computer command:

net help computer
```
The syntax of this command is:
NET COMPUTER \\computername {/ADD | /DEL}
NET COMPUTER adds or deletes computers from a domain database. This command
    is available only on Windows NT Servers.
\\computername    Specifies the computer to add or delete from the domain.
/ADD              Adds the specified computer to the domain.
/DEL              Removes the specified computer from the domain.
```

The same result can be obtained by typing:

net computer /help

Get only the syntax of net computer:

net computer /?
```
The syntax of this command is:
NET COMPUTER \\computername {/ADD | /DEL}
```

See Also

net helpmsg

---

net helpmsg

Provides information on net command error messages.

Syntax

```
net helpmsg message#
```

Options

message#
> Four-digit error-message number from a net command

Examples

View a nonexistent share on the server (spelling mistake):

```
net share pubb
This shared resource does not exist.
More help is available by typing NET HELPMSG 2310.
```

Find out what error message 2310 means:

```
net helpmsg 2310
This shared resource does not exist.
EXPLANATION
The share name you specified does not exist.
ACTION
Check the spelling of the share name.
To display a list of resources shared on the server, type:
    NET SHARE
```

See Also

net help

---

net localgroup

Creates local groups or modifies their membership.

Syntax

```
net localgroup [groupname [/comment:"text"] ] [/domain]
net localgroup groupname {/add [/comment:"text"] | /delete} [/domain]
net localgroup groupname username [...] {/add | /delete} [/domain]
```

Options

None
> Lists local groups on the server.

groupname
> Shows the name of a group to create, delete, or modify the membership of.

/comment:"text"
> Describes a group (up to 48 characters).

/domain
> If omitted, performs the command on the local computer (which must be a domain controller). To manage groups from a workstation, use this switch.

username[...]
> Adds or removes user account(s) from the group (separate with spaces).

/add
> Creates a new group or adds existing users to an existing group.

/delete
> Deletes a group or removes users from a group.

Examples

List all local groups in the domain:

```
net localgroup
Aliases for \\TEST
```

```
--------------------------------------------------------
*Account Operators    *Administrators          *Backup Operators
*DHCP Administrators   *DHCP Users              *DnsAdmins
*Guests                *NetShow Administrators  *Pre-W2K Compatible
*Print Operators       *RAS and IAS Servers     *Replicator
*Server Operators      *Users                   *WINS Users
The command completed successfully.
```

Create a new local group called Color Printers:

net localgroup "Color Printers" /add
```
The command completed successfully.
```

Add the Domain Users global group to the Color Printers local group:

net localgroup "Color Printers" "domain users" /add
```
The command completed successfully.
```

List the members of Color Printers:

net localgroup "Color Printers"
```
Alias name      Color Printers
Comment
Members

--------------------------------------------------------
Domain Users
The command completed successfully.
```

Notes

- net localgroup can also be typed **net localgroups**.
- Use double quotes around group names with embedded spaces, such as "domain users."
- In the output of the command, an asterisk preceding a group name indicates that it includes both users and groups.

See Also

Groups, net accounts, net group, net user

---

net name

Adds or removes an alias for the computer. ↘

Syntax

```
net name [alias [/add | /delete] ]
```

Options

None
> Displays a list of names for which the computer accepts messages.

alias
> Specifies an alias (up to 15 characters).

/add
> Adds an alias. (This switch is optional, as it is implied.)

/delete
> Removes an alias.

Examples

Display the names that your computer responds to for messages sent over the network using the Messenger service:

net name
```
Name
-----------------------------------------------
TEST
NETSHOWSERVICES
The command completed successfully.
```

Add the alias hellothere for the computer:

net name hellothere /add
```
The message name HELLOTHERE was added successfully.
```

Notes

- Aliases must be unique to the network and may not be the same as a computer name or username elsewhere on the network. If an alias duplicates an existing computer name and either machine is rebooted, the Messenger service will fail to start on the restarted machine.
- The Messenger service must be running.

See Also

net send

---

net pause

Pause a service.

Syntax

    net pause *service*

Options

service
    The service to pause

Examples

Pause the Server service:

net pause server
```
The Server service was paused successfully.
```

Restart (continue) the paused Server service:

net continue server
```
The Server service was continued successfully.
```

Notes

- Services whose names have embedded spaces must be enclosed in quotes:
  net pause "Net Logon"
- If a service is paused, users previously connected to resources managed by the service remain connected. The same isn't true of stopping a service, which

forcibly disconnects users from resources. However, not all services can be paused (e.g., the Remote Procedure Call service), and the effect of pausing a service depends on the service involved. For example:

Server service
> Pausing this service prevents users from forming new connections to shared resources on the server (existing connections are unaffected). Administrators can still connect to the server even if the Server service is paused.

Workstation service
> Pausing this service has no effect on the user's logon session and network connections. However, if the user tries to print to a network printer, the request will be redirected to a local printer.

Netlogon service
> Pausing this service prevents the affected computer from processing logon requests.

• You should pause services on a server before stopping them. This gives the user time to save work and disconnect from resources. After pausing a service, send connected users a message indicating that you will soon be stopping it and that they should save their work (see net send later in this chapter).

See Also
net continue, net send, net start, net stop, *Services*

---

net print

Manages printer queues and print jobs.

Syntax
```
net print \\computername\sharename
net print [\\computername] job# [/hold | /release | /delete]
```

Options
computername
> Indicates the print server

sharename
> Indicates share name of the printer

job#
> Represents identification number of print job

/hold
> Holds a print job waiting in a queue and lets other jobs bypass it (use with job#)

/release
> Releases a job that is on hold

/delete
> Deletes a job from the queue

Examples
Display jobs in print queue of printer *HPLASERJ* on print server *TEST*:

```
net print \\test\hplaserj
Printers at \\test

Name              Job #   Size      Status
------------------------------------------------------
hplaserj Queue    1 jobs            *Printer Active*
     administrator    3   17500     Printing
The command completed successfully.
```

Look at details of job 3 earlier:

```
net print \\test 3
Print job detail

Job #              3
Status             Printing
Size               17500
Remark             Untitled - Notepad
Submitting user    administrator
Notify             administrator
Job data type      NT EMF 1.
Job parameters
Additional info
The command completed successfully.
```

Delete job 3 from the queue:

```
net print \\test 3 /delete
The command completed successfully.
```

Notes

- To find the share name of your shared printer, type **net share** at the command line.
- If a print server has multiple shared printers, each printer has its own print queue. However, jobs in different print queues on the same server can't have the same job ID number.

See Also

Printing

---

net send

Sends a message to users or computers on the network.

Syntax

```
net send {name | * | /domain[:name] | /users} message
```

Options

name

Sends the message to a specific recipient, which can be:

A logged-on user
   user logon name

A computer name
 NetBIOS name

A computer alias
 see net name earlier in this chapter

* Broadcasts the message to all registered NetBIOS names in the domain or workgroup

/domain[:name]
 Broadcasts the message to all names in the local domain or a specified domain

/users
 Sends the message to all users connected to the server

message
 Is the actual message sent (no quotes required)

Examples

Send the message "Save your work--rebooting in 5 minutes" to all users who have open sessions with the server:

```
net send /users Save your work--rebooting in 5 minutes
```

Notes

- In order for a user to receive messages, the Messenger service must be running.

- Use quotation marks for computer names or usernames that have embedded spaces in them.

- Messages can be up to 128 characters in length.

- The message queue, which temporarily stores messages for the Messenger service, can store a maximum of only six messages; any further messages are ignored if the previous ones aren't acknowledged.

- net send * is the same as net send /domain.

- Broadcast messages (* and /domain options) are sent over all network protocols. For example, if you have both TCP/IP and NWLink installed, messages will appear twice on receiving machines. Messages sent to specific recipients are received only once, however.

- Broadcast messages are received only on the local subnet unless routers are specifically configured to forward NetBIOS Name Query packets.

- Messages sent using the /user option are sent to each session established with the server. If a user has three sessions open with the server, the message will be received three times.

See Also

Shared Folders

---

net session

Manages sessions between a server and connected clients.

Syntax

```
net session [\\computername] [/delete]
```

Options

None
> Displays information about all sessions on the server.

\\computername
> Specifies the client whose sessions with the server you want to manage.

/delete
> Terminates the session between the server and the specified client or between the server and all clients if *computername* is unspecified. Files that were opened during the session are closed.

Examples

View current sessions on the server:

```
net session
Computer    usernames    Client Type   Opens Idle time
------------------------------------------------------
\\172.16.11.100  BACH$   W2K    1    07:04:11
\\172.16.11.104  TEST$   W2K    0    00:00:00
\\BACH    ADMINISTRATOR   W2K    1    07:02:32
\\TEST    ADMINISTRATOR   W2K    0    05:01:42
\\TEST    ADMINISTRATOR   W2K    0    07:16:08
The command completed successfully.
```

View details of the session between client *BACH* and server *TEST*:

```
net session \\bach
usernames       ADMINISTRATOR
Computer        BACH
Guest logon     No
Client type     W2K 2195
Sess time       07:04:06
Idle time       07:02:40

Share name     Type     # Opens
-----------------------------------------------
pub            Disk     1
The command completed successfully.
```

Terminate the session with *BACH*:

```
net session \\bach /delete
The session from BACH has open files.
Do you want to continue this operation? (Y/N) [N]: y
The command completed successfully.
```

Notes

- net sessions is equivalent to net session.
- A session is initiated when a client machine successfully contacts a server—for example, to access a shared folder or printer.
- A client can establish only one session with a server but can have many connections to resources on the server.
- Use net send to warn clients to save their work before terminating their connections with the server.

See Also

net file, net share, net use, net view, *Shared Folders*

---

net share

Manages shared resources.

Syntax

```
net share sharename

net share sharename=drive:path [/users:number | /unlimited]
[/remark:"text"] [/cache:Manual | Automatic | No]

net share sharename [/users:number | /unlimited] [/remark:"text"]
[/cache:Manual | Automatic | No]

net share {sharename | devicename | drive:path} /delete
```

Options

None
> A list of information about all shares on the server

sharename
> The name of the share (may differ from actual name of folder or printer shared)

drive:path
> Absolute path of a folder to share or unshare

/users:number
> Maximum number of users who can simultaneously connect to the share

/unlimited
> No limit to number of users who can simultaneously connect to the share

/remark:"text"
> Description of share

/cache
> Undocumented option for configuring share caching for offline folders

/delete
> Used to unshare (stop sharing) the share

Examples

List all shared resources on the local machine:

```
net share
Share name   Resource                    Remark
-------------------------------------------------------------
C$           C:\                         Default share
IPC$                                     Remote IPC
print$       C:\WINDOWS\System32\        Printer Drivers
             spool\drivers
H$           H:\                         Default share
ADMIN$       C:\WINDOWS                  Remote Admin
G$           G:\                         Default share
F$           F:\                         Default share
E$           E:\                         Default share
```

CertConfig	C:\CAConfig	Certificate Services configuration
CertEnroll	C:\WINDOWS\System32\ CertSrv\CertEnroll	Certificate Services share
NETLOGON	C:\WINDOWS\ sysvol \sysvol\ mtitcanada.com\SCRIPTS	Logon server share
pub	G:\pub	
SYSVOL	C:\WINDOWS\sysvol\sysvol	Logon server share
Tool	E:\Tool	
BROTHER	\\SELKIRK\BROTHER	Spooled \\SELKIRK\BROTHER
HPLaserJ	LPT1:	Spooled HP LaserJet 5L

The command completed successfully.

View details of PUB share:

net share pub

Share name	pub
Path	G:\pub
Remark	
Maximum users	No limit
Users	

The command completed successfully.

Unshare the PUB share:

net share pub /delete
Users have open files on pub. Continuing the
   operation will force the files closed.
Do you want to continue this operation? (Y/N) [N]: **y**
pub was deleted successfully.

Reshare PUB:

net share pub=G:\pub
The command completed successfully.

Notes

- Enclose the absolute path in quotes if it contains embedded spaces.
- If you delete a shared folder using net share /delete, the share may still be visible in My Computer and Windows Explorer even if you reboot. The workaround is to press F5 to flush the cached information.
- The /cache option can configure the share-caching mode to be used when offline folders are implemented (see *Files and Folders* in Chapter 4). For a full description of this option, see Knowledge Base article 214738 on Microsoft TechNet.

See Also

Files and Folders, net file, net session, net use, net view, *Shared Folders*

net start

Manages services.

Syntax

net start *service*

Options

None
> A list of services currently running on the machine

service
> The service you want to start

Examples

Display the services running on the local machine:

```
net start
These Windows services are started:
   Alerter
   Application Management
   Certificate Services
   COM+ Event System
   Computer Browser
   DHCP Client
   DHCP Server
   Distributed File System
   Distributed Link Tracking Client
   Distributed Link Tracking Server
   Distributed Transaction Coordinator
   DNS Client
   DNS Server
   Event Log
   File Replication Service
   File Server for Macintosh
   FTP Publishing Service
   IIS Admin Service
   Indexing Service
   Internet Authentication Service
   Intersite Messaging
   IPSEC Policy Agent
   Kerberos Key Distribution Center
   License Logging Service
   Logical Disk Manager
   Logical Disk Manager Administrative Service
   Message Queuing
   Messenger
   Microsoft Search
   Net Logon
   Network Connections
   Network News Transport Protocol (NNTP)
   NT LM Security Support Provider
   Plug and Play
   Print Server for Macintosh
   Print Spooler
   Protected Storage
   Remote Access Connection Manager
   Remote Procedure Call (RPC)
   Remote Procedure Call (RPC) Locator
   Remote Registry Service
   Remote Storage Engine
```

```
                  Remote Storage File
                  Remote Storage Media
                  Removable Storage
                  RunAs Service
                  SAP Agent
                  Security Accounts Manager
                  Server
                  Simple Mail Transport Protocol (SMTP)
                  Simple TCP/IP Services
                  Site Server ILS Service
                  SNMP Service
                  Still Image Service
                  System Event Notification
                  Task Scheduler
                  TCP/IP NetBIOS Helper Service
                  TCP/IP Print Server
                  Telephony
                  Windows Installer
                  Windows Internet Name Service (WINS)
                  Windows Management Instrumentation
                  Windows Management Instrumentation Driver Extensions
                  Windows Media Monitor Service
                  Windows Media Program Service
                  Windows Media Station Service
                  Windows Media Unicast Service
                  Windows Time
                  Workstation
                  World Wide Web Publishing Service
            The command completed successfully.
```

Start the Fax service:

net start "Fax Service"
```
The Fax Service service is starting.
The Fax Service service was started successfully.
```

Notes

- Use quotation marks to enclose service names containing embedded spaces.
- Starting services can have unexpected effects due to service dependencies.
- The GUI tool for managing services is the Services console.

See Also

net continue, net pause, net stop, *Services*

---

net statistics

Displays statistics for the Workstation or Server service.

Syntax

```
net statistics {workstation | server}
```

Options

None
> Lists services running for which statistics can be displayed

workstation
> Displays statistics for Workstation service

server
> Displays statistics for Server service

Examples

Display statistics for Server service:

```
net statistics server
Server Statistics for \\TEST
Statistics since 6/14/2003 4:21 PM

Sessions accepted               6
Sessions timed-out              0
Sessions errored-out            2
Kilobytes sent                  4056
Kilobytes received              7421
Mean response time (msec)       0
System errors                   0
Permission violations           0
Password violations             0
Files accessed                  3149
Communication devices accessed  0
Print jobs spooled              0
Times buffers exhausted
  Big buffers                   0
  Request buffers               0
The command completed successfully.
```

Display statistics for Workstation service:

```
net statistics workstation
Workstation Statistics for \\TEST
Statistics since 6/14/2003 4:21 PM

Bytes received                             7848390
Server Message Blocks (SMBs) received      80932
Bytes transmitted                          33602893
Server Message Blocks (SMBs) transmitted   80791
Read operations                            8338
Write operations                           70
Raw reads denied                           0
Raw writes denied                          0
Network errors                             0
Connections made                           3024
Reconnections made                         0
Server disconnects                         1
Sessions started                           214
Hung sessions                              1
Failed sessions                            0
Failed operations                          0
```

```
        Use count                          1693
        Failed use count                   3
     The command completed successfully.
```

Use more to display Server service statistics one screen at a time:

net statistics server | more

Notes

- net stats has the same result as net statistics.
- Use the net statistics command to display performance information for the specified service.

See Also

Services

---

net stop

Stops a service.

Syntax

net stop *service*

Options

service

The service you want to stop. See net start earlier in this chapter for a list of services you can start and stop.

Examples

Stop the Server service:

```
net stop server
These workstations have sessions on this server:
172.16.11.100       TEST            TEST
BACH                BACH            172.16.11.104
Do you want to continue this operation? (Y/N) [Y]: y
These workstations have sessions with open files on this server:
172.16.11.100          172.16.11.104
Do you want to continue this operation? (Y/N) [N]: y
The following services are dependent on the Server service.
Stopping the Server service will also stop these services.
   Net Logon
   Message Queuing
   Distributed File System
   Computer Browser
Do you want to continue this operation? (Y/N) [N]: n
```

Stop the Net Logon service:

```
net stop "net logon"
The Net Logon service is stopping.
The Net Logon service was stopped successfully.
```

Restart Net Logon:

```
net start "net logon"
The Net Logon service is starting.........
The Net Logon service was started successfully.
```

Notes

- Stopping a service removes its associated resources from memory.

- Whenever possible before stopping a service, pause the service first and then send a message to connected users that the service is about to be stopped. This gives users time to save their work and disconnect. See net pause and net send earlier in this chapter.

- You can't stop the Fax service as this service functions on demand and stops automatically when there are no faxes to send or receive.

See Also

net continue, net pause, net send, net start, *Services*

---

net time

Synchronizes the clock on the local machine with a time server.

Syntax

```
net time [\\computername | /domain[:domainname] |  /rtsdomain[:domainname] ]
[/set]
net time [\\computername] /querysntp
net time [\\computername] /setsntp[:ntp server list]
```

Options

None
> A display of the current date and time on the time server

\\computername
> The time server for the domain (can be any WS2003 computer)

/domain[:domainname]
> The domain where the time server resides

/rtsdomain[:domainname]
> The domain where a Reliable Time Server resides

/set
> An option forcing synchronization to occur

/querysntp
> The name of the Network Time Protocol (NTP) server for the domain

/setsntp[:ntp server list]
> A list of IP addresses or DNS names of NTP time servers for the domain

Examples

Synchronize the clock on the local machine with time server *BACH*:

```
net time \\bach /set
Current time at \\bach is 6/26/2003 11:18 PM
```

```
The current local clock is 6/26/2003 11:16 PM
Do you want to set the local computer's time to match
  the time at \\bach? (Y/N) [Y]: y
The command completed successfully.
```

Verify that the previous command worked:

net time
```
Current time at \\TEST is 6/26/2003 11:18 PM
The command completed successfully.
```

Notes

- Synchronization of clocks is important for activities such as directory replication to function properly. (Updates are timestamped to resolve collisions.)

- Use net time *timeserver* /set /yes in a logon script to synchronize the clocks of all machines with *timeserver*, which should have a reliable clock itself.

- /s no longer works for /set as it did in Windows NT.

See Also

date, time

---

net use

Manages connections with shared resources.

Syntax

```
net use [devicename | *] [\\computername\sharename[\volume]
[password | *] ] [credentials] [ [/delete] | [/persistent:{yes | no}] ]
```

where credentials represents one of:

```
[/user:[domainname\]username]
[/user:[dotted domain name\]username]
[/user:[username@dotted domain name]
net use {devicename | *} [password | *] /home
net use [/persistent:{yes | no}]
```

Options

None

A list of current network connections.

devicename

The resource to connect/disconnect. (Specify D: to Z: for drives and LPT1: to LPT3: for printers, or use an asterisk to assign the next available device name.)

computername\sharename[\volume]

The shared resource to connect/disconnect. volume represents a NetWare volume to connect/disconnect (requires Client Service for NetWare or Gateway Service for NetWare).

*[password | *]*

Password required for the resource. An asterisk causes a prompt for the password when the command is run.

/user:[domainname\]username

Domain to connect from and username to use for establishing the connection (if required). If *domainname* is omitted, the current logon domain is used.

/delete

Termination of the connection. (If an asterisk is used for the connection, all network connections are disconnected.)

*/home[password | *]*

Connection of a user to the home directory.

/persistent:[yes | no]

yes makes the connection being made and subsequent connections persistent (saves them and restores them at next logon). no makes the connection being made and subsequent connections nonpersistent, but existing persistent connections remain so (use /delete to remove persistent connections).

Examples

Display a list of currently connected mapped network drives:

```
net use
New connections will be remembered.
Status  Local  Remote           Network
-------------------------------------------------
OK      I:     \\leonardo\swynk    Microsoft Windows Network
OK      J:     \\leonardo\transfer  Microsoft Windows Network
The command completed successfully.
```

Notice that all connections are currently persistent.

View details of *I.* connection.

```
net use I:
Local name      I:
Remote name     \\leonardo\swynk
Resource type   Disk
Status          OK
# Opens         0
# Connections   1
The command completed successfully.
```

Display a list of connections on server *BACH*:

```
net view \\bach
Shared resources at \\bach
Share name  Type  Used as  Comment
-------------------------------------------------
NETLOGON    Disk           Logon server share
one         Disk
source      Disk
SYSVOL      Disk           Logon server share
test2       Disk
test3       Disk
y1          Disk
y2          Disk
y3          Disk
The command completed successfully.
```

Map the drive letter *P:* to the share TEST2 on *BACH*:

net use p: \\bach\test2
The command completed successfully.

Disconnect mapped drive *P:* previously connected:

net use p: /delete
p: was deleted successfully.

Notes

- Use quotes to enclose *computername* if it contains embedded spaces.
- You can't disconnect from a share if it is your current drive or if it is locked by an active process.

See Also

net file, net session, net share, net view, *Shared Folders*

---

net user

Manages user accounts.

Syntax

```
net user [username [password | *] [options] ] [/domain]
net user username {password | *} /add [options] [/domain]
net user username [/delete] [/domain]
```

Options

None
> Lists user accounts on computer or domain (see /domain later in this list).

*username [password | *] [options]*
> Indicates user account (up to 20 characters long) and password (up to 127 characters long) to manage. An asterisk prompts for a password when the command is run. *options* specifies account options, which can include:

/active:[no | yes]
> Enables or disables the account (enabled is default).

/comment:"text"
> Indicates a descriptive comment up to 48 characters long.

/countrycode:nnn
> Uses country/region codes to specify language file for user's Help and error messages (use 0 for default country/region code).

/expires:[date | never]
> Represents the account expiration date (use mm/dd/yy, dd/mm/yy, or mmm,dd,yy format depending on the country/region code).

/fullname:"name"
> Indicates the user's full name.

/homedir:path
> Indicates path to user's home directory.

/passwordchg:[yes | no]
> Specifies whether users can change their password (default is yes).

/passwordreq:[yes | no]
> Specifies whether a password is required (default is yes).

/profilepath:[path]
> Indicates path to user's logon profile.

/scriptpath:path
> Indicates path to user's logon script, which must be relative to:
>
> `%Systemroot%\System32\Repl\Import\Scripts`

/times:[times | all]
> Represents logon hours allowed. Use:
>
> `day[-day][,day[-day]] ,time [-time][,time[-time]]`
>
> in one-hour time increments with days spelled out or abbreviated as `M,T,W,Th,F,Sa,Su` and hours in 12- or 24-hour notation). Using a null (blank) value means the user can never log on.

/usercomment:"text"
> Specifies the "user comment" for the account.

*/workstations:{computername[,...] | *}*
> Specifies up to eight workstations from which the user can log on (separate using commas). An asterisk means the user can log on from any machine.

/domain
> Manages domain accounts.

/add [options]
> Adds the account (see earlier in this list for options).

/delete
> Removes the account.

Examples

Display a list of user accounts on a domain controller *TEST*:

```
net user
User accounts for \\TEST

-------------------------------------------------------
Administrator        Guest            ILS_ANONYMOUS_USER
IUSR_MS3             IUSR_TEST        IWAM_MS3
IWAM_TEST            krbtgt           mktulloch
NetShowServices      sally            TsInternetUser
The command completed successfully.
```

If you execute the previous command on a WS2003 machine, you need to add the /domain switch.

View details of user account Sally:

```
net user sally
usernames            sally
Full Name            sally
Comment
User's comment
Country code         000 (System Default)
Account active       Yes
```

```
Account expires          Never
Password last set        6/23/2003 11:56 AM
Password expires         8/5/2003 10:44 AM
Password changeable      6/23/2003 11:56 AM
Password required        Yes
User may change password Yes
Workstations allowed     All
Logon script
User profile
Home directory
Last logon               Never
Logon hours allowed      All
Local Group Memberships
Global Group memberships *support            *Domain Users
The command completed successfully.
```

Add user account *fredp* (for Fred Penner) with high security password KDj59Pw8, allowing the user to log on between 8 a.m. and 5 p.m. from Monday to Friday, prohibiting the user from changing his password himself, and restricting the user to logging on from the workstation named *PRO115*:

net user fredp KDj59Pw8 /add /fullname:"Fred Penner"
    /times:M-F,8am-5pm /passwordchg:no
    /workstations:PRO115
The command completed successfully.

Since you entered a different password from the one Fred requested, you need to change it:

net user fredp *
Type a password for the user:********
Retype the password to confirm:********
The command completed successfully.

Generate a report listing all users in the computer's primary domain:

net user /domain > users.txt

Notes

net users has the same effect as net user.

See Also

net accounts, net group, net localgroup, *Users*

---

net view

Lists domains, computers, and shared resources.

Syntax

```
net view [\\computername [/cache] | /domain[:domainname] ]
net view /network:nw [\\computername]
```

Options

None
    Lists computers in current domain.

\\computername

Represents the computer whose shared resources you want to display.

/domain[:domainname]

Represents the domain whose available computers you want to display. (To display all domains on the network, just omit *domainname*.)

/network:nw

Shows available servers on a NetWare network or, if a computer name is specified, the resources available on that computer.

Examples

List all available computers in current domain:

```
net view
Server Name            Remark
---------------------------------------------
\\TEST                 Hello
The command completed successfully.
```

List all available domains:

```
net view /domain
Domain
---------------------------------------------
MTIT
MTITCANADA
MTITCORP
MTITWORLD
The command completed successfully.
```

List available computers in *MTITWORLD* domain:

```
net view /domain:mtitworld
Server Name            Remark
---------------------------------------------
\\BACH
The command completed successfully.
```

List shared resources on *BACH* in *MTITWORLD* domain:

```
net view \\bach
Shared resources at \\bach
Share name   Type    Used as   Comment
---------------------------------------------
NETLOGON     Disk              Logon server share
one          Disk
source       Disk
SYSVOL       Disk              Logon server share
test2        Disk
test3        Disk
y1           Disk
y2           Disk
y3           Disk
The command completed successfully.
```

You can get the same result with:

```
net view \\bach.mtitworld.com
```

You can also use the computer's IP address.

Command Reference

Notes

If you try to view the shared resources on a computer and get a System Error 51 or 53 message, File and Printer Sharing for Microsoft Networks isn't enabled on the computer or its appropriate network interface.

See Also

net file, net session, net share, net use, *Shared Folders*

---

netsh

Configures networking services from the command line.

Description

This group of commands enables command-line administration of networking services such as DHCP, DNS, Routing and Remote Access, and WINS. NetShell (*netsh.exe*) is a command-line scripting tool that can administer these services on local or remote computers in both interactive and batch mode. It provides a shell from which you can enter different contexts for administering each service. Contexts are provided by helper DLLs, which extend NetShell's functionality by providing service-specific command sets. Some contexts have subcontexts as well, which are described in the following entries.

NetShell supports two kinds of commands:

Global commands
> These can be run within any context and provide general functionality to the shell.

Context-specific commands
> These are commands specific to a given context (see later in this section and in the following entries).

The various contexts and subcontexts currently supported by NetShell include the following:

AAAA
> Configures the AAAA component that is used by both Routing and Remote Access and Internet Authentication Service

DHCP
> Configures DHCP servers

> *Server*
>> Subcontext for configuring a specific DHCP server

Interface
>> Configures demand-dial interfaces

> *IP*   Subcontext for configuring IP demand-dial interfaces

RAS   Configures remote-access servers

> *IP, IPX, NETBEUI, Appletalk, AAAA*
>> Possible subcontexts for configuring RAS

Routing
> Configures IP and IPX routing

> *IP, IPX*
>> Possible subcontexts for configuring routing

WINS
> Configures WINS servers

NetShell can be run in two command modes:

Interactive (online) mode
> Commands typed at the NetShell prompt (netsh>) are executed immediately.

Batch (offline) mode
> Commands typed at the NetShell prompt are collected and then run as a batch job using the commit command. Note that this is only for router-configuration commands in the routing context.

In addition, you can create a text file containing a script of NetShell commands and then run the script using the -f switch or exec command (see netsh–Global Context).

Syntax

```
netsh [-a Aliasfile] [-c Context] [-r RemoteComputer] [command |
    -f Scriptfile]
```

Options

-a Aliasfile
> Specifies an alias file to use. It is a file containing a list of NetShell commands together with an alias to allow the commands to be used by just typing the alias name (useful for mapping commands on other platforms, such as Unix, to specific NetShell commands).

-c Context
> Opens the NetShell shell and switches immediately to the specified context.

-r RemoteComputer
> Specifies the remote computer on which NetShell commands are to be executed. The computer can be specified using its computer name (NetBIOS or DNS name) or IP address. If this option is omitted, the commands are executed on the local computer.

command
> Specifies any NetShell global command to be executed immediately (see the following "*Examples*" section).

-f Scriptfile
> Runs the NetShell commands found in the file *Scriptfile* (include path).

Examples

Open the NetShell shell:

```
C:\>netsh
netsh>
```

Open the NetShell shell in the DHCP context to configure DHCP interactively:

```
C:\>netsh -c dhcp
dhcp>
```

Open the NetShell shell, switch to the IP subcontext of the Interface context, obtain IP address information about the network interface, and return to the command shell:

```
C:\>netsh -r 172.16.11.104 -c interface ip show address
Configuration for interface "Local Area Connection"
```

Command Reference

```
      DHCP enabled:           No
      IP Address:             172.16.11.104
      SubnetMask:             255.255.255.0
      Default Gateway:        172.16.11.196
      GatewayMetric:          1
      InterfaceMetric:        1
 C:\>
```

netsh/Global Context

Commands available in every NetShell context.

Subcontexts

AAAA
DHCP
Interface
RAS
Routing
WINS

Commands

..   Returns to previous context.

?   Displays help for this context.

aaaa
> Enters the AAAA context (see the next entry).

abort
> Discards any changes made while in offline mode.

add helper DLLfilename
> Installs a new helper DLL to extend the functionality of NetShell. The DLLs included are:

> *Aaaamon.dll*
>> AAAA component DLL

> *Dhcpmon.dll*
>> DHCP server DLL

> *Ifmon.dll*
>> Interface DLL

> *Ipmontr.dll*
>> Routing DLL

> *Rasmontr.dll*
>> Remote-access server DLL

> *Winsmon.dll*
>> WINS server DLL

alias [aliasname [[string]...]]
> Displays all aliases or the specified alias, or assigns string values to the specified alias.

bye
> Exits the shell (can also use quit or exit).

commit
> Commits NetShell router commands collected in offline mode and sends them to the router.

delete helper DLLfilename
> Removes an installed Helper DLL.

dhcp
> Enters the DCHP context (see below).

dump filename
> Dumps or appends the configuration to the specified text file.

exec scriptfile
> Executes a text file containing a series of NetShell commands.

interface
> Enters the Interface context (see below).

offline
> Changes to offline mode. All router commands entered into the shell are collected and can later be sent to the router using the commit or online commands.

online
> Changes to online mode. All commands entered into the shell are executed immediately.

popd
> Pops a context from the stack.

pushd
> Pushes current context onto the stack.

ras
> Enters the RAS context (see below).

router
> Enters the Routing context (see below).

set machine
> Sets the current machine on which to operate.

set mode [mode=[offline | online]]
> Changes the NetShell mode.

show [alias | helper | mode]
> Shows all defined aliases, installed Helper DLLs, or the current NetShell mode.

unalias aliasname
> Removes an alias.

wins
> Enters the WINS context (see below).

Examples

First use Notepad to create a text file called *Script.txt*, containing the following NetShell commands, to display the authentication mode and types currently enabled on a remote-access server:

```
ras
show authmode
show authtype
..
```

Now start the NetShell shell:

```
C:>netsh
```

Check that you are in Online mode:

```
netsh>show mode
online
```

Run the script:

```
netsh>exec C:\script.txt
authentication mode = standard
Enabled Authentication Types:
Code            Meaning
------------------------------------------
MSCHAP          Microsoft Challenge-Handshake
   Authentication Protocol.
MSCHAPv2        Microsoft Challenge-Handshake
   Authentication Protocol version 2.
netsh>
```

If you are in the command shell, you can run the script directly:

```
C:\>netsh -f Script.txt
```

Notes

- There is supposed to be a flush command for removing commands collected in offline mode, but it doesn't seem to work in the current release.
- The dump command outputs the current configuration of NetShell-configurable services on the machine as a series of NetShell commands. The dumped file can then be run on a different machine using the exec command to configure that machine identically to the first. The only problem is that a number of the configuration settings aren't dumped properly! See Knowledge Base article 254252 on Microsoft TechNet for how to edit the dump file manually to fix it.

netsh/AAAA context

Configures Internet Authentication Services (IAS), which is the Microsoft implementation of Remote Authentication Dial-In User Service (RADIUS). The AAAA stands here for "authentication, authorization, auditing, and accounting" (and has nothing to do with the AAAA record of DNS as defined in RFC 1886!).

Subcontexts

None

Commands

In addition to global context commands, the following additional commands are available in this context:

set config blob=data
   data sets the configuration of the aaaa engine and must be in Base64 format (as, for instance, that dumped by the show command)

show [config | version]
   Dumps the configuration of the aaaa engine in Base64 form or displays the version of the engine (currently Version 0)

Examples

```
C:\>netsh
netsh>aaaa
aaaa>show config

# aaaa configuration script.
# Known Issues and limitations:
# Import/Export between different versions is not be supported.
# IAS.MDB Version = 0
pushd aaaa
set config blob=\
/bEAAAEAAFNOYW4AZGFyZCBKZXQIIERCAZAAtW4DAGJgCcJV6alnAHJAPwCcfp+QAP+FmjHF\
ebrtADC838ydY9nkAMOfRvuKvE7nAHTsNzzLnPqnANEo5nI5imA1ABt7NpT937EWAHsTQ64g\
...
...
A7ACI/wD\
\
*
popd
# End of aaaa show config
aaaa>
```

netsh/DHCP Context

Configures DHCP servers.

Subcontexts

> Server
> Scope
> Mscope

Commands

list
> Lists available DHCP commands (more verbose than help).

dump
> Dumps the configuration of the DHCP server as a series of NetShell commands.

add server [servername | serveraddress]
> Adds a DHCP server to the list of authorized DHCP servers stored in Active Directory. You can specify either the DNS name or IP address of the server.

delete server [servername | serveraddress]
> Removes a DHCP server from the list of authorized DHCP servers.

show server
> Lists all authorized DHCP servers in the current domain.

server [\\servername | serveraddress]
> Enters the subcontext for the specified DHCP server, which enables you to configure the DHCP server using the add, delete, initiate, scope, mscope, set, and show commands. These commands and their options are summarized in Table 5-8.

Note that the scope and mscope commands enter new subcontexts. The Scope context configures a specific scope on the server, and Mscope configures multicast scopes. The commands available in these subcontexts are shown in Tables 5-9 and 5-10.

You can tell what context you are currently in by the command prompt during a NetShell session. For example:

```
C:\>netsh
netsh>dhcp
dhcp>server \\mydhcp
dhcp server>
```

In the previous example, you move from the Windows command shell to the NetShell global context (netsh>), then to the DHCP context (dhcp>), and finally to the DHCP server context (dhcp server>), which is a subcontext for a particular DHCP server. From here, you could move deeper into the subcontext of a particular scope on the specified server and so on.

Table 5-8. Commands available in DHCP Server subcontext

Command	Option	Description
add	class	Adds a new class
	mscope	Adds a new multicast scope
	optiondef	Adds a new option
	scope	Adds a scope
delete	class	Deletes a class
	mscope	Deletes a multicast scope
	optiondef	Deletes an option
	optionvalue	Deletes an option value
	scope	Deletes a scope
	superscope	Deletes a superscope
initiate	auth	Reauthorizes the server
	reconcile	Reconciles the DHCP database
mscope	mscope-name	Switches to specified mscope
scope	scope-ip-address	Switches to specified scope
set	auditlog	Configures audit log settings
	databasebackupinterval	Specifies database backup interval
	databasebackuppath	Specifies database backup path
	databasecleanupinterval	Specifies database cleanup interval
	databaseloggingflag	Resets flag for database logging
	databasename	Specifies name of database file
	databasepath	Specifies path of database file
	databaserestoreflag	Resets flag for database restore
	detectconflictretry	Specifies conflict detection attempts
	dnsconfig	Configures Dynamic DNS settings
	optionvalue	Configures global option value

Table 5-8. Commands available in DHCP Server subcontext (continued)

Command	Option	Description
	server	Specifies the current DHCP server
	userclass	Specifies the global user class name
	vendorclass	Specifies the global vendor class name
show	all	Displays all DHCP server settings
	auditlog	Displays the audit log settings
	bindings	Displays bindings
	class	Lists available classes
	detectconflictretry	Displays detect-conflict-retry settings
	dnsconfig	Displays Dynamic DNS settings
	mibinfo	Displays MIB information
	mscope	Lists multicast scopes
	optiondef	Displays DHCP options
	optionvalue	Displays configured option values
	scope	Lists all available scopes
	server	Displays current server
	dbproperties	Displays database configuration
	serverstatus	Shows current status of server
	userclass	Displays current user class name
	vendorclass	Displays current vendor class name
	version	Displays server version number
	optiondef	Deletes an option

Table 5-9. Commands available in DHCP Server Scope subcontext

Command	Option	Description
add	excluderange	Specifies an exclusion
	iprange	Specifies an IP address range
	reservedip	Creates a new reservation
delete	excluderange	Removes an exclusion
	iprange	Removes an IP address range
	optionvalue	Deletes a scope option value
	reservedip	Deletes a reservation
	reservedoptionvalue	Deletes a reservation option value
initiate	reconcile	Reconciles current scope
set	comment	Specifies a comment
	name	Specifies scope name
	optionvalue	Specifies an option value
	reservedoptionvalue	Specifies a reserved option value
	scope	Specifies the current scope
	state	Toggles current scope active/inactive
	superscope	Specifies the current superscope
show	clients	Lists available Version 4 clients

Command Reference

Table 5-9. Commands available in DHCP Server Scope subcontext (continued)

Command	Option	Description
	clientsv5	Lists available Version 5 clients
	excluderange	Lists configured exclusions
	iprange	Lists configured IP address ranges
	optionvalue	Lists configured option values
	reservedip	Lists configured reservations
	reservedoptionvalue	Lists configured reserved option values
	scope	Displays current scope
	state	Displays state of current scope

Table 5-10. Commands available in DHCP Server Mscope subcontext

Command	Option	Description
add	excluderange	Specifies an exclusion
	iprange	Specifies an IP address range
delete	excluderange	Removes an exclusion
	iprange	Removes an IP address range
initiate	reconcile	Reconciles current scope
set	comment	Specifies a comment
	lease	Specifies lease duration
	mscope	Specifies the current scope
	name	Specifies scope name
	state	Toggles current scope active/inactive
	ttl	Specifies time-to-live (TTL) value
show	clients	Lists available clients
	excluderange	Lists configured exclusions
	iprange	Lists configured IP address ranges
	lease	Shows current lease duration
	mibinfo	Displays MIB information
	mscope	Displays current scope
	state	Displays state of current scope
	ttl	Displays time-to-live (TTL) value

Examples

Configure the scope on the DHCP server with IP address 172.16.11.104:

```
C:\>netsh
netsh>dhcp
dhcp>server 172.16.11.104
dhcp server>show scope
=========================================================
Scope Address  - Subnet Mask   - State   - Scope Name
=========================================================
172.16.11.0    - 255.255.255.0  -Active   -Building 14
```

```
        Total No. of Scopes = 1
        Command completed successfully.
```

Switch to subcontext of the defined scope:

```
    dhcp server>scope 172.16.11.0
    Changed the current scope context to 172.16.11.0 scope.
```

Show the range of IP addresses in the current scope:

```
    dhcp server scope>show iprange
    ===========================================================
    Start Address    -    End Address    -    Address Type
    ===========================================================
    172.16.11.220    -    172.16.11.240    -    DHCP ONLY
    No. of IPRanges : 1 in the Scope : 172.16.11.0.
    Command completed successfully.
```

Show addresses excluded from the scope:

```
    dhcp server scope>show excluderange
    =========================================
       Start Address    -    End Address
    =========================================
       172.16.11.233    -    172.16.11.233
    No. of ExcludeRanges : 1 in the Scope : 172.16.11.0.
    Command completed successfully.
```

To exclude the addresses 172.16.11.236 through 172.16.11.238 from the scope, first check the syntax for adding an exclusion range:

```
    dhcp server scope>add excluderange ?
    To exclude a range of IP addresses from distribution by the scope.
    Syntax:
      add excluderange StartIP EndIP
    Parameters:
      StartIP        - The starting IP address of the
                       exclusion range.
      EndIP          - The ending IP address of the
                       exclusion range.
    Example:       add excluderange 10.2.2.10 10.2.2.20
    This command excludes IP addresses in the range 10.2.2.10 to 10.2.2.20 from
    distribution in the scope.
```

Exclude the addresses:

```
    dhcp server scope>add excluderange 172.16.11.236 172.16.11.238
    Command completed successfully.
```

Verify the results:

```
    dhcp server scope>show excluderange
    =========================================
       Start Address    -    End Address
    =========================================
       172.16.11.233    -    172.16.11.233
       172.16.11.236    -    172.16.11.238
    No. of ExcludeRanges : 2 in the Scope : 172.16.11.0.
    Command completed successfully.
```

Quit the NetShell shell:

```
    dhcp server scope>quit
    C:\>
```

Notes

- You must be a member of the Enterprise Admins group to configure DHCP servers.
- NetShell's DHCP context is particularly useful for managing remote DHCP servers over slow WAN links where using the remote-administration Terminal Server mode to run the GUI DHCP management tool would result in poor performance.

See Also

DHCP

netsh/Interface Context

Configures router interfaces for Routing and Remote Access Service.

Subcontexts

IP

Commands

add interface name=iname type=[tunnel | full]
Adds an interface to the router, specifying its name (*iname*) and type (tunnel for VPN interfaces and full for demand-dial interfaces). The name of the interface must be in quotes if it contains spaces.

delete interface name=iname
Removes the specified interface.

dump
Dumps the configuration of the interfaces for the Routing and Remote Access Service as a series of NetShell commands.

ip   Switches to the IP subcontext to further configure IP interfaces on the router. The commands available in this subcontext are listed in Table 5-11.

reset all
Resets the router configuration by deleting all interfaces.

set credentials name=iname user=username domain=domainname password=password
Specifies the credentials needed to connect to an interface.

set interface name=iname admin=[enabled | disabled] connect=[connected | disconnected] [newname=newiname]
Sets the current state of the WAN interface called iname to either enabled or disabled. If connected is specified, the interface is automatically enabled. newiname is used only for renaming the default LAN interface.

show credentials name=iname
Displays the credentials needed to connect to each interface.

show interface [name=iname]
Displays the name, type, and current state of each interface on the router. If no name is specified, all interfaces are displayed.

Table 5-11. Commands available in Interface IP subcontext

Command	Option	Description
add	address	Adds IP address
	dns	Adds static DNS server address
	wins	Adds static WINS server address
delete	address	Deletes IP address or default gateway
	arpcache	Flushes ARP cache
	dns	Removes DNS settings
	wins	Removes WINS settings
dump		Dumps configuration as netsh commands
set	address	Specifies IP address or default gateway
	dns	Specifies DNS server mode and addresses
	wins	Specifies WINS server mode and addresses
show	address	Lists all addresses
	config	Lists IP addresses and configuration settings
	dns	Lists addresses of DNS servers
	icmp	Displays ICMP statistics
	interface	Displays interface statistics
	ipaddress	Lists IP addresses
	ipnet	Lists net-to-media mappings
	ipstats	Displays statistics for IP addresses
	joins	Lists joined multicast groups
	offload	Lists offload information
	tcpconn	Lists TCP connections
	tcpstats	Displays TCP statistics
	udpconn	Lists UDP connections
	udpstats	Displays UDP statistics
	wins	Lists addresses of WINS servers

Examples

Display interfaces on router:

```
C:\>netsh
netsh>interface
interface>show interface
Admin State     State       Type            Interface Name
-------------------------------------------------------
Enabled     Connected   Loopback        Loopback
Enabled     Connected   Internal        Internal
Enabled     Connected   Dedicated       Local Area Connection
```

Switch to IP subcontext and view details of interfaces:

```
interface>ip
interface ip>show interface
MIB-II Interface Information
-------------------------------------------------------
```

Command
Reference

```
        Index:                          1
        User-friendly Name:             Loopback
        GUID Name:                      Loopback
        Type:                           Loopback
        MTU:                            32768
        Speed:                          10000000
        Physical Address:
        Admin Status:                   Up
        Operational Status:             Operational
        Last Change:                    0
        In Octets:                      0
        In Unicast Packets:             0
        In Non-unicast Packets:         0
        In Packets Discarded:           0
        In Erroneous Packets:           0
        In Unknown Protocol Packets:    0
        Out Octets:                     0
        Out Unicast Packets:            0
        Out Non-unicast Packets:        0
        Out Packets Discarded:          0
        Out Erroneous Packets:          0
        Output Queue Length:            0
        Description:                    Internal loopback interface for
                                        127.0.0 network


        Index:                          2
        User-friendly Name:             Local Area Connection
        GUID Name:                      {54414D01-02DA-4783-B931-C9AC7A70EDDD}
        Type:                           Ethernet
        MTU:                            1500
        Speed:                          10000000
        Physical Address:               00-00-B4-A0-47-74
        Admin Status:                   Up
        Operational Status:             Operational
        Last Change:                    0
        In Octets:                      4722820
        In Unicast Packets:             16263
        In Non-unicast Packets:         6698
        In Packets Discarded:           0
        In Erroneous Packets:           0
        In Unknown Protocol Packets:    8151
        Out Octets:                     2970151
        Out Unicast Packets:            21769
        Out Non-unicast Packets:        3745
        Out Packets Discarded:          0
        Out Erroneous Packets:          0
        Output Queue Length:            0
        Description:                    Realtek RTL8029(AS) Ethernet Adapt
        (Microsoft's Packet Scheduler)
```

Display IP address info for "Local Area Connection" interface:

```
        interface ip>show address "Local Area Connection"
        Configuration for interface "Local Area Connection"
```

```
DHCP enabled:                    No
IP Address:                      172.16.11.104
SubnetMask:                      255.255.255.0
Default Gateway:                 172.16.11.196
GatewayMetric:                   1
InterfaceMetric:                 1
```

Before adding a second IP address for this interface, first check the syntax for the add address command:

```
interface ip>add address ?
Usage: add address [name=]string [[addr=]IP address
  [mask=]IP subnet mask][[gateway=]IP address
  [gwmetric=]integer]
Parameters:
    name       - The name of the IP interface.
    addr       - The IP address to be added for
                 the interface.
    mask       - The IP subnet mask for the
                 specified IP address.
    gateway    - The default gateway for the
                 specified IP address.
    gwmetric   - The metric to the default
                 gateway.
Remarks: Adds IP addresses and default gateways to an interface configured
with static IP addresses.
Examples:
add address "Local Area Connection" 10.0.0.2 255.0.0.0
add address "Local Area Connection" gateway-10.0.0.3
  gwmetric=2
The first command adds a static IP address of 10.0.0.2 with a subnet mask of
255.0.0.0 to the Local Area Connection interface. The second command adds
the IP address of 10.0.0.3 as a second default gateway for this interface
with a gateway metric of 2.
```

Add a second IP address 172.16.11.105 for this interface:

```
interface ip>add address "Local Area Connection" 172.16.11.105 255.255.255.0
Ok.
```

Verify the result:

```
interface ip>show address "Local Area Connection"
Configuration for interface "Local Area Connection"
    DHCP enabled:                No
    IP Address:                  172.16.11.104
    SubnetMask:                  255.255.255.0
    IP Address:                  172.16.11.105
    SubnetMask:                  255.255.255.0
    Default Gateway:             172.16.11.196
    GatewayMetric:               1
    InterfaceMetric:             1
interface ip>
```

You can also verify that the address was successfully added by accessing the TCP/IP properties sheet for this interface in the GUI:

Right-click on My Network Places → Properties → right-click on Local-Area Connection → Properties → select Internet Protocol (TCP/IP) → Properties → Advanced

Command Reference

See Also

Connections, Routing and Remote Access

---

netsh/RAS Context

Configures a remote-access server.

Subcontexts

> AAAA
> Appletalk
> IP
> IPX
> NETBEUI

Only commands for the IP subcontext are covered in this section. For a list of commands in a different subcontext, switch to that subcontext and type **help**.

Commands

aaaa
> Switches to AAAA subcontext.

add authtype type=[PAP | SPAP | MD5CHAP | MSCHAP | MSCHAPv2 | EAP]
> Specifies additional types of authentication the RAS server can negotiate.

add link type=[SWC | LCP]
> Specifies additional link properties that can be used for PPP negotiation.

add multilink type=[MULTI | BACP]
> Specifies additional multilink types that can be used for PPP negotiation.

add registeredserver name=domainname server=RASservername
> Registers the RAS server in Active Directory.

appletalk
> Switches to Appletalk subcontext.

delete [authtype | link | multilink | registeredserver] [options]
> Removes a RAS authentication, PPP link, or PPP multilink type or unregisters a RAS server in Active Directory (see the add commands earlier in this list for the syntax).

dump
> Dumps the configuration of the remote-access server as a series of NetShell commands.

ip   Switches to IP subcontext. The commands available in this subcontext are listed in Table 5-12.

ipx   Switches to IPX subcontext.

netbeui
> Switches to NETBEUI subcontext.

set authmode mode=[STANDARD | NODCC | BYPASS]
> STANDARD means all clients must be authenticated, NODCC bypasses authentication for direct cable connections, and BYPASS means authentication isn't required for any type of device.

set tracing component=componentname state=[ENABLED | DISABLED]
> Turns extended tracing on or off for the specified component (use an asterisk to represent all components).

set usernames=username dialin=[PERMIT | DENY | POLICY] [cbpolicy=[NONE | CALLER | ADMIN] cbnumber=callbacknumber]
> Configures the RAS properties for the specified user, including whether the user is specifically allowed or denied the right to dial in, whether this is determined by the remote-access policy, and whether the user can use callback when dialing in.

show activeservers
> Causes the server to listen for RAS server advertisements.

show authmode
> Displays the current authentication mode of the RAS server.

show authtype
> Displays the authentication types currently enabled on the server.

show client
> Lists RAS clients currently connected to the server.

show link
> Displays the types of link properties that the server currently uses for PPP negotiation.

show multilink
> Displays the types of multilink types that the server currently uses for PPP negotiation.

show registeredserver domain=domainname server=RASservername
> Verifies whether the specified RAS server is registered in Active Directory for that domain.

show tracing component=componentname
> Displays whether extended tracing is enabled for the specified component. (If no component is specified, then the state of tracing is displayed for all components.)

show usernames=username mode=[PERMIT | REPORT]
> Displays the RAS settings for the specified user—or for all users, if no username is specified. PERMIT displays only those users whose dial-in setting is currently set to PERMIT, while REPORT displays all users in the current domain.

Table 5-12. Commands available in RAS IP subcontext

Command	Option	Description
add	Range	Specifies address ranges for static address pool
delete	Pool	Removes all ranges from static address pool
	Range	Removes specified range from static address pool
dump		Dumps configuration as netsh commands
set	Access	Gives RAS clients access to network beyond RAS server
	Addrassign	Specifies method RAS server assigns addresses to RAS clients
	Addrreq	Allows RAS clients to request addresses from RAS server
	Negotiation	Enables IP negotiation for RAS client connections
show	Config	Displays current configuration of RAS server

Examples

Enter RAS context of NetShell:

```
C:\>netsh
netsh>ras
ras>
```

Display the authentication mode and types currently configured on the server:

```
ras>show authmode
authentication mode = standard
ras>show authtype
Enabled Authentication Types:
Code            Meaning
-------------------------------------------
MSCHAP          Microsoft Challenge-Handshake
                    Authentication Protocol.
MSCHAPv2        Microsoft Challenge-Handshake
                    Authentication Protocol version 2.
```

Check whether the RAS server *test.mtitcanada.com* is registered in Active Directory:

```
ras>show registeredserver domain=mtitcanada.com server=test
The following RAS server is registered:
  RAS Server:  test
  Domain:      mtitcanada.com
```

Check if user Sally is currently allowed to dial in to the RAS server:

```
ras>show usernames=sally
usernames:              sally
Dialin:                 policy
Callback policy:        none
Callback number:
```

The default remote-access policy denies all users RAS dial-in permission, so specifically assign Sally this permission and enable callback:

```
ras>set usernames=sally dialin=permit cbpolicy=admin cbnumber=555-777-1212
usernames:              sally
Dialin:                 permit
Callback policy:        admin
Callback number:        555-777-1212
```

Switch to the IP subcontext:

```
ras>ip
ras ip>
```

Show the IP configuration of the RAS server (this isn't the IP address of the server's interface, but rather how it provides clients with IP addresses when they connect):

```
ras ip>show config
RAS IP config
  Negotiation mode:     allow
  Access mode:          all
  Address request mode: deny
  Assignment method:    auto
  Pool:
```

Notes

Use the set user command in a batch file or script to automatically configure RAS dial-in settings for a collection of users.

See Also

Connections, Routing and Remote Access

netsh/Routing Context

Configures a router (a multihomed computer with the Routing and Remote Access Service installed and enabled).

Subcontexts

IP   autodhcp

        dnsproxy

        IGMP

        NAT

        OSPF

        Relay

        RIP

IPX   NETBIOS

        RIP

        sap

Only commands for the IP subcontext are covered in this section. For a list of commands in the IPX subcontext, switch to that subcontext and type **help**.

Commands

dump
> Dumps the configuration of the router as a series of NetShell commands.

ip   Switches to IP subcontext. The commands available in this subcontext are listed in Table 5-13. Within the IP subcontext are the following deeper subcontexts: autodhcp, dnsproxy, IGMP, NAT, OSPF, Relay, and RIP. The commands for these subcontexts are listed in Tables 5-14 through 5-20.

ipx   Switches to IPX subcontext.

reset
> Resets the IP address configuration of the router to a clean state.

show helper
> Details IP and IPX Helper DLLs for the routing context.

Table 5-13. Commands available in Routing IP subcontext

Command	Option	Description
add/delete/ set/show	interface	Adds/deletes/specifies/displays routing settings
	filter	Adds/deletes/specifies/displays packet filters
	rtmroute	Adds/deletes/specifies/displays nonpersistent routes

Table 5-13. Commands available in Routing IP subcontext (continued)

Command	Option	Description
	persistentroute	Adds/deletes/specifies/displays persistent routes
	preference- forprotocol	Adds/deletes/specifies/displays preference level
	scope	Adds/deletes/specifies/displays multicast scope
add/delete/ show	boundary	Adds/deletes/displays multicast boundary settings
add/set	ipiptunnel	Adds/specifies IP-in-IP interface
autodhcp		Switches to routing IP autodhcp subcontext (see Table 5-14)
dnsproxy		Switches to routing IP dnsproxy subcontext (see Table 5-15)
igmp		Switches to routing IP IGMP subcontext (see Table 5-16)
nat		Switches to routing IP NAT subcontext (see Table 5-17)
ospf		Switches to routing IP OSPF subcontext (see Table 5-18)
relay		Switches to routing IP relay subcontext (see Table 5-19)
rip		Switches to routing IP RIP subcontext (see Table 5-20)
set/show	loglevel	Specifies/displays global logging level
show	helper	Lists all netsh subcontexts for IP
	protocol	Lists all running IP routing protocols
	mfe	Shows multicast forwarding entries
	mfestats	Displays entry statistics for multicast forwarding
	boundarystats	Lists all IP multicast boundaries
	rtmdestinations	Lists destinations in routing table
	rtmroutes	Lists routes in routing table

Table 5-14. Commands available in Routing IP autodhcp subcontext

Command	Option	Description
set/show	global	Specifies/displays global DHCP allocator settings
	interface	Specifies/displays DHCP allocator settings for specified interface
add/delete	exclusion	Adds/deletes an exclusion

Table 5-15. Commands available in Routing IP dnsproxy subcontext

Command	Option	Description
set/show	global	Specifies/displays global DNS proxy settings
	interface	Specifies/displays DNS proxy settings for specified interface

Table 5-16. Commands available in Routing IP IGMP subcontext

Command	Option	Description
set/show	global	Specifies/displays IGMP global settings
add/delete/ set/show	interface	Adds/deletes/specifies/displays IGMP settings on specified interface
add/delete	staticgroup	Adds/deletes static multicast group
show	grouptable	Displays IGMP host-groups table
	ifstats	Displays IGMP statistics

Table 5-16. Commands available in Routing IP IGMP subcontext

Command	Option	Description
	iftable	Displays IGMP host groups per interface
	proxygrouptable	Displays IGMP group table for proxy interface
	rasgrouptable	Displays IGMP group table for internal interface used by RAS server

Table 5-17. Commands available in Routing IP NAT subcontext

Command	Options	Description
set/show	global	Specifies/displays global NAT settings
add/delete/ set/show	interface	Adds/deletes/specifies/displays NAT settings for specified interface
add/delete	addressrange	Adds/deletes address range for public address pool
	addressmapping	Adds/deletes NAT address mapping
	portmapping	Adds/deletes NAT port mapping

Table 5-18. Commands available in Routing IP OSPF subcontext

Command	Option	Description
set/show	global	Specifies/displays global OSPF settings
add/delete/ set/show	interface	Adds/deletes/specifies/displays OSPF settings for specified interface
	area	Adds/deletes/specifies/displays an area
	virtif	Adds/deletes/specifies/displays a virtual interface
add/delete/ show	range	Adds/deletes/specifies/displays a range for an area
	neighbor	Adds/deletes/specifies/displays a neighbor
	protofilter	Adds/deletes/specifies/displays routing information sources for external routes
	routefilter	Adds/deletes/specifies/displays route filtering for external routes
show	areastats	Displays area statistics
	lsdb	Displays link-state database
	virtifstats	Displays virtual-link statistics

Table 5-19. Commands available in Routing IP Relay subcontext

Command	Option	Description
set	global	Specifies global settings for DHCP relay agent
add/delete/set	interface	Adds/deletes/specifies DHCP relay agent settings
add/delete	dhcpserver	Adds/deletes IP address for DHCP server
show	ifbinding	Displays bindings
	ifconfig	Displays DHCP relay agent settings
	ifstats	Displays statistics

Command Reference

Table 5-20. Commands available in Routing IP RIP subcontext

Command	Option	Description
set/show	flags	Specifies/displays advanced settings
	global	Specifies/displays global settings
add/delete/ set/show	interface	Adds/deletes/specifies/displays settings
add/delete	peerfilter	Adds/deletes a peer filter
	acceptfilter	Adds/deletes a route filter to/from list of accepted routes
	announcefilter	Adds/deletes a route filter to/from list of announced routes
add/delete/ show	neighbor	Adds/deletes/displays a neighbor
show	globalstats	Displays global settings
	ifbinding	Displays bindings
	ifstats	Displays statistics

Examples

Reset routing tables in router to clean configuration:

```
C:\>netsh
netsh>routing
routing>reset
routing>
```

Switch to IP subcontext and display routing table:

```
routing>ip
routing ip>show rtmroutes

Prefix  Protocol  Prf  Met  Gateway  Vw  Interface
---------------------------------------------------
0.0.0.0/0        NetMgmt  10    1  172.16.11.196  UM
   Local Area Connection
127.0.0.0/8      Local    1     1  127.0.0.1      U
   Loopback
127.0.0.1/32     Local    1     1  127.0.0.1      U
   Loopback
172.16.11.0/24   Local    1     1  172.16.11.104  UM
   Local Area Connection
172.16.11.0/24   Local    1     1  172.16.11.105  UM
   Local Area Connection
172.16.11.104/32 Local    1     1  127.0.0.1      U
   Loopback
172.16.11.105/32 Local    1     1  127.0.0.1      U
   Loopback
172.16.255.255/32 Local   1     1  172.16.11.104  UM
   Local Area Connection
172.16.255.255/32 Local   1     1  172.16.11.105  UM
   Local Area Connection
224.0.0.0/4      Local    1     1  172.16.11.104  U
   Local Area Connection
224.0.0.0/4      Local    1     1  172.16.11.105  U
   Local Area Connection
```

```
255.255.255.255/32 Local  1    1  172.16.11.104   U
    Local Area Connection
255.255.255.255/32 Local  1    1  172.16.11.105   U
    Local Area Connection
```

Show IP protocols used:

```
routing ip>show protocol
Type        Vendor       Protocol
----------------------------------------------------
General     -            Protocol Priority
General     -            Multicast Boundaries
General     -            Global Info
Multicast   Microsoft    IGMP
Unicast     MS-0000      DHCP
```

Switch to Relay subcontext, and show DHCP Relay global settings:

```
routing ip>relay
routing ip relay>show global
DHCP Relay Global Configuration Information
----------------------------------------------------
Logging Level                   : Errors Only
Max Receive Queue Size          : 1048576
Server Count                    : 0
```

See Also

Routing and Remote Access

netsh/WINS Context

Configures a WINS server.

Subcontexts

Server

Commands

dump

Dumps the configuration of the WINS server as a series of NetShell commands.

list

Lists available WINS commands (more verbose than help).

server [\\servername | serveraddress]

Enters the subcontext for the specified WINS server, which enables you to configure the WINS server using the add, check, delete, init, reset, set, and show commands. These commands and their options are summarized in Table 5-21.

Table 5-21. Commands available in WINS Server subcontext

Command	Option	Description
add	name	Registers name of WINS server
	partner	Specifies a replication partner
	pngserver	Specifies *persona non grata* servers
check	database	Verify WINS database consistency

Table 5-21. Commands available in WINS Server subcontext (continued)

Command	Option	Description
	name	Verifies a list of name records against specified servers
	version	Verifies version number consistency
delete	name	Removes a registered name from database
	partner	Removes a replication partner
	records	Removes or tombstones specified records
	owners	Removes list of owners and their records
	pngserver	Removes specified *persona non grata* servers
init	backup	Performs backup of database
	import	Imports an *lmhosts* file
	pull	Sends a pull trigger to specified server
	pullrange	Pulls specified records from specified server
	push	Sends a push trigger to specified server
	replicate	Replicates with replication partners
	restore	Restores database from a file
	scavenge	Initiates database scavenging
	search	Searches database for specified server
reset	statistics	Resets server statistics
set	autopartnerconfig	Configures automatic-replication partner- configuration settings
	backuppath	Configures backup settings
	burstparam	Cnofigures burst-handling settings
	logparam	Configures database and event-logging settings
	migrateflag	Sets migration flag
	namerecord	Configures interval and timeout settings
	periodicdbchecking	Configures periodic database-checking settings
	pullpartnerconfig	Configures settings for specified pull partner
	pushpartnerconfig	Configures settings for specified push partner
	pullparam	Configures default pull settings
	pushparam	Configures default push settings
	replicateflag	Sets replication flag
	startversion	Specifies start version ID
show	browser	Displays active domain master browser
	database	Lists records in database
	info	Displays configuration settings
	name	Displays detailed info for a specified record
	partner	Lists pull or push (or both) partners
	partnerproperties	Displays default partner configuration
	pullpartnerconfig	Displays configuration settings for pull partner
	pushpartnerconfig	Displays configuration settings for push partner
	reccount	Displays number of records owned by specified server
	recbyversion	Displays records owned by specified server
	server	Displays current WINS server

Table 5-21. Commands available in WINS Server subcontext (continued)

Command	Option	Description
	statistics	Displays statistics
	version	Displays current version counter value
	versionmap	Displays owner ID-to-maximum version number mappings

Examples

Open a NetShell shell, and switch to the subcontext of a WINS server with IP address
172.16.11.104:

```
C:\>netsh
netsh>wins
wins>server \\172.16.11.104
***You have Read and Write access to the server 172.16.11.104***
```

Display configuration settings of WINS server:

```
wins server>show info

WINS Database backup parameter
~~~~~~~~~~~~~~~~~~~~~~~~~~~~~~~~~~~~~~~~~~~~~~~~~~~~~~~~
Backup Dir                          : Not Set
Backup on Shutdown                  : Not Set

Name Record Settings(day:hour:minute)
~~~~~~~~~~~~~~~~~~~~~~~~~~~~~~~~~~~~~~~~~~~~~~~~~~~~~~~~
Refresh Interval                    : 006:00:00
Extinction(Tombstone) Interval      : 004:00:00
Extinction(Tombstone) TimeOut       : 006:00:00
Verification Interval               : 024:00:00

Database consistency checking parameters :
~~~~~~~~~~~~~~~~~~~~~~~~~~~~~~~~~~~~~~~~~~~~~~~~~~~~~~~~
Periodic Checking                   : Disabled

WINS Logging Parameters:
~~~~~~~~~~~~~~~~~~~~~~~~~~~~~~~~~~~~~~~~~~~~~~~~~~~~~~~~
Log Database changes in Jet.Log     : Not Set
Log details events to event log     : Not Set

Burst Handling Parameters :
~~~~~~~~~~~~~~~~~~~~~~~~~~~~~~~~~~~~~~~~~~~~~~~~~~~~~~~~
Burst Handling State                : Not Set
```

Display records in WINS server's database:

```
wins server>show database {172.16.11.104}
Description of different fields in the Record Table
~~~~~~~~~~~~~~~~~~~~~~~~~~~~~~~~~~~~~~~~~~~~~~~~~~~~~~~~
NAME            = Name of the Record. Up to 16
                  characters
T               = Type of Record : D - Dynamic,
                  S - Static
S               = State of the Record : A - Active,
                  R - Released, T - Tombstoned
```

```
VERSION        = LowPart ( in Hex)
G              = Address Group : U - Unique,
                 N - Group, I - Internet,
                 M - Multihomed, D - Domain Name.
IPADDRESS      = List of IP Addresses associated
                 with the Name.
EXPIRATION DATE = Expiration Time Stamp for the Name
                 Record.


~~~~~~~~~~~~~~~~~~~~~~~~~~~~~~~~~~~~~~~~~~~~~~~~~~~~~
NAME    -T-S- VERSION -G- IPADDRESS - EXPIRATION DATE
~~~~~~~~~~~~~~~~~~~~~~~~~~~~~~~~~~~~~~~~~~~~~~~~~~~~~
Retrieving database from the Wins server 172.16.11.104
??__MSBROWSE__?[01h]-D-A- 1        -N- 172.16.11.104  -
                                   7/8/2000 3:40:31 PM
MTITCANADA    [1Bh]-D-A- 1f8        -U- 172.16.11.104  -
                                   7/7/2000 8:57:56 AM
IS~TEST       [00h]-D-A- 2          -U- 172.16.11.104  -
                                   7/8/2000 6:24:33 PM
Total No. of records retrieved for server 172.16.11.104 : 3
Total No. of records displayed : 3
Command completed successfully.
```

Note that some WINS records may contain characters that can't be displayed, which are represented in the example by question marks.

See Also

WINS

---

netstat

Displays statistics and current connections for TCP/IP.

Syntax

```
netstat [-a] [-e] [-n] [-s] [-p protocol] [-r] [interval]
```

Options

-a   Lists all TCP/IP connections and their current statuses.

-e   Displays frame statistics for network adapters (can be used with -s option).

-n   Lists addresses and port numbers as numbers instead of trying to resolve them using DNS. This is useful if DNS isn't working properly, and you want to avoid long timeouts when using netstat.

-o   Displays process ID associated with each listening port.

-s   Displays statistics and connections for all TCP/IP protocols.

-p protocol
      When used in conjunction with -s option, displays statistics for the specified protocol, which can be either TCP, UDP, ICMP, or IP.

-r   Displays the routing table.

interval
    Causes the output to be refreshed each specified number of seconds until Ctrl-C
    is pressed.

Examples

Show statistics for Ethernet frames:

```
netstat -e
Interface Statistics
```

	Received	Sent
Bytes	48446148	43795441
Unicast packets	195267	207067
Non-unicast packets	12311	6830
Discards	0	0
Errors	0	0
Unknown protocols	15400	

Show statistics for TCP protocol and the current state of TCP connections:

```
netstat -s -p tcp
TCP Statistics
    Active Opens                 = 7631
    Passive Opens                = 4689
    Failed Connection Attempts   = 269
    Reset Connections            = 380
    Current Connections          = 23
    Segments Received            = 160892
    Segments Sent                = 173884
    Segments Retransmitted       = 680


Active Connections
```

Proto	Local Address	Foreign Address	State
TCP	test:ldap	test.mtitcanada.com:4208	ESTABLISHED
TCP	test:ldap	test.mtitcanada.com:4216	ESTABLISHED
TCP	test:ldap	test.mtitcanada.com:4229	ESTABLISHED
TCP	test:ldap	test.mtitcanada.com:4233	ESTABLISHED
TCP	test:1110	test.mtitcanada.com:ldap	CLOSE_WAIT
TCP	test:4208	test.mtitcanada.com:ldap	ESTABLISHED
TCP	test:4216	test.mtitcanada.com:ldap	ESTABLISHED
TCP	test:4229	test.mtitcanada.com:ldap	ESTABLISHED
TCP	test:4233	test.mtitcanada.com:ldap	ESTABLISHED
TCP	test:ldap	test.mtitcanada.com:3993	TIME_WAIT
TCP	test:ldap	test.mtitcanada.com:3994	TIME_WAIT
TCP	test:ldap	test.mtitcanada.com:4001	TIME_WAIT
TCP	test:ldap	test.mtitcanada.com:4007	TIME_WAIT
TCP	test:ldap	test.mtitcanada.com:4232	ESTABLISHED
TCP	test:microsoft-ds	test.mtitcanada.com:4009	ESTABLISHED
TCP	test:1026	test.mtitcanada.com:1233	ESTABLISHED
TCP	test:1026	test.mtitcanada.com:1334	ESTABLISHED
TCP	test:1224	test.mtitcanada.com:ldap	CLOSE_WAIT
TCP	test:1227	test.mtitcanada.com:3268	CLOSE_WAIT
TCP	test:1233	test.mtitcanada.com:1026	ESTABLISHED

TCP	test:1298	LEONARDO:netbios-ssn	ESTABLISHED
TCP	test:1300	BACH:1026	ESTABLISHED
TCP	test:1334	test.mtitcanada.com:1026	ESTABLISHED
TCP	test:3712	test.mtitcanada.com:ldap	CLOSE_WAIT
TCP	test:3936	test.mtitcanada.com:ldap	CLOSE_WAIT
TCP	test:3995	BACH:ldap	TIME_WAIT
TCP	test:3996	BACH:microsoft-ds	TIME_WAIT
TCP	test:3998	test.mtitcanada.com:microsoft-ds	TIME_WAIT
TCP	test:4001	test.mtitcanada.com:ldap	TIME_WAIT
TCP	test:4008	BACH:ldap	TIME_WAIT
TCP	test:4009	test.mtitcanada.com:microsoft-ds	ESTABLISHED
TCP	test:4010	test.mtitcanada.com:epmap	TIME_WAIT
TCP	test:4011	test.mtitcanada.com:1026	TIME_WAIT
TCP	test:4012	test.mtitcanada.com:epmap	TIME_WAIT
TCP	test:4013	test.mtitcanada.com:1026	TIME_WAIT
TCP	test:4232	test.mtitcanada.com:ldap	ESTABLISHED

Notes

- The -o switch is new to WS2003.
- The fields in the output of netstat are:

Proto
> The name of the protocol used for the connection.

Local Address
> The name (or IP address) and port number (or descriptor) for the connection on the local machine. An asterisk means that the port has not yet been established.

Foreign Address
> The name (or IP address) and port number (or descriptor) for the connection on the remote machine. An asterisk means that the port has not yet been established.

State
> The connection state (TCP only). This is typically either:

> *LISTEN*
> > TCP is waiting for a connection at this port.

> *ESTABLISHED*
> > An active TCP connection has been established at this port.

> If the state is any of the following, the TCP/IP connection is in the process of being established or torn down using a three-way TCP handshake:

> CLOSED

> CLOSE_WAIT

> FIN_WAIT_1

> FIN_WAIT_2

> LAST_ACK

> SYN_RECEIVED

> SYN_SEND

> TIME_WAIT

See Also

TCP/IP

nslookup

Diagnostic utility that displays information stored in DNS servers.

Modes

nslookup has two modes of operation:

Interactive
>In this mode, an nslookup shell is opened so that any sequence of nslookup commands can be run one at a time. Enter interactive mode by typing:
>
>>**nslookup**

Noninteractive
>In this mode, only a single nslookup command is run, after which you return to the command prompt. The syntax is:
>
>>nslookup -*command host DNSserver*

>*-command*
>>One of the nslookup commands in the following list. The hyphen is part of the syntax.

>*host*
>>The IP address or hostname of the host whose DNS information you want to obtain from the DNS server. If you use a hyphen, the prompt changes to nslookup interactive mode.

>*DNSserver*
>>The IP address or hostname of the DNS server you want to query. (If omitted, the default DNS server for the local machine is used.)

Commands

exit
>Quits the interactive mode of nslookup.

finger [username]
>Fingers the current computer for a list of currently logged-on users. If you specify username, then the information for that user is obtained.

ls [option] dnsdomain [[> | >>] filename]
>Lists (or redirects to a file) different subsets of resource records for the specified DNS domain depending on the option selected, specifically:

>*-t querytype*
>>Lists all records of the specified type (see Table 5-22)

>*-a* Lists aliases of hosts in the DNS domain (same result as using -t CNAME)

>*-d* Lists all records for the DNS domain (same result as using -t ANY)

>*-h* Lists operating-system information for the DNS domain (same result as using -t HINFO)

>*-s* Lists well-known services of host in the DNS domain (same result as using -t WKS)

lserver dnsdomain

    Sets the default server to the specified DNS domain using the initial server.

root

    Sets the default server to the DNS root server ns.nic.ddn.mil (same result as using lserver ns.nic.ddn.mil). Use set root to change the default root server.

server dnsdomain

    Sets the default server to the specified DNS domain using the current default server.

set all

    Displays the configuration of nslookup (how it performs lookups).

set class=value

    Modifies the query class, which can be IN (Internet class), CHAOS (Chaos class), HESIOD (MIT Athena Hesiod class), or ANY (any class). The default is IN (the other classes are obsolete).

set [no]d2

    Enables or disables exhaustive debugging mode, which is incredibly verbose (default is no).

set [no]debug

    Enables or disables debugging mode, which is very verbose (default is no).

set [no]defname

    Appends the default DNS domain name to each query (default is yes).

set domain=dnsdomain

    Switches the default DNS domain to the one specified. This name is appended to all nslookup queries if defname is specified.

set [no]ignore

    Reports or ignores packet errors (default is ignore).

set port=value

    Modifies the default TCP/UDP port for the DNS name server port. (This is port 53 by default.)

set querytype=value

    Specifies the types of resource records to obtain from the DNS server (see Table 5-22). The default is Address (A) record.

set [no]recurse

    Enables or disables recursion, i.e.,whether the DNS server should query other DNS servers if it can't respond with the requested information. (Default is yes.)

set retry=number

    Specifies the number of retries that can be performed by nslookup when querying a DNS server until it gives up (default is four times).

set root=DNSserver

    Specifies the root server (affects the root command earlier in this list). The default is ns.nic.ddn.mil.

set [no]search

    Toggles whether each DNS domain name in the search list should be appended to a request until a response is received (default is yes).

set srchlist DNSdomain1[/DNSdomain2/...]

    Specifies the DNS domain name search list (up to six DNS servers can be specified).

set timeout=seconds

    Modifies the initial time in seconds that `nslookup` waits for a response to its first request (default is five seconds).

set type=value

    Specifies the type of records to be requested from a DNS server (see Table 5-22).

set [no]vc

    Specifies that a virtual circuit should be used when sending requests to a DNS server (default is no).

view filename

    Displays the output of any previous commands that have been redirected to files.

Table 5-22. Values for querytype parameter for nslookup commands

Value	Description
A	Computer's IP address
ANY	All types of data
CNAME	Canonical name for an alias
GID	Group identifier of a group name
HINFO	Computer's CPU and operating-system type
MB	Mailbox domain name
MG	Mail group member
MINFO	Mailbox or mail-list information
MR	Mail rename domain name
MX	Mail exchanger
NS	DNS name server for the named zone
PTR	Hostname (if the query is an IP address) or pointer to other info
SOA	DNS domain's start-of-authority record
TXT	Text information
UID	User identifier
UINFO	User information
WKS	Well-known service description

Examples

Start `nslookup` in interactive mode:

```
C:\>nslookup
Default Server:  izzy.mtitworld.com
Address:  172.16.11.99
>
```

Switch default DNS server to *BACH*:

```
> server bach.mtitworld.com
Default Server:  bach.mtitworld.com
Address:  172.16.11.100
```

Specify that only Address (A) records should be queried:

```
> set query=A
```

Command Reference

Resolve host *BEETHOVEN* in domain *mtitworld.com* into its IP address:

```
> beethoven.mtitworld.com
Server:  bach.mtitworld.com
Address: 172.16.11.100
Name:    beethoven.mtitworld.com
Address: 172.16.11.101
```

Query default DNS server for all records in its database:

```
> ls mtitworld.com
[bach.mtitworld.com]
mtitworld.com.                 A     172.16.11.100
mtitworld.com.      NS    server=bach.mtitworld.com
gc._msdcs                      A     172.16.11.105
gc._msdcs                      A     172.16.11.103
gc._msdcs                      A     172.16.11.104
gc._msdcs                      A     172.16.11.100
bach                           A     172.16.11.100
beethoven                      A     172.16.11.101
chopin                         A     172.16.11.102
distrib                        A     172.16.11.103
franck.distrib                 A     172.16.11.103
handel                         A     172.16.11.70
chopin.vancouver               A     172.16.11.102
```

Notes

- nslookup commands must be 255 or fewer characters.
- To look up a computer not in the current DNS domain, append a period to the name. For example, type **beethoven.otherdomain.com.** at the interactive nslookup prompt.
- Use exit or Ctrl-C to escape from an nslookup session.
- An unrecognized command is interpreted as a hostname.
- For more information on using nslookup, see *DNS on Windows Server 2003* (O'Reilly).

See Also

DNS

---

openfiles

Displays or disconnects files opened by local or network users.

Syntax

```
openfiles /command switches
```

Options

command
    Specifies the action to perform, which can be:

query
> Displays all open files

disconnect
> Disconnects one or more open files

The full syntax for these two commands is:

```
/query [/s Computer [/u Domain\User [/p Password]]]
    [/fo {TABLE | LIST | CSV}] [/nh] [/v]
```

and:

```
/disconnect [/s Computer [/u Domain \ User [/p Password]]] {[/id OpenFileID]
    | [/a UserName] | [/o OpenMode]} [/op OpenFileName]
```

The various switches are:

/s Computer /u [Domain\]User /p [Password]
> Name or IP address of a remote computer (if omitted, defaults to local computer) and credentials for running the script (if omitted, defaults to System built-in identity).

/fo {TABLE | LIST | CSV}
> Format for displaying driver properties (if omitted, default is TABLE).

/nh   Omits header row from displayed information if /fo is set to TABLE or CSV.

/v   Displays verbose information.

/id OpenFileID
> Disconnects an open file with a specific numeric ID (use openfiles /query to find the ID). A wildcard (*) can also be used to disconnect all open files.

/a UserName
> Disconnects all open files for a specific user. A wildcard (*) can also be used.

/o OpenMode
> Disconnects all open files by OpenMode value (Read, Write or Read/Write). A wildcard (*) can also be used.

/op OpenFileName
> Disconnects all open file connections created by a specific OpenFile name. The wildcard (*) disconnects all open files on the specified computer.

Examples

List open files on member server with IP address 172.16.11.230:

```
openfiles /query /s 172.16.11.230 /fo list
```

```
ID:                       41
Accessed By:              ADMINISTRATOR
Type:                     Windows
Open File (Path\executable): C:\caps

ID:                       104
Accessed By:              ADMINISTRATOR
Type:                     Windows
Open File (Path\executable): \PIPE\srvsvc
```

Disconnect open file with ID 41:

```
openfiles /disconnect /s 172.16.11.230 /id 41
```

```
SUCCESS: The connection to the open file "C:\caps" has been terminated.
```

Verify the result (verbose mode):

```
openfiles /query /s 172.16.11.230 /fo list /v
```

```
Hostname:                          ESRV230D
ID:                                111
Accessed By:                       ADMINISTRATOR
Type:                              Windows
#Locks:                            0
Open Mode:                         Write + Read
Open File (Path\executable):       \PIPE\srvsvc
```

See Also

Files and Folders

---

pathping

Combines the features of ping and tracert to trace packet loss due to routers over a routed path through an internetwork. pathping gives additional information that neither of these commands provides.

Syntax

```
pathping [-n] [-h maxhops] [-g hostlist] [-p msec] [-q queries] [-w msec] [-T] [-R] target
```

Options

-n Does not resolve IP addresses to hostnames

-h maxhops
Specifies maximum number of hops to traverse (the default is 30 hops)

-g hostlist
Permits consecutive hosts to be separated by intermediate gateways along *hostlist*

-p msec
Specifies how many milliseconds to wait between consecutive pings (default is 250 msec, or 0.25 sec)

-q queries
Specifies number of queries issued to each host along the route (default is 100 queries)

-w msec
Specifies how many milliseconds to wait for a reply (default is 3,000 msec or 3 seconds)

-T Checks which routers don't have layer-2 priority configured

-R   Checks which routers support Resource Reservation Setup Protocol (RSVP)

target
> Identifies hostname or IP address of remote target host

Examples

Use pathping to check for congestion along the route from *test.mtitcanada.com* to *www.gov.mb.ca*:

```
pathping -n www.gov.mb.ca
Tracing route to www.gov.mb.ca [198.163.12.46]
over a maximum of 30 hops:
  0   205.200.52.64
  1   205.200.52.1
  2   205.200.52.6
  3   205.200.28.66
  4   205.200.27.54
  5   192.35.252.242
  6   198.163.12.46


Computing statistics for 150 seconds...
                    Source to Here   This Node/Link
Hop   RTT     Lost/Sent = Pct   Lost/Sent = Pct   Address
0                                                  205.200.52.64
                                 0/ 100 =  0%        |
1     128ms   0/ 100 =  0%       0/ 100 =  0%      205.200.52.1
                                 0/ 100 =  0%        |
2     122ms   0/ 100 =  0%       0/ 100 =  0%      205.200.52.6
                                 0/ 100 =  0%        |
3     138ms   0/ 100 =  0%       0/ 100 =  0%      205.200.28.66
                                 15/ 100 = 15%       |
4     132ms   5/ 100 =  5%       6/ 100 =  6%      205.200.27.54
                                 0/ 100 =  0%        |
5     124ms   7/ 100 =  7%       0/ 100 =  0%      192.35.252.242
                                 1/ 100 =  1%        |
6     127ms   6/ 100 =  6%       0/ 100 =  0%      198.163.12.46
Trace complete.
```

Notes

pathping first displays the route taken to the remote target in the fashion of the `tracert` command. After an indicated period of time during which `pathping` collects necessary statistics, it displays the efficiency of the route by showing:

Hop
> Local host 0. Each remote host along the route increments the hop count by 1.

RTT
> Round-trip time along the route.

Source to Here—Lost/Sent = Pct
> Cumulative packets lost by this point along the route, expressed as both a fraction and a percentage. pathping sends 100 ICMP packets to each host along the route, so the results are statistical (and therefore don't add up when comparing different hops).

Command
Reference

This Node/Link—Lost/Sent = Pct
Packets lost on this hop (between this host and the previous one), expressed as both a fraction and a percentage. There are actually two sets of results here:

- Loss rates for routers (indicated with the IP address in the Address column). When this is high, the router is congested.
- Loss rates for links (indicated with | in the Address column). When this is high, the link is congested.

Address
IP address of each host along the route.

See Also

ping, *TCP/IP*, tracert

---

ping

Tests TCP/IP connectivity with a remote host.

Syntax

```
ping [-t] [-a] [-n number] [-l bytes] [-f] [-i TTL] [-v TOS] [-r number]
[-s hops] [ [-j hostlist] | [-k hostlist] ] [-w msec] host [...]
```

Options

-t   Continues pinging the host until interrupted using Ctrl-C.

-a   Resolves IP addresses to hostnames.

-n number
Specifies the number of ICMP ECHO packets to send. (The default is four packets.)

-l bytes
Indicates number of bytes in each ECHO packet. (The default is 32 bytes, and the maximum is 65,527 bytes.)

-f   Sets the Do Not Fragment flag in the packets to prevent them from being fragmented by routers along the route.

-i TTL
Sets the time-to-live field in the packets.

-v TOS
Sets the Type of Service field in the packets.

-r number
Records the route of the outgoing packet and the returning packet in the Record Route field. (The minimum number of hosts you can specify is one, and the maximum is nine.)

-s hops
Specifies the timestamp for the number of hops specified by number.

-j hostlist
Routes packets using the specified list of remote hosts (up to nine). Consecutive hosts can be separated by intermediate gateways (loose source routing).

-k *hostlist*

    Routes packets using the specified list of remote hosts (up to nine). Consecutive hosts can't be separated by intermediate gateways (loose source routing).

-w *msec*

    Specifies timeout interval in milliseconds.

host

    Indicates IP address or hostname of remote host(s) being pinged.

Examples

ping a remote host:

```
ping www.gov.mb.ca
Pinging www.gov.mb.ca [198.163.12.46] with 32 bytes of data:

Reply from 198.163.12.46: bytes=32 time=140ms TTL=250
Reply from 198.163.12.46: bytes=32 time=130ms TTL=250
Reply from 198.163.12.46: bytes=32 time=120ms TTL=250
Reply from 198.163.12.46: bytes=32 time=110ms TTL=250

Ping statistics for 198.163.12.46:
Packets: Sent = 4, Received = 4, Lost = 0 (0% loss),
Approximate round trip times in milli-seconds:
Minimum = 110ms, Maximum =  140ms, Average =  125ms
```

Notes

- By default, ping sequentially sends four 32-byte ICMP ECHO packets to the remote host and waits one second for a reply.
- If you can ping the remote host by IP address but not by hostname, there is probably a DNS problem.

See Also

pathping, *TCP/IP*, tracert

popd

Changes back to the directory stored by pushd (see pushd later in this chapter).

Syntax

    popd

Options

None.

Examples

Here's a simple example of how popd together with pushd can be used in a batch file to return to the directory in which the batch file was started:

```
@echo off
' Batch file to delete all .TXT files in a specified directory
pushd %1
```

```
    del *.txt
    popd
```

Notes

The pushd/popd buffer is cleared each time after the command is used.

See Also

pushd

---

prncnfg

Displays information about printers and configures them.

Syntax

```
prncnfg -g -s RemoteComputer -p PrinterName
prncnfg -t -s RemoteComputer -p PrinterName [-r PortName] [-h ShareName]
    [-i DefaultPriority] ... [{+ | -}{direct | published | shared |
    workoffline ...}]
```

Options

-g   Displays printer settings

-s *RemoteComputer*
    Name of print server.

-t   Configures printer.

-p *PrinterName*
    Name of printer.

-r *PortName*
    COM, LPT, or TCP/IP port of printer.

-h *ShareName*
    Share name of printer.

-i *DefaultPriority*
    Default priority for new jobs.

direct
    Prints directly to printer (doesn't spool).

published
    Publishes printer in Active Directory.

shared
    Shares printer on network.

workoffline
    Users can submit jobs to print queue even if their computers are offline.

Examples

Display information about printer named *SalesPrinter* managed by local computer:

```
prncnfg -g -p SalesPrinter
Microsoft (R) Windows Script Host Version 5.6
Copyright (C) Microsoft Corporation 1996-2001. All rights reserved.
```

```
Server name
Printer name SalesPrinter
Share name
Driver name HP Color LaserJet
Port name LPT1:
Comment
Location
Separator file
Print processor WinPrint
Data type RAW
Parameters
Priority 1
Default priority 0
Printer always available
Attributes local shared published enable_bidi do_complete_first

Printer status Idle
Extended printer status Unknown
Detected error state Unknown
Extended detected error state Unknown
```

Share *SalesPrinter* with share name *SPRT*:

prncnfg -t -p SalesPrinter -h SPRT +shared
```
Microsoft (R) Windows Script Host Version 5.6
Copyright (C) Microsoft Corporation 1996-2001. All rights reserved.

Configured printer SalesPrinter
```

Verify the result:

prncnfg -g -p SalesPrinter
```
Microsoft (R) Windows Script Host Version 5.6
Copyright (C) Microsoft Corporation 1996-2001. All rights reserved.

Server name
Printer name SalesPrinter
Share name SPRT <---NOTE
Driver name HP Color LaserJet
Port name LPT1:
Comment
Location
Separator file
Print processor WinPrint
Data type RAW
Parameters
Priority 1
Default priority 0
Printer always available
Attributes local shared enable_bidi do_complete_first

Printer status Idle
Extended printer status Unknown
Detected error state Unknown
Extended detected error state Unknown
```

Notes

- This command is a *.vbs* script and requires CScript to run. You can make CScript your default script host by typing the following at the command prompt:

  cscript //h:cscript //s

- This command requires Administrator credentials. If logged on with different credentials, use -u *UserName* -w *Password* to specify suitable credentials.

See Also

Printing, prndrvr, prnjobs, prnmngr, prnport, prnqctl

---

prndrvr

new in WS2003

Manages printer drivers.

Syntax

```
prndrvr {-l | -x} [-s RemoteComputer]
prndrvr -d [-s RemoteComputer] -m DriverName   -v {0 | 1 | 2 | 3} -e
Environment
prndrvr -a [-s RemoteComputer] [-m DriverName] [-v {0 | 1 | 2 | 3}] [-e
Environment]
   [-h Path] [-i FileName.inf]
```

Options

-l   Lists all printer drivers on the print server.

-x   Deletes all unused printer drivers from the print server.

-s RemoteComputer
    Name of print server.

-d   Deletes a printer driver.

-m DriverName
    Name of printer driver.

-v {0 | 1 | 2 | 3}
    Version of driver to install, where:

    0   Windows 95/98/Me

    1   Windows NT 3.51

    2   Windows NT 4.0

    3   W2K/XP/2003

    If omitted, the version for the OS on the printer server is used.

-e Environment
    The environment for the driver, which can be:

    "Windows NT x86"
    "Windows NT Alpha_AXP"
    "Windows IA64"
    "Windows NT R4000"
    "Windows NT PowerPC"
    "Windows 4.0"

    If omitted, the environment of the print server is used.

-a   Adds (installs) a printer driver.

-h Path
> Path to printer driver.

-i FileName.inf
> Printer driver file (if omitted, *ntprint.inf* is used).

Examples

List the printer drivers installed on the local print server:

```
prndrvr -l
Microsoft (R) Windows Script Host Version 5.6
Copyright (C) Microsoft Corporation 1996-2001. All rights reserved.

Server name
Driver name HP Color LaserJet,3,Windows NT x86
Version 3
Environment Windows NT x86
Monitor name PJL Language Monitor
Driver path C:\WINDOWS\system32\spool\DRIVERS\W32X86\3\UNIDRV.DLL
Data file C:\WINDOWS\system32\spool\DRIVERS\W32X86\3\HPCLJ.GPD
Config file C:\WINDOWS\system32\spool\DRIVERS\W32X86\3\UNIDRVUI.DLL
Help file C:\WINDOWS\system32\spool\DRIVERS\W32X86\3\UNIDRV.HLP
Dependent files
 C:\WINDOWS\system32\spool\DRIVERS\W32X86\3\PCL5ERES.DLL
 C:\WINDOWS\system32\spool\DRIVERS\W32X86\3\TTFSUB.GPD
 C:\WINDOWS\system32\spool\DRIVERS\W32X86\3\UNIRES.DLL
 C:\WINDOWS\system32\spool\DRIVERS\W32X86\3\STDNAMES.GPD

Server name
Driver name HP LaserJet 1200 Series PCL 6,3,Windows NT x86
Version 3
Environment Windows NT x86
Monitor name
Driver path C:\WINDOWS\system32\spool\DRIVERS\W32X86\3\hpbf312G.dll
Data file C:\WINDOWS\system32\spool\DRIVERS\W32X86\3\hpbf312I.pmd
Config file C:\WINDOWS\system32\spool\DRIVERS\W32X86\3\hpbf312E.dll
Help file C:\WINDOWS\system32\spool\DRIVERS\W32X86\3\hpbf312I.hlp
Dependent files
 C:\WINDOWS\system32\spool\DRIVERS\W32X86\3\hpbftm32.dll
 C:\WINDOWS\system32\spool\DRIVERS\W32X86\3\hpbafd32.dll
 C:\WINDOWS\system32\spool\DRIVERS\W32X86\3\hpbf312F.dll
 C:\WINDOWS\system32\spool\DRIVERS\W32X86\3\hpbf312H.dll
 C:\WINDOWS\system32\spool\DRIVERS\W32X86\3\hpbf312I.dll
 C:\WINDOWS\system32\spool\DRIVERS\W32X86\3\hpbf312J.dll
 C:\WINDOWS\system32\spool\DRIVERS\W32X86\3\hpbf312K.dll

Number of printer drivers enumerated 2
```

Notes

- This command is a *.vbs* script and requires CScript to run. You can make CScript your default script host by typing the following at the command prompt:

```
cscript //h:cscript //s
```

- This command requires Administrator credentials. If logged on with different credentials, use -u *UserName* -w *Password* to specify suitable credentials.

See Also
Printing, prncnfg, prnjobs, prnmngr, prnqctl

---

prnjobs   new in WS2003
Manages print jobs.

Syntax
    prnjobs {-l | -m | -x | -z} [-s *RemoteComputer*] -p *PrinterName* -j *JobNumber*

Options
-l   Lists all jobs in the print queue

-m   Resumes a paused print job

-x   Cancels a print job

-z   Pauses a print job

-s RemoteComputer
    Name of print server

-p PrinterName
    Name of printer

-j JobNumber
    ID number of print job

Examples
List print jobs pending in print queue on *SalesPrinter*:

    prnjobs -l -p SalesPrinter
    Microsoft (R) Windows Script Host Version 5.6
    Copyright (C) Microsoft Corporation 1996-2001. All rights reserved.

    Job id 9
    Printer SalesPrinter
    Document Budget.rtf
    Data type NT EMF 1.008
    Driver name HP Color LaserJet
    Description SalesPrinter, 9
    Machine name \\ESRV210D
    Notify Administrator
    Owner Administrator
    Pages printed 0
    Parameters
    Size 131000
    Status Job is printing
    Time submitted 03/27/2003 10:24:32

    Job id 10
    Printer SalesPrinter
    Document Report.rtf

```
Data type NT EMF 1.008
Driver name HP Color LaserJet
Description SalesPrinter, 10
Elapsed time 00:00:00
Machine name \\ESRV210D
Notify Administrator
Owner Administrator
Pages printed 0
Parameters
Size 152292
Status
Time submitted 03/27/2003 10:24:40

Job id 11
Printer SalesPrinter
Document Resume.rtf
Data type NT EMF 1.008
Driver name HP Color LaserJet
Description SalesPrinter, 11
Elapsed time 00:00:00
Machine name \\ESRV210D
Notify Administrator
Owner Administrator
Pages printed 0
Parameters
Size 87928
Status
Time submitted 03/27/2003 10:24:47

Number of print jobs enumerated 3
```

Pause job 10:

prnjobs -z -p SalesPrinter -j 10
```
Microsoft (R) Windows Script Host Version 5.6
Copyright (C) Microsoft Corporation 1996-2001. All rights reserved.

Success Pause Job id 10 Printer SalesPrinter
```

Verify the result:

prnjobs -l -p SalesPrinter
```
Microsoft (R) Windows Script Host Version 5.6
Copyright (C) Microsoft Corporation 1996-2001. All rights reserved.

Job id 9
Printer SalesPrinter
Document Budget.rtf
Data type NT EMF 1.008
Driver name HP Color LaserJet
Description SalesPrinter, 9
Machine name \\ESRV210D
Notify Administrator
Owner Administrator
Pages printed 0
Parameters
```

Size 100220
Status Job is printing
Time submitted 03/27/2003 10:24:32

Job id 10
Printer SalesPrinter
Document Report.rtf
Data type NT EMF 1.008
Driver name HP Color LaserJet
Description SalesPrinter, 10
Elapsed time 00:00:00
Machine name \\ESRV210D
Notify Administrator
Owner Administrator
Pages printed 0
Parameters
Size 152292
Status Job is paused **<---NOTE**
Time submitted 03/27/2003 10:24:40

Job id 11
Printer SalesPrinter
Document Resume.rtf
Data type NT EMF 1.008
Driver name HP Color LaserJet
Description SalesPrinter, 11
Elapsed time 00:00:00
Machine name \\ESRV210D
Notify Administrator
Owner Administrator
Pages printed 0
Parameters
Size 87928
Status
Time submitted 03/27/2003 10:24:47

Number of print jobs enumerated 3

Resume job 10:

prnjobs -m -p SalesPrinter -j 10
Microsoft (R) Windows Script Host Version 5.6
Copyright (C) Microsoft Corporation 1996-2001. All rights reserved.

Success Resume Job id 10 Printer SalesPrinter

Cancel job 10:

prnjobs -x -p SalesPrinter -j 10
Microsoft (R) Windows Script Host Version 5.6
Copyright (C) Microsoft Corporation 1996-2001. All rights reserved.

Success Cancel Job id 10 Printer SalesPrinter

Notes

- Unfortunately, you can pause, resume, or cancel only one job at a time using this command. See prnqctl later in this chapter to pause or resume a printer or cancel all jobs in a print queue.
- This command is a *.vbs* script and requires CScript to run. You can make CScript your default script host by typing the following at the command prompt:

  ```
  cscript //h:cscript //s
  ```

- This command requires Administrator credentials. If logged on with different credentials, use -u *UserName* -w *Password* to specify suitable credentials.

See Also

Printing, prncnfg, prndrvr, prnmngr, prnqctl

---

prnmngr

new in WS2003

Manages printers.

Syntax

```
prnmngr -a [-s RemoteComputer] -p PrinterName -m DriverName -r PortName
prnmngr -d [-s RemoteComputer] -p PrinterName
prnmngr {-l | -x} [-s RemoteComputer]
prnmngr {-ac | -t} -p PrinterName
prnmngr -g
```

Options

-a Adds a local printer

-d Deletes a printer

-l Lists all printers

-x Deletes all printers

-ac Adds a printer connection

-t Specifies the default printer

-g Displays the default printer

-s RemoteComputer
   Name of print server

-p PrinterName
   Name of printer

-m DriverName
   Name of printer driver

-r PortName
   COM, LPT, or TCP/IP port of printer

Examples

List all printers on the local computer:

```
prnmngr -l
Microsoft (R) Windows Script Host Version 5.6
Copyright (C) Microsoft Corporation 1996-2001. All rights reserved.
```

```
        Server name
        Printer name HP LaserJet 1200 Series PCL 6 on dizzy (from SNOOPY) in session
        1
        Share name
        Driver name HP LaserJet 1200 Series PCL 6
        Port name TS005
        Comment
        Location
        Print processor WinPrint
        Data type RAW
        Parameters
        Attributes 33348
        Priority 1
        Default priority 0
        Average pages per minute 0
        Printer status Idle
        Extended printer status Unknown
        Detected error state Unknown
        Extended detected error state Unknown

        Server name
        Printer name SalesPrinter
        Share name SPRT
        Driver name HP Color LaserJet
        Port name LPT1:
        Comment
        Location
        Print processor WinPrint
        Data type RAW
        Parameters
        Attributes 2632
        Priority 1
        Default priority 0
        Average pages per minute 0
        Printer status Idle
        Extended printer status Unknown
        Detected error state Unknown
        Extended detected error state Unknown

        Number of local printers and connections enumerated 2
```

Display the default printer:

```
prnmngr -g
Microsoft (R) Windows Script Host Version 5.6
Copyright (C) Microsoft Corporation 1996-2001. All rights reserved.

The default printer is HP LaserJet 1200 Series PCL 6 on dizzy (from SNOOPY)
in
session 1
```

Change the default printer to *SalesPrinter*:

```
prnmngr -t -p SalesPrinter
Microsoft (R) Windows Script Host Version 5.6
```

```
          Copyright (C) Microsoft Corporation 1996-2001. All rights reserved.

          The default printer is now SalesPrinter
```

Notes

- This command is a *.vbs* script and requires CScript to run. You can make CScript your default script host by typing the following at the command prompt:

  cscript //h:cscript //s

- This command requires Administrator credentials. If logged on with different credentials, use -u *UserName* -w *Password* to specify suitable credentials.

See Also

Printing, prncnfg, prndrvr, prnjobs, prnqctl

---

prnqctl   new in WS2003

Clears a print queue, prints a test page, and pauses/resumes a printer.

Syntax

```
          prnqctl -e | -m | -x | -z [-s RemoteComputer] -p PrinterName
```

Options

-*e*   Prints a test page

-*m*   Resumes a printer

-*x*   Cancels all jobs in a print queue

-*z*   Pauses a printer

-*s RemoteComputer*
         Name of print server

-*p PrinterName*
         Name of printer

Examples

Pause the *SalesPrinter* printer on the local computer:

```
          prnqctl -z -p SalesPrinter
          Microsoft (R) Windows Script Host Version 5.6
          Copyright (C) Microsoft Corporation 1996-2001. All rights reserved.

          Success Pause Printer SalesPrinter
```

Resume the printer:

```
          prnqctl -m -p SalesPrinter
          Microsoft (R) Windows Script Host Version 5.6
          Copyright (C) Microsoft Corporation 1996-2001. All rights reserved.

          Success Resume Printer SalesPrinter
```

Clear the print queue of all jobs:

```
          prnqctl -x -p SalesPrinter
          Microsoft (R) Windows Script Host Version 5.6
```

```
Copyright (C) Microsoft Corporation 1996-2001. All rights reserved.

Success Purge Printer SalesPrinter
```

Use prnjobs to verify the queue is empty:

prnjobs -l -p SalesPrinter
```
Microsoft (R) Windows Script Host Version 5.6
Copyright (C) Microsoft Corporation 1996-2001. All rights reserved.

Number of print jobs enumerated 0
```

Notes

- This command is a *.vbs* script and requires CScript to run. You can make CScript your default script host by typing the following at the command prompt:

  cscript //h:cscript //s

- This command requires Administrator credentials. If logged on with different credentials, use -u *UserName* -w *Password* to specify suitable credentials.

- It may take a few seconds for the last job to clear when using the -x switch. Don't run the prnqctl -x command again before the queue is cleared or a printing error may result and the final job may be stuck in the queue.

See Also

Printing, prncnfg, prndrvr, prnjobs, prnmngr

---

pushd

Stores the name of the current directory and then changes to the specified directory (for use by the popd command earlier in this chapter).

Syntax

```
pushd [path | ..]
```

Options

path
> The directory to make the current directory

Examples

Store the current directory (here *C:*) and change to *C:\pub*:

pushd C:\pub
```
C:\pub>
```

See popd to see what you can do with this.

Notes

pushd supports relative paths and accepts either a network path or a local drive letter and path. If a network path is specified, a temporary drive letter is created, and pushd then switches the current drive and directory to the specified directory on the temporary drive. popd then deletes the temporary drive letter when it is used.

See Also

popd

---

rcp

Stands for remote copy command, which copies files between the client and a host running the *rshd* daemon.

Syntax

```
rcp [-a | -b] [-h] [-r] [hostname][.username:]source [hostname]
[.username:]destination
```

Options

-a   Switches to ASCII mode (the default), which converts end-of-line control characters between MS-DOS and Unix format.

-b   Switches to binary mode (used to copy binary files such as images).

-h   Also copies hidden files.

-r   Recursively copies all subdirectories and their contents.

hostname[.username]
Specifies the destination host running the *rshd* daemon and the credentials used for accessing the server (need to be specified only if different from those of logged-on user). If hostname is omitted, the destination is the local machine. If hostname is specified as a full DNS name such as *george.mtit.com*, the username must be specified; otherwise, the last part of the DNS name (here *.com*) is interpreted as the username.

source
Indicates files or directories to be copied (include path if needed).

destination
Specifies target directory on *rshd* machine (path can be absolute or relative).

Examples

Recursively copy the *pub* directory and its contents from the local machine to a remote Unix machine as user *mitcht*:

```
rcp -r C:\pub bongo.mitcht:/tmp
```

This command creates the directory */tmp/pub* on *BONGO* and copies the contents of *C:\pub* to this directory.

Notes

- WS2003 doesn't include a *rshd* daemon, so rcp is used mainly to copy files between Windows and Unix machines.

- rcp doesn't prompt for a password before copying. You get around this by using the *.rhosts* file in the user's home directory on the *rshd* server to specify which remote hostnames and usernames are allowed to use rcp to copy files to or from the *rshd* server.

See Also

rexec, rsh, telnet

recover

Tries to recover a file from a defective disk.

Syntax

```
recover [drive:][path]filename
```

Options

[drive:][path]filename
   The file you want to recover

Examples

Recover the file *doc1.txt* in the root of the *H:* drive:

recover H:\doc1.txt
```
The type of the file system is NTFS.
Press ENTER to begin recovery of the file on drive H:

459264 of 459264 bytes recovered.
```

Notes

- recover reads the specified file sector by sector and recovers data on good sectors. (Data on bad sectors is lost.)
- You can't use wildcards.

See Also

chkdsk, chkntfs, convert, defrag, diskpart, *Disks*, format, label, mountvol

---

rexec

Stands for remote execute command, which runs commands on remote machines running the rexec service.

Syntax

```
rexec remotehost [-l username] [-n] command
```

Options

remotehost
   The remote machine running the rexec service.

-l username
   The credentials used to run the command on the remote host.

-n   Redirection of standard input of rexec to null. (Try using this for commands that run interactively.)

command
   The command to remotely execute (enclose in quotes if there are embedded spaces).

Examples

Perform a directory listing on the Unix machine *BONGO* as user *mitcht* by remotely executing the ls command:

```
rexec bongo -l mitcht "ls ~"
Password (bongo:): ********
doc
fig
read.ps
```

Note that rexec prompts for a password before executing the command remotely.

Notes

- rexec copies standard input to the remote command.
- rexec terminates when the remote command has been executed.
- rexec can't be used to run some common interactive Unix commands such as emacs (use telnet to do this instead).

See Also

rcp, rsh, telnet

---

route

Displays and modifies the routing table on the local machine.

Syntax

```
route [-f] [-p] [command [destination] [MASK netmask] [gateway]
[METRIC metric] [IF interface]
```

Options

-f   Flushes all routes (gateway entries) from the routing table. (If combined with other options, this causes the table to be flushed prior to executing the other options.)

-p   When used with the add command, causes the added route to be persistent across reboots; when used with the print command, lists only persistent routes.

Commands

print
    Displays the contents of the routing table.

add destination MASK netmask gateway METRIC metric IF interface
    Adds a new route to the routing table using the following parameters:

    destination
        The IP address of the host or network, which can be reached by using the gateway.

    netmask
        The subnet mask used for packets going to the previously mentioned destination.

gateway
> The IP address of the router interface used for routing packets to the previously mentioned destination.

metric
> The cost metric, usually the number of hops between the local machine and destination, or any arbitrary number to represent the degree of preference of this route when many routes to destination are possible. (The default is 1, and maximum is 9,999.)

interface
> The interface to add the route to on multihomed machines.

delete [destination MASK netmask gateway METRIC metric IF interface]
> Removes an entry from the routing table. (Specify enough parameters to make the result unique.)

change [destination MASK netmask gateway METRIC metric IF interface]
> Modifies an existing route in the routing table. (Specify enough parameters to make the result unique.)

Examples

Display the routing table on the local machine:

```
route print
===========================================================
Interface List
0x1 ........................... MS TCP Loopback interface
0x1000003 ...00 40 95 d1 29 6c ...... Novell 2000 Adapter.
===========================================================
===========================================================
Active Routes:
Destination      Netmask          Gateway          Interface        Metric
0.0.0.0          0.0.0.0          172.16.11.1      172.16.11.100    1
127.0.0.0        255.0.0.0        127.0.0.1        127.0.0.1        1
172.16.11.0      255.255.255.0    172.16.11.100    172.16.11.100    1
172.16.11.100    255.255.255.255  127.0.0.1        127.0.0.1        1
172.16.255.255   255.255.255.255  172.16.11.100    172.16.11.100    1
224.0.0.0        224.0.0.0        172.16.11.100    172.16.11.100    1
255.255.255.255  255.255.255.255  172.16.11.100    172.16.11.100    1
Default Gateway:       172.16.11.1
===========================================================
Persistent Routes:
  None
```

Add a persistent route to the class B network 133.16.0.0, which is accessible through the local router interface 172.16.11.2:

```
route -p add 133.16.0.0 MASK 255.255.0.0 172.16.11.2 METRIC 3
```

Verify the result:

```
route print
===========================================================
Interface List
0x1 ........................... MS TCP Loopback interface
0x1000003 ...00 40 95 d1 29 6c ...... Novell 2000 Adapter.
===========================================================
===========================================================
```

```
Active Routes:
Destination     Netmask         Gateway        Interface      Metric
0.0.0.0         0.0.0.0         172.16.11.1    172.16.11.100  1
127.0.0.0       255.0.0.0       127.0.0.1      127.0.0.1      1
133.16.0.0      255.255.0.0     172.16.11.2    172.16.11.100  3
172.16.11.0     255.255.255.0   172.16.11.100  172.16.11.100  1
172.16.11.100   255.255.255.255 127.0.0.1      127.0.0.1      1
172.16.255.255  255.255.255.255 172.16.11.100  172.16.11.100  1
224.0.0.0       224.0.0.0       172.16.11.100  172.16.11.100  1
255.255.255.255 255.255.255.255 172.16.11.100  172.16.11.100  1
Default Gateway:        172.16.11.1
==========================================================
Persistent Routes:
Network Address Netmask         Gateway Address  Metric
133.16.0.0      255.255.0.0     172.16.11.2      3
```

Notes

- If you use route -f indiscriminately on a server, you could interrupt network communications between the server and other computers on the network, causing users to lose work. However, rebooting the server restores the default gateways defined in Network in the Control Panel.

- You can use the symbolic names contained in the *Hosts* and *Networks* files instead of IP addresses for destination or gateway parameters in the route command.

- The delete and print commands support wildcards for the destination and gateway parameters.

- The change command is useless; it's easier to delete a route and then add the new one than to modify an existing one.

See Also

TCP/IP

---

rsh

Runs commands on remote machines running the rsh service.

Syntax

    rsh *remotehost* [-l *username*] [-n] *command*

Options

remotehost
 The remote machine running the rsh service.

-l username
 The credentials used to run the command on the remote host.

-n Redirection of standard input of rexec to null. (Try using this for commands that run interactively.)

command
 The command to remotely execute (enclose in quotes if there are embedded spaces).

Examples

Perform a directory listing on the Unix machine *BONGO* as user *mitcht* by remotely executing the ls command:

```
rsh bongo -l mitcht "ls ~"
doc
fig
read.ps
```

Notes

- WS2003 includes only the client-side rsh command, so this command is typically used to remotely execute processes on Unix machines.
- Unlike the rexec command discussed earlier, rsh doesn't prompt for a password before executing the command remotely. rsh uses the same authentication mechanism used by rcp, namely the *.rhosts* file on the remote machine.

See Also

rcp, rexec, telnet

---

runas

Runs a program using alternate credentials than those currently being used.

Syntax

```
runas [/profile] [/env] [/netonly] /user:credentials program
```

Options

program
: Program to be run.

/profile
: User's profile (may need to be loaded for some programs).

/env
: Current network environment instead of user's local environment.

/netonly
: For remote access.

/user:credentials
: User credentials for running the program. (The syntax is user@domain or domain\user for domain accounts and user@computer or computer\user for local accounts.)

Examples

Open a command shell using the default Administrator account for the domain while logged on as an ordinary domain user:

```
runas /user:administrator@mtitworld.com cmd
Enter password for administrator@mtitworld.com: ********
Attempting to start "cmd" as user
    "administrator@mtitworld.com"...
```

A second command shell now opens with the following in the titlebar:

```
cmd (running as administrator@mtitworld.com)
```

Run Computer Management using the administrator account *JaneD* from the domain *mtitworld.com*:

```
runas /user:janed@mtitworld.com "mmc %windir%\system32\compmgmt.msc"
```

Open a command shell to administer a server in a different forest using credentials in that forest:

```
runas /netonly /user:<credentials> cmd
```

runas can also be invoked from the GUI. For example, to open the Display utility in the Control Panel using alternate credentials, select:

Start → Settings → Control Panel → hold down Shift → right-click Display → Run as → enter credentials

This is easier than remembering how to do it from the command line:

```
runas /user:<credentials> "control %windir%\system32\desk.cpl"
```

Notes

- It's a good idea for administrators to have two accounts: an ordinary user account for performing daily tasks, such as checking email or writing reports, and an administrator account for performing administrative tasks. The usefulness of runas is that administrators can perform tasks requiring Administrator credentials while logged on as an ordinary user, making it unnecessary to log off and then on again.

- Another term for using runas is *using the secondary logon*.

- runas works with programs (**.exe*), saved MMC consoles (**.msc*), and Control Panel items.

- runas can't be used to start items, such as Windows Explorer, the *Printers* folder, and desktop items. However, you can work around this by using the Processes tab of Task Manager to kill the current shell (*Explorer.exe*) and then the New Task button on the Applications tab to run the following command:

```
runas /user:domain\administrator explorer.exe
```

- You can create a shortcut to an item such as a saved MMC console and configure it to always run using a specific set of credentials.

- runas may not be able to run programs stored on a network share since the credentials used to start the program may be different from the credentials used to connect to the network share. This may make runas unable to gain access to the share.

- The runas service must be running in order to use the runas command.

- If you use runas at the command line without the /profile option, the default user profile is used instead of the profile of the user being impersonated. For example, if the command being invoked by runas saves a file in My Documents; it saves it in My Documents for the default user, not the user being impersonated by runas. If you use the runas option from the shortcut menu in Windows Explorer, the /profile option is specified by default.

See Also

cmd, *Logon*

schtasks

new in WS2003

Schedules tasks (commands or programs) to run on a computer at a specified time/
date and manages scheduled tasks.

> In WS2003, the schtasks command replaces the at command for
> managing and scheduling tasks from the command line (the at
> command remains only for backward compatibility with W2K/
> NT).

Syntax

General syntax:

```
schtasks /command switches [/s Computer [/u [Domain\]User [/p Password]]]
```

Syntax for each type of command:

```
schtasks /create /sc ScheduleType /tn TaskName /tr TaskRun
    [/ru {[ Domain \] User | SYSTEM}] [/rp Password]
    [/mo Modifier] [/d Day[,Day...] | *] [/m Month[,Month...]]
    [/i IdleTime] [/st StartTime] [/ri Interval] [{/et EndTime
        | /du Duration}   [/k]]
    [/sd StartDate] [/ed EndDate] [/it] [/z] [/f]

schtasks /change /tn TaskName    [/ru {[ Domain \] User | SYSTEM}]
    [/rp Password] [/tr TaskRun] [/st StartTime] [/ri Interval]
    [{/et EndTime |
/du Duration} [/k]]
    [/sd StartDate] [/ed EndDate] [/{ENABLE | DISABLE}] [/it] [/z]

schtasks /run /tn TaskName

schtasks /end /tn TaskName

schtasks /delete /tn { TaskName | *} [/f]

schtasks [/query] [/fo {TABLE | LIST | CSV}] [/nh] [/v]
```

Options

Here are the commands for schtasks:

create
    Creates a scheduled task

change
    Modifies properties of a scheduled task

run
    Runs a scheduled task immediately

end
    Stops a running task

delete
    Deletes a scheduled task

query
> Displays all scheduled tasks (can omit /query)

The remaining switches for schtasks are:

/sc ScheduleType
> Type of schedule, choose from:

> MINUTE
> HOURLY
> DAILY
> WEEKLY
> MONTHLY
> ONCE
> ONSTART
> ONLOGON
> ONIDLE

/tn TaskName
> Gives the task a name (in quotation marks if there are spaces).

/tr TaskRun
> The full path program, script, batch file, or command to run (if path is omitted, defaults to \System32 directory).

/s Computer /u [Domain\]User /p Password
> The /s switch specifies the name or IP address of the remote computer on which the scheduled task should run (if omitted, defaults to local computer). The /u and /p switches run schtasks using the specified credentials (if omitted, defaults to currently logged-on user on local computer). Note that the specified credentials are used for both scheduling and running the task—if desired you can run the task with different credentials by using the /ru switch.

/ru {[Domain\]User | SYSTEM} /rp Password
> Runs the task using the specified credentials (if omitted, defaults to currently logged-on user on local computer or credentials specified by /u switch if present). Unlike the /u switch, which can schedule tasks only on remote computers, the /ru switch can schedule tasks on both the local and remote computers.

/mo Modifier
> How often a scheduled task runs. Values defined by /sc set the schedule for how the task runs, e.g., hourly. *Modifier* describes how frequently it runs; every hour (i.e., *Modifier* of 1, which is the default), every 2 hours (*Modifier* of 2), and so on. Allowed values for *Modifier* are:

> *MINUTE*
>> Every *N* minutes (1–1439)

> *HOURLY*
>> Every *N* hours (1–23)

> *DAILY*
>> Every *N* days (1–365)

> *WEEKLY*
>> Every *N* weeks (1–52)

> *ONCE*
>> Only once

ONSTART
> Every time the system starts

ONLOGON
> Every time a user logs on

ONIDLE
> When the system has been idle for number of minutes specified by /i switch

MONTHLY
> Every *N* months (1–12)
>
> LASTDAY (run on the last day of the month)
>
> FIRST, SECOND, THIRD, FOURTH, LAST (requires /d Day switch)

/d Day[,Day...] | *
> Specifies one or more days of the week/month when WEEKLY or MONTHLY is used. Allowed values for Day are:
>
> *With WEEKLY*
> MON-SUN[, MON-SUN...] | * (if omitted, defaults to MON, while wildcard (*) means every day)
>
> *With MONTHLY (if 1–12)*
> 1–31 (if omitted, defaults to 1)
>
> *With MONTHLY (if FIRST, SECOND, THIRD, FOURTH, or LAST)*
> MON-SUN

/m Month[,Month...]
> One or more months during which the scheduled task runs (select from JAN to DEC or use * for every month). Works only with MONTHLY and, if omitted, defaults to * (every month).

/i IdleTime
> Number of minutes computer must be idle before task starts (select from 1 to 999). Works only with ONIDLE.

/st StartTime
> Specifies the time of day that the task starts (each time it starts) in HH:MM 24-hour format. The default value is the current time on the local computer. The /st parameter is valid with MINUTE, HOURLY, DAILY, WEEKLY, MONTHLY, and ONCE schedules. It is required for a ONCE schedule.

/ri Interval
> Repetition interval in minutes (select from 1 to 599,940 minutes). Doesn't apply for MINUTE, HOURLY, ONSTART, ONLOGON, or ONIDLE, and defaults to 10 minutes if /et or /du are used.

/et EndTime
> Time of day in HH:MM 24-hour format that a MINUTE or HOURLY task schedule ends (if omitted, defaults to no end time)

/du Duration
> Maximum time interval in HHHH:MM 24-hour format for a MINUTE or HOURLY schedule (if omitted, defaults to no maximum duration).

/k
> Kills the program associated with the task at time specified by /et or /du (if omitted, schtasks doesn't restart program again when it reaches the time specified by /et or /du, and it doesn't stop the program if it's still running).

/sd StartDate

Date when task schedule starts (if omitted, defaults to current date on local computer). Format for date depends on Regional and Language Options in the Control Panel on local computer, for instance, MM/DD/YYYY for English (United States).

/ed EndDate

Date when task schedule ends (if omitted, no ending date). Format for date depends on Regional and Language Options in the Control Panel on local computer, for instance, MM/DD/YYYY for English (United States).

/it Runs the task only if the user account under which the task runs is logged on to the computer (has no effect if task runs with SYSTEM identity). This user account is either:

- The current user on the local computer when the task was scheduled
- The account specified by the /u parameter
- The account specified by the /ru parameter

/z Delete the task once its schedule is completed.

/f Create the task and suppress warnings even if the task already exists.

/fo {TABLE | LIST | CSV}

Format for displaying tasks (if omitted, default is TABLE).

/nh

Omits header row from displayed information if /fo is set to TABLE or CSV.

/v Displays verbose information.

Table 5-23 summarizes which switches are allowed for each *ScheduleType* parameter.

Table 5-23. Switches that work with different ScheduleType parameters

ScheduleType	Allowed switches										
	/mo	d	/m	/i	/st	/ri	/et	/du	/k	/sd	/e
MINUTE	√	—	—	—	√	√	√	√	√	√	√
HOURLY	√	—	—	—	√	√	√	√	√	√	√
DAILY	√	—	—	—	√	—	—	—	—	√	√
WEEKLY	√	√	—	—	√	—	—	—	—	√	√
MONTHLY	√	√	√	—	√	—	—	—	—	√	√
ONCE	—	—	—	—	√	—	—	—	—	√	—
ONSTART	—	—	—	—	—	√	—	—	—	√	—
ONLOGON	—	—	—	—	—	√	—	—	—	√	—
ONIDLE	—	—	—	√	—	√	—	—	—	√	—

Examples

Schedule the script *testscript.vbs* located in *\System32* to run every five minutes:

```
schtasks /create /sc minute /mo 5 /tn "First Task" /tr testscript.vbs
The task will be created under current logged-on usernames
("MTIT\Administrator").
Please enter the run as password for MTIT\Administrator: ********

SUCCESS: The scheduled task "First Task" has successfully been created.
```

Schedule the script to run every 2 hours for 12 hours starting at midnight:

> **schtasks /create /sc hourly /mo 2 /tn "Second Task" /tr testscript.vbs**
> **/st 00:00 /du 0012:00 /ru MTIT\Administrator /rp Passw0rd**
> SUCCESS: The scheduled task "Second Task" has successfully been created.

Schedule the script to run daily at 6 a.m. until June 30, 2005:

> **schtasks /create /sc daily /tn "Third Task" /tr testscript.vbs /st 06:00**
> **/ed 06/30/2005 /ru MTIT\Administrator /rp Passw0rd**
> SUCCESS: The scheduled task "Third Task" has successfully been created.

Schedule the script to run every Monday:

> **schtasks /create /sc weekly /tn "Fourth Task" /tr testscript.vbs /d MON**
> **/ruMTIT\Administrator /rp Passw0rd**
> SUCCESS: The scheduled task "Fourth Task" has successfully been created.

Schedule the script to run on the last day of each month:

> **schtasks /create /sc monthly /tn "Fifth Task" /tr testscript.vbs**
> **/mo lastday /m * /ru MTIT\Administrator /rp Passw0rd**
> SUCCESS: The scheduled task "Fifth Task" has successfully been created.

Display scheduled tasks in table format:

```
schtasks /query
TaskName                          Next Run Time              Status
=================================== ==================== ===================
Fifth Task                        3:31:00 PM, 3/31/2003
First Task                        3:35:00 PM, 3/27/2003
Fourth Task                       3:28:00 PM, 3/31/2003
Second Task                       12:00:00 AM, 3/28/2003
Third Task                        6:00:00 AM, 3/28/2003
```

List scheduled tasks using verbose option:

```
C:\>schtasks /query /fo list /v

HostName:                          ESRV210D
TaskName:                          Fifth Task
Next Run Time:                     3:31:00 PM, 3/31/2003
Status:
Logon Mode:                        Interactive/Background
Last Run Time:                     Never
Last Result:                       0
Creator:                           Administrator
Schedule:                          At 3:31 PM on day 31 of every month,
starting 3/27/2003
Task To Run:                       C:\WINDOWS\system32\testscript.vbs
Start In:                          testscript.vbs
Comment:                           N/A
Scheduled Task State:              Enabled
Scheduled Type:                    Monthly
Start Time:                        3:31:00 PM
Start Date:                        3/27/2003
End Date:                          N/A
Days:                              31
Months:
JAN,FEB,MAR,APR,MAY,JUN,JUL,AUG,SEP,OCT,NOV,DEC
Run As User:                       MTIT\Administrator
```

```
Delete Task If Not Rescheduled:          Disabled
Stop Task If Runs X Hours and X Mins: 72:0
Repeat: Every:                           Disabled
Repeat: Until: Time:                     Disabled
Repeat: Until: Duration:                 Disabled
Repeat: Stop If Still Running:           Disabled
Idle Time:                               Disabled
Power Management:                        No Start On Batteries, Stop On Battery
Mode

HostName:                                ESRV210D
TaskName:                                First Task
etc...
```

Delete the task named "Fifth Task":

schtasks /delete /tn "Fifth Task"
```
WARNING: Are you sure you want to remove the task "Fifth Task" (Y/N )? y
SUCCESS: The scheduled task "Fifth Task" was successfully deleted.
```

Run the task named "First Task" immediately:

schtasks /run /tn "First Task"
```
SUCCESS: Attempted to run the scheduled task "First Task".
```

Kill the program just started:

schtasks /end /tn "First Task"
```
SUCCESS: The scheduled task "First Task" has been terminated successfully.
```

Disable "Third Task" to temporarily prevent it from running:

schtasks /change /tn "Third Task" /disable /ru MTIT\Administrator /rp Password
```
SUCCESS: The parameters of scheduled task "Third Task" have been changed.
```

Notes

- The user account specified by the /u switch must belong to the Administrators group on the remote computer specified by the /s switch, and the local computer must belong to the same domain as the remote computer or be in a domain trusted by the remote computer's domain. In other words, only Administrators can schedule tasks. You can however specify that the program started by the scheduled task should run under different credentials (even non-Administrator credentials) by using the /ru switch.

- If you use /ru SYSTEM, you don't need to use /rp to specify a password.

- If you run a task using System credentials, users will not be able to view or interact with the program started by the task. This is because System doesn't have interactive logon rights.

- schtasks doesn't verify the program filename or password for a user account specified by /u, and if either of these is wrong the task simply won't run.

- To check for errors in running scheduled tasks, view the *SchedLgU.txt* log file in the *\Windows* directory.

- schtasks works the same as Scheduled Tasks in the Control Panel.

See Also

at, *Tasks*

set

Set local environment variables.

Location
Internal

Syntax
    set *Variable* = *String*

Options
None
>   Displays current environment variables and their settings

Variable
>   The environment variable to set

String
>   The string to be associated with the environment variable

Examples
Create an environment variable named *APPVAR* and assign it the string value C:\
stuff:

set appvar=c:\stuff

Use the echo command to display the value of the variable:

echo %appvar%
c:\stuff

Use the variable just created in a dir command:

dir %appvar%
    Volume in drive C has no label.
    Volume Serial Number is D405-058E

    Directory of c:\stuff

    03/27/2003 07:28 PM   <DIR>   .
    03/27/2003 07:28 PM   <DIR>   ..
    03/27/2003 10:23 AM   12,307 Budget.rtf
    03/27/2003 10:23 AM   20,677 Report.rtf
    03/27/2003 10:23 AM   11,767 Resume.rtf
                   3 File(s)   44,751 bytes
                   2 Dir(s)   8,023,367,680 bytes free

Notes
- The set command can be used at the Recovery Console; see *Recovery Console* in Chapter 4 for more info.
- Environment variables set using set are available only for the current console session. To set persistent variables, use setx instead.

See Also
cmd, setx

setx

Sets local or system environment variables.

Syntax

```
setx [/s Computer [/u [Domain\]User [/p [Password]]]] Variable Value [/m]
setx [/s Computer [/u [Domain \] User [/p [Password]]]] [Variable]
    /k Path [/m]
```

Options

/s Computer /u [Domain\]User /p [Password]
> Name or IP address of a remote computer (if omitted, defaults to local computer) and credentials for running the script (if omitted, defaults to SYSTEM built-in identity)

Variable
> Name of environment variable to set

Value
> Value to assign the variable

/k Path
> Registry value to assign the variable (use \HIVE\KEY\...\Value format)

/m   The environment variable is a system variable (if omitted, it is a local variable)

Examples

Set the system environment variable MYOS to the value WS2003:

```
setx MyOS "WS2003" /m
```

Set the local environment variable BootDevice to the registry value SystemBootDevice in HKLM\System\CurrentControlSet\Control:

```
setx BootDevice /k HKLM\System\CurrentControlSet\Control\SystemBootDevice
```

See Also

cmd, set

---

shutdown

Shut down or restart the local computer or a remote computer.

Syntax

```
shutdown [/i | /l | /s | /r | /a | /p | /h | /e] [/f] [/m \\ComputerName]
    [/t seconds] [/d [p:] XX:YY [/c "Comment"]]
```

Options

/i   Displays the Remote Shutdown Dialog box (if included, all other switches following it are ignored).

/l   Logs off the current user immediately (can't be used with /m or /t).

/s   Shuts the computer down.

/r   Restarts the computer.

/a   Cancels a shutdown if done during the timeout period.

/p   Shuts down the local computer immediately with no warning (requires /d). This switch doesn't work with remote computers.

/h   Sends local computer into hibernation (if supported). Requires /f.

/e   Lets you document the reason for the unexpected shutdown.

/f   Forces running applications to close without warning users (may result in data loss).

/m *ComputerName*
> Specifies the target computer (can't use with /l).

/t *seconds*
> Specifies a delay in seconds (from 0 to 600) before shutdown (a warning is displayed on the local console). If omitted, delay defaults to 30 seconds.

/d [p:]*XX:YY*
> Specifies a reason for shutdown, where:
>
> *p:*   The shutdown was planned
>
> *XX*
> > Major reason number (0–255)
>
> *YY*
> > Minor reason number (0–65,535)

/c *"Comment"*
> Specifies details concerning reason for shutdown (when used with /d). Maximum of 127 characters.

Examples

Display the remote shutdown dialog box:

```
shutdown /i
```

Using this dialog box, you can specify:

- Which computer(s) to shut down or restart.
- Whether to perform a shutdown, restart, or annotated unexpected shutdown of the specified computers.
- Whether to warn users of the impending action and how long to display the warning to give users time to save their work.
- Whether the shutdown is planned or unplanned. If planned, the type of shutdown and an optional comment can be specified.

Restart the remote computer 172.16.11.230 in 15 seconds, forcing the restart if users have open applications, displaying the reason "We're under attack, duck!":

```
shutdown /r /t 15 /f /m \\172.16.11.230 /c "We're under attack, duck!"
```

A dialog box appears on the remote computer warning users of the impending shutdown.

See Also

Logon

start

Runs a program or command.

Syntax

```
start ["title"] [/d path] [/i] [/min] [/max] [/separate | shared]
[/low | /normal | /high | /realtime | /abovenormal | /belownormal]
[/wait] [/b] [program] [parameters]
```

Options

None
> Opens a new command-shell window.

"title"
> Displays in titlebar.

/d path
> Indicates startup directory.

/i Passes the startup environment for cmd to the new window.

/min
> Starts window minimized.

/max
> Starts window maximized.

/separate
> Indicates a 16-bit Windows program run in separate memory.

/shared
> Indicates a 16-bit Windows program run in shared memory.

/low
> Runs application using idle priority.

/normal
> Runs application using normal priority.

/high
> Runs application using high priority.

/realtime
> Runs application using real-time priority.

/abovenormal
> Runs application using above-normal priority class (between normal and high).

/belownormal
> Runs application using below-normal priority class (between normal and low).

/wait
> Starts application and waits for it to end.

/b When executing a Windows command using start, prevents a new command-interpreter window from being opened to run the command. In this case use Ctrl-Break instead of Ctrl-C to interrupt the application.

program [parameters]
> Specifies a program or command to run, with optional parameters.

Examples

To start a new command-shell window with the title "Testing Connection" and continuously ping host 172.16.11.39 until Ctrl-C is pressed:

```
start "Testing Connection" ping -t 172.16.11.39
```

To start Computer Management from the command line:

```
start mmc %windir%\system32\compmgmt.msc
```

or simply:

```
mmc %windir%\system32\compmgmt.msc
```

Notes

- Using start to run a Windows command (such as dir, chkdsk, and so on) opens a new command-interpreter (cmd) window to execute the command. This window implicitly runs using the /k option, which means that the new window stays open after the command is run. See cmd earlier in this chapter for more info.

- When executing a 32-bit GUI application using start, control is returned to the command prompt immediately. When a Windows command or command script is run, however, the command or script must first terminate before control is returned to the command shell.

- If command extensions are enabled (as they are by default), you can use start to open a document or file using its associated application. For example, to open *readme.doc* using Word, you can type:

```
start readme.doc
```

See Also

cmd

---

systeminfo   new in WS2003

Displays system information including operating system, product ID, and hardware settings.

Syntax

```
systeminfo [/s Computer [/u Domain\UserName [/p Password]]] [/fo {TABLE |
LIST | CSV}] [/nh] [/v]
```

Options

/s Computer
Name or IP address of a remote computer (if omitted, defaults to local computer)

/u [Domain\UserName [/p [Password]]]
Credentials for running the command (if omitted, defaults to currently logged-on user)

/fo {TABLE | LIST | CSV}
Format for displaying information (if omitted, default is TABLE)

/nh   Omits header row from displayed information if /fo is set to TABLE or CSV

/v   Displays verbose information

Examples

Display system info for computer 172.16.11.230:

```
systeminfo /s 172.16.11.230 /u MTIT\Administrator /p Password
```

```
Host Name:                 ESRV230D
OS Name:                   Microsoft(R) Windows(R) Server 2003, Enterprise
Edition
OS Version:                5.2.3763 Build 3763
OS Manufacturer:           Microsoft Corporation
OS Configuration:          Member Server
OS Build Type:             Uniprocessor Free
Registered Owner:          me
Registered Organization:   me
Product ID:                55039-116-0117345-32669
Original Install Date:     2/12/2003, 1:31:27 PM
System Up Time:            0 Days, 0 Hours, 3 Minutes, 18 Seconds
System Manufacturer:       System Manufacturer
System Model:              System Name
System Type:               X86-based PC
Processor(s):              1 Processor(s) Installed.
                           [01]: x86 Family 6 Model 7 Stepping 3
GenuineIntel ~5
01 Mhz
BIOS Version:              ASUS   - 30303031
Windows Directory:         C:\WINDOWS
System Directory:          C:\WINDOWS\system32
Boot Device:               \Device\HarddiskVolume1
System Locale:             en-us;English (United States)
Input Locale:              en-us;English (United States)
Time Zone:                 (GMT-06:00) Central Time (US & Canada)
Total Physical Memory:     512 MB
Available Physical Memory: 391 MB
Page File: Max Size:       1,762 MB
Page File: Available:      1,549 MB
Page File: In Use:         213 MB
Page File Location(s):     C:\pagefile.sys
Domain:                    mtit.local
Logon Server:              N/A
Hotfix(s):                 1 Hotfix(s) Installed.
                           [01]: Q147222
Network Card(s):           1 NIC(s) Installed.
                           [01]: 3Com EtherLink XL 10/100 PCI For Complete
PC Management NIC (3C905C-TX)
                               Connection Name: Local Area Connection
                               DHCP Enabled:    No
                               IP address(es)
                               [01]: 172.16.11.230
                               [02]: 172.16.11.231
                               [03]: 172.16.11.232
                               [04]: 172.16.11.233
                               [05]: 172.16.11.234
```

See Also

Devices

---

takeown

new in WS2003

Lets an administrator take ownership of a file.

Syntax

```
takeown [/s Computer [/u [Domain\User [/p [Password]]]] /f FileName [/a] [/r]
   [/d {Y | N}]
```

Options

/s Computer
>   Name or IP address of a remote computer (if omitted, defaults to local computer)

/u [Domain\User[/p [Password]]]
>   Credentials for running the command (if omitted, defaults to currently logged-on user)

/f FileName
>   A file or directory name pattern (wildcard character * and ShareName\FileName format are supported)

/a   Assigns ownership to Administrators group instead of current user

/r   Recursive operation on all files in the specified directory and subdirectories

/d {Y | N}
>   Default prompt to use when current user doesn't have permission to view folders in a directory (Y takes ownership and N suppresses confirmation prompt)

Examples

Take ownership of the folder *C:\docs* and the files within it on the remote computer with IP address 172.16.11.230:

takeown /s 172.16.11.230 /f C:\docs /r /d N

SUCCESS: The file (or folder): "\\172.16.11.230\C$\docs" now owned by user "MTIT\Administrator".

SUCCESS: The file (or folder): "\\172.16.11.230\C$\docs\resume.txt" now owned by user "MTIT\Administrator".

See Also

cacls, *Permissions*

---

taskkill

new in WS2003

Kills running processes.

Syntax

```
taskkill [/s Computer] [/u Domain\UserName [/p Password]] [/fi FilterName]
   {[/pid ProcessID] | [/im ImageName]} [/f] [/t]
```

Options

/s Computer
> Name or IP address of a remote computer (if omitted, defaults to local computer).

/u [Domain\UserName [/p [Password]]]
> Credentials for running the command (if omitted, defaults to currently logged-on user).

/fi FilterName
> Filters the types of process(es) to kill using:
>
> Status *{eq | ne} {RUNNING | NOT RESPONDING | UNKNOWN}*
>
> Imagename *{eq | ne}*
> > Any valid string
>
> PID *{eg | ne | gt | lt | ge | le}*
> > Any valid positive integer
>
> Session *{eg | ne | gt | lt | ge | le}*
> > Any valid session number
>
> CPUTime *{eg | ne | gt | lt | ge | le}*
> > Valid time in format HH:MM:SS
>
> Memusage *{eg | ne | gt | lt | ge | le}*
> > Any valid integer
>
> Username *{eq | ne}*
> > Any valid username in format *Domain\UserName*
>
> Services *{eq | ne}*
> > Any valid string
>
> Windowtitle *{eq | ne}*
> > Any valid string
>
> Modules *{eq | ne}*
> > Any valid string

Be sure to put the filter in quotes.

/pid ProcessID
> Process ID of process to kill

/im ImageName
> Image name of process to kill (can use * to kill all processes)

/f Forces termination of process

/t Terminates the specified process and any child processes spawned by that process

Examples

Kill the instance of Notepad running on the local machine:

```
taskkill /fi "Imagename eq Notepad.exe"
SUCCESS: Sent termination signal to the process with PID 308.
```

Notes

Use tasklist to obtain the process ID of running processes you wish to kill.

See Also

tasklist, *Tasks*

tasklist

Lists running processes.

Syntax

```
tasklist [/s Computer] [/u Domain\User [/p Password]] [{/m Module
| /svc | /v}] [/fo {TABLE | LIST | CSV}] [/nh] [/fi FilterName [/fi
FilterName2 [ ... ]]]
```

Options

/s Computer
Name or IP address of a remote computer (if omitted, defaults to local computer).

/u [Domain\User[/p [Password]]]
Credentials for running the command (if omitted, defaults to currently logged-on user).

/m Module
Lists tasks having DLLs loaded that match the pattern.

/svc
Lists service information for each process without truncation (requires TABLE).

/fo {TABLE | LIST | CSV}
Format for displaying driver properties (if omitted, default is TABLE).

/nh
Omits header row from displayed information if /fo is set to TABLE or CSV.

/v Displays verbose information.

/fi FilterName
Filters the types of process(es) to kill (be sure to put the filter in quotes):

Status {eq | ne} {RUNNING | NOT RESPONDING | UNKNOWN}

Imagename {eq | ne}
Any valid string

PID {eg | ne | gt | lt | ge | le}
Any valid positive integer

Session {eg | ne | gt | lt | ge | le}
Any valid session number

CPUTime {eg | ne | gt | lt | ge | le}
Valid time in format HH:MM:SS

Memusage {eg | ne | gt | lt | ge | le}
Any valid integer

Username {eq | ne}
Any valid username in format Domain\UserName

Services {eq | ne}
Any valid string

Windowtitle {eq | ne}
Any valid string

Modules {eq | ne}
Any valid string

Examples

Display all running processes:

tasklist

```
Image Name                     PID Session Name        Session#    Mem Usage
========================= ========= ================== ========== =========
System Idle Process              0 Console                     0        16 K
System                           4 Console                     0       220 K
smss.exe                       280 Console                     0       484 K
csrss.exe                      356 Console                     0     3,092 K
winlogon.exe                   380 Console                     0     5,500 K
services.exe                   424 Console                     0     3,052 K
lsass.exe                      436 Console                     0    22,168 K
svchost.exe                    664 Console                     0     3,048 K
svchost.exe                    796 Console                     0     3,948 K
svchost.exe                    812 Console                     0     2,044 K
svchost.exe                    840 Console                     0    21,448 K
spoolsv.exe                   1080 Console                     0     7,696 K
msdtc.exe                     1104 Console                     0     3,708 K
dfssvc.exe                    1172 Console                     0     3,668 K
dns.exe                       1208 Console                     0     5,128 K
svchost.exe                   1256 Console                     0     1,628 K
ismserv.exe                   1292 Console                     0     3,332 K
ntfrs.exe                     1304 Console                     0       820 K
svchost.exe                   1400 Console                     0     1,224 K
tcpsvcs.exe                   1436 Console                     0     8,564 K
svchost.exe                   1652 Console                     0     3,968 K
alg.exe                       1688 Console                     0     3,444 K
svchost.exe                   1904 Console                     0     3,344 K
wmiprvse.exe                  2208 Console                     0     4,208 K
csrss.exe                     2384 RDP-Tcp#1                   1       964 K
winlogon.exe                  2412 RDP-Tcp#1                   1     3,092 K
rdpclip.exe                   2636 RDP-Tcp#1                   1     2,280 K
explorer.exe                  2696 RDP-Tcp#1                   1    10,312 K
HelpCtr.exe                   2836 RDP-Tcp#1                   1    17,140 K
HelpSvc.exe                   2888 Console                     0     8,368 K
cmd.exe                       3012 RDP-Tcp#1                   1       564 K
logon.scr                     4008 Console                     0     1,348 K
wmiprvse.exe                   704 Console                     0     4,588 K
notepad.exe                   2548 RDP-Tcp#1                   1     1,748 K
tasklist.exe                  2644 RDP-Tcp#1                   1     3,036 K
```

List verbose info for process with ID 840:

tasklist /fi "PID eq 840" /fo list /v

```
Image Name:   svchost.exe
PID:          840
Session Name: Console
Session#:     0
Mem Usage:    21,440 K
Status:       Unknown
usernames:    NT AUTHORITY\SYSTEM
```

```
CPU Time:      0:00:08
Window Title: N/A
```

List service info for this process:

tasklist /fi "PID eq 840" /fo list /svc

```
Image Name:   svchost.exe
PID:          840
Services:     Browser
              CryptSvc
              dmserver
              EventSystem
              helpsvc
              lanmanserver
              lanmanworkstation
              Netman
              Nla
              RasMan
              RemoteAccess
              Schedule
              seclogon
              SENS
              ShellHWDetection
              W32Time
              winmgmt
              wuauserv
              WZCSVC
```

Notes

tasklist replaces the *tlist* support tool.

See Also

taskkill, *Tasks*

---

telnet

Runs an interactive shell session on a remote host running the *telnet* daemon.

Syntax

```
telnet [hostname [portnumber] ]
```

Options

telnet [hostname [portnumber]]

Starts a client-side *telnet* session by opening a Microsoft *telnet* shell within the command shell on the local machine.

hostname is the name (DNS or NetBIOS, depending on the network) or IP address of the remote *telnet* server. If *hostname* is omitted, the *telnet* client starts but doesn't connect to a *telnet* server (use the open command in that case to connect).

portnumber is required only if the default port (TCP port 23) isn't used by the *telnet* server.

Commands

close
> Terminates the current *telnet* session but keeps the *telnet* shell open on the client

display
> Displays the operating parameters (see set *option* later in this list)

open
> Establishes a connection with a *telnet* server

quit
> Exits the *telnet* shell and returns to the command prompt

set option
> Enables different settings, specifically:

> *NTLM*
>> Authenticates telnet sessions using NTLM (challenge/response) authentication

> *LOCAL_ECHO*
>> Displays typed keystrokes on the screen

> *TERM [ANSI | VT100 | VT52 | VTNT]*
>> Specifies the terminal mode to use

> *CRLF*
>> Sends both a carriage return and linefeed when Enter is pressed

status
> Displays the status of the connection

unset option
> Disables different settings, specifically:

> *NTLM*
>> Authenticates *telnet* sessions using basic authentication (clear text) instead of NTLM (challenge/response) authentication

> *LOCAL_ECHO*
>> Causes typed keystrokes not to be displayed on the screen

> *CRLF*
>> Sends only a carriage return (and not a carriage return plus a linefeed) when Enter is pressed

Examples

Start the *telnet* client on the local machine:

```
C:\>telnet
Microsoft (R) WS2003
Welcome to Microsoft Telnet Client
Telnet Client Build 5.00.99201.1

Escape Character is 'CTRL+]'

Microsoft Telnet>
```

Display the current client settings:

```
Microsoft Telnet> display
Escape Character is 'CTRL+]'
WILL AUTH (NTLM Authentication)
```

Command Reference

```
LOCAL_ECHO off
Sending both CR & LF
WILL TERM TYPE

Preferred Term Type is ANSI
```

Open a session with the *telnet* server 172.16.11.100:

```
Microsoft Telnet> open 172.16.11.100
*========================================================
Welcome to Microsoft Telnet Server.
*========================================================
C:\>
```

Determine the IP address configuration of the remote *telnet* server:

```
C:\> ipconfig /all
Windows IP Configuration

Host Name . . . . . . . . . . . . : bach
Primary DNS Suffix  . . . . . . . : mtitworld.com
Node Type . . . . . . . . . . . . : Hybrid
IP Routing Enabled. . . . . . . . : No
WINS Proxy Enabled. . . . . . . . : No
DNS Suffix Search List. . . . . . : mtitworld.com

Ethernet adapter Local Area Connection:

Connection-specific DNS Suffix  . :
Description . . . . . . . . . . . : NE2000 Compatible
Physical Address. . . . . . . . . : 00-40-95-D1-29-6C
DHCP Enabled. . . . . . . . . . . : No
IP Address. . . . . . . . . . . . : 172.16.11.100
Subnet Mask . . . . . . . . . . . : 255.255.255.0
Default Gateway . . . . . . . . . : 172.16.11.1
DNS Servers . . . . . . . . . . . : 172.16.11.100
                                    172.16.11.104
Primary WINS Server . . . . . . . : 172.16.11.50
```

Notes

- Unlike NT before it, WS2003 includes a *telnet* service and can function as a *telnet* server that provides a new way of performing remote administration on WS2003 servers. Note that the *telnet* service must be manually started on the server or have its startup setting changed to Automatic before a *telnet* client can connect to it.

- While the *telnet* client on NT was a GUI utility (*telnet.exe*), the WS2003 version runs in console mode instead. This client also supports NTLM authentication to provide more secure authentication between *telnet* clients and servers. However, one feature that was provided by the GUI *telnet.exe* on NT, which isn't supported in the new command-line version, is session logging.

See Also

rcp, rexec, rsh

tftp

Stands for trivial file-transfer protocol, which copies files between the client and a host running the TFTP service.

Syntax

```
tftp [-i] hostname [get | put] source [destination]
```

Options

-i   Switches to binary (octet) mode for bytewise transfers of binary files. (Otherwise, the default ASCII mode is used.)

hostname
   Indicates the destination host running the TFTP service.

get | put
   Downloads or uploads the file as specified.

source
   Specifies the local file you want to transfer. If you use a hyphen, the destination file is printed out on STDOUT (when getting) or is read from STDIN when putting).

destination
   Renames the file after transferring it (destination is optional).

Examples

Transfer the file *C:\pub\smiley.gif* from the local machine to the remote Unix host called *BONGO*:

```
tftp -i bongo put C:\pub\smiley.gif
Transfer successful: 386 bytes in 1 second, 386 bytes/s.
```

Notes

TFTP doesn't support user authentication, so the user transferring the file must be logged on and must have permission to write to the remote directory. TFTP also uses UDP to transfer files and is therefore not guaranteed as reliable. Use FTP instead for a more reliable method that supports basic authentication.

See Also

ftp

---

time

Displays or modifies system time.

Syntax

```
time [/t] [Hours:[Minutes[:Seconds[.Hundredths]]] [{A | P}]]
```

Options

None
   Displays the system time and prompts you to modify it

/t   Displays the current system time without prompting you to modify it

Examples

Display the current system date and time:

```
date /t & time /t
Thu 03/27/2003
09:29 PM
```

See Also

date

---

tracert

Traces the route from the local machine to a remote host.

Syntax

```
tracert [-d] [-h maxhops] [-j hostlist] [-w msec] remotehost
```

Options

-d   To speed things up, don't resolve IP addresses into hostnames

-h maxhops
   Maximum number of hops for the trace

-j hostlist
   Loose source route along the list of hosts

-w msec
   Timeout for replies in milliseconds

remotehost
   IP address or DNS name of host at remote end of route

Examples

Trace route from local machine to *www.umanitoba.ca* (my alma mater):

```
tracert www.umanitoba.ca
Tracing route to spica.cc.umanitoba.ca [130.179.16.50] over a maximum of 30
hops:
1    120 ms    281 ms    140 ms  wnpgas01.mts.net [205.200.52.1]
2    121 ms    150 ms    130 ms  wnpgbr00-f00-303.mts.net [205.200.52.7]
3    131 ms    120 ms    200 ms  wnpgbr01-f000-101.mts.net [205.200.28.66]
4    140 ms    110 ms    140 ms  wnpgin-c14out.mts.net [205.200.27.54]
5    120 ms    150 ms    140 ms  207.161.242.34
6    120 ms    141 ms    130 ms  atrouter.cc.umanitoba.ca [207.161.242.18]
7    120 ms    131 ms    140 ms  bbrouter.cc.umanitoba.ca [130.179.0.1]
8    140 ms    140 ms    150 ms  spica.cc.umanitoba.ca [130.179.16.50]
Trace complete.
```

Determine route to Beijing University in China:

```
tracert www.pku.edu.cn -d
Tracing route to sun1000e.pku.edu.cn [202.112.7.12] over a maximum of 30
hops:
1    121 ms    130 ms    100 ms  205.200.52.1
2    110 ms    111 ms    110 ms  205.200.52.7
3    120 ms    110 ms    110 ms  205.200.28.66
```

```
 4   110 ms   100 ms   120 ms   206.108.110.5
 5   100 ms   120 ms   120 ms   206.108.102.81
 6   130 ms   131 ms   150 ms   206.108.98.85
 7   130 ms   140 ms   141 ms   206.108.98.50
 8   130 ms   140 ms   151 ms   206.108.97.21
 9   180 ms   180 ms   241 ms   206.108.97.6
10   150 ms   130 ms   170 ms   207.45.208.133
11   290 ms   210 ms   211 ms   207.45.223.89
12   230 ms   220 ms   221 ms   207.45.223.174
13   180 ms   230 ms   211 ms   207.45.223.154
14   250 ms   201 ms   210 ms   207.45.214.190
15   791 ms   881 ms     *       202.112.61.222
16     *      801 ms   851 ms   202.112.36.194
17   781 ms   801 ms   801 ms   202.112.1.62
18     *      761 ms   801 ms   202.112.1.218
19   761 ms     *      802 ms   202.112.1.66
20   761 ms  1061 ms   902 ms   202.112.6.22
21   801 ms   781 ms   741 ms   202.112.6.194
22   821 ms   961 ms   871 ms   202.112.7.12
Trace complete.
```

The asterisks indicate ICMP Echo packets whose reply was not received in the timeout period (default is one second).

Notes

- tracert is a troubleshooting tool used to identify failed or congested routers along a route.
- Use the -d option to speed the trace by disabling DNS resolution.

See Also

pathping, ping

---

ver

Displays OS version info.

Syntax

ver

Examples

ver
```
Microsoft Windows [Version 5.2.3763]
```

See Also

Devices

Resources

Appendix: Useful Sites

If you administer the Windows Server 2003, you may find these sites useful:

Find Knowledge Base articles
support.microsoft.com/default.aspx?pr=kbinfo

Windows Server 2003 home
www.microsoft.com/windowsserver2003/

Lots of useful stuff. Take the time to browse the site and become familiar with what's there.

Windows Server 2003 downloads
www.microsoft.com/windowsserver2003/downloads/

Check this site out regularly for new add-ons and enhancements for the platform.

Windows Server 2003 support center
support.microsoft.com/default.aspx?scid=fh;EN-US;winsvr2003

Microsoft Product Support Services (PSS) site for Windows Server 2003 issues and fixes.

Search Microsoft.com
search.microsoft.com

General newsgroup for Windows Server 2003 discussion and questions
microsoft.public.windows.server.general

This is the most active of the *windows.server* newsgroups on the *msnews. microsoft.com* news server.

Paul Thurrot's Supersite for Windows
www.winsupersite.com

The latest news about upcoming Windows platforms.

myITforum.com
www.myitforum.com

The top site on managing Windows platforms, run by SMS guru Rod Trent.

Windows & .NET Magazine Network
www.win2000mag.net

News and content about the Windows platforms.

Acronyms

For your reference, here is a brief list of acronyms used in this book.

ACL
Access control list

ACPI
Advanced Configuration and Power Interface

ADMT
Active Directory Migration Tool

ADSI
Active Directory Services Interface

APIPA
Automatic Private IP Addressing

ASR
Automatic System Recovery

ATAPI
AT Attachment Packet Interface

ATCP
AppleTalk Control Protocol

BDC
Backup domain controller

BITS
Background Intelligent Transfer Service

CAL
Client-access license

DC
Domain Controller

DFS
Distributed File System

DHCP
Dynamic Host Configuration Protocol

DNS
Domain Name System

EFS
Encrypting File System

EMS
Emergency Management Services

EULA
End User License Agreement

FQDN
Fully qualified domain name

FRS
File Replication Service

FSMO
Flexible single master of operations

GPMC
Group Policy Management Console

GPO
Group Policy Object

GPOE
Group Policy Object Editor

GPT

GPT
Group Policy Template

GUID
Globally unique identifier

HCL
Hardware Compatibility List

ICF
Internet Connection Firewall

ICS
Internet Connection Sharing

IDE
Integrated device electronics

IIS
Internet Information Services

IRQ
Interrupt request

L2TP
Layer Two Tunneling Protocol

MMC
Microsoft Management Console

NAT
Network Address Translation

NC
Naming Context

NLB
Network Load Balancing

NT
NT LAN Manager

OEM
Original equipment manufacturer

OU
Organizational unit

PDC
Primary domain controller

PnP
Plug and Play

PPPoE
Point-to-Point Protocol over Ethernet

PPTP
Point-to-Point Tunneling Protocol

RAID
Redundant array of independent disks

RID
Routing Information Daemon

RIS
Remote Installation Services

RRAS
Routing and Remote Access Service

RSoP
Resultant Set of Policy

SID
Security identifier

SUS
Software Update Services

UDB
Uniqueness database file

UDMA
Ultra direct memory access

UPN
User Principal Name

VPN
Virtual private network

VSS
Volume Shadow Copy Service

WFP
Windows File Protection

WINS
Windows Internet Naming Service

WMI
Windows Management Instrumentation

WPA
Windows Product Activation

Index

A

A (address) record, DNS, 171
Account Lockout Policy, 35
account policies, configuration, 6
accounts
    built-in, 77
    disabling, 76
    password reset, 76
    renaming, 76
    restrictions, 76
    user accounts
        disabling, 400
        naming conventions, 402
    users
        copying, 400
        deleting, 400
        finding, 401
        password reset, 401
        renaming, 401
        unlocking, 401
ACLs (access control lists), displaying
        and modifying, 431
Action menu (Active Directory Users
        and Computers tool), 88
activation, 6
    DHCP, 145
    Windows Product Activation, 78
Active Directory, 35
    administrative authority,
        delegation, 84

    auditing, 89
    comma-delimited text files,
        importing/exporting, 446
    compacting, 93
    connections, sites and, 379
    diagnostic logging, enabling, 94
    domain controllers, connection
        issues, 92
    Group Policy, 7, 84
    groups
        adding, 462–464
        finding, 52
    implementation, 6
    installation, 90
        troubleshooting, 94
    LDAP queries, 94
    log files, 86
    logical structure, 82
        deployment planning, 83
        DNS names, 83
        schemas, 85
    multiple platform-based networks,
        Active Directory Client
        Extensions, 93
    NCs (naming contexts), 85
    objects
        auditing, 36, 105
        creating, 60, 90
        deleting, 60, 473
        displaying properties, 464–467

We'd like to hear your suggestions for improving our indexes. Send email to *index@oreilly.com*.

external trusts, 391
  creating, 392
  revoking, 393

F

failure events, security log, 201
FAT filesystem
  converting to NTFS, 445
  partitions, 44
file associations, 50
file attributes, displaying, modifying,
    removing, 417
file extension associations, displaying/
    modifying, 413, 484
file management, Windows
    Explorer, 50
File Server Management, shared folders
    and, 70, 363
file sharing, 371
file system
  compression, 50
  copy files/folders, 50
  Group Policy and, 50
  move files/folders, 50
files
  Active Directory physical
      structure, 86
  archives, 204
  associations, 211
  attributes, 50, 204, 213
    display, 210
  auditing, 36
  compressed, expanding, 50
  compression, 205, 209, 213
  copying, 50, 209
    rcp command, 583
  decryption, 211
    EFS, 49
  encryption, 205–207, 210
    EFS, 49
  Indexing Service, 204
  moving, 209
  offline
    configuration, 61
    shared folders, 61
  opening, 50, 212
    displaying or disconnecting, 566
  ownership, 50
    takeown command, 602
  permissions
    display, 60
    special permissions, 59

properties, 50
recovery
  defective disks, 584
  EFS and, 49
securing, 212
sending, 212
transferring, 50
  ftp command, 481–484
  Windows Explorer, 207
filesystems
  converting, FAT to NTFS, 445
  installation and, 266
  maintenance
    chkdsk command, 433
    scheduling automatic, 435
  objects, auditing, 105
filtering, Group Policy objects, 53
filters
  event logs, 49
  GPOs, 248
  TCP/IP, 389
Find Knowledge Base articles, 615
finger command, 478
folders
  archives, 204
  attributes, 50, 204, 213
    display, 210
  auditing, 36
  backups, 37
  compression, 205, 209, 213
  copying, 50, 209
  custom, 210
  decryption, 211
    EFS, 49
  encryption, 205–207, 210
  Indexing Service, 204
  moving, 209
  Network Connections folder, 114
  NT/WS2003 comparison, 4
  opening, 50, 212
  ownership, 50
  permissions
    assign, 59
    display, 60
  Printers folder, 315
  properties, 50
  recovery, EFS and, 49
  redirection, 51
    Group Policy, 235
  security, 212
  sending, 212

About the Author

Mitch Tulloch is a well-known author, trainer and consultant based in Winnipeg, Canada. In addition to the three Nutshell books he has written for O'Reilly, Mitch is also the author of the *Microsoft Encyclopedia of Networking* and the *Microsoft Encyclopedia of Security,* both from Microsoft Press, plus a string of best-selling IIS books from Osborne/McGraw-Hill. *Windows Server 2003 in a Nutshell* is only his thirteenth book, so Mitch still has a long way to go to catch up with his childhood hero, Isaac Asimov. And although Mitch has an encyclopedic (yea, even "Asimovian") interest in all things technical, his advice to aspiring young authors is, "Don't ever try to write an encyclopedia!"

Mitch has also written for magazines such as *NetworkWorld* and *MCP Magazine* and contributes regularly to *myITforum.com,* a popular knowledge and information forum for IT professionals. Mitch maintains a weblog on the O'Reilly Network (*weblogs.oreillynet.com*) where he soapboxes on all sorts of issues, and a techblog on BlogSpot (*mitchtulloch.blogspot.com*) containing random thoughts, ideas, suggestions, tips, and resources for network and system administrators. If you're interested (and who wouldn't be?), you can find out more about Mitch at *www.mtit.com* and can contact him at *info@mtit.com.*

Colophon

Our look is the result of reader comments, our own experimentation, and feedback from distribution channels. Distinctive covers complement our distinctive approach to technical topics, breathing personality and life into potentially dry subjects.

The animal on the cover of *Windows Server 2003 in a Nutshell* is an American white pelican (*Pelecanus erythrorhynchos*). It inhabits the coastal regions, freshwater marshes, lakes, and rivers of North America, and winters in the Gulf States of the southern United States and Mexico.

Sometimes confused with the whooping crane, the American white pelican is a huge white bird with black primary and outer secondary feathers, sporting a wingspan of over 9 feet and an average weight of 16 pounds. Unlike the brown pelican, which plunge-dives into water from the air, the white pelican feeds while swimming, ingesting fish and straining out frogs, salamanders, and aquatic invertebrates from its pouch.

White pelicans prefer to nest on low, bare islands, sandbars, or remote peninsulas, especially on freshwater lakes. Egg laying begins in mid-May in the colonies, and both parents incubate a brood of two chalky-white eggs, which hatch about a month later. The parents incubate the eggs with their feet because they don't have a brood patch of bare skin on the belly. The chicks are helpless when they hatch and eat by scooping digested food out of the adult's pouch. As the chicks mature, they join a pod and feed in large groups until they are ready to fly, at approximately 10 weeks.

American white pelicans are one of the most social of the avian species: the flocks forage cooperatively, by encircling fish or driving them into shallows where they are more easily caught. Colonies of a hundred or more birds are often seen nesting, roosting, foraging, and sunbathing together.

In medieval heraldry, the pelican is a symbol representing maternal protectiveness and piety.

Mary Anne Weeks Mayo was the production editor, and Norma Emory was the copyeditor for *Windows Server 2003 in a Nutshell*. Mary Anne Weeks Mayo and Matt Hutchinson proofread the book. Mary Brady and Claire Cloutier provided quality control. James Quill and Mary Agner provided production assistance. Tom Dinse and Johnna Van Hoose Dinse wrote the index.

Emma Colby designed the cover of this book, based on a series design by Edie Freedman. The cover image is a 19th-century engraving from the Dover Pictorial Archive. Emma produced the cover layout with QuarkXPress 4.1 using Adobe's ITC Garamond font.

David Futato designed the interior layout. This book was converted by Joe Wizda to FrameMaker 5.5.6 with a format conversion tool created by Erik Ray, Jason McIntosh, Neil Walls, and Mike Sierra that uses Perl and XML technologies. The text font is Linotype Birka; the heading font is Adobe Myriad Condensed; and the code font is LucasFont's TheSans Mono Condensed. The illustrations that appear in the book were produced by Robert Romano and Jessamyn Read using Macromedia FreeHand 9 and Adobe Photoshop 6. The tip and warning icons were drawn by Christopher Bing. This colophon was written by Reg Aubry.

Other Titles Available from O'Reilly

Windows 2000 Administration

Active Directory Cookbook

By Robbie Allen
1st Edition October 2003
624 pages, ISBN 0-596-00464-8

Active Directory Cookbook contains hundreds of step-by-step solutions for both common and uncommon problems that you might encounter with Active Directory on Windows 2003 Server or Windows 2000—including recipes to deal with the Lightweight Directory Access Protocol (LDAP), multi-master replication, Domain Name System (DNS), Group Policy, the Active Directory Schema, and many other features. Each recipe includes a discussion to explain how and why the solution works, so you can adapt the problem-solving techniques to similar situations.

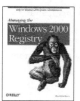

Managing the Windows 2000 Registry

By Paul Robichaux
1st Edition August 2000
558 pages, ISBN 1-56592-943-8

The Windows 2000 Registry is the repository for all hardware, software, and application configuration settings. *Managing the Windows 2000 Registry* is the system administrator's guide to maintaining, monitoring, and updating the Registry database. A "must-have" for every 2000 system manager or administrator, it covers what the Registry is and where it lives on disk, available tools, Registry access from programs, and Registry content.

Securing Windows NT/2000 Servers for the Internet

By Stefan Norberg
1st Edition November 2000
200 pages, ISBN 1-56592-768-0

In recent years, Windows NT and 2000 systems have emerged as viable platforms for Internet servers, but securing Windows for internet use is a complex task. This concise guide simplifies the task by paring down installation and configuration instructions into a series of security checklists for security administration, including hardening servers for use as "bastion hosts," performing secure remote administration with OpenSSH, TCP Wrappers, VNC, and the new Windows 2000 Terminal Services.

Active Directory, 2nd Edition

By Robbie Allen
& Alistair G. Lowe-Norris
2nd Edition April 2003
720 pages, ISBN 0-596-00466-4

Active Directory, 2nd Edition, provides system and network administrators, IT professionals, technical project managers, and programmers with a clear, detailed look at Active Directory for both Windows 2000 and Windows Server 2003. *Active Directory*, 2nd Edition will guide you through the maze of concepts, design issues and scripting options enabling you to get the most out of your deployment.

Windows 2000 Administration in a Nutshell

By Mitch Tulloch
1st Edition February 2001
798 pages, ISBN 1-56592-713-3

Anyone who installs Windows 2000, creates a user, or adds a printer is a 2000 system administrator. This book covers all the important day-to-day administrative tasks, and the tools for performing each task are included in a handy easy-to-look-up alphabetical reference. What's the same and what's different between the Windows 2000 and Windows NT platform? Has the GUI or the networking architecture changed, and if so, how? *Windows 2000 Administration in a Nutshell* addresses the problems associated with bridging the gap between the Windows NT and Windows 2000 platforms.

DNS on Windows 2000

By Matt Larson & Cricket Liu
2nd Edition September 2001
35 pages, ISBN 0-596-00230-0

This special Windows-oriented edition of the classic *DNS and BIND* is a guide to one of the Internet's fundamental building blocks: the distributed host information database responsible for translating names into addresses, routing mail, and many other services. Covers server setup and maintenance along with Windows-specific topics like integration between DNS and Active Directory, conversion from BIND to the Microsoft DNS server, and registry settings.

O'REILLY®

To order: *800-998-9938* • *order@oreilly.com* • *www.oreilly.com*
Online editions of most O'Reilly titles are available by subscription at *safari.oreilly.com*
Also available at most retail and online bookstores.

How to stay in touch with O'Reilly

1. Visit our award-winning web site

http://www.oreilly.com/

★ "Top 100 Sites on the Web"—PC Magazine
★ CIO Magazine's Web Business 50 Awards

Our web site contains a library of comprehensive product information (including book excerpts and tables of contents), downloadable software, background articles, interviews with technology leaders, links to relevant sites, book cover art, and more. File us in your bookmarks or favorites!

2. Join our email mailing lists

Sign up to get email announcements of new books and conferences, special offers, and O'Reilly Network technology newsletters at:

http://elists.oreilly.com

It's easy to customize your free elists subscription so you'll get exactly the O'Reilly news you want.

3. Get examples from our books

To find example files for a book, go to:

http://www.oreilly.com/catalog

select the book, and follow the "Examples" link.

4. Work with us

Check out our web site for current employment opportunites:

http://jobs.oreilly.com/

5. Register your book

Register your book at:
http://register.oreilly.com

6. Contact us

O'Reilly & Associates, Inc.
1005 Gravenstein Hwy North
Sebastopol, CA 95472 USA
TEL: 707-827-7000 or 800-998-9938
        (6am to 5pm PST)
FAX: 707-829-0104

order@oreilly.com
For answers to problems regarding your order or our products. To place a book order online visit:

http://www.oreilly.com/order_new/

catalog@oreilly.com
To request a copy of our latest catalog.

booktech@oreilly.com
For book content technical questions or corrections.

corporate@oreilly.com
For educational, library, government, and corporate sales.

proposals@oreilly.com
To submit new book proposals to our editors and product managers.

international@oreilly.com
For information about our international distributors or translation queries. For a list of our distributors outside of North America check out:

http://international.oreilly.com/distributors.html

adoption@oreilly.com
For information about academic use of O'Reilly books, visit:

http://academic.oreilly.com

O'REILLY®

To order: *800-998-9938* • *order@oreilly.com* • *www.oreilly.com*
Online editions of most O'Reilly titles are available by subscription at *safari.oreilly.com*
Also available at most retail and online bookstores.